Harding Families

of the Northern Neck of Virginia
Rockingham Co., North Carolina
Giles and Williamson Cos., Tennessee

New: The Combs Connection

With emphasis on families
originating in early
Northumberland & Stafford Co., Virginia

Leland E. Pound
Laguna Woods, California
lee@leepound.com
Phone 949-246-8580

Harding Families of the Northern Neck of Virginia

This version contains many corrections and additions to previous versions. If you own an earlier version of this book, you should purchase this one to get the latest research.

© 2022 Leland E. Pound
All Rights Reserved

First edition published July 1998
Second Edition published June 2022
Revised April 2023
Revised February 2025
Third Edition September 2025
Published by Solutions Press

All rights reserved. Except as permitted by applicable copyright laws, no part of this book may be reproduced, duplicated, sold, or distributed in any form or by any means, either mechanical, by photocopy, electronic, or by computer, or stored in a database or retrieval system, without the express written permission of the publisher, except for brief quotations by reviewers.

ISBN: 979-8-9864517-1-8
Printed in the United States of America

This is a work of non-fiction. The conclusions presented are those of the author alone and are based solely on original records. With a few identified exceptions, all references given are to original public records either in identified local record repositories or online sites. Record extracts presented in this book have in all cases been created from original records and not from published secondary sources.

Table of Contents

Table of Contents iii
Introduction xiii
Chapter 1   Corrections to Errors in Published Sources 1
    George Harding and Mary Orley are NOT the Parents of Thomas Harding (1-1) of Northumberland County, Virginia 1
    Thomas Harding (1-1) had six children, none of them named Mary or George .. 7
    Thomas Harding II (1-3) first wife was not named Martha 9
    Thomas Harding III (1-8) was not the man who married Mary Giles 11
    Henry Moseley's wife was not Ann Knott 12
    William Harding (2-1), grandfather of Hopkins Harding (2-15) was not the son of Henry Harding (1-6) and Jane Arledge. 14
    William Harding (4-2) is not the son of Charles Harding (2-2) of Stafford County, Virginia. He is the son of Joseph Combs I (4-1) of Stafford 15
    Joseph Harding (4-21) of Loudoun County Virginia, is the son of Joseph Combs II 16
    Parentage of Henry Harding (3-1) and Family of Henry Harding (1-6) 17
    William Harding (2-27) of Clarke Co., Iowa was not the son of Joseph Harding (4-21) of Loudoun County, Virginia 18
    Thomas Harden (1-23) of Rockingham Co., NC and his family 20
    The True Ancestry of Hiram Harden (1-88) of Shelby Co., Tennessee, and William Presley Harden (1-87) of Boone Co., Arkansas 24
    The Ashby Connection 27
Chapter 2   DNA Results Analysis 31
    Results from the Harding DNA Projects 31
Chapter 3   Family Genealogies with References 47
    Family 1: Thomas Harding of Northumberland Co., VA 47
    Family 2: William Harding of Northumberland County, VA 74
    Family 3: Henry Harding of Stafford County, Virginia 89
    Family 4: Joseph Combs, William Harden and Clarissa Million of Stafford County, Virginia 110
    Family 5: Mark Hardin and Mary of Northumberland Co., VA 135
    Unrelated Hardin Families of the Northern Neck of Virginia 146
Chapter 4   Virginia County Records 150
    Virginia Military Records 150
    Land Grants of the Northern Neck of Virginia 151
    Arlington County, Virginia Records 151
        Will Books 151
        Marriage Records 151
    Culpeper County, Virginia Records 152

    Deed Records 152
    Probate Records 153
    Federal Census Records 153
    Marriage Records (from marriage register) 153
    Personal Property Tax Lists 153
Essex County, Virginia Records 154
    Will and Deed Book 1 1664-1677 154
    Deed Book 2 1656-1664 (Film # 1929926) 154
    Deed Book 3 1664-1668 155
    Deed Book 4 1668-1672 155
    Deed Book 5 1672-1676 156
    Deed Book 6 1676-1682 157
    Deed Book 7 1682-1687 157
    Deed Book 8 1686-1692 157
    Deed Book 9 1695-1699 157
    Deed and Will Book 10 1699-1702 157
    Deed and Court Book 13 1707-1711 158
    Deed and Will Book 14 1711-1716 159
    Deed and Will Book 14 1711-1716 159
    Will Book 4 159
Fairfax County, Virginia Records 159
    Deed Books 159
    Will Books 161
    Court Order Books 1749-1753 162
    Court Order Books 1754-1755 162
    Court Order Books 1757-1762 163
    Court Order Books 1763-1764 163
    Court Order Books 1768-1769 164
    Court Order Books 1770-1771 164
    Court Order Books 1772-1774 164
    Court Order Books 1783-1787 164
    Court Order Books 1788-1791 164
    Tax Lists 1782-1795 165
Fauquier County, Virginia Records 166
    Court Order Books Volume 1 1759-1762 166
    Court Order Books Volume 2 1763-1764 167
    Court Order Books Volume 3 1764-1768 167
    Will Books 167
    Deed Books 167
    Marriage Records 168
    1784 Personal Property Tax Lists 169

Frederick County, Virginia Records 169
    Will Books 169
    Deed Books 169
    Court Order Book 1 1743-1745 170
    Court Order Book 2 1745-1748 171
    Court Order Book 3 1748-1749 171
    Court Order Book 4 1750-1753 171
    Court Order Book 5 1753-1754 171
    Court Order Book 6 1754-1755 171
    Court Order Book 7 1755-1758 171
    Court Order Book 8 1758-1760 172
    Court Order Book 9 1760-1762 172
    Personal Property Tax Lists 172
Halifax County, Virginia Records 173
    Will and Probate Records 173
    Deed Records 173
Hampshire County, Virginia Records 173
    Land Tax Lists 173
    Personal Property Tax Lists 174
    Deed Books 174
    Will Books 177
    From Find A Grave Index 178
Lancaster County, Virginia Records 178
    Deed Book 178
    Will Book 178
    Court Order Books 178
    Court Order Book 178
    Order Book 8 1729-1743 178
Loudoun County, Virginia Harding Records 179
    Personal Property Tax Lists (SLC 975.528 R4h) 179
    Marriage Records 1751-1880 180
    Will Books 180
    Court Order Books 182
    Order Book A 1757-1762 182
    Order Book B 1762-1765 182
    Order Book C 1765-1767 182
    Order Book E 1770-1773 182
    Order Book F 1773-1776 182
    Order Book G 1776-1783 183
    Order Book H 1783-1785 183
    Order Book I 1785-1786 183

- Order Book K 1787-1788 184
- Order Book L 1788-1790 184
- Order Book N 1790-1791 184
- Order Book P 1792-1794 184
- Order Book Q 1794-1796 184
- Order Book 7 1813-1815 184
- Minute Book 1 1815-1817 185
- Minute Book 2 1817-1819 185
- Minute Book 3, 4, 5, 6, 7 1819-1826 185
- Minute Book 8 1826-1828 185
- Minute Book 1a 1829-1830 186
- Minute Book 1 1830-1832 187
- Minute Book 4 1834-1836 187
- Deed Books Index 188
- Federal Census Records 190

Middlesex County, Virginia Records 191
- Deed Books 191
- Will Books 192
- Christ Church Parish Register 192
- Marriage Records 192

Northumberland Co., Virginia Records 193
- Deeds and Wills A 1650-1652 193
- Deeds and Wills B 1652-1658 193
- Deeds and wills C 1658-1666 193
- Deeds and Wills D 1666-1672 195
- Deeds and Wills E 1707-1720 (re-recorded) 196
- Deeds and Wills F 1710-1713 196
- Deeds and Wills G 1718-1725 196
- Deeds and Wills H 1726-1729 198
- Deeds and Wills I 1737-1743 199
- Deeds and Wills J 1743-1747 199
- Deeds and Wills K 1747-1749 200
- Deeds and Wills Book 1 1750-1751 200
- Deeds and Wills Book 2 1752-1754 200
- Deeds and Wills Book 3 1754-1756 200
- Deeds and Wills 4 1756-1758 201
- Wills and Deeds 5 1758-1762 201
- Wills and Deeds 6 1762-1766 202
- Wills and Deeds 7 1766-1770 203
- Wills and Deeds 8 1770-1772 204
- Wills and Deeds 9 1772-1776 204

    Wills and Deeds 10 1776-1780 204
    Wills and Deeds 12 1782-1785 204
    Wills and Deeds 13 1785-1787 204
    Wills and Deeds 14 1787-1793 205
    Wills and Deeds 15 1794-1799 205
    Wills and Deeds 17 1803-1808 206
    Wills and Deeds 19 1811-1815 206
    Wills and Deeds 22 1819-22 206
    Wills and Deeds 25 1831-1833 206
Northumberland County VA Order Books 207
    Order Book 1 1652-1657 207
    Book 2 1657-1661 208
    Book 3 1661-1666 208
    Book 4 1666-1678 208
    Book 5 1678-1698 209
    Book 6 1699-1713 213
    Book 7 1713-1719 214
    Book 8 1719-1729 217
    Book 9 1729-1737 218
    Book 10 1737-1743 219
    Book 11 1743-1749 221
    Book 12 1750 to 1753 222
    Book 13 1753-1756 223
    Book 14 1756-1758 224
    Book 15 1758-1762 Partial Index from Page 362 225
    Census Records 225
    Personal Property Tax Lists 226
    Northern Neck Land Grants 229
    Marriage Records of Northumberland 230
    St. Stephens Parish Register 230
Orange County, Virginia Records 232
    Court Records 232
    Deed Abstracts 234
    Northern Neck Land Grants 235
Prince William County, Virginia Records 235
    Northern Neck Land Grants 235
    Will and Deed Abstracts 235
    Deed Abstracts 236
    Court Order Books 237
Richmond Co., VA Records 238
    North Farnham Parish 238

Deeds Book 8 238
Court Order Book 9 1721-1732 238
Will Book 2 238
Will Book 7 239
Russell County, Virginia Records 239
United States Census Records 239
Marriage Records 241
Probate Records 242
Revolutionary War Pension Filed Russell Co. 242
Shenandoah Co., Virginia Records 242
Will and Probate Records 242
Deed Books 243
Marriage Records 246
Personal Property Tax Lists 247
Spotsylvania County, Virginia Records 249
Probate Records 250
Census Records 250
Stafford County, Virginia Records 250
Military Pension Records 254
Northern Neck Land Grants 255
From the St. Paul's Parish Register 255
From the Overwharton Parish Register 255
Miscellaneous Records 257
Index to lost Deed and Will books 257
Will and Deed Book M 1729-1767 258
Will and Deed Book P 1755-1764 259
Deeds and Wills Book S 1780-1787 259
Deeds and Wills Book AA 1810-1813 259
Deeds and Wills Book GG 1825-1827 260
Court Order Book 1790-1793 261
Land Tax Records 261
Westmoreland Co., VA Records 277
"Virginia Colonial Soldiers" by L D Bookstruck 277
Court Order Book 278
Court Order Book 1698-1705 278
Court Order Books 278
Deed and Will Book 279
Deed and Will Book 11 279
Deed and Will Book 12 279
Deed and Will Book 13 279
Deed and Will Book 14 280

  Deed and Will Book 14 280
Chapter 5 North Carolina County Records 281
  Caswell Co., NC Records 281
    Federal Census Records 281
    Deed Records 281
  Guilford Co., NC Records 284
    Federal Census 284
    Deed Books Index 285
    Will Books 285
    Marriage Records 285
  Johnston Co., NC Records 286
    Deed Books 286
  Orange Co., NC Records 287
    1790 Federal Census 287
    Marriage Records 287
    Deed Records 288
    Will and Probate Records 288
  Randolph Co., NC Records 290
    Federal Census Records 290
    Deed Books 291
  Rockingham Co., NC Records 291
    Federal Census Records 291
    Marriage Record Index 292
    Deed Records 292
    Will Records 293
Chapter 6 Tennessee County Records 296
  Giles Co., Tennessee Records 296
    Federal Census Records 296
    Deed Records 296
  Shelby Co., Tennessee Records 297
    Probate Records 297
    Deed Records 297
    Marriage Records 297
    Taxation Records 298
    Federal Census Records 298
  Williamson Co., Tennessee Records 299
    Taxation Records 299
    Census Records 299
    Marriage Records 299
    Deed Records 300
    Will and Probate Records 301

Chapter 7   Alabama, Arkansas, Georgia County Records 303
- Lauderdale County, Alabama Records 303
  - Will and Probate Records 303
  - Gravestone Records 304
- Arkansas County Records 304
  - Federal Census Records 304
- Warren County, Georgia Records 305
  - Will and Probate Records 305

Chapter 8   Indiana County Records 306
- Clark Co., Indiana Records 306
  - Census Records 306
  - Marriage Records 307
  - Cemetery Records 307
- Dearborn Co., Indiana Records 307
  - From History of Dearborn County 307
  - Marriage Records 307
  - Federal Census Records 308
- Marion Co., Indiana Records 308
  - Revolutionary War Pension Records 308

Chapter 9   Kentucky County Records 310
- Anderson Co., Kentucky Records 310
  - Personal Property Tax Records 310
  - Deed Records 310
- Bath Co., Kentucky Records 311
  - Will and Probate Records 311
- Clark Co., Kentucky Records 312
  - Deed Records 312
- Franklin Co., Kentucky Records 314
  - Federal Census Records 315
  - Court Records 315
  - Deed Records 317
  - Marriage Bond Records 317
  - Personal Property Tax Lists 318
- Henry Co., Kentucky Records 322
  - Federal Census Records 322
  - Marriage Records 323
  - Revolutionary War Pension Applications 323
  - Will Records 324
  - Deed Records 324
  - Personal Property Tax Lists 326
- Hopkins Co., Kentucky Records 327

- Federal Census Records 327
- Deed Records 328
- Will Records 329
- Jefferson Co., Kentucky Records...329
  - Federal Census Records 330
  - Will Books 330
  - Deed Books 331
  - Court Records 335
  - Federal Census Records 336
  - Marriages 336
  - Personal Property and Land Tax Records......................................339
- Livingston Co., Kentucky Records...347
  - Will Books 347
- Mercer Co., Kentucky Records 347
  - Will and Probate Records...347
  - Marriage Records 347
  - Personal Property Tax Lists 349
- Nelson Co., Kentucky Records 350
  - Will and Probate Records...350
  - Personal Property Tax Lists 350
- Oldham Co., Kentucky Records 351
  - Deed Records 351
  - Personal Property tax lists 355
  - Will and Probate Records...356
  - Marriage Records 357
  - Federal Census Records 358
- Owen Co., Kentucky Records..360
  - United States Census Records 360
  - Personal Property Tax Books 362
  - Will Books 367
  - Deed Books 367
  - Marriage Records..371
  - Find A Grave Index 371
- Washington Co., Kentucky Records..372
  - Marriage Records 372
  - Deed Records 372
  - Wills and Inventories 373
  - Federal Census Records 374
  - Personal Property Tax Lists 375

Chapter 10   Missouri County Records 379
- Pike Co., Missouri Records 379

- Federal Census Records 379
- Marriage Records 381
- Will and Probate Records 382
- Cemetery Records 383

Chapter 11   Ohio and South Carolina County Records 384
- Belmont Co., Ohio Records 384
  - Census Records 384
- Guernsey Co., Ohio Records 384
  - Marriage Records 384
  - Probate Records 384
  - Census Records 384
- Laurens Co., South Carolina Records 386
  - Will and Probate Records 386
  - Deed Records 386

Chapter 12   Comments on published articles 388
- Article 1: Mrs. O. A. Keach, Tyler's Quarterly 388
- Article 2: Eva Hardin Benning, Francois Benin 400
- Article 3: Lucy Lemoine Waring, "Hardings of Northumberland Co., VA" 401
- Article 4: Fredna Tweedt Irvine, "Henry Hardin of California" 402
- Article 5: J. Oran Hardin, "Hardin USA" 402
- Article 6: Dorothy Ford Wulfeck, "Hardings in Virginia and Kentucky" 403

Index   Including Individual Numbers 404

Introduction

For the last fifty years, I have attempted to trace the ancestry of Thomas Harden (1-23), who died in Rockingham Co., North Carolina in 1809. His daughter, Jane Harden (1-42), who married William Hornbuckle (1-42), is my ancestor.

I traced him from Rockingham and Caswell counties back to Fairfax County, VA, where Jane Harden (1-42) and William Hornbuckle (1-42) married, and back to Cople Parish, Westmoreland Co., VA, where he lived in the 1750s.

Among his sons were Peter (1-50) and Presley Harden (1-43), names that appear together almost exclusively among the descendants of the daughters of William and Peter Presley of Northumberland Co., VA, who had no male descendants.

This led me to consider the Harding families in the Northern Neck of Virginia as possible ancestors for Thomas Harden (1-23) of Rockingham. Further research led to his possibly being the son of John Harden (1-10) of Westmoreland Co., Virginia, and his wife Jane Barecraft, whose brother married a descendant of the Presley family. Furthermore, Peter Harden, a man near Thomas Harden's age, lived in Westmoreland in the 1750s. This Peter witnessed a deed for Ann Washington, widow of Augustine Washington, in 1762 in Fairfax County, but is heard from no further.

However, I could find no proof that this is my line.

I started with research on the most prominent Harding family in Northumberland County, the descendants of Thomas Harding (1-1) and Anne Moseley (1-1). Their connections and descendants are the subject of numerous publications ranging from 1920 to the 1970s and 1980s.[1] Most researchers accepted the results of that early research. (100 years ago)

However, when I researched the family in detail, I noticed many statements of family relationships in these published works that had no proof behind them. I accepted them because most family researchers accepted them.

Still, the contradictions were frustrating. Many names appeared in families and were never heard from again. Others appeared to be duplicates. In many cases, two ancestries were supplied for the same man and in others two individuals were combined in one.

---

[1] See reviews at the end of this book for Mrs. O. A. Keach, Fredna Tweedt Irvine, Eva Harding Benning, Lucy Lemoine Waring, and Dorothy Ford Wulfeck.

I had to sort this out if there was a chance of success in tracing my own line.

In the late 1990s, I went to Salt Lake City to do research in the wonderful genealogical library there. At the time there was little genealogy on the Internet, so microfilm was the only avenue open. Almost on a whim, I decided to look at the three documents mentioned in a then seventy-year-old article on the Harding family I'd found years earlier in Tyler's Quarterly by Mrs. O. A. Keach that traced the immigrant Thomas Harding (1-1) of Northumberland County, Virginia back to George and Mary Harding of London based on the will of Thomas Orley and two subsequent court records. This article at the time was the gold standard for the family and remains so today. Everyone followed her theories, including many later writers. Why would anyone ever doubt her work?

First, I read the will of Thomas Orley and discovered he left his estate to George and Mary Harding of London, his sister and brother-in-law, but never mentioned Thomas Harding (1-1) of Northumberland or any of his children, which Mrs. Keach claimed were Thomas Orley's relatives. The aha moment came when I read the lawsuit filed in Northumberland Co., Virginia by a representative of George and Mary Harding of London, again with no mention of the Northumberland Harding family, the opposite of what Mrs. Keach claimed.[2]

I still remember my exact thoughts. "This is the London family collecting the estate, not the Northumberland family of Thomas Harding (1-1). Mrs. Keach was wrong, the Orley and Harding families of London are not connected to Thomas Harding (1-1) of Northumberland and never were!"

I remember reading the document a few times, then I unrolled the reel and put it back on the shelf. "If she's wrong on this, how much else is wrong with her article? What do the records really say?"

After I got home, I reread the article. At the time I worked in Beverly Hills, near the LDS Temple Genealogy Library, which had almost all the microfilm of the records of Northumberland, Westmoreland, Fairfax, and other Virginia counties. Okay, I decided, I'm going to read through every one of these films, copy out the records word for word, and see how much of the material in the published works could be proven from the original records.

Since all the Northumberland County records were on film five minutes from where I worked, the job was easy, if time consuming. I expected four

---

[2] See complete text of these documents in Chapter 1

or five pages of records to emerge from this research. I also expected a better picture of how the family fits together.

I abstracted word for word most of the court, will and deed records of Northumberland County, except for the later ones, which are summaries. I also added, either word for word or in summary, all the records I could find for Stafford, Westmoreland, Prince William, Fairfax, and Loudoun counties.

After two months of research, I found that virtually every family connection in print was wrong. First to go was the English ancestry of Thomas Harding I (1-1) of Northumberland. Second were the four sons of his son Henry Harding (1-6), who married Jane Arledge (1-6). Next was William, an imaginary son of his son William (1-5). Among the mass of original records, I found incorrect published dates, missing children, connections that had been totally missed, and people who never existed.

I originally published the results of my research in 1998 but that book did not reach a wide audience. Now, 20 years later and after more major research on these families in Virginia, North Carolina, Kentucky, Tennessee, Alabama, Arkansas, Ohio, and Missouri., I have filled out the descendants of my own ancestor, Thomas Harden (1-23), who died in Rockingham Co., NC after May 25, 1809,[3] and found Y-DNA results that confirm my conclusion 20 years ago that five separate families existed in Northumberland County, Virginia, including a previously unknown family grouping.

In this book, as I did in the first edition, I have assigned a unique number to each person connected to the five families and their spouses. Husbands and wives have the same number to make their connection clear. The first number is the family number, one through five, followed by a dash, then the individual number. When you see the number (2-5), this means the individual is person #5 in Family #2.

In the first chapter, I present detailed discussions of major corrections to the family relationships in the five different Hardin-Harden-Harding families. Many researchers will be shocked to discover they are not descended from the Thomas Harding (1-1) and Anne Moseley (1-1) family at all. Others will dispute my conclusions without reading them. Read these discussions carefully and you will see that major changes are needed in the thousands of family trees published on the Internet.

In the second chapter of the book, I discuss the DNA results relevant to the families covered in this book, which require major realignment of the Northern Neck Harding families.

---

[3] Rockingham County, North Carolina Wills. Full text in the records section.

In the third chapter I present a detailed genealogy of each family, including children as known, followed by a detailed listing of the records pertaining to each person by county and in date order, giving each a timeline for their life. Each brief record includes the book and page reference to the full record by state and county presented in chapters four to twelve. I personally extracted all these records from microfilm copies of the originals, so each person's family record is based on original records. I numbered the Northumberland record books for ease of reference although no numbers exist for the early books. I have carried the lines down into the 1800s, in some cases as late as 1850, so descendants should be able to connect to their correct lines without difficulty.

The extracted records in chapters four to eleven are the heart of the book. Each record, except later deeds and court records, contains the full text with reference to its location in the original books so the researcher can easily check them. I marked each person I identified as a member of one of the five families with their unique number for easy reference. The detailed index also includes these unique numbers and the name of their spouse. For married people, both spouses have the same number. Persons with no number are not members of one of the five families or I am uncertain which individual they are.

In Chapter 12 I include extensive comments on Mrs. Keach's article so you can see the errors she made and how the original records correct them. I also review several later Harding works which draw on Mrs. Keach's article and show how unreliable most of the existing secondary research resources are.

With few exceptions that are noted in the records section, I extracted all the records in this book myself from digital or microfilm copies of original courthouse records to ensure their accuracy.

Finally, a note on spelling. At various times all these families used the spelling Hardin, Harden, or Harding interchangeably, sometimes even using different spellings in the same document. As a convention, I have used the most common spelling for each family in the index but have left the variant spellings in the extracted records. If you can't find the person you want, check each spelling in the index.

I make no claim that my reconstruction of the families involved is the final word on the subject. I present this material so other researchers will have a solid base from which to proceed. All comments are welcome.

Lee Pound
September 2025

Chapter 1
Corrections to Errors in Published Sources

George Harding and Mary Orley are NOT the Parents of Thomas Harding (1-1) of Northumberland County, Virginia

This is a strong statement to make given the thousands of people who have accepted this parentage over the last hundred years. This error and many others started with an article in Tyler's Quarterly[4] by Mrs. O. A. Keach in 1920 which purported to prove Thomas Harding's (1-1) ancestry and at least three generations of his descendants.

As I stated in the Introduction, this article contains numerous errors, misquotations, and blatant changes of dates in some records to make her theory fit.

These errors have become so deeply embedded in the mythology of the Harding family's origins that researchers now give them as facts with no further research.

The belief that George Harding, grocer of London, and his wife Mary (Orley) Harding were the parents of the immigrant Thomas Harding I (1-1) of Northumberland Co., VA is based on Mrs. Keach's statement in her article that two records in Northumberland Co., Virginia, and a power of attorney in London prove the connections. This statement is not true.

In this chapter I will prove that her interpretation is wrong. We will begin with the actual deed, court, and will records involved both in England and in Northumberland County, Virginia. First is the Orley and Harding

---

[4] This article is reprinted in full, with detailed comments in the reviews section at the end of this book.

family timeline of the births and deaths in Thomas Orley's family and George Harding's family.

Timeline for Thomas Orley and George Harding families[5]

1615, 30 Apr, **Thomas Orley** (Sr.) married Anne Wing, in St. Mary Whitechapel, London, England

1619, 30 March 1619 **Thomas Orley (Jr.)**, son of Thomas and Anne Orley, baptized in St. Mary Whitechapel, Stepney, London, England.

1622, 25 April, **Mary Orley**, daughter of Thomas and Anne Orley, baptized in St. Mary Whitechapel, Stepney, London, England.

1647, 27 February, **Anne Harding,** daughter of George and Mary, baptized in St. Mary Whitechapel, Stepney, London, England

1651, 25 October, **Mary Harding,** daughter of George and Mary, baptized in St. Mary Whitechapel, Stepney, London, England

1655, 1 July, **Elizabeth Harding,** daughter of George and Mary, baptized in St. Mary Whitechapel, Stepney, London England

1661, 2 February, **Samuel Harding**, son of George and Mary, baptized in St. Mary Whitechapel, Stepney, London England

1662, 11 September, **Thomas Orley (Sr)**, buried, St. Mary Whitechapel, Stepney, London, England

1662, 11 Aug **Thomas Orley (Jr)** wrote his will.[6] He died between 11 Aug. 1662 and 8 Oct. 1662 in Cherry Point, Northumberland Co., Virginia

1663, 28 February, **Samuell Hardine** buried St. Mary Whitechapel, London, England

1664, 22 September, London, England, **George Harding, and Mary** his wife, get a Power of Attorney to collect their portion as heirs of Thomas Orley's estate in Cherry Point, Northumberland Co., Virginia

1665, 7 March, **John Harding,** son of George and Mary, baptized in St. Mary Whitechapel, Stepney, London, England

1675/6, 19 January in Northumberland Co., Virginia court,[7] Richard Parrott, attorney for Ann Harding, Mary Harding, George Harding, Mary Harding, and Thomas Orley, heirs of Thomas Orley, deceased sued the estate of William Jolland, who married Thomas Orley's widow.

---

[5] All dates in England are from the Parish Register of St. Mary Whitechapel, London, England
[6] Northumberland County, Virginia wills, in full on the next page
[7] Northumberland County, Virginia Court records, Book 4 Page 126

Correction of Errors in Published Sources

This proves that the London Hardin family consisted of the following persons at the time Thomas Orley wrote his will: George Harding and Mary his wife, who was Thomas Orley's sister, daughters Anne Harding, Mary Harding, Elizabeth Harding, and son Samuel Harding. Their son John Harding was not yet born.

Mrs. Keach based her entire argument on three documents which she quotes in part, the will of Thomas Orley, a power of attorney issued in London to the London Harding family, and a court case in Northumberland County, Virginia where the London family sued to collect the legacy of Thomas Orley that they were owed. on the assumption that Thomas Orley was the uncle of Thomas Harding (1-1) of Northumberland County, Virginia. She uses the similarity of names in the London George Harding family and the Virginia Thomas Harding (1-1) family to make these three documents relate to the Virginia family. These documents, quoted in full on the next page, make no reference to Thomas Harding. There is also no mention of any of his children in these documents. They refer solely to the London family and not to anybody in Northumberland except Thomas Orley, his widow Rebecca, and her new husband William Jollins.

In the Power of Attorney dated 1664, George and Mary Harding and their daughters Anne and Mary Harding, all of London, attempted to collect the estate left to them.

In Northumberland County, Virginia, at the same time, Thomas Harding (1-1) and his wife Anne had only two children, Anne (1-2) born about 1662 and Thomas (1-3), born in 1664.

Mrs. Keach read the documents wrong, assumed the Thomas Harding (1-1) family of Virginia was the petitioner and so stated without qualification, and added Mary Harding to her list of Thomas Harding's children to make the family match the document. Every researcher since then has copied her. Mrs. F. F. Everett Bowen, quoted in Wulfeck, added a son George to the list of Thomas Harding's children.

The children Mary Harding and George Harding never existed in Thomas Harding's (1-1) family and are a figment of Mrs. Keach's and Mrs. Bowen's imagination.

Following are the full texts of the three documents in question, the will of Thomas Orley, the Power of Attorney signed by George and Mary Harding in London, England, and the court hearing in Northumberland granting the Harding family of London their portion of the estate of Thomas Orley.

The will of Thomas Orley is badly damaged, which Mrs. Keach's article fails to make clear. In fact, only about one quarter of the bequest section has survived and is written exactly as follows. Each line in the bequest section except the first is missing about six to ten words:

The Will of Thomas Orley 1662

IN THE NAME OF GOD Amen I **Thomas Orley** in CHERRY POINT NECK in the County of Northumberland in Virginia, Planter, beinge of sound & perfect memory praised bee God for the same, yet knowinge the weake & fraile condition of mans body and the uncertainty of mans life, doe make this my Last Will and Testament in manner & forme followinge: Imprs. I doe give & bequeath my Soule unto God my Creator hopeinge by the merits of Jesus Christ my Redeemer after the expiracon of my time here to obtaine an eternall waight of glory wth : him in heaven hereafter; And my body I committ to the earth from whence it came: to be buryed in Christian buryall and for my worldly Estate, I dispose of it as followeth, It. I give & bequeath unto my deare & loveinge Wife, Rebeckah Orley, after paymt. of my just debts, all that messuage or tenement whereon I now live, together with all the land & priviledges thereunto belonginge, to have & to hold to her and the heires of her body lawfully to bee begotten under the same tenure by which I doe at pr:sent enjoy the same. Next, I doe herein give unto my deare Sister, Mary Harden, ye Wife of George Harden, Foure hundred tobco. is
to bee carefully
decease & deprt:
the first& soe in case of more
moreover it is my
from my Wife as heires
Unto John Harden's Sonne
Of Mary Harden his Wife
want of such issue unto
Orley Of Whitechappell Middlesex & his heyres;
It. I desire & bequeath
all my goods chattels
else under the rest
mediately after m
estate bee inventoried
ent men & that the
use without controversy I
the time of her wi
should intermarry

Correction of Errors in Published Sources

that such Husband
good caution forth
sd. personal Estate
appraysed after my decease
to succeed in the
land, alsoe I doe hereby appoynt,
John Tingey, Nicholas Owen & Walter Weekes to bee my Exrs. of this my last Will &Testamt., In Wittness whereof I have hereunto set my hand & seale this eleventh day of August 1662 Signed & delivered in the sight of Jno. Garner. Rich: Browne

Tho: Orley, ye Seale

The 8th 8ber [October] 1662. This Will was proved in Court by the oathes of the sd, Jno: Garner & Richd. Browne & is recorded.

The Power of Attorney of George and Mary Harding of London 1664

22 7ber 1664 By this Publick Instrumt: of procuracon or Lre. of Atorney. Be it Knowne unto all people yt: on ye 22th day ye month 7ber: Anno Dom: 1664, . . . before me Frederick Ixem, sole Notary and Tabellion Publlet to & for ye sd. Soveraigne Lord ye King, admitted and sworne, dwelling in this City of London, in ye p:sence of ye witnesses hereafter named p:sonally appeared Geo: Hardinge. Citizen & Grocer of London, & Mary Hardinge his Wife, Daughter of Tho: Orley & Anne his Wife, deced., & Sister of Tho: Orley late of Cherry Poynt in Potomack. Planter. deced., have made & doe make Capt. William Ball of London, Mariner, there & either of there lawfull Attorneys giveinge unto him special charge to receive from Rebecca Orley, late Wife & Exrx. of ye Last Will and Testamt: of the sd. Tho: Orley of Cherry Poynt aforesd. deced., & of & from William Jollins of Cherry Poynt aforesd:. Planter, her now Husband, or of either of them or there heyres or: goods whereso they shall be found all summes of money debts goods & things wt:soever as ye sd: William : Jollins & Rebecca his Wife or either of them noe doe or hereafter shall owe & be indebted unto ye sd: Constituants by Bill Book Legacy specialty or other wayes . . . In Witnesses whereof the sd. Constituants have put there hands & seales. This was thus don & passed in the Citty of London in ye p:sence of William : Scorey & Robt: Barson in Clarkes. Signed: Geo: Hardinge, Mary Hardinge (the mke: of). Witnesses Toby Michell, John Frodskain, Jam: Syer. P:sence William : Scorey, Robt. Barson in Clarkes Witnesses Toby Michell Geo Hardinge, John Frodskain, Jam: Syer The Mks; Of Mary Hardinge P:Sence William : Scorey, Robt:

5

Barson To all yt; shall see this p:sents Know yee that I Sr. ant: Bateman Knt., Lord ye Citty of London doe hearby make yt. Frederick Ixem who hsth signed ye Instrumt, before goeing, Notary &Tabellion Publick to & for ye admitted sworn. dwelling. in this to acts & other Writinges by him signed & attested in full fayth & creditt given in Corts; & out; In Fayth & Testamoney whereof we ye sd: Lord Maior & Aldermen of ye sd. Citty of London ye Seale of Mayoralty of ye same City to the presence have caused to be put & affixed, dated in London ye 20th 7br: Anno Dom 1664 & in ye 16th year. of ye Reigne of or: Soveraigne Lord Charles ye 2d. by ye Grace of God of England &c. The Seale[12]

The Order granting George Harding and Mary Orley their part of the Thomas Orley's estate in 1676.

Northumberland County, Virginia Court Order Book 4 Page 126, 19 January 1675/6 states: "Whereas it appears to this court that there is due unto Mr. Rich Parrott Esq Attorney for Ann Harding, Mary Harding, George Harding, Mary Harding and Thomas Orley, the heires of Thomas Orley, late of this County decd an estate according to appraisement amounting to the sum of fourteen thousand five hundred twenty-four pounds of tobacco, judgment is granted the said Mr. Richard Parrott, attorney as aforesaid for ye yet same agst the estate of William Jolland decd who married the Relict of ye said Thomas Orley and ordered ye the Sheriff possess ye said Mr. Parrott with the ---- of the sd Thomas Orley in right of the said prayers."

From the context of these documents, all refer to claims by the family of George and Mary Harding of London, England to Thomas Orley's estate.

Nobody in the family of Thomas Harding (1-1) is mentioned in these documents and nobody in the Thomas Harding family attempted to claim anybody's estate.

In Thomas Orley's will, the key bequest is to his sister Mary Harden, ye wife of George Harden. He also mentions John Harden's son, and Mary Harden, wife of unknown, and Orley of Whitechapel. None of the children of Thomas Harding I of Northumberland County, Virginia appears in this record, not Thomas, not Henry, not William, not John. This record cannot refer to his family.

The second document, the Power of Attorney issued in 1664 in London, makes it clear that George Harding and Mary his wife, sister of Thomas Orley of Cherry Point, with daughters Anne and Mary, are the London family and that the London family are the heirs of Thomas Orley.

The third document is the successful attempt by the London family to collect the legacy owed to them.

To repeat, in the court record above, George and Mary Harding, Ann Harding, Mary Harding and Thomas Orley hired an attorney in London to collect their estate. The heirs listed in the court record match the London family and the heirs listed in Thomas Orley's will.

In addition, there is no mention of Thomas Harding (1-1), or any of Thomas Harding's sons in the court record or in any other record pertaining to Thomas Orley. Mrs. Keach admits this in the first part of the following quote but proceeds with her conclusion anyway to end the quote with an unfounded, undocumented false assertion. *"He does not mention his nephew, Thomas Harding, in his will and had doubtless made generous provision for him."*

Far from proving that Thomas Harding (1-1)'s family claimed the legacy, these records prove that the London family claimed it and that Thomas Harding's family had no part in the legacy and no connection with the London family.

Thomas Harding (1-1) had six children, none of them named Mary or George

Thomas Harding (1-1), Sr. had six children. The names and order vary from that given by Mrs. Keach and by most other researchers. Mrs. Keach had most of the family correct except that she left out John (1-7) and added Mary. Mrs. Bowen added George. Both children were figments of the imagination derived from the records discussed in the previous section.

Mrs. Keach also added four children (*"probably Henry, William, Thomas, John" to quote Mrs. Keach*) to the family of Henry Harding (1-5).[8] The first two of these children were proven by DNA evidence to be unrelated to each other and the last two belong in other branches of the family. (See discussion in the segments on Henry and William Harding later in this Chapter.)

See the genealogy for Family 1 for references for the following table.

Thomas Harding's (1-1) only known children and grandchildren were:

1. Thomas[1] **Harding** (1-1) was born in England about 1630. He arrived in Northumberland County Virginia prior to 1658, when he received land from Richard Rice. He married **Anne Moseley** (1-1) about 1661 in

---

[8] See full text of her article at the end of this book.

Northumberland County, Virginia and died by 16 June 1675 in Northumberland Co., VA.

Children of Thomas[1] Harding and Anne Moseley:

 2 i. ANNE[2] HARDING (1-2) born about 1662 mentioned in the will of her Uncle John Moseley and in a deed of gift from her step-grandfather John Tyngey.

+ 3 ii. THOMAS HARDING (1-3) born 4 Sept 1664 St. Stephen's Parish, Northumberland Co., Virginia, married Miss Haynie and Ann, died 1691 Northumberland County, Virginia

 4 iii. John Harding (1-4) born by 6 Sept 1665 died after August 1667. John Tyngey mentions Thomas Harding's (1-1) oldest son and a younger son in August 1667. Since none of the other sons of Thomas Harding I (1-1) were[9] born before 1669, this must refer to a child who did not survive.

+ 5 iv. WILLIAM HARDING (1-5) born 20 July 1669 St. Stephen's Parish, Northumberland Co., Virginia, married Elizabeth Price, died 1696 Northumberland County, Virginia

+ 6 v. HENRY HARDING (1-6) born about 1672, married Jane (perhaps Arledge), died 1697 Northumberland County, Virginia

+ 7 vi. JOHN HARDING (1-7) born about 1674, married Anne Bennett, died 1714 Northumberland County, Virginia

3. Thomas[2] Harding II (Thomas[1]) (1-3) was born 4 Sept 1664 in St. Stephen's Parish, Northumberland Co., VA. He married first **Miss Haynie** about 1686 and second **Anne** (MNU) about 1689. He died before 2 September 1691 Northumberland Co., VA. His widow (1-3) married Luke Rowland (1-3) around 1694/5.

Children of Thomas[2] Harding II and Miss Haynie:

+ 8 i. THOMAS[3] HARDING III (1-8) born about 1688 in Northumberland County, Virginia, married Mary Berry 1707, died 1722 Northumberland County, Virginia

Children of Thomas[2] Harding II and Anne (MNU)

+ 9 ii. WILLIAM HARDING (1-9) born 15 Feb 1690 St. Stephen's Parish, Northumberland Co., Virginia, married and had two children. No further information

5. William[2] Harding (Thomas[1]) (1-5) was born 20 Jul 1669 in St. Stephen's Parish, Northumberland Co., VA. He married **Elizabeth**, possibly Price. Records show he admitted having an illegitimate child with her. He died by 16 December 1696 Northumberland Co., VA.

Children of William[2] Harding and Elizabeth:

+ 10 i. JOHN[3] HARDING (1-10) born October 1692 Northumberland Co., Virginia, married 1717 Jane (Barecraft) Trussell, died 1734 Northumberland County, Virginia

6. Henry[2] Harding (Thomas[1]) (1-6) was born about 1672 in Northumberland Co., VA. He married **Jane** about 1694. Her name is often

---

[9] See bios of Henry and John Harding in Family 1 for proof of approximate birth dates.

given as Arledge but no known records support that. He was still underage in August 1691, according to court rec3ords. (Northumberland CO 1678-98 p 529 and 564). He died by 8 August 1697 in Northumberland Co., VA. He had no known children.

7. John² Harding (Thomas¹) (1-7) was born about 1672 in Northumberland Co., VA. He married **Anne Bennett** before 1701 and died in Northumberland Co., VA before 15 Sept 1714. Anne was born 20 September 1676 in Northumberland County, Virginia, the daughter of Edward Bennett. After John Harding died, she married William Humphries. As her brother Cuthbert Bennett's next of kin, she administered Cuthbert's estate in 1718.

Children of John² Harding and Anne Bennett:

11   i. THOMAS³ HARDING (1-11) born about 1698, lived in Stafford County, Virginia in 1720. See later in Family #1.
12   ii. JOHN HARDING (1-12) born after 1701. On 30 March 1720 he, an orphan, was bound to Henry Garner by the Westmoreland County Court (CO 1720 Page 386) We have no record of his marriage whether he had any children or where he lived.
13   iii. WILLIAM HARDING (1-13) born after 1701. As an orphan, he was bound to Edmund Jeffries by Westmoreland County Court (CO 1720 Page 286). We have no record of his marriage or of any children or where he lived after 1720.

Thomas Harding II (1-3) first wife was not named Martha

One of the great disputes among descendants of Thomas Harding II (1-3) is the name of the daughter of John Haynie that Thomas Harding II (1-3) married and whether he was married once or twice. In most sources her name, when given at all, is given as Martha or Martha Ann Haynie.

The problem comes from several researchers making unwarranted assumptions about the family of John Haynie. Most of the speculation arises from two deeds in 1659 in which gifts are made to Martha and Elizabeth Haynie, daughters of John Haynie, and Susanna Warre, John Haynie's daughter-in-law (stepdaughter).[10]

The assumption is that since Elizabeth Haynie's marriage is known, Thomas Harding II (1-3) must have married Martha Haynie. Then, since

---

[10] All references in this segment can be found in Chapter 3, Family 1 and in the Northumberland County Court records in the records section for Virginia.

Harding Families of the Northern Neck of Virginia

Thomas Harding II (1-3) had a widow Anne (1-3), many speculate that Martha was Martha Anne or that Anne was Susanna Warre.

In fact, here is what is known about John Haynie's family:

By 1659 John Haynie had daughters Martha and Elizabeth.

By 1659 John Haynie had a "daughter-in-law" Susanne Ware (Warre).

A man named John Warre died by 1651 and left debts.

By 1660 Jane, the daughter of Nicholas Morris, was married to John Haynie and had a son Richard Haynie.

A daughter of John Haynie married Thomas Harding II (1-3), had a son Thomas, and died before 2 September 1692.

Anne (1-3), the executor of Thomas Harding II (1-3), married Luke Rowland (1- 3) before mid-1696.

John Haynie had a son John Haynie Jr.

Elizabeth Newman was related in some manner to John Haynie and his wife.

We do not know the birth dates of any of John Haynie's children.

So, cutting all the speculation out of what the Haynie researchers say, this is the most likely scenario for how the family developed:

John Warre, or a relative, married Jane Morris, daughter of Nicholas sometime before 1649-50 and had a daughter by him named Susannah, born 1650-51.

The widow Jane married John Haynie about 1653 or 1654.

John Haynie and Jane Morris had at least four children: Martha, Elizabeth, Richard, and John, the first three born before 1660, based on the two deeds of gift and the will of Nicholas Morris.

There is no reason that John Haynie and Jane Morris could not have had more daughters after 1660, perhaps more sons as well. Certainly, John was born after 1660.

Martha and Elizabeth would have been well over 30 at the time Thomas Harding II (1-3) married the daughter of John Haynie. Thomas was barely 22 and it would seem to me that he would marry a younger woman. Thus, the name of the daughter of John Haynie who married Thomas Harding II (1-3) remains unknown but is not Martha.

John Haynie's daughter died shortly after the birth of her son Thomas Harding. Note the language in John Haynie's 1692 request for guardianship in which he states he has sustained the child since birth three years earlier.

Thomas Harding married second about 1689 a woman named Anne --, whose maiden name is not known and who was almost certainly not related to John Haynie, and had a son William in 1690, who was not claimed by John Haynie as his grandson.

After Thomas died, Anne was named his executor (no record of this until the 1696 items). Anne Harding (1-3), his widow, married Luke Rowland (1-3) by 1696 and he died shortly thereafter.

In 1698 Anne Rowland (1-3), widow of Luke Rowland (1-3), administered Luke Rowland's (1-3) estate.

In summary:

John Haynie (c 1624-1697) married the widow Jane (Morris) Warre as his first wife.

Martha Haynie born by 1659 married unknown.

Elizabeth Haynie born by 1659 married Elliston.

Richard Haynie born by 1660.

John Haynie Jr.

Daughter Haynie born about 1663-1665 died about 1689 married Thomas Harding II (1-3) and had one son, Thomas Harding III (1-8) born 1688-89 died 1722.

(Note: Thomas Harding II (1-3) married second Anne ---- and had a son William Harding (1-9) born 1690. Anne (1-3) married Luke Rowland (1-3) and died by 1697-8. Anne is unrelated to John Haynie.)

Thomas Harding III (1-8) was not the man who married Mary Giles

Over 6,000 trees on Ancestry are based on the claim that the Thomas Harding (c 1685-1737), who married Mary Giles and whose will was recorded in Book 1725-1737 on Page 272, Inventory Page 299, Settlement Page 326 in Henrico County, Virginia, was identical to Thomas Harding III (1-8) of Northumberland County, Virginia.

Thomas of Henrico had two sons, Thomas and William, and one daughter Mary, all of whom received land in Goochland and Henrico counties.

In this book I have documented the life and death and children of Thomas Harding III (1-8), son of Thomas Harding II (1-3) and a daughter of John Haynie in Family #1. He is clearly not the same man who lived in Henrico County.

In addition, over 1,000 researchers on Ancestry.com placed this same Thomas Harding who married Mary Giles as a son of Henry Harding (1-6) who I have proven in this book had no children.

In fact, the parentage of Thomas Harding who married Mary Giles in unknown at this time.

Both connections are incorrect and need to be removed from any tree where they appear.

Henry Moseley's wife was not Ann Knott

In several sources, the wife of Henry Moseley and mother of Anne Moseley (1-1), who married Thomas Harding I (1-1), is given as Ann Knott, the daughter of George and Elizabeth Knott. This identification does not appear in Mrs. Keach's article. However, it does appear in most other sources. Its origin appears to be from a genealogist, Kathryn Gottschalk, who is quoted in Wulfeck.

This identification is totally erroneous. According to deed and will abstracts, Henry Moseley was about 40 when he gave a deposition 20 November 1654. This means he was born about 1614. According to the same records, George Knott was age 36 on 20 August 1655, making him born about 1619.

On 18 November 1655 George Knott made his will, naming wife Elizabeth, son George, son John, son William, daughter Ann and brother George Berry. On 25 Feb 1660, Elizabeth Bennett, widow of John Bennett, mentions her children George Knott when he comes of age, John Knott and Ann Knott. On 28 May 1660, the will of John Bennett mentions godson John Knott and says Ann Knott to have no legacy from him. On 1 Jan 1664, the will of Sam Mann mentions daughter Mary, Wife Elizabeth, George Nott one cow and John Knott half of the land.

Elizabeth then married John Tyngey about 1665 or 1666 and Tyngey died in 1667. Tyngey's wife before Elizabeth was the widow of Henry Moseley, Ann --- Moseley, who was dead by 1666.

From the above it is clear that in 1655, when Henry Moseley died, Ann Knott, the daughter of George Knott was most likely barely into her teens, if that, and was still single five years after Henry Moseley died.

It is also clear that George Knott was younger than Henry Moseley and could not be his father-in-law and that Ann Knott, daughter of George, was slightly younger than her supposed daughter Ann Moseley.

The graphic below and the following genealogies show the exact connections between all these families in an easy-to-read format. Children of each couple are in connected gray boxes.

Correction of Errors in Published Sources

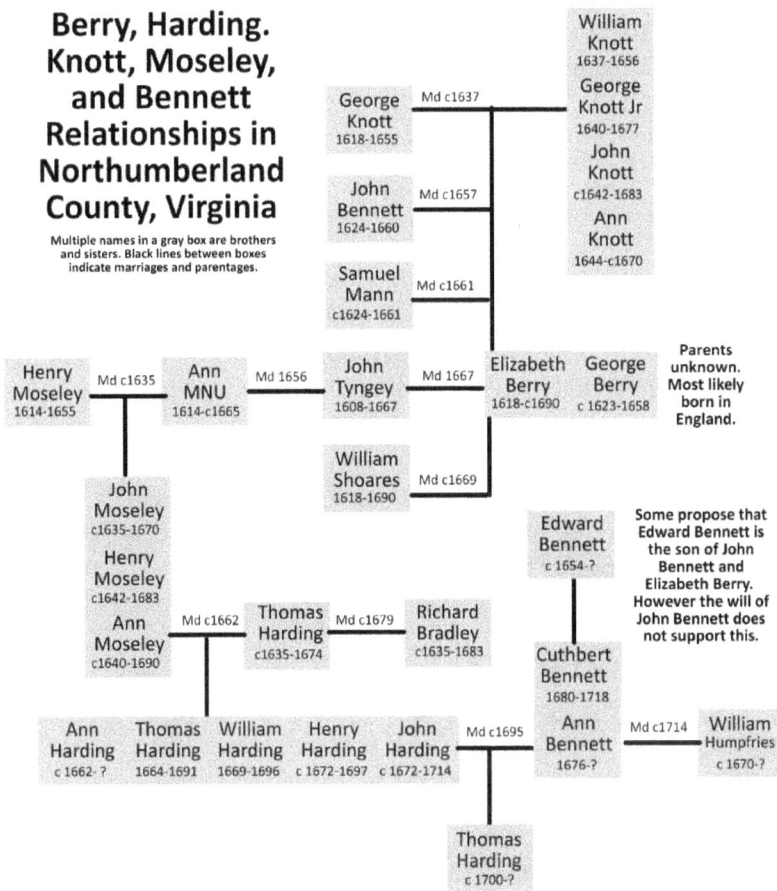

1. **Henry¹ Moseley** was born about 1614 in England. He married **Ann (MNU)** about 1634 in Virginia. He died 20 January 1655/56 in Northumberland County, Virginia. Ann married second **John Tingey** (1608-1667) before 23 March 1656/57.

    2   i. John² Moseley born about 1635, died 20 May 1670 Northumberland County, VA
    3   ii. Henry Moseley about 1642 to after 1664 Northumberland County
    4   iii. Anne Moseley about 1643 died after 1683 Northumberland. She married Thomas Harding (1-1) about 1662 in Northumberland and married second Richard Bradley about 1679. See Family 1 for their children.

1. **Elizabeth¹ Berry** was born about 1618 in England. She married **George¹ Knott** (1618-1655) about 1637. He died 20 March 1655/56 in Northumberland County Virginia. Elizabeth Berry married second **John Bennett** (1624-1660) in Northumberland Co., VA. After he died, she married

Samuel Mann (c1624-1665) about 6 June 1661. After he died, she married **John Tingey** (1608-1667) in early 1667. After he died, she married **William Shoares** before 22 June 1669. He died 28 August 1695 in Northumberland County, Virginia.

    2   i. William² Knott born about 1637, died 1656 Stafford County VA
    3   ii. George Knott born about 1640, died 1677 in Northumberland County, Virginia
    4   iii. John Knott born about 1642 died 1683 in Northumberland County, Virginia
    5   iv. Anne Knott born about 1644, died after 1670.

Note that Anne Knott, daughter of George Knott and Elizabeth Berry, was born about 1644, while Ann the wife of Henry Moseley was born about 1618 or so. As you can see from the graphic, the only connection between these two families is that John Tingey married the widow of Henry Moseley and the widow of George Knott in sequence, creating the records that have confused genealogists ever since.

Full transcripts of the records pertaining to each person in this chart are available in published sources and on the website www.colonialsettlers-md-va.us. Search by name for the records.

William Harding (2-1), grandfather of Hopkins Harding (2-15) was not the son of Henry Harding (1-6) and Jane Arledge.

This family was the most difficult to construct since its existence is poorly reported in the sources. I have looked at the St. Stephen's Parish Register in high magnification, making it clear that William Harding (2-1) had sons Charles Harding (2-2) and Francis Harding (2-3) born in 1704 and son Thomas Harding (2-4) born in 1706. This requires me to propose the existence of a William Harding (2-1) not related to Thomas Harding I (1-1) of Northumberland Co. since this William Harding (2-1) must have been born by about 1683, when no Northumberland Harding men were having children.

Some points:

DNA shows that William Harding (2-1) is not related to his purported brother Henry Harding. (3-1) (See DNA discussion in Chapter 3) The DNA, along with the earlier birthdates for both William Harding (2-1), discussed in this section, and Henry Harding (3-1), discussed in the next section, prove that neither man could be the son of Henry Harding (1-6).

Correction of Errors in Published Sources

Francis Harding (2-3) witnessed a will in 1721 and proved it in 1726. There is no other Francis Harding (2-3) who could have done so except this one.(5-1)

Moses Lunsford, father-in-law of Charles Harding (2-2), sold property in Northumberland Co., VA to Thomas Harding (2-4) in 1741. Hopkins Harding (2-15) sold the same land in 1759.

The name Charles appears only in the families of Charles Harding (2-2) of Stafford County, VA and in the Hopkins Harding (2-15) and Mark Harding (2-16) families. It also appears in the family of William Harding (2-5) of Stafford and Fairfax counties, who died in 1781, who I now believe, based on DNA results, is a younger son of William (2-1) Harding and his second wife Frances Waddington.

See the family chart for the connections of the Waddington, Robinson, and Harding families in section three under Family 2.

A particular problem in this family is that Lucy Waring stated that Hannah, who married Thomas Harding (2-4) and who was the mother of Mark Harding (2-16) and Hopkins Harding (2-15), was the daughter of Robert Hopkins of Lancaster County. This conflicts with the deed from John Harding (2-19) in 1765 (WD 4-613) in Northumberland in which he states that his grandfather was John Waddington and that he had an older brother John Harding (2-14) who first inherited the land. It's clear that John Harding (2-19) was young, perhaps not born before the early 1740s, after his elder brother John Harding (2-14) died. I believe that the Hopkins connection is incorrect.

Note that in Lancaster County, an Edmund Denny died in 1735, leaving a widow named Hannah. He left no will so there is no mention of a son Samuel Denny. He is, however, the most likely husband for Hannah Harding (2-4) and father of Samuel Denny.

William Harding (4-2) is not the son of Charles Harding (2-2) of Stafford County, Virginia. He is the son of Joseph Combs I (4-1) of Stafford

For many years researchers have believed that Charles Harding (2-2) of Stafford County, Virginia, and son of William Harding (2-1) of Northumberland County, was the father of William Harding (4-2) who married Clarissa Million (4-2) about 1760 in Stafford County. This was a logical conclusion since Charles Harding (2-2) had a son William (2-6) recorded in the Overwharton Parish Register born in 1738. Virtually all researchers (with a few exceptions) have accepted this identification as an incontrovertible fact.

However, recent Y-DNA and Y-700 DNA studies (See DNA Chapter) have revealed that William Harding, (4-2) who married Clarissa Million, (4-2) has at least two Y-DNA descendants whose DNA test shows no connection to William Harding Sr., (2-1) Charles Harding's (2-2) father. The Y-DNA says that he was married prior to Clarissa Million, (4-2) and that he may have been born as early as 1720. Y-DNA also connects five men who settled in western Virginia in the 1760s and 1770s, Enos Harding, (4-7) Benjamin Harding, (4-9) Evangelist Harding, (4-6) and James Harding, (4-8) whose parentage is not clearly established, with William Harding (4-2). William Harding's (4-2) descendants are part of a separate Y-DNA group discussed in the DNA chapter later in this book. For a discussion of his mother see The Ashby Connection at the end of this chapter.

Y-700 DNA results for two of William's descendants prove that William Harding (4-2) was an illegitimate son of Joseph Combs I of Stafford County, Virginia. (See next section.) They also show that Joseph Harding (4-21) was an illegitimate son of Joseph Combs II of Stafford County. This means that we now know the name of the father of William Harding (4-2) who married Clarissa Million. (4-2), and the parents of Joseph Harding. To find a full discussion of this new discovery, see the DNA chapter referenced above and the biography of William Harding (4-2) in Family #4 of the Family Genealogies Chapter.

Joseph Harding (4-21) of Loudoun County Virginia, is the son of Joseph Combs II

This Joseph Harding (4-21) has again long been an enigma to researchers. A few have tried to tie him to English families. Some just say unknown. One or two tried to tie him and some of his children to my ancestor Thomas Harden (1-23) but that effort was disproved.

Now Y-700 DNA testing at Family Tree DNA has proven that this Joseph is an illegitimate son of Joseph Combs II (4-4), son of Joseph Combs I (4-1) of Stafford County, Virginia. Two testers, proven descendants of Joseph Harding (4-21), tested into Haplogroup R-FTG39316, which is a descendant of Haplogroup R-FTD20575, which includes Joseph Combs II,

Correction of Errors in Published Sources

the son of Joseph Combs I above, whose haplogroup is R-FTD86565., the parent of R-FTD20575 See discussion in the DNA test results Chapter 2.

In addition (more details in the genealogies for Family One), Joseph Harding (4-21) did not have a son Jeremiah Harding, (1-86) as many Ancestry trees claim. This Jeremiah Harding (1-86) is the son of Thomas Harding (1-48) and grandson of Thomas Harden (1-23)

Joseph Harding's (4-21) mother was not recorded at the time. However, autosomal DNA testing revealed that one descendant had DNA matches with 30 descendants of Mark Hardin (5-1) and Mary Hogue (5-12) (see Family 5). That couple had four daughters of the right age who were never married. One of them, based on the DNA results is the likely mother of Joseph Harding.

Parentage of Henry Harding (3-1) and Family of Henry Harding (1-6)

This is likely the most controversial proposal, that Henry Harding (3-1) of Stafford Co., Virginia was a recent immigrant and that Henry Harding (1-6), son of Thomas Harding (1-1) and Ann Moseley(1-1) of Northumberland Co., Virginia had no children.

In summary, the facts are as follows:

Henry Harding (1-6) (1671-1697) was a minor as late as August 1691.[11]

Henry Harding (1-6) was dead by 8 August 1697, when his widow was granted administration of his estate,[12] which includes no mention of children. No guardianship or apprenticeship is recorded. His estate was dealt with quickly, indicating it was small. His widow remarried Charles Ashton, who was dead by 15 January 1700.[13] No further mention of Jane (Arledge) Harding (1-6) appears.

Henry Harding (3-1) of Stafford Co., VA married Anne Beltcher by 1708,[14] indicating a birthdate of 1686 or 1687 at the latest.

---

[11] On 21 November 1690, he and John Harding chose their brother Thomas Harding as guardians CO 5-529. On 20 August 1691 his brother William filed a suit on his behalf CO 5-564.

[12] Northumberland County Court Orders 5-781.

[13] Northumberland Court Orders 5-814. No page number for second order, find by date.

[14] Northumberland County Court Orders 6-412 and 6-519

Henry Harding (3-1) is mentioned as a servant of John Cockrell in 1700, indicating an even earlier birth date.[15]

Henry Harding (3-1) was transported to Virginia prior to 1704. See the detailed timelines for both Henrys in Chapter 3.[16]

Henry Harding (3-1) is not a DNA match with William Harding (2-1). (See DNA discussion in Chapter 3.)

An analysis of the purported other children of Henry Harding (1-6) and Jane Arledge appears in the notes to the Keach article at the end of this book. A detailed list of the references given here will be found after the biographies of each person in Families 1 and 2.

From these and following discussion, the William (2-1) and Henry Harding (3-1) usually placed in this family cannot be here because both men were too old to be sons of Henry Harding (1-6). There is no evidence he had a son Thomas or a son John and indeed such sons are not necessary. We know that the older John Harding, (1-4) born about 1674, was still underage in 1691. He married Anne Bennett and had children. Records show that he was a son of Thomas Harding (1-1), not a grandson. Thomas is most likely the son of William Harding (2-1), born in 1707. (See Family #2). I will discuss the descendants of Henry Harding (3-1) in the Genealogy section in their individual biographies. The younger John Harding (1-10) was the son of William Harding (1-5) and Elizabeth Price, (1-5) married Jane (Barecraft) Trussell and had one son Willoughby, proven by court records in Westmoreland County, Virginia.

William Harding (2-27) of Clarke Co., Iowa was not the son of Joseph Harding (4-21) of Loudoun County, Virginia

Over 250 trees posted on Ancestry.com have mixed up these two families. It is true that Joseph Harding (4-21) of Loudoun County, Virginia, who died in 1806, did have a son named William (4-82) and it is also true that William Harding (2-27) of Clarke Co., Iowa did live in Stafford County, Virginia and did fight in the War of 1812. By not paying attention to the

---

[15] Northumberland Court Orders 6-128
[16] Northumberland Court orders Book 6. Many of the transportations happened well before the grant was recorded.

Correction of Errors in Published Sources

records, researchers grafted the Stafford County William Harding (2-27) onto the Loudoun County William Harding (4-82). In this book I have included records that clearly show the life pattern of each of these men in the records section and in the genealogies in Chapter 3, Families 2 and 4.

First, let's look at the William Harding (4-82) of Loudoun County, Virginia. As you can see there is a long list of records in his name. His wife was named Elizabeth Harding (4-82) and he did have children, all clearly spelled out in the records. The one record everyone missed was that on 13 December 1824, an inventory was taken of the William Harding (4-82) estate, clear proof that he died at that time in Loudoun County, Virginia. The relationships are clear. He was mentioned in his mother Elizabeth Harding (4-21)'s will, his heirs divided the estate of his parents with his brothers, and his children with his wife Elizabeth (4-82) were named and provided for. From this data is clear that William Harding (4-82) of Loudoun County died in 1824 and could not be the man who later lived in Stafford County, Virginia and Clarke County, Iowa, who lived to the age of over 94.

Who was this second William Harding (2-27)? The answer lies in the confused state of the records of Stafford County, Virginia, most of which were lost during the Civil War in the 1860s. A few scattered deeds and wills remain as well as all the land tax and personal property tax lists, which start only in 1783. When I explored the records of family #2, descendants of William Harding (2-1) and especially his son Charles Harding (2-2), I found literally thousands of trees with misidentified family members with at least two sons coopted into unrelated families.

The key is John Scott Harding (2-10), born 3 August 1747 in Overwharton Parish, Stafford County. The Stafford County records for this man aren't hard to find. However, they are buried, leaving him fair game for those trying to find a John Hardin to parent their ancestor. There are elaborate trees, almost a thousand, saying John Scott Harding (2-10) married Nancy Cloud and went to Guilford County, North Carolina. Yes, one John Harding did marry Nancy Cloud and lived in Guilford. He just wasn't the John Scott Harding (2-10) of Stafford County.

To follow John Scott Harding (2-10), it is necessary to inspect the Personal Property Tax lists year by year. First, we look at the land tax records, which show ownership of land. In 1782 and 1783 John Harden (2-10) is listed with 70 acres. Then in 1784 he is listed as John Scott Harden (2-10) with 70 acres. From 1785 to 1794, he is John Harding (2-10), still with 70 acres. In 1795 Lucy Harding (2-10) is listed as holding the land of John S. Harding (2-10). This would happen if John Scott Harding (2-10) died. To make it even more clear, Lucy is holding the land for J Scott Harding (2-10) in 1795. She then owns the same 70 acres until 1816, when she is listed as deceased. In the personal property tax list, he is variously listed as John Harding, John S. Hardin, and John Scott Harding (2-10). In 1795 John S. Harding (2-10) disappears and Lucy Harding (2-10) appears.

In 1793, John S. Harding (2-10) has two males over 16 in the household. After he died Lucy showed one male of 16. In 1801, Lucy had no males in her household, about the same time William Harding (2-27) married Elizabeth Doggett in Culpeper County, Virginia. He returned to Stafford County about 1814 and had a large family there. In the 1814 personal property tax lists he is named as the son of Scott Harding (2-10), clearing up who his parents were. From there we can follow him through the records in Stafford to his enrollment in the company of Elijah Harding (4-14), in the War of 1812, through census records, all the way to Clarke County, Iowa, where he applied for his War of 1812 Pension.

Therefore, the William Harding (4-82), son of Joseph Harding (4-21) of Loudoun County, married and had three children by his wife Elizabeth and died in 1824 never having left Loudoun County.

Thomas Harden (1-23) of Rockingham Co., NC and his family

I descend from this family. This book was inspired by my search for his ancestry, a search that is finally over. From the records presented in this book, Thomas Harden (1-23) married first Sarah Cox. (See DNA discussion later in this section), lived in Westmoreland Co., VA until about 1758, in Fairfax Co., VA until about the 1780s and Rockingham after that. In Fairfax, he married a daughter of Henry Taylor, who might be his widow, Eleanor.

In published and Internet sources, his family has been badly misrepresented. He appeared in Stafford County, Virginia with no records to back that up. His children and grandchildren have been added into various other families. His son Presley Harden (1-43) has been confused with Presley Hardin (4-83) of Loudoun Co., Virginia and Bath County, Kentucky, whose actual ancestry will be discussed later in this book.

In the next section I will present a complete account of his children and grandchildren down four generations, complete with detailed records from all the counties involved. Thomas' children scattered across North Carolina and Tennessee, making them difficult to trace. However, they were active

Correction of Errors in Published Sources

landowners and almost all left wills naming not only their children but also nephews and nieces in the various counties where they lived.

Thomas Harden (1-23) appears to have had children by both wives since his children were separated into two groups in his will.

Thomas Harden (1-23) had sons Peter Harden (1-50) and Presley Harden (1-43), indicating a connection with the descendants of the Presley family of Northumberland County. Among the daughters of Peter and William Presley, the names Peter and Presley are common, particularly in the Cockrell, Neale, Cox, Bearcraft and Thornton families.

My search for his ancestry first led me to John Harding (1-10) (1693-1734), the son of William Harding (1-5) and Elizabeth Harding (1-5) and grandson of Thomas Harding (1-1) and Anne Moseley. John Harding (1-10) lived and died in Westmoreland County, Virginia, where in the 1750s we find Thomas Harden (1-23), later of Rockingham County, North Carolina. John Harding (1-10) married Jane Bearcraft, daughter of Thomas Bearcraft and sister of John Bearcraft, who had a son Presley Bearcraft. This seemed to be a good connection to the Presley family. However, John Harding (1-10) died in 1834, when his children would have been in their teens. One son, Willoughby Harding (1-22), was apprenticed out but I found no record of my Thomas Harden being apprenticed, as was the normal way to take care of fatherless children. Therefore, I have found no evidence of an actual connection with this John Harding (1-10)'s family.

The only other possibility for his father is Thomas Harding (1-11), born about 1700, the son of the above John Harding (1-10)'s uncle, also named John Harding (1-7), the youngest son of Thomas Harding (1-1) and Anne Moseley. This Thomas Harding (1-11) inherited land from his grandfather Thomas Harding (1-1) and father John Harding (1-7) in Richmond County, Virginia and sold that land in 1720 to his cousin Thomas Harding (1-8) while living in Stafford County, Virginia. We know nothing further about this Thomas Harding (1-11) and, since Stafford County records are mostly lost, we may never know more. He could have had a son named Thomas Harding but no record of this exists. See The Ashby Connection at the end of this chapter for more information

Autosomal DNA results also indicate a genetic connection between Thomas Harden (1-23) and this Thomas Hardin (1-11), whose father John Harding (1-7) married Ann Bennett. Both my sister and I show DNA connections to 14 descendants of Edward Bennett, Ann Bennett's father, through her brother Cuthbert and her sister Mary. This indicates a connection and opens other research lines.

This preponderance of evidence leads me to place Thomas Harden (1-23) in Family #1.

So far, no proven male descendants of Thomas Harding (1-1) and Anne Moseley have taken a Y-DNA test. I also cannot find any other male line descendants of Thomas Harding (1-1) and Anne Moseley after about 1800, which means they most likely have no male descendants carrying the Harding name unless Thomas Harden (1-23) of Rockingham belongs in this family.

As I show in the genealogical chapter on Family One, We have DNA tests from three descendants of Thomas Harding (1-23) of Rockingham, but the results match no other Hardin family. This leaves open the probability that Thomas Harden (1-23) of Rockingham Co., North Carolina, who first appears in Westmoreland County, Virginia near where Thomas Harding (1-11) lived, was the only descendant of Thomas Harding (1-1) to leave male line descendants..

As outlined in the next chapter, we have Y-DNA test results from descendants of Henry Harding (3-1) and William Harding (2-1), purported grandchildren of Thomas Harding (1-1) and Anne Moseley. Those tests show conclusively that Henry Harding (3-1) and William Harding (2-1) are not related to each other. They also are unrelated to the descendants of Thomas Harden (1-23) of Rockingham County, North Carolina.

I also prove in the sections on their families that Henry Harding (3-1) and William Harding (2-1) cannot be descended from Thomas Harding (1-1) and Anne Moseley because of their ages.

The Wives of Thomas Harden

A close reading of the records indicates that Thomas Harden (1-23) had two wives who each had children with him.

The first key record is his will.[17] He spends four paragraphs on bequests to his wife Eleanor Harden (1-23) and his sons Henry Harden (1-49) and Peter Harden (1-50) and his daughter Peggy Harden (1-51), including distribution of land and slaves.

Then he adds a fifth paragraph where he divides "the remainder of my Negroes equally among my other children." Of these, Ann Reed (1-46), Jeremiah Harden (1-45), and John Harden (1-44) were already deceased. Presley Harden (1-43), Thomas Harden (1-48), Sarah Rogers (1-47), and

---

[17] Rockingham County North Carolina Wills Book A, Page 86, 1809.

Correction of Errors in Published Sources

William Hornbuckle (1-42), (a son-in-law and husband of his daughter Jane) were still living.

This indicates a clear division in the family between the heirs of his second wife Eleanor and those of his first wife, who are almost an afterthought. A second indication is that he made his younger sons Henry Harden (1-49) and Peter Harden (1-50) his executors.

His last three children were born around or after 1770 in Fairfax County, Virginia. The first seven were born between 1750 and about 1765. None of the birth dates are exact.

In his will[18] in Loudoun County, Virginia in March 1770, Henry Taylor mentions his sons-in-law William Cotton, William Williams, Thomas Harden (1-23) and Notley Williams. Some of these men later lived in and around Rockingham and Caswell counties in North Carolina and appear in various deed records together. This indicates that Thomas Harden (1-23) married a Taylor before 1770. Her name is not given in Henry Taylor's will, but clearly Eleanor was the mother of his last three children and so she is the best candidate for Thomas Harden's (1-23) second wife.

This leaves open the question of his first wife's identity. According to records in Westmoreland County, Virginia, her first name was Sarah, a very common name. In 1753 Thomas Harden (1-23) bought 50 acres of land in Cople Parish, Westmoreland County[19] and in 1755 witnessed a deed from Edwin Turner to Peter Presley Cox[20] also for 50 acres, also in Cople Parish. In October 1759 Thomas Harden (1-23) and Sarah Harden (1-23) sold his 50 acres[21] in Cople Parish to John Brown. He later shows up in Fairfax County, Virginia, for several years then moved to North Carolina. I believe Sarah died around 1765 or so, leaving him with seven children.

What was Sarah's maiden name? My first major clue was in the naming of his children. Thomas Harden (1-23) named his eldest son Presley (1-43) and his second eldest by his second wife Peter Hardin (1-50).

The names Peter and Presley are very common among the descendants of William Presley (1608-1657) and Jane Newman of Northumberland County, Virginia. William, a very prominent planter, had two sons, William and Peter. William Junior had one son, Peter. Their other children were female. The male line died out with the passing of his grandson Peter, but

---

[18] Loudoun County, Virginia Wills Book A Page 318 1770
[19] Westmoreland County, Virginia Deeds Book 11, Page 482
[20] Westmoreland County, Virginia Deeds Book 12
[21] Westmoreland County, Virginia Deeds Book 13 Page 253

the names Peter and Presley continued to be used for generations among the descendants of his daughters.

I spent hours searching my DNA matches at Ancestry to see if any members of the Presley family were among them. I found 150 matches with centiMorgan amounts well within the range of distant relationships. Since Mary Presley married Charnock Cox, I also checked the Cox family and found another 25 matches among descendants of the immigrant Vincent Cox from his children other than Charnock Cox. In addition, I found 32 matched descendants of Charnock Cox and Mary Presley.

This indicated a strong probability that Thomas Harden's wife Sarah was descended from the Presley and Cox families.

One of Charnock Cox's children, Peter Cox, died in 1748 in Westmoreland County, leaving among others, a daughter Sarah mentioned in his will. Peter Cox married Mary, possibly Mary Lewis, daughter of James Lewis and Hannah Lovelace.

There are strong DNA matches that includes the Lewis, Garner and Keene families of Northumberland. When I checked the DNA for relatives among those families, I found another 65 matches.

Since I have no other matches with any of these families, this is good circumstantial and physical evidence that the Presley, Cox, Lewis, Garner and Keene families are among my ancestors through Sarah Cox, who married Thomas Harden (1-23).

I might also mention that the Peter Presley Cox, whose deed Thomas Harden (1-23) witnessed, was a nephew of Peter Cox and a cousin of his daughter Sarah Cox (1-23). For references to all the records discussed in this section, see Chapter 3, Family 1.

The True Ancestry of Hiram Harden (1-88) of Shelby Co., Tennessee, and William Presley Harden (1-87) of Boone Co., Arkansas

For many years, researchers have believed that Hiram Harden (1-88) (1797-1864), who lived in Shelby Co., Tennessee and later Navarro Co., Texas, and William Presley Harden (1-87) (1795-1865), who lived in Shelby Co., Tennessee and Boone Co., Arkansas, were older sons of Moses Harden and Orpha Hassell of Lincoln Co., Tennessee. Over 400 trees on Ancestry and other sites currently show this connection.

Correction of Errors in Published Sources

Recent research has uncovered records that show this connection is incorrect and that both men were sons of Thomas Harden (1-48) (c 1762-bef 1820) and Elizabeth Powell, born c 1768, died after 1850, of Giles Co., Tennessee.

Why Moses Harden cannot be their father.

Moses Harden was born in 1772 in Burke County, North Carolina, according to most researchers, but lived most of his life in Lincoln Co, Tennessee, which is located on the Tennessee-Alabama border and is the next county east of Giles Co., Tennessee.

The first reason he cannot be the father of Hiram Harden (1-88) and William Presley Harden (1-87) is that he married Orpha Hassell after June 16, 1803, in Sumner Co., Tennessee.[22] Both Hiram[23] (1-88) and William Presley Harden[24] (1-87) were born in North Carolina prior to that date.

The second reason is that Moses is enumerated in the 1810 Census in Burke Co., North Carolina with two males under age 10 and four females under age 10 and in the 1820 Census in Lincoln Co., Tennessee, with 2 males 10 to 16 and five males under 10, one female under 10 and one female age 16-26. No older males or females born before 1800 are listed.

The third reason is that neither man is listed in Moses Hardin's will.[25] There is no indication that either Hiram Harden (1-88) or William Presley Harden (1-87) were at any time a member of Moses Harden's family.

The fourth reason is that Moses Harden is in Haplogroup I on Family Tree DNA while Hiram is in Haplogroup R, which means the two are not related within up to 10,000 years.

Hiram Harden's father and connections

Next door to Lincoln Co., Tennessee, in Giles Co., Tennessee, Thomas Harden (1-48) lived with his wife Elizabeth (1-48). Thomas Harden (1-48) was born about 1762 in Fairfax Co., Virginia, son of Thomas Harden (1-23) and his wife Sarah (1-23), and came with his father to North Carolina in the

---

[22] Sumner County, Tennessee marriage bonds, loose papers file.
[23] United States Census, 1850, Upshur Co., Texas, Hiram Harden age 53, born in 1797, North Carolina, Page 189
[24] United States Census, 1850, Jefferson, Carroll Co., Arkansas, page 172, Age 55, born in North Carolina, 1860 Washington Carroll Co., Arkansas, page 64, age 65 born North Carolina.
[25] Lincoln County, Tennessee Will Book 1-2 page 370, dated May 12 1849.

1780s, where he married Elizabeth Powell (1-48) December 20, 1791 in Orange County, North Carolina.[26] In the early 1800s, Thomas Harden (1-48) and his wife Elizabeth (1-48) moved to Giles Co., Tennessee, where on August 27, 1818, he executed a deed of gift to "my son Hiram Hardin (1-88) of Giles Co., Tennessee."[27]

Thomas Harden (1-48) also had a son Joshua Harden (1-90), born about 1811, proven when Joshua's (1-90) mother Elizabeth Harden (1-48) of Giles Co., Tennessee filed a suit[28] on November 4, 1830, to summon John Harden (1-79) of Orange Co., North Carolina to Court. She claimed that when her husband Thomas Harden (1-48)'s brother Peter Harden (1-50) died without children, he divided his estate in his will[29], among all his nieces and nephews.

In Elizabeth Harden's (1-48) suit, she claimed that John Harden (1-44), also a brother of Peter Harden (1-50) and his executor, failed to pay her son Joshua Harden (1-90) his portion of the estate of Peter Harden (1-50) due to him.

It is more difficult to prove that William Presley Harden (1-87) was also one of Thomas Harden's (1-48) sons. However, in the 1820 Census, after Thomas Harden (1-48) died, Elizabeth Harden (1-48) is listed in the 1820 Census in Pulaski, Giles Co., Tennessee with one male age 16-26, most likely Hiram Harden (1-88), one male 10 to 16, most likely Joshua (1-90), and one female age 10 to 16, name unknown.

Listed a few lines above Elizabeth Harden (1-48) is William Harden (1-87) with one male 16 to 26 and one female age 16-26, most likely William Presley Harden (1-87). This record is difficult to read on the original microfilm but on detailed examination appears to be and is indexed as William Hardin (1-87).

Another indication is the middle name Presley. Thomas Harden (1-48) Jr. above had a brother named Presley Harden (1-43). I believe Thomas Harden (1-23)'s wife Sarah was descended from the Presley family of Northumberland Co., Virginia, where the Harden family originated. Presley is a common first and middle name in all other branches of this Harden family. However, it never appears in Moses Harden's family. In addition, William Presley Harden (1-87) named his only son Thomas Presley Harden (1-127). Thomas Presley Harden (1-127) named a son Hiram Harden.

---

[26] Marriage bonds of Orange County, North Carolina
[27] Giles Co., Tennessee Deed Book C, page 378 Aug 27, 1818
[28] Orange County, North Carolina probate packets, Estate of Thomas Harden
[29] Rockingham Co., North Carolina will packets Jan 27, 1819

In 1837 and 1838[30] Joshua Harden (1-90), Hiram Harden (1-88), and William Harden (1-87) are listed in the tax lists of Shelby Co., Tennessee together. By 1840 William Presley Harden (1-87) was living in Van Buren Co., Arkansas, to the north and west of Shelby Co., Tennessee.

In the 1840 Census, Hiram Harden (1-88) and Joshua Harden (1-90) are listed in Shelby Co., Tennessee near each other. Living with Joshua Harden (1-90) was his mother Elizabeth Harden (1-48), noted as a female age 70 to 80.

In 1850, Joshua Harden (1-90) and his mother Elizabeth Harden (1-48), now aged 82, are enumerated together in Shelby Co., Tennessee.

Conclusion

Hiram is a rare name in the Harden families. Only two are known to have lived in Tennessee in the early 1800s. The name occurs often in this Harden family only.

The records show that Thomas Harden (1-48) Jr. of Caswell and Rockingham Counties, North Carolina, relocated to Giles County, Tennessee in the early 1800s with three sons, Jeremiah Harden (1-86), Hiram Harden (1-88), and William Presley Harden (1-87), and had another son Joshua Harden (1-90) while living there. After he died, Joshua, Hiram, and William and their mother Elizabeth moved to Shelby Co., Tennessee together, Hiram Harden (1-88) married there in 1838, and by 1850 Hiram Harden (1-88) moved to Texas and William Presley Harden (1-87) to Arkansas, leaving Joshua Harden (1-90) in Shelby Co., Tennessee.

The Ashby Connection

The Hardin and Combs families are intertwined with the Ashby family of Stafford County, Virginia in many ways. The first known member of the family is Thomas Ashby born about 1690, died 1754 in Frederick County, Virginia. His ancestry is unknown although some researchers claim he is connected to the South Carolina Ashbys, a claim not supported by DNA.

We do know that from records preserved in Stafford County, in the Overwharton Parish Register, that Thomas most likely had a brother Robert Ashby, whose records appear there. Some daughters have been theorized but not proven.

---

[30] Shelby Co., Tennessee tax lists

Harding Families of the Northern Neck of Virginia

In my DNA research on Ancestry, while searching for the ancestry of my ancestor Thomas Harden (1-23), I found that in autosomal DNA, I matched over 90 people who descended from various branches of the Ashby family. In most cases, I saw no other common ancestor with these matches, suggesting a strong Ashby ancestral connection.

To narrow down the possible place this connection could take place you must understand my own ancestry. For instance my mother is half German from immigrants in the 1850s. Her other half is New England families Watson from Rhode Island and Walker from Vermont and Massachusetts, all traced back to the 1600s. No Southern lines.

My father's family, Pound, traces half it's ancestry back to Quaker families in New Jersey and the Norton and Minor families of New England. No Virginia there.

His mother, my grandmother, Erna Sacre Pound, traces back to Virginia. The Sacres are an obscure family that lived in central and southern Virginia, where many records were destroyed. They were never in northern Virginia.

My grandmother's mother was Madeline Currance Hornbuckle, who descends from William Hornbuckle and Jane Harden. The Hornbuckle lines have been thoroughly researched and published by me and other family members in the 800-page book, *Hornbuckles in America*, which covers the family in detail starting in the late 1600s.

The only ancestral line not completed was Jane Harden, daughter of Thomas Harden (1-23) and Sarah Cox (1-23).

After many years of research, I determined through autosomal DNA the ancestors of Sarah Cox, which left Thomas Harden (1-23) the only avenue for Ashby to enter my ancestral lines. (see Graphic on Page 45 for details of the number of matches for the Cox and Ashby families).

The graphic on the next page shows my proposed relationships for the Harding, Ashby, and Combs families. My ancestry comes from the Thomas Harding (1-23) in the lower center right of the graphic.

As you can see, this is complicated. However, it shows how the very large family of descendants of Thomas Ashby can match my DNA. I also have strong autosomal DNA matches among the descendants of William Harding and Clarissa Million since both descend from the Bennett family of Northumberland County. I especially want to clarify the possible mother of William Harding (4-2) who is much in dispute. At this time we know of only a few Hardings living in Stafford County near Joseph Combs I (4-1), who first appears there in 1723, a few years after William Harding's birth.

We know that Charles Harding,(2-2), who was born in 1704 in Northumberland County, lived there after about 1730, when he married and had children. None of his family was old enough to be the mother of William Harding in 1720.

The other family was Henry Harding Sr, (3-1) from Northumberland County, married about 1708 but had children born from 1714 on, too young to have any children with Joseph Combs I in 1720.

Harding, Combs, Ashby, Bennett, Million Relationships in Northumberland County, Virginia

Multiple names in a gray box are brothers and sisters. Black lines between boxes indicate marriages and parentages.

- Edward Bennett c 1654-?
- Thomas Harding c1630-1675 (1-1)
- Robert Million c 1680 — Md c1705
- Grace Bennett c 1680
- Cuthbert Bennett 1680-1718
- Ann Bennett 1676-?
- Md c1695
- John Harding c 1674-1714 (1-7)
- Robert Million c1710
- Mark Hardin c1681-1735 (5-1)
- Joseph Combs I c1690-1753 (4-1)
- With c 1720
- Miss Harding c 1697
- Thomas Harding c 1700-? (1-11)
- Md c 1720
- Miss Ashby c1680-?
- Thomas Ashby c 1680-?
- Miss Hardin One of 5 Daughters (5-7-11)
- Joseph Combs II 1728-1781 With c 1750 (4-4)
- Thomas Harden 1725-1809 (1-23)
- Joseph Harding 1750-1806 (4-21)
- Clarissa Million c1730 — Md c1761
- William Harding 1720-1780 (4-2)
- Md c1744
- Elizabeth Ashby c 1725-c1759
- Thomas Ashby Jr c 1714-
- Jesse Ashby Jr c 1738-c1823
- Benjamin Harding 1753-1834 (4-9)
- Evangelist Harding 1742-1830 (4-6)
- James Harding 1748-1843 (4-8)
- Enos Harding 1745-1826 (4-7)
- Martha Ashby c 1771-c1823

This leaves a possible daughter of John Harding (1-7) and Ann Bennett (see chart on page 28) as being of age enough to be the mother of William Harding. There is nobody else who meets the parameters spelled out here. I emphasize that there is no hard evidence for this reconstruction except for the amount of Ashby DNA matches and the DNA matches between me and

Harding Families of the Northern Neck of Virginia

the Bennet, Million and Ashby families, which make this the most reasonable reconstruction possible given the lack of records in Stafford County, Virginia.

See the records for families One and Four in Chapter 3 for detailed extant records that confirm this analysis. The graphic below shows the number of Ancestry.com matches who have trees by ancestor or family for myself and my sister. As you can see, the numbers are quite high. Note that only a small portion of matches on Ancestry have trees.

Leland and Lynne Pound	
Autosomal DNA Matches with Descendants of:	
Thomas Ashby and Rosanna Berry Children	
John Ashby	13
Stephen Ashby	8
Thomas Ashby Jr	22
Robert Ashby	18
Elizabeth Ashby	2
Henry Ashby	11
Benjamin Ashby	3
Sarah Ashby	5
	82
Robert Ashby and Elizabeth Botts	
Robert Ashby Jr	12
Thomas Ashby	11
Winifred Ashby	15
John Ashby	1
	39
Total Ashby Matches	121
Ancestors of Sarah (Cox) Harden	
Wife of Thomas Harden (1-23)	
Presley/Cox	189
John Lewis	18
John Garner	34
Thomas Keene	25
Total Presley Matches	266

Chapter 2
DNA Results Analysis

Results from the Harding DNA Projects

There are two projects at Family Tree DNA that include members of the Harding families of the Northern Neck. The first, the Harding-Harden-Hardin Y-DNA project at Family Tree DNA is one of the most important sources of data showing how the various Harding families, and there are many of them, are related or not related. The second, which is source of the extended Y-700 DNA test data that proves many of the lines presented in this book, particularly the Harding-Combs connection in Family Number 4, is the Combs & Harding et al under R-FT86565, DNA Project, which is also referenced in this chapter.

It is important to remember that Y-DNA analysis is not an exact science except in one area. The Y-DNA chromosome is passed unchanged from father to son in the direct male line only, except for rare mutations. The more markers on the Chromosome tested, the sharper the results get. Thirty-seven is considered the minimum for good results. All the tests used in this study have 37 markers tested.

In addition, we do Haplogroup testing. The deeper the testing, the sharper the result. Most of the results in the HHHDNA Project (I'll call it HHHDNA from here on) test down three or four levels although it is possible to go down 12 to 15 levels to get increasing Haplogroup accuracy.

You can read much more about all this at the Family Tree DNA website.

The concept of genetic distance is also important for two reasons. If all the markers in a DNA test are the same at the 37-marker level, the two testers are closely related, and the genetic distance is zero. Genetic distance counts all the markers that differ between two individuals with a few exceptions. Distance up to three indicates a relationship, four a possible relationship, and five a possible relationship. Above five means no or very distant relationship.

I will include genetic distance charts for each group in this analysis. They show in some cases that people we expect from research in records to be related are unrelated and in others that people we expect to be unrelated are in fact related. This happens most often when research is not rigorous, or trees are copied without verification. Much Hardin research is afflicted with this problem as you will see from the DNA results.

HHHDNA breaks all the tested individuals into related groups by both DNA matches and by haplogroup. Most tests have come back as being in the R Haplogroup, the most common one in Western Europe and the British Isles, where most HHHDNA families originated. A few are in other scattered Haplogroups.

In the HHHDNA database on Family Tree DNA, all the men who took the y-DNA test are distributed into categories or Haplogroups based on closeness of their genetic distance, the prime indication two or more men are closely related genetically. Group R has 24 separate Haplogroups lettered from A to X. In this analysis I will concentrate on five groups, A, D, F, H, and N. Many included an early ancestor as shown in the first table.

For a century, most researchers have believed that all Northumberland County Hardens except Mark Hardin (5-1) and Mary (MNU) (5-1) were related through Thomas Harding (1-1) (c 1630-1674) and Anne Moseley.

My analysis of the HHHDNA site shows that to not be true. I identified five unrelated groups that connect back to the Harding families of Northumberland County, Virginia.

These five unrelated ancestral family groups are:
1. Haplogroup D. Thomas Harding (1-1) (c 1630-1675) and Ann Moseley (1-1) of Northumberland Co., Virginia. Thomas Harden (1-23) (c1725-1809) and Sarah (1-23), of Westmoreland Co Virginia and Rockingham Co., North Carolina, most likely to descend from Thomas Harding (1-1) and Anne Moseley (1-1) and he and his descendants are included in that family in this book. Several male line descendants of Thomas Harden (1-23) have been tested for DNA.
2. Haplogroup F: William Harding (2-1) (c 1680 to unknown) and an unknown wife of Northumberland Co., Virginia.
3. Haplogroup H: Henry Harding (3-1) (c1680-1737) and Ann Belcher of Northumberland and Stafford Counties in Virginia.
4. Haplogroup N: Joseph Combs I, (4-1) his natural son William Harding (4-2) who married Elizabeth Ashby as his first wife and Clarissa Million (4-2) as his second wife, brothers Benjamin (4-9) and Enos Hardin (4-7), Joseph Combs II (4-4) and his natural son, Joseph Hardin (4-21) of Loudoun Co., Virginia, all of whom belong to the same y-DNA group.

DNA Results Analysis

5. Haplogroup A: Mark Hardin (5-1) and Mary (MNU) (5-1) of Northumberland, King George, and Prince William Counties. The genealogy of this family is filled with numerous errors.

I will use this numbering system to differentiate the families throughout the book, where each family will be identified by these family numbers. DNA results exist for families 2 through 6. However, here comes the big question. Does the first family, the descendants of Thomas Harding (1-1) and Anne Moseley (1-1), have any male line descendants? Many people erroneously claim descent from him through William and Henry Hardin (families 2 and 3) which the research presented in this book shows is not correct.

When these two men are eliminated from Family Group 1, Thomas Harding (1-1) and Ann Moseley's (1-1) family, we find that no male line descendants have taken a y-DNA test and furthermore that no male line descendants after about 1800 are known and none may exist. It is probable that Thomas Harden (1-23), is one of their descendants, therefore I have included his descendants in this Group One.

Results for Group One TVY9C R1B Haplogroup D

Descendants of Thomas Harden (c 1725-1809) (1-23) of Rockingham County, North Carolina (Family #5):

#	Name of Participant	Earliest Ancestor on HHHDNA
1	Donnie Lee Hardin	Hiram Hardin 1796 TN or NC to 1864 TX
2	Curtis Hardin	Thomas J. Harden 1825 TN to 1879 MO
3	Daniel Conrad Hardin	Thomas J. Harden 1825 TN to 1879 MO
4	Brian David Armstead	Monroe Armstead Sr 1854- 1935 TX

Genetic Distance Chart for Group One TVY9C				
Name	Donnie	Curtis	Daniel	Brian
Donnie		2	2	1
Curtis	2		1	0
Daniel	2	1		1
Brian	1	0	1	

The first table shows the four men in Group TVY9C and the earliest known ancestor before my research. These four men are in Haplogroup R1b1. The second shows the genetic distance between them. As you can see, the distances are 0, 1, and 2, which indicates a close relationship between them.

It appears at first to be an easy research problem. The earliest known ancestors have birthdates close to each other. However, descendants of both men attempted in the past but failed to make a connection because of two problems: Nobody knew for certain the parents of Hiram Hardin (1-88), and nobody knew the grandparents of Thomas J. Harden. (1-126)

For many years researchers believed that Hiram Harden (1-88) was the son of Moses Harden of Lincoln Co., Tennessee. However, DNA from a descendant of Moses tested into Haplogroup I and is therefore not related to Hiram within thousands of years.

Later I will show that Hiram Harden (1-88) was a son of Thomas Harden Jr. (1-48) and Elizabeth Powell (1-48) of Giles County, Tennessee, and grandson of Thomas Harden Sr. (1725-1809) (1-23), who died in Rockingham Co., North Carolina, my ancestor. I've reconstructed his family later in this book. Later I will show why these may be the only male descendants of Thomas Harding (1-1) (c 1630-1674) of Northumberland County, Virginia and his wife Ann Moseley (1-1) to take a DNA test.

I will also show that Thomas J. Harden (1-126) was the son of Jeremiah Harden and Sally McCutchin of Williamson and Giles Co., Tennessee, the grandson of Thomas Harden Jr. (1-48) and Elizabeth Powell (1-48) of Giles Co., Tennessee, and great-grandson of Thomas Harden Sr. (1725-1809) (1-23) of Rockingham County, North Carolina.

Thus, Hiram Hardin (1-88) and Thomas J. Harden (1-126) in this group are first cousins once removed and the relationship problem has been solved.

Results for Group Two HYRT9, Haplogroup 1B Haplogroup F

Descendants of William Harding (2-1) (c 1680- ?) of Northumberland Co., Virginia (Family #2)

#	Name of Participant	Earliest Ancestor on HHHDNA
1	Richard W. Harding	Thomas Harding born 1831
2	Robert Harding	William Harding (c 1680-?)
3	James Everett Hardin	Charles Wesley Hardin c1827
4	Roger Alan Harding	Joseph (or Andress) Harding d 1806 VA
5	Tommy Hardin	John F. Hardin 1805 GA Father born VA
6	Dennis Dean Hardin	Henry Hardin 1814-1816
7	David Marion Hardin	Moses Harding c 1751
8	Larry Dean Hardin	Benjamin J Harden 1807 to 1890
9	Eric Harden	John William Harden c 1836
10	Arthur Eugene Hardin	John Hardin 1804-1861

DNA Results Analysis

Genetic Distance Chart for Group Two HYRT9										
	Ric	Rob	Jam	Rog	Tom	Den	Da	La	Eric	Art
Richard		7	5	5	5	5	5	4	4	4
Robert	7		5	3	3	4	4	4	4	4
James	5	5		2	2	3	2	2	2	2
Roger	5	3	2		1	2	2	2	2	2
Tommy	5	3	2	1		1	2	2	2	2
Dennis	5	4	3	2	1		1	1	1	1
David	5	4	2	2	2	1		1	1	1
Larry	4	4	2	2	2	1	1		0	0
Eric	4	4	2	2	2	1	1	0		0
Arthur	4	4	2	2	2	1	1	0	0	

Descendancy Chart For William Harding (2:1)

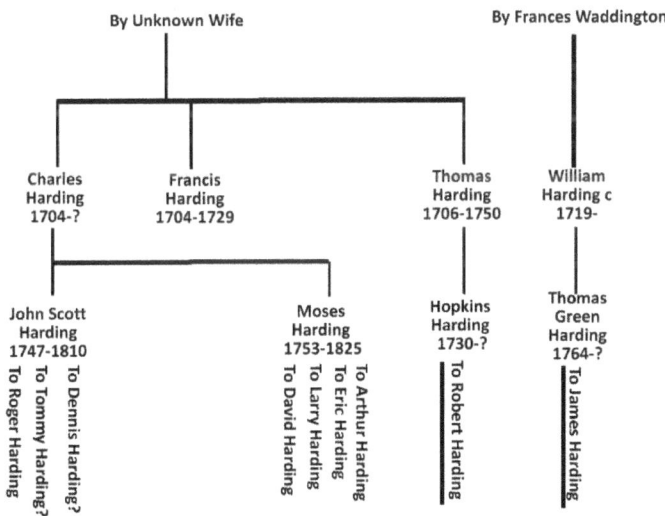

This group at first seems to be the most diverse of all the groups and was also the one with the fewest lines leading back before 1800.

Richard W. Harding was the only one whose line must connect to the others before 1600. He descends from Robert Harding of Dorchester Co., Maryland, whose ancestry is otherwise unknown. The genetic distance of 5 and 4 from the rest of the group indicates a much earlier connection.

Robert Harding provided a pedigree that goes directly back to William Harding (2-1) (c 1680-?) of Northumberland Co., Virginia (Family #Two). The line is documented and appears to be correct. This gives us a baseline for the rest of the chart. This line goes back furthest before connecting with the others, to William's son Thomas Harding. (2-4).

Dennis Dean Hardin can only be traced back to Henry Hardin who was born before 1810 in Kentucky and whose pedigree I was unable to extend further back. However, based on the genetic distance chart above, he is closely related to Tommy Hardin in the next paragraph and to Roger Harding, a descendant of John Scott Harding (2-10), discussed in the following paragraph. I expect this means Tommy and Dennis will most likely be descended from John Scott Harding (2-10). We have no proof since the other possible children of John Scott Harding (2-10) are unknown.

Tommy Hardin goes back to John F. Hardin born in 1805 in Georgia. Some trees list is father as Nicholas Harding, who is said to have died in Washington County, Georgia in 1814, but for which I have seen no proof.

Roger Harding descends from William Harding (2-27), born in 1777 in Virginia and died in Clarke Co., Iowa in 1875. He guessed that Andress Harding, who I can find no evidence for, or Joseph Harding, (4-21) who died in 1806, might be his ancestor. However, as I show in Chapter 1, This William Harding is descended from William Harding (2-1) through Charles Harding (2-2) and John Scott Harding (2-10) and not Joseph Harding (4-21), who lived in Loudoun Co., VA and had a son William Harding (4-82) born about 1770, who belongs to Group #4 at the end of this chapter.

David, Larry, Eric, and Arthur change this pattern. They descend from Moses Harding (2-12), born 1753, through three different sons, which accounts for the close genetic distance we see in their lines, 0, 1, or 2. The line runs back through Moses Harding (2-12) to his father Charles Harding (2-2) of Stafford Co., VA, the son of William Harding (2-1), born about 1680, the head of Family #2. Note that eight of the ten men are separated by a genetic distance of 0, 1, or 2, including Roger and the unknown ancestries of Dennis, and Tommy.

James Hardin goes back through a different line, through Thomas Green Harden (2-26), his father William Hardin (2-5) and mother Patty Green (2-5), to William Hardin (2-1) (Family #2). Since six of the ten men tested have

DNA Results Analysis

lines back to William Hardin of Family #2, we can confidently say that all the men in this group will eventually connect to William.

Results for Group Three, R1B Haplogroup H.

Descendants of Henry Harding (3-1) (c 1680 to 1737) and Ann (MNU) Belcher (3-1) of Northumberland Co., Virginia (Family #3

#	Name of Participant	Earliest Ancestor on HHHDNA
1	Edgar Silvester Hardin	George W. Harding b 1835 VA d af 1900
2	Delmar Harding	John Hardin born 1833 VA d 1894 WV
3	H. Harding	William Harding b c 1740 VA d 1809 SC
4	Bobby N. Harding	William Harding b c 1740 VA d 1809 SC
5	Randall Moon	Unknown
6	David C. Hardin	John Harding b 1565 England
7	David John Harding	Henry Harding (1690-1737)
8	Anthony Hardin	Unknown

Genetic Distance Chart for Group Three								
	Edg	Delm	H	Bob	Rand	DavC	DavJ	Anth
Edgar		2	5	4	2	4	4	4
Delmer	2		3	2	5	4	6	5
H	5	3		5	3	3	8	5
Bobby N	4	2	5		0	4	6	4
Randall	2	5	3	0		2	3	3
David C	4	4	3	4	2		4	2
David J	4	6	8	6	3	4		2
Anthony	4	4	5	4	3	2	2	

On first look, this group seems more diverse than expected. The first two testers only go back to the early 1800s before the line stops. Then we have two lines going back to a William Harding (3-9) who died in South Carolina and one who traces back to England and one to Henry Harden I (3-1) of Northumberland County, Virginia. Two others did not add trees or a common ancestor to their profile.

Further research established that the first four on the list, Edgar, Delmar, H and Bobby Harding, descend from William Harding (3-9), who moved from Virginia to South Carolina in the 1780s. This chart shows the relationships by generation of these four men. All dates are approximate. My research also established through probate records that William was the son of George Harding (3-3). Edgar, Delmar, and H are descended from William Harding (3-9) through his son Abner (3-33) while Bobby descends through William's (3-9) son William (3-36) and Bobby are related to each other. See Family #3 for detailed timelines.

David C. Hardin supplied a pedigree showing his descent from Henry Hardin (3-1) (c 1680-1737) and Anne Belcher (3-1) of Northumberland County, Virginia, Family #3 in this book. David John Harding did not supply a pedigree but did state he was descended from the same Henry Hardin (3-1) and Anne Belcher (3-1).

These two proven pedigrees indicate a strong connection between the descendants of William Harding (3-9) who died in South Carolina in 1809 and the descendants of Henry Harding (3-1).

In his will, William Harding (3-9) names eight children, named in order in the will, Abner, Abraham, Salley, William, Elizabeth, Nicholas, George, and Henry. (See Chapter 15, South Carolina County Records.)

Nicholas is a rare name in the Hardin families. Henry Harden (3-1) (c 1680 to 1737) had a son Henry (3-2) and a son George (3-3). His son Henry Jr (3-2) married Wilmouth George, daughter of Nicholas George and named one of his sons Nicholas (3-6). The presence of the names George, Nicholas, and Henry in William Harding (3-9) of South Carolina's family along with DNA results indicates a likely relationship to that family.

I now believe that William Harding (3-9) (c 1740-1809) is an older son of George Harding (3-3), son of Henry Harden (3-1) and Ann Belcher (3-1). When George Harding (3-3) died in 1768, William Harding (3-9) was his executor, proving that George Harding had a relative, most likely a son, named William (3-9). Although William is not in the Stafford County birth records with the rest of the family, his connection is proven by several probate records referenced in his personal record in Chapter 4.

This group also proves that Henry Hardin (3-1) who married Ann Belcher (3-1) and William Hardin (2-1) of Northumberland Co. (Family #2), the ancestor of Group Two, cannot be related within thousands of years. The genetic distance between the two sets of descendants is between 18 and 23, far too distant for any possible connection. They also have a genetic distance in the same range from our fifth group, the family of Thomas Harden (1-23), who died in Rockingham Co., North Carolina.

Results for Group Four, R1B Haplogroup N.

This is an already extensive discussion. However recent Y-700 testing with Family Tree DNA (Group Combs & Harding etal under R-FT86565) paints an entirely new picture of this family, including the exact parentage of two previously unattached families, Joseph Harding (4-21) and William Harding (4-2)

DNA Results Analysis

Y-700 DNA is different from the lower-level testing discussed in this chapter. The earlier testing levels, both autosomal and lower-level Y-DNA tests used in earlier analysis work on a broad spectrum. However, Y-700 can provide in many cases a generation-by-generation tree if enough testers are found. Detailed discussions of these tests can be found on the Family Tree DNA web site, www.familytreedna.com. In short, each person tested is assigned a unique Haplogroup number, which ties into the huge family tree of man created by FTDNA. The Haplogroup changes when two or more people in the same generation are tested. The Haplogroup is then tied to the next distance ancestor. At times this can be hundreds of years. If enough people test, it will show a generation-by-generation pattern that indicates the parental line. The chart below shows how the Combs and Harding families are connected. The number below each name is the Family Tree DNA Y-700 Haplogroup Number that applies to each generation. Joseph Combs I is the parent generation. Joseph Combs II and William Harding are the child Haplogroups and Joseph Harding and Robert A Combs are the grandchild haplogroups. As you can see, there is a direct line link for all three generations, proving that William Harding and Joseph Harding belong in the Combs family. We also tested two descendants of another son of Joseph Combs II, Robert Ashby Combs, Haplogroup R-FTF65434, which finally proved he was the son of Joseph Combs II and father of Robert Aythelle Combs in the next generation, a huge breakthrough for that line.

Harding-Combs Connection From Family Tree DNA Project: Combs & Harding etal under R-FT86565		
	Joseph Combs I	
	R-FTD86565	
Joseph Combs II		William Harding
R-FTD20575		R-BY90511
Joseph Harding	Robert A Combs	
R-FTG39136	R-FTF65434	

In the case of William Harding (4-2), who was born about 1720, two men were tested for Y-700 DNA, Joe Richard in the chart below and K.W., a new tester. The Haplogroup for both, whose common ancestor was a son of William Harding (4-2) showed both men in Haplogroup R-BY90511, which a sub group of Haplogroup R-FTD86565, which to our surprise, is the Haplogroup of Joseph Combs I of Stafford County, Virginia (c 1695-1754), which proves that William Harding (4-2) is the son of this Joseph Combs I, most likely by a female Harding who lived in Stafford County at the time. He will be discussed further in the chapter on Family Number 4.

In the second group, Joseph Harding (4-21), who was born about 1750 in Virginia, whose ancestry had never been proven, we found again two testers. One, Boyd Hardin is in the chart below. The other is Gilbert. Both descend from a grandson of Joseph Harding (4-21). The Y-700 test showed that both men were in Haplogroup R-FTG39136, which is a descendant of Haplogroup R-FTD20575, which includes Joseph Combs II, the son of Joseph Combs I above, whose haplogroup R-FTD86565. This shows a direct connection from Joseph Combs I to his son William Harding and his son Joseph Combs II. Then the next generation shows the connection to Joseph Hardin. Of interest is the fact that a court order from Loudoun County in 1774 refers to Joseph Harding as Joseph Harding alias Combs, a common way of referring to men (and women) who were illegitimate. Harding refers to the mother, Combs to the father.

This group includes five autosomal testers. Genealogical research currently available says that these five people belong to three to five unrelated Harding families. However, the Y-DNA result given below shows that all five are members of one closely tied Harding family connected to William Harding (4-2) and Clarissa Million (4-2). I will discuss these results after presenting the following table.

#	Name of Participant	Earliest Ancestor on HHHDNA
1	Howard Harding	Lewis G. Harding b 1812 Mark, Charles
2	Boyd Wayne Harding	Joseph Harding b c 1750
3	John Oliver Harding	Benjamin Hardin b 1753 Virginia
4	Jeffrey Hardin	Benjamin Hardin b 1753 Virginia
5	Joe Richard Harding	John Bennett Harding b 1761 d 1847

Genetic Distance Chart for Group Four					
	Howard	Boyd W	John Oliver	Jeffrey	Joe R
Howard		0	1	1	3
Boyd W	0		2	1	3
John O	1	2		0	3
Jeffrey	1	1	0		2
Joe R	3	3	3	2	

This small group is filled with trouble spots. The five men who tested submitted lines going back to three early immigrant families. Unfortunately,

DNA Results Analysis

all five lines go back to families with separate HHDNA Haplogroups on FTDNA that are separated from each other by a genetic distance of 27.

These five men have never been placed in the same group in any published pedigrees. Yet the DNA places them tightly together. Published pedigrees must be incorrect.

Howard Harding in his tree shows descent from William Harding (2-1) of Group Two. After much research, when I analyzed his line, it goes back to Mark Harding (4-19), one of the sons of William Harding (4-2) and Clarissa Million of Stafford County, Virginia.

Joe Richard Harding traces back to John Bennett Harding in a direct line which appears correct. John Bennett Harding is the older son of William Harding(4-2) and Clarissa Million, whose mother was Martha Bennett.

This William Harding (4-2) has long been considered to be the William Harding born in 1738 to Charles Harding (2-2) and Rachel Lunsford (2-2) recorded in the Overwharton Parish Register in Stafford County, Virginia. Charles Harding (2-2) is the son of William Harding (2-1) (Family #2), which creates a DNA conflict. Howard and Joe Richard Harding are at a genetic distance of 20 from Charles Harding's other descendants in Family #2, which means that William Harding (4-2) who married Clarissa Million cannot descend from William Harding (2-1), Family #2. The younger William (4-2) must be placed in a family of his own, where he is DNA connected. We now know WilliM (4-2) is a natural son of Joseph Combs I.

Boyd Wayne Harding, mentioned earlier, traces back to Joseph Harding (1750-1808) (4-21) of Loudoun County, Virginia,

The last two men, John Oliver and Jeffrey, both have a well-established line back to Benjamin Hardin (4-9) of Henry Co., Kentucky, born 1753 in Virginia, a reputed Revolutionary War soldier most researchers place in the family of Mark Hardin (5-1) and Mary (MNU) (5-1) through their son Mark Hardin (5-4).

Unfortunately, Mark and Mary Hardin's descendants are already in the R1B Haplogroup A on the HHHDNA site, which has an average genetic distance of about 20 from this group so Benjamin (4-9) cannot belong there.

Records in Kentucky and Virginia, included in this book, prove that Benjamin Hardin (4-9) had a brother Enos Hardin (4-7) and probably brothers Evangelist Hardin (4-6) and James Hardin (4-8). Based on DNA evidence I believe that William Hardin (4-2) who married Clarissa Million (4-2) is the father of Enos, Evangelist, Benjamin, and James, by his first wife, now known to be Elizabeth Ashby. See genealogies in Chapter 3. DNA from Boyd Wayne Harding and others indicates that Joseph Harding (4-21) of

Loudoun County, VA must be a son of Joseph Combs II and nephew of William Harding. (4-2).

After much consideration, I have proposed in Family #4 that the first wife of William Harding (4-2) was Elizabeth Ashby (4-2) from Stafford County, Virginia. I will discuss who she is in Chapter 3, Family 4. An indication of the family connection is that names such as Lewis and Mark and Enos (or Ennis) show up in all branches of the family and that the sons of William Harding (4-2) and his first wife have very close ties to the Ashby family. I will further discuss this and show detailed references for this family in Family #4.

Finally, we look at autosomal DNA research, which at this generational distance is usually not helpful for proving relationships. Anything above an eight centimorgan length of common autosomal DNA can indicate a true relationship in genealogical time while below that number is likely to be genetic noise and not actual proof. In this case we have an unusual circumstance when comparing the descendants of William Harding's first wife and his second wife. Since both sides only inherit common autosomal DNA from William, this cuts the amount of inherited DNA between the two families in half, making any comparison at this level difficult since the results fall below the normal relationship level.

However, an unusual circumstance in one family, which is descended from two of William's children, adds back autosomal DNA and gives us a comparison between a descendant of Benjamin Hardin and his half brother and sister Enoch and Celia Harding easier. A GedMatch comparison shows a common 20 centimorgan connection between the two lines, enough to confirm that yes, they are closely related. Comparisons of other lines showed the expected distant connections. Combining Y-DNA and autosomal DNA proves the genetic connection between the two families beyond a reasonable doubt.

As you can see from the chart, all the tested men have a close genetic distance to each other, which indicates a connection no more than a generation or two before the soldier Benjamin Hardin. This proves that they all belong to the same close family, descended from Joseph Combs I (4-1) and William Harding (4-2). They are unrelated to anybody else in the HHDNA database. Current research on these families must be reconsidered. Y700 DNA now proves the ancestry of William Harding (4-2), , son of Joseph Combs I of Stafford County, Virginia. See Chapter 3, Family 4 for a deeper discussion.

DNA Results Analysis

Results for Group Five R1B Haplogroup A

Descendants of Mark Hardin (5-1) and Mary (MNU) (5-1) of Northumberland County Virginia (Family #6):

#	Participant	Earliest Ancestor on HHHDNA
1	James Hardin	John Hardin 1790-1867 VA-KY
2	Michael Hardin	John Hardin born 1763
3	David W. Hardin	John Hardin 1828-1894 Kentucky
4	Thomas Hardin	Mark Hardin 1681-1736 VA
5	William Hardin	Mark Hardin
6	Paul Hardin	Jean Pierre Hardouin 1635-1685
7	Justin Hardin	Richard Hardouin 1605
8	Joseph Hardin	George Hardin 1812 PA to 1854 IN
9	Ronald Hardin	Joseph Hardin b 1756 VA
10	A W Hardin	Joseph Hardin b 1756 VA
11	Stamey Hardin	Mark Hardin 1740-50-1797 NC
12	C J Hardin	Not stated
13	Robert Hardin	Mark Hardin 1681-1736 VA (25 Marker)
14	Francis Hardin	Not Stated (12 Marker DNA Test)
15	David L. Hardin	Daniel Hardin Kentucky

Genetic Distance Chart for Group Six 37 Markers Only												
	Ja	Mi	Dw	St	CJ	AW	Ro	Ju	Wm	Pa	Jo	Th
James		1	1	2	2	3	3	3	3	3	4	4
Michae	1		1	2	2	3	2	3	3	4	4	5
Dav W	1	1		2	1	2	2	2	4	3	4	4
Stamey	2	2	2		0	1	1	1	3	2	2	3
CJ	2	2	1	0		1	1	1	3	2	2	3
A W	3	3	2	1	1		0	2	4	3	3	4
Ronald	3	2	2	1	1	0		2	4	3	3	4
Justin	3	3	2	1	1	2	2		4	2	3	3
Will	3	3	4	3	3	4	4	4		3	4	4
Paul	3	4	3	2	2	3	3	2	3		4	3
Joseph	4	4	4	2	2	3	3	3	4	4		5
Thoma	4	5	4	3	3	4	4	3	4	3	5	

When I started to write this book, I wasn't sure I wanted to add the family of Mark Hardin (5-1) and Mary (MNU) (5-1) to my studies for several reasons. First it is a very complicated family which is hopelessly messed up on the Internet and in books. Nobody seems to agree on which families the dozens of Johns, Marks, Martins, Henrys, and Benjamins belong to, and which people don't belong in the family at all or aren't included when they should be. In addition, there is no evidence that the maiden name of the wife of Mark Hardin (5-1) is Hogue. I will use the abbreviation (MNU), maiden name unknown, for her throughout this book.

Then I discovered Kay Haden's website on this Hardin family. She went back through all the records for each descendant and restructured the family into what appear to be the correct generations. Although she has sorted out most of the family, she still left a few ambiguous connections where the evidence was not sufficient for a clear connection.

The analysis of the DNA for this family may clear up a few of these ambiguities in the families of Henry (5-5) and Mark Hardin (5-31) that Kay left unclear. Her incredibly detailed web site, which should become a book, is at http://freepages.rootsweb.com/~katy/genealogy/hardin/. The records she amassed are incredible.

Of the 14 men whose DNA was tested, 11 used the 37-marker test, which gives the most detailed information. I've divided these eleven men into five groups in the order they appear in the two tables above.

Before we begin, I will reiterate that this family is a genealogical mess. Kay Haden's site is one of the few relatively trustworthy sites on the Internet. Even there, do your own research.

The Founding Legend

Even the founding legend of the French ancestry of Mark Hardin (5-1) cannot be trusted as there is little evidence to support it. In brief, a man named Martyn Hardewyn was said to have escaped France and went to Staten Island, New York, where he married Madeleine Madame du Sauchoy and baptized five children in the 1670s and 1680s, Abraham, Isaac, Elizabeth, Jacob and Mark or Marcus. Many researchers have added Benjamin B. Hardin of Richmond, Henrico County, Virginia to this family on no evidence whatsoever. See WikiTree profiles for recent research.

To dispose of Benjamin, his descendants are listed in the FTDNA Hardin project as Haplogroup R, Group C. This family is not connected with the Mark Hardin (5-1) and Mary (MNU) (5-1) family in Group A, which we are analyzing here. In addition, there is no evidence whatsoever that the Mark Hardin (5-1) who bought land in Northumberland County, Virginia was in any way connected to the Staten Island family. No other descendants are known for the other four children born in Staten Island. This Mark Hardin is also unrelated to the other Northumberland County Harding families as shown by the DNA results.

DNA Results Analysis

The Brick Walls

Let's start with the first three men in the chart, James, Michael, and David W. All three descend from a man named John Hardin, born 1790, died 1867 in Kentucky. This line has been a brick wall for the family for a long time. Nobody has a clue where this John originated. The DNA says he is connected to the Mark Hardin (5-1) and Mary (MNU) (5-1) family with a genetic distance of one from each other.

The next two men, Stamey and CJ, also have brick walls. They are also closely related to each other but are a genetic distance of only two from the men in the previous paragraph. Their line goes back to Mark Hardin, who died in 1797, and Hannah Holder of Randolph County, North Carolina. This man had a son Mark, who left quite a few descendants in North Carolina. The DNA says they are part of the Mark Hardin (5-1) and Mary (MNU) (5-1) family.

The next two men, A.W. and Ronald, descend from Joseph Hardin, born about 1756 in Virginia and died in 1838 In Greenville, South Carolina. Joseph has been placed in several families, including as a descendant of Benjmain B. Hardin mentioned above. However, there is no evidence for his actual place of birth or his family connections. Although no connection has been found between this Joseph and Mark Hardin's (5-1) family, the DNA places them among the descendants of Mark Hardin (5-1) and Mary (MNU) (5-1). They are at a genetic distance of three from the first group, two from the second group and zero to one from each other.

The next two men, Justin and William, are proven descendants of Mark Hardin (5-1) and Mary (MNU) (5-1) through their son Henry Hardin (5-5). They are a genetic distance of two to three from the first group, one to three from the second group and two to four from the third group, again indicating a close relationship.

The next three are proven descendants of Mark Hardin (5-1) and Mary (MNU) (5-1) through their oldest son John Hardin (5-2) and his wife Catherine Marr. Their genetic distance is two to four from the previous groups, again indicating a close relationship.

Of the final three men, who I have not included in this analysis, Francis tested only 12 markers and does not have a submitted pedigree, so his ancestry is not known. Robert and Mark have proven lines from Mark Hardin (5-1) and Mary (MNU) (5-1) through their eldest son John (5-2) and his wife Catherine Marr

In summary, the DNA ties the three brick wall ancestries to the same family as the seven proven descendants of Mark Hardin (5-1) and Mary (MNU)? (5-1). It is possible that the three brick walls descend from Mark

Hardin (5-4), the son of Mark Hardin (5-1) and Mary (MNU) (5-1), whose children are unknown at this point. Mark Hardin (5-4) is known to have married Elizabeth (MNU) about 1751 and divorced her by 1753. After that he vanishes from the records. It is possible he married again later in life and lived in another part of the state. However, no records I have found can connect any children to him unless he is or connects with the Mark Hardin who married Hannah Holder mentioned in the second paragraph of this section.

These three brick walls are the only unknown lines that can be tied to Mark Hardin (5-1) and Mary (MNU) (5-1) by DNA testing. Further research is needed to determine how all these families connect.

Conclusion

When I compared the genetic distance between these five groups, the distance ranged from 7 to 10 for Group Five and Group Three and 18 to 23 between the rest of the groups, indicating no relationship between the five groups.

These results show that my original conclusion is correct. Henry Harding (3-1) who married Ann Belcher (3-1) (Family #3) was not a brother of William Harding (2-1) (Family #2). William was born about 1680 and married twice with children Charles (2-2), Thomas (2-4), and Francis (2-3) by his first wife and William (2-5) by his second wife. They belong in two separate unrelated families.

The DNA results also indicate that Thomas Harden (1-23) (c 1725-1809) (Family #5) is not related to either Henry or William but is from a separate family.

So far, my theories of the origin of Thomas Harden (1-23) who died in Rockingham County, North Carolina, indicate a connection to the family of Thomas Harding (1-1) and Ann Moseley (1-1) of Northumberland County, Virginia. It appears that no male line descendants of this couple except those possibly descended from Thomas Harden (1-23) (c 1725-1809) have been tested. It is also possible that this family has no other male line descendants to test when we remove the families of William Harding (2-1) and Henry Harding (3-1) from the family.

Chapter 3
Family Genealogies with References

The following records give references to the county records presented in detail in Parts 5 to 11. The following abbreviations are used: CO-court order books; DW-deed and will books; PPTL-personal property and land tax lists. Following the prefix is the book and page number where available. Records are separated by county and sorted by year to show the progression of the person's life. Book and page numbers are given where available. If I give no book and page number, the references will be found in date order. Either a full transcription or a detailed abstract of each record is given in Chapter Four.

Family 1: Thomas Harding of Northumberland Co., VA

1. Thomas¹ Harding (1-1) was born in England about 1630. He arrived in Northumberland County Virginia prior to 1658, when he received land from Richard Rice. He married **Anne Moseley** (1-1) about 1661 in Northumberland County, Virginia and died by 16 June 1675 in Northumberland Co., VA. See Family 7 for discussion of the purported Fauntleroy connection.

Children of Thomas¹ Harding and Anne Moseley:

    2   i. ANNE² HARDING born about 1662. In 1665 John Tyngey gave her one cow calf. In 1667 John Moseley calls her his cousin in his will.

+   3   ii. THOMAS HARDING (1-3) born 4 Sept 1664 St. Stephen's Parish, Northumberland Co., Virginia, married Miss Haynie and Ann, died 1691 Northumberland County, Virginia

    4   iii. JOHN HARDING (1-4) born by 6 Sept 1665 Northumberland County, Virginia and died after August 1667. John Tyngey mentions Thomas Harding's (1-1) oldest son and a younger son in August 1667. Since none of the other sons of

Harding Families of the Northern Neck of Virginia

Thomas Harding I (1-1) were[31] born before 1669, this must refer to a child who did not survive.

+ 5 iv. WILLIAM HARDING (1-5) born 20 July 1669 St. Stephen's Parish, Northumberland Co., Virginia, married Elizabeth Price, died 1696 Northumberland County, Virginia
+ 6 v. HENRY HARDING (1-6) born about 1672, married Jane (perhaps Arledge), died 1697 Northumberland County, Virginia
+ 7 vi. JOHN HARDING (1-7) born about 1674, married Anne Bennett, died 1714 Northumberland County, Virginia

Northumberland County, Virginia Records

1658 22 Nov: Richard Rice Patent recorded DW C-13

1658 22 Nov: Richard Rice signs patent to Thomas Harding and James Johnson DW C-13

1661 24 Aug: Witness deed James Johnson to James Claughton DW C-63

1661 09 Sep: With wife Anne assigns Rice land to James Johnson DW C-63

1661 09 Sep: Buys 150 acres from James Johnson DW C-63

1661 09 Sep: Buys 100 acres from James Claughton DW C-64

1663 12 Mar: Witnesses deed William Metcalf to John Tyngey DW C-125a

1664 04 Sep: Son Thomas born (St. Stephen's Parish Register)

1665 18 Aug: Wife Anne Harding acknowledges dower right DW C-170a

1665 19 Aug: James Claughton sells 100 acres to him DW C-170a

1665 06 Sept: John Tyngey gives Thomas Harding's daughter Ann Harding one cow calf DW C

1667 01 Aug: Will of John Tyngey mentions his eldest and youngest sons, no names DW D-30

1667 18 May: Will of John Moseley mentions cozens Thomas and Ann Harding DW D-126

1668/9 27 Jan: Serves on jury CO 4

1668/9 27 Jan: Gives evidence for John Saffin CO 4

1669 06 Apr: Guardian to John Moseley CO 4-31

1669 20 Jul: Son William born (St. Stephen's Parish Register)

1669 26 Dec: Serves on jury CO 4

1670 10 Oct: Serves on a jury CO 4

1670 27 Oct: Granted 575 acres on Mattapony River Land Grants

1671 15 Nov: Serves on a jury CO 4

1672 17 April: Named constable for Mattapony CO 4

1673/4 13 Feb: Thomas Harding, executor of Stephen Thomas, buys property. Land later passed to his son John and grandson Thomas. Essex Co., VA Deed Book 5 Page 196

1675 16 Jun: Widow Anne Harding granted administration of estate CO 4-116b

1675 16 Jan: Inventory of estate ordered CO 4-116b

---

[31] See bios of Henry and John Harding in Family 1 for proof of approximate birth dates.

1675 16 Jun: Appraisers of estate appointed CO 4-116b
1679 20 Aug: Widow is married to Richard Bradley CO 5-41
1679 20 Aug: Widow Anne Bradley named guardian to son Thomas Harding CO 5-41
1683 19 Aug: Anne Bradley named executor of estate of Richard Bradley CO 5-198

    3. **Thomas² Harding II** (Thomas¹) (1-3) was born 4 Sept 1664 in St. Stephen's Parish, Northumberland Co., VA. He married **Anne Haynie** about 1686. After the birth of her first son, her father took over raising her son Thomas. He died before 2 September 1691 Northumberland Co., VA. His widow (1-3) married Luke Rowland (1-3) around 1694/5.

    Children of Thomas² Harding II and Miss Haynie:

+ 8   i. THOMAS³ HARDING III (1-8) born about 1688 in Northumberland County, Virginia, married Mary Berry 1707, died 1722 Northumberland County, Virginia
+ 9   ii. WILLIAM HARDING (1-9) born 15 Feb 1690 St. Stephen's Parish, Northumberland Co., Virginia, married and had two children. No further information

Northumberland County, Virginia Records
1664 04 Sep: Born, son to Thomas Harding (St. Stephen's Parish Register)
1667 01 Aug: John Tyngey
1679 20 Aug: At age of fourteen chooses mother Anne Harding (now Bradley) as guardian CO 5-41
1689 18 July: Files suit against James Claughton CO 5-476
1690 19 Nov: Asks that 100 acres owned by his father be surveyed CO 5-525
1690 19 Nov: Sues Luke Rowland (1-3) for 4000 pounds of tobacco CO 5-528
1690 21 Nov: Chosen as guardian to brothers Henry and John Harding CO 5-529
1690 17 Dec: Damages awarded against Luke Rowland (1-3) CO 5-534
1690/1 19 Mar: Rowland dismissal order quashed CO 5-549
1691 02 Sep: Inventory of his estate ordered CO 5-566
1691 02 Sep: John Haynie guardian of his son Thomas Harding by Haynie's deceased daughter CO 5-566
1691/2 19 Feb: Accounting of William Harding estate and other orphans of his ordered. CO 5-581
1692 10 May: Appraisal of estate ordered CO 5-592
1696 22 May: John Haynie guardian of orphan Thomas Harding III vs Luke Rowland (1-3). who married his widow Anne (1-3). CO 5-728
1696 16 July: John Haynie guardian of the orphans vs Luke Rowland (1-3), who married his widow Anne (1-3) CO 5-736
1696 17 Sep: John Haynie guardian of the orphans vs Luke Rowland (1-3), who married his widow Anne (1-3) CO 5-742

Harding Families of the Northern Neck of Virginia

5. William² Harding (Thomas¹) (1-5) was born 20 Jul 1669 in St. Stephen's Parish, Northumberland Co., VA. He married **Elizabeth Price**, since records show he admitted having an illegitimate child with her. He died by 16 December 1696 Northumberland Co., VA.

Children of William² Harding and Elizabeth:
+ 10   i. JOHN³ HARDING (1-10) born October 1692 Northumberland Co., Virginia, married 1717 Jane (Barecraft) Trussell, died 1734 Northumberland County, Virginia

Northumberland County, Virginia Records
1691 20 Aug: Sues Luke Rowland (1-3) on behalf of John & Henry Harding, orphans of Thomas Harding dec CO 5-564
1691 20 Aug: Bond Luke Rowland (1-3) to answer suit of William Harding CO 5-564
1692 10 Oct: Elizabeth Price swears he is the father of her illegitimate child CO 5-603
1696 16 Dec: Henry Harding granted administration of his estate CO 5-753
1696 17 Dec: on Henry Harding's motion appraisal is ordered. CO 5-754
1697 21 Apr: Estate owes Henry Harding 800 pounds of tobacco CO 5-761
1697 22 Apr: James Johnson vs Henry Harding, his administrator CO 5-764
1697 22 Apr: John Cralle vs Henry Harding his administrator CO 5-765
1697 20 May: Johnson vs Harding continued CO 5-774
1697 20 May: Cralle vs Harding continued CO 5-774
1697/8 19 Feb: Charles Ashton and Jane his wife granted administration of his estate CO 5-814
1698 19 May: Carpentry work done for Richard Thompson to be valued CO 5-825
1698 21 Jul: Estate owes John Cralle 304 pounds tobacco CO 5-835
1698 21 Jul: Estate owes James Johnson 712 pounds of tobacco CO 5-835

6. Henry² Harding (Thomas¹) (1-6) was born about 1672 in Northumberland Co., VA. He married **Jane** about 1694. Her name is often given as Arledge but no known records support that. He died by 8 August 1697 in Northumberland Co., VA. He had no known children.

Northumberland County, Virginia Records
1690 21 Nov: Chooses brother Thomas Harding as guardian CO 5-529
1691 20 Aug: William Harding files suit against Luke Rowland (1-3) on his behalf CO 5-564
1696 16 Dec: Granted administration of William Harding estate CO 5-753
1696 17 Dec: Makes motion to appraise William Harding estate CO 5-754
1697 21 Apr: William Harding estate owes him 800 pounds tobacco CO 5-761
1697 22 Apr: James Johnson vs Henry Harding, William's administrator CO 5-764
1697 Apr: John Cralle vs Henry Harding, William's administrator CO 5-765 22
1697 20 May: Johnson vs Harding continued CO 5-774
1697 20 May: Cralle vs Harding continued CO 5-774

1697 08 Aug: His widow Jane Harding granted administration of his estate CO 5-781
1697 08 Aug: Appraisal of estate ordered CO 5-781
1697/8 19 Feb: Charles Ashton and Jane his wife to administer William Harding CO 5-814
1700/1 15 Jan: Charles Ashton dies, will proved by Trigue Allen and Charles Carpenter CO 6 (no page #)

7. **John² Harding** (Thomas¹) (1-7) was born about 1672 in Northumberland Co., VA. He married **Anne Bennett** before 1701 and died in Northumberland Co., VA before 15 Sept 1714. Anne was born 20 September 1676 in Northumberland County, Virginia, the daughter of Edward Bennett. After John Harding died, she married William Humphries. As her brother Cuthbert Bennett's next of kin, she administered Cuthbert's estate in 1718.

Children of John² Harding and Anne Bennett:

+ 11   i. THOMAS³ HARDING (1-11) born about 1698, lived in Stafford County, Virginia in 1720.
   12   ii. JOHN HARDING (1-12) born after 1701. On 30 March 1720 he, an orphan, was bound to Henry Garner by the Westmoreland County Court (CO 1720 Page 386) We have no record of his marriage whether he had any children or where he lived.
   13   iii. WILLIAM HARDING (1-13) born after 1701. As an orphan, he was bound to Edmund Jeffries by Westmoreland County Court (CO 1720 Page 286). We have no record of his marriage or of any children or where he lived after 1720.

Richmond County, Virginia Records
1678 02 Jun: Stephen Thomas wills him 200 acres in Richmond Co., VA Richmond Co. deeds 8-15
Northumberland County, Virginia Records
1676 20 Sep: Ann Bennett born. St. Stephens Parish Register
1680 15 Jan: Cuthbert Bennett born St. Stephens Parish Register
1690 21 Nov: Chooses brother Thomas as Guardian CO 5-529
1691 20 Aug: William Harding sues Luke Rowland (1-3) on his behalf CO 5-564
Westmoreland County, Virginia Records
1693 John Harding gives evidence CO
1698 Witnesses will of Philip Hearn CO
1703 Owes debt to William Clark Estate CO
1704 6 Jul: Guardian to nephew John, son of William and Elizabeth CO 231a
Northumberland County, Virginia Records
1714 15 Sep: William Humphries and Anne his wife grant son Thomas Harding to Grant Jewsbury CO 7-73
1717 21 Aug: Son Thomas (age over 14) chooses as guardian his cozen Thomas Harding CO 7-234

1718 20 Aug: William Humphries and wife Anne, next of kin, administered estate of Cuthbert Bennett CO 7-276

8. Thomas³ Harding III (Thomas², Thomas¹) (1-8) was born about 1688 in Northumberland Co., VA. He married **Mary Berry** about 1707. He died between 17 Oct 1722 and 19 Dec 1722 in Northumberland Co., VA

Children of Thomas³ Harding III and Mary Berry:

+ 14   i. WILLIAM⁴ HARDING (1-14) born about 1708 married Sarah Ball 1731 in Richmond County, Virginia, died 1762 Northumberland County, Virginia
+ 15   ii. THOMAS HARDING IV (1-15) born 21 Feb 1710/11 St. Stephen's Parish, Northumberland County, Virginia, married Jane Gibbons, died 1761 Northumberland County, Virginia
   16   iii. SAMUEL HARDING (1-16) was born about 1712 in Northumberland Co., Virginia. It is not known whether he married. He died before 12 May 1740 when Northumberland County Court ordered his estate to go to his sister Judith Harding. (DW I-77) No children are known.
   17   iv. JANE HARDING (1-17) was born about 1715 in Northumberland Co., Virginia. She married by 23 November 1733, when George Humphries, her husband, asked the Northumberland County Court for her portion of Thomas Harding's estate. (CO 9-129) It is not known when she died or whether she had children.
   18   v. JUDITH HARDING (1-18) was born about 1718 in Northumberland Co., Virginia. On 10 March 1739/40 a case she filed against George Ball was continued for report. (CO 10-125). On 12 May 1740 She received her share of estate of father Thomas Harding and brother Samuel Harding (DW I-77). On 13 May 1740, her part of estate of her father Thomas Harding was ordered partitioned (CO 10-139). We don't know if she married or had children.
   19   vi. MARY HARDING (1-19) was born about 1722 in Northumberland Co., VA. On 18 August 1725 from Northumberland County Court, she received land from her mother Mary Betts, late Harding, inherited from William Berry. (DW G-404) It is not known when she died or whether she ever had children.

Northumberland County, Virginia Records
1691 02 Sep: Age 3, Grandfather John Haynie named his guardian CO 5-566
1693/4 19 Jan: William Harvey arrested at land of John Haynie, guardian of Thomas Harding CO 5-646
1706/7 19 Mar: thought he paid his taxes but didn't through John Haynie Jr. CO 6-433
1713/14 12 Mar: Eliza Callan, age 7, apprenticed to him until age of 18 CO 7-21
1717 16 May: Appointed Constable for St. Stephen's Parish CO 7-215
1718 00 Nov: John Haynie deed to him acknowledged CO 7-296 19
1719 28 Apr: Witnessed will of William Nelms. DW G-53
1720 16 Jun: Judgment against Frances Harding Dec granted 300 pounds tobacco CO 8-19

1721 27 Sep: Buys 50 acres from John Bird of Stafford Co., VA DW G-253
1722 17 Oct: Wrote will DW G-290
1722 19 Dec: Will probated DW G-290
1722 19 Dec: Inventory of estate ordered, execs Mary Harden, George Ball DW H-19
1722/3 16 Jan: Inventory presented to court. CO 8-95
1722/3 20 Feb: Judgment for Richard Vanlandegam against estate for 400 pounds tobacco CO 8-99
1722/3 20 Feb: Judgment for Elizabeth Nelms against estate for 9-2-10 Sterling CO 8-99
1723 17 Jul: Added inventory filed with court. Approximate date. DW G-408
1724 24 May: Mary Harden, daughter of William Berry, land division surveyed DW H-4
1725 18 Aug: Widow Mary, wife of Rosten Betts Land to her daughter Mary Harding DW G-404

Richmond County, Virginia Records
1720 Jan 25: Bought 200 acres from Thomas Harding of Stafford County, Virginia Deeds 8-16
1722 03 Oct: Sold 200 acres purchased from Thomas Harding of Stafford 8-152

9. William³ Harding (Thomas², Thomas¹) (1-9) was born 15 February 1690 St. Stephen's Parish, Northumberland Co., VA. It is not known who he married or when he died.

Children of William³ Harding:
- 20   i. THOMAS⁴ HARDING (1-20) born 6 Oct 1717 St. Stephen's Parish, Northumberland Co., Virginia. No further information.
- 21   ii. JUDDAYDAH HARDING (1-21) born 16 July 1721 St. Stephen's Parish, Northumberland Co., Virginia. No further information.

Northumberland County, Virginia Records
1691/2 19 Feb: Audit of accounts of William Harding, orphan of Thomas, ordered. CO 5-581
1713 19 May: Sells land from his father Thomas Harding to Samuel Robinson DW F-283

10. John³ Harding (William², Thomas¹) (1-10) was born October 1692 in Northumberland Co., VA. After his father died, he was raised by his uncle John Harding (1-7). He married by 19 Sept 1717 Northumberland Co., VA **Jane (Barecraft) Trussell**, widow of John Trussell. He died before April 1734 Westmoreland Co., VA. He had one known son but no known descendants.

Children of John³ Harding and Jane Barecraft:
- 22   i. WILLOUGHBY⁴ HARDEN (1-22) born 23 Feb 1726/7 in Westmoreland Co., VA. On 25 May 1736 he was bound by the Westmoreland County

Court to George Jeffries, having turned nine the last February 23. (CO) It is not known whether he married or had children.

Northumberland County, Virginia Records

1717 19 Sep: With wife Jane, widow of John Trussell, administer John Trussell's estate CO 7-241

1717 19 Sep: With wife Jane to take inventory of John Trussell estate. CO 7-241

1724 24 Sep: 1724 Jane Hardin named as daughter of Thomas Barecraft in his will DW G-390

Westmoreland County, Virginia Records

1704 06 Jul: Bound to uncle John Harden CO 231a

1733/4 Jan: Witnessed will of William Butler DW 18

1734 26 Mar: Matthew Trussell to administer estate CO-131

1734 28 May: Matthew Trussell files inventory CO-137

1736 25 May: Orphan son Willoughby bound to George Jeffries CO-197a

11 Thomas³ Harding (John², Thomas¹) (1-11) was born about 1698 and was living in Northumberland County, Virginia as late as 1717 when he chose his cousin Thomas Harding as his guardian. He was living in Stafford County, VA in 1720 when he sold land inherited from his grandfather Thomas Harding through his father John Harding. We do not know his wife's name or family although he may have married a sister of Thomas Ashby (c 1690-1754), later found further west. As one of Thomas Harden's descendants, my sister I have many matches (over 80) with people descended from Thomas Ashby. This means that this Thomas Harding is a strong candidate for of being the father of Thomas Harding who died in 1809 in Rockingham County, North Carolina.

Northumberland County, Virginia Records

1714 15 Sep: William Humphries and Anne his wife granted him, their son, to Grant Jewsbury CO 7-73

1717 21 Aug: Chooses as guardian his cozen Thomas Harding CO 7-234

1720 25 Jan: Sells 200 acres to Thomas Harding of Northumberland Co. Was of Stafford County. Land from his father John Harding. Richmond Co. deeds 8-15

Children of Thomas Harding⁴ and Miss Ashby:

+ 23   i. THOMAS⁴ HARDING (1-23) born about 1725 perhaps Stafford County, Virginia, Married Sarah Cox, Died 1809 in Rockingham Co., North Carolina

14. William⁴ Harding (Thomas³, Thomas², Thomas¹) (1-14) was born about 1708 Northumberland Co., VA, He married **Sarah Ball**, born 10 March 1714, daughter of Joseph Ball and Mary Spencer, 14 Feb 1730/31 N. Farnham

Parish, Richmond Co., VA. He died Between 15 November 1761 and 8 February 1762 in Northumberland Co., VA.

Children of William[4] Harding and Sarah Ball:

+ 24   i. JUDITH[4] HARDING (1-24) born about 1732 Northumberland County, Virginia, married Joseph Wildey Jr. in 1757, John Anderson 1774.
   25   ii. BETTY HARDING (1-25) born about 1735 married Griffin Fauntleroy
   26   iii. HANNAH HARDING (1-26) married John Lewis
   27   iv. SARAH HARDING (1-27) married --- Humphrey, John Cralle Jr.
   28   v. MARY HARDING (1-28) married Matthew Neale
   29   vi. MOLLY HARDING (1-29)
   30   vii. JANE HARDING (1-30) married Parrish Garner
   31   viii. FRANCES HARDING (1-31) married Samuel Lewis
+ 32   ix. WILLIAM HARDING (1-32) born about 1754 married Milly Glasscock, died 1786 Northumberland County, Virginia

Northumberland County, Virginia Records

1732 06 Aug: Requests valuation of negroes belonging to Father Thomas' orphans CO 9-64

1739 12 Jun: Sues Henry Dawson for 434 pounds tobacco, wins. CO 10-99

1739/40 10 Mar: serves as processioner in 1st pct St. Stephen's Parish CO 10-124

1744 07 Oct: Witnesses deed from George Ball to sons Richard and John Ball DW J-52

1745 09 Jul: Sues Richard Gorham for 2-4-2 Sterling and wins. CO 11-74

1744 07 Oct: Witnesses a deed George Ball to his sons Richard and John Ball. DW J-52

1746 06 Mar: Spencer Ball deed to William Harding ordered recorded CO 11-179

1747 13 Apr: Spencer Ball to brother-in-law William Harding and sister Sarah negroes to go to children of William and Sarah DW J-193

1747 15 Sep: Buys 393 acres in Northumberland County from William and Mary Hughlett. DW J-245

1747 09 Nov: Deed from William and Mary Hughlett ordered recorded CO 11-260

1747/8 14 Mar: Bond to Spencer Ball ordered recorded CO 11-281

1750 10 Sept: Appointed guardian to Mary Appleby, orphan of John Appleby CO 12-80

1750 10 Sep: He gets Mary Appleby's part of her father's estate. CO 12-81

1750 10 Dec: Appraises estate of Timothy Paydon CO 12-111

1751: Buys land from John Evins DW 2-66

1751 12 Nov: Sues Samuel Partridge CO 12-245

1752: Gift to daughter Sarah provided he has no son by present wife. DW 2-105

1752 13 Apr: Bond to Sarah Humphries ordered recorded CO 12-268

1752 14 April: Suit against John Evins dismissed CO 12-276

1752 25 Sep: Sued by Richard Jackson, judgment granted 1-18-11 Sterling CO 12-344

1753 09 Jul: Attachment against him CO 13-14

1753 14 Aug: Attachment against estate of William Hughlett CO 13-42

1754 13 Mar: Attachment against estate of William Hughlett CO 13-91
1754 14 Oct: As inspector, gives report CO 13-226
1755 10 Mar: Bond to Matthew Neale ordered recorded CO 13-273
1755 13 Oct: Witness for James Crane, earns 25 pounds tobacco CO 13-381
1755 11 Nov: Gift to daughter Mary, wife of Mathew Neale DW 3-251
1755 13 Nov: Deed to Matthew Neale ordered recorded CO 13-410
1756 10 Mar: Witness for James Wilkins, earns 100 pounds tobacco CO 13-
1756 10 May: Produces inspection report for Coan Warehouse CO 14-62
1757 10 Oct: Filed report on Coan Warehouse CO 14-228
1758 19 Oct: Swore to his inspector's report CO 14-348
1758-19 Oct: Case vs Jonathan Edwards continued
1761 13 Apr: Administers estate of Thomas Harding DW 5
1761 15 Nov: Writes will DW 5-496
1762 08 Feb: Will proved. DW 5-496
1762 12 Apr: Thomas Harding and William Harding estates separated. DW 6-19
1762 12 Apr: Widow Jane Harding files bond with court CO 15-367
1762 10 May: His will proved in court CO 15-377-8
1762 13 Sep: Report on value of slave from his estate filed 15-515
1763 13 Jun: Widow Sarah writes will DW 6-316
1763 Dec: Widow Sarah will probate DW 6-316 12.
1763 12 Dec: Spencer Ball negroes divided among 9 children DW 6-360
1764 09 Jan: Widow Sarah inventory recorded. DW 6-340
1765 12 Aug: Inventory ordered 8 Feb 1762 is recorded DW 6-590
1765 12 Aug: Sale list of estate recorded DW 6-591

15. Thomas⁴ Harding IV (Thomas³, Thomas², Thomas¹) (1-15) was born 21 Feb 1710/11 St. Stephen's Parish, Northumberland Co., VA. He married **Jane Gibbons** about 1732. He died by 13 Apr 1761 Northumberland Co., VA

Children:
- 33 i. JOHN⁵ HARDING (1-33) born 21 Apr 1734 Northumberland Co., VA
- 34 ii. THOMAS HARDING (1-34) born 9 Sep 1737 Northumberland, VA
- 35 iii. FRANCES HARDING (1-35) born 9 Sept 1737 Northumberland Co., VA
- 36 iv. JEMAYMA HARDING (1-36) born 3 May 1739 Northumberland, VA, married James Hudnall (1-36) 20 March 1771 in Northumberland County, Virginia.
- 37 v. MARY HARDING (1-37) born 6 Apr 1741 Northumberland Co., VA
- + 38 vi. SAMUEL HARDING (1-38) born 6 Mar 1744 Northumberland Co., Virginia, died 1819 Northumberland County, Virginia. Never married.
- + 39 vii. JUDITH HARDING (1-39) born 18 July 1745 Northumberland Co., VA, Married Ellis Hudnall (1-39) 27 May 1765 Northumberland County, Virginia
- 40 ix. HATTE HARDING (1-40) born 5 Apr 1748 Northumberland Co., VA
- 41 x. JANE HARDING (1-41) born about 1750

Northumberland County, Virginia Records

Family Genealogies with References

1710 21 Feb: Born, son to Thomas Jr, St Stephens Parish Register
1722 19 Dec: Buys (with mother, Mary) 120 acres in Northumberland Co. from James Palmer DW G-296
1733 16 Aug: Request valuation of negroes who belong to orphans of father Thomas Harding CO 9-111
1739 08 Oct: Sues Thomas Machen CO 10-109
1739 10 Dec: Wins case against Thomas Machen for 1275 pounds tobacco CO 10-116
1739 10 Dec: Morris Gibbons wins case against Thomas Machen for 1275 pounds tobacco CO 10-116
1739/40 10 Mar: Processioner for St. Stephen's Parish 6th precinct CO 10-124
1746: Will of Morris Gibbons mentions Daughter Jane Harding DW J-165
1749 13 Jun: Suit by Colson dismissed CO 11-481
1749 11 Jul: Jury out on suit by John Smith, exec of John Smith decd. CO 11-500
1749 12 Jul: Suit by John Smith in Detinue CO 11-509?
1752 18 Jun: Appointed Overseer for road in Room of Thomas Dameron CO 12-299
1752 15 Jul: Suit against William Johnston continued CO 12-320
1753 13 Feb: Suit against William Johnson dismissed CO 12-383
1753 13 Feb: Suit by William Johnson dismissed CO 12-383
1753 13 Aug: Appointed surveyor of highway from Smith Oldfield to Coan Warehouse CO 13-36
1753 14 Aug: Suit by Thomas Ball, judgment granted CO 13-42
1754 11 Feb: Appraises estate of Robert Rowland CO 13-74
1754 04 Jul: Witness for Spencer Haynie, earns 150 pounds tobacco for 6 days at court CO 13-173
1756 08 Mar: Administrator of estate of Joseph Robinson WD 3
1757 14 Feb: To process part of Robinson movable estate CO 14-120
1757 01 Mar: As executor, gets possession of Joseph Robinson Jr. part of father's estate WD 4-48
1757 14 Mar: Processing Robinson estate filed CO 14-121
1758 11 Sep: Suit vs Jonathan Edwards CO 14-341
1761 13 Apr: Estate administered by Jane and William Harding WD 5 ??
1762 12 Apr: Jean Harding takes over administration of estate of husband WD 6-19
1762 10 May: Appraisal of estate ordered. WD 6-36

23 Thomas[4] Harden (1-23) (Thomas[3], John[2], Thomas[1])was born about 1725 in Virginia. The county is not known. He first appears in the records in Westmoreland County, Virginia, when he purchased land from Thomas Blundell 27 March 1753. He married first, **Sarah Cox,** about 1750. They lived in Westmoreland County. By 1758 he and Sarah had moved to Fairfax County, Virginia, where he first appears as a juror. Sarah died about 1767 in

Harding Families of the Northern Neck of Virginia

Fairfax County, and he married before 1770 **Eleanor Taylor**, daughter of Henry Taylor of Fairfax County, who mentioned him as a son-in-law in his 1770 will.

Prior to 1786, he moved to Caswell County, North Carolina with his family. By 1789 he was living in Rockingham County, North Carolina. In May 1809 he wrote his will and died soon thereafter.

In his will, Thomas Harden split his bequests into two segments, the longest one dealing with his wife Eleanor and his youngest three children. In a much shorter paragraph at the end of the will, he left bequests to his older children, almost certainly from his first wife Sarah.

Thomas Harden's origin is corrected here. I no longer think he was a son of John Harden and Jane Bearcraft as I have previously stated because there is no guardian record for him while there is for another of John Harden's sons. We do have Y-DNA results for three of his descendants, but he does not share any other Harden-Hardin-Harding test results. See www.hhhdna.com for more information and updated results

Children of Thomas[4] Harding and Sarah (Cox?) :

+ 42   i. JANE[5] HARDEN (1-42) born about 1752 Westmoreland County, Virginia, married William Hornbuckle
+ 43   ii. PRESLEY HARDEN (1-43) born about 1753 Westmoreland County, Virginia, married Susannah Williams, died in Williamson County, Tennessee.
+ 44   iii. JOHN HARDEN (1-44) born about 1754, Westmoreland County, Virginia married Sarah Holt, died in 1808 in Orange County, North Carolina.
+ 45   iv. JEREMIAH HARDEN (1-45) born about 1756 Westmoreland County, Virginia, married Sarah Wiley, died by 1798 in North Carolina.
    46   v. ANN HARDEN (1-46) born about 1758, Fairfax Co., Virginia and died before 1809, when her father's will was written. She married John Reid. It is not known if she had any children.
    47   vi. SARAH HARDEN (1-47) born about 1760 Fairfax Co., Virginia She died after 1809, when her father's will was written. She married Mr. Rogers. It is not known whether she had children.
+ 48   vii. THOMAS HARDEN (1-48) born about 1762 Fairfax County, Virginia m Elizabeth Powell, died by 1819 in Giles County, Tennessee.

Children of Thomas[1] Harden and Eleanor Taylor:

+ 49   viii. HENRY HARDEN (1-49) born about 1772 Fairfax County, Virginia married Elizabeth Hornbuckle, died about 1815 in Rockingham County, North Carolina
+ 50   ix. PETER HARDEN (1-50) born about 1775 Fairfax County Virginia, never married, died 1819 Rockingham Co., NC
+ 51   x. PEGGY HARDEN (1-51) born about 1776 Fairfax County, Virginia, never married, died 1840 Rockingham Co., NC

Westmoreland County, Virginia Records

Family Genealogies with References

1753 27 Mar: Bought 50 acres from Thomas Blundell DW 11-482
1754 28 May: Paid by Abraham Garrard for appearing in court CO
1755 01 Mar: Witnessed deed Edwin Turner to Peter Presley Cox DW 12-
1759 24 Oct: Sold 50 acres to John Brown DW 13-253

Fairfax County, Virginia Records
1758 18 May: Served on a jury CO
1761 19 Mar: Served on a jury CO
1761 16 Jun: Sued by Bryan Alliston, trespass CO
1761 16 Jun: Sued Clement Atchison, dismissed CO
1761 15 Sep: Charged with received counterfeit bill CO
1762 16 Jun: Sued by Robert Bogges Jr. CO
1763 18 Mar: Alliston suit Bryan pleads not guilty CO
1763 22 Jul: Awarded costs as a witness CO
1764 20 Mar: Appointed surveyor CO
1764 24 Sep: Witness for defendant Boggess, paid for three days CO
1768 19 Sep: Deed from William Fitzhugh ordered recorded CO
1768: Leased land from William Fitzhugh (deed book lost) Deed H-262
1768 20 Sep: Served as juror CO
1768 23 Nov: Witness for William Gardner and Thomas Carson CO
1770 29 Mar: Henry Taylor calls him his son-in-law in will, Wills
1770 21 May: Replaced as surveyor CO
1770 18 Jun: On case with Frances Poston CO
1773 21 Jun: Witnessed deed William Fitzhugh to Thomas Kirby Deed
1773 25 Jun: Witnessed deed William Fitzhugh to Edward Potter Deed
1774 May: Appraised estate of Benoni Kent Will

Loudoun County, Virginia Records
1783 listed as a tithable.

Caswell County, North Carolina Records
1786 07 Jun: Witnessed will of William Johnson to Thomas Hornbuckle Deeds
1786 10 Oct: Of Rockingham, Buys 188 acres from James and Mary Scott Deeds E-144
1786 01 Jun: Witnessed deed Daniel Johnston to John Hardin Deeds E-288
1789 14 Aug: Of Guilford Co., Bought 158 acres from Daniel Gwynn Deeds F-322
1794 02 Dec: Of Rockingham Co. Sells 145 acres to son Henry Harden Deeds H-433
1795 18 Jan: of Rockingham Co. Sells 100 acres to son Thomas Harden Jr. Deeds H-417
1799 15 Apr: Of Rockingham Co., buys 168 acres from Jesse Dickens Deed L-61

Rockingham County, North Carolina Records
1787 17 May: Owns land near William Hall Deeds
1789 28 Aug: Owns land by William Williams Deeds B-250
1790: Federal Census Listed in Salisbury District
1790: Buys 60 acres from Peter O'Neal Deeds C-40
1793: 05 Jun: Witnessed deed Andrew Wilson to Thomas Hornbuckle Deeds D-12

1795 16 Nov: William Hornbuckle sells land near him. Deeds
1797: Owns land near land sold by A Harvey to Peter Harden Deeds E-236
1800: Federal Census 00011 00011
1809: 25 May: 1809 Wrote his will. Wills A-86

24. Judith[5] Harding (William[4], Thomas[3], Thomas[2], Thomas[1]) (1-24) was born about 1732 in Northumberland County, Virginia. She married **Joseph Wildey Jr** in December 1757. Joseph died between 10 September 1769. when he made his will, and 11 December 1769, when the will was proved. She married **John Anderson** on 12 December 1774.

Children of Joseph Wildey Jr and Judith[5] Harding:
- 52   i. SARAH[6] WILDEY (1-52) born 2 Sept 1758 Northumberland Co., VA
- 53   ii. WILLIAM WILDEY (1-53) born 9 April 1760 Northumberland, VA
- 54   iii. MOLLY WILDEY (1-54) born 14 Sept. 1761 Northumberland VA
- 55   iv. JUDITH WILDEY (1-55) born 17 Mar 1763 Northumberland VA
- 56   v. JOSEPH WILDEY (1-56) born about 1765
- 57   vi. HELI WILDEY (1-57) born about 1766 married Betty Nelms 26 April 1790
- 58   vii. JANE WILDEY (1-58) born about 1767
- 59   viii. ELIZABETH WILDEY (1-59) born about 1768

Northumberland County, Virginia Records
1757 Dec: Joseph Wildey and Judith Harding were married
1769 10 Sep: Joseph Wildey wrote his will WD 7-443
1769 11 Dec: Joseph Wildey will is proved. WD 7-443

32. William[5] Harding (William[4], Thomas[3], Thomas[2], Thomas[1]) (1-32) was born about 1754 in Northumberland County, Virginia, and married **Milly Glasscock**. He died in 1786 in Northumberland County, Virginia.

Children of William[5] Harding and Milly Glasscock:
- + 60   i. JAMES[6] HARDING (1-60) born 18 Nov 1775 in Northumberland Co., Virginia. He married Ann.
-    61   ii. WILLIAM HARDING (1-61) born 7 Jan 1778 in Northumberland Co., Virginia
-    62   iii. THOMAS HARDING (1-62) born 7 Jan 1778 in Northumberland Co., Virginia
-    63   iv. SARAH HARDING (1-63)
-    64   v. ANN HARDING (1-64)
-    65   vi. EASTER HARDING (1-65)
-    66   vii. ALCEY HARDING (1-66)
-    67   viii. MILLY HARDING (1-67)

Northumberland County, Virginia Records
1777 03 Nov: Sold 50 acres to Thomas Downing WD 12-238
1782-1796: On Personal Property Tax List, estate 1787-1796

1784 05 Feb: Will of William Glascock mentions son-in-law William Harding and daughter Milly Harding. WB 7:459
1785 05 Mar: Purchases 210 acres from William Neale WD 12-409
1786 11 Mar: Will of William Harding written WD 13-198
1786 12 Jun: Will of William Harding proved WD 13-158

38. Samuel^5 Harding (Thomas^4, Thomas^3, Thomas^2, Thomas^1) (1-38) was born 6 March 1744 St. Stephen's Parish, Northumberland Co., VA. It is not known whether he married. He died in 1820 in Northumberland Co., Virginia. No wife or children are mentioned in his will. He did leave bequests to his grand-nephews, William Jett, Joseph Jett, and John H. Jett.

Northumberland County, Virginia Records
1769 Feb: Witnesses will of Jesse Ball DW 1
1770 14 May: Administered estate of William Greenwood DW
1783-1802: On Personal Property Tax Lists
1810: Appears in 1810 Federal Census
1819 15 Jun: Will written DW 21-447
1820: Appears in 1820 Federal Census
1820 11 Dec: Will proved DW 21-447

39. Judith^5 Harding (Thomas^4, Thomas^3, Thomas^2, Thomas^1) (1-39) was born 18 July 1745 Northumberland Co., VA, She married **Ellis Hudnall** (1-39) 27 May 1765 in Northumberland County, Virginia.

Children of Ellis Hudnall and Judith Harding:
+ 68   i. ELIZABETH^6 HUDNALL born 1764 in Northumberland County, Virginia
   69   ii. FRANCES HUDNALL (1765-1823)
   70   iii. ELLIS HUDNALL 1770-
   71   iv. JOHN HUDNALL 1790

42. Jane^5 Harden (Thomas^4, Thomas^3, John^2, Thomas^1)) (1-42) also known as Sarah Jane Harden (1-42), was born about 1752 Westmoreland Co., VA. She married about 1770 Fairfax Co., VA **William Hornbuckle** (1-42). She had a large family, lived in Kentucky and later in Callaway County, Missouri, where she died in 1831.

NOTE: This is my ancestor. I have compiled over 1,500 of her descendants as part of my book *Hornbuckles In America*, published in 2000. Anyone interested in the Hornbuckle family should contact me directly for more information.

43. Presley^5 Harden (Thomas^4, Thomas^3, John^2, Thomas^1) (1-43) was born about 1753 in Westmoreland County, Virginia and moved with the rest of his family to Fairfax County VA and later to Caswell Co., North Carolina, where he lived until about 1805, when he moved to Williamson County, Tennessee, where he spent the rest of his life. He married **Susannah Williams** about 1773.

Children of Presley⁵ Harden and Susannah Williams:
- \+ 72   i. JOHN⁶ HARDEN (1-72) born 1775 in North Carolina, married Susannah Appleton, and Mary Tilman, died 1846 in Lauderdale County, Alabama.
- \+ 73   ii. PEGGY HARDEN (1-73) born about 1776 North Carolina, married Samuel Shelborne.
- 74   iii. THOMAS HARDEN (1-74) born about 1778 North Carolina
- \+ 75   iv. JEREMIAH HARDEN (1-75) born about 1780 North Carolina, married Elizabeth Click, died in 1828 in Williamson County, Tennessee.
- 76   v. SALLY HARDEN (1-76) born about 1785 Caswell Co NC. She died about 1835 in Dyer Co., Tennessee and married Gregory Wilson 17 August 1815 in Williamson Co., Tennessee. She is listed with her husband in the 1820 Census of Williamson Co., Tennessee
- 77   vi. POLLY HARDEN (1-77) born about 1790 North Carolina. She wrote her will 19 September 1831 and died unmarried before 17 August 1837 Lauderdale Co., Alabama.
- 78   vii. SUSANNAH HARDEN (1-78) born about 1792 North Carolina. She was mentioned in Polly Harden's Will, but nothing further is known about her.

Caswell County, North Carolina Records
1786: State Census 1786 Listed with 2 males 21-60 and 3 males 0-21 and 3 females.
1786 10 Oct: Witnessed deed James Scott to Thomas Harden Deed E-144
1790: Listed in Federal Census Hillsborough District.
1790 30 Nov: Witnessed deed Jeremiah Harden to Lewis Pike Deed H-80
1795 19 Jul: Witnessed division of Waddy Tate estate Deed Books
Williamson County, Tennessee Records
1803 14 Mar: Leased land from James Anderson Deeds A-325
1804 09 Jul: Bought land from Reuben Parks. Deeds A-522
1805: On Personal Property Tax List PPTL
1807 25 Jul: Sold land to John Harden. Deeds B-514
1807 25 Jul: Sold land to Jeremiah Harden. Deeds B-515
1815 Jan: Bought a bed at estate sale Wills
1816 Apr: Bought items at estate sale. Wills
1820: Listed in Federal Census Page 646
Rockingham County, North Carolina Records
1826 29 July Mentioned in sister Peggy Harden's will, Wills B-235
Lauderdale County, Alabama Records
1844 27 Mar: Harden Cemetery Widow Susannah buried

44. John⁵ Harden (Thomas⁴, Thomas³, John², Thomas¹) (1-44) was born about 1754 in Westmoreland Co., Virginia and died 14 July 1808 in Orange

Family Genealogies with References

County, North Carolina. He married **Sarah Holt** on 14 December 1783 in Orange County, North Carolina. Sarah died in Orange County after 20 September 1814, when she made her will.

Children of John^5 Harden and Sarah Holt:

+ 79   i. John Harden^6 (1-79) born 28 September 1790 in North Carolina He married Rebecca Holt and died in 1875 in Graham, Alamance County, North Carolina.
- 80   ii. Mary (Polly) Harden (1-80) born about 1795 Orange Co., NC. She died 1 June 1860 in Missouri. She married John Prather (1790-1828) on 26 November 1812 in Orange County, North Carolina.
- 81   iii. Sally Harden (1-81) born 4 March 1797 in Orange Co., NC. She died 27 July 1877 in North Carolina. She married James Clay Wren.
- 82   iv. Elizabeth Harden (1-82) born 22 April 1799, Orange Co. and died 19 June 1825. She married Lewis Holt.
- 83   v. Margaret Harden (1-83) born 7 January 1807 Orange Co., NC. She married George Thomas Hurdle.
- 84   vi. Jane Harden (1-84) married William Whitsitt

Caswell County, North Carolina Records
1786 01 Jun: Buys 600 acres from Daniel Johnston Deed E-288
1786 04 Nov: Witnesses deed John Murphy to Jeremiah Harden Deed F-312
1789 22 Sep: Of Orange Co., sells 20 acres to Thomas Hornbuckle Deed H-151
1790 04 Nov: Witnesses deed Rowland Hughes to William Brown Deed

Orange County, North Carolina Records
1790: Federal Census, listed in Chatham District
1798 23 Jan: Will of Michael Holt mentions Sarah Hardin. Wills
1807 24 Oct: Writes will. Wills D-235
1808 Aug: Will probated. Wills D-235
1814 20 Sep: Wife Sarah writes will, Wills D-418
1814 Nov: Wife Sarah's will probate Wills D-418

45. Jeremiah^5 Harden (Thomas^4, Thomas^3, John^2, Thomas^1) (1-45) was born about 1756 in Westmoreland County, Virginia and died about 1797 in Tennessee. He married **Sarah Wiley** on 3 December 1789 in Orange County, North Carolina. She was born about 1770 and died in 1865 in Columbia County, Georgia.

Children of Jeremiah^5 Harden and Sarah Wiley:

- 85   i. MARGARET^6 HARDEN, (1-85) born 4 March 1797 in Tennessee and died 2 December 1882 in Talbot County, Georgia. She married William B. Binion (1-85) 15 August 1813 in Columbia County, Georgia.

Fairfax County, Virginia Records
1782-1784: On Personal Property Tax Lists
1783 18 Jun: Served as a juror CO
1783 19 Jun: Defendant on charge of trespass CO

1784 Jul: Witnessed eight leases for William Fitzhugh Deeds
1785 19 Jan: Paid 650 pounds tobacco for guarding prisoners to Richmond. CO
Caswell County, North Carolina Records
1786 10 Oct: Witnessed deed James Scott to Thomas Harden Deed E-144
1786 04 Nov: Of Caswell Co., Buys 200 acres from John Murphy and wife Deed F-312
1790 30 Nov: Of Caswell Co. Sells 20 acres to Lewis Pike Deed H-80
1795 08 Jan: Witnessed deed John Lenox to Lewis Pike Deed
Rockingham County, North Carolina Records
1793 14 Oct: Witnessed deed George Hornbuckle to William Hornbuckle Deed

48. Thomas[5] Harden Jr. (Thomas[4], Thomas[3], John[2], Thomas[1]) (1-48) was born about 1762 in Fairfax County, Virginia and died before 1820 in Giles County, Tennessee. He married **Elizabeth Powell** on 20 December 1791 in Orange County, North Carolina. She was born about 1768 in North Carolina and died after 1850 in Shelby County, Tennessee.

Children:

+ 86 i. JEREMIAH[6] HARDEN (1-86) born about 1793 North Carolina, married Sally McCutchin, died after 1840 in Poinsett County, Arkansas.
+ 87 ii. WILLIAM PRESLEY HARDEN (1-87) born about 1795 North Carolina, married Agnes Hale, died about 1870 in Boone County, Arkansas.
+ 88 iii. HIRAM HARDEN (1-88) born 1797 North Carolina, married Cynthia Estill and Frances Smith, died in Navarro County, Texas in 1864.
  89 iv. THOMAS HARDEN (1-89) born about 1811 Tennessee. He was enumerated in 1850 in Shelby County, Tennessee. At the time he was unmarried. It is not known whether he had children.
+ 90 v. JOSHUA HARDEN (1-90) born about 1812 Tennessee, married Lucy Woodson, and Eliza O'Quin and lived in Shelby County, Tennessee.

Caswell County, North Carolina Records
1795 18 Jan: Buys 100 acres from his father Thomas Harden Deeds H-417
1796 15 Sep: Of Caswell Co. Sells 100 acres to Samuel Cobb Deeds K-9
Williamson County, Tennessee Records
1805: Personal Property tax list PPTL
1811 05 Oct: Samuel Shelburne sold land to Thomas Harden of Williamson Co, TN. Deeds Book B-670
1815 05 Nov: Sold land to John Harden. Deeds Book D-125
Giles County, Tennessee Records
1818 27 Aug: Makes deed of gift to his son Hiram Harden. Deeds C-378
1820: Federal Census Giles County, Tennessee, Elizabeth on Page 17
Shelby County, Tennessee Records
1850: Federal Census Elizabeth Age 82 born N Carolina

49. Henry[5] Harden (Thomas[4], Thomas[3], John[2], Thomas[1]) (1-49) was born about 1772 in Fairfax County, Virginia and died about 1815 in Rockingham

Family Genealogies with References

County, North Carolina. He married **Elizabeth Hornbuckle** about 1795 in Caswell County, North Carolina. She was the daughter of Thomas and Nancy Ann Hornbuckle.

Children:
- \+ 91   i. NANCY^6 HARDEN (1-91) was born about 1796 in North Carolina. She married James Foster and died about 1818 in Rockingham County, North Carolina.
- \+ 92   ii. DEBORAH HARDEN (1-92) was born in 1798 in North Carolina, married John Patman Freeman. They later lived in Logan County, Kentucky.
- \+ 93   iii. THOMPSON HARDEN (1-93) was born in Rockingham County, North Carolina in 1802, married Margery Lackland and died in 1880 in Logan County, Kentucky.

Rockingham County, North Carolina Records
1789 28 Aug: Witnessed deed William Hall to William Williams Deed B-250
1790: Witnessed deed Peter O'Neal to Thomas Harding Deed C-40
1793 05 Jun: Witnessed deed Andrew Wilson to Thomas Hornbuckle Deed D-12
1793 14 Oct: Witnessed deed George Hornbuckle to William Hornbuckle Deed
1797: Witnessed deed Absalom Harvey to Peter Harden Deed E-236
1797 16 Oct: Witnessed deed Henson Humphrey to Absalom Harvey Deeds E-236

Caswell County, North Carolina Records
1789 22 Sep: Witnessed deed John Harden to Thomas Hornbuckle Deed H-151
1790: Listed in 1790 Federal Census
1794 02 Dec: Buys 145 acres from father Thomas Harden Deed H-433
1795 18 Jan: Witnessed deed Thomas Harden Sr. to Thomas Harden Jr. Deed H-417
1796 15 Sep: Thomas Harden sells land adjacent to his property Deed K-9
1799 07 Jan: Buys 200 acres from father-in-law Thomas Hornbuckle Deed L-18
1800: Federal Census listed 00010 30010
1806 29 Jul: Witnessed deed John Windsor Jr. to Aaron Simpson Deed
1810: Federal Census listed 10010 03010
1816 29 Nov: Lands owned by estate allocated to children. Deed S-34

50. Peter^5 Harden (Thomas^4, Thomas^3, John^2, Thomas^1) (1-50) was born about 1775 in North Carolina. He died in 1819 in Rockingham County, North Carolina. He never married and had no children.

Caswell County, North Carolina Records
1792 14 Jan: Witnessed deed Hugh Larimore to George Hornbuckle Deeds
1794 02 Dec: Witnessed deed Thomas Harden to Henry Harden Deed H-433
1796 15 Sep: Witnessed deed Thomas Harden to Samuel Cobb Deed K-9
1799 15 Apr: Witnessed deed Jesse Dickens to Iverson Gwynn Deed
1813 03 Jun: Of Rockingham, buys 100 acres from Samuel Cobb Deed R-32
1816 27 Dec: Of Rockingham Co., buys 162 acres from John Harden Deed S-25
Rockingham County, North Carolina Records

1797: Buys 45 acres from Absalom Harvey Deed E-236
1797 16 Oct: Witnessed deed Henson Humphrey to Absalom Harvey Deed
1798 09 Feb: Witnessed will of Hedgebeth White Will OW-202
1801: Buys 62 acres from Charles Sillivan Deed H-40
1803: Buys 404 acres from Robert Williams Deed L-167
1806: Buys 96 acres from Hugh Gwyn Deed M-142
1808: Buys 96 acres from Hugh Gwyn Deed N-2
1819 27 Jan: Writes his will, Wills A-179
1819 Feb: Will probated Wills A-179
Rowan County, North Carolina Records
1801 10 Jan: Witnessed will of James Beam Rowan NC Wills D-117

51. Peggy^5 Harden) (Thomas^4, Thomas^3, John^2, Thomas^1) (1-51) was born about 1776 in North Carolina and died in May 1840 in Rockingham County, North Carolina. She never married and had no children.
Caswell County, North Carolina Records
1827 12 May: Of Rockingham Co., sells Negro girl Julia to Frances Hornbuckle Deed X-304
1837 29 Apr: Of Rockingham Co., sells 25 acres to Bernard Boswell Deed DD-276
Rockingham County, North Carolina Records
1826 29 Jul: Wrote will, Wills B-235
1840 May: Will probated Wills B-235

60. James^6 Harding (William^5, William^4, Thomas^3, Thomas^2 Thomas^1) (1-60) was born 18 November 1775 in Northumberland County, Virginia. Prior to 1797, he married **Ann Glasscock**, also called Nancy 13 May 1794 Richmond County, Virginia.
 Children of James Harding and Ann:
 94   i. WILLIAM^7 HARDING (1-57) born about 1796
Northumberland County, Virginia Records
1786 11 Mar: Mentioned in will of William Harding WD 13-198
1797 31 Mar: Gives land where he lives to son William WD 15-372
1797 11 Sep: Sells Catesby Jones personal property WD 15-408
1798 14 Feb: Sells 58 acres to Charles Fallin WD 15-464
1798 13 Feb: Sells land to James Cox WD 15-467
1799 03 Mar: Gives 150 acres to John Glasscock WD 15-618
1804 22 Apr: Sells land to William Claughton WD 17 181

69. Elizabeth^6 Hudnall (Judith Harding^5, William^4, Thomas^3, Thomas^2, Thomas^1) was born about 1764 in Northumberland County, Virginia, and married William Jett 27 April 1785 in Northumberland County, Virginia.
 Children:
 95   i. WILLIAM^7 JETT (1-95), md Nancy Davenport 5 Dec 1815

Family Genealogies with References

96   ii. JOSEPH H. JETT (1-96) md Harriet Hudnall 19 Aug 1829
97   iii. JOHN H. JETT (1-97) married three times
98   iv. THOMAS HARDING JETT (1-99) md Elizabeth Edwards 9 Apr 1808
100   v. JANE JETT (1-100) md Samuel Edwards
101   vi. JUDITH JETT (1-101) md William Wildy 20 October 1823

72 John^6 Harden (Presley^5, Thomas^4, Thomas^3, John^2, Thomas^1) (1-72) was born 30 Sept 1775 in North Carolina, died 15 August 1846 Center Hill, Lauderdale Co., Alabama. Married first **Susanna Appleton** 29 Dec 1815 in Williamson Co., Tennessee. He married second Mary Tilman 19 January 1818 in Williamson Co., Tennessee.

Children of John^6 Harden and Susanna Appleton:
102   i. PRESLEY^7 W. HARDEN (1-102) born about 1817 in Williamson Co., Tennessee, died 1878 Center Hill, Lauderdale Co., Alabama. Married Mary S. Williams 23 September 1839 Williamson Co., Tennessee.

Children with John^6 Harden and Mary Tilden:
103   ii. EMMA R. HARDEN (1-103) born about 1820 died 1898 Married John Williams

Williamson County, Tennessee Records
1807 25 Jul: Bought land from Presley Harden Deeds B-514.
1815 05 Nov: Bought land from Thomas Harden. Deeds D-125
1818 19 Jan: Married Mary Tilman. Bond was James Nowlen.
1819 28 May: Bought land from David McElwee. Deeds F-100
1819 29 Sep: Filed plat of land in Williamson Co., TN Deeds F-321
1819 Apr: Guardian settlement for children of John Appleton, Wills
1820 23 Apr: Sold land to Henry Cook. Deeds G-59
1820: Listed in Federal Census Page 646
1821 29 Dec: Sold land to Jeremiah Harden. Deeds G-154
1823 11 Oct: Sold land to Thomas A. Jones Deeds G 438
1824 10 Oct: Sold land to Jacob Halfacre. Deeds H-70
1824 13 Oct: Sold land to Thomas A Jones Deeds H-71
1825 Dec: Sold land to Thomas Old. Deeds H-534
1825 Dec: Sold land to Thomas Old Deeds H-666

Lauderdale County, Alabama Records
1831 19 Sep: Executor of sister Polly's will.
Gravestone from Hardin Cemetery Lauderdale Co., Alabama for both John Harden and his mother Susan Hardin

73. Peggy^6 Harden (Presley^5, Thomas^4, Thomas^3, John^2, Thomas^1) (1-73) was born about 1776 North Carolina, and married **Samuel Shelborne** 25 September 1812, Williamson Co, Tennessee.

Children of Samuel Shelborne and Peggy^6 Harden:
103   i. JEREMIAH^7 H. SHELBORNE (1-103)

104   ii. POLLY SHELBORNE (1-104)
105   iii. NANCY SHELBORNE (1-105)
106   iv. THOMAS R. SHELBORNE (1-106)
107   v. PEGGY TAYLOR SHELBORNE (1-107)

Williamson County, Tennessee Records
1811 05 Oct: Samuel Shelburne sold land to Thomas Harden Deeds
1831 19 Sep: Husband and family mentioned in sister Polly's will, Wills 5-126

75. Jeremiah⁶ Harden (Presley⁵, Thomas⁴, Thomas³, John², Thomas¹) (1-75) was born about 1780 North Carolina and married **Elizabeth Click** 3 January 1821 Jefferson Co., Alabama. He died in December or January 1828. His wife later married Lewis Baldwin.

Children of Jeremiah⁷ Harden and Elizabeth Click:
108   i. SUSAN TAYLOR⁷ HARDEN (1-108) born about 1822 Williamson Co., Tennessee
109   ii. JOHN CLICK HARDEN (1-109) born about 1823 Williamson Co., Tennessee, died July 1849 Ouachita County, Arkansas married Louisa M. Moore 22 Jan 1846 Carroll Co., Tennessee.
110   iii. PETER HARDEN (1-110) born 14 November 1824 in Tennessee died 5 April 1903 Henderson Co., Texas, married Rebecca Moss
111   iv. MARGARET JANE HARDEN (1-111) born 24 October 1826 in Tennessee died 6 May 1903 Falcon, Nevada Co., Arkansas Married John Lightfoot 31 Aug 1841 Henry Co., Tennessee

Williamson County, Tennessee Records
1807 25 Jul: Bought land from Presley Harden. Deeds B-515
1820: Federal Census of Williamson Co., TN Page 534
1821 29 Dec: Sold land to Gregory Wilson. Deeds G-134
1821 29 Dec: Bought land from John Harden. Deeds G-154)
1828 21 Oct: Sold land to Alfred Gee Deeds J-427
1828 24 Nov: He wrote his will. Wills
1829 07 Jan: Will presented for probate.

79. John⁶ Harden Jr. (John⁵, Thomas⁴, Thomas³, John², Thomas¹) (1-76) was born 28 September 1790. He died 18 August 1868 in Graham, Alamance County, North Carolina He married **Rebecca Holt** 26 October 1812 in Orange County, North Carolina She was born 14 December 1794 in North Carolina and died 26 July 1875 in Graham, Alamance County, North Carolina.

Children of John⁷ Harden Jr. and Rebecca Holt:
112   i. DANIEL CLAPP⁷ HARDEN (1-112), born 15 November 1815 in North Carolina, died 20 January 1902 in Morven, Anson Co., North Carolina. He married Rebecca Caroline Mebane 7 February 1843 in Alamance County, North Carolina. She was born 2 August 1816 in Guilford

County, North Carolina and died 21 November 1848 in Alamance County, North Carolina

113 ii. JEREMIAH HOLT HARDEN (1-113) was born 1 January 1818 in Orange County, North Carolina. He died 25 June 1871 in Graham, Alamance County, North Carolina. He married Lucy Ann Royster 19 December 1844 in Mecklenburg County, Virginia. She was born in 1827 and died in 1858.

114 iii. SALLY H. HARDEN (1-114) was born 6 December 1819 in Orange County North Carolina and died 24 October 1844 in Alamance County, North Carolina. She never got married.

115 iv. PETER RAY HARDEN (1-115) was born 3 January 1822 in Orange County, North Carolina and died 23 June 1889 in Alamance County, North Carolina. He married Sarah Elizabeth Holt (1830-1903). They lived in Alamance County, North Carolina.

116 v. MARGARET JANE HARDEN (1-16) was born 26 March 1824 in Guilford County, North Carolina and died 10 December 1902 in Newton, Catawba County, North Carolina. She married William Milton Mebane (1821-1898) 12 November 1844 in Orange County, North Carolina.

117 vi. BARBARA HOLT HARDEN (1-117) was born 6 October 1826 in Orange County, North Carolina. She died in 1885.

118 vii. MARY CATHERINE HARDEN (1-118) was born 6 February 1829 and died 26 May 1830 in Orange County, North Carolina.

119 viii. REBECCA ADELINE HARDEN (1-119) was born 5 April 1831 in Graham, Alamance County, North Carolina and died 26 August 1894 in Reidsville, Rockingham County, North Carolina.

120 ix. JOHN WILLIAM HARDEN (1-120) was born 22 July 1833 in Orange County, North Carolina and died 3 October 1906 in Alamance County, North Carolina. He married Emma Ann Reade (1841-1910)

121 x. GEORGE MONROE HARDEN (1-121) was born 24 March 1836 in Orange County, North Carolina and died 17 March 1897. He married Margaret Turrentine.

122 xi. NANCY ANN HARDEN (1-122) 1839-1851

Orange County, North Carolina Records
1807 24 Oct: Mentioned in will of his father John Harden Orange NC Wills D-235
1814 20 Sep: Executor of Mother Sarah's will Orange NC Wills D-418
1819 14 Mar: Witness to will of Benjamin Whidbee Wills

Caswell County, North Carolina Records
1816 27 Dec: of Orange Co., sells 162 acres to Peter Harden Caswell NC Deed S-25
1831 24 Jan: Summoned to appear in case of Joshua Harden inheritance not paid

Rockingham County, North Carolina Records
1819 27 Jan: Named executor of Uncle Peter Harden's will Rockingham NC Wills A-179
1826 29 Jul: Executor of Aunt Peggy Harden's will Rockingham NC Wills

86. Jeremiah[6] Harden (Thomas[5], Thomas[4], Thomas[3], John[2], Thomas[1]) 5-26) was born about 1793 in North Carolina and died after 1840 in Poinsett Co., Arkansas. He married **Sally McCutchin**, daughter of James M. McCutchin and Martha Elizabeth Petterson. She was born about 1793 and died after 1840 in Poinsett County, Arkansas. In 1820 he is listed in the Federal Census of Giles County, Tennessee next to wife's father and next to his mother.

Children of Jeremiah[6] Harden and Sally McCutchin:

- 123   i. JAMES M[7]. HARDEN (1-123) born about 1815 in Tennessee and died in March 1870 in Poinsett County, Arkansas.
- 124   ii. MARGERY HARDEN, (1-124) born about 1817 in Giles County, Tennessee and died in 1863 in Lawrenceville, Marshall County, Alabama
- 125   iii. JOHN HARDEN, (1-125) born bout 1820 in Giles County, Tennessee. he married Emily and lived in Poinsett County, Arkansas.
- 126   iv. THOMAS JEFFERSON HARDEN (1-126) was born about 5 July 1825 in Tennessee and died 16 January 1879 in Ozark County, Missouri. He married Frances Spencer about 1851 in Poinsett County, Arkansas.

87. William Presley[6] Harden (Thomas[5], Thomas[4], Thomas[3], John[2], Thomas[1]) (1-87) was born about 1795 in North Carolina and died 15 April 1865 in Bellefonte, Boone County, Arkansas. He married **Agnes Hale** (or Hole) in about 1820. She was born about 1800 in Arkansas and died about 1870 in Bellefonte, Boone County, Arkansas. William lived first in Giles County, Tennessee, where he is listed in the 1820 Census next to his mother. By 1837 he had moved to Shelby County, Tennessee, where he is listed in the personal property tax lists with his brothers Hiram and Joshua in 1837 and 1838.

Children:

- 127   i. THOMAS[7] PRESLEY HARDEN, (1-127) born about 1820 in Giles County, Tennessee and died about 1856 in Bellefonte, Boone Co., Arkansas. He married Minerva Jane Starkey on 4 December 1850 in Shelby County, Tennessee

88. Hiram[6] Harden (Thomas[5], Thomas[4], Thomas[3], John[2], Thomas[1]) (1-88) was born about 1797 in North Carolina and died 4 April 1864 in Navarro County, Texas. In 1818 his father deeded him a grist mill, livestock, and personal property as a gift. He married first an unknown wife about 1826 in Giles County, Tennessee. No record survives of her identity. He married second **Cynthia Estill** on 29 October 1838 in Shelby County, Tennessee. She was born about 1806 and died 11 February 1843 in Bowie County, Texas. He married the widow **Frances Smith** on 3 March 1849 in Navarro County,

Texas. She was born in 1806 in Illinois, married first a Mr. Smith, and died 3 March 1859 in Pursley, Navarro County, Texas.

Children of Hiram[6] Harden and Unknown wife:

128   i. MARY LYDDY[7] HARDEN (1-128) born about 1827 in Tennessee, died after 1900 in Bosque County, Texas. She married Sterling Mann Yancey about 1843 in Upshur County, Texas. He was born 12 May 1815 in Granville County, North Carolina and died about 1866 in Upshur County, Texas. They had four children.

Children of Hiram[3] Harden and Cynthia Estill:

129 ii. WILLIAM PRESLEY HARDEN (1-129) was born 30 August 1839 in Shelby County, Tennessee and died 12 October 1895 in Pursley, Navarro County, Texas.

130 iii. THOMAS JEFFERSON HARDEN (1-130) was born 29 September 1842 in Bowie County, Texas and died in August 1886 in Navarro County, Texas. He married Mary and had three children.

Giles County, Tennessee Records:
1818 27 Aug: Received deed of gift from his father Thomas Harden Deeds C-378
1843 10 Apr 1843 Giles Co., TN Grant made to D.A. Alexander, assignee of Hiram Harden.

Shelby County, Tennessee Records
1837: Shelby Co., TN on Personal Property Tax List
1838: Shelby Co., TN on Personal Property Tax List
1840: Federal Census Shelby County, TN Page 39 Next to Josh Harden

90. Joshua[6] Harden (Thomas[5], Thomas[4], Thomas[3], John[2], Thomas[1]) (1-89) was born about 1812 in Giles County, Tennessee and lived in Shelby County, Tennessee. It is not known where or when he died. He married first **Lucy Woodson** (1813- before 1856) on 15 June 1848 in Shelby County, Tennessee and had a daughter with her who died young. He married **Eliza O'Quin** 7 February 1857 in Shelby County, Tennessee but had no children with her. They were listed in the 1880 Census of Shelby County, Tennessee.

Shelby County, Tennessee Records
1837: On Personal Property Tax List PPTL
1838: Shelby Co., TN On Personal Property Tax List PPTL
1840: Federal Census Shelby County, TN Page 39 Next to Hiram Harden
1845 13 Jun: Received grant of land. Grants 3-59
1845 13 Jun: Married Mary Woodson Marriages 1-191
1850: Federal Census Shelby Co., TN Age 38 Born Tennessee
1852 13 Jan: Sold part of land to George W. Williams
1856 26 Sep: Mentioned in John Woodson's will, Wills
1857 02 Feb: Married Eliza O'Quin Marriages 1-410
1860: Federal Census Shelby Co., TN Age 51 Farmer born Tennessee.
1870: Federal Census Shelby Co., TN Age 61 Farmer born Tennessee.
1880: Federal Census Shelby Co., TN Age 68 Farmer born Virginia.

91. Nancy[6] Harden (Henry[5], Thomas[4] Thomas[3], John[2], Thomas[1]) (1-91) born about 1796 in North Carolina and died about 1818 in Rockingham County, North Carolina. She married **James Foster** 4 September 1812 in Caswell County, North Carolina. He was born 7 June 1783 in Virginia and died 21 May 1867 in Simpson, Johnson County, Missouri. It is not known if she had children.
Caswell County, North Carolina Records
1816 29 Nov: Received 64.8 acres from father Henry Harden's estate Deed S-34
1818 02 Sep: James Foster received 146 acres from James Simpson estate. Deed

92. Deborah[6] Harden (Henry[5], Thomas[4] Thomas[3], John[2], Thomas[1]) (1-92) born 24 January 1798 in Caswell County, North Carolina and died 20 August 1852 in Corinth, Logan County, Kentucky. She married **John Patman Freeman** 1 February 1815 in Caswell County, North Carolina. He was born 17 September 1791 in Granville County, North Carolina and died 24 August 1853 in Logan County, Kentucky. They had one son who died at the age of 20.
Caswell County, North Carolina Records
1816 29 Nov: Allocated 64.8 acres from her father Henry Harden's estate Deed S-34
1819 07 Oct: Of Caswell Co., sell 64.8 acres to John Windsor Deed
Rockingham County, North Carolina Records
1826 29 Jul: Mentioned in her aunt Peggy Harden's will, Wills B-235

93. Thompson[6] Harden (Henry[5], Thomas[4] Thomas[3], John[2], Thomas[1]) (1-93) was born 4 April 1802 in Rockingham County, North Carolina and died 14 December 1880 in Logan County, Kentucky. He married **Margery Lackland**, who was born in about 1807 in Maryland and died in 1855 in Logan County, Kentucky.
Children of Thompson Harden and Margery Lackland:
- 131 i. HENRY ROGER[7] HARDEN, (1-131) born 22 October 1827 in Logan County, Kentucky and died 13 April 1878 in Logan County, Kentucky.
- 132 ii. WALTER ELIAS HARDEN (1-132) born 16 May 1829 in Logan County, Kentucky. He married Lucretia J. Hayden about 1852.
- 133 iii. WILLIAM THOMPSON HARDEN, (1-133) born 8 February 1830 in Logan Co., Kentucky. He died 19 June 1907 in Logan County, Kentucky. He married Mary E. Merritt and had four daughters.
- 134 iv. MARGARET ELEANOR HARDEN (1-134) was born 13 April 1832 in Logan County, Kentucky and died 17 March 1892 in Simpson County, Kentucky. She married Bushrod Duval Taylor (1825-1869) 18 May 1848 in Logan County, Kentucky.

135   v. MARY ELIZABETH HARDEN (1-135) was born 15 October 1833 in Logan County, Kentucky and died 29 April 1884 in Logan County, Kentucky.
136   vi. JOHN MILTON HARDEN (1-136) born 25 November 1835 in Logan County, Kentucky and died 7 November 1902 in Logan County, Kentucky. He married Belle Merritt.
137   vii. AMERICA LACKLAND HARDEN (1-137) was born 27 March 1837 in Logan County, Kentucky. She died 20 July 1918. She married John Maddox Conn.
138   ix. GEORGE WASHINGTON HARDEN (1-138) born 15 November 1838 in Logan County, Kentucky and died 16 April 1894. He married Lucy J. Monday.
139   x. CAROLINE HARDEN (1-139) was born 18 May 1840 in Logan County, Kentucky and died 25 August 1911. She married Joseph Herndon Conn.
140   xi. PHILIP HARDEN (1-140) was born 4 December 1843 in Logan County, Kentucky and died 4 January 1918 in Adairville, Logan County, Kentucky. He married Mary Elizabeth MacDonald (1849-1936) on 21 November 1871 in Franklin, Simpson County, Kentucky.

Caswell County, North Carolina Records
1816 29 Nov: Received 64.8 acres from father Henry Harden's estate Deed S-34
1823 10 Oct: John Windsor, his guardian, sold property in Tennessee Deed
1826 18 Oct: Of Logan Co., KY Power of atty. to John Windsor Deed
1831 31 Dec: Of Logan Co., KY, John Windsor his atty. sells property Deed

Rockingham County, North Carolina Records
1819 27 Jan: Named executor of uncle Peter Harden's will, Wills A-179
1826 29 Jul: Named executor of Aunt Peggy Harden's will, Wills

Logan County, Kentucky Records
1850 Census lists all but his eldest child.

Family 2: William Harding of Northumberland County, VA

1. **William¹ Harding** (2-1) was born, probably in England, sometime around 1680. There is no record of his arrival in Virginia. He married before 1702 but his first wife's name is unknown. He married for the second time after June 1716 to **Frances (Waddington) Robinson**, widow of Richard Robinson, He died after 1719 in Northumberland Co., VA. Most researchers give the birth dates of his children as 1714 and 1716 to make it possible for this William to be the son of Henry Harding (3-1), which he is not. A close reading at magnification of the St. Stephens Parish Register shows the handwritten dates to be 1704 and 1706. The zero is narrow but very distinct from the 1 in the handwriting.

Children of William¹ Harding and Unknown:

+ 2 i. CHARLES² HARDING (2-2) born 2 July 1704 St. Stephen's Parish, Northumberland Co., Virginia, married Rachel Lunsford about 1737 in Stafford County, Virginia. He died between 1767 and 1783.
  3 ii. FRANCIS HARDING (2-3) was born 2 July 1704 St. Stephen's Parish, Northumberland Co., VA On 20 November 1721 he Witnessed the will of Richard Smith Sr. (DW H-35a). On 18 January 1726/7 he proved the will of Richard Smith Jr. in court. (DW H-35a). It is not known whether he married or had children. He died after 18 January 1726/7.
+ 4 iii. THOMAS HARDING (2-4) born 2 Feb 1706 St. Stephen's Parish, Northumberland Co., Virginia, married 1737 Hannah (Waddington) Denny, died 1748 Northumberland County, Virginia

Children of William¹ Harding and Frances (Waddington) Robinson:

+ 5 iv. WILLIAM HARDING (2-5) born about 1718, married Patty Green in 1746, died 1781 Fairfax County, Virginia

Northumberland County, Virginia Records
1716 15 Sep: Frances Robinson executor of will of Richard Robinson CO 7-188
1719/20 20 Jan: Samuel Robinson admin estate of Frances Harding, late Robinson CO 7-353
1719/20 17 Feb: Inventory of Frances Harding, formerly Robinson, recorded CO 8-1
1719/20 17 Feb: Appraisal of estate of Frances Harding, formerly Robinson recorded DW G-96
1720 16 Jun: Thomas Harding judgment against estate of Frances Harding deceased CO 8-19
1720 16 Jun: Judgement for Charles Hobson against estate of Frances Harding. CO 8-20

Family Genealogies with References

2. Charles² Harding (William¹) (2-2) was born 2 July 1704 St. Stephen's Parish, Northumberland Co., VA. He married by July 1737 in Stafford Co., VA **Rachel Lunsford**, daughter of Moses Lunsford. He died between 1767 and 1783 Stafford Co., VA

Children of Charles² Harding and Rachel Lunsford:
- 6   i. WILLIAM³ HARDING (2-6) born 12 March 1738 Overwharton Parish, Stafford Co., VA Probably died young. For many years, researchers believed that he is the same man who married Clarissa Million about 1760 in Stafford County. As the DNA results discussed in Group Four reveal, the man who married Clarissa Million cannot be this child since he is not a DNA match for this family and is therefore placed in Family Four where he is shown to be a son of Joseph Combs I.
- 7   ii. ANN HARDING (2-7) born 3 February 1740 Overwharton Parish, Stafford Co., VA
- 8   iii. JANE HARDING (2-8) born 9 November 1742 Overwharton Parish, Stafford Co., VA
- 9   iv. CHARLES HARDING (2-9) born 6 April 1745 Overwharton Parish, Stafford Co., Virginia. The name of his wife is not known. Some researchers have claimed that he went to Guilford County, North Carolina by 1779, where Charles Harding received a land grant and where he married Jean Stewart and had a family. This Jean is unlikely to be the Jean Stewart who married Charles Hardin in 1760 in Abington, Pennsylvania since this Charles Harding was only 15 at the time and his children don't appear until 10 or 15 years after the marriage. I cannot find any evidence that the Guilford Charles is the same as this man and therefore am not including his descendants here. Stafford County, Virginia records show tax list entries for Charles Hardin in the Personal Property Tax Lists from 1783 to 1786, then he vanishes.
- + 10   v. JOHN SCOTT HARDING (2-10) born 3 August 1747 Overwharton Parish, Stafford Co., Virginia, married Lucy, died by 1795 Stafford County, Virginia
- + 11   vi. THOMAS HARDING (2-11) born 11 August 1749 Overwharton Parish, Stafford Co., Virginia, married Elizabeth Strother
- + 12   vii. MOSES HARDING (2-12) born 19 March 1752 Overwharton Parish, Stafford Co., Virginia, married Mary Ball about 1777, died 1826 in Washington County, Kentucky
- + 13   viii. GEORGE HARDING (2-13) born 3 July 1754 Overwharton Parish, Stafford Co., Virginia, married Nancy Bland about 1775. No further information.

Stafford County, Virgina Records
1734 14 Aug: Inventory of Thomas Timmons lists him as servant man WD Book M
1740 11 Nov: Is owned money from estate of Elias Hore dated 1734 WD Book M
1741/42 17 Feb: Witnesses the will of Thomas Bowts WD Book M
1742 17 Aug: witnessed the will of William Brent WD Book M
1744 05 Apr: Appraised the estate of John Holliday WD M

Harding Families of the Northern Neck of Virginia

1746: Estate of William Mason paid money due to Charles Hardin WD M
1749: William Jackson estate owed money to Charles Hardin WD M
1750: 14 Aug: Estate of Ann Parson paid Charles Hardin WD M
1750: was on an appraisal list In 1750 WD M
1750: Estate of William Brent received money for corn sold to Charles Hardin WD M
1754 11 Jun: appraised the estate of James Starke WD M
1760 21 Feb: Witnessed deed from William Fitzhugh to Richard Bristoe M
1762 11 Mar: Goods of estate of Robert Burgess sold to Charles Hardin Stafford WD M
1773-1779 WD Book R-209 A grantor deed filed. Index to a lost book
1767-1783 WD W-N 385 Will filed. Index to a lost book

4. Thomas² Harding (William¹) (2-4) was born 2 February 1706 in St. Stephen's Parish, Northumberland Co., VA. He married, about 1737, **Hannah (Waddington) Denny**. He died before 13 March 1748/9 in Northumberland Co., Virginia.

Children of Thomas² Harding and Hannah Waddington:

+ 14   i. JOHN³ HARDING I (2-14) born about 1738 died after 1765. No children.
+ 15   ii. HOPKINS HARDING (2-15) born about 1739, married Jemima Everett, died 1812, Northumberland County, Virginia.
+ 16   iii. MARK HARDING (2-16) born about 1741, married Mary Pritchard, died by 1775 in Northumberland County, Virginia.
  17   iv. WINIFRED HARDING (2-17) was born about 1743. On 13 February 1748/9 she was bound to Maximilian Haynie until age 18 by Northumberland County Court (CO 11-416). It is not known whether she married or had children.
  18   v. FRANCES ANN HARDING (2-18) was born about 1745. On 13 March 1748/9 she was bound to Benjamin Haynie by Northumberland County Court until age 18 (CO 11-429). On 18 March 1756 she asked the Court for her part of her father Thomas Harding's estate in hands of Presley Thornton (CO 13-464). It is not known whether she married or had children.
+ 19   vi. JOHN HARDING II (2-19) was born about 1746, died after 1765.
  20   vii. SARAH HARDING (2-20) was born about 1747. On 13 May 1755 in Northumberland County Court, as an Orphan of Thomas Harding deceased, she chose Joseph Robinson Jr. as her guardian (CO 13-324). It is not known whether she married or had children.
  21   viii. HANNAH HARDING (2-21) was born about 1748. On 13 May 1755 as an Orphan to Thomas Harding dec, she chose Joseph Robinson Jr. as guardian (CO 13-324). It is not known whether she married or had children.

Northumberland County, Virginia Records
1726/7 06 Mar: Witnessed will of Pitts Curtis DW H-143a

Family Genealogies with References

** 1734 16 May: Nelms vs Thomas Harding judgment to Nelms for 400 pounds tobacco CO 9-149
** 1737 11 Apr: Gave evidence for Robert Clark, paid for 11 days at court CO 9-255
** 1737 10 Oct: Buys indenture contract of Hester Flood CO 10-6
** 1738 11 Jul: Hornby sues, gets judgment for 320 pounds tobacco CO 10-57
1741 28 Jul: Buys 50 acres in Wicomico Parish from Moses Lunsford DW I-134, 173
1742/3 25 Jan: Accused of burning down Joseph Robinson's outhouse, 1742/3: insufficient evidence CO 10-321
** 1743: Judgment for John Gorham 334 pounds tobacco CO 11-28
1744: Martha Lunceford, wife of William Lunceford, brother Joseph Robinson, Godchild Hannah Harding DW
** 1746 11 Mar: Cornelius Todd awarded judgment for 291 pounds tobacco CO 11-168
1748/9 13 Feb: Orphan Winifred Harding bound to Maximilian Haynie CO 11-416
1748/9 13 Mar: Orphan Frances Ann Harding bound to Benjamin Haynie CO 11-429
1750 06 Aug: Will of Samuel Denney: brothers Mark and Hopkins Harding, mother Hannah Harding DW 1-229
1750 10 Dec: Estate administered by Hannah Harding DW 1-???
1750 10 Dec: Hannah Harding granted admin of estate CO 12-111
1751 May: Inventory ordered recorded CO 12-162 13
1751 13 May: Inventory of Samuel Denney ordered recorded CO 12-162
1755 12 May: John, orphan of Thomas, bound to Peter Chapman CO 13-312
1755 13 May: Sarah, John and Hannah Harding, orphans of Thomas, gdn Joseph Robinson Jr. CO 13-324
1756 08 Mar: Frances, daughter of Thomas, asks for her part of estate. CO 13-464
NOTE: Items marked ** may refer to Thomas Harding IV, Family 1, No. 1212

5. William² Harding (William¹) (2-5) was born about 1718 in Northumberland County, Virginia. DNA from a descendant of Thomas Green Harding matches the DNA of other descendants in this family. He first married **Patty Green** 28 Jan 1746 in Stafford Co., VA and married second **Anastasia Ball**, date unknown. He died before 18 May 1781 in Fairfax Co., VA, where his will was probated.

Children of William² Harding and Patty Green:

+ 22 i. HALL³ HARDING (2-22) born 25 Oct 1746 Overwharton Stafford County, Virginia, Married Elizabeth. He lived in Fairfax and Fauquier Counties, Virginia.
  23 ii. CHARLES HARDING (2-23) was born about 1750 in Stafford County, VA. It is not known whether he married. Some trees say that he married Hannah and that he died about 1794 in Loudoun County. He

is said to have sons William, Charles, and Wesley, who lived in Franklin County, Kentucky but I have no proof they are from this Charles Harding. On 18 May 1781, he was mentioned in the will of his father William Harden (WB D1-236). On 19 November 1782, he posted a bond as guardian of Thomas Green Harden (WB D1-306).

24 iii. MARYANN HARDING (2-24) married Mr. Ball

25 iv. ANTHONY HARDING (2-25) was born about 1760 in Stafford County, VA. On 8 May 1781 he was mentioned in will of his father William Harden in Fairfax County, Virginia (WB D1-236). On 12 March 1788 he filed a lawsuit in Loudoun County Court against Richard Gower (CO K-370). It is not known whether he married.

+ 26 v. THOMAS GREEN HARDEN (2-26) born about 1764 in Virginia, married Mary Sinclair about 1802. He died in Alexandria, Virginia in 1815.

Fairfax County, Virginia Records
1749: Inventoried estate of Joseph Boliny CO 1749-53
1754 02 Mar: Witnessed deed Panoply Bowling to son DB C-798
1754 21 Nov: Complaint against Charles Story litigated. CO 1754-55
1758 10 Dec: Inventoried estate of Hooper Gwyn CO 1757-62
1759 19 Jun: Lease from Jabez Downman ordered recorded CO 1757-62
1759 05 Feb: Bought 525 acres from Jabez Downman Deed Book D-626
1759: Served on jury CO 1757-1762
1760: Served on jury CO 1757-176
1761: Served on jury CO 1757-176
1761: Owned 525 acres Deed Book
1764: Owned 525 acres Deed Book
C 1770: Bought land from John Alexander Jr. Deed Book H-238
1767: Bought from estate of Daniel Jennings Will Book
1769 18 Jul: Gave bail CO 1768-69
1769: Served as juror CO 1768-69
1770: Owned 525 acres Deed Book
1770: Surveyed a road by James Green CO 1770-71
1771: Owned 525 acres Deed Book
1771: Took inventory of John Lowe Jr. CO 1770-1771
1771 Aug: Appraised estate of John Lowe Will Book
1772: Owned 525 acres Deed Book
1781 18 May: Wrote will. Will Book D1-236
1782: Patty Harden on Personal Property Tax List.
1784 19 Mar: est divided between widow and Thomas Green Harden WB D1-334

10. John Scott[3] Harding (Charles[2], William[1]) (2-10) was born in Stafford County Virginia 3 August 1747. He married **Lucy** about 1770 in Stafford County. No record of this marriage exists but it is clear from the property tax and land tax lists that they were married and had some children in Stafford County, Virginia. He died before 1795 in Stafford County. Lucy

Harding continued to appear in the Land Tax Lists until 1816, when she was listed as deceased. Other researchers have posted family trees showing him as the John Scott Hardin who had a family in Guilford County, North Carolina. However that John is never known there by the name John Scott, just John. I believe the Scott came from a researcher who added the middle name from the birth record of the man who stayed in Stafford County, Virginia.

Children of John Scott^3 Harding and Lucy:
+ 27 i. WILLIAM^4 HARDING (2-27) born 1 July 1777 in Stafford County, Virginia, married Elizabeth Doggett 1802 in Culpeper County, Virginia, died 1875 in Clarke County, Iowa.

Stafford County, Virgina Records
1782-1794: John Harding on land tax list with 70 acres of land
1795-1815: Lucy Harding listed on land tax lists with 70 acres for John Scott Harding
1783-1794: On Personal Property Tax Lists
1795-1809: Widow Lucy Harding listed on Personal Property Tax Lists
1810: Widow Lucy listed in Federal Census
1810 25 Dec: Owned land by Fristoe, was deceased DW 1810-13
1814 03 Mar: William Harding appears in personal property tax lists as "son of Scott" to distinguish him from William Harding Sr on same list.
1816: Lucy Harding listed on Land tax list as deceased

11. Thomas^3 Harding (Charles^2, William^1) (2-11) was born 19 March 1749 in Stafford Co., Virginia, and married **Elizabeth Strother**.

Children of Thomas^3 Harding and Elizabeth Strother:
28 i. PHILIP^4 HARDING (2-28) born about 1772 Stafford Co., VA
29 ii. BYRAM HARDING (2-29) born about 1775 Stafford Co., VA
30 iii. JOEL HARDING (2-30) born about 1779 Stafford Co., VA
31 iv. STROTHER B. HARDING (2-31) born about 1781 Stafford Co., VA
32 v. ELIZABETH HARDING (2-32) born about 1784 Stafford Co., VA

Stafford County, Virgina Records
1782-1818: On Land Tax lists
1783-1820: On Personal property tax lists
1783-1786 11 Sep: Got land from William Fitzhugh DW 1780-335
1791 Nov: Ordered to pay witnesses in court case CO 1790-216
1792 Jun: Named Commissioner for valuation CO 1790-274
1810 25 Dec: Owned land near Fristoes DW 1810-13
1810: Listed in 1810 Federal Census Stafford Co., VA
1810: Son Joel listed in Federal Census Stafford Co., VA
1820: Listed in 1820 Federal Census Stafford Co., VA
1820: Son Philip listed in Federal Census Stafford Co., VA
1820: Son Byram listed in Federal Census Stafford Co., VA

Harding Families of the Northern Neck of Virginia

1830: Listed in 1830 Federal Census Stafford Co., VA
1830: Son Byram listed in Federal Census Stafford Co., VA

12. Moses³ Harding (Charles², William¹) (2-12) was born 19 March 1753 in Stafford County, Virginia. He married **Mary Ball** about 1777 in Stafford Co., VA. From 1782 to 1790 he lived in Fairfax County, Virginia. He died in 1826 in Washington Co., Kentucky. Mary Ball was born about 1756 in Virginia and died before 1826 in Washington Co., Kentucky.

Children of Moses³ Harding and Mary Ball:
- 33   i. BAILEY⁴ HARDIN (2-33) 1777-1824
- 34   ii. JOHN STEPHEN HARDIN (2-34) 1778-1845 married Jenny Keeling
- 35   iii. ELIZABETH HARDIN (2-35) 1780-1840
- 36   iv. MARY HARDIN (2-36) 1782-1852 married Richard Pyburn
- 37   v. WILLIAM HARDIN (2-37) 1784-1861 married Margaret Keeling
- 38   vi. JANE HARDIN (2-38) 1787-1851 married James Thompson
- 39   viii. JAMES HARDIN (2-39) 1788-1876 married Susannah Tubman
- 40   ix. SARAH HARDIN (2-40) born about 1791-1879 married John Hendrickson
- 41   x. ANNA HARDIN (2-41) 1797-1867 married Daniel Cheatham

Fairfax County, Virginia Records
1782-1790: On Personal Property Tax Lists

Washington County, Kentucky Records
1796 03 Mar: Bought 100 acres from Anthony Hundley Deeds A-323
1802 03 Aug: Bought 200 acres from Anthony Hundley Deeds B-579
1811 19 Feb: With son John Hardin bought 134 acres from William Meredith Deeds C-513 (501 in the typescript)
1814 19 Oct: Sold 31 acres to William Hardin Deeds D-522
1817 14 Apr: Bought 127 acres from Matthew Walton Deeds E-337
1818 09 Aug: With John sold 134 acres to Daniel Cheatham Deeds F-38
1819 02 Oct: Bought 18 acres from Henry Bayne Deeds F-304
1821 01 Jul: Bought 19 acres from John Pope Deeds G-209
1821 Jun: Bought 19 acres from John Pope Deeds G-299
1821 20 Jan: Sold 38 acres to James Harding G-371
1821 20 Jan: Sold 86 ½ acres to John Harding G-372
1822 12 Dec: Sold 120 acres to William Hardin Deeds H-139
1822 12 Dec: Bought 31 acres from William Hardin Deeds H-142
1823 14 July: Sold land to John Pope Deeds H-248
1826 06 Apr: Inventory of Moses Hardin Wills D-181
1826 13 Apr: Sale list of Moses Hardin filed Wills D-176
1826 11 Nov: Second sale list of Moses Hardin

13. George³ Harding (Charles², William¹) (2-13) was born 3 July 1754 in Stafford County Virginia. He married **Nancy Bland** about 1775. He lived in Stafford County, Virginia. He owned land until 1805, then disappeared.

Children of George³ Harding and Nancy Bland:
42   i. GEORGE⁴ HARDING JR. (2-42) was born about 1775 in Stafford County, Virginia. There is no record of a marriage, but he is listed in the personal property tax lists of Stafford County, Virginia from 1794 until 1799. Nothing further is known of him.

Stafford County, Virgina Records
1782-1805: On land tax records with 65 acres
1783-1798: On personal property tax lists
Prince William County, Virginia Records
1785:02 May: Thomas Bland to Nancy Hardin, wife of George Hardin of Stafford County, one negro boy. Deeds W-109

14. John³ Harding (Thomas², William¹) (2-14) was born about 1738 and died after 1765. He had no known children.
Northumberland County, Virginia Records
1745 10 Feb: Suit by Elizabeth Gawkins was dismissed CO 11-171
1758 17 Nov: John Harding guardianship account was filed
1762 11 Oct: Bond from John Harding and Jane his wife filed CO 15-538
1765 02 Sept: Inherited land from his grandfather John Waddington, died with no children DW 6-613

15. Hopkins³ Harding (Thomas², William¹) (2-15) was born about 1739 and married about 1757 **Jemima Everett**. He died in 1812. Most online sources include many short-lived children. However, I cannot prove that any of these children existed. The only four I can confirm are those he mentioned in his will.

Children of Hopkins³ Harding and Jemima Everett:
+   43   i. CYRUS⁴ HARDING (2-43) born in 1765 married Mary Goodridge, died by 1806 in Northumberland County, Virginia.
     44   ii. MALE HARDING (2-44) born about 1767 died young
+   45   iii. WILLIAM (BILLY) HARDING (2-45) was born in 1769, married Sally Coppedge Sutton, died in 1833 in Northumberland County, Virginia.
     46   iv. THOMAS EVERETT HARDING (2-46) 1772-1790
     47   v. JOHN HARDING 1774-1797 (2-47) married Sally Basye
     48   vi. SAMUEL HOPKINS HARDING (2-48) 1779-1781
     49   vii. DAUGHTER (2-49) born and died 1781
     50   viii. RICHARD HARDING (2-50) born and died 1783
     51   ix. LUCY HARDING (2-51) 1780- married Edward Pitman

Northumberland County, Virginia Records
1750 06 Aug: Mentioned as brother of Samuel Denney in Denney's will WD 1-229
1756 10 May: Chose Swan Pritchard as guardian CO 14-7
1757 09 May: Paid 25 pounds tobacco for attending court CO 14-150
1757 10 Oct: Swan Pritchard did not file guardianship report CO 14-228

1759 09 Apr: Sells 50 acres in Wicomico bought by father Thomas Harding WD 5-62
1760 01 Mar: Possessed with Mark Harding's part of father's estate WD 5-186
1762 13 Jul: Ordered that he possess the estate of Aron Nelms CO 15-455
1762 09 Aug: Report on possesses the estate of Aron Nelms CO 15-466
1762 10 Aug: Takes over estate of Aaron Nelms, orphan of Aaron Nelmes dec WD 6-96
1763 13 Jun: Deed to Joseph Moore 50 acres in Wicomico WD 6-229
1770 23 Apr: Mentioned in brother Mark Harding's will WD????
1775 12 Jun: Deed from Hopkins Harding and wife Jemima WD????
1782-1802: On Personal Property Tax Lists
1810: On Federal Census for 1810
1812 12 Oct: Wrote his will, Wills 19-278
1812 14 Dec: Will proved in court Wills 19-278

16. Mark[3] Harding (Thomas[2], William[1]) (2-16) was born about 1741 and married **Mary Pritchard** (1745-1775), daughter of Swanson Pritchard and Mary Coppage. He died by 13 February 1775 Northumberland Co., VA.

Children of Mark[3] Harding and Mary Pritchard:
52   i. THOMAS[4] HARDING (2-52) born about 1768
53   ii. BETTY HARDING (2-53) born about 1770
54   iii. CHARLES HARDING (2-54) b about 1772
55   iv. MARK HARDING (2-55) born about 1773
56   v. CHILD NOT BORN IN (2-56) 1774

Northumberland County, Virginia Records
1750 06 Aug: Will of Samuel Denney, mentioned as brother DW 1-229
1758 13 Mar: Bound to Robert Balvard
1760 01 Mar: Hopkins Harding takes Mark Harding's part of father's estate DW 5-186
1762 Jun: Paid for attendance at court CO 15-428
1765 21 –: Deed Mark Harding from John Tiffee DW 6-585
1774 Apr: Writes will DW --23
1775 13 Feb: Will probated. DW --

19. John[3] Harding (Thomas[2], William[1]) (2-19) was born about 1746. It is now known whether he married or had children.

Northumberland County, Virginia Records
1755 12 May: Bound to Peter Chapman until age 21. Orphan of Thomas Harding dec CO 13-312
1755 13 May: Orphan of Thomas Harding dec, chooses Joseph Robinson Jr. as guardian CO 13-324
1759 10 Sep: Expenses of John Harding, orphan, by Samuel Blackwell. Guardian WD 5-122

Family Genealogies with References

1765 02 Sep: Sells 198 ½ acres of land inherited from grandfather John Waddington through uncle Ralph Waddington, elder brother John Harding and her aunt Sarah Ann, wife of Isaac Palmer. WD 6-613

22. Hall³ Harding (William², William¹) (2-22) was born 25 October 1746 in Overwharton Parish, Stafford Co., VA. He married **Elizabeth** and later settled in Fairfax County, Virginia. It is not known when he died.

Children of Hall³ Harding and Elizabeth:
- 57   i. AMNAH⁴ HARDIN (2-57) married Daniel Shackelford 8 Jan 1793
- 58   ii. GEORGE HARDIN (2-58)
- 59   iii. FRANCES HARDIN (2-59) married Selah Shackelford 5 Dec 1797
- 60   iv. SUSANNA HARDEN (2-60) married William Pope 8 March 1808
- 61   v. PHILIP HARDING (2-61) married Frances Pope 24 May 1815
- 62   vi. NANCY HARDIN (2-62) married John Daniel 8 January 1795

Fairfax County, Virginia Records
1772 22 Mar: Presented a petition CO
1782 to 1791: Tax Lists Listed each year Tax Lists
1789 22 Sep: Listed on road CO
1789 With wife Elizabeth made deed to William Wilson CO
1792 With wife Elizabeth deed to Jesse Taylor CO
Fauquier County, Virginia Records
Records 1793 to 1815 show marriages of his daughters. Marriage Bonds

26. Thomas Green³ Harden (William², William¹) (2-26) was born about 1764 in Virginia. He married **Mary Sinclair** (1782-1815) about 1802. She died in 1815 in Alexandria, Virginia. He died February 1815 in Alexandria, Virginia.

Children of Thomas Green³ Hardin and Mary Sinclair:
- 63   i. SUSANNAH⁴ HARDING (2-63) born about 1795 married Dickerson Sarratt
- 64   ii. WILLIAM HARDEN (2-64) born about 1800-1828 married Ann Elizabeth Adams
- 65   iii. NANCY HARDEN (2-65) born about 1807
- 66   iv. THOMAS SINCLAIR (2-66) Harden about 1809
- 67   v. HARRIET ELIZABETH (2-67) Harden about 1811
- 68   vi. MARY ANN HARDEN (2-68) born about 1813

Fairfax County, Virginia Records
1781 18 May: mentioned, will of his father William Harden WB D1-236
1782 19 Nov: Charles Harden gets a bond as his guardian. WB D1-306
1784 19 Mar: Father's estate split between he & mother WB D1-334
1789 15 Jun: Deed to John Dowdall Land from his father DB R-390
1789: On Personal Property Tax List
1791-1795: On Personal Property Tax Lists
Arlington County, Virginia Records

1813 25 Aug: Daughter Susannah married
1815 18 Jan: Thomas G. Harding wrote will.
1815 27 Feb: Guardians for children appointed.
1821 25 Apr: Guardians bond for orphans filed.

27. **William**[4] **Harding** (John Scott[3], Charles[2], William[1]) (2-27) was born 1 July 1777 in Stafford County, Virginia. He married **Elizabeth Doggett** on 2 September 1802 in Culpeper Co., Virginia. In July 1814 he was drafted into the Army and served about 4 months. He lived in Stafford County until about 1865, when he moved to Clarke County, Iowa, where he applied for a War of 1812 Pension. He died 3 January 1875 in Clarke County, Iowa. Over 250 trees on Ancestry have this man confused with William Harding of Loudoun County, Virginia, who died in 1826, according to county records. See discussion in Chapter 1.

Children of William[4] Harding and Elizabeth Doggett:
- 69   i. THOMAS SHARP[4] HARDING (2-69) born 30 July 1803 in Stafford Co., VA, died 21 December 1880 Clarke County, Iowa. Married Mary Timms Robertson
- 70   ii. GEORGE R. HARDING (2-70) born 1804 in Stafford County, Virginia, married Catherine Sash 22 April 1841 Allegheny Co., Maryland. He lived in Stafford in 1850, Hampshire County VA in 1860 and in Mineral County, West Virginia in 1870.
- 71   iii. WILLIAM H. HARDING (2-71) 1807-
- 72   iv. RICHARD HARDING (2-72) 1814-1860
- 73   v. ELIZABETH HARDING (2-73) 1814-
- 74   vi. PHILLIP HARDING (2-74) 1817-
- 75   vii. FEMALE BORN (2-75) born about 1818

Stafford County, Virgina Records
1782-1801: On Personal Property Tax Lists.
1812-1820: On Personal Property Tax List
1814 04 Sep: Served in the War of 1812 under Capt. Elijah Harding, from Military Pension Application
1820: on Federal Census for 1820 Page 178
1830: On Federal Census for 1830
1840: On Federal Census for 1840
1850: On Federal Census for 1850

43. **Cyrus**[4] **Harding** (Hopkins[3], Thomas[2], William[1]) (2-43) was born about 1765 in Northumberland County, Virginia. He married **Mary Goodridge** after 13 September 1791. Cyrus died before 3 June 1806 in Northumberland County, Virginia.

Children of Cyrus[4] Harding and Mary Goodridge:
- 76   i. REBECCA K[5] HARDING (2-76) born about 1797-1820 married Thomas Everett Harding (2-80) 25 September 1815 Northumberland Co, VA

77   ii. MARY (POLLY) G. HARDING (2-77) born about 1799-c 1830 married Thomas Everett Harding 26 February 1822 in St. Mary's County, Maryland
78   iii. NANCY HARDING (2-78) born about 1806

Northumberland County, Virginia Records
1792-1802: On Personal Property Tax Lists
1805 16 Jan: Wrote his will
1806 03 Jun: His will was proved

45. William⁴ (Billy) Harding (Hopkins³, Thomas², William¹) (2-45) was born about 1769 in Northumberland County, Virginia and died 14 February 1833 in Northumberland County. He married **Sally Coppedge Sutton** (1775-1813) on 13 June 1792 in Northumberland County, Virginia.

Children of William⁴ (Billy) Harding and Sally Coppedge Sutton:
79   i. HIRAM⁵ WILLIAM HARDING (2-79) 1793-1873
80   ii. THOMAS EVERETT HARDING 2-80) 1796-1830 married his cousin Rebecca K. Harding (2-76)
81   iii. WILLIAM HARDING (2-81) 1797-1878
82   iv. SALLY COPPEDGE HARDING (2-82) 1799-1818
83   v. ELIZABETH HARDING (2-83) 1801-1862
84   vi. JOHN HOPKINS HARDING (2-84) 1803-1873
85   vii. HOPKINS HARDING (2-85) 1805-1807
86   vi. CYRUS HARDING (2-86) 1807-1873
87   vii. JAMES ORION HARDING (2-87) 1809-1873

Northumberland County, Virginia Records
1793-1802: On Personal Property Tax Lists
1810: Listed on 1810 Federal Census
1820: Listed on 1820 Federal Census
1827 13 Mar: Wrote his will WD 25-316
1830: Listed on 1830 Federal Census
1833 11 Mar: His will was proved
1784 19 Mar: estate divided between widow and Thomas Green Harden WB D1-334

Waddington Robinson Harding Chart

Reconstructed from court orders, wills, and deeds in the following section. Note that the names Waddington and Warrington were both used in reference to this family. Robinson, Robertson and Roberson were all used as well.

1. **Ralph¹ Waddington** of Northumberland County, VA died about 1695
Children of Ralph¹ Waddington:

	1	i. GEORGE² WADDINGTON
+	2	ii. FRANCES WADDINGTON (??-1719) married 1) Richard Robinson (1670-1716) William Harding (2-1)
	3	iii. RALPH WADDINGTON
+	4	iv. JOHN WADDINGTON (??- about 1714) married Frances Gill, who married second, about 1714, Joseph Robinson Sr.

2. Frances² Waddington (Ralph¹) (??-1719) married first before 16 Feb 1697/8 **Richard Robinson** (1670-1716), second about 1718 **William Harding** (2-1).

Children of Richard Robinson and Frances² Waddington:
- 5   i. JANE³ ROBINSON 27 Nov 1698
- 6   ii. JOHN ROBINSON 26 February 1700
- 7   iii. WINIFRED ROBINSON 29 May 1704 died young
- 8   iv. WINIFRED ROBINSON 24 September 1708
- 9   v. RICHARD ROBINSON 25 September 1713
- 10   vi. WADDINGTON ROBINSON 25 September 1713
- 11   vii. RICHARD ROBINSON 5 December 1716

Children of William Harding (2-1) and Frances² (Waddington) Robinson
- 12   ix. WILLIAM HARDING born about 1719

4. John² Waddington (Ralph¹) (??- about 1714) married **Frances Gill**, who married second about 1714 Joseph Robinson Sr.

Children of John² Waddington and Frances² Gill:
- 13   i. RALPH³ WADDINGTON (?? – 1735)
- 14   ii. SARAH ANN WADDINGTON (??-by 1748) married Isaac Palmer (??-1748)
- + 15   iii. HANNAH WADDINGTON (?? – after 1751) married 1) --- Denney married second Thomas Harding (1706-c 1748)

Children of Frances Gill² and Joseph Robinson Sr.
- 15   iv. FRANCES ROBINSON born 1715
- 16   v. JOSEPH ROBINSON JR. born 1720
- 17   vi. JOHN ROBINSON born 1726
- 18   viii. LUCRETIA ROBINSON born 1729

15. Hannah³ Waddington (Ralph¹, John²) (?? – after 1751) married 1) --- **Denney** and married second **Thomas Harding** (1706-c 1748)

Children of Mr. Denney and Hannah³ Waddington:
- 19   i. SAMUEL⁴ DENNEY (??-1751)

Children of Thomas Harding (2-4) and Hannah³ Waddington:
- 20   ii. JOHN HARDING I
- 21   iii. MARK HARDING (??-1774)
- 22   iv. HOPKINS HARDING (??-1792)
- 23   v. HANNAH HARDING
- 24   vi. SARAH HARDING
- 25   vii. JOHN HARDING II

26   viii. FRANCES ANN HARDING
27   ix. WINIFRED HARDING

Northumberland County, Virginia Records

1671 10 Oct: Ralph Waddington bought land from Francis Roberts DW D-200

1678 20 Oct: Deed Ralph Waddington to son Ralph, mentions son George DW E-118

1695: Will of Ralph Waddington proved CO 5-660

1697/8 18 Feb: Richard Robinson and Frances his wife claim part of estate of Ralph Warrington CO 5-809

1700/1 13 Jan: Will of John Robinson mentions all sons DW E-108

1703 26 Mar: Will of Joseph Palmer of Wicomico mentions son Isaac Palmer DW E-9

1707/8 10 Feb: Will of Thomas Gill mentions daughters Susanna Robinson, Frances Waddington DW E-97

1713 19 May: William Harding sells land to Samuel Robinson DW F-283

1713/4 18 Mar: Joseph Robinson and wife Frances, relict of John Waddington, granted probate CO 7-24

1714 19 May: Inventory of John Waddington filed CO 7-34

1716 16 Jun: Will of Richard Robinson presented by Frances Robinson CO 7-188

1717 05 May: Joseph and Frances Robinson deed to John Lunsford CO 7-209

1719/20 20 Jan: Samuel Robinson granted administration of Frances Harding dec CO 7-353

1719/20 17 Feb: Estate of Frances Harding, formerly Robertson (Robinson) DW G-96

1719/20 17 Feb: Samuel Robinson files inventory of Frances Harding deceased DW G-96

1719/20 17 Feb: Inventory of estate of Frances Harding, formerly Robinson, filed CO 8-1

1720 16 Jun: Thomas Harding judgment vs estate of Frances Harding, in hands of Samuel Robinson CO 8-19

1720 16 Jun: Charles Hobson judgment vs estate of Frances Harding in hands of Samuel Robinson CO 8-20

1724 16 Sep: Joseph Robinson named guardian of Warrington Robinson CO 8-160

1726/7 15 Mar: Sarah Ann, wife of Isaac Palmer, to get her part of father John Warrington's estate CO 8-256

1728 13 Jul: Alice Palmer deed to Isaac Palmer and Rebecca wife of Samuel Snow DW H-99

1735 19 Nov: Will of Ralph Waddington was probated by adm Joseph Robinson CO 9-202

1737: Suit, Samuel Snow vs Isaac and Thomas Palmer CO 10-48

1742 13 Apr: Robert Warrington, Joseph Robinson give evidence for Isaac Palmer CO 10-259

1746 13 Oct: Isaac Palmer of Wiccomico deed to Rebecca Snow DW J-156

Harding Families of the Northern Neck of Virginia

1748 14 May: Will of Isaac Palmer DW K-148
1748 18 Aug: Will of Isaac Palmer is ordered recorded CO 11-368
1748/9 18 Feb: Isaac Palmer inventory ordered recorded CO 11-411
1757 01 Mar: Inventory of Estate of Joseph Roberson dec DW 4-51
1765 02 Sep: John Harding sells land inherited from grandfather John Waddington, brother John Harding, cozen Ralph Waddington, cozen Sarah Ann Waddington who married Isaac Palmer DW 6-613

Family 3: Henry Harding of Stafford County, Virginia

1. **Henry¹ Harding** (3-1) was born, probably in England, about 1675. He married **Anne Beltcher**, most likely the widow of William Belcher Jr., between 23 November 1706 and 20 May 1708. By 1722, they were living in Stafford Co., Virginia. He died prior to January 1737, when his widow and executors filed an inventory of his estate.

Children of Henry¹ Harding and Ann Beltcher:
+ 2   i. HENRY² HARDING (3-2) born about 1714 Stafford County, Virginia, married Wilmouth George by 1736, died 1779 in Shenandoah County, Virginia.
+ 3   ii. GEORGE HARDING (3-3) born about 1717 Stafford County, Virginia, married Jane Bunbury in 1740, died in 1768 in Stafford County, Virginia.

Northumberland County, Virginia Records
1700 23 Aug: As servant of John Cockrell testifies in court case CO 6-128
1705/6 21 Mar: George Eskridge gets 250 acres for transporting Henry Harding CO 6-???
1706 23 Nov: Anne Beltcher vs Fergus continued CO 6-412
1708 20 May: Henry and Anne Harding administer estate of William Beltcher Jr. decd. CO 6-519
1708/9 08 Feb: Witnesses deed Thomas Leachman to Thomas Smith. DW E-91

Stafford County, Virginia Records
1722 07 Mar: Valentine Payton sells land by his tract WD M-???
1723 Valentine Payton sells land by his tract. WD M-???
1724 Feb: Listed as a tobacco tender
1726 11 May: Buys 60 acres from William Allen WD M-???
1726 03 Nov: Buys 100 acres from Joseph Allen WD M-???
1731 10 May: Inventoried estate of William Mason WD M-???
1733 16 Nov: Witnessed a bond WD M-???
1737 Jan: Inventory filed by widow and executors. WD M-???
1740 15 May: Second appraisal filed
1754 13 September: Anne Harding died Overwharton Parish

2. **Henry² Harding Jr** (Henry¹) (3-2) was born about 1714 in Stafford County, VA. He married by 1736 in Stafford Co., VA **Wilmouth George**. They later lived in Frederick County, Fauquier County, and Shenandoah Co., Virginia. Before he died in Shenandoah in 1779, he divided his property among his five children.

Children of Henry² Harding and Wilmouth George:

+ 4   i. GEORGE³ HARDING (3-4) b about 1738 Stafford Co., Virginia, married Margaret and died in 1810 in Jefferson County, Kentucky.

   5   ii. WILMOUTH HARDING (3-5) born 14 April 1741 Overwharton Parish, Stafford Co., Virginia. She married John Smith by 1779 in Shenandoah County, Virginia. On 25 November 1775, her father gave her 386 acres of land (Shenandoah County, Virginia Deed Book B Page 269) She was mentioned in her father's will in 1779 and in her mother's will in 1794.

+ 6   iii. NICHOLAS HARDING (3-6) born 6 July 1743 Overwharton Parish, Stafford Co., Virginia. He married Ann Ashby in 1776 and died April 1833 in Hopkins County, Kentucky.

   7   iv. NANNY HARDING (3-7) born about 1745 in Stafford Co., VA. She married John Combs. She was mentioned in her father's will in 1779 and her mother's will in 1794, both in Shenandoah County, Virginia.

+ 8   v. HENRY HARDING (3-8) was born about 1746 in Stafford County, Virginia, married Rebecca Netherton about 1765 and died in 1796 in Jefferson County, Kentucky.

Stafford County, Virginia Records
1724 Feb: Listed as a tobacco tender, age 10
1736 16 Oct: Wilmot Harding named as daughter in will of Nicholas George WD M-???
1755 Sold to George Harding (3-3) 200 acres on Acquia Creek

Frederick County, Virginia Records
1743 10 Mar: Suit against William Hurst dismissed CO 1-55
1749 06 Dec: Leases land for ten years from Jeremiah Cloud Deeds 2-80
1760 04 DEC: Henry Hardin case vs James McKay settled CO 9-237
1761 20 Aug: Leased 2000 acres from Mathusalem Evans Deeds 4-316

Fauquier County, Virginia Records
1762 28 May: Sells to Nicholas George 180 acres bought of William Allen
1762 28 May: Sells to John Nelson 180 acres bought of William Allen

Shenandoah County, Virginia Records
1775 27 Nov: Gives 250 acres to son Nicholas Harding DB B-266
1775 27 Nov: Gives 386 acres to s)on-in-law John Smith DB B-269
1775 27 Nov: Gives 400 acres to son George Harding DB B-271
1775 27 Nov: Gives 556 acres to son Henry Harding Jr. DB B-302
1778 13 Dec: Leases 100 acres to Reuben Padgit Jr for one year DB C-349
1778 14 Dec: Sells land to Reuben Padgit DB C-440
1779 28 Sep: Henry Harding makes his will Book A-33
1782 to 1794: Wilmouth his widow Listed in Personal Property Tax Lists
1794 14 Dec: Wilmouth Harding makes her will, Wills D-474

3. George² Harding (Henry¹) (3-3) was born about 1717 in Stafford Co., VA. He married **Jane Bunbury** 3 December 1740 in St. Paul's Parish.

All his children were born in Stafford County as recorded in the Overwharton Parish Register. After 1758 he moved to Halifax County, Virginia but maintained business activities in northern Virginia. He died before 5 February 1768 in Stafford Co., VA when the Virginia Gazette reported his death while there on business. His estate was administered by William Harding in Halifax County, Virginia. This George Harding's family has been badly represented in online trees. Several proofs exist for placing him here. First, in Stafford County, Virginia, all these children are listed as children of George Harding and Jane or a variation of the name Jane. Second, when George Harding died, the man who paid for his coffin in Halifax County, Virginia was Francis Bunbury, likely a relative of his wife. Third, proof that the George Harding of Stafford County was the same as the George Harding who died in Halifax comes from his son Henry's Revolutionary War Pension application, in which he states that he was born in Stafford County in 1753 and grew up in the Hico Creek area of Halifax County on the border with North Carolina. Fourth, DNA from several of the descendants of William Harding (3-9), who lived in Laurens County, South Carolina, match the DNA of descendants of Henry Harding (3-1) of Stafford County, Virginia. This same William Harding (3-9) is closely associated with the settling of the estate of George Harding in Halifax County, North Carolina.

Children of George^2 Harding and Jane Bunbury:
+ 9   i. WILLIAM^3 HARDING (3-9) was born about 1741 in Virginia. Died 1809 in Laurens County, South Carolina. His wife's name is not known.
   10   ii. FRANKY HARDING (3-10) was born 7 March 1743 Overwharton Parish, Stafford Co., VA
   11   iii. WINNY HARDING (3-11) was born 1 Dec 1746 Overwharton Parish, Stafford Co., VA
   12   iv. ANN HARDING (3-12) was born 29 May 1749 Overwharton Parish, Stafford Co., VA
+ 13   v. HENRY HARDING (3-13) was born 29 August 1753 Overwharton Parish, Stafford Co., Virginia. He married Delilah Allensworth in 1782 in Shenandoah County, Virginia and died in 1835 in Marion County, Indiana.
   14   vi. SARAH HARDING (3-14) was born 23 March 1758 Overwharton Parish, Stafford Co., VA

Stafford County, Virginia Records
1745 Jul: Bought from estate of Anthony Linton WD M-???
1747: Debt to estate of Thomas Hampton recorded WD M-???
1750: Listed on appraisal list WD M-???
1751: Listed as a Negro Slave owner in Overwharton Parish
1755 13 May: Valued the estate of George Allen WD M-???
1755 14 Oct: Bought 200 acres Acquia Creek from Henry Harding II WD M-86
       Valued the estate of H. Bussey WD M-??
1768 06 Feb: Virginia Gazette says he died in Stafford Co. while there on business
Fauquier County, Virginia Records

1768 29 Jun: Executor of his estate William Harding sued Wm Hammett CO Book 1

Halifax County, Virginia Records
1768 19 Apr: Inventory and sale list filed. Wills O-254
1771 15 Aug: Estate settled by William Harding, Francis Bunbury paid for buying George Harding's coffin. Wills O-334

4. **George³ Harding** (Henry², Henry¹) (3-4) was born about 1738 in Stafford Co., VA. He married **Margaret** and had children in Shenandoah Co., Virginia. About 1798 he moved to Jefferson County KY where he died in 1810. That this George Harding was the son of Henry Harding (3-4) is proven by the fact that his father gave him 400 acres of land in 1775 among other land gifts to his other children, land that George and his wife Margaret sold to Henry Harding Jr (4-19) in 1794. In 1796 this same Henry sold this same parcel to William Allen. His two sons are proven by the 1787 Personal Property Tax lists in which he states two men in his household are 16-21, George and Henry. When his two daughters married, they stated their father was George Harding.

Children of George³ Harding and Margaret:
+ 15   i. GEORGE⁴ HARDING (3-15) born about 1761 Virginia. He died in Jefferson County Kentucky.
+ 16   ii. HENRY HARDING (3-16) born about 1765 in Virginia He married Mary Allensworth in 1788 and died in 1830 in Oldham County, Kentucky.
    17   iii. WINIFRED HARDING (3-17) born about 1766 married John Netherton 3 Oct 1786 in Shenandoah County, Virginia
    18   iv. NANCY HARDING (3-18) married Henry Netherton 15 May 1798 Jefferson Co., Kentucky

Frederick County, Virginia Records
1758 04 Apr: Bought 130 acres from John Harrold Deeds 4-316
1782-1783: On Personal Property Tax Lists
1783 03 Mar: Buys half acre from George Dromgoole Deeds 19-390
1783 01 Nov: Sells half acre to Philip Bower

Shenandoah County, Virginia Records
1782-1794: Listed on Personal Property tax lists
1775 27 Nov: Given 400 acres by father Henry Harding DB B-271
1779 28 Sep: Mentioned in father's will
1779 05 Oct: Mortgages land received from father 131 acres
1782 to 1790: Listed in Personal Property Tax Lists
1787 25 Apr: Sells 130 acres bought from John Harrell DB F-328
1794 13 Aug: Sells 316 acres to Thomas Allen DB I-409
1794 08 Sep: Sells 121 acres to Henry Harding Jr. DB I-407
1800 21 Jan: John Netherton of Jefferson Co KY sells 200 acres DB M-714

Jefferson County, Kentucky Records

1798 15 May: Nancy Harding married Henry Netherton Mg Register 1-30
1799 29 May: On personal property tax list no land as George Sr
1800 29 May: On Personal property tax list no land as George Sr
1801-1809: On Personal Property Tax Lists no land as George Sr
1808 02 Jan: Henry Netherton witnessed wedding of William Harding and Rhoda Wilhoit Marriage Register 1:59
1810: Listed in 1810 Federal Census
Oldham County, Kentucky Records
1830: Son-in-law Henry Netherton listed in 1830 Federal Census

6. Nicholas^3 Harding (Henry^2, Henry^1) (3-6) was born 6 July 1743 in Overwharton Parish, Stafford Co., VA. He married **Ann Ashby**, daughter of Henry and Ellen Ashby, 21 November 1776 in Shenandoah County, Virginia. He died in Hopkins Co., Kentucky before April 1833, when his will was probated.

Children of Nicholas^3 Harding and Ann Ashby:
- 19   i. SARAH^4 HARDING (3-19) about 1777 married Jones
- 20   ii. GEORGE HARDING (3-20) born about 1779
- + 21   iii. MARY HARDING (3-21) born about 1780 married John Ashby. She died in 1826 in Hopkins County, Kentucky.
- 22   iv. NATHANIEL HARDING (3-22) born about 1785 died 1850 Hopkins Co KY
- 23   v. HEROD HARDING (3-23) born about 1787
- 24   vi. NANCY HARDING (3-24) about 1789 married Robert Downey
- 25   viii. ELIZABETH HARDING (3-25) born about 1791
- 26   ix. WILMOUTH HARDING (3-26) born about 1793 married James Prather
- 27   x. ELINOR HARDING (3-27) born about 1795

Shenandoah County, Virginia Records
1775 27 Nov: Given 250 acres by father Henry Harding Sr
1776 21 Nov: Marries Ann Ashby
1777 05 Jan: Mortgages land received from his father
1779 28 Sep: Mentioned in father's will
1782 to 1792: Listed in Personal Property Tax Lists
22 May 1786: Appraised estate of Joseph Fetheringill Wills B-250
1785 21 Nov: Owned land bordering Henry Hardin (3-8) Deeds E-406
1787 19 Feb: Leases 250 acres to Alexander Machie DB G-11-12
1789 09 May: Buys personal property from John Netherton
1792 27 Sep: Sells 572 acres to Henry Ashby and Nicholas Jones DB H-446
1792 07 Oct: Sells land to Joseph Stover and Philip Spangler DB I-248
Hopkins County, Kentucky Records
1810: Listed in 1810 Federal Census
1820: Listed in 1820 Federal Census
1821 10 May: Got a bank mortgage for six months
1825 05 Feb: Deeds daughter Elizabeth one negro girl

1826 24 Mar: He wrote his will
1833 Apr: His will probated

8. Henry³ Harding III (3-8) (Henry², Henry¹) was born about 1746 in Stafford Co., VA. He is also known as Henry Harding Senior in tax and deed records. He married **Rebecca Netherton** about 1765. He died in Jefferson County, Kentucky before 1 November 1796. He had five children according to his will. Rebecca died in 1823 in Jefferson County, Kentucky

Children of Henry³ Harding and Rebecca Netherton:

- 28   i. JOHN⁴ HARDING (3-28) was born about 1765. He appears in the 3 June 1796 Tax Lists. Nothing further is known about him.
- 29   ii. WILMOUTH HARDING (3-29)
- + 30   iii. SARAH HARDING (3-30) born about 1766, married William Hancock in 1785 in Shenandoah County, Virginia. She died about 1825 in Oldham County, Kentucky.
- + 31   iv. HENRY HARDING (3-31) born about 1768 in Shenandoah County, Virginia. He married Mary Smith about 1795 and died in 1823 in Jefferson County, Kentucky.
- 32   v. CATHERINE (CATY) HARDING (3-32) born about 1770 and married William Shrader 23 January 1797 in Jefferson County, Kentucky (marriage register 1-25). He was born in 1774 in Westmoreland County, Pennsylvania and died in 1855 in Oldham County, Kentucky. She was mentioned in her father's will in 1790 and in her mothers in 1822.

Shenandoah County, Virginia Records
1775 27 Nov: Given 556 acres by father Henry Harding Sr. DB B-302
1779 28 Sep: Mentioned in his father's will, Wills A-33
1782: 1785 20 Nov: Leases 181 acres to James Roy Deeds E-404-404, 406
1785 24 Nov: Leases 266 acres to Theophilus Padget E-409
1794 14 Dec: Mentioned in mother's will, Wills D-474
1782 to 1795: On Personal Property Tax Lists

Jefferson County, Kentucky Records
1796 03 Jun: On Personal Property Tax List
1796 12 Oct: Writes his will, Wills 1-70
1796 01 Nov: Will probated. Wills 1-70 CO 5-30
1797-1822: Widow Rebecca on Personal Property Tax Lists
1822 21 Aug: Widow Rebecca writes her will, Wills 2-241
1823 12 Oct: Widow Rebecca Will probated. Wills 2-241

9. William Harding (George², Henry¹) (3-9) was born in Virginia sometime around 1740. Records in Halifax County, Virginia show that George Harding most likely had a son, William, who administered his estate. Several of his descendants connect with other Descendants of Henry Harding (Family #2) in DNA results, so he is placed here. He moved to

South Carolina early and died there in 1809. The name of his wife is not known.

Children of William[3] Harding and Unknown:
+ 33   i. ABNER[4] HARDING (3-33) born about 1773 South Carolina, married Susanna Skeen
   34   ii. ABRAHAM HARDING (3-34)
   35   iii. SALLEY HARDING (3-35)
+ 36   iv. WILLIAM HARDING (3-36) born c. 1773 South Carolina.
   37   v. ELIZABETH HARDING (3-37)
   38   vi. NICHOLAS HARDING (3-38)
   39   viii. GEORGE HARDING (3-39)
   40   ix. HENRY HARDING (3-40)

Halifax County, Virginia Records
1768 19 Apr: Purchased many items in George Harding estate sale Wills O-254
1771 15 Aug: Settled his administration of George Harding's estate Wills O-334
Fauquier County, Virginia Records
1768 29 Jun: As executor of George Harding sued William Hammett
Orange County, Virginia Records
1769 22 Jun: As executor of George Harding sued Thomas Kendall CO 8-14
Laurens County, South Carolina Records
1808 22 May: Wrote his will. Wills

13. Henry[3] Hardin (George[2], Henry[1]) (3-13) was born 29 August 1753 in Stafford Co., Virginia. He served in the Revolutionary War from Halifax County, Virginia twice and from Shenandoah County, Virginia after 1780. He married **Delilah Allensworth** on 14 October 1782 in Shenandoah County, Virginia. He is known as Long Henry in tax records. In 1796, he sold his property and he and his wife went west to Dearborn County, Indiana. His brother-in-law William Allensworth also came then. He died in Marion County, Indiana in 1835. His Revolutionary War Application gives details of his early adulthood in Hico Creek, Halifax County, Virginia, his move to Shenandoah County, Virginia to join relatives after his father died and his move to Dearborn County, Indiana in 1796. Note that his six children, including William, are listed in the Dearborn County History Published in 1915.

Children of Henry[3] Harding and Delilah Allensworth:
   41   i. MARY ANN[4] HARDIN (3-41) born 20 June 1785 Shenandoah Co., VA died 30 December 1865 Marion Co., Indiana. She married Elijah Dawson (781-1858) 3 December 1805 in Dearborn County, Indiana.
   42   ii. WILLIAM ALLENSWORTH HARDIN (3-42) was born 8 January 1791 in Virginia and died 9 February 1863 in Hendricks Co., Indiana. He married Mary Anderson 25 April 1815 in Dearborn Co., Indiana

43   iii. JAMES HARDIN (3-43) married Catherine Cloud 16 Sept 1813 in Dearborn Co., Indiana. He was born 26 January 1792 in Virginia and died 13 April 1847 in Henry County, Iowa. Catherine was born 24 January 1793 in Boone Co., Kentucky and died 9 October 1879 in Henry County, Iowa Data from Find a Grave Index

44   iv. JOHN HARDIN (3-44) born 16 January 1794 in Virginia, died 11 September 1871 Franklin Co Indiana married Jane Cloud (1786-1869)

45   v. CATHERINE HARDIN (3-45) born about 1795 in Virginia married Jacob Dennis by 1824

46   vi. PHILIP HARDIN (3-46) born about 1795 in Virginia. Married Sarah Housley

47   vii. HENRY HARDIN (3-47) 1801-1891 married Catherine Ludwick.

48   viii. ELIZABETH HARDIN (3-48) married John St. Clear by 1824

49   ix. NANCY HARDIN (3-49) married Ephraim Morrison by 1824

Shenandoah County, Virginia records
1783- 1789 Listed on Personal property Tax Lists
1792 25 Oct: Buys 132 acres from John Mathis Deeds I-165
1794-1786: Listed in personal property tax lists as Long Henry
1795 08 Sep: Henry and Delilah sell 132 acres to James Stinson Deeds K-13

Dearborn County, Indiana Records
1796: Henry Hardin with children William, Mary, James, Catherine, John, and Philip settled in Hardinsburg along with William Allensworth. History of Dearborn County Page 110, Published 1915.

Marion County, Indiana Records
1832 13 Sep: Applied for Revolutionary War Pension and was approved.

15. GEORGE⁴ HARDIN JR (George³, Henry², Henry¹) (3-15) was born about 1761, most likely in Stafford County, Virginia. The name of his wife is not known. By 1801 he was living in Jefferson County, Kentucky with his father George Hardin. He is in the personal property tax lists as George Hardin Jr.

Children of George⁴ Hardin Jr:
+ 50.   i. WILLIAM⁵ HARDIN (3-50) born 15 March 1788 in Shenandoah County, Virginia. He married Rhoda Wilhoit in 1808 and died in 1865 in Clark County, Indiana.

Shenandoah County, Virginia Records
1787: Listed in George Hardin Sr tax list as between 16 and 21.

Jefferson County, Kentucky Records
1801-1809: On personal property Tax Lists as George Jr.
1808 03 Aug: Witnessed deed Henry Harding to Edward Dorsey Deeds 8-357
1810: Listed with his father George in 1810 Federal Census
1810-1813: On personal property tax lists as George. Not present in 1814. No lists 1815-1816
1814 07 Feb: Bought ½ acre in Transylvania from Samuel Luckett Deeds 10-444

1814 09 Aug: Bought 50 acres on Harrods Creek from John Dicken Deeds H-310
1815 20 Jun: Sold ½ acre lot in Transylvania to Samuel Luckett Deeds I-364
1815 30 Aug: Sold to William Hardin land on Harrods Creek Deeds M-310
1817 04 Aug: Bought Lot 15 in Transylvania from Paul Skidmore Deeds M-269
1817-1821: On personal property tax lists
1826 18 Apr: Sold Lot 15 on Ohio Street to Christian Barrell

16 **Henry**[4] **Hardin** (George[3], Henry[2], Henry[1]) (3-16) was born about 1765 in Virginia. He is known as Henry Harding Jr in deeds and tax lists. He died in July 1830 in Oldham County, Kentucky. He married **Mary (Polly) Allensworth**, daughter of Philip Allensworth 27 November 1788. In the 1788 personal property tax list he is listed as son of George Harding. About 1802 he moved to Jefferson County, Kentucky. He died in June or July 1830 in Oldham Co. Kentucky.

Children of Henry[4] Hardin and Mary Allensworth:

+ 51   i. WILLIAM ALLENSWORTH[5] HARDIN (3-51) was born 8 February 1791 in Shenandoah County, Virginia, married Sarah Trigg, died in 18754 in Oldham County, Kentucky.
+ 52   ii. JONATHAN HARDIN (3-52) was born 7 June 1792 in Shenandoah County, Virginia, Virginia. He married Lucy Wilhoite and died in Oldham County, Kentucky in 1869.
   53   iii. JAMES A. HARDIN (3-53) born 10 February 1797 died 1 October 1831
   54   iii. KATHARINE HARDIN (3-54) born 23 February 1799 in Shenandoah County, Virginia. She married Abraham Souther 27 February 1823 in Jefferson Co., KY. She died 2 January 1864 Moultrie Co., Illinois
+ 55   iv. ROWLEY HARDIN (3-55) born about 1804 and died in 1843 in Oldham County, Kentucky.
+ 56   v. WARNER HARDIN, (3-56) born 1806 Virginia, married Catherine Ann Hitt.
   57   vi. BUTLAR HARDIN (3-57)

Shenandoah County, Virginia Records
1788: Listed as son of George on Personal Property Tax List (PPTL)
1789-1798: Listed on Personal Property Tax Lists PPTL
1794 08 Sep: Buys 121 acres on Gooney Run from father George Harding DB I-407
1795 01 Oct: Sells 121 acres on Gooney Run to Thomas Allen DB K-40
1796 13 Jul: Buys 154 acres on Dry Run from William Dyer DB K-509
1799 04 Mar: Sells 154 acres on Dry Run to Michael Rosenberger DB L-300

Jefferson County Kentucky Records
1800 26 May: Henry Harding Sr. 614 acres Floyds Fork Patent to James Catlett 1 male 1 horse PPTL
1801 16 July: Henry Harding Sr Land: 272 acres Jefferson County, Floyds Ford Entered Surveyed Patented Robert Catlett. 1 over 21 2 livestock PPTL
1802 10 June: Henry Hardin 150 acres Jefferson Co Floyds Creek Entered, Surveyed, Patented James Catlett PPTL

Harding Families of the Northern Neck of Virginia

1803 19 Jan: Bought 100 acres from John Gwathney Deeds 5-392

1803 21 June: Henry Harding Sr 100 acres Jefferson County Harrods Creek Enter Survey Patent Joel Stephens; PPTL Henry Harding Sr 98 acres Jefferson County Floyd's Fork Enter Survey Patent James Catlett

1804 30 June: Henry Harding Sen 100 acres Jefferson County Harrods Creek Enter Survey Patent David Williams 1 male 3 livestock PPTL

1804 03 Sep: Henry and Polly sell to Thomas Mason 106 acres Floyds Creek Patent Catlett PPTL

1805 25 Aug: Henry Harding Sr 100 acres Jefferson County Harrods Creek Enter Survey Patent David Williams PPTL

1806 31 July: Henry Harding Sr 100 acres Jefferson Co Harrods Creek Enter Survey Patent David Williams PPTL

1807 04 Aug: Henry Harding Sr 100 acres Jefferson County Harrods Creek Enter Survey Patent David Williams PPTL

1808 27 July: Henry Harding Sr 100 acres Jefferson County Harrods Creek Entry Survey Patent David Williams PPTL

1808 30 Aug: Sold 61 ½ acres on Floyds Creek to heirs of Edward Dorsey Deeds 8-357

1809 28 July: Henry Hardin Sr. 100 acres Jefferson Co Harrods Creek Entry Survey Patent David Williams PPTL

1810: Listed in 1810 Federal Census

1810 23 July: Henry Hardin Sr. 213 acres Jefferson County Harrods Creek Entry Survey Patent Samuel Beall PPTL

1811: No Day Henry Harding 100 acres no details 1 male 1 black 4 livestock PPTL

1812: No Date Henry Hardin 180 acres Jefferson County Harrods Creek Patent etc. D Williams PPTL

1812 07 Dec: Bought 96 acres from Owen Gwathney border on William Hardin Deeds 9-495

1813: 01 Aug: Harry Hardin 140 acres Jefferson County Harrods Creek Patent etc. David Williams 1 over 21 2 16-26. 4 livestock PPTL

1814: Henry Harden 180 acres Jefferson County Harrods Creek Patent David Williams 1 male 3 livestock PPTL

1817: Henry Hardin Jr 213 acres Jefferson County Harrods Creek Patent David Williams PPTL

1817: George Hardin Jun, Henry Hardin, Henry Tanback? 250 acres Jefferson County, Harrods Creek Patent N B Beall 1 male 10 blacks 3 livestock

1818: Henry Hardin Sr 215 acres Jefferson County Harrods Creek Patent D Williams 1 male 1 black 2 livestock PPTL

1819: Henry Harding 200 acres PPTL

1819-1823: Son James on Personal Property Tax Lists

1821: Henry Hardin 200 acres Jefferson Co Harrods Creek patent Williams

1822: Henry Harden Sr 200 acres Jefferson Co Harrods Creek D Wiliamson

1823: Henry Hardin Sr 200 acres Jefferson Co Harrods Creek PPTL

Family Genealogies with References

Oldham County, Kentucky Records
1825-1827: Son James on Personal Property Tax Lists PPTL
1825: Henry Harding 210 acres Harrods Creek Patent Williams PPTL
1826: Henry Hardin 200 acres Harrods Creek Patent D Williams PPTL
1826 04 Apr: Bought 81 acres from Eliab White Harrods Creek (Beall) Deeds A-225
1827: Henry Hardin 180 acres Harrods Creek Entered Williams Survey Hite
1827: Son Rowley on Personal Property Tax List PPTL
1828: Henry Harding Senior 200 acres Harrods Creek Williams PPTL
1829 12 Nov: He wrote his will, Wills 1-167
1830: Son James listed in 1830 Federal Census
1830 16 Jan: Sold 35 acres to William Harding, part of 100 acres bought of John Gwathney. Deeds B-167
1830 19 Jul: His will probated. Wills 1-167
1830: Widow Mary Hardin listed in 1830 Federal Census
1843 05 Apr: Son Rowley wrote his will. Probated 5 May 1843

21. Mary³ Harding (Nicholas², Henry², Henry¹) (3-21) was born about 1780 in Shenandoah County, Virginia. She married **John Ashby** in Mercer Co., Kentucky 10 April 1797. She died 24 March 1826 in Hopkins Co., Kentucky. John Ashby was born 1753 in VA and died 11 Jan 1841 in Hopkins Co., KY

Children of Mary³ Harding and John Ashby:
- 58   i. NANCY JANE⁵ ASHBY (3-58) born 13 Jan 1798 Mercer Co., KY died 19 Sept 1857 Hopkins Co., KY married Vincent Howel 15 Jan 1818 Hopkins Co., KY
- 59   ii. ENOS JOHN ASHBY (3-59) born 17 Jan 1800 Hopkins Co Ky died 4 Sep 1873 Hopkins Co Ky married Tabitha Ashby
- 60   iii. STEPHEN JOHN ASHBY (3-60) born 16 May 1802 Hopkins Co., KY died 18 April 1872 Hopkins Co., KY married Malinda Crabtree 25 Dec 1834 Hopkins Co., KY
- 61   iv. WILLIAM JOHN ASHBY (3-61) born 23 April 1804 Kentucky died 12 August 1877 Hopkins Co., KY married Mary Charlotte Ashby 1814-1863 daughter of Stephen Ashby and Elizabeth Robertson
- 62   vi. LUCINDA ASHBY (3-62) born 4 July 1807 Mercer Co., KY die 8 Oct 1853 Hopkins Co., KY married John Crabtree married John Crabtree 17 Nov 1831 Hopkins Co., KY
- 63   vii. EMILY ASHBY (3-63) born 24 June 1812 KY died 13 Aug 1852 Hopkins Co KY married Enos G. Ashby, son of Stephen Ashby Jr and Elizabeth Robertson
- 64   v. SALLY ASHBY (3-64) born about 1814 died 1870 Married Daniel S. Ashby 24 Dec 1826 Hopkins Co., KY married Daniel Ashby
- 65   ix. ELIZABETH ASHBY (3-65) born 7 Mar 1815 Hopkins Co KY died about 1878 KY married John Stodghill 12 May 1836 Hopkins Co., KY

Harding Families of the Northern Neck of Virginia

66   x. MATILDA (3-66) ASHBY born 30 Dec 1818 in Kentucky died 11 Sept 1883 Hopkins Co., KY married Edwin Robertson 9 April 1840 in Hopkins Co., KY

Records of Mercer Co., Kentucky
1797 10 Apr: Married John Ashby
1797 10 Apr: Father Nicholas Harding made bond for the marriage.
1847: Heirs of Nicholas Harding sell land to Herod Harding Deeds 12-414

30. **Sarah⁴ Harding** (Henry³, Henry², Henry¹) (3-30) was born about 1766 and married **William Hancock** 11 October 1785 in Shenandoah County, Virginia. He was born about 1768 in Goochland Co., Virginia and died 4 February 1822 in Mercer Co., Kentucky. She died about 1825 in Oldham Co., Kentucky.

Shenandoah County, Virginia Records
1785 11 Oct: Married William Hancock
1790 12 Oct: Mentioned in father's will

Jefferson County, Kentucky Records
1810: 23 July: Personal Property Tax List William Hancock 150 acres Jefferson County Harrods Creek Entry Survey Patent Samuel Bealle
1811: No Day Personal Property Tax List William Hancock 150 acres Harrods Creek Entry Survey Patent E Stevens
1812: No Date Personal Property Tax List William Hancock 140 acres Patent etc. Edward Stephens 1 male 5 livestock
1817: William Hancock Personal Property tax List 135 acres Jefferson County Harrods Creek Patent M Kuykendall
1819: William Hancock Sr Personal Property Tax List 135 acres
1821: William Hancock Personal Property Tax List 135 acres Jefferson County Harrods Creek Patent to Stephens
1822 21 Aug: Mentioned in mother's will

Oldham County, Kentucky Records
1825: William Hancock Personal Property Tax List 100 acres Harrods Creek

31. **Henry⁴ Harding IV** (Henry³, Henry², Henry¹) (3-1) was born about 1768 in Shenandoah County, Virginia. He married **Mary Smith** about 1795. He died before 13 October 1823 in Jefferson County, Kentucky.

Children of Henry⁴ Harding and Mary Smith:
+ 67 i. JOHN⁵ HARDING (3-67) born about 1797 in Shenandoah County, Virginia, married Nancy Phillips, died before 1836 in Oldham County, Kentucky.
+ 68 ii. HENRY HARDING V (3-68) born 1801 in Jefferson County, Kentucky. He married Mary Phillips in 1821 in Jefferson County Kentucky and died in 1859 in Sebastopol, Sonoma County, California.
   69 iii. NANCY HARDING (3-69) was born about 1804 in Jefferson County, Kentucky. She married Thomas Callahan

Family Genealogies with References

    70   iv. EMILY POLLY (MARY) HARDING (3-70) born about 1804

    71   v. WILMOUTH HARDING (3-71) born about 1805 married William H. Brown 22 September 1825.

+   72   vi. WILLIAM JOHN HARDING (3-72) born 15 June 1807 in Jefferson County, Kentucky, married Emily Brown and died in 1889 in McLean County, Kentucky.

    73   vii. JAMES ALLEN HARDIN (3-73) born about 1814 Jefferson County, KY married Ann Lucinda Ellston, died 25 November 1886 Tulare Co., California.

    74   viii. ELIZA HARDING (3-74) born 1815 Jefferson Co., KY, married Isaac Ritter. Died about 1840 in Rollington, Oldham Co., KY.

    75   ix. REBECCA JANE HARDING (3-75) born about 1819 Jefferson Co., Kentucky. Married Richard Jobe 28 Nov 1836 Oldham Co KY. She died in McLean County, Kentucky

    76   x. JUNE AMANDA HARDING (3-76) born 6 June 1822 Jefferson Co., Kentucky, married Gibson Wilhoit 5 June 1835. She died in 1888 in Missouri.

    77   xi. MILDRED ANN HARDIN (3-77) born 20 August 1823 Jefferson Co., Kentucky, died 1853 Kansas City, Jackson Co., Missouri. Married Simeon Wilhite 20 February 1837 in Oldham County, Kentucky.

Shenandoah County, Virginia Records

1796 13 Jul: Buys 154 acres from William Dyer DB K-509

1799 04 Mar: Sells 154 acres to Michael Rosenberger DB L-300

Jefferson County, Kentucky Records

1797 12 May: On Personal Property Tax List no land PPTL

1799 13 Jun: On Personal Property Tax List no land PPTL

1800 06 Jun: Henry Harding Jr, 100 acres Jefferson Co on Harrods Creek, Entered Survey Patented to Samuel Beale 1 over 21 2 Livestock PPTL

1801 16 Jul: Henry Harding Jr No land 1 male 4 livestock PPTL

1802 15 Jul: Henry Hardin Jr 100 acres Jefferson Co Harrods Creek Entered Surveyed Patented to Samuel Beale PPTL

1803 23 Jun: Henry Harding Jr 100 acres Jefferson County Harrods Creek Enter Survey Patent Samuel Beall PPTL

1804 30 Jun: Henry Harding Jr 150 acres Jefferson County, Goose Creek Enter Survey Patent John Willis 1 male 2 livestock PPTL

1805 19 Jun: Henry Harding Jr 150 acres Jefferson County Goose Creek Enter Survey Patent Willis 1 male 3 livestock PPTL

1806 16 Aug: Henry Harding Jr 130 acres Jefferson County Goose Creek Enter Survey Patent John Willis; Henry Harding Jr 100 acres Harrods Creek Enter Survey Patent Samuel Beale PPTL

1807 12 Aug: Henry Harding Jr 10 acres Jefferson County Harrods Creek enter survey patent Samuel Beall PPTL

1807 12 Aug: Henry Harding Jr 130 acres Jefferson County Goose Creek Enter Survey Patent John Willis PPTL

1808 13 Aug: Henry Harding Jr 100 acres Jefferson County Harrods Creek Entry Survey Patent Samuel Beall; Henry Harding Jr 120 acres Jefferson County Goose Creek Entry Survey Patent John Willis PPTL

1809 12 Jul: Henry Hardin Jr 100 acres Jefferson County Harrods Creek Entry Survey Patent Samuel Beall 1 male 3 livestock; Henry Hardin Jr 130 acres Jefferson County Goose Creek Entry Survey Patent John Willis PPTL

1810 23 Jul: Henry Hardin 100 acres Jefferson County Harrods Creek Entry Survey Patent Samuel Beall 1 male 1 male over 16 2 Blacks 4 livestock: 1810 July 23 Henry Hardin 130 acres Jefferson County Goose Creek Entry Survey Patent John Willis PPTL

1811 20 Jul: Henry Harden 130 acres Jefferson County Goose Creek Entry Survey Patent Willis 1 male 2 black 7 livestock; Henry Hardin 100 acres Jefferson County Harrods Creek Entry Survey Patent S Beall PPTL

1812 12 Apr: Henry Hardin sold 11 ¾ acres to John Wilhoit

1812 08 Aug: Henry Hardin 130 acres Jefferson County Goose Creek Patent Willis 1 male 2 blacks 6 livestock: Henry Hardin 100 acres Harrods Creek Patent etc Beall PPTL

1813 26 Jun: Henry Harden 100 acres Jefferson County H Creek Patent etc. Beall 1 over 21, 1 16-21 2 black 6 livestock PPTL

1814: Harry Hardin 50 acres Jefferson County Harrods Creek Patent Beall 1 over 21 8 blacks 5 livestock PPTL

1815 09 May: Benja Smith heirs sold estate to Stephen Smith Deed I-251

1818: Henry Hardin 250 acres Jefferson County Harrods Creek Patent N B Beall 1 male 11 black 4 livestock PPTL

1819: Henry Harding 250 acres PPTL

1821 12 Sep: Daughter Nancy married Thomas Callahan Register 1-122

1822: Henry Harden Sr 100 acres Jefferson Co Harrods Creek Beall PPTL

1822: Bought 50 acres Harrods Creed from Beale and Galt. Deeds U-398

1822 21 Aug: He writes his will. Wills 2-249

1823 13 Oct: His will proved. Wills 2-249

Oldham County, Kentucky Records

1816 15 Apr: Bought 286 acres from Robert Maupin Deeds C-121

1825: Widow Mary Hardin 150 acres Curry Fork Patent N Beall Personal Property Tax List

1826: Widow Mrs. Polly Harding 157 acres Harrods Creek Patent S Beall Personal Property Tax List

1827: Widow Miss Polly Harding 157 acres Harrods Creek entered Beall Personal Property Tax List

1828: Widow Mary Hardin 150 acres Beall Personal Property Tax List

33. Abner[4] Harding (William[3], George[2], Henry[1]) (3-33) was born about 1770. He married **Susannah Skeen**, born about 1764.

Children of Abner[4] Harding and Susannah Skeen:

Family Genealogies with References

+ 78   i. WILLIAM⁵ HARDING (3-78) was born 1802 in South Carolina. He lived with Arreta Monk in Russell County, Virginia but never married her. He married Eliza about 1855.
79   ii. ABNER HARDING (3-79) Jr was born 1804 South Carolina
80   iii. SUSAN HARDING (3-80) was born 1806 South Carolina
81   iv. PHEBE HARDING (3-81) was born 1809 South Carolina

Laurens County, South Carolina Records
1800: Listed in Federal Census for Laurens County SC
Russell County, Virginia Records
1848 09 Aug: Wife Susannah Testified in court for brother Peter Skeen's Revolutionary War Pension Application. Age was 84.

36. William⁴ Harding (William³, George², Henry¹) (3-36) was born about 1773 in South Carolina.
    Children of William⁴ Harding:
    82   i. WILLIAM⁵ HARDING (3-82) born about 1800 South Carolina

Laurens County, South Carolina Records
1802 30 Jan: Bought 100 acres from Thomas Broughton Deeds J-269
1805 05 Nov: Sold 75 acres to John McClure Deeds H-238
1812 20 Jun: Sold 100 acres to Northam Vance Deeds J-269
1819 03 Aug: As executor to William Johnson sold land Deeds K-256

50. William⁵ Hardin (George⁴, George³, Henry², Henry¹) (3-50) was born 15 March 1788 in Shenandoah Co., Virginia. He married **Rhoda Wilhoite**, daughter of John Wilhite, on 2 January 1808 in Jefferson County, Kentucky. In an 1814 deed he is called the son of George. He died in 1865 in Clark County, Indiana. Finding this man's parentage was extremely difficult. Researchers have placed him in five or six different families with little actual evidence. I have placed him here based on the deed evidence and in other records below where you can see his movements and connections. He is a first cousin of Jonathan Harding, (3-52) who married the sister of his wife, Lucy Wilhoit.
    Children of William⁵ Hardin and Rhoda Wilhoite:
    83   i. LUCY⁶ HARDIN (3-83) born about 1809 married John B. Rankin
    84   ii. LEWIS HARDIN (3-84) born about 1811 and married Margaret Clore 20 August 1840 in Oldham County, Kentucky. They are listed in the 1850 Census of Oldham County, Kentucky.
    85   iii. OWEN G. HARDIN (3-85) born about 1815-
    86   iv. PRESLEY HARDIN (3-86) born about 1817 died 1847
    87   v. MARY ANN HARDIN (3-87) 10 Apr 1820 married Hartwell Pate
    88   vi. REBECCA JANE HARDIN (3-88) born about 1822- married Peter Mitchell
    89   vii. EMILY HARDIN about 1825- (3-89) married Lawrence Barrickman
    90   viii. PAULINA HARDIN (3-90) July 1826 married Eli Burt

91   ix. JAMES HARDIN (3-91) born about 1831-

Jefferson County, Kentucky Records

1805 19 June: William Harding 1 male 2 livestock PPTL
1806 01 Aug: William Harding Jr 1 male 3 livestock PPTL
1808 02 Jan: Married Rhoda Wilhoit Marriage Register 1-59
1808 12 Aug: William Harding 1 male 1 livestock PPTL
1809 07 July: William Hardin Jun 1 male 1 livestock PPTL
1810: Listed in 1810 Federal Census
1810 23 July: William Hardin 1 male 2 livestock PPTL
1811: No Date William Hardin 1 over 21 3 livestock PPTL
1812: No Date William Hardin 1 male 2 livestock PPTL
1812 07 Dec: Bought 34 acres bordered by Henry Harding from Owen Gwathney Deeds 9-494
1813 01 Aug: William Hardin 44 acres Jefferson County Harrods Creek Patent etc. Leavin Powell PPTL
1814 Apr: Purchases 46 ½ acres on Harrods Creek from Reuben Ross and the property is bounded by John Wilhoit. He is identified in this deed "son of George." Deeds 10-497
1814: William Hardin 34 Acres Jefferson County Harrods Creek Patent Samuel Hoke; 1814 William Hardin 80 acres Jefferson County Harrods Creek 1 male 2 black 9 livestock PPTL
1815 30 Aug: Buys land on Harrods Creek from Geoge Hardin Deeds M-310
1817: William Hardin, son of George 200 acres Jefferson County, Harrods Creek Patent M Kuykendall PPTL
1818: William Hardin 177 acres Jefferson County Harrods Creek Patent Kirkpatrick 1 male 2 black 2 livestock PPTL
1818: William Harding 58 ¾ acres 1 male 2 blacks PPTL
1820: William Hardin Sr 300 acres PPTL
1820: Listed in 1820 Federal Census
1821: William Hardin 300 acres Jefferson County Harrods Creek Patent Kirkpatrick PPTL
1823: William Hardin 200 acres Jefferson Co Harrods Creek PPTL

Oldham County, Kentucky Records

1825-1828: On Personal Property tax lists, Owns land on Harrods Creek with cousin Jonathan Harding. PPTL
1830: Listed in 1830 Federal Census
1837 16 Jan: Daughter Lucy married John B. Rankin Marriage Bonds
1837 29 Apr: Sells 106 1/2 acres on Harrods Creek to Henry Netherton Deeds D-99
1850: Listed in 1840 Federal Census
1840 31 Mar: Daughter Mary Ann married Hartwell Pate Mg Bonds
1842 31 Mar: Daughter Emily married Larence Barrickman Mg Bonds
1846 13 Dec: Son Lewis buys 206 acres from James Clore
1847 17 Feb: Sells 102 ½ acres on Harrods Creek to Jesse Y Clore DB F-310

1847 05 Apr: Daughter Rebecca Ann married Peter Mitchell Mg Bonds
1848 12 Dec: With Jesse Clore 20 ½ acres on Harrods Creek Deeds G-26
Clark Co., Indiana Records
1788 15 Mar: Born. Cemetery Records Burtt Cemetery
1865 23 Aug: Died. Cemetery records Burtt Cemetery

51. William⁵ Allensworth Hardin (Henry⁴, George³, Henry², Henry¹) (3-51) was born about 8 February 1791 in Shenandoah County, Virginia. He married **Sarah Trigg** 10 March 1824 in Oldham Co., Kentucky. He died in Oldham County, Kentucky 13 August 1874.

Children of William Allensworth⁵ Hardin and Sarah Trigg:
92   i. ALBERT⁶ WILLIAM HARDIN (3-92) born about 1830, died 1899

Jefferson County, Kentucky records
1817: William Hardin Jr no land 1 white PPTL
1818: William Hardin Jr 1 male 1 livestock PPTL
1819 01 Jan: Bought 165 acres from Elizabeth Wilhoit Deeds U-341
1819: William A Harding On Personal Property Tax Lists PPTL
1822 11 May: Bought 165 acres from Lewis Wilhoit Deeds V-381
1824 10 Mar: Married Sarah Trigg

Oldham County, Kentucky Records
1825-1828: On Personal Property tax lists, Owns land on Harrods Creek with cousin William. PPTL
1830: Listed in 1830 Federal Census Page 274
1834 21 Feb: Bought 150 acres from Jonathan Hardin Deeds C-213
1836 16 Feb: Bought one acre from Allen Yewell Deeds C-453
1836 13 Feb: Bought estate of Thomas Trigg from William Trigg Deeds 6-505
1837 29 Apr: Sold 10 acres Harrods Creek to Henry Netherton Deeds D-90
1837 29 Apr: Bought 5 acres from Henry Netherton Deeds D-101
1838 11 Jun: Sold 1 acre Harrods Creek to John B. Rankin Deeds D-289
1840: Listed in the 1840 Federal Census
1843 08 Apr: Sold 30 acres to John B. Rankin Deeds F-9
1846 16 Mar: Bought one negro boy from John F., Locke Deeds F-166
1850: Listed in 1850 Federal Census

52. Jonathan⁵ Hardin (Henry⁴, George³, Henry², Henry¹) (3-52) was born 7 June 1792 in Shenandoah County, Virginia. He married **Lucy Wilhoit** 28 January 1813 Jefferson Co., Kentucky died 29 March 1869 Oldham Co., Kentucky.

Children of Jonathan⁵ Hardin and Lucy Wilhoite:
93   i. ELEANOR ANN⁶ HARDIN (3-93) was born 20 October 1813 in Jefferson County, Kentucky. She married Allen Clore 28 February 1833 in Oldham County, Kentucky. She died 8 March 1877 Moultrie County, Illinois (find a Grave Index).

94	ii.	CATHERINE ANN HARDIN (3-94) was born 2 May 1816 in Jefferson Co KY and died 26 August 1838. She married Richard Hart Clore 20 October 1836.
95	iii.	WILLIAM TEMPLE HARDING (3-95) was born 6 January 1819 in Jefferson County, Kentucky. He married Eleanora Young 27 November 1844 in Shelby Co., KY He died 22 January 1891 in Kentucky.
96	vi.	ELIZABETH HARDING (3-96) was born 16 March 1825 in Oldham Co., KY. She married Abraham Clore Yager 4 May 1840 in Oldham County, Kentucky. She died 14 February 1891 in Oldham Co., KY
97	vii.	MARY JANE HARDIN (3-97) was born 14 February 1827 in Oldham Co., KY. She married Presley Nevil Yager 23 November 1843 in Oldham County, Kentucky. She died 27 June 1846 in Oldham Co KY. She had one daughter, Elizabeth Onorah Yager
98	viii.	ABRAHAM HENRY HARDING (3-98) was born 1 December 1829 in Oldham Co., KY. He married Louisa F. Yager 29 November 1854. He died 9 March 1911 Jefferson County, KY.
99	ix.	JOHN WARNER HARDING (3-99) was born 1 February 1832 in Oldham Co., KY He died about 1860.
100	x.	SUSAN FRANCES HARDING (3-100) was born 11 February 1834 in Oldham Co K. She married Presley Nevel Yager 21 January 1851 in Oldham Co KY. She died 17 October 1908 in Brownsboro, Oldham Co KY.
101	xi.	JAMES HARDIN (3-101) born December 1837 died 26 December 1837.

Jefferson County, Kentucky Records
1813 19 Jan: Married Lucy Wilhoite Marriage Reg 1-74
1814: Jonathan Hardin 1 male 1 livestock PPTL
1817: Jonathan Hardin 95 acres Jefferson County Harrods Creek Patent Moses Kirkpatrick PPTL
1818: Jonathan Hardin 20 acres Jefferson Co Harrods Creek Patent Kirkpatrick 1 male 2 black 2 livestock PPTL
1819: Jonathan Harding 155 acres PPTL
1819 01 Jan: Bought 165 acres from Elizabeth Wilhoit Deeds U-341
1821: Jonathan Hardin 155 acres Jefferson County Horrods Creek Patent Williams PPTL
1822: Jonathan Harden 150 acres Jefferson Co Harrods Cr Ross PPTL
1822 11 May: Bought 165 acres from Lewis Wilhoit Deeds V-381

Oldham County, Kentucky Records
1830: Listed in 1830 Federal Census
1831 04 Jan: Buys 149 ½ acres from William Ingram Deeds B-217
1834 21 Feb: Sold 150 acres to William A. Hardin Deeds C-213
1834 30 Oct: Bought 145 acres Harrods Creek from Jacob Souther Deeds D-339
1840: Listed in the 1840 Federal Census
1850: Listed in 1850 Federal Census
1867 22 May: Writes his will, Wills 5-288
1869 April: His will probated.

55. Rowley⁵ Hardin (Henry⁴, George³, Henry², Henry¹) (3-55) was born in Kentucky about 1804. He died in Oldham County Kentucky in May 1843.

Oldham County, Kentucky Records
1843 13 Mar: Sold 88 acres to Warner Hardin Deeds E-411
1843 13 Mar: Bought 88 acres from Rowley Hardin Deeds E-413
1843 05 Apr: Sold 90 acres to Warner Hardin Deeds E-484
1843 05 Apr: Writes his will, Wills 2-405
1843 15 May: Will probated Wills 2-405

56. Warner⁵ Hardin (Henry⁴, George³, Henry², Henry¹) (3-56) was born in Shenandoah Co., Virginia in 1806. He married **Catherine Ann Hitt** 21 March 1838 in Oldham Co., Kentucky.

Children of Warner⁵ Hardin and Catherine Ann Hitt:
- 102   i. JOEL HENRY⁶ HARDING (3-102) born 18 December 1838 in KY. Died 16 November 1922 Harrods Creek, Jefferson Co., Kentucky. (From Death Certificate)
- 103   ii. JAMES LEANDER HARDIN (3-103) J born 1841 KY

Oldham County, Kentucky Records
1838 21 Mar: Married Catherine Ann Hitt
1840: Listed in the 1840 Federal Census
1843 13 Mar: Bought 88 acres from Rowley Hardin Deeds E-411
1843 13 Mar: Sold 88 acres to Rowley Hardin Deeds E-413
1843 05 Apr: Bought 90 acres from Rowley Hardin Deeds E-484
1848 05 Jul: Buys 6 ¾ acres from Presley Yeager Deeds F-497
1850: Listed in 1850 Census of Oldham Co., Kentucky

67. John⁵ Hardin (Henry⁴, Henry³, Henry², Henry¹) (3-67) was born about 1797 in Shenandoah County Virginia. He married **Nancy Phillips** 16 May 1816 in Jefferson County, Kentucky. He died before 1836 in Oldham County, Kentucky.

Children of John⁵ Hardin and Nancy Phillips:
- \+   104   i. HENRY⁶ HARDIN (3-104) born 14 February 1816 in Jefferson County, Kentucky. He married Emily Ritter in 1840 and died in 1844 in Oldham County, Kentucky.
- 105   ii. SARAH ANN HARDIN (3-105) married Edmund A. Buckner
- \+   106   iii. JOHN W. HARDIN (3-106) born about 1821 Jefferson Co., Kentucky, married Azberine Antle in 1840 in Oldham County, Kentucky.
- 107   iv. MARY J HARDIN (3-107)
- 108   v. AMANDA HARDIN (3-108) born about 1823 Jefferson Co KY. Married David Flint 6 February 1846 Oldham Co., KY. She died 1897 Oldham Co KY
- 109   vi. OLDHAM HARDIN (3-109)
- 110   vii. AMERICA HARDIN (3-110)

111 viii. EMALINE F. HARDIN (3-111)
112 ix. CATHERINE A. HARDIN (3-112) born 16 July 1825 Oldham Co Kentucky, married Thomas Coakley Brown 3 October 1844. Died 3 January 1861 McLean Co., Kentucky

Jefferson County, Kentucky Records
1816 16 May: He married Nancy Phillips Register 1-87
1818: John Hardin 1 male 4 livestock Personal Property Tax List
1819: John Harding 200 acres Personal Property Tax List
1821: John Hardin 100 acres Jefferson County Harrods Creek Beall Personal Property Tax List
1822: John Harden 202 acres Jefferson Co Floyds Fork Nichols Personal Property Tax List

Oldham County, Kentucky Records
1825: John Hardin 100 acres Curry Fork Patent Norbonne Beall Personal Property Tax List
1826: John Harding 181 acres Harrods Creek S Beall Personal Property Tax List
1827 John: Harding 180 acres Harrods Creek Beall Personal Property Tax List
1830: Listed in 1830 Federal Census
1836 12 May: Bought 100 acres from William J Hardin Deeds C-531
1836 18 Jul: Railroad construction damages to his land determined. All children named. He was deceased. Deeds C-625
1839 21 Mar: Daughter Sarah Ann married Edmund A. Buckner
1840: Widow Nancy Harding listed in 1840 Federal Census
1845 25 Jul: Land divided among heirs. Deeds F-120
1850: Son Henry's widow Emily listed in 1850 Federal Census

68. Henry^5 Harding (Henry^4, Henry^3, Henry^2, Henry^1) (3-68) was born 19 January 1801 in Jefferson County, Kentucky and married **Mary Phillips**, daughter of Samuel Phillips 27 February 1821 in Jefferson County, Kentucky. He died 6 October 1859 in Sebastopol, Sonoma County, California. Mary was born 1 March 1803 in Jefferson Co., KY and died 4 January 1866 in Sonoma Co., California. They moved to Johnson County Missouri about 1839 and to California before 1860.

Children of Henry^5 Harding and Mary Phillips:
113   i. WILLIAM JEFFERSON^6 HARDIN (3-113) 1821-1900
114   ii. IRENE FRANCES HARDIN (3-114) 1822-1901
115   iii. SARAH ANN HARDIN (3-115) 1828-1915
116   iv. JAMES ALLEN HARDIN (3-116) 1830-1905
117   v. HENRY ANDREW HARDIN (3-117) 1833-1920
118   vi. JULIA ANN HARDIN (3-118) 1835-1909
119   vii. MARY JANE HARDIN (3-119) 1838-1902
120   ix. ANN ELIZA HARDIN (3-120) 1841-1932

Jefferson County, Kentucky Records
1821 27 Feb: Married Mary Phillips Register 1-122

1821: Henry Hardin Jr 130 acres Jefferson County Harrods Creek Beall PPTL
1821: Henry Hardin 50 acres Jefferson Co Harrods Creek Beall PPTL
1822: Henry Harden 50 acres Jefferson Co Harrods Creek Beall PPTL
1823: Henry Hardin 50 acres Jefferson Co Goose Creek Beall PPTL
1823: Henry Hardin
Oldham County, Kentucky Records
1825: Henry Harding Jr 50 acres Harrods Creek Patent Beall PPTL
1826: Henry Harding 50 acres Harrods Creek Patent S Beall PPTL
1827: Henry Harding 120 acres Harrods Creek Beall PPTL
1828: Henry Hardin 130 acres Harrods Creek Beall PPTL
1830: Listed in 1830 Federal Census
1834 05 May: Sold 19 acres Floyds Fork to William Yager Deeds C-209
1835 01 Aug: Sold 175 acres Floyds Fork to Henry N Brown Deeds C-419
1836 17 May: Sold 2 acres to Charity Boulware. On Flat Rock Deed C-544
1839 01 Oct: Sold 263 acres Floyds Ck to Joseph Beard. Deeds E-138

72. William^5 J. Harding (Henry^4, Henry^3, Henry^2, Henry^1) (3-72) was born 15 June 1807 in Jefferson County KY and married **Emily Brown** 22 December 1826 in Jefferson County, Kentucky. He died 6 June 1889 in McLean Co., Kentucky. She died 24 September 1843 in Oldham Co., Kentucky. He married second **Mary Shake** and lived in 1850 in Daviess County, Kentucky

Children of William J.^{5} Harding and Emily Brown:
121   i. FRANCIS MARION^6 HARDING (3-121) about 1830 Kentucky
122   ii. WILLIAM MCCLELLAND HARDING (3-122) 1832-1915
123   iii. MARY E. HARDING (3-123) born about 1834 Kentucky
124   iv. JAMES A HARDING (3-124) born about 1836 Kentucky
125   v. SARAH A. HARDING (3-125) born about 1838 Kentucky
126   iv. EMILY J. HARDING (3-126) born about 1840 Kentucky
127   v. ANN L. HARDING (3-127) born about 1842 Kentucky

Children of William J.^{5} Harding and Mary Shake:
128   vi. CATHERINE HARDING (3-128) born about 1845 Kentucky
129   vii. BENJAMIN A. HARDING (3-129) born about 1846 Kentucky
130   viii. JOHN J. HARDING (3-130) born about 1848 Kentucky

Oldham County, Kentucky Records
1834 06 Sep: Agrees to pay debt from father's estate Deeds C121
1836 12 May: Sold 100 acres to John Hardin Deeds C-531
1836 30 Mar: Sold 100 acres Harrods Creek to C Stoddard Deeds C-537
1836 17 May: Sold land Harrods Creek to Calvin Stoddard Deeds C-534
1836 05 Apr: Bought lot in Rollington from Rosanna Smith Deeds C-545
1836 18 Nov: Sold ¼ acre in Rollington to William K Allen Deeds D-217

78. William^5 Harding (Abner^4, William^3, George^2, Henry^1) (3-78) was born about 1802 in South Carolina. He moved with his parents and family to Russell Co., Virginia about 1810 or later. William had two sons with **Arreta Monk** in Virginia. They originally went by the name Monk per census records but by 1860 assumed the name Harding for their father. William then had two children with **Eliza** before he married her about 1855 and accepted the children as his own.

Children of William[5] Harding and Retta Monk:
- 131   i. JOHN G.[6] HARDING (3-131) born 1833 Russell Co., VA married Amanda Fields
- 132   ii. GEORGE W. HARDING (3-132) born 1835 Russell Co., VA

Children William[5] Harding and Eliza:
- 133   iii. EDWARD K. HARDING (3-133) born 1847 Russell Co., VA
- 134   iv. ELIJAH HARDING (3-134) born 1852 Russell Co. VA
- 135   v. HENRY HARDING (3-135) born 1858 Russell Co., VA

104. Henry[6] Hardin (John[5], Henry[4], Henry[3], Henry[2], Henry[1]) (3-104) was born 14 February 1816 in Jefferson County, KY. He married **Emily Ritter** after 26 October 1840 in Oldham Co KY. He died 20 April 1844 in Oldham Co., KY. Emily married second James Featheringill 3 February 1852.

Children of Henry[6] Hardin and Emily Ritter:
- 136   i. ABNER[7] HARDING (3-136) born 15 Jan 1842 Oldham Co KY

Oldham County, Kentucky Records
1840 25 Oct: Married Emily Ritter
1852 03 Feb: Widow Emily married Janes A Featheringill Mg Bonds

106. John[6] W. Hardin (John[5], Henry[4], Henry[3], Henry[2], Henry[1]) (3-106) was born about 1821 in Jefferson Co., Kentucky. He married **Azberine Antle**, daughter of James Antle, 17 December 1840 in Oldham County, Kentucky.

Oldham County, Kentucky Records
1840 17 Dec: Married Azberine Antle
1841 10 May: Mortgage from John Antle paid off Deeds E-117
1841 10 May: Satisfaction of debt from James Antle recorded
1851 04 Feb: Sells two tracts to William White

Jefferson County, Kentucky Records
1850: Listed in Division 2 Jefferson Co., KY Federal Census

Family 4: Joseph Combs, William Harden and Clarissa Million of Stafford County, Virginia

I discussed the Y-700 DNA results for this family in Chapter 2, Group 4, which show that William Harden (4-2) is the son of Joseph Combs I of

Family Genealogies with References

Stafford County, Virginia and a Harding woman, who I suspect is the sister of my Thomas Harden (1-23). This reorganizes this chapter in several ways to account for the revelation of the ancestry of both William Harden, (4-2) and Joseph Harden (4-21).

In earlier versions of this chapter, based on the DNA results, I proposed for the first time that William Harding (4-2), who has for many years been considered a son, born in 1738, of Charles Harding (2-2) and Rachel Lunsford, (2-2), was not his son, was born many years earlier, and first married Elizabeth Ashby (4-2), a daughter of Thomas Ashby of Stafford County, Virginia and later Federick County, Virginia.

Current Y-DNA research now proves this statement to be correct and shows his actual parentage and true structure of his family. The largest change is that Joseph Harden (4-21) is no longer his son but is the proven son of Joseph Combs II, and a daughter of Mark Hardin Sr (5-1) perhaps Elizabeth. . Therefore, I will start with the family of Joseph Combs I in some detail and include references for more information.

Two of the sons of this proposed couple, William Harding (4-2) and Elizabeth Ashby (4-2), Benjamin (4-9) and Enos, (4-7) are closely DNA related and Benjamin (4-9) and Enos (4-7) are known to be brothers from later land records in Kentucky detailed later in this book. Evangelist (4-6) and James (4-8) are almost certainly brothers of Benjamin (4-9) and Enos (4-7) and are placed here because the records closely associate them with the other three. Joseph Hardin (4-21) is now given as the son of Joseph Combs II.

Benjamin, (4-9) Enos, (4-7) Evangelist, (4-6) and James (4-8) all have a clear connection with the Thomas Ashby family of Frederick County Virginia, who married Rose Berry.

Researchers have claimed for years that one of Thomas Ashby's daughters, Elizabeth Ashby (4-2), married Mark Harden Jr. (5-4) from Family #5, the descendants of Mark Hardin (5-1) and Mary (MNU) (5-1) family. Thomas Ashby Sr. died in 1752 in Frederick County, Virginia and mentioned Elizabeth Harding (4-2) in his will.

Elizabeth Ashby (4-2) did not marry Mark Hardin, (5-4). Although Mark Hardin appears to have had a wife, named Betty or Elizabeth in the records, no maiden name is ever given for this Elizabeth, who cannot be the daughter named in Thomas Ashby's will. In Mark Hardin's divorce record in December 1753, no children are mentioned. In most recent sources, Mark Hardin (5-1) is mentioned as the father of either one son or no children.

Further, Elizabeth Ashby's) (4-2) children, Enos, Benjamin, and Evangelist, who as proven by DNA, are not children of Mark Hardin (5-4) and Elizabeth, who appear to have been married for a little over a year and were divorced before 1753. The problem of whether Mark Hardin (5-4) had any children is a problem for another book. Some say he had a son, Mark, born in 1757 but by then he was divorced and without a wife.

Since all four sons of William Harding's (4-2) first marriage emerge into the records in western Virginia and much later in time, I suspect they might have been orphans since I have found no possible male relatives in counties where they are known to have lived but have found a lot of connections with the Ashby family, which makes sense if his first wife was an Ashby. The following genealogical stories give all the details I have found about each man. There is also no record of when Elizabeth (Ashby) Hardin (4-2) may have died although I believe it was before William Hardin's marriage to Clarissa Million (4-2).

First, let's look at what we know about the emergence of each man into history. William Harding (4-2) is first seen in the 1783 tax lists of Stafford County, Virginia and in a deed in 1784, when he leased property from Marquis Calmes of Hampshire County, Virginia. We know he married Clarissa Million (4-2) before the early 1760s but have no idea where they married. Her parents, Robert Million and Grace Bennett, lived in Northumberland County early but his children were born in Stafford County. How William met Clarissa is unknown as well as where they spent the first 20 years of their marriage.

Benjamin Hardin (4-9) was born in 1753, we even have the exact date, but we have no idea where he was born. In this section, I propose for the first time here that he was born in Stafford County, Virginia. He first appears in the records when he married Nancy Routt in Fauquier County, Virginia in 1785. He claimed to have served in the Revolutionary War in Captain Stephen Ashby's company and that he joined in Hampshire County, Virginia, but no records or muster rolls confirm this. In his pension application, he says nothing about his background or where he came from. The first tax lists he shows up in are from 1794 in Clark County, Kentucky.

Enos Harden (4-7) is known to be Benjamin's brother according to an 1827 deed in Henry County, Kentucky which says they were brothers. Enos Hardin (4-7) first appears as a soldier in Captain Stephen Ashby's company muster rolls from 1777 to 1778. He is on the Hampshire County Tax rolls from 1782 to 1785 and by 1793 was in Clark County, Kentucky. He married Martha Ann Ashby in 1793 in Mercer County, Kentucky. There is no record of his origin.

Evangelist Harding (4-6) is closely associated with Enos Harding (4-7) and James Harding (4-8). He first appears as one of the people who spent time in Harrodsburg, Kentucky after 11 March 1775. Next, he appears on the Hampshire County Tax Lists in 1782 and was there until 1785, when Benjamin Ashby in Clark County, Kentucky sold 200 acres to him and Enos Harding (4-7) in the same deed. One of the witnesses was James Hardin (4-8). The name of his wife is unknown, and his origin is unknown. He seems to be a wealthy landowner but very shadowy, appearing very few records. He is known to have two daughters and one son. Nothing is known about him before 1784, when he emerged in Hampshire County, Virginia.

James Hardin (4-8) is closely associated with this family in a lot of ways. He first appears in the records in 1795, when he married Hanna Berry, a relative of Thomas Ashby's wife, in Mercer County Kentucky. He appraised the estates of Benjamin Hardin's two sons who died young and one of Evangelist's sons, who also died young. He also administered Enos Hardin's estate in 1818.

Finally, Joseph Harding (4-21), now proven to be a nephew of William through Joseph Combs II, was born around 1750 and first appears in the records in 1772 in Loudoun County, Virginia Tax lists. He married and had a family of four sons and a daughter in Loudoun County and died there in 1806 after writing his will.

All of this makes sense if William Harding's first wife died soon after the birth of her last child and William in the mid 1750s sent his orphan sons to live with their Ashby relatives in the northwest of Virginia, where they all appear in the 1770s and 1780s, seemingly from nowhere. That nowhere now appears to be the homes of various Ashby relatives who lived in the area.

Several names, Lewis, Mark and Enos, are common among the descendants of these men, which gives a clue to their ancestry. One thing for certain, proven by DNA, is none of them descend from the family of Mark Hardin (5-1) and Mary (MNU) (5-1) (Family #5) or any other Virginia Hardin family. All we can say is that Benjamin, (4-9) Enos, (4-7) William, (4-2) and Joseph (4-21) are DNA cousins, closely related to each other and that Evangelist (4-6) and James (4-8) are so close to them for so many years that they must be relatives.

1. Joseph Combs I (4-1) is an enigma. His birthdate and place are unknown. The best guess is that he was born around 1695. He is first found in Stafford County, Virginia in 1723. However, because of the condition of Stafford County records, we cannot say that he was not present there from an earlier date. His ancestry is also unknown. The name of his wife is unknown. Y-700 DNA places him in a separate haplogroup with no recent

Combs connections since about 1100 AD. He died about 1765 in Stafford County. For more detailed information see the Combs Family website: https://combs-families.org/combs/families/c-jos1.htm.

Children of Joseph¹ Combs I and unknown mothers:

+ 2 i. WILLIAM² HARDING born about 1720.
   3 ii. JOHN COMBS md SETH BULLITT
+ 4 iii. JOSEPH COMBS II md ELIZABETH HARRISON
   5 iv JANE COMBS md JOHN ASHBY, son of THOMAS ASHBY

2. William² Harding (4-2) (Joseph¹ Combs I) was born about 1720 in Virginia and died in Stafford County, Virginia in 1796.

For many years most researchers identified him with William, the son of Charles Harding (2-2) in Family #2, who was born in 1738 according to the Overwharton Parish Register. However, this William's (4-2) descendants are not a DNA match with any member of Family #2, so he cannot be placed in that family. Descendants of two of his children by Clarissa Million are DNA matches with descendants of Benjamin Hardin so must be placed in this family with him and his brother Enos Hardin.

For the first time, I'm proposing a radical reconstruction of the families presented here and a major change in the connections with the Ashby family and to Family #5, the descendants of Mark (5-1) and Mary Harding (5-1).

Currently, most sources say that Mark Hardin) (5-4) married Elizabeth Ashby. One web source (Stickels) even gives a date of 1 January 1752 in Prince William County, Virginia, which I have never been able to verify. The only original source I have found is Thomas Ashby's will, which mentions his daughter Elizabeth Hardin and says she shall get no part of his estate. He does not name her husband.

An Elizabeth Hardin is mentioned several times in the records, only once with reference to a husband:

1. Prince William County, Virginia, 27 November 1753 Betty Hardin sued Mark Harden for alimony, not divorced him as many claim.
2. Frederick County, Virginia Court 6 April 1757 Elizabeth Harden vs Mark Hardin (5-4) over debt.
3. Frederick County, Virginia Court 9 August 1759 Elizabeth Harden sued John Hardin (5-2). She paid for a witness.

It is true that Mark Hardin and his brother John Hardin lived in the same area as Thomas Ashby in the 1740s and 1750s and various members of the Ashby family interacted with various members of the Hardin family. This is not proof of Mark's marriage. Circumstantial evidence suggests it.

Family Genealogies with References

Prior to the 1740s Thomas Ashby lived in Overwharton Parish, Stafford County, Virginia. Many Ashbys, relatives of Thomas are recorded in the parish registers, which started in 1724.

The key point here is that we do not know who Elizabeth or Betty Hardin was although it seemed to early researchers that she was most likely the Elizabeth Hardin mentioned in Thomas Ashby's will dated 6 April 1752 and proved 4 August 1752. It just seemed to make sense. However, we have only these three records that mention Elizabeth or Betty Hardin and none of them connect Elizabeth Ashby directly to Mark Hardin. Mark's marriage appears to have been short and childless. His wife's maiden name remains unknown.

I propose here for the first time, based in DNA evidence and many later connections with the Ashby family, that William Harding (4-2) married Elizabeth Ashby, daughter of Thomas Ashby, about 1740 in Stafford County, Virginia and had four sons with her, Evangelist, (4-6) Enos, (4-7) James, (4-8) and Benjamin. (4-9) I also propose either that some years after 1753, his first wife died, and a devastated William Harding sent the children to live with their mother's relatives until they grew up. They lived in Prince William County and counties to the west, where all five appear in various places, almost always associated with Ashby family, during their lives. This answers the question of who these five men were, how they connected, and affirms the DNA record saying they were all close relatives.

Some time later, about 1761 or 1762, William Harding (4-2) married **Clarissa Million**, daughter of Robert Million and Martha Bennett of Stafford County, Virginia. She was born about 1740 and died in 1826. We do not know where he lived before 1784, when he leased land in Stafford County, Virginia from Marquis Calmes of Hampshire Co., Virginia, who is also associated with the Ashby family. William Harding (4-2) is listed in the Stafford County, Virginia tax lists from 1784 until 1798, when William Harding's executors are in the tax lists. After that Clarissa (Clarky) is listed until 1826, when Clarky Harding made her will in which she mentions *her* children. No mention of her husband or his other children, since he was long dead.

Children of William[2] Harding (Joseph Combs[1]) and Elizabeth Ashby:

+ 6   i. EVANGELIST[3] HARDIN[3] (4-6) about 1742 Virginia
+ 7   ii. ENOS (ENNIS) HARDIN (4-7) born about 1745 Virginia
+ 8   iii. JAMES HARDIN (4-8) about 1748 Virginia
+ 9   v. BENJAMIN HARDIN (4-9) born December 1753 Virginia

Children of William[2] Harding (Joseph Combs[1]) and Clarissa Million:

Harding Families of the Northern Neck of Virginia

+ 10   i. JOHN³ BENNETT HARDING (4-10) born 1763 in Virginia, married Elizabeth Bennett, died in 1848 in Knox County, Ohio
+ 11   ii. CUTHBERT HARDING (4-11) born c 1766 Virginia, married Winifred McInteer and died in 1842 in Kentucky.
+ 12   iii. ENOCH HARDING (4-12) born about 1767 Virginia, married Sarah Kendall, died 1849 in Stafford County, Virginia.
    13   iv. FRANCES HARDING (4-13) born about 1770 in Virginia. She died in Alexandria, Virginia in 1855. She married Mr. Shackelford
+ 14   v. ELIJAH HARDING (4-14) born about 1772 in Virginia, married Philadelphia, died in Stafford County Virginia in 1816.
    15   vi. CELIA HARDING (4-15) born about 1775 Virginia md James Stark
    16   vii. NANCY HARDING (4-16) born about 1780 Virginia
    17   x. ADAH HARDING (4-17) born about 1790 Stafford Co., Virginia married William McInteer. She died in 1805.
    18   viii. LEWIS HARDING (4-18) born about 1785, Stafford Co., Virginia
+ 19   ix. MARK HARDING (4-19) born about 1788 Stafford Co., Virginia, married Nancy Young and Agnes Hord and died in Spotsylvania County, Virginia after 1873.

Stafford County, Virginia Records
1784 William Harding of Stafford leased land from Marquis Calmes of Hampshire Co VA
1783 to 1797 William Harding listed in personal property tax lists PPTL
1798 William Harding Executor listed in personal property tax lists PPTL
1798 – 1819: Clarkey Harding Listed on Personal Property Tax Lists PPTL
1810: Federal Census Clarka Harding listed
1820 Federal Census Clarky Harding listed
1826 Will of Clarky Harding DW GG-278

    4. **Joseph² Combs II** (Joseph Combs¹) (4-4) was born about 1725 in Stafford County, Virginia. He married Elizabeth Harrison about 1752 and had several children with her. Prior to his marriage, about 1748, he fathered an illegitimate son, Joseph Harding (alias Combs) with a Hardin woman, perhaps one of the daughters of Mark Hardin (5-1) and Mary Hogue,(5-1) who has not been identified. About 1749 he fathered an illegitimate son, Robert Ashby Combs with Sarah Ashby. A year alter he fathered another illegitimate son, Joseph Hardin, (4-21) possibly by a daughter of Mark Hardin (5-1) and Mary Hogue. By 1756 he was living in Frederick County, Virginia by 1755 at the latest. By 1765 he was living in Loudoun County, Virginia. He was living in Loudoun County as late as 1790, when he sold land. The number of children he fathered is uncertain. You will find considerable detailed information at the Combs Family website: https://combs-families.org/combs/families/c-jos1.htm. The following list of his children is the best we have.
    Children of Joseph Combs II:

Family Genealogies with References

   20   i. ROBERT ASHBY COMBS³ born c 1749 (by Sarah Ashby)
+ 21   ii. JOSEPH HARDIN born c 1750 (by unknown Harding)
   22   iii. JOSEPH COMBS III born c 1753 married Mary McMakin
   23   iv STEPHEN COMBS born c 1755 married Barbara Allen

6. Evangelist³ Hardin (William², Joseph Combs¹) (4-6) was born about 1742. He is first mentioned in the History of Kentucky, 1845, by Lewis Collins as one of the 54 men who were present in Harrodsburg, Kentucky after 11 March 1775. By 1782 he was living in Hampshire County, Virginia and returned to Kentucky by 1795. He married but the name of his wife is not known. He died in Owen Co., Kentucky in the 1830s.

Children:
   24   i. JOHN HARDIN⁴ (4-24) born about 1790-1813
   25   ii. ELIZABETH HARDIN (4-25) Elizabeth Hardin was born about 1794 and married Jacob Kelly (4-25) 21 March 1814 in Franklin Co., Kentucky. There are two marriages of a Jacob Kelly and Elizabeth Hardin. I believe this Jacob Kelly is the one most people say died in 1831 although I have found no record to confirm this. Their children are not known for certain.
   26   iii. SARAH HARDIN born about 1797 (4-26) married Orlando Dorsey Lindsey in 1814 and has many descendants

Hampshire County, Virginia Records
1782: Hampshire Co., VA Personal Property Tax List PPTL
1783: Hampshire Co., VA Personal Property Tax List PPTL
1784: Hampshire Co., VA Personal Property Tax List PPTL
1785: Hampshire Co., VA Personal Property Tax List PPTL
Clark County, Kentucky Records
1795 26 Nov: Benjamin Ashby Power of Attorney to Nathaniel Ashby to sell 200 acres to Evangelist Hardin
1795 27 Nov: Evangelist Hardin witnesses Power of Attorney from Benjamin Ashby to Enos Hardin. Deed Book 1 Page 591
Franklin County, Kentucky Records
1803 to 1814 On Franklin Co., KY Personal Property Tax Lists PPTL
1810: US Census shows Enos Hardin next to Evangelist and James Hardin
1814 21 Mar: Daughter Sarah married Orlando Lindsay
1813 20 Sep: To administrate estate of John Hardin dec.
1814 18 Apr: Inventory of the estate of James Hardin returned CO E-398
Owen County, Kentucky Records
1819: On personal property Tax Lists
1823 25 Dec: Robert Ashby to George, James, Thomas Hardin, and Ann Hawkins Land on Kentucky River
1856 16 May: Deed notes land bordering Evangelist Hardin DB M-510
Henry County, Kentucky Records

1826 18 Sep: Heirs of Enos Hardin sell land he held to Evangelist Hardin. Deed Book 12 Page 185.

7. Enos³ Hardin (William², Joseph Combs¹) (4-7) was born about 1745 in Virginia. He married first Sophia (4-7), MNU about 1783. He does not appear in any personal property tax lists from 1785-1793 and since his daughter states she was born in Maryland, he may have lived there for several years. After Sophia died, he married **Martha Ann Ashby** (4-2) in 1793 in Mercer Co., Kentucky. He died before 18 September 1826 in Henry Co., Kentucky.

Children of Enos³ Hardin and Sophia:
- 27 i. REBECCA⁴ HARDIN (4-27) was born about 1785, married Jeremiah Bunnel (4-27) 27 November 1804 in Mercer County, Kentucky. She died 7 March 1856 in Hart County, Kentucky. Her death record says she was born in Maryland.

Children of Enos² Hardin and Martha Ann Ashby:
- + 28 i. GEORGE HARDIN (4-28) born about 1793 in Virginia, married Jemima Hawkins, died after 1860 in Pike Co MO
- + 29 ii. ENOS HARDIN (4-29) born about 1797 in Kentucky, married Elizabeth Guthrie, died in Owen County, Kentucky by 1862.
- + 30 iii. THOMAS HARDIN (4-30) 1801 in Kentucky, married Rachel Allen, died in 1855 in Owen County, Kentucky.
- + 31 iv. ANN HARDIN (4-31) was born about 1803, married Benjamin T. Hawkins by 1820 and died before 1833 in Pike County, Missouri.

Virginia Military Records
Mar 1777 to May 1778 Pvt Capt. Stephen Ashby Company 12th VA Regiment
July 1778 to Sep 1778 Pvt Lt Col John Neville's Company 4th Virginia Regiment
Oct 1778 to Sep 1779 Col James Woods Company 8th Virginia Regiment

Hampshire County, Virginia Records
1782: Hampshire Co., VA on Personal Property Tax List
1785: Hampshire Co., VA Personal Property Tax List

Loudoun County, Virginia Records
1790 Loudoun Co., VA files suit against Joseph Combs and Daniel Tuagan

Mercer County, Kentucky Records
1793 30 Jan: Marriage Bonds, married Martha Ann Ashby, George Ashby bond
1804 27 Nov: Daughter Rebecca married Jeremiah Bunnel

Clark County, Kentucky Records
1793: Listed on Clark County, Kentucky Personal Property Tax List PPTL
1794: Listed on Clark County, Kentucky Personal Property Tax List PPTL
1795: Listed on Clark County, Kentucky Personal Property Tax List Has 1000 acres on Stoner Creek in Clark County. PPTL
1795 26 Nov: Buy 200 acres from Benjamin Ashby. Deeds Bk 1 Page 592
1795 27 Nov: Gets Power of Atty from Benjamin Ashby of Frederick Co VA Deeds Bk 1 Page 591

1796: Listed on Clark County, Kentucky Personal Property Tax List. See table of lands owned. PPTL
1802 09 Mar: Benjamin Ashby Power of Atty revoked Deeds Bk 4 Page 357
1803 03 Sep: Of Franklin Co., KY Deed Bk 7 Page 417 and 419
1805 22 Apr: Of Franklin Co., KY Resolved real estate issue with Peter Scholl. Deeds Bk 7 Page 85
1810 27 Jun: Of Franklin Co., KY sells 100 acres in Clarke Co to John Johnson. Deeds Bk 7 Page 410, 414

Franklin County, Kentucky Records
1801-1818: Listed on personal property tax lists. PPTL
1810: US Census shows Enos Hardin next to Evangelist and James Hardin
1811 02 Mar: Buys land in Franklin County from Benjamin Ashby Book C Page 139
1811 02 Mar: Benjamin Ashby sells him 318 ¾ acres in Franklin Co. Deed Books
1813 21 June: To appraise estate of James Hardin Dec. CO E-335
1813 21 June: To appraise estate of Benjamin Hardin Dec. C E-335
1813 20 Sep: To appraise the estate of John Hardin dec. CO E-345

Henry County, Kentucky Records
1826 18 Sep: Heirs of Enos Hardin sell land he held to Evangelist Hardin. Deeds, Bk 12 Page 185.

Owen County, Kentucky Records
1825 03 Aug: Swapped Land with Benjamin Hardin of Owen County DB B-49
1825 12 Sep: Heirs of Enos Hardin Emancipate Tom Frazier DB B-77

8. James³ Hardin (William², Joseph Combs¹) (4-8) was born about 1748 in Virginia and married **Hanna Berry** (4-8), daughter of Reuben Berry, in 1795 Mercer Co., Kentucky. He died in Owen Co., Kentucky before March 1843.

Children of James³ Hardin and Hanna Berry:

- 32   i. LUCY⁴HARDIN (4-32) born 10 April 1796 Franklin Co., KY She married Silus B. Calvert 2 April 1814 in Franklin Co., Kentucky. She died 21 August 1840 in Owen Co., Kentucky.
- 33   ii. ENOS HARDIN (4-33) born about 1797, died 1818 in Franklin Co., Kentucky
- 34   iii. LEWIS HARDIN (4-34) born about 1800 Kentucky, He lived in Owen County, Kentucky, where he was listed on the personal property tax lists from 1819 to 1845. He sold his interest in his father's property to the Branhams 1 July 1843 (Owen County Deed Book I-33)
- + 35   iv. HARRIET HARDIN (4-35) born about 1802 Kentucky, married John R. Hawkins, died after 1870 in Pike County, Missouri.
- + 36   v. ABSOLOM HARDIN (4-36) born about 1804 in Kentucky. He married Eleanor Warner in 1827 and Catherine Henderson in 1833 in Owen County, Kentucky. He died after 1860 in Texas.
- 37   vi. SARAH HARDIN (4-37) Sarah Hardin was born about 1806 in Kentucky. She married William P. Thornton (1796-1865) on 4 August 1828 in Owen Co., Kentucky. They are listed in the 1850 Census of

Owen County, Kentucky. She died about 1855 in Owen Co., Kentucky.

38   vii. MARY HARDIN (4-38) born about 1806 Kentucky Mary Hardin was born about 1806 in Kentucky. She married Israel Ellis 6 December 1824 Owen Co., Kentucky. Died 1846 Mattoon, Coles Co., Illinois.

+ 39   viii. BAYLIS G. HARDIN (4-39) born about 1817 Owen Co., Kentucky. He married Sarah Spires in 1844 in Owen County, Kentucky.

40   ix. JAMES B. HARDIN (4-40) was born about 1820 in Kentucky. He appears on personal property tax lists after 1839 in Owen County, Kentucky.

Henry County, Kentucky Records
1795 14 Aug: Marriage of James Hardin and Hanna Berry

Clark County, Kentucky Records
1795 Nov: Witnesses Power of Attorney to Nathaniel Ashby.
1795 27 Nov: James Hardin witnesses Power of Attorney from Benjamin Ashby to Enos Hardin. Deed Book 1 Page 591
1795: Listed on Personal Property Tax List. No Land. PPTL

Franklin County, Kentucky Records
1801 to 1819 Listed on Franklin County, KY Personal Property Tax Lists
1810: US Census shows Enos Hardin next to Evangelist and James Hardin
1813 21 June: To appraise estate of James Hardin Dec. CO E-335
1813 21 June: To appraise estate of Benjamin Hardin Dec. CE E-335
1813 20 Sep: To appraise the estate of John Hardin dec. CO E-345
1813 16 Nov: Judgement for Breach of the peace CO H-367
1814 19 Sep: Renews bond as constable for county CO F-27
1816 19 Aug: Given leave to renew bond as constable for county CO F-199
1818 15 Jun: Administrator of estate of Enos Hardin decd CO F-397
1818 15 Jun: Appraisers selected for estate of Enos Hardin CO F-397
1818 17 Aug: Leave given to renew bond as constable. CO F-412

Owen County, Kentucky Records
1819-1842: Listed in Personal Property Tax Lists
1820: Listed in Federal Census
1820: Son Lewis Hardin Listed in Federal Census
1823-25 Dec: Robert Ashby to George, James, Thomas Hardin, and Ann Hawkins Land on Kentucky River
1829 27 Aug: Buys from William Warner estate by sheriff DB C-366
1830: Listed in Federal Census
1830: Son Lewis listed in Federal Census
1840: Listed in Federal Census Owen Co., Kentucky
1840: Son Lewis listed in Federal Census
1840 11 Apr: Buys land from William Cave DB G-181
1840 10 Aug: Buys personal property from William Ball DB G-119
1843 18 Feb: He writes his will WB C-127l
1843 Mar: His will proved in court. WB C-127
1846 28 Jan: Executor sells estate to John Smith DB K-31

Family Genealogies with References

1850 16 Apr: Final settlement of his estate WB D-223

9. Benjamin³ Hardin (William² Joseph Combs¹) (4-9) was born in 1753 in Virginia and died in 1834 in Henry Co., Kentucky. He is known to be a brother of Enos Hardin from deed records. He is also a brother to James and Evangelist Hardin. He first married **Nancy Routt** in 1785 in Fauquier County, Virginia and second the widow **Rebecca Jackson** (c 1777-February 1821) 22 January 1815 in Henry County, Kentucky.

Children of Benjamin³ Hardin and Nancy Routt:

- 41   i. DANIEL⁴ HARDIN (4-41) 1790-1845
- 42   ii. JAMES HARDIN (4-42) born about 1793-1813 Franklin Co., KY
- 43   iii. BENJAMIN HARDIN (4-43) Jr about 1795-1813 Franklin Co., KY
- 44   iv. WILLIAM HARDIN (4-44) 1799-1844
- 45   v. MARK HARDIN (4-45) 1800-1877 married Lucinda Douthitt
- 46   vi. ELIZABETH HARDIN (4-46) 1805-1879 married Jacob Kelly This Elizabeth Hardin married Jacob Kelly, (4-46) according to her father's will, before 1827. Since she was born about 1804, she is not the same Elizabeth Hardin who married Jacob Kelly in Franklin Co., KY in 1814. Per that marriage bond, that Elizabeth (4-25) was the daughter of Evangelist Hardin (4-6). This Elizabeth Hardin and Jacob Kelly are listed in the 1830 Census in Owen Co., Kentucky and lived in Illinois after 8 December 1840, per a deed where they sell land purchased from her father Benjamin Hardin. So far, I have not been able to find Jacob and Elizabeth in Illinois or Indiana or Kentucky after 1840.
- 47   vii. NATHANIEL HARDIN (4-47) 1807-1884 married Sarah Sanford
- 48   viii. HENRY HARDIN (4-48) 1808-

Children of Benjamin² Hardin and Rebecca Jackson:

- 49   ix. REBECCA ANN HARDIN (4-49) 1815-
- 50   x. GEORGE WASHINGTON HARDIN (4-50) 1818-1895 married Martha Sanford
- 51   xi. NANCY HARDIN (4-51)1821-1881

Fauquier County, Virginia Records

1785 16 Mar: Marriage Bond to marry Nancy Routt. Marriage Records Book 1 Page 139

Clark County, Kentucky Records

1794: Clark Co., Kentucky Listed on Personal Property Tax List PPTL
1795: Clark Co., Kentucky Listed on Personal Property Tax List PPTL
1796: Clark Co., Kentucky Listed on Personal Property Tax List PPTL
1797: Clark Co., Kentucky Listed on Personal Property Tax List PPTL

Scott County, Kentucky Records:

1820 02 Oct: Revolutionary War Pension application

Franklin County, Kentucky Records

1813 21 Jun: Administrator of estate of James Hardin, deceased CO E-335
1813 21 Jun: Administrator of estate of Benjamin Hardin Jr dec. CO-E335
1814 18 Apr: Inventory of the estate of James Hardin returned CO E-398

1814 18 Apr: Inventory of the estate of Benjamin Hardin Jr. returned CO E-398
1817 19 May: Turned in his list of taxable property for 1816. CO F-288
1822 12 Oct: Son Mark Hardin married Loucinda Douthitt 12 October 1822 from Marriage Records
Henry County, Kentucky Records
1812 09 Jun: Son Daniel married Rebecca Kelly
1815 22 Jan: Married Rebecca Jackson. Marriages
1823 01 Sep: Further Revolutionary Pension Application
1827 05 Nov: Sells 900 acres purchased with his brother Ennis Hardin to his children. Deed Book 12 Page 410
1830: In Federal Census for 1830
1830: Sons Daniel and Mark in 1830 Federal Census
1832 Aug: Declaration for Pension for Revolutionary War Service
Owen County, Kentucky Records
1820: On Federal Census for 1820
1820: Listed on Personal Property Tax Lists PPTL
1825 03 Aug: Swapped Land with Enos Hardin of Owen County DB B-49

10. John[3] Bennett Harding (William[2] Joseph Combs[1]) (4-10) was born about 1761 in Virginia, lived first in Culpeper Co., Virginia, then later moved to Kentucky and then Knox Co., Ohio, where he died in 1848. He married **Elizabeth Bennett**.

Children of John Bennett[2] Harding and Elizabeth Bennett:

- 52   i. MASON[4] HARDING (4-52) born about 1784
- 53   ii. BENNETT HARDING (4-53) born 1786
- 54   iii. LARKIN HARDING (4-54) 1788-
- 55   iv. DANIEL HARDING (4-55) 1790-1869
- 56   v. LEWIS HARDING (4-56) 1790-c 1840
- 57   vi. JOHN HARDING (4-55) 1792-
- 58   vii. NELSON HARDING (4-58) 1794-1865
- 59   viii. JAMES HARDING (4-59) 1795-
- 60   ix. ELIZABETH HARDING (4-60) 1796-
- 61   x. SARAH HARDING (4-61) 1796-1874

Stafford County, Virginia Records
1784-1812: On Personal Property Tax Lists PPTL
1805-1810: Son Mason on Personal Property Tax Lists PPTL

11. Cuthbert[3] Harding (William[2] Joseph Combs[1]) (4-11) was born about 1766 in Virginia. He died in 1842 in Kentucky. He married **Winifred McInteer,** daughter of Alexander McInteer and Miriam Belcher. He appears in Stafford County, Virginia personal property tax lists from 1785-1792.

Children of Cuthbert[3] Harding and Winifred McInteer:

- 62   i. MARCUS[4] HARDING (4-62) 1785-1859 Barren Co KY married Judith Shockley

63	ii.	WILLIAM A. HARDING (4-63) born about 1787 VA
64	iii.	AMY HARDING (4-64) 1790-1863 married James Whitworth
65	iv.	MARTIN HARDING (4-65) 1793-1850 married Isabella Beard
66	v.	GARLAND HARDING (4-66) 1793-c 1870 married Martha Votaw
67	vi.	MARTHA HARDING (4-67) born 1799
68	vii.	MARY HARDING (4-68) 1799-1876 married Samuel Whitworth
69	viii.	JOHN SAMUEL HARDING (4-69) 1802-1880 married Sarah Clements

12. Enoch³ Harding (William² Joseph Combs¹) (4-12) was born about 1767 in Virginia. He married **Sarah Kendall**, daughter of John Kendall and Catharine Kees before 1794. He died in Stafford Co., Virginia in September 1849.

Children of Enoch³ Harding and Sarah Kendall:

70	i.	MARISSA⁴ HARDING (4-70)1793-1864
71	ii.	FRANCES HARDING (4-71) 1799-1883
72	iii.	HENRY WILDY HARDING (4-72) 1801-1878
73	iv.	GILBERT HARDING (4-73) 1805-1890
74	v.	ENOCH HARDING (4-74) 1807-1874
75	vi.	MARY HARDING (4-75) 1808-1886
76	vii.	STROTHER HARDING (4-76) 1812-1880

Stafford County, Virginia Records
1792-1818: Appears in land tax lists PPTL
1791-1820: Appears in personal property tax lists PPTL
1810: In Federal Census Falmouth Stafford County VA
1811 27 Nov: Enoch, Elijah, Lewis, and Mark Harding sell land they bought in 1801. DW
1820: In 1820 Federal Census Stafford County, VA
1830: In 1830 Federal Census Stafford County, VA
1840: In 1840 Federal Census Stafford County, VA
1850: In 1850 Federal Mortality Schedule, died Sept 1849 Age 55

14. Elijah³ Hardin (William² Joseph Combs¹) (4-14) was born before 1772 and married **Philadelphia** --- by 1811. He was an officer in the War of 1812. He died by 1816 in Stafford County, Virginia

Children of Elijah³ Harding and Philadelphia:

77	i.	PHILIP⁴ HARDING (4-77) was born in 1795. He married Frances Humphrey. He died in Stafford Co., Virginia in 1869

Stafford County, Virginia Records
1800: On personal Property Tax Lists PPTL
1806-1814: On Personal Property Tax Lists PPTL
1810: In 1810 Federal Census Falmouth, Stafford Co., VA
1811 07 Nov: Enoch, Elijah, Lewis, and Mark Harding sell land they bought in 1801. DW
1813-1816: On Land Tax Lists PPTL

Harding Families of the Northern Neck of Virginia

1816: Widow Philadelphia on Personal Property Tax Lists PPTL
1817-1818: Heirs of Elijah Harding on Land Tax Lists PPTL

19. Mark³ Harding (William² Joseph Combs¹) (4-19) was born about 1788. He married first **Nancy Young** and Second **Agnes Hord**. He died in Spotsylvania Co., VA after September 1873.

Children of Mark³ Harding and Nancy Young:
78   i. LEWIS⁴ G. HARDING (4-78) 1812 to 1896
79   ii. JANE AMANDA HARDING (4-79) 1817-1856
80   iii. ELIJAH PARKINSON HARDING (4-80) 1828-1887

Children of Mark³ Harding and Agnes Hord:
81   iv. ADA ENGEDI HARDING (4-81) 1823-1905 married Foster

Stafford County, Virginia Records
1810: In Federal Census Aquia, Stafford Co., VA
1809-1820: On Personal property Tax List
1811 27 Nov: Stafford Co., VA DW Enoch, Elijah, Lewis, and Mark Harding sell land they bought in 1801.
1820: In Federal Census Stafford County, VA
1830: In Federal Census Stafford County, VA
1840: In Federal Census Stafford County, VA
1850: In Federal Census Stafford County, VA Age 63 with Agnes Age 55

Spotsylvania County, Virginia Records
1860 Census Berkeley Parish, Spotsylvania Co., VA age 71 born VA
1870 Census Livingston, Spotsylvania Co., VA Age 83 Retired
1872 26 Mar: He made his will. Will Book Y Page 433
1873 Sep: His will proved in court.

21. Joseph³ Harding (Joseph Combs² Joseph Combs¹,) (4-21) has been an enigma for many years. Trees on Ancestry give him various parents or named none. Recent DNA testing of two of his male descendants proves that he is the natural son of Joseph Combs Jr of Stafford County, Virginia. He was born around 1750 probably in Stafford County and lived in Loudoun County. by 1765. In a court record there he is called Joseph Hardin Alias Combs, a way at the time of identifying his father as a Combs. He is said to have married **Elizabeth Pressley** although a record of that marriage has never been found. He did name one of his sons Presley Harding. That son moved later to Bath County, Kentucky, where he left a large family. He left a will in Loudoun Co., Virginia in 1806 that mentions four sons and his wife. He left 1000 acres on the Rolling Fork River in Kentucky to his four sons. I have found no clue to where or when he purchased this land. He never had a son Jeremiah, (1-86) as many trees suggest. That Jeremiah (1-86) was a grandson of Thomas Hardin,(1-23)

Family Genealogies with References

Children of Joseph[3] Harding and Elizabeth Pressley:

+ 82   i. WILLIAM HARDING[4] (4-82) was born about 1770 in Loudoun County, Virginia, married Elizabeth, and died in 1824 in Loudoun County, Virginia.
+ 83   ii. PRESLEY HARDING (4-83) born about 1772 in Loudoun County, Virginia. He married Sarah Sears in 1803 in Loudoun County, Virginia. He died in 1858 in Bath County, Kentucky.
+ 84   iii. LEWIS HARDING (4-84) was born about 1774 in Loudoun County, Virginia and married Edy Thatcher. Later he lived in Bath County, Kentucky.
+ 85   iv. HENRY HARDING (4-85) born about 1776 in Loudoun County, Kentucky, married Margaret Sears in 1803 and died in 1835 in Loudoun County, Virginia.
   86   v. FRANCES HARDING (4-86) born about 1780

Loudoun County, Virginia Records
1765: Loudoun Co VA tax Lists PPTL
1772 to 1775: Loudoun Co VA Tax Lists PPTL
1774 10 Oct Page 504 Joseph Hardin alias Combs ordered to work on the road CO Book F
1780 09 Oct: Paid debts of the estate of William Musgrave Will Book.
1784 10 May Peter Bower sued him and Joseph Combs CO Book H
1784 12 May: Attended court for James McKinney CO Book H
1785 08 Aug Sued with Benjamin Ethell by Catherine Combs CO Book I
1786 10 May: Attended court for Joseph Cummings CO Book I
1786 13 Aug: Attended court for John Walker CO Book
1791 16 Feb: Appointed overseer of the road CO Book N
1791 17 Mar: Recovered money from Travis Wrenn CO Book N
1794 16 Apr: Deposition taken against Robert Sears CO Book P
1794 10 Sep: won judgement against Robert Sears CO Book Q
1795 15 Sep: Suit against Robert Sears. CO Book Q
1795 19 Oct: Robert Sears Case Continued CO Book Q
1796 09 Feb: Robert Sears Case dismissed CO Book Q
1796 09 Aug: Paid for attendance as witness CO Book Q
1806 21 Dec: Wrote his will
1806 15 Apr: His will probated
1807 04 Apr: With son William bought land from Mary Taylor Deed 21-134
1810 Federal Census, Elizabeth, Henry, Pressley, and Lewis Harden
1820: Listed in 1820 Federal Census
1830 12 Aug: Will of Elizabeth Harden filed WB T-22
1830 12 Oct: Will of Elizabeth Harding presented to court CO 1a-470

Fairfax County Virginia Records
1791 16 August: Accused of trespassing CO

28. George[4] Hardin (Enos[3], William[2] Joseph Combs[1]) (4-28) was born about 1793 in Virginia and died after 1860 in Pike Co., Missouri. He married

Jemima Hawkins, most likely daughter of Herman Hawkins, 3 May 1818 Franklin Co., Kentucky.

Children of George^3 Hardin and Jemima Hawkins:
- \+ 87   i. JESSE E.^{5} HARDIN (4-87) was born 1820 in Owen County, Kentucky, married Nancy Ann Hardin (4-103) in 1847, later lived in Pike County, Missouri.
- 88   ii. MALINDA HARDIN (4-88) 1821-1876
- 89   iii. ELIZABETH HARDIN (4-89) 1826-
- 90   iv. MARTHA ANN HARDIN (4-90) 1828 married Jessie Allen Hardin (4-98)
- \+ 91   v. WILLIAM E. HARDIN (4-91) was born about 1829 in Missouri, married Susan Jones in 1856 and married Mollie Gray in 1863. He died in Owen County, Kentucky in 1907.
- 92   vi. MARIA HARDIN (4-92)) 1832-
- 93   vii. AILSIE HARDIN (4-93) 1836-

Franklin County, Kentucky Records
1818 28 Apr: Married Jemima Hawkins

Owen County, Kentucky Records
1819-1827: Listed in Personal Property Tax Lists PPTL
1820: Listed in Federal Census
1823 25 Dec: Robert Ashby to George, James, Thomas Hardin, and Ann Hawkins Land on Kentucky River DB A-416
1825 12 Sep: Heirs of Enos Hardin Emancipate Tom Frazier DB B-77

Henry County, Kentucky Records
1826 18 Sep: Heirs of Enos Hardin sell land he held to Evangelist Hardin. Deeds, Bk 12 Page 185.

Pike County, Missouri Records
1840: Listed in 1840 Federal Census
1850 11 Jun: Son Jesse E. Hardin guardian of George Hardin (unsound mind) WB 4-147

29. Enos^4 Hardin (Enos^3, William^2 Joseph Combs^1) (4-29) was born about 1797 in Kentucky and married **Elizabeth Guthrie** 12 June 1823. He died in Owen County, Kentucky before January 1862, when his will entered probate.

Children of Enos^4 Hardin and Elizabeth Guthrie:
- 94   i. ALEXANDER LIVINGSTON^5 HARDIN (4-94) born 1824 Kentucky
- 95   ii. MARTHA HARDIN (4-95) born about 1828 married John Montgomery
- 96   iii. AMANDA ANN HARDIN (4-96) 1832- married Thomas P. Daily
- 97   iv. SALLY ANN HARDIN (4-97) 1838- married Thornburg
- 98   v. GEORGE THOMAS HARDIN (4-98) 1838-
- 99   vi. ENOS HARDIN (4-99) 1843-
- 100   vii. AMERICA ELIZABETH HARDIN (4-100) 1846-1918

Henry County, Kentucky Records

1826 18 Sep: Heirs of Enos Hardin sell land he held to Evangelist Hardin. Deed Book 12 Page 185.

Owen County, Kentucky Records
1819-1850: Listed in Personal Property Tax Lists PPTL
1823 12 Jun: Married Elizabeth Guthrie Owen Co KY Marriages
1825 12 Sep: Heirs of Enos Hardin Emancipate Tom Frazier DB B-77
1830: Listed in Federal Census of 1830
1835 01 Jun: Heirs of Alexander Guthrie sell land DB E-232
1837 25 Apr: Sells land to Johnson Ballard DB F-53
1839 03 Jan: Buys Land from Robert Ashby DB F-333
1839 01 Oct: Buys land from James Ross DB F-331
1840: Listed in Federal Census
1841: 11 Sep: Loans money to Henley Roberts and J Bennett DB G-382
1842 03 Aug: Buys land from William Spires DB H-316
1849 08 Mar: Buys land from William Sanford DB J-476
1850: Listed in Federal Census with family
1852 25 Sep: Enos and son A. L. et al sell land to James Long DB L-294/6
1856 15 Feb: Sells land to heirs of Thomas Hardin Deceased. DB M-338
1856 10 May: Heirs of Ann Hardin of Pike Co, MO and Enos Hardin of Owen Co KY sell land to heirs of Thomas Hardin deceased DB M-510
1856 10 Mar: Heirs of Thomas Hardin and Ann Hawkins sell land to Enos Hardin of Owen County, Kentucky DB M-512.
1857: Buys land from W. Bates DB N-332
1859 05 Dec: He writes his will
1862 22 Jan: His will probated.

30. Thomas[4] Hardin (Enos[3], William[2] Joseph Combs[1]) (4-30) was born 24 November 1801 and died October 6, 1855, in Owen Co., Kentucky. He married **Rachael Allen**, 1804-1876, in 1823.

Children of Thomas[4] Hardin and Rachael Allen:
+ 101   i. ENOS[5] HARDIN JR. (4-101) born 18 October 1824 died 1 November 1901 Buried in Hardin Cemetery. Married Eliza A. (16 Oct 1830 to 31 October 1902 buried Harden Cemetery
+ 102   ii. JESSIE ALLEN HARDIN (4-102) born 18 March 1827 died 22 January 1906 buried Harden Cemetery. He married Martha Ann Hardin (4-90) in Pike County, Missouri 6 March 1851 and died in 1906 in Owen County, Kentucky.
  103   iii. NANCY ANN HARDIN (4-103) born about 1829 married Jessie E. Hardin (4-87)
  104   iv. GEORGE W. HARDIN (4-104) 1832-1905
  105   v. THOMAS JEFFERSON HARDIN (4-105) 1834-1906
  106   vi. MARTHA ELIZABETH HARDIN (4-106) 1836-1916 married Hughes
  107   vii. ADELINE HARDIN (4-107) 1840-1906 married Lawrence
  108   viii. WILLIAM DAVID HARDIN (4-108) 1842-1909
  109   ix. MARY ALICE HARDIN (4-109) 1847-1926 married Head

Owen County, Kentucky Records
1823-1851: Listed on Personal Property Tax Lists PPTL
1823 09 Jun: Married Rachel Allen Owen County KY. Marriages
1823-25 Dec: Robert Ashby to George, James, Thomas Hardin, and Ann Hawkins Land on Kentucky River DB A-416
1825 12 Sep: Heirs of Enos Hardin Emancipate Tom Frazier DB B-77
1826 18 Sep: Heirs of Enos Hardin sell land he held to Evangelist Hardin. Deed Book 12 Page 185.
1829 27 Aug: Buys from William Warner estate by sheriff DB C-366
1840: Listed in Federal Census
1843 26 Apr: Land sold by commissioners to pay debt DB H-448
1850: Listed on Federal Census
1851 26 Apr: Buys Lot 23 from Enos Hardin Jr Hardin DB K-428
1855: 06 Oct: Thomas Hardin died Buried Hardin Cemetery, Owen Co., KY Find a Grave Index.
1855 30 Nov: Inventory of his estate WB D-524
1855 01 Dec: Sale bill filed WB D-542
1856 15 Feb: Thomas Hardin Heirs buy land from Enos Hardin DB M-338
1856 11 Aug: John S. Smith power of atty to son JAA Hardin DB M-608
1856 20 Sep: Buys land from Theodore Bates DB M553
1857 08 Sep: Son G W Hardin buys 3 acres DB N-308
1876 19 Dec: Rachel Allen Harden died, born 23 December 1804, Bourbon Co., KY Find a Grave Index Hardin Cemetery, Owen Co., KY

31. Ann⁴ Hardin (Enos³, William², Joseph Combs¹) (4-31) was born about 1803. She married **Benjamin T. Hawkins** (1793-1866) before 1820. She died prior to 1833, when Benjamin Hawkins married Alcey Lowry 6 June 1833 in Pike County, Missouri She was born about 1805 and died in November 1866 in Pike Co., Missouri. She had four children. Alcey had no children with Benjamin Hawkins.

Children of Benjamin T. Hawkins and Ann³ Hardin:
110 i. MARTHA ANN⁴ HAWKINS (4-110) 1820-1882 married James Humphrey
111 ii. JANE HAWKINS (4-111) born about 1824 married Zachariah T. Emerson
112 iii. AMANDA M. HAWKINS (4-112) born about 1825 married John S. Smith
113 iv. ENNIS HAWKINS (4-113) born about 1828 married Cassandra Doyle

Owen County, Kentucky Records
1823-25 Dec: Robert Ashby to George, James, Thomas Hardin, and Ann Hawkins Land on Kentucky River
1825 12 Sep: Heirs of Enos Hardin Emancipate Tom Frazier DB B-77
1856 10 May: Heirs of Ann Hardin of Pike Co, MO and Enos Hardin of Owen Co KY sell land to heirs of Thomas Hardin deceased DB M-510

1856 10 Mar: Heirs of Thomas Hardin and Ann Hawkins sell land to Enos Hardin of Owen County, Kentucky DB M-512.
1856 11 Aug: John S. Smith power of atty to JAA Hardin DB M-608
Pike County, Missouri Records
1830: Listed in Federal Census of 1830
1833 06 Jun: Benjamin Hawkins married second Ailsey Lowry
1837 17 May: Benjamin Hawkins guardian of James Humphrey WB 2-152
1841 30 Aug: Daughter Martha married James Humphrey Mgs Book 2
1849 24 Dec: Son Ennis married Cassandra Doyle. Mgs 2-259
1850 12 Sep: Daughter Jane married Zachariah T. Emerson Mgs 2-274
1852 22 Dec: Daughter Amanda married John S. Smith Mgs
1856 17 Mar: Bond to administer Susan Hardin estate WB 4-506
1866 23 Apr: Estate administered WB 6-56, 57
1866 27 Oct: Will of wife Alcy Hawkin administered WB 6-92
1869 22 Aug: Son Enos Hawkins admin estate of Benjamin T. Hawkins, minor. WB 6:453

35. Harriet⁴ Hardin (James³, William², Joseph Combs¹) (4-35) was born about 1802 in Kentucky and married **John R. Hawkins**, son of Herman Hawkins, 26 September 1821 in Owen Co., Kentucky. She later moved to Pike Co., Missouri, where she died after 1870.

Children of John R. Hawkins and Harriet³ Hardin:
- 114   i. WILLIAM⁵ HAWKINS (4-114) born about 1827 in Missouri, married Catherine Jasper 1849 Pike Co., Missouri
- 115   ii. NANCY HAWKINS (4-115) born about 1828 Kentucky
- 116   iii. SALLY HAWKINS (4-116) born about 1830 Kentucky
- 117   iv. JOHN S. HAWKINS (4-117) born about 1832 Missouri
- 118   v. BENJAMIN S. HAWKINS (4-118) born about 1834 Missouri
- 119   vi. REBECCA A. HAWKINS (4-119) born about 1836 Missouri
- 120   vii. GEORGE HAWKINS (4-120) born about 1840 Missouri
- 121   viii. LUCY JANE HAWKINS (4-121) born about 1842 Missouri

Owen County, Kentucky Records
1821 27 Sep: Married John Hawkins Owen Co., KY Marriages

Pike County, Missouri Records
1849 08 Apr: Son William Hawkins married Catherine Jasper
1850: United States Census, Cuivre, Pike Co., Missouri
1850: Son William listed in Federal Census Pike Co Missouri
1860: United States Census, Bowling Green, Pike Co., Missouri

37. Absolem⁴ Hardin (James³, William², Joseph Combs¹) (4-36) was born about 1804 in Kentucky. He married **Eleanor Warner** 29 October 1827 in

Owen Co., Kentucky and married **Catherine Henderson** 20 September 1833 in Owen Co., Kentucky. By 1860 he was living in Robertson Co., Texas.

Children of Absolem[4] Hardin and Eleanor Warner:
- 122   i. JAMES[5] HARDIN (4-122) born about 1829 Owen Co., Kentucky

Children of Absolem Hardin and Catherine Henderson:
- 123   ii. LUCY HARDIN (4-123) born 1839 Owen Co., Kentucky
- 124   iii. WILLIAM CREGG HARDIN (4-124) 1842-1860
- 125   iv. GEORGE WASHINGTON HARDIN (4-125) 1845-1921
- 126   v. SAMUEL LEE HARDIN (4-126) 1847-1900
- 127   vi. SIMEON T. HARDIN (4-127) 1849-1929
- 128   vii. MARTHA E. HARDIN (4-128) 1851-1889
- 129   viii. RICHARD CALVIN HARDIN (4-129) 1852-? Robertson Co Texas

Owen County, Kentucky Records
1824 to 1851: Listed on Personal Property Tax Lists PPTL
1827 29 Oct: Married Eleanor Warner Owen Cc., KY Marriages
1830: Federal Census Owen Co., Kentucky
1833 20 Sep: Married Catharine Henderson Owen Co KY Marriages
1843 19 Jul: Sold all interest in Father James Estate DB H-448
1860: Federal Census Robertson Co., Texas

39. Baylis[4] G. Hardin (James[3], William[2], Joseph Combs[1]) (4-39) was born about 1817 in Kentucky. He married **Sarah (Spires) Sparks**, born about 1819, on 16 December 1844 in Owen Co., Kentucky.

Children of Baylis G.[4] Hardin and Sarah Spires:
- 130   i. WILLIAM[5] HARDIN (4-130) born about 1847 Kentucky
- 131   ii. HENRY S. HARDIN (4-131)

Owen County and Hardin County, Kentucky Records
1839-1851: Listed on Personal Property Tax Lists PPTL
1844 16 Dec: Married Sarah Sparks Owen Co., KY Marriages
1848 25 Jan: Agreement with Branham re Sparks children. DB J-261
1849 22 Aug: Filed report as guardian of Milton Sparks heirs. WB D-150
1853 21 Mar: Final settlement of Milton Sparks guardian estate WB D-403
1850: Census Owen Co., Kentucky (Bayless G. Hardin)
1850: Census Hardin Co., Kentucky (Sarah Hardin)
1860: Census Owen Co., Kentucky (Sarah and William Hardin)
1869 16 Feb: Married Mary E. Evans Owen Co KY Marriages

82. William[4] Harding (Joseph[3] Joseph Combs II[2], Joseph Combs[1]) (4-82) was born about 1770 in Loudoun County, Virginia. He married **Elizabeth**. He died in Loudoun County in 1824. This man has often been confused with the William Harding (2-27) who settled in Clarke County, Iowa. (See discussion in Chapter 1)

Children of William[4] Harding and Elizabeth:

132 i. WILLIAM[5] L. HARDING (4-132) born about 1805
133 ii. ELIZABETH HARDING (4-133) born about 1807
134 iii. SARAH ANN HARDING (4-134) born about 1809

Loudoun County, Virginia Records
1807 04 Apr: With mother purchased land from Mary Taylor Deed 21-134
1820: Listed in 1820 Federal Census
1815 09 Dec: Judgment in court case CO 1-274
1819 11 Feb: Case vs John Nuson continued CO Book 2-350
1822 24 May: Sell slaves to Silas Garrett Deeds 3E-262
1822 09 Sep: Bought six acres from William Randall Deeds 3F-252
1824 13 Dec: Inventory of William Harding filed. WB P-204
1827 08 Jan: Administration account filed with court WB R-155
1827 15 Feb: Elizabeth Haden to Townshend McVeigh CO 8-96
1827 14 May: Elizabeth Harden negroes except from tax CO 8-163
1827 11 Sep: Elizabeth releases land to pay note. Deeds 3P-223
1828 04 Jan: Elizabeth Harden to E Tyler Trust CO 8-383
1829 10 Aug: William Hardin estate account continued CO 1a-76
1829 11 Aug: Elizabeth Hardin vs children CO 1a-85
1829 12 Sep: William Harden estate account received CO 1a-133
1830: Listed in 1830 Federal Census
1830 12 Aug: Mentioned in Will of Elizabeth Harden WB T-22
1830 15 Dec: Division of land between heirs and brother Deeds 3Z-158
1832 09 Jan: Administration account ordered to be settled CO 4-67
1832 11 Jun: Further administration account filed WB U-97
1834 10 Mar: Ordered to settle account CO 4-67
1835 11 May: Further administration account filed WB W-159.
1835 08 Jun: Administration account ordered recorded CO 4-211
1837 09 May: Further administration account filed, and WB X-299 account distributions made to widow and children.
1839 12 Oct: William L Harding sells land to Joseph Garrett 4N-394
1840: Elizabeth listed in 1840 Federal Census
1842 08 Sep: Inventory of Estate of Elizabeth Harden ordered WB AA-306

83. Presley[4] Harding (Joseph[3] Joseph Combs II[2], Joseph Combs[1]) (4-83) was born about 1772 in Loudoun County, Virginia. He married **Sarah Sears** 27 September 1803 in Loudoun County, Virginia. He later moved to Bath County, Kentucky, where many of his children lived, and died there in 1858. He is often confused with the Presley Harden (1-43) who lived in Williamson County, Tennessee.

Children of Presley[4] Harding and Sarah Sears:
135 i. JOSEPH SANFORD[5] HARDIN (4-135) 1804-1888 married Kitty Myers
136 ii. LEWIS HARDIN (4-136) 1805-1884 married Mary McElhenney
137 iii. ROBERT WESLEY HARDIN (4-137) 1807-1881 married Philadelphia Carden

138   iv. ELIZABETH HARDIN (4-138) married Rice Burnes 1808-1835
139   v. SARAH HARDIN (4-139) married Ratliff Baird 1810-1859
140   vi. PRESLEY HARDIN (4-140) 1810-1880
141   vii. EMILY HARDIN (4-141) 1813-1885 married William Amos
142   viii. LOUISA JANE HARDIN (4-142) 1815-1892 married Hardaman Baird
143   ix. MILDRED HARDIN (4-143) 1818-1912 married John R. Baird
144   x. WILLIAM EDGAR HARDIN (4-144) 1822- married Caroline Rogers

Loudoun County, Virginia Records
1803 27 Sep: Married Sarah Sears
1810: Listed in Federal Census of 1810
Bath County, Kentucky Records
1849 04 May: Presley Harden writes his will. Wills F-54
1858 20 Mar: Presley Harden's will proved. Wills F-54

84. Lewis^4 Harding (Joseph^3 Joseph Combs II^2, Joseph Combs^1) (4-84) was born about 1774. He married **Edy Thatcher** on 18 March 1807. In the 1830s he moved to Bath County, Kentucky.

Children of Lewis^4 Harding and Edy Thatcher:
145   i. WILLIAM^5 HARDIN (4-145) 1808-1874
146   ii. MANLEY HARDIN (4-146) 1810-1880
147   iii. FIELDING HARDIN (4-147) 1811-1893
148   iv. JOSEPH S. HARDIN (4-148) 1818
149   v. LUCINDA HARDIN (4-149) 1819- married David B. Young
150   vi. PRESLEY THATCHER HARDIN (4-150) 1822-1892
151   vii. JAMES HARDIN (4-151) 1824-1912
152   viii. GEORGE WASHINGTON HARDIN (4-152) 1828-1912
153   ix. JOHN EDGAR HARDIN (4-153) 1832-1890

Loudoun County, Virginia Records
1807 18 Mar: Married Edy Thatcher
1810: Listed in Federal Census of 1810
1830 12 Oct: Henry Harding vs Lewis Harding CO 1a-474
Bath County, Kentucky Records
1849 09 Sep: Lewis Harden writes his will. Wills E-128
1849 Oct: Lewis Harden's will proved. Wills E-128

85. Henry^4 Harding (Joseph^3 Joseph Combs II^2, Joseph Combs^1) (4-85) was born about 1780 in Loudoun County, Virginia, and married **Margaret Sears** in 1803. He died in 1835 in Loudoun County, Virginia, where his large family and numerous descendants are well documented.

Children of Henry^4 Harding and Margaret Sears:
154   i. JOSEPH^3 HARDEN^5 (4-154) born about 1810
155   ii. ENOS DAVID HARDIN (4-155) 1815-1896 married Louisa Branham
156   iii. ALBERT HARDING (4-156) 1817-1884
157   iv. MARIA HARDING (4-157) 1818

158   v. MILDRED HARDING (4-158) born about 1820
159   vi. ROBERT HENRY HARDING (4-159) born about 1821
160   vii. JOHN RAMEY HARDING (4-160) about 1827 Ann Amanda Wortman
161   viii. ELIZABETH ELLEN HARDING (4-161) born about 1828
162   ix. ELIZA JANE HARDING (4-162) born about 1829
163   x. SUSAN ANN HARDING (4-163) born about 1829
164   xi. MARTHA FRANCES HARDING (4-164) born about 1830 married Cornelius Wyncoop
165   xii. LEWIS BARD HARDING (4-165) born about 1830 married Patsy Garrison

Loudoun County, Virginia Records
1803 27 Sep: married Margaret Sears
1810: Listed in Federal Census of 1810
1820: Listed in 1820 Federal Census
1822 24 May: Sell slaves to Silas Garrett Deeds 3E-262
1827 11 Sep: Elizabeth Hardin releases land to pay note. Deeds 3P-223
1830 12 Aug: Mentioned in Will of Elizabeth Harden WB T-22
1830 12 Oct: Henry Harding vs Lewis Harding CO 1a-474
1830 15 Dec: Land division between brother's heirs Deeds 3Z-158
1832 01 Oct: Sells land to Stephen Garrett Deeds 4A-230
1835 11 May: mentions payments to Henry Harden WB-159
1835 14 Sep: Henry Harding administration bond recorded CO 4-285
1835 13 Oct: Margaret Harding guardian of orphans CO 4-308
1840: Albert Harding listed in 1840 Federal Census
1840: Margaret Harding listed in 1840 Federal Census
1850: Margaret and children listed in 1850 Federal Census
1852 29 May: Lewis B. Harding married Patsy Garrison
1852 19 Oct: John R. Harding married Ann Amanda Wortman
1852 26 Dec: Martha F. Harden married Cornelius B. Wyncoop

87. Jesse E.^{5} Hardin (George^4, Enos^3, William^2, Joseph Combs^1) (4-87) was born in Owen County, Kentucky in 1820. He married **Nancy Ann Hardin** (4-103) 1 April 1847 in Owen County, Kentucky. By 1850 he was living in Cuivre, Pike County, Missouri.

Owen County, Kentucky Records
1847 01 Apr: Married Nancy Ann Hardin

Pike County, Missouri Records
1850 11 Jun: Made guardian of father George Hardin (unsound mind) WB 4-147

91 William E.^{5} Hardin (George^4, Enos^3, William^2, Joseph Combs^1) (4-91) was born about 1829 in Missouri. He married **Susan Jones** 1 December 1853 in Pike Co., Missouri. Susan died before 17 March 1856, leaving a daughter. William married second **Mollie Gray** 17 November 1863 in Pike County Missouri. By 1880 he moved back to Owen County, Kentucky, where he and

Mary were listed in the 1880 Census of Monterey, Owen Co., Kentucky, Page 187 Family #25. He died in 1907 and was buried in the Monterey Cemetery.

Note: A second William E. Hardin lived in Pike County. The other was born in Virginia and married Louisa Beasley in Pike County in 1849. He died in 1861 and Louisa administered his estate. His relationship is not known.

Children of William E^5. Hardin and Susan Jones:
166 i. SUSAN O.^{6} HARDIN (4-166) born about 1854

Pike County, Missouri Records
1853 01 Dec: Married Susan Jones Mgs 3-55
1856 17 Mar: Administered estate of Susan Hardin WB 4-506

101. ENOS^5 HARDIN JR (Thomas^4, Enos^3, William^2, Joseph Combs^1) (4-101) was born 18 October 1824 died 1 November 1901 Buried in Hardin Cemetery. Married **Eliza A.** (16 Oct 1830 to 31 October 1902) buried Harden Cemetery in Owen Co., Kentucky.

Owen County, Kentucky Records
1850 25 Aug: Bought Lot 23 from G C Branham DB K-238
1851 26 Apr: Sells Lot 23 to Thomas Hardin DB K-428

102. Jesse Allen A^5 Hardin (Thomas^4, Enos^3, William^2, Joseph Combs^1) (4-102) known in most records as J A. A. Hardin, was born 18 March 1827 in Kentucky and died 22 January 1906. He is buried in the Harden Cemetery in Owen County, KY. He married **Martha Ann Hardin**, (4-90) his cousin, in Pike Co., Missouri 6 March 1851. Martha died in 1896 and is buried in the Hardin Cemetery in Owen County, Kentucky.

Pike County, Missouri Records
1850-1851: Listed in Personal Property Tax Lists PPTL
1851 06 Mar: Married Martha Ann Hardin, daughter of George Hardin Mgs 2-288
1860: Listed in Federal Census

Family 5: Mark Hardin and Mary of Northumberland Co., VA

1. **Mark**[1] **Hardin** (5-1) was born about 1681, location unknown. He has been identified in many pedigrees with the Mark Hardin born on Staten Island, New York, son of Martyn Hardewyn and Madame de Sauchoy but no evidence except a few family stories has ever surfaced to prove this. He first appears in Northumberland County, Virginia in 1707, when he lived in Wicomico Parish and purchased land there. He later moved into the area that became Prince William County and died there in 1735, leaving a will. He married **Mary** (maiden name unknown) about the time he emerged in Northumberland County. Her name has been given as Hogue in most genealogies but there is no evidence to prove this identification. I will not attempt to provide all the record sources for this family since others have already done so but will include relevant ones I found in my own research. His children are well documented in his will.

Children of Mark[1] Hardin and Mary:

+ 2   i. JOHN[2] HARDIN (5-2) was born about 1710 Northumberland Co, Virginia. He married Catherine Marr and died in 1789 in Nelson County, Kentucky.
+ 3   ii. MARTIN HARDIN (5-3) was born about 1716 Northumberland Co., Virginia, married Lydia Waters, and died in 1779 in Monongalia County, Virginia.
+ 4   iii. MARK HARDIN (5-4) was born about 1720 Northumberland Co., Virginia, married Elizabeth about 1751 and divorced her a year later. It is not known when or where he died.
+ 5   iv. HENRY HARDIN (5-5) was born about 1722 Northumberland Co., Virginia. He married Judith Lynch and died in 1797 in Pittsylvania County, Virginia.
  6   v. MARTHA HARDIN (5-6) married McDonhill
  7   vi. ABIGAIL HARDIN (5-7)
  8   vii. MARY HARDIN (5-8)
  9   viii. ANN HARDIN (5-9)
  10   ix. ALIS HARDIN (5-10)
  11   x. ELIZABETH HARDIN (5-11)

Northumberland County, Virginia Records

1707 07 Apr: Mark Hardin purchased 50 acres in Wicomico Parish from John Mutton heirs DW Book E Page 116

1713 18 Mar: Mark Harding examined for evidence CO Book 7 Page 26

1718 18 Sep: Mark Harding vs Curtis dismissed CO Book 7 Page 294

1720 14 Nov: Mark Harding and wife Mary of Richmond Co sold 50 acres to John Pope DW Book G Page 145

Prince William County Records
1733 02 Oct: Lease and release land James McDonnell Deeds B-173-80
1734 16 Mar: Will of Mark Hardin written Will Book C-36
1734 10 Jun: Release of lease to James McDonnell Deeds B-174
1735 05 May: Will of Mark Harden Proved Will Book C-36

2. **John² Hardin** (Mark¹) (5-2) was born about 1710 in Northumberland Co., VA and died 13 October 1789 in Nelson County Kentucky. He was a militia captain in the French and Indian War and in 1782 built boats during the Revolutionary War. He married **Catherine Marr**. By 1740 he was living in Frederick County, VA Extensive material on his land purchases and movements is available on Kay Haden's web site.

Children of John² Hardin and Catherine Marr:

+ 12   i. JOHN³ (MILLER) HARDIN (5-12) born 1733 Prince William Co Virginia, married Isabella Strawbridge, died in 1803 in Fayette County, Pennsylvania.
+ 13   ii. MARK HARDIN (5-13) born about 1735 Prince William Co Virginia. He married Ann Hartley and died in 1792 in Nelson County, Kentucky.
+ 14   iii. BENJAMIN HARDIN (5-14) born about 1739 Prince William Co Virginia, married his cousin Sarah Hardin (5-23), died 1816 in Washington County, Kentucky.
+ 15   iv. WILLIAM HARDIN (5-15) born about 1745 Frederick Co Virginia, married Winifred Ann Holtzclaw, died 1821 in Breckinridge County, Kentucky.
+ 16   v. JESSE HARDIN (5-16) born about 1749 Frederick Co VA
  17   vi. ABIGAIL HARDIN (5-17) born about 1753 married Lynch
  18   vii. MARY HARDIN (5-18) born about 1735 married Owen Thomas
  19   viii. CATHERINE HARDIN (5-19) married Burnett
  20   ix. ELIZABETH HARDIN (5-20) born about 1757 married Martin
  21   x. SUSANNAH HARDIN (5-21) born about 1759 married Walker

Orange County, Virginia Records
1740 22 Nov: Leases 300 acres from Nathaniel Thomas Deeds 5-182
1741 28 Nov: Suit against James Scott dismissed. CR 3-89
1741 28 Feb: Allowed to clear roads to top of ridges CR 3-113
1742 25 Sep: Suit against him continued CR 3-287
1744 28 Jun: John Grant sues for trespass CR 4-145
1746 23 May: Case vs James Brown dismissed CR 4-481
1746 23 May: Pays Marquis Calmes as a witness CR 4-481
1753 26 Apr: Sued for trespass against Henry Franklin CR-5-415

Frederick County, Virginia Records
1743 to 1745: Many court suits mostly money owed to him. CO Book 1
1744/5 06 Mar: Witnessed deed Thomas Ashby Jr to John Ashby Deeds 1-197
1749 15 Nov: Makes mortgage to Thomas Ashby for land he lives on Deeds 2-47

Family Genealogies with References

1752 06 Apr: Mentioned in the will of Thomas Ashby Sr. Wills 2:53
1753 05 Sep: Redevise mortgage to Thomas Ashby recorded CO 5-162
1754 05 Sep: John Ashby paid for attending court five days in case of Mark Hardin vs John Hardin CO 6-70
1757 06 Apr: Garnishee in case of Elizabeth Hardin vs Mark Hardin CO 7-229
1759 09 Aug: Elizabeth Hardin vs John Hardin case dismissed. James Catlet paid as witness CO 8-303
1760 09 May: John Hardin vs William Shepherd Debt CO 9-51
1760 03 Sep: John Hardin vs Daniel Purcell settled CO 9-143
1760 03 Dec: John Harding vs James Irwin Debt CO 9-224

Hampshire County, Virginia Records (Now WV)
1762 09 Nov: John Harden lease and release from Benjamin Rutherford Deed 1-145, 1-146
1768 02 Mar: John Hardin lease and release from Benjamin Rutherford Deed 2-51, 2-52
1769 06 Feb: John Hardin lease and release from Rutherford's Deed 2-119, 2-120
1771 09 Mar: John Hardin to Thomas Fairly of York PA Deed 2-228, 2-229
1773 08 Mar: John Hardin to Mark Hardin Lease and release 2-141 2-142
1773 06 Oct: John Hardin to William Blackburn lease and release 4-23, 4-24
1774 03 Mar: John Hardin to William Blackburn lease and release 4-25, 4-26
1780 09 May: John Hardin to Joseph House lease and release 5-108, 5-109

Shenandoah County, Virginia Records
1778 9 Jan: Sold 290 acres in Shenandoah to Thomas Allen.

Nelson County, Kentucky Records
1788 04 Jun: He wrote his will
1789 13 Oct: His will proved.

3. **Martin² Hardin** (Mark¹) (5-3) was born about 1716 in Northumberland County, Virginia. He died 20 November 1779 in Monongalia County, Virginia. He is often called "Ruffled Shirt" Hardin. He married **Lydia Waters**.

Children of Martin² Hardin and Lydia Waters:

- 22   i. MARY³ HARDIN (5-22) born 4 Oct 1741 Prince William County Va. She married Robert Wickliffe in 1759 and William Robinson in 1785
- 23   ii. SARAH ELLEN HARDIN (5-23) born 10 Mar 1743 married Benjamin Hardin, (5-14) her first cousin. She died 13 October 1826 Washington County, Kentucky
- 24   iii. HANNAH HARDIN (5-24) born 10 September 1745 Prince William County, Virginia. Married James Neal about 1764.
- 25   iv. LYDIA HARDIN (5-25) born 10 Apr 1748 Prince William County Virginia. She married Charles Wickliffe
- + 26   v. MARK HARDIN (5-26) born 1 Dec 1750 Prince William Co. Virginia, married Susannah Stull, died 1835 in Marion County, Kentucky.

+ 27 vi. JOHN HARDIN (5-27) born 1 Oct 1753 Prince William Co Virginia married Jane Davies, died 1792 in Ohio.
28 vii. CATHERINE HARDIN (5-28) born about 1755 Stafford Co VA, married John Remy
+ 29 viii. MARTIN HARDIN (5-29) born 1 February 1757 Prince William Co Virginia, married Letitia Stull, died 1848 in Washington County, Kentucky.
30 ix. ROSANNA HARDIN (5-30) born 9 March 1760 Fauquier Co. VA died November 1789 KY married John McMahon

Prince William County, Virginia Records
1751 08 Aug: Sued Frances Ball adm John Ball 1-51
1752-1755 Several court cases
Fauquier County, Virginia Records
1759 08 Jun: Settles suit against William Robinson over his daughter's marriage CO 1-7
1759 07 Aug: License to keep an ordinary granted. CO 1-23
1759 20 Aug: Bond with Robert Whicliffe for daughter's marriage.
1760: Will of Tillman Weaver mentions land sale WB 1760
1761 Jan: Petition against George Wheatley continued CO 1-123
1761 25 Mar: Two Tithables discharged from clearing road. CO1-138
1762 26 Aug: Appraised estate of Thomas Seaman
Culpeper County, Virginia Records
1762 17 Jun: Sold 66 acres in Culpeper Co to Edward Tinsley Deeds D-51
1762 13 Aug: Sold 250 acres to John Grayson Deeds D-91
1762 20 Aug: Sold 350 acres to John Lillard Deeds D-114
1769 01 Sep: Sold 360 acres to Fisher Rice Deeds F-121
1773 09 Aug: Lease bond to John Strother Deeds G-429
Prince William County, Virginia Records
1775 11 Sep: Deeded two lots to son John Hardin Deeds T-167

4. Mark² Hardin (Mark¹) (5-4) was born about 1720 died unknown after 1753 married **Elizabeth** (birth name unknown) about 1751 and was sued for divorce in 1753. The marriage did not last long enough for there to be any children. There is also no evidence that she was Elizabeth Harden, the daughter of Thomas Ashby mentioned in Ashby's will, and there are no proven children by her or anyone else. It is possible that he lived in southern Virginia in later years. Several Mark Hardins are found in the area but there is little to distinguish them from each other.

Prince William County, Virginia
1753-27 Nov: Sued for alimony by Betty Harding
1754 27 Nov: Acknowledged lease deeds for Martin Hardin CO 2-186
Frederick County, Virginia Records
1754/5 05 Mar: Robert Ashby vs Mark Hardin dismissed CO 5-325
1754/5 06 Mar: Robert Ashby vs. Mark Hardin case dismissed CO 5-326

Family Genealogies with References

1754 05 Sep: John Ashby paid for attending court five days in case of Mark Hardin vs John Hardin CO 6-70
1757 06 Apr: Elizabeth Hardin vs Mark Hardin Garnishment discharged. CO 7-229
1759 09 Aug: Elizabeth Hardin vs John Hardin Case dismissed. Elizabeth ordered to pay for witness CO 8-303
1760 06 Aug: Robert Ashby vs Mark Hardin for trespass and battery CO 9-103

5. Henry² Hardin (Mark¹) (5-5) was born about 1712 In Northumberland County, Virginia and died in 1797 in Pittsylvania County, Virginia. He married **Judith Lynch** about 1736 died 1797 Pittsylvania County VA.
  Children:
+ 31   i. MARK³ HARDIN (5-31) born about 1735 in Virginia, married Mary Hunter and Frances Newsom and died in Warren County, Georgia in 1794.
  32   ii. MARY HARDIN (5-32) born about 1737-1796 married John Taliaferro
+ 33   iii. WILLIAM EVERETT HARDIN (5-33) born about 1741 to 1810 married Sarah Bledsoe, died 1810 Franklin County, Georgia.
  34   vi. ELIZABETH HARDIN (5-34) born about 1748, died in 1845 and married Mr. Wilson
  35   vii. JUDITH HARDIN (5-35) married Burgess
+ 36   viii. MARTIN HARDIN (5-36) born in 1755 in Virginia, married Mary Burgess, died in 1848 in Marshall County, Tennessee.
+ 37   ix. HENRY HARDIN (5-37) born about 1757 in Virginia married Alice, later lived in Wilkes County, Georgia.
  38   x. AVARILLA HARDIN (5-38) married Wright
  39   xi. SARAH HARDIN (5-39) married Buckhalter

Halifax County, Virginia Records
1762 20 May: Henry Hardin from William Byrd 1000 acres Winns Creek
1764 06 Apr: Sold 250 acres on Wynns Creek to Richard Brooks
Pittsylvania County, Virginia Records
Many more records of this Henry Hardin are found in Pittsylvania County, Virginia. I have not done an exhaustive search of them since others have published many of these records.

12. John³ Hardin (John², Mark¹) (5-12) also called Miller John, was born 2 June 1733 in Prince William County, VA and died before 3 June 1803 in Fayette Co., Pennsylvania. He married **Isabella Strawbridge** about 1757. She died 17 May 1814 in Fayette Co., PA. He had extensive military experience during the Revolutionary War.
  Children of John³ Hardin and Isabella Strawbridge:
  40   i. JOHN (JACK)⁴ HARDIN (5-40) born 1752 in Frederick Co VA, died 1818 in Washington Co KY. He was an illegitimate son of John Harding. He married Mary Harding, daughter of John Harding and Mary Moss. Served in the Revolutionary War

	41	ii. NESTOR HARDIN (5-41) born 1759, died 18 November 1839 Barbour Co., VA Married Kate Hardin, daughter of Benjamin and Sarah Hardin, his cousin.
+	42	iii. JOHN HARDIN (5-42) born 1762, died 1853 Fayette Co., PA married Barbara Rowner
	43	iv. ABSOLOM HARDIN (5-43) born about 1764, died July 1851 Livingston Co., KY. Married Elizabeth Powell
	44	v. WILLIAM HENRY HARDIN (5-44) born 1765 PA died 5 October 1825 Nicholas Co., KY married Catherine Hoagland
	45	vi. MARIAM HARDIN (5-45) married Isaac Hoagland
	46	vii. MARY ANN HARDIN (5-46) married Francis Mitchell
	47	viii. ELIZABETH HARDIN (5-47)
	48	ix. ISABEL HARDIN (5-48)
	49	x. MATILDA HARDIN (5-49)
	50	xi. HECTOR HARDIN (5-50) married Hannah
	51	xii. ALICE HARDIN (5-51) born about 1782 Fayette Co., PA died 9 September 1823 Ohio. Married Daniel Duvall
	52	xiii. GEORGE HARDIN (5-52) born 1776 Fayette Co., VA died 5 January 1854 Fayette Co., PA married Jane Cunningham and Mary Lambert
	53	xiv. CATO HARDIN (5-53) married Susan Cunningham

Livingston County, Kentucky Records
1839 17 Sep: Son Absolom Hardin made his will. Wills B-126
1851 07 Apr: Son Absolom will proved in court Wills B-126

13. Mark³ Hardin (John², Mark¹) (5-13) was born about 1735 in Prince William County VA. He died in 1792 in Nelson County, Kentucky. He married **Ann Hartley** in Frederick County VA and lived for a while in Hampshire Co., VA.

Children of Mark³ Hardin and Ann Hartley:

	54	i. ANN⁴ HARDIN (5-54)
	55	ii. HENRY HARDIN (5-55) born 1764 Hampshire Co VA married Mary Davis and Mary Head.
	56	iii. JOHN HARDIN (5-56) was born 14 August 1767 in Hampshire Co., VA and died 3 April 1850. He married Elizabeth Payne.
	57	iv. CATHERINE HARDIN (5-57) married Thomas Hollett
	58	v. HANNAH HARDIN (5-58) born about 1767 VA, died 1792 in Kentucky. Married Henry Stalcup
	59	vi. MARK HARDIN (5-59) Lived in Henry Co., KY. Never married
	60	vii. BENJAMIN (STILLER BEN) HARDIN (5-60) born 3 April 1776 in VA died about 1820 in Kentucky. He married Elizabeth Clark.
	61	viii. MARY HARDIN (5-61) married John Summers
	62	ix. LYDIA HARDIN (5-62) married Jacob Rounder. Died 1824 in Indiana
	63	x. SARAH HARDIN (5-63)

Records of Hampshire County, Virginia (Now WV)
1773 08 Mar: John Hardin to Mark Hardin Lease and release Deeds 2-141 2-142
1782-1788: On Personal Property Tax Lists

Family Genealogies with References

1789 17 Aug: Mark Hardin and Ann to Jacob Brookhart 126 acres Deeds 9-22
Nelson County, Kentucky Records
1790 31 Mar: He wrote his will.
1792 08 May: His will proved
Mercer County, Kentucky Records
1792 15 Jun: Marriage of son Henry Hardin to Mary Davis

14. Benjamin³ Hardin (John², Mark¹) (5-14) was born about 1739 in Prince William Co., Virginia and died 1 December 1816 in Washington County, Kentucky. He married **Sarah Hardin**, (5-23) daughter of Martin Hardin and Lydia Waters, his cousin.

Children of Benjamin³ Hardin and Sarah Hardin:
- 64   i. CATHERINE (KATE)⁴ HARDIN (5-64) born about 1766 died 1839 Barbour Co VA married her cousin Nestor Hardin
- 65   ii. LYDIA HARDIN (5-65) born 29 December 1768, married Thomas Tobin
- 66   iii. SARAH HARDIN (5-66) born 17 December 1770 Married Robert Tobin
- 67   iv. ROSANNA HARDIN (5-67) born 5 March 1773, married James McElroy. No Children
- 68   v. MARY HARDIN (5-68) born 15 August 1775. Married Andrew Barnett. No children
- 69   vi. CASSANDRA HARDIN (5-69) born 5 September 1778, married William Hardin Jr., her cousin. She died before March 1799.
- 70   vii. MARTIN L. HARDIN (5-70) born 25 May 1780 died 1848 in Texas Married Juliet Calhoun 1799
- 71   viii. JAMES HARDIN (5-71) born 10 August 1782 died 1782
- 72   ix. BENJAMIN HARDIN (5-72) born 29 February 1784, died 24 September 1852 Nelson Co., KY. Married Elizabeth Pendleton Parker
- 73   x. WARREN HARDIN (5-73) born 30 November 1786 Washington Co PA, Died 12 March 1866 Meade Co., KY. Married Elizabeth Calhoun

15. William³ Hardin (John², Mark¹) (5-15) was born about 1745 in Frederick Co., VA and served in the Revolutionary Way. He died 22 July 1821 in Hardinsburg, Breckinridge Co., KY me married **Winifred Ann Holtzclaw**, daughter of Henry Holtzclaw and Ann Hardin.

Children of William³ Hardin and Winifred Ann Holtzclaw:
- 74   i. AMELIA⁴ HARDIN (5-74) married Horatio Merry
- 75   ii. JEHU HARDIN (unmarried) (5-75)
- 76   iii. JOHN E. HARDIN (5-76) born about 1774 died 1850 Fayette Co., PA
- 77   iv. WINNIE ANN HARDIN (5-77) born 1775 married William Comstock
- 78   v. ELIJAH HARDIN (5-78) born about 1776 died 1805 in KY
- 79   vi. HENRY HARDIN (5-79) born 8 June 1778 Hardinsburg Ky married Rachel Biddle Walker
- 80   vii. MELINDA ANN HARDIN (5-80) born 2 February 1780 married William H. Crawford

81 viii. WILLIAM HARDIN JR. (5-81) born 1781 married Cassandra Hardin, Mary Biddle, Caroline C. Innes,
82 ix. MARY HARDIN (5-82) born about 1770 married Benjamin Huff
83 x. CELIA HARDIN (5-83) born 1794 married William Davison
84 xi. DANIEL HARDIN (5-84) born about 1770 married Alice Jolly

16. Jesse³ Hardin (John², Mark¹) (5-16) is a shadowy figure who may or may not have been a son of John Hardin. His wife may have been named **Margaret**.

It is possible his children were the following:
85 i. POLLY⁴ HARDIN (5-85)
86 ii. DANIEL HARDIN (5-86)

26. Mark³ Hardin (Martin², Mark¹) (5-26) was born 1 December 1750 in Prince William Co., VA and died 3 September 1835 in Marion Co., KY. He married **Susanna Stull**. He served in the Revolutionary War. He is also known as "Horse Racer" Hardin.

Children of Mark³ Hardin and Susanna Stull:
87 i. MARTIN⁴ HARDIN (5-87) born December 1781 died 1838 married Jenny Thomas
88 ii. JOHN HARDIN (5-88) born 1 May 1783
89 iii. DANIEL STULL HARDIN (5-89) born 28 April 1785 died 18 August 1824 Bourbon County, KY He married Mary Chinn
90 iv. SARAH WHITE STULL HARDIN (5-90) born 17 February 1787
91 v. MARK HARDIN (5-91) born 28 March 1789
92 vi. THOMAS HARDIN (5-92) born 15 March 1791, died 1871 Hickman Co KY married Nancy Elizabeth Davis
93 vii. DAVIS HARDIN (5-93) born 15 February 1793
94 viii. WILLIAM HARDIN (5-94) born 2 October 1795
95 ix. LEWIS T. HARDIN (5-95) born 3 January 1799 married Elizabeth Sheets
96 x. LATITIA S. HARDIN (5-96) born 30 January 1802
97 xi. SUSANNAH MARY HARDIN (5-97) born 10 February 1808

Jefferson County, Kentucky Records
1799 07 Feb: Sold 501 acres in Culpeper County to John Strother DB 5-24 and Culpeper County, Virginia DB U-403
1801 04 Dec: Bought 200 acres on Prather Creek Deeds 6-245

Franklin County, Kentucky Records
1818 29 Dec: Son Lewis married Elizabeth Sheets
Culpeper County, Virginia Records

27. John³ Hardin (Martin², Mark¹) (5-27) was born 1 October 1753 in Prince William Co VA. He died in May 1792 in Ohio. He married **Jane Davies**.

Children of John³ Hardin and Jane Davies:

Family Genealogies with References

98   i. SARAH⁴ HARDIN (5-98) born 4 May 1774 Pennsylvania died 16 June 1833. Married Barnabas McHenry
99   ii. MARTIN DAVIS HARDIN (5-99) born 21 June 1780 PA died 8 Oct 1823 Franklin County, KY married Elizabeth Logan
100   iii. MARK HARDIN (5-100) born 14 March 1782, died 1875. Married Mary Adair and Elizabeth Hall
101   iv. DAVIS HARDIN (5-101) born 5 April 1784 in PA. He married Elizabeth Simpson.
102   v. MARY HARDIN (5-102) born 7 July 1786, married Wallace Estill
103   vi. LYDIA ANN HARDIN (5-103) born 28 December 1788 in KY, died 11 February 1790
104   vii. ROSANNAH HARDIN (5-104) born 8 June 1791 Kentucky married Curtis Field

Prince William County, Virginia Records
1775 11 Sep: Received two lots from father Martin Hardin Deeds T-167
1780 02 Feb: Deeded two lots to William Carr, Deeds U-180
1784 10 Sep: and wife Jane, Deeded two lots to W. McDaniel Deeds W-76
Mercer County, Kentucky Records
1806 14 Oct: Marriage of son Mark to Mary Adair

29. Martin³ Hardin (Martin², Mark¹) (5-29) was born 1 February 1757 in Prince William County, Virginia. He died in 1848 in Washington Co., KY. He married first **Letitia Stull**, who died in 1798. He married second about 1810 **Elizabeth Truman**.

Children of Martin³ Hardin and Letitia Stull:
105   i. JOHN⁴ HARDIN (5-105) was born about 1791, died before 1838. He married Sarah Boyce
106   ii. MARTIN HARDIN (5-106) born 26 January 1781, died 2 April 1877, married Rosannah Fisher.
107   iii. SALLY HARDIN (5-107) died before 1843. She married William Torrance.
108   iv. LYDIA HARDIN (5-108) born in 1789. She married Josiah H. Yeager
109   v. LETITIA HARDIN (5-109) died before 1838. She married Andrew Fite.
Mercer County, Kentucky Records
1806 30 Jun: Son Martin Hardin married Rosannah Fisher

31. Mark³ Hardin (Henry², Mark¹) (5-31) was born about 1735 in Virginia. He died in 1817 in Warren Co., GA He married **Mary Hester Hunter** about 1759 in Johnston, NC. He lived in Pittsylvania County VA and perhaps Surry Co., North Carolina before leaving for Georgia. He married second Frances Newsom in Warren County, GA in 1794. She was the mother of his last three children.

Children of Mark³ Hardin and Mary Hester Hunter:

110 i. HENRY EDWARD⁴ HARDIN (5-110) born 12 April 1761 in Johnston Co NC and died 12 November 1843 in Walton Co GA. He married Sarah Effie Cook

111 ii. WILLIAM HARDIN, (5-111) born about 1762 in North Carolina. He lived in Caswell County North Carolina and later in Rockingham County, North Carolina, where he died after 1794. He married Elizabeth Guinn, but they had no children. He wrote his will 9 October 1794, leaving his estate to his wife and to his brother Mark.

112 iii. MARK HARDIN (5-112) born about 1763 North Carolina, died in 1839 in Rockingham Co., North Carolina. He married Frances Hill

113 iv. MARTIN HARDIN (5-113) born about 1765 in North Carolina, died 1837 in Decatur Co., GA Never married

114 v. JAMES HARDIN (5-114) was born about 1767 in North Carolina, He died 28 November 1820 in Georgia. He married Nancy Morgan in 1801 in Warren County, Georgia.

115 vi. MARY HUNTER HARDIN (5-115) was born about 1769 in Rockingham County, North Carolina. She died 29 May 1861 in Jones County, Georgia. She married James Rufus George.

116 vii. JUDITH HARDIN (5-116) was born about 1770 in North Carolina. She died in Georgia after 1850 She married James Willis, Jacob Bull and William Young

117 viii. JOHN HARDIN (5-117) was born about 1771 in North Carolina. He died in 1847 in Leon, Floria. He married Sukey Mullins in Georgia.

118 ix. SARAH HARDIN (5-118) was born about 1775 in North Carolina and died after 1845.

119 x. MARTHA HARDIN (5-118) was born in Georgia about 1796 and died after 1860

120 xi. NANCY HARDIN (5-119) was born about 1798 in Warren County, Geogia and died after 1832 in Jones Co Georgia

121 xii. WILLIAM S. HARDIN (5-120) was born about 1800 in Warren Co., Georgia and died in 1868 in Georgia.

Records for Mark Hardin (5-31)
1759 11 Jun: Sold 10 acres to Thomas Robertson Johnston Co., NC Deeds Book A1 Page 77,
1810-1826: Mark Hardin made his will. Warren Co., Georgia Wills Book Page 43

Records for William Hardin (5-111)
1783 13 Oct: Received Grant for 257 acres. Caswell Co., NC Deeds B 299
1786 13 Jan: Sold 100 acres to Henry Graves. Caswell Co., NC Deeds D-13
1787 20 Feb: Sold 511 acres to Joseph Beadles. Caswell Co NC Deeds E-168
1790: Federal Census Caswell County, NC
1794 09 Oct: Wrote his will WB Old Page 35

Records for Mark Hardin (5-112)
1786 25 Mar: Witnessed deed Henry Harden to Watson Gentry. Rockingham Co., NC Deed Book A-144
1790: Federal Census of Rockingham County, NC
1795: Bought 500 acres from John Hill. Rockingham Co., NC Deed Book H-50

Family Genealogies with References

1796 26 Jan: Married Frances Hill. Rockingham Co., NC Marriages
1799: Bought 133 ½ acres from Elizabeth and John Glenn Jr Rockingham Co., NC Deed book F-106
1821 09 Mar: witnessed will of Elizabeth Black. Rockingham Co., NC Will Book A-135
1834 14 Jan: Wrote his will. Rockingham Co., NC Will Book B-213. Probated November 1839.

33. William Everett³ Hardin (Henry², Mark¹) (5-33) was born 25 April 1741 in Prince William County, Virginia and died 4 March 1810 in Franklin County, Georgia. He married **Sarah Bledsoe**. Children from his will.
   Children of William Everett³ Hardin and Sarah Bledsoe:
   121   i. HENRY⁴ HARDIN (5-121) was born 18 September 1765 in Wake County, North Carolina. He died in 1856 in Ashe County, North Carolina. He married Catherine Cox.
   122   ii. SWAN HARDIN (5-122) was born 10 March 1773 in Johnston Co., North Carolina and died in 1829 in Liberty Co., Texas. He married Jerusha Blackburn.
   123   iii. MARK HARDIN (5-123) was born about 1775 and died in 1843. He married Nancy Callaway.
   124   iv. MARTIN HARDIN (5-124)
   125   v. SUSAN HARDIN (5-125)
   126   vi. RICHARD HARDIN (5-126)
   127   vii. CYNTHIA HARDIN (5-127) married Toney.
   128   viii. BLEDSOE HARDEN (5-128)

36. Martin³ Hardin (Henry², Mark¹) (5-36) was born in 1755 in Virginia. He died in 1848 in Marshall County Tennessee. He married **Mary Burgess**.
   Children of Martin³ Hardin and Mary Burgess:
   129   ix. CLARA⁴ HARDIN (5-129) 1793-1830 married John Larue
   130   x. JOHN L. HARDIN (5-130) born about 1795-1878 Rebecca
   131   ix. BURGESS HARDIN (5-131) born about 1786 to 1848

37. Henry³ Hardin Jr (Henry², Mark¹) (5-37) was born about 1757 in Virginia. His wife was named **Alice**. He first appears in Pittsylvania County VA in the 1780s but soon went to Rockingham County, North Carolina, just across the county line from Pittsylvania. By 1793 he sold his land and moved to Wilkes Co., Gorgia, where he lived the rest of his life.
Rockingham County, North Carolina Records
1783 25 Mar: Purchased 50 acres from Watson Gentry. Deed Book A-144
1786: Purchased 200 acres from Zachariah Stanley. Deed Book A-123
1787 10 Nov: Purchased 100 acres from Benjamin Cook Deed Book C-135
1793 12 Oct: Of Wilkes Co., Ga, sold 200 acres to Mark Hardin. Deed Book C-331

1793: of Wilkes Co., Georgia, sold through attorney M Hardin 150 acres to John Mathews. Deed Book D-166

42. John⁴ Hardin (John³, John², Mark¹) (5-42) was born in 1762 and died in 1853 in Fayette Co., Pennsylvania. He married **Barbara Rowner**.
Children of John⁴ Hardin and Barbara Rowner:
132   i. PETER⁵ HARDIN born about 1790 married Sally Hardin.

Unrelated Hardin Families of the Northern Neck of Virginia

In my research, I have found several Harden-Hardin-Harding families in the Northern Neck of Virginia who can't be connected to the five families discussed in this book. They are presented here to avoid confusion between these families and the five main families presented in this book.

Family 7: Thomas Harding of Old Rappahannock (later Essex) County Virginia

1. This Thomas Harding¹ (7-1) appears early. In July 1660 his son Leroy Harding was given a black cow by Coll. Fauntleroy. Although the record does not say so explicitly, many have assumed this means Thomas married a daughter of Colonel Fauntleroy, which is not necessarily true. Research on Coll. Fauntleroy shows he arrived 1643 as a widower and married again and lived in what is now Richmond County. He married shortly thereafter and had one son William. It is unlikely there was a family relationship between this Thomas Harding and the Fauntleroy family. In 1650 in Pioneers and Cavaliers by Nugent (2018 Page 194-95), one Thomas Harding was listed as transported from England to Virginia by Coll. Fauntleroy. It is likely this man is the Thomas Harding in that list. Many researchers have assumed that this man is the same as the Thomas Harding (1-1) who settled in Northumberland County by 1658. That is not likely because as late as the end of 1662, this Thomas Harding (7-1) is noted as being of Rappahannock County in a deed. (See the records following this sketch.) Thomas Harding continued to show up in Rappahannock County records as late as 1668 then he vanishes from the records. No children are known.

Children of Thomas¹ Harding:
2. LEROY HARDING born before July 1660, Nothing further known.

Old Rappahannock (Essex) County, Virginia Records
1660 Jul: Son Leroy given a black cow by Capt. Fauntleroy DB 2-125
1660 20 Dec: Buys 100 acres from Samuel and Elizabeth Perry DB 2-167
1660/61 13 Feb: Witnesses deed from Francis Brown to Wm Richards DB 2-182
1661 Oct: Page 135 Witnessed gift deed (recorded 21 August 1677 DB 6-135
1662 05 Nov: Relinquishes land bought of Samuel Perry DB 2-62
1662 05 Nov: Witnesses deed from Richard Stokes to Thomas Jewll DB 2-264
1663 06 May: Witnesses sale from Ann Young to Richard Maccabone DB 2-283
1667 10 Apr: Witnessed power of attorney for Richard Spurling DB 3-170
1668 27 Jul: Witnesses deed Henry Woodnut to Roger Smith DB 3-506
1668 04 Jan: Witnesses deed Henry Woodnut to Thomas Warwan DB 4-231

Family 8: Harding of Old Rappahannock (later Essex) County Virginia

1. The progenitor of this Harding family is unknown and may have never emigrated to Virginia from England. We know some of the relationships as indicated below since deeds and will give us some clues. We know that William Harding (9-2) had a cousin (or nephew) Peter, a child and that Nicholas Harding has a son Peter Harding born in Middlesex County.

Children of Unknown Harding:
+   2   i   WILLIAM^2 HARDING, born about 1646, most likely in England.
+   3   ii   NICHOLAS HARDING, born about 1655, most likely in England

2. William Harding^2 (8-2) was born about 1646 and first appears in Old Rappahannock County, Virginia in July 1667, when he witnessed a deed. Later, a will he witnessed in 1675 gives his age as about 28. in 1723. He does, however, mention a cousin Peter Harding, an infant. His wife Martha has a long and interesting history. She was born in the late 1640s because she already had a son by 1672. She was the daughter of Mr. Bollin and Rebecca his wife, who married second John Cabell who died before 1661. Martha married first Mr. Harood or Harwood and had a son Peter (c1670-1707). After Mr. Harwood died, she married William Harding but had no children with him. See the deeds and wills of Essex County for the Bollin and Harwood records.

Old Rappahannock (Essex) County, Virginia Records
1667 02 Jul: Witnessed deed Richard Holt to John Soper DB3-276
1670 10 Oct: given power of attorney to record deed, witnesses deed DB 4-458
1670 10 Oct: Buys 200 acres from William and Catherine Richards DB 4-471
1670/1 06 Feb: Sells 200 acres to Edmund Pagett DB 5-3

1674/5 20 Feb: Witnesses the will of Henry Cox of Rappahannock. Says he his age about 28 WB 1-194
1675 17 Apr: Witnesses deed of Daniel Mackonnell DB 5-407
1675 15 Apr: Witnessed power of attorney DB 5-407
1677 02 Mar: Witnesses power of attorney DB 6-163
1685/6 10 Feb: Mentioned as debtor in estate of George Boyce DB 7-97
1687/8 03 Feb: Attended court for two days. DB 8-51
1697 11 Oct: Appraised estate of William Creamer DB 9-125
1699 12 Aug: Appraised estate of John Eyles DB 10-5
1699 12 Jul: Appraised estate of John Clarke DB 10-8
1709 10 Aug: Peter Harood leaves clothing to him DB 13-230
1709 10 Aug: Mentioned in a deed from Edmund Pagett to son DB 13-231
1712 04 Apr: Sells interest in land to Owen Owens DB 14-40
1712 10 Apr: Acknowledges deed to Owens DB 14-40
1720/1 08 Feb: Witnessed deed Gilpin to Amoorson DB 14-282
1723 28 Mar: Writes his will. Mentions cousin Peter Harding infant WB 4-32
1723 18 Sep: Will proved WB 4-32

3. Nicholas² Harding's birthdate and date of arrival in Virginia are unknown. We do know that he married Elizabeth, whose maiden name is not known. He died in 1709 in Middlesex County, Virginia shortly after his son was born.

Children of Nicholas² Harding:
4 i PETER³ HARDING born 27 April 1709 in Christ Church Parish, Middlesex County. It is not known where he lived.

Old Rappahannock (Essex after 1692)) County, Virginia Records
1708 25 Jan: Witnessed will of James Osman with Owen Owens
1709 10 Jan: Estate administered by John Callicote
1710 11 May: Inventory of estate presented

Family 9 George Harding of Middlesex County Virginia

1. This George¹ Harding (9-1) was born about 1680 to 1690, location unknown but probably England. He first appears in Middlesex County when his son Thomas Harding was born in 1712. He married Elizabeth (possibly Keeble) probably about 1710 and lived in Middlesex County the rest of his life. He died before 2 April 1745, when his will was probated. In his will he mentioned a niece, Eizabeth Stapleton. Lucy Hardin married William Stapleton in 1733 in Middlesex County, Virginia. She is most likely a younger sister.

Children of George¹ and Elizabeth Harding:
+ 2 i THOMAS² HARDING born 3 May 1712 Middlesex County, Virginia

Family Genealogies with References

+ 3 ii ANNE HARDIN born 21 December 1716 Middlesex County Virginia. Died before 1744. Married Mr. Keeble and had daughter Elizabeth.
+ 4 iii MARY HARDING born 7 November 1722 Middlesex County, Virginia. Married Charles Blacknall and had three daughters listed in mother's will.

Middlesex County, Virginia Records
1709 18 Sep: Files bond as executor of Thomas Baynes Will
1712 03 May: Son Thomas Born Parish Register Page 73
1716 21 Dec: Daughter Anne Born Parish Register Page 96
1722 07 Nov: Daughter Mary Born Parish Register page 111
1744 10 Oct: Writes his will
1745 02 Apr: Will probated
1759 20 Jan: Wife Elizabeth write her will
1759 05 Jun: Wife Elizabeth will probated

Spotsylvania County, Virginia Records
1733 04 Sep: Bought 1020 acres from William Johnston

2. Thomas Hardin was born 3 May 1712 in Middlesex County, Virginia. He married Lucy Billups 5 January 1747 in Middlesex County, Virginia. He died before 4 December 1759, when his will was probated. He owned land in Orange County, Virginia patented by his father. He had no children.

Middlesex County, Virginia Records
1747 05 Jan: Married Lucy Billups
1759 07 Nov: Wrote his will
1759 04 Dec: His will probated.

Orange County, Virginia Records
1745 25 Nov: Power of attorney for corn and animal delivery DB 10-258
1748 25 Jul: Lease 1000 acres granted to his father to John Boutwell DB 11-60
1748 27 Jul: Lease and release filed

Chapter 4
Virginia County Records

Virginia Military Records

Captain Stephen Ashby's (Capt. since Sept 1776) Company of the 12th Virgnia Regiment of foot, Stribling 1st Lt Richard Routt 2nd Lt

March 1777 Ennis Enos Hardin (4-7) Pvt
June 1777 Enos Hardin (4-7) Pvt
July 1777 Ennis Enos Hardin Pvt (4-7)
August 1777 Ennis Enos Hardin (4-7) Pvt
September 1777 Enos Hardin (4-7)
November 1777 Enis Enos Hardin (4-7) Pvt
December 1777 Enos Hardin (4-7) Pvt
February 1778 Innis Enos Hardin (4-7) Pvt
March 1778 Enos Hardin Pvt (4-7)
April 1778 Eanus Enos Hardin Pvt (4-7)
May 1778 Eanus Enos Hardin Pvt (4-7)

Lt Col John Neville's Company 4th Virginia Regiment Commanded by Colonel James Woods

July 1778 Ennis Enos Hardin (4-7)
August 1778 Ennis Hardin Waggoner (4-7)
September 1778 Ennis Hardin (4-7)

Colonel James Woods Company of the 8th Virginia Regiment Abraham Hite Captain, Joseph Hite, Lieutenant

October 1778 Ennis Enos Hardin (4-7)
November 1778 Ennis Enos Hardin (4-7)
December 1778 Ennis Enos Hardin (4-7)
January 1779 Ennis Enos Hardin (4-7)
February 1779 Ennis Enos Hardin (4-7)
March 1779 Ennis Enos Hardin (4-7)
April 1779 Ennis Enos Hardin (4-7)
May 1779 Ennis Enos Hardin (4-7)
July 1779 Ennis Enos Hardin (4-7)
August 1779 Ennis Enos Hardin (4-7)

September 1779 Ennis Enos Hardin (4-7)

October 1779 Ennis Enos Hardin (4-7)

Land Grants of the Northern Neck of Virginia

1793 14 Aug: Book W Page 493 Treasury Warrant 19,716 4 October 1783 Lewis Ashby 140 ½ A (8 May 1792) in Frederick County on Howells Run of Shenandoah R., adj the Manor of Leeds, Francis Berry formerly Thomas Ashby the Younger 4 Sept 1793.

Arlington County, Virginia Records

Will Books

1815 18 Jan: Will Book 2, Page 2 Will of Thomas G. Harding (2-26) To son William Harding (2-64) the farm he lives on and if he dies without heirs, the farm to go to Sinclair Harding (2-66). $300 to raise and school the two youngest daughters Harriet Eliza Harding (2-67) and Mary Ann Harding (2-68). To daughter Susanna Harding (2-63) three barrels of corn and 50 wt of pork. After sale balance of estate to be divided among them all. Executor Thomas Sinclair. Proved 16 February 1815.

1815 27 Feb: Will Book 2 Page 7 Bond for Guardians for Thomas Harding (2-26) Orphans. Thomas Sinclair, guardian for William Harding (2-64), Nancy Harding (2-65), Thomas Sinclair Harding (2-66), Harriet Eliza Harding (2-67), and Mary Ann Harding (2-68).

1821 25 Apr: Will Book 2, Page 432 Bond for William Hardin (2-64), Simon Daine and Benjamin Donaldson, guardians for Thomas Sinclair Hardin (2-66), Harriet Eliza Harden (2-67) and Mary Ann Harden (2-68), orphans of Thomas Green Harden (2-26) late of Alexandria County deceased.

Marriage Records

1805 16 Feb: Richard Harding married Lucretia Catterton

1806 26 Mar: Sarah Harding married Joseph Hughes

1808 10 Jul: Elizabeth Harden married Stephen Woden

1810 21 Nov: Lettice Harding married Henry Joachim Daughter of George Harding

1813 25 Aug: Susannah Harden (2-63) married Dickerson Sarratt (2-63) (daughter of Thomas G. Harden (2-26)

Harding Families of the Northern Neck of Virginia

Culpeper County, Virginia Records

Formed 1749 from Orange County, Virginia

Deed Records

1753 29 May: Book B Page 99. William Beverly of Blanfield Parish Essex County to George Harding of Culpeper County Farm lot where he now lives and 100 acres in Culpeper County.to hold through the natural lives of George Harding and his two sons Charles and George, rent to be paid in tobacco.

1762 17 Jun: Book D Page 51 Martin Hardin (5-3) of Fauquier County, Virginia to Edward Tinsley, land in Brumfield Parish, Culpeper County, named Campbells land, 66 acres

1762 13 Aug: Book D Page 91 Martin Hardin (5-3) of Fauquier County, Virginia to John Grayson of Culpeper County, for 30 Pounds, 250 acres bounded by John Roberts, Francis Thornton, and Martin Hardin (5-3)

1762 20 Aug: Book D Page 114, very hard to read. Martin Hardin (5-3) of Fauquier County Virginia to John Lillard. For 43 pounds 350 acres in Culpeper County by Thornton. This is the date the deed was proved. The deed itself has no date in it.

1769 01 Sep: Book F Page 121 Martin Hardin (5-3) of Fauquier County, Virginia to Fisher Rice of Culpeper County, Virginia. For 50 Pounds, 367 acres in Brumfield Parish, part of 400 acres granted to Martin Hardin Thomas Lord Fairfax 2 June 1748. Witnessed by Robet Stuart Jr, John Hardin, Ammon Bohannon, Susannah Hardin, Benj Pulliam, Thomas Pulliam, Thomas Cave.

1773 09 Aug: Book G Page 429 Martin Hardin (5-3) of Westmoreland County, Pennsylvania, bond to John Strother of Culpeper County, Virginia in sum of 200 Pounds. Lease for a term of 90 years a parcel of land in Culpeper County in the east end o Pignut Ridge adjoining John Minifee, Nicholas Battle, and Joseph Bryant.

1782 27 Sep: Book L Page 324 Philip Weaver and Ann his wife to George Hardin, both of Culpeper County for 20 Pounds. 240 acres in Bromfield Parish on the Rappahannock River

1794 15 Jan: Book S Page 90 George Hardin and his wife Catherine of Culpeper County to Augustine Cowns of same county, for 30 pounds 100 acres of land on Triplett's line.

1799 07 Feb: Book U Page 403 Mark Hardin (5-26) and Susanna his wife of Washington County, Kentucky to John Strother of Culpeper County, consideration two negroes, 501 acres. On Pignut Ridge bound by John Battie and Thornton.

1809 23 Sep: Book QQ Page 460 George Hardin and Catherine his wife of Culpeper County, Virginia to Francis Mauzy of the same. For $760 land in Culpeper County 200 acres

Probate Records

1780 15 May: Book B Page 381. Inventory of the estate of George Hardin submitted

1787 17 Dec: Book C Page 275 administrative account of George Harding estate settled. Report made by George Thomas, John Peper, Brian McGrath

Federal Census Records

Culpeper County, Virginia Census of 1810
Page 41 Culpeper Geo Hardin 50010 01010

Marriage Records (from marriage register)

1786 17 Nov: Page 79 Sarah Hardin married James Stevenson by John Pickett

1788 15 Feb: Page 63 Elizabeth Hardin married Robert Level by William Mason

1792 20 Aug: Page 53 Martin Hardin married Jane Aynes by William Mason

1796 27 Oct: Page 5 Frances Hardin Jr married Joshua Burkland by John Swindler

1802 02 Sep: Page 54 William Hardin (2-27) married Elizabeth Doggett by Frederick Kabler

1802 28 Sep: Page 41 Sarah Hardin married Thomas Doggett by Frederick Kabler

1808 03 May: Page 13 Robert Hardin married Elizabeth Oder by William Mason

Personal Property Tax Lists

1782: List of Elijah Hirtley: James Hardon 1 tithe
1782: List of William McClanahan George Harden 1 tithe 1 horse 2 cow
1803: George Hardin
1804: George Hardin 1 son over 16
1805-1810 books are missing
1811: George Hardin and William Hardin next to each other
1812: George Hardin and William Hardin next to each other
1813: George Hardin and William Hardin next to each other
1814: George Hardin alone

1815: George Hardin alone
1817: George Hardin alone
1818: George Hardin alone

Essex County, Virginia Records

Old Rappahannock formed 1656 from Lancaster Co., VA, Became Essex 1692

The indexes and Book numbering for Old Rappahannock County and Essex County are very confused with different book numbers, page numbers, and years given in different indexes. You will need to be patient when attempting to find these records.

Will and Deed Book 1 1664-1677

1672 27 Jan: Probate 27 Jan 1674. Will of John Bollin. In the name of God Amen, I John Bollin being sick in body but of sound mind and perfect memory do make this my last will and testament in manner following. Item I doe give and bequeath my soul to almighty God which giveth to me in hope of a resurrection at the last day and my body to the burying of my dearest friends. I doe give and bequeath all my land unto Mathew Harwood and her heirs after the death of my mother to Martha Harod and her heirs forever. I do give unto Peter Harod one yearling heifer and her increase forever, I do give my cattle unto my dear mother making her my lawful Executrix this being my last will and testament as witness my hand and seal this 27th of January in the year of our lord 1674.

1674/5 22 Feb: Page 194 probate 2 Nov 1675 Will of Henry Cox of Rappahannock, witness was William Harding (8-2), age about 28.

Deed Book 2 1656-1664 (Film # 1929926)

(NOTE: Although some have claimed that this Thomas Harding (7-1) is the same as the Thomas Harding (1-1) of Northumberland County who married Anne Moseley, I believe this is not the case. Thomas Harding of Northumberland received land in 1658 and was married to Anne Moseley by 1661 whereas this Thomas Harding (7-1) was still living in Rappahannock County in 1662.)

1660 Jul: Page 125 A black cow with a white foot behind and slitt on the left ear the right Ear ( ) given by Coll Moore Fauntleroy unto Leroy Hardinge (7-2) son of Thomas Hardinge (7-1) to be recorded for the said Leroy Harding (7-2) the said Thomas Hardinge (7-1) to have ( ) be fifteen years of age.

Fauntleroy's first name is almost torn out, but one can see the beginning of an M and the end of an E with the title Coll before the name.

1660 20 Dec: Page 167 Samuel and Elizabeth Parry of Rappahannock Co. deed to Thomas Harding (7-1). 100 acres, witnesses were Will Johnson and Francis Browne.

1660 13 Feb: recorded 1661 Page 182 Thomas Harding (7-1) witnesses deed from Francis and Elizabeth Brown to William Richards

1662 05 Nov: recorded 1662 Page 263 (first line is on page 262) Know all men by these presents that I Thomas Harding (7-1) of the County of Rappahannock planter doth acknowledge and relinquish of One Conveyance of Land containing one hundred acres bought of Samuel Parry his heirs or assigns which said conveyance of land the (missing portion) Harding my heirs or assigns do wholly relinquish as witness my hand this 5th day of November 1662. Signed Thomas Harding his seal.

1662 05 Nov: rec 1662 Page 264 Thomas Harding (7-1) witnesses deed from Richard Stokes of Rappahannock Co. to Thomas Powell

1663 06 May: rec 1663 Page 283 Thomas Harding (7-1) witnessed sale from Ann Young of Rappahannock Co. to Richard Mattabone, one cow.

Deed Book 3 1664-1668

1667 02 Jul: rec 12 December 1667 Page 276 (signature on Page 277) William Harding (8-2) witnessed deed 200 acres Richard Holt to John Soper.

1667 10 Mar: Page 372 This is to certify that I Marmaduke Hazelwood did upon Satterday the Last of February in presence of Rich Taylor Mrs. Harding and others Execute the within written warrant as witness my hand this second day of March 1667. Case was Pattison vs Corbin referenced in preceding filings on the same page.

1667 10 Apr: Page 432 rec 12 May 1668 Thomas Harding (7-1) witnessed power of attorney Richard Spurling to Henry Woodnut

1668 27 Jul: Page 506 rec 10 November 1668 Thomas (7-1) Harding witnessed deed 114 acres Henry Woodnut of Rappahannock Co. to Roger Smith

Deed Book 4 1668-1672

1668 04 Jan: Page 231 rec 10 March 1669 Thomas Harding (7-1) witnessed deed 114 acres Henry Woodnut of Rappahannock Co. to Thomas Warwan of Rappahannock Co.

1670 10 Oct: Page 458 rec 5 July 1671 Dorothy Coventon appoints William Harding (8-2) as her lawful attorney to acknowledge her right title and interest in 300 acres in Dragon Swamp unto William Richards of Pascatoque sold by husband William Coventon and Thomas Bay Warton to said Richards. record deed of 300 acres Thomas Hayworton to William Richards Haywarten is spelled two different ways in the deed.

1670 10 Oct: Page 458 William Hardin (8-2) witnesses deed from William Coventon and Dorothy his wife to Thos Haywarton of Rappahannock County.

1670/1 26 Feb: Page 471, recorded 5 July 1671 Katherine Richards appoints Thomas Hayworton as attorney to acknowledge deed for 200 acres at head of Piscaqua Creek to William Harding.

1670 18 Oct: Page 471 recorded 5 July 1671. William Richards of Rappahannock County and Katherine his wife for valuable consideration assigns all Estate title and Interest of within written conveyance unto William Harding. (8-2), 200 acres of land.

Deed Book 5 1672-1676

1671 06 Feb: Page 3 rec 26 Apr 1672 William Harding (8-2) of Rappahannock County Bill of Sale 200 acres Piscatacon to Edmund Pagett.

1672 15 Apr: Page 27 rec 6 May 1672 Mathew Wilcox to Stephen Thomas, 200 acres, Rappahannock County, Begins at northwest corner at R. S. Path, runs along path to northwest, then southwest, then southeast to land of Samuel Griffin.

1673 12 Apr: Page 142 rec 7 May 1673 Stephen Thomas of Northumberland Co., VA "acknowledges to have sold from my heirs Executors administrators unto Robert Bradley and Richard Browne and to their heirs, 200 acres bought of and from Mathew Wilcox of Totasky Mill in Rappahannock River". Witnesses were Adam King and John Browne

1673/4 10 Feb: Page 283 rec 17 Apr 1674 Bill of Sale Robert and Anne Bradley and Richard and Mary Browne to Thomas Harding (1-1) "Whereas I Robert Bradley and one Richard Brown did formerly lay off from Stephen Thomas the quantity and Tract of land accordingly as is Expressed in a bill of sale under the hand and seal of the said Stephen Thomas before his decease and acknowledged also in Rappa County Court. Knowe ye whose presence this present writing shall Come before that we the said Bradley and Browne do hereby lett sett and sell and by these presents doe let vet of assigne from us our heirs Executors administrators or assigns all our Rights titles or Interest forever of this above said land to Thomas Hardin who is the sold executor unto the said Stephen Thomas decd wee do herein surrender unto the said Harding by our act and deed to him his heirs as above expressed being for and in Consideration of the Delivery and Surrendering back again until the said Bradley and Browne our own proper obligations that we doth both Confess to have received upon our subscribing hereunto the said obligations being the consideration we were expected to pay unto the abovesaid Stephen deceased moreover it is here acknowledged by us Ann Bradley and Mary Brown" (their wives) Stephen Thomas deceased, 200 acres. Witnesses James Claughton, Horlins Anerson, John Herbert, Adam Booth, William Howard. (*This was the same property Robert Bradley and Richard Browne bought from Stephen Thomas page 142 above.*)

1675 17 Apr: Page 407 rec 15 May 1675 13 William Hardin (8-2) witnessed deed Daniel Mackonnell to Neale Peterson

1675 15 Apr: Page 407 rec 17 May 1675 William Hardin (8-2) witnessed power of attorney Daniel Mackonnell to Thomas Gaines

Deed Book 6 1676-1682

1661 Oct: Page 135 rec 21 Aug: 1677 Thomas Harding (7-1) witnessed gift from Robert Hopkins to William Talbut Jr.

1677 02 Mar: Page 163 rec 27 Mar 1678 William Hardin (8-2) witnessed a power of atty. from Elizabeth Bush to John Bagwell

1681 30 May: Page 310 rec 13 June 1681 John Hardin gave gift of one cow to Jane Elmore, daughter of Peter Elmore.

Deed Book 7 1682-1687

1685 10 Feb: Page 97 recorded 22 Apr 1686 William Hardin (8-2) mentioned as a debtor to the estate of Geo Boyce

Deed Book 8 1686-1692

1687 03 Feb: Page 51 Court order, William Hardin (8-2) attended court for two days.

Deed Book 9 1695-1699

1697 11 Oct: Page 125 Wm. Harding (8-2) Appraised estate of William Creamer

Deed and Will Book 10 1699-1702

1699 12 Aug: Page 5 William Harding (8-2) Appraised estate of John Eyles

1699 12 Jul: Page 8 William Harding (8-2) Appraised the estate of John Clarke

1701 09 Mar: Page 96 Proved 10 March 1701 in court. Peter Harwood Planter of South Farnham Parish, Essex County, VA (only son and heir apparent of Martha Harding late of same place) to Francis Moore Merchant of Sittingbourne Parish, Essex County, VA. Consideration 600 pounds of tobacco. 125 acres in South Farnham Parish, on Piscataway Creek, along land of Thomas Green. Land patented to John Cabell by Patent dated 4 October 1653. On petition of Rebecca Cabell, widow of John Cabell, land was granted and confirmed to Rebecca Cabell 24 March 1661 and afterwards granted to John Bullen, son and heir of the said Rebecca Cabell on 26 March 1664. Then along with 83 acres more, in all 333 acres, granted unto Martha Harding, sister and heir of the said John Bullen 25 October 1687 and now doth of right belong unto the said Peter Harwood, only son and heir of the said Martha Harding.

1709 Thomas Harding filed a bond.

1710 the inventory of Richard Harding was filed.

Deed and Court Book 13 1707-1711

1708 25 Jan: Page 48 Nicholas Harding (8-3) and Owen Owens witnessed will of James Osman

1709 10 Aug: Page 230 Will of Peter Harood of South Farnham Parish, Essex County. "I give & bequeath unto William Harding (8-2) all my wearing apparel my longest Gumme? after all my debts are to be satisfied and paid. Balance of estate to wife Mary Witnessed by Owen Owens, dated 20 Mar 1709

1709 10 Aug: Page 231 Deed Edmund Pagott of South Farnham, Essex Co Virginia, to Son Ephraim Pagott of same, 200 acres in the same county. Formerly belonged to Francis Browne of same county, who with wife Elizabeth sold it to William Richards by deed dated 17th March 1667 and by said Richards and Katherine his wife assigned to William Harding (8-2) by assignment made on the back of the deed dated 18 Oct 1670, and by the said Harding sold to the aforesaid Edmund Paget by deed dated 6 February 1671.

1709 Jan: 10 Page 273 Nicholas Harding (8-3) Estate Administered by John Callicote

1710 May: 11 Page 342 Nicholas Harding (8-3) Inventory

1711, 14 Sept 1708 Page 437 Filed September 14 Edward Ellis Mariner has a boat at Andrew Harding's Landing.

Deed and Will Book 14 1711-1716

1712 4 Apr:, Page 40, William Harding (8-2) of South Farnham Parish sells land to Owen Owens and Mary his wife of same Par, "Whereas Peter Harrood late of the said county was in his lifetime seized of a plantation xx and by his last will xx Devised the same to the said Mary then his wife for and during her natural life, the reversion of which said land is Vested in the said William Harding and his heirs" Harding disposes of his interest to the Owens for ½ of the land.

1712 Apr: 10 Page 40 William Harding (8-2) to Owen Owens and wife Mary Acknowledgment

1716 Jul: 15 Page 632 Thomas Harding of the County of Accomack Debtor to Buckingham Brown for 34 pounds Bond Dated 15 July 1709

Deed and Will Book 14 1711-1716

1720/21 08 Feb: Page 282 (8-2) William Harding witnessed a deed from Richard Gilpin of Middlesex Co VA to Joseph Amoorson

Will Book 4

1723 28 Mar: Page 32 Will of William Harding (8-2) of South Farnham Parish Essex County mentions cousin Peter Harding, an infant, one shilling. Friend John Turrell all my lands, 75 acres, to Robert Moody clothing, to friend Joseph Anderson bed guns and 15 shillings, balance to Elisabeth Ward. Proved 18 September 1723

Fairfax County, Virginia Records

Formed 1742 from Prince William County

Deed Books

(NOTE: Edward Hardin's origin is not known although he may have some from Maryland. He and his family are unrelated to the Northumberland Harding families. Two of his sons were Elihu Harden and William Hanby Harden mentioned below.)

1743 19 May: Book A Page 43 George Taylor of Fairfax County lease from William Clifton for life of his wife Elizabeth and daughter Keziah. 200 acres.

Harding Families of the Northern Neck of Virginia

1747 15 Jun: Page B-186 Power of attorney, Samuel Taylor of Frederick Co., VA to William Yeardley

1750 09 Jun: Book C Pages 329-331 Edward Hardin deed to Mahlon Kirkbride

1754 02 Mar: Book C Page 798 William Harding (2-5) witnessed the deed from Panalopy Bowling to son William Bowling.

1755-61 Book D Page 111-113 Edward Hardin of Fairfax County deed to Mahlon Kirkbride of Bucks Co., PA 405 acres.

1755 16 Oct: Book D Page 225-227 Robert Carter of Westmoreland Co., VA to Henry Taylor, lease for 295 acres of land on Goose Creek in Fairfax Co., VA to have during the lives of Joshuah Taylor, second son of Margaret Taylor, Henry Taylor, third son by same woman, and William Whitely, eldest son by my present wife by a former husband.

1759 5 Feb: Book D Page 626-29 Jabez Downman and Ann his wife of Prince William Co. to William Harding (2-5) of Fairfax County, for 59 pounds, 525 acres on Four Mile Run, north side of Upper Long Branch

1761 17 Mar: Book D Page 845 Joseph Stephens and Ann his wife of Truro, Fairfax County to John Taylor and Thomas Wellman Culverhouse 80 Pounds 456 acres

1762 25 May: Book F Page 131 Peter Harding witnessed the deed of Will Booth and Elizabeth Booth of Cople Parish, Westmoreland Co., VA to Ann Washington, widow of Augustine Washington, to John Turberville of Cople Parish, land in Fairfax County.

1767 10 Apr: Book G Page 188 William Fitzhugh to William Williams, 216 acres Truro Parish, lease for the lives of said Williams and his sons James and William. Witness Thomas Harden (1-23).

Book H Page 262 William Fitzhugh deed (lost) to Thomas Harden (1-23)

Book H Page 238 John Alexander Jr. deed (lost) to William Harding (2-5)

1773 21 Jun: Book M1 Page 118 William Fitzhugh to Thomas Kerby, Witness Thomas Harden (1-23).

1773 25 Jun: Book M1 Page 124 William Fitzhugh to Edward Potter, one witness is Thomas Harden (1-23)

1784 Jul: Book O Pages 380-417 Jeremiah Harden (1-45) with William Lewis and Ben Gwinn witnessed eight leases for William Fitzhugh

1787 17 Jul: Book Q1 Page 451 Edward Harden bond to the Governor. Obligation is to collect duties on tobacco crossing the Potomac River.

1789 15 Jun: Book R1 Page 390 Thomas Green Harden (2-26) deed to John Dowdall. Thomas Green Harden of Fairfax Co to John Dowdall of same. 150 pounds. Land devised to Thomas Green Harden by William Harden (2-5) and his wife Stacy (2-5) in his will in Fairfax County 200 acres.

1789 16 Mar: Book S1 Page 6 Hall Harden (2-22) of Fairfax County and Elizabeth his wife deed to William Wilson of same. 140 acres on Subber Branch, land devised to Hall Harden by his father William Harden in his will dated 18 May 1781. Hall Harden was sued by William Dunlop and Company of Glasgow, Scotland for 40 Pounds 15 Shillings and 3 pence and won. The debt is property of William Wilson. Deed agrees Hall Harden will pay to William Wilson the debt due with interest before 16 March 1793 to redeem the property.

Will Books

1740 01 May: Book A1 Page 229 probated 17 May 1747 Will of John Taylor, names son George, daughters Elizabeth Smith and Hannah Taylor, executor son Henry Taylor, witnesses Daniell Sampson, John Shereden, John Snoden

1767 20 May: Book C1 Page 6 William Harding (2-5) bought from the estate of Daniel Jennings

1771 19 Aug: Book C-1 Page 115 William Harding (2-5) appraised the estate of John Lowe.

1774 16 May: Book C-1 Page 212 Thomas Harding (1-23) appraised the estate of Benoni Kent

1781 18 May: Book D1 Page 236 Will of William Harding (2-5), mentions wife Stacy (2-5) 300 acres, 5 negroes and half the stock, Son Thomas Green Harden (2-26), son Charles (2-23), son Hall Harden (2-22), daughter Maryan Ball (2-24) 100 acres, son Charles (2-23) leased plantation where he lives, son Anthony Harden (2-25) 5 negroes and leased plantation, Alexander Williams' children, Martha Harden's children. Witnesses William Carlin and Joseph Birch Inventory 546-11-9, 611-10-10 Proved 16 October 1781.

1782 17 Jun: Book D1 Page 259 Bond by Henry Garrett and Henry Garrett Jr., guardians of Ann, Charles, William and Daniel Harden. Says orphan rather than orphans.

1782 19 Nov: Book D1 Page 306 Bond by Charles Harden (2-23) and Moses Ball, condition is that Charles Harden, guardian of Thomas Green Harden (2-26), performs his duties.

1784 19 Mar: Book D1 Page 334 Estate of William Harding (2-5) split between widow and Thomas Green Harden (2-26).

1800 16 May: Book I1 Page 161 Will of James Hopper mentions mother Mary Hopper, John Hopper at 21, four sisters Nancy, Betsy, Mary, Sarah, Robert Hopper, Daniel McCarty's son James, Martha Harden one mare, and Amelia Harden six Pounds. Daniel Lewis executor Probated 20 October 1800,

Court Order Books 1749-1753

1751 25 Jun: Page 157 Edward Hardin received lease and release from John Hanby. Witnesses Edward Norton, Richard Roach, Edmond Sands

In 1749 William Harding (2-5) inventories estate of Joseph Boliny

1751 26 Sep: Page 170 Isaac Hardin summoned to testify against James Smith for horse stealing.

1752 17 Jun: Page 206 Isaac Hardin ordered to work on road under Edmund Sands, overseer

1752 17 Jun: Page 206 Edward Hardin leases land to Mahlon Kirkbride. Witnesses Francis Hague, John ---, --- Yates

1753 William Harding (2-5) inventories estate of Joseph Boliny

1753 23 Mar: Page 328 Edward Hardin defendant on petition vs John Carlyle, Gent, to pay 300 pounds tobacco and costs.

1753 20 Jun: Isaac Hardin plaintiff on petition vs Richard Freeman, continued

1753 22 Nov: Page 482 Isaac Hardin plaintiff on a petition vs Richard Freeman, awarded 3 pounds 40 and costs.

Court Order Books 1754-1755

Isaac Hardin several items

William Harding (2-5) three items

1754 21 Nov: Page 188 In the complaint of William Harding (2-5) against Charles Storey and Mary his wife it is ordered that that the said Charles do give Security for his and her good behaviour Viz himself in ten pounds and two Securities in five pounds each.

1755 17 Feb: George Hardin's wife Mary (also named Mary Duncan 21 Nov 1754) adm of Blanche Flower Duncan, dec, ordered to give administration of estate to Guy Broadwater and William Shortridge

1755 19 Aug: Edward Harden transferred with wife Mary indentures of lease and release to Samuel Russell

1756 15 Jun: Edward Harden Administered the estate of James Green, decd.

Court Order Books 1757-1762

(The index is badly damaged, so no page numbers are available for this book.)

In 1756 and 1757 Edward Harden administration of estate of James Green, dec

In 1757 Edward Harden inventoried the estate of Thomas Davies, dec.

1758 18 May: Thomas Harden (1-23) served on Jury

In 1758 Isaac Hardin mentioned

In 1758 John Hardin Gent, trespass defendant

1758 10 Dec: William Harding (2-5) inventoried estate of Hooper Gwyn, decd.

1759 19 Jun: William Harding (2-5) lease from Jabez Downman

1759, 1760, 1761 William Harding (2-5) a grand juror

In 1760 John Hardin Gent, trespass deft

1761 19 Mar: Thomas Harden (1-23) served as juror

1761 16 Jun: Thomas Harden (1-23) defendant vs Bryan Alliston, trespass

1761 16 Jun: Thomas Harden (1-23) plaintiff vs Clement Atchison dismissed

1761 15 Sep: Thomas Harden (1-23) charged with receiving a counterfeit three-pound bill with intent to pass. Thomas Harden (1-23), Henry Boggess Jr., and Joseph Cockerel bound to King George, Thomas for 50 Pounds, others for 25 Pounds, on condition that Thomas be of good behavior towards all his majesties subjects for a year and a day.

1762 16 Jun: Thomas Harden (1-23) defendant vs Robert Bogges Jr.

1762 19 Oct: Page 789 Peter Harden witnessed indenture from William Brotherton and wife Elizabeth and Ann Washington to John Turberville.

1763 18 Mar: Thomas Harden (1-23) Defendant vs Alliston, Bryan pleads not guilty

1763 22 Jul: Thomas Harden (1-23) awarded costs. Witnesses were John Taylor, Thomas Harden (1-23) and John Gound

Court Order Books 1763-1764

1764 20 Mar: Thomas Harden (1-23) appointed surveyor to clear road between Thomas Harden (1-23) and Daniel McCarty gent

1764 24 Sep: Thomas Harden (1-23) witness for defendant Boggess for three days

Court Order Books 1768-1769

1768 19 Sep: Thomas Harden (1-23) lease from William Fitzhugh, witnesses Frances Whiting, John Sarter, James Appleton

1768 23 Nov: Thomas Harden (1-23) witness seven days for William Gardner and Thomas Carson

1768 20 Sep: Thomas Harden (1-23) a juror

1769 18 Jul: William Harding (2-5) gave bail

In 1769 William Harding (2-5) served as a juror

Court Order Books 1770-1771

1770 21 May: Thomas Harden (1-23) replaced as surveyor

1770 18 Jun: Thomas Harden (1-23) with Frances Poston

In 1770 William Harding (2-5) surveyed road by James Green

In 1771 Edward Harden was a defendant

In 1771 William Harding (2-5) took inventory of John Lowe Jr.

Court Order Books 1772-1774

1772 22 Mar: Hall Harden (2-22) presented a petition

In 1773 Edward Harden was a defendant

In 1773 Edward Harden was a juror

Court Order Books 1783-1787

18 Jun: 1783 Jeremiah Harden (1-45) served as a juror

19 Jun: 1783 Jeremiah Harden (1-45) defendant vs Vincent Kirk, charge of trespass, assault and battery, awarded costs. Witnesses paid were William Rogers $1, Thomas Hornbuckle $2, Thomas Alliston $3

19 Jan: 1785 Jeremiah Harden (1-45) paid 650 pounds of tobacco by county for guarding criminals to Richmond

Court Order Books 1788-1791

In 1788 Green Harden (2-26) an injunction

22 Sep: 1789 Hall Harden (2-22) listed on road

22 Sep: 1789 Elisha Harden listed on road

22 Sep: 1789 Moses Hardin (2-12) listed on road

In 1789 Elisha Harden served as a juror

In 1789 Hall Harden (2-22) and Elizabeth Harden deed to William Wilson

19 Nov: 1789 Edward Harden mentioned

23 Dec: 1789 Elihu Harden and John Harden

18 Jul: 1791 Elihu Harden listed on road

16 Aug: 1791 Joseph Harden (4-21) trespass

In 1791 Moses Hardin (2-12) gets bail.

In 1792 Hall Harden (2-22) and Elizabeth Harden (2-22) deed to Jesse Taylor

Tax Lists 1782-1795

Fairfax County Rent Holders
1764 Rents in Fairfax County, William Harding (2-5) 525 acres
1761 rents in Fairfax and Loudoun Co., VA: William Harding (2-5) 525 acres. Will
    Kirtland executors, 110 acres now owned by James Hardin pr: William
1770, 1771, 1772 landholders: William Harding (2-5) 525 acres.

Personal Property Tax Lists
Edward Harden 1782 1783 1784 1785 1786 1787 1788 (unrelated)
Elihu Harden 1784 1785 1787 1788 1789 1790 1791 (son of Edward)
Elisha Harden 1783 1786
George Harden (2-58) 1792 1793 1794 1795
Hall Harden (2-22) 1782 1783 1784 1785 1786 1787 1788 1789 1790 1791
Jeremiah Harden (1-45) 1782 1783 1784
Job Harden 1789 (son of Edward)
Martha Harden 1784
Moses Hardin (2-12) 1782 1783 1785 1786 1787 1788 1789 1790
Patty Harden 1782
Sarah Harden 1787 1788
Stacy Harding (2-5) 1782 (second wife)
Thomas G Harden (2-26) 1791 1792 1793 1794 1795
William Harden 1784 (son of Edward)
Notes to tax lists:
1789: T. G. Harden (2-26) and Hall Harden (2-22) living with Hall Harden (2-22)
1790: Moses and Bailey Harden living with Moses Hardin (2-12)
1790: Elihu Harden and Thomas Tucker living with Elihu Harden
1791: Hall Harden (2-22) and George Harden (2-58) living with Hall Harden.

Harding Families of the Northern Neck of Virginia

Fauquier County, Virginia Records

Formed 1759 from Prince William County

Court Order Books Volume 1 1759-1762

1759 08 Jun: Book 1 Page 7 Mary Hardin (5-22) by Martin Hardin (5-3) her next Friend against William Robinson (Taylor) This suit is abated by the Plt marriage, and it is ordered that Pltf pay unto Deft his costs Robinson

1759 07 Aug: Book 1 Page 23 License is granted Martin Hardin (5-3) to keep an Ordinary at his house he having with Maximillion Berryman his secy entered into and acknowledged Bond

1760 28 Nov: Book 1 Page 123 The petition of Martin Hardin (5-3) vs George Wheatley is continued until the next court.

1761 26 Mar: Book 1 Page 136 The Tithables belonging to Martin Hardin (5-3), John Ashby, Edward Humston, John Orear, Davis Holder, John Moorehead and John Morehead Jr 's be discharged from clearing the road from Elk Run to Marrs Bridge.

1761 28 Mar: Book 1 Page 153 Martin Hardin (5-3) vs George Wheatley Judgement for Martin Hardin

1762 27 May: Book 1 Page 244 Martin Hardin (5-3) vs Davis Holder Judgement against Defendant

1762 28 May: Book 1 Page 252 Henry Hardin (3-2) Wife Wilmouth (3-2)'s deed to Nicholas George Lease and release ordered recorded

1762 28 May: Book 1 Page 252 Henry Hardin (3-2) and Wilmouth (3-2) his wife deed to John Neilson ordered to be recorded

1762 24 Jun: Book 1 Page 272 Martin Hardin (5-3) vs Richard Bryant Decided in favor of plaintiff.

1762 25 Jun: Book 1 Page 294 Martin Hardin (5-3) vs James Bashan

1762 23 Jul: Book 1 Page 304 Martin Hardin (5-3) vs Duncan

1762 23 Jul: Book 1 Page 313 Martin Hardin (5-3) vs Markham Beard Parker Luttrell

1762 27 Aug: Book 1 Page 324 Martin Hardin (5-3) vs Begam and Duncan

1762 27 Aug: Book 1 Page 333 Martin Hardin (5-3) vs Burdit Clifson

1762 23 Sep: Book 1 Page 353 Martin Hardin (5-3) vs Daniel Hogarn

1762 23 Sep: Book 1 Page 356 Martin Hardin (5-3) Rodham Tullos

1762 23 Sep: Book 1 Page 366 Martin Hardin (5-3) vs John Duncan Jr

1762 28 Oct: Book 1 Page 371 Martin Hardin (5-3) vs Robert Scott

Court Order Books Volume 2 1763-1764

1763 25 Aug: Book 2 Page 190-191 Martin Hardin (5-3) vs Joshua Tullos, Joseph Bradford, Rodham Tullos, Hugh Snelling, Daniel Hogain, Absolom Ramey, Moses Hayes

1764 26 Nov: Book 2 Page 249 Martin Hardin (5-3) vs Tullos

Court Order Books Volume 3 1764-1768

1766 30 Jul: Book 3 Page 194 Joseph Williams vs Martin Hardin (5-3) Martin Hardin (5-3) to pay Sarah and Lydia Hardin (5-3) 50 pounds of tobacco each for attending court 2 days as witness for him.

1767 24 Nov: Book 3 Page 339 Martin Hardin (5-3) vs John Ariss

1768 24 May: Book 1 Page 368 William Harding (3-9), executor of John Harding, plaintiff against John Pope

1768 29 Jun: William Harding (3-9), executor of George Harding (3-3), plaintiff against William Hammett. Act of limitations pleaded and dismissed.

Will Books

Written 1759, Probated 1760, will of Tillman Weaver mentions use of land bought of Martin Hardin (5-3) and taken up by John Hardin (5-2)

1762 26 Aug: Martin Hardin (5-3) appraised estate of Thomas Seaman

Deed Books

1762 28 May: Book 1 Page 316 Henry Harding (3-2) and Wilmoth Harding (3-2) of Frederick Co., VA deed to John Nelson of Fauquier Co., VA 180 acres, starts at land of William Allen at tree in Fork of Elk Run, along Allan's to Elk Run that divides Harding from John Delashmute's land. To line of Nicholas George.

1762 28 May: Book 1, Page 317 Henry Harding (3-2) and Wilmoth Harding (3-2) deed to Nicholas George of Stafford Co., VA 180 acres land bought of William Allen.

1762 27 May: Book 1 Page 320 Henry Harding (3-2) and Wilmouth Harding (3-2) of Frederick County, VA to Nicholas George of Stafford County for 5 shillings, 180 acres, part of 360 acres purchased by Henry Harding (3-1), father of the said Henry Harding (3-2) from William Allen to whom the same was granted by patent from the proprietor's office 5 March 1718/19, Lease for the term of one year.

1762 28 May: Book 1 Page 321. Henry Harding (3-2) and Wilmouth Harding (3-2) of Frederick Co., VA to Nicholas George of Stafford County, release of land in above deed.

Marriage Records

1759 27 Aug: Book 1 Page 2 Martin Hardin (5-3) and Robert Whickliffe bond for marriage of Robert Whickliffe to Mary Hardin (5-22) spinster.

1785 16 Mar: Book 1 Page 139 Benjamin Hardin (4-9) and Lewis Grigsby bond for the marriage of Benjamin Hardin (4-9) and Nancy Routt (4-9)

1785 18 Mar: Book 1 Page 441 John Monroe certifies he married Benjamin Hardin (4-9) and Nancy Rout 18 March 1785.

1793 04 Jan: Book 1 Page 377 Daniel Shackelford and Benjamin Glover bonds to marriage of Daniel Shackelford (2-57) to Amnah Harden (2-57) January 1793 Hall Harden (2-22) gives permission for marriage.

1795 8 Jan: Book 1 Page 451 Ephraim Abell certifies he married John Daniel and Nancy Hardin (2-62) 8 January 1795.

1795 02 Jan: Book 2 Page 1 John Daniel and George Hardin (2-58) bond for the marriage of John Daniel and Nancy Hardin (2-62). Hall Harden (2-22) grants permission for John Daniel to get license. George Hardin (2-58), brother of Nancy certifies she is over 21.

1797 05 Dec: Book 2 Page 107 Selah and Solomon Shackelford bond for marriage of Selah Shackelford and Frances Harden (2-59). Her father Hall Harden (2-22) gives permission. Witness George Hardin (2-58)

1808 08 Mar: Book 3 Page 69 William Pope and William Harden bond for marriage of William Pope to Susanna Harden (2-60). Hall Harden (2-22) gives permission for the marriage of his daughter.

1815 24 May: Book 3 Page 250 Philip Harding (2-61) and Churchill Shackelford bond for marriage of Philip Harding (2-61) to Frances Pope. Humphrey Pope made oath that Frances Pope is over 21 years of age.

1784 Personal Property Tax Lists

John Hardin (1 over 21) 1 horse

Frederick County, Virginia Records

Formed 1743 from Orange County, Virginia

Will Books

1752 06 Apr: Book 2 Page 53 Will of Thomas Ashby Thomas Ashby of Frederick Co., Virginia. Son Thomas Ashby one shilling. Son Benjamin Ashby land on Goose Creek where Enoch Berry now lives. Son Henry Ashby land where he now lives laid off by James Guin decd. Son Stephen Ashby land on which he now lives after death of his mother. Daughter Elizabeth Hardin (4-2) one shilling sterling. Daughter Sarah Ashby one shilling sterling. Daughter Rose Ashby one shilling sterling. Daughter Ann Ashby one shilling sterling. Cozen Reuben Berry one cow and calf at age 21. Cousin Ann Berry one cow and calf at age 18 or marriage. The land whereon John Hardin (5-2) is now living that is mortgaged. Instructions if payment is not received. To wife Ann Ashby his house he bought of John Ashby. Executors: sons Robert, John, and Henry Ashby. Proved 4 August 1752.

Deed Books

6 Mar: 1744/5 Book 1 Page 197 Thomas Ashby Jr of Frederick County, VA deed of gift to his loving brother John Ashby of same county 50 acres in the same county Part of a parcel "purchased by me of Thomas Branson Sr. Witnesses John Hardin (5-2), John Stone, Thomas Doftgate.

4 Aug: 1747 Book 1 Page 311 Indenture. Between Richard Murrah of Frederick Co., Virginia and Thomas Ashby of same, Term of six years five months to serve in such service or Employment as the said Thomas Ashby or his Assigns shall Employ him. Ashby to provide clothing. Witnesses Thomas Hooper, Sam Hooper.

15 Nov 1749 Book 2 Page 47 John Hardin (5-2) of Frederick County, Virginia to Thomas Ashbey of same county. Mortgage. John Hardin (5-2) received 84 Pounds from Thomas Ashby for Mortgage on 84 acres of land purchased from Jacob Pennington on which John Hardin (5-2) now lives. Condition that the said John Hardin (5-2) will pay 84 Pounds with interest two years from the date of this indenture.

6 Dec: 1749 Book 2 Page 80 Jeremiah Cloud of Frederick Co., VA to Henry Hardin (3-2) of same. Lease for term of Ten Years at 500 pounds tobacco per year. Adjoins Jeremiah Cloud's plantation. Witnesses Marquis Calmes, Reuben Paxson, Thomas Wood. Filed 13 February 1749/50

4 Apr: 1758 Book 4 Page 316 John Harrold of Frederick Co to George Hardin (3-4) of Frederick Co. 130 acres south side of Shenando River Term of one year,

20 Aug: 1761 Book 6 Page 423 Mathusalem Evans of Frederick Co to Henry Hardin (3-2) of same county Lease land on Shenando River 2000 acres.

3 Mar: 1783 Book 19 Page 390 George Dromgoole and Margaret Elizabeth his wife of Winchester Frederick County VA to George Hardin (3-4) of same, ½ acre in town of Winchester Lot 161. Lease term one year

1 Nov: 1783 Book 20 Page 140 George Hardin (3-4) of Winchester, Frederick Co to Philip Bower of same, half of Lot 161 in Winchester Land purchased from George Drumgoole 3 and 4 May 1783

Court Order Book 1 1743-1745

1743 10 Mar: Book 1 Page 55 Henry Hardin (3-2) vs Willm Hurst Dismissed
1743 10 Mar: Book 1 Page 55 Samuel Earle vs John Hardin (5-2)) Continued
1743 10 Mar: Book 1 Page 55 John Hardin (5-2) vs Samuel Earle Continued
1743 10 Mar: Book 1 Page 55 William Reugh vs John Hardin (5-2) Continued
Page 80 Bounds vs Hardin
Page 107 Peugh vs Hardin agreed
Page 123 Walsh vs Hardin dismissed
13 Jul: 1744 Book 1 Page 134 John Hardin (5-2) vs Christopher Hersey Dismissed
John Hardin vs Earle 1 175
Earle vs John Hardin 1 175
Earle vs John Hardin 1 469
John Hardin vs Peck order 1 215
Hardin vs Stuart 251 in 250s
Hardin vs Walson 250s
John Hardin vs W Gartin 256
Hardin vs Davis 259
Hardin vs Wilford 27-
Hardin vs Oneal 314
John Hardin vs Christoper Gibson 329
John Hardin vs six people 339
Henry Hardin vs Christopher Marr 360
John Hardin vs Gibson 362
Hardin vs Hammon 373
Hardin vs Bounds 390
Hardin vs Cain agreed 419

Stites vs Hardin 1 429 judgement
Hardin vs Hamman 433
Hardin vs 439, 442
Bealy vs Hardin 478
Hardin vs 466 468 471

Court Order Book 2 1745-1748

Court Order Book 3 1748-1749

Court Order Book 4 1750-1753

Court Order Book 5 1753-1754

1753 05 Sep: Book 5 Page 162 John Hardin (5-2) to Thomas Ashby redevise of mortgage. A receipt and redevise on the back of a mortgage from John Hardin to Thomas Ashby being proved by the oath of Gabriel Hones a witness therein is admitted to record.

1754 05 Feb: Book 5 Page 300 Ordered the Church Wardens of Frederick Parish Bind Reuben Berry and Ann Berry two Bastard Children to Rose Ashby according to law.

1754 05 Mar: Book 5 Page 325 Robert Ashby vs Mark Hardin (5-4) In Case. This Case being agreed is ordered to be dismissed.

1754 06 Mar: Book 5 Page 326 Robert Ashby vs Mark Hardin (5-4) In Trespass assault etc. This case being agreed is ordered to be dismissed.

Court Order Book 6 1754-1755

1754 06 Jun: Book 6 Page 18 John Ashby in open court made oath that he has attended five days as witness for Peter Rout at the suit of Henry Brinker ordered Peter pay him 125 pounds of tobacco.

1754 05 Sep: Book 6 Page 70 John Ashby attended five days as witness for Mark Hardin (5-4) against John Hardin (5-2), ordered to be paid 120 pounds of tobacco.

Court Order Book 7 1755-1758

1757 06 Apr: Book 7 Page 229 Elizabeth Hardin (5-4) vs Mark Hardin (5-4), on attachment. John Hardin (5-2) a garnishee in this cause being sworn declared that he had in his hands before the attachment was served

Twenty Pounds Six sheep and Six shoats that he had assets to pay the debts due from the dft to Mr. Knox and others more than the value of what in his hands. Ordered that the garnishee be discharged, and nothing being attached whereon to found a judgment the Suit is dismissed.

Court Order Book 8 1758-1760

1759 09 Aug: Book 8 Page 303 Elizabeth Hardin (5-4) vs John Hardin (5-2) The witnesses being sworn and the arguments of the Parties heard and considered by the Court Ordered that the suit be dismissed and that the 0Dft pay Cost.

1759 09 Aug: Book 8 Page 303 Ordered that Elizabeth Hardin (5-4) pay to James Catlet Five Hundred and Twenty-five pounds of Tobacco for attending Twenty-one days a witness for her agst John Hardin (5-2) on petition.

Court Order Book 9 1760-1762

1760 09 May: Book 9 Page 51 John Hardin (5-2) vs William Shepherd Debt

1760 03 Jun: Book 9 Page 55 Nimrod Ashby v Barnaby Nowland

1760 14 May: Book 9 Page 59 Thomas Ashby and wife Betty to Thomas Cooper Deed Acknowledged

1760 06 Aug: Book 9 Page 103 Robert Ashby vs Mark Hardin (5-4) for trespass and Battery Discontinued two cases

1760 03 Sep: Book 9 Page 143 John Hardin (5-2) vs Daniel Purcell Settled

1760 03 Dec: Book 9 Page 224 John Hardin (5-2) vs James Irwin Debt

1760 04 Dec: Book 9 Page 237 Henry Hardin (3-2) vs James McKay Case settled and dismissed

1762 05 Mar: Book 9 Page 413 William Gant pay David Ashby 50 pounds tobacco for giving evidence against Benjamin Berry

Personal Property Tax Lists

1782 Personal Property Tax Lists
Thrustons List: Robert Ashby 1 over 21 6 slaves 4 horse 4 cows
Dowdalls List: George Hardin (3-4) 1 over 21 1 slave 2 horse 1 cow
Williams List Thomas Bennett 1 over 21 1 horse
Williams List Nathl Ashby 1 over 21 4 slave 3 horse 11 cows
Williams List: John Ashby 0 over 21 5 slave 5 horse 37 cows
Williams List Henry Ashby 1 over 21 8 slave 2 horse 9 cow
Williams List George Ashby 1 over 21 2 slave 1 horse 3 cow

Williams List Lucy Calmes 0 over 21 12 slave 6 horse 30 cow
Nobles List: Thomas Ashby 1 over 21 2 horse 4 cow
Nobles List David Ashby 1 over 21 2 slave 3 horse 10 cow
Nobles List: Marquis Calmes 1 over 21 6 slave 9 horse 25 cow

1783 Personal Property Tax Lists
McGuires List: George Hardin (3-4) 1 over 21 1 horse 1 cow

Halifax County, Virginia Records

Formed 1752 from Lunenburg County

Will and Probate Records

1768 19 Apr: Book O Page 254 Inventory and sale list of the estate of George Hardin (3-3). One purchaser was William Harding (3-9), who bought a lot of items. Sale list received and ordered recorded 16 March 1769.

1771 15 Aug: Book O Page 334 The estate of George Harding (3-3) Dec. To pay the Sheriff of Halifax To Cash paid Francis Bunbury for George Harding's coffin. To Larkin Cason in part of his ag the admr. By Balance in the hands of the Admr as settled Sept 18 1769 agreeable to the annexed Total 26 Pounds. In obedience to an order of the worshipful court Halifax County we have settled William Harding (3-9)'s account current of his administration of George Harding (3-3)'s Estate agreeable to the above certified under our hands this 17th of July (no year). At court 15 August 1771 This account current was returned and ordered to be recorded.

Deed Records

1762 20 May: Book 3 Page 320 William Byrd of Charles City County to Henry Hardin (5-5) of Halifax County. For 7 pounds 10 shillings, land on Winns Creek 1000 acres

1764 06 Apr: Book 5 Page 133 Henry Hardin (5-5) of Halifax County to Richard Brooks of Lunenburg County 250 acres on Wynn's Creek

Hampshire County, Virginia Records

Formed 1754 from Frederick and Augusta Counties

Land Tax Lists

1782 Land Tax Lists
Mark Hardin (5-13) 126 acres

Personal Property Tax Lists

1782 Personal Property Tax List
Page 3 Mark Hardin (5-13) (1 over 21) 0 slaves 6 Horses 13 cattle
Page 25 Ennis Harding (4-7) (1 over 21) 0 slaves 4 horses 2 cattle
Page 25 Evangelist Harding (4-6) (1 over 21) 0 slaves 5 horses 7 cattle Listed after Peter, Henry, Thomas, and Stephen Ashby, Listed before Mordecai Batson Sr and Jr

1783 Personal Property Tax List
Page 4 Evangelist Harding (4-6) (2 over 21 1 under 21) Slaves 12 horse 17 cattle Listed near Mordecai Batson
Page 29 John Hardin (5-56) (1 over 21) 1 cattle
Page 29 Mark Hardin (5-13) (1 over 21, 1 over 16) 8 horse 15 cattle

1784 Personal Property Tax List
Page 5 Evangelist Harding (4-6) (1 over 21 1 over 16) 4 horse 13 cattle Next to Peter, Jesse, and Henry Ashby
Page 11 Mark Hardin (5-13) (1 over 21 2 over 16) 5 horses 12 cattle Next to John And Henry Stalcup
Page 12 John Hardin (5-56) (1 over 21) no animals or slaves

1785 Personal Property Tax List
Page 11 Vingalist Harden (4-6) (1 over 21 1 over 16) 6 horses 11 cattle
Page 11 (next line) Ennis Harding (4-7) (1 over 21) 4 horse 1 cattle Henry, Peter and Jesse Ashby on next lines.
Page 16 Mark Hardin (5-13) (one over 21 2 under 21) 5 horse 17 cattle

1786 Personal Property Tax List
Page 26 Mark Hardin (5-13) (1 over 21 1 over 16) 4 horse 18 cattle

1787 Personal Property Tax List
Page 9 Mark Hardin (5-13) (1 over 21 1 under 21) 6 horse 10 cattle

1788 Personal Property Tax List
Page 9 Mark Hardin (5-13) (3 over 16) 6 cattle

Deed Books

Virginia County Records

1762 09 Nov: Book 1 Page 145 Benjamin Rutherford of Frederick Co., VA to John Hardin (5-2) of same Lease 5 shillings Leased On the Drain of Pattersons Creek in Hampshire Co VA Start at land of James McCracken Decd Land granted to Benjamin Rutherford by Thomas Lord Fairfax 21 January 1762 Total of 83 acres One year lease No Witnesses

1762 09 Nov: Book 1 Page 146 Benja Rutherford to John Hardin (5-2) Release of property to him. No witnesses

1767 08 Apr: Book 2 Page 11 and 12 Enoch Innis from Gabriel Cox Lease Both of Hampshire County VA land on north branch of Patomac River 162 acres granted to Gabriel Cox 4 Jan 1764

1767 08 Aug: Book 2 Page 50 Thomas Lord Fairfax to Benjamin Rutherford late of County of Hampshire but now of Frederick Co, Number 4 tract on Pattison's Creek Manor 520 acres. Term during the natural lives of Benjamin Rutherford, Robert Rutherford Jr, James Rutherford. Witnesses Ga Jones, Pet Hog, Enoch Innis, Edward McGiver

1767 Book 2 page 57 James Livingston of Frederick Co MD to Enoch Innis, merchant of Hampshire Co VA power of atty to purchase and sell land in Virginia and Pennsylvania.

1768 02 Mar: Book 2 Page 51 Benjamin Rutherford, Robert Worthington, Margaret McEachern of Frederick Co., VA to John Hardin (5-2) of Hampshire Co VA Lease land on Pattison's Creek 201 acres, another parcel on Patterson's Creek 306 acres Term One Year Witnesses: Jas Keith, Enoch Innis, Richd Hougland, Job Pearsall.

1768 02 Mar: Book 2 Page 52 Benjamin Rutherford to John Hardin (5-2) Release of land Witnesses Jas Keith, Enoch Innis, Richd Hougland, Job Pearsall

1769 06 Feb: Book 2 Page 119 Benjamin Rutherford, Robert Worthington, Jane McCracken, Margaret McCracken of Frederick Co VA to John Hardin (5-2) of Hampshire County Land on Pattersons Creek Lot 17 201 acres. Term One Year. Witnesses Jas Keith, Edward McGuiver, Alexr White, Pat Hog

1769 06 Feb: Page 120 Rutherford to John Hardin (5-2) Release

1771 Book 2 Page 232 John Lewis to Thomas Lewis John Lewis bought three tracts of land from Samuell Pritchard 223 ¼ acres Deeds weren't acknowledged but he wants them acknowledged to his son Thomas Lewis.

1771 09 Mar: Book 2 Page 228 John Hardin (5-2) to Thomas Fairly of York Co., Pennsylvania Lease 83 acres + 106 acres originally Benjamin Rutherfords. Term One Year

1771 09 Mar: Book 2 Page 229 John Hardin (5-2) to Thomas Fairly Release

Harding Families of the Northern Neck of Virginia

1773 08 Mar: Book 3 Page 141 John Hardin (5-2) Sr of Bedford Co., PA to Mark Hardin (5-13) of Hampshire County, Virginia Lease 125 acres originally owned by Benjamin Rutherford, transferred to John Hardin (5-2) 7 February 1769

1773 08 Mar: Book 3 Page 142 Mark Hardin (5-13) from John Hardin (5-2) Sr Release

1773 06 Oct: Book 4 Page 23 John Hardin (5-2) of Westmoreland County PA to William Blackburn Lease of Hampshire County VA 127 acres

1773 Book 4 Page 24 John Hardin (5-2) to W Blackburn Release

1774 03 Mar: Book 4 Page 25 John Hardin (5-2) to William Blackburn Lease 100 acres in Hampshire Co, VA surveyed for John Hardin 121 May 1763

1773 Book 4 Page 26 John Hardin (5-2) to W Blackburn Release

1774 Book 4 Page 29 Lohn Lewis from Simon Doyle Lease

1774 Book 4 Page 57 John Lewis to Samuel Doyle Mortgage

1778 10 Nov: Book 4 Page 258 Enoch Innis of Hampshire Co VA to Michael Heaton of Washington County MD Lease land on North Branch of Potomac 162 acres granted to Gabriel Cox. Another tract adjoining this one, 128 acres. Term of lease one year. 128 acres granted to Enoch Innis from Lord Fairfax dated 5 June 1765 registered in Book M Page 386

1778 10 Nov: Book 4 Page 259 Enoch Innis to Michael Heaton Release

1779 Book 5 Page 40 John Lewis to William Jackson Deed

1779 Book 5 Page 82 John Lewis land for Mill Valuation

1780 09 May: Book 5 Page 108 John Hardin (5-2) and Catherine his wife of Monongala Co. VA to Joseph House of Hampshire Co VA Lease 211 acres

1780 Book 5 Page 109 John Hardin (5-2) to Joseph House Lease Release

1782 Book 6 Page 42 John Lewis to William Barber Lewis Power of atty, both of Hampshire Co VA. Witness Samuel Lewis.

1782 Book 6 Page 57 Power of Atty John Lewis of Hampshire Co to William Harding (1-32) of Northumberland Co to collect sums of money tobacco slaves or lands that are his just right and due

1780 Book 6 Page 72 John Lewis from Joseph Colville Vance Deed

1785 Book 7 Page 52 Deed John Lewis to George Hammas?

1790 Book 8 Page 32 John Lewis to Adam Hinds Lease

1790 Book 8 Page 37 John Lewis to William B Lewis POA

1789 17 Aug: Book 9 Page 22 Mark Hardin (5-13) and Ann his wife of Hampshire County to Jacob Brookhart of same. Land on Pattison Creek Lott #18 126 acres granted by deed from the proprietors of the Northern Neck of Virginia to Benjamin Rutherford, Robert Worthington, Jane McCracken, and Margaret McCracken 22 Oct: 1766 306 acres conveyed to John Hardin 7 Feb 1769 then conveyed to Mark Hardin 9 March 1773

1801 Book 12 Page 442 John Lewis from William Cornell and wife

1803 Book 13 Page 369 John Lewis (John) to William Cowan Deed

1809 Book 16 Page 364 John Lewis from Abraham Weaver Deed

1810 Book 16 Page 362 John Lewis and wf to Abraham Weaver Deed

1807 Book 14 Page 397 Henry Hardin to Adam Hidden Power of atty

1821 Book 22 Page 274 Henry Harden Trustee to Ephraim Dunn

Will Books

1774 09 May: Misc Wills #380 Will of Henry Lewis of Hampshire County, Virginia. To wife Mary one-third of Plantation Profits. Son Henry Lewis 20 Pounds current money paid by his three brothers Samuel, Evan and John Lewis, when John comes to the age of 21. To son Samuel Lewis half of a survey of land in Frederick Co VA 200 acres on Sleysy Creek. To son Evan Lower half of same survey. Daughter Sidney Rees, Daughter Ellinor Cook. Daughter Elizabeth Lewis. Son John Lewis the Plantation I live on. Executors: wife Mary and son Samuel. Proved 14 November 1775

1780 01 Mar: Book 2, Page 1 Enoch Innis, Sheriff of County of Hampshire, Bond. Innis is appointed to collect taxes for the county.

1780 10 May: Book 2, Page 12 Enoch Innis bound to collect taxes due in Hampshire County.

1778 10 Feb: Book 2 Page 60 Will of Enoch Innis Jr. of Hampshire County VA. Order that "all his lands in Virginia and a lot which I hold in the addition to George Town in Maryland, also all the Negro's and all personal estate be sold to pay debts and expenses." To Loving wife Sarah. Mentions Mother and Father still living. To brother James Innis two of my best Suits and Cloathes. 5 Pounds to each of my sisters. Executor his loving wife, which gives her full power to convey as well lands and lot which Major James Livingston empowered him to purchase. Will was Proved 12 August 1783

1783 10 Sep: Book 2 Page 84 Inventory of estate of Enoch Innis Gent, late of Hampshire County

1783 08 Oct: Book 2 Page 85 Enoch Innis Estate Sale list filed by Sarah Innis Executor.

From Find A Grave Index

From Find A Grave Index:

Enoch Innis born 1735 King George Co., VA, died 1783 Hampshire Co., VA, Buried Oldtown Cemetery, Oldtown, Allegany Co., MD. Unmarked Grave

Wife Sarah Cresap, d/o Thomas CRESAP & Hannah Johnson b. 21 August 1740 in Frederick Co. MD. (Maryland, Births and Christenings Index, 1662-1911) Miss Sarah Cresap 1st m. Enoch Innis Jr. Mrs. Sarah Innis (widow) m. 2nd to the Rev. John Foster December 20, 1783. Died unknown date Pike Co., Ohio, buried Foster Cemetery.

Lancaster County, Virginia Records

Formed 1651 from Northumberland and York Counties

Deed Book

1670 19 Dec: William Hardin of Rappahannock County, Power of attorney to Henry Hartloe to collect debts.

Will Book

1698/9 12 Jan: Will Book 10 Page 169 Inventory of Thomas Hardin presented

Court Order Books

1653, Thomas and Martha Harding were witnesses

1653, Thomas Harding was a witness twice

1655, Thomas Harding was a witness, and was owed 800 lbs tobacco

1663, Thomas Harding was owed 394 lbs tobacco

Court Order Book

1669/70 26 Jan: Certificate John Chym for Transport of Will Harding

Order Book 8 1729-1743

1732 11 May: Page 57 Ordered that Thomas Chetwood be forwarded to the next court to answer the --- of Peter Hardin.

1732 14 Jun: Page 60 In the suit between Peter Hardin and Thomas Chetwood defendant by petition for --- the parties being heard, Judgment is that Chetwood owes 10 bushels of Indian corn to Peter Hardin.

1734/5 12 Feb: Page 119 Margaret Denny says William Denny died with no will and is granted administration of his estate.

1734/5 12 Mar: Page 121 Inventory presented by Margaret Denny.

1735 02 Nov: Page 132 Hannah Denny (2-4) came into court and made oath that Edmond Denny (2-4) late of this county Decd. departed this life without making any will as far as she knows or believes and on her motion and giving security for her just and faithful administration of the said decd., Estate certificate is granted her for obtaining letters of administration thereof in due form.

1735 02 Nov: Page 132 Benjamin George Jr., William Hadon, Thomas Haydon, and Clement Lattimer to take inventory of Edmond Denny (2-4) decd.

1735/6 11 Feb: Page 135 Inventory returned and recorded on Hannah Denny (2-4) oath.

1737 09 Sep: Page 181 John Harding vs William Crane, judgment for plaintiff for 3 pounds money and 350 pounds of tobacco. Seven shillings six pence for lawyer's fee.

Loudoun County, Virginia Harding Records

Formed 1757 from Fairfax County

Personal Property Tax Lists (SLC 975.528 R4h)

William Harding 1749
July 30 1758 Henry Taylor
1759 Thomas Lewis on Difficult, John Lewis Thomas Lewis Jr.
1759 Richard Vallandigham
1760 John Hardin (difficult to read)
1760 William Winns
1760 Edward Harden 1760, 1761, 1762
Notley Williams 1760
William Williams 1760, 1764, 1765, 1767, 1768
Joseph Harden (4-21) 1765, 1772, 1773,1774, 1775
1774 John Lewis, Joel Lewis

Charles Harding 1783
Thomas Harding 1783

Marriage Records 1751-1880

1803 27 Sep: Pressley Harden (4-83) married Sarah Sears (4-83)

1807 18 Mar: Lewis Harden (4-84) married Edy Thatcher (4-84)

1810 23 May: John H Harding married Darcus S. Davis (from Maryland)

1832 13 Sep: Elizabeth Harden married William Smallwood

1834 20 May: Rachel Harding married Sampson Hutchison (granddaughter of Job Harding)

1835 07 May: Harriet Harding married Dr. Francis W. Powell at the house of her father John I Harding Leesburg VA (from Maryland)

1852 29 May: Lewis B Harden (4-165) married Patsy Garrison. Albert Harden present

1852 02 Sep: Sarah Jane Harding married John W. Gover

1852 19 Oct: John R. Harden (4-160) married Ann Amanda Wortman. Isaac Wortman proved ages.

1852 26 Dec: Martha F. Harden (4-164) married Cornelius B. Wyncoop. Henry Harden proved ages.

1856 24 Dec: Frances Anne Harding, 15, daughter of Thomas I and Susan (Latham) Harding, of Fauquier, married Alexander Pierson, 25, Fauquier, son of Whittington and Frances Ann (Jordan) Pierson.

1857 10 Mar: Mary E. D. Harding, 16, daughter of Albert and Ann E. Harding, married P. S. Beach, 25, son of John and Priscilla Beach.

1866 24 Jul: Samuel D. Harding married Sallie Jenkins

1872 16 May: Harry C. Harding married Nettie B. Meyers

1877 03 May: Luther F Harding married Martha Dosson

Will Books

1770 29 Mar: Book A Page 318 Probated 12 August 1771 Will of Henry Taylor mentions wife Susannah, sons Walter, Joshua and Henry Taylor, sons-in-law William Cotton, William Williams, Thomas Harden (1-23), 5 shillings, and Notley Williams. Executor is wife and youngest son John Taylor.

1780 09 Oct: Estate of William Musgrave, debts paid by George Taylor, Henry Taylor and Joseph Harding (4-21).

1788 On 23 Apr: Will of Thomas Green mentions his son-in-law Elihu Harden

1793 Jul: Elihu Harden witnessed the will of James Mahue

1796 14 Sep: Book E Page 133 Appraisal of estate of Charles Harden, deceased. Value 562 Pounds 10 shillings 7 pence

1805 21 Dec: Probated 15 Apr 1806 Book G Page 470 Will of Joseph Harding (4-21) mentions wife Elizabeth, sons William Harding (4-82), Pressley Harding (4-83), Lewis Harding (4-84) and Henry Harding (4-85), to sons 1000 acres of land on the Rolling Fork, state of Kentucky, located by James McCullock, to equally divided among them subject to dower. Daughter Frances Harding (4-86). Wife Elizabeth to be executor. Witnesses, Simon Triplett, Silas Rose, Martha Triplett.

1808 14 Nov: Book H Page 290 Estate accounting of Charles Harding filed. The Estate of Charles Hardin in acct with Garrison Loy who is intermarried with Hannah Harding his (widow).

1819 09 Feb: Book N Page 86 On motion of Sanford Ramey Guardian of Ann A. Harding one of the legatees of John A Binns decd ordered that James Moore Asa Moore Thomas Philips and Alexander Cordell or any three of them appointed commissioner to examine the guardianship account of said Ramey agt his said Ward and make report thereof to the court.

1824 13 Dec: Book P Page 204 Inventory of William Harding (4-82) filed. Administrator Stephen Garrett.

1827 08 Jan: Book R Page 155, administration account of William Harden (4-82) filed with court.

1830 12 Aug: Book T Page 22. Will of Elizabeth Harden (4-21) written. Gives her son Henry Harden (4-85) all her lands, it being the half of a tract of land purchased by myself and my Son William Harden (4-82) of Mary Taylor. Son Henry Harden (4-85) executor. Proved 11 Oct: 1830.

1832 11 Jun: Book U Page 97 Administration account of William Harden (4-82) filed with court.

1835 11 May: Book W Page 159 Administration account of William Harden (4-82) Filed with court. Mentions payments to Henry Harden (4-85) for difference allotted him for negroes and for one half of two and three/quarters acres of land in Swarts field.

1837 09 May: Book X Page 299 Administration account of William Harden (4-82). Among items: Cash paid Margaret Harding (4-85) adm of Harding decd (4-85) and expense of division of land and slaves. Distribution of estate to

Elizabeth Harden (4-82), widow, one third, to William Harden (4-132), to Joseph Garrett, and to Robert Rose, guardian of Sarah Ann Harden (4-134).

1838 09 Apr: Book Y Page 142 Undated will of Thomas Harden Sr of Loudoun County, Virginia. Leaves everything to his wife Mary. Filed 9 April 1838

1842 14 Jun: Book AA Page 306 Inventory of the estate of Elizabeth Hardin (4-82) ordered by court. Inventory dated 8 September 1842, filed with court 14 February 1843.

Court Order Books

Order Book A 1757-1762

Page 184 Edward Harding vs Bolding
Page 186 Edward Harding vs. Ambury
Page 246 John Hardin Gent vs Davis
Page 308 Edward Hardin vs Galachan
Page 319 Edward Hardin vs Galachan
Page 435 Edward Hardin vs Gladon
Page 647 John Hardin Gent vs Davis

Order Book B 1762-1765

Page 14, 27 Hardin vs Claphan
Page 371 Hardin vs Herryford

Order Book C 1765-1767

1767 13 Aug: Page 304 John Hardin vs John Davis Claim affirmed

Order Book E 1770-1773

Page 391 Edward Harding to Henry McCabe Lease and release

Order Book F 1773-1776

1773 16 Jun: Page 104 Harding to McCabe Indentures approved (Edward Harding)

1774 10 Oct Page 504 Ordered that the following hands work on the road whereof Isaac SANDERS is appointed Surveyor to wit: Apollas COPPER's hands, Ann WILLIAMS, John SIMMS, Bernard SIMMS, John SIMMS Junr, Joseph McGEE, Francis TRIPLETT, Reuben TRIPLETT, John CHAMBERLAIN, Ferdinando ONEALE, CHELTON's Quarter, Sarah SANDERS, Simon TRIPLETT's, William SMITH, John ONEALE, Alexander McMULLIN, John

LUKE, John VANHORN, Andrew BURNSIDE, Thomas THOMPSON, Valentine CORNGIVER, Thomas HUNT, Michael GAHAGAN, Joseph HARDING (alias COMBS) (4-21), John McWICKER, William McNABB.

Loudoun County Road Orders (no date) Joseph Hardin alias Combs appears.

Order Book G 1776-1783

5 Jun: 1780 Page 251 Ordered that the Churchwarden of Shelburne Parish bind Thomas Hardin a base born child of Catherine Hardin to William Hutchison.

Order Book H 1783-1785

1784 10 May page 273 Peter BOWER against Joseph COMBS & Joseph HARDIN (4-21) – in debt – Nathaniel WEEDON came into Court and undertook for the Defendant that if convicted he shall pay the condemnation or surrender his body to prison or WEEDON would do it for him

1784 12 May: Page 289 Ordered that James McKinny pay unto Joseph Hardin (4-21) fifty pounds of Tobacco according to Law for attending court two days as a Witness for him at the suit of Jacob Moore. James McKinny lost the case.

Order Book I 1785-1786

8 Aug 1785 Page 5 Catherine Combs Adm. Exe. of John Combs deceased, plaintiff vs. Benjamin Ethell & Joseph HARDEN (4-21) , defendants...motion upon a replevy bond...this day came the plaintiff, and the defendants having legal notice of this motion were solemnly called but came not. It is therefore considered by the court that the plaintiff recover against them twelve pounds nineteen shillings and ten pence current money and her costs by her in this behalf expended, and the said defendants in mercy, etc...But this judgement is to be discharged by the payment of six pounds nine shillings and eleven pence like money (include debt and costs) with interest thereon, to be computed after the rate of 5 per cent per annum from the 22nd of July 1784, till paid, and her costs.

1786 10 May: Page 228 Ordered that Joseph Cummings pay unto Joseph Hardin (4-21) Fifty Pounds of Tobacco according to law for attending court two days so a Witness for John Walker an infant against him the suit being continued at his Coste.

1786 13 Aug: Page 298 Ordered that John Walker pay unto Joseph Hardin (4-21) Eight Hundred Pounds of tobacco according to law for attending court thirty-two days as a Witness for him against Joseph Cummings.

1786 09 Oct: Page 345 Deed of mortgage from Charles Harden to Joseph Gardner and John Davis was acknowledged by the said Charles and ordered to be recorded.

Order Book K 1787-1788

1788 12 Mar: Page 370 Anthony Harden (2-25) vs Richard Gowin and Harper. Plaintiff Harden to recover money.

Order Book L 1788-1790

1789 11 Jun: Page 219 Edward Harden vs Henry Lowe. Judgement for Plaintiff

1790 10 Mar: Page 375 Ennis Harden (4-7) vs Joseph Combs and Daniel Tuagan. Plaintiff won.

Order Book N 1790-1791

1791 16 Feb Page 89 Joseph Hardin (4-21) appointed overseer of the road.

1791 P 17 Mar: age 140 Joseph Hardin (4-21) vs Travis Wrenn Plaintiff recovers.

Order Book P 1792-1794

1794 16 Apr: Page 399 Joseph Harden (4-21) vs Robert Sears, depositions

Order Book Q 1794-1796

1794 10 Sep: Page 23 Joseph Harding (4-21) vs Robert Sears, judgement for plaintiff.

1794 08 Dec: Page 60 Hannah Harding bond to get letters of administration for Charles Harding, deceased.

1795 14 Sep: Page 238 Inventory of Charles Harding deceased was returned and filed.

1795 15 Sep: Pages 252 Joseph Harding (4-21) vs Robert Sears Agreed on having several people make the judgement.

1795 19 Oct: Page 273 Joseph Harding (4-21) vs Robert Sears Case continued.

1796 09 Feb: Page 335 Case of Joseph Harding (4-21) vs Robert Sears dismissed

09 Aug: 1796 Page 454 William Gregg pay Jos Harding (4-21) for attendance as a witness. (Might be Job Harding)

Order Book 7 1813-1815

Book 7 Page 14 Harding's adm vs Woodford

Book 7 Page 39 Harding vs Sheppard

Minute Book 1 1815-1817

1815 09 Oct: Book 1 Page 52 John J Harding vs Samuel Noland

1815 10 Oct: Book 1 Page 57 John J Harding vs Noland

1816 12 Mar: Book 1 Page 119 John J Harding vs Dade P. Noland

1816 13 May: Book 1 Page 143 John Harding vs Walter Bozzall

1816 09 Dec: Book 1 Page 274 Francis Warder vs William Harding (4-82) Notice proved and judgement for.

1816 09 Dec: Book 1 Page 274 John J Harding vs Clemmons. Wildman, Hixon Notices provided

Minute Book 2 1817-1819

1818 10 Nov: Book 2 Page 276 John J Harding & Others vs Shepherd's Admin Agreed

1818 12 Nov: Book 2 Page 285 John J Harding Overseer of the Poor vs Watson continued

1819 11 Jan: Book 2 Page 318 Harding vs Taylor Notice proved and continued to tomorrow

1819 12 Jan: Book 2 Page 321 John J Harding vs Ann Taylor & Jesse Gover Several cases noted but no action.

1819 9 Feb: Book 2 Page 341 Committee appointed to examine the guardianship account of Sanford Remy guardian of Ann A Harding and report back.

1819 11 Feb: Book 2 Page 350 William Harding (4-82) vs Geo Nusan's Executor continued

1819 10 May: Book 2 Page 419 Guardian Account of A B Harding with Sanford Remy her guardian. Guardian acct recorded.

Minute Book 3, 4, 5, 6, 7 1819-1826

No Index

Minute Book 8 1826-1828

1826 15 Nov: Book 8 Page 21 John J Harding vs Jacob Waltman

1827 08 Jan: Book 8 Page 55 Stephen Garrett adm of William Hardin (4-82) decd. Edmund Tyler and Jesse McVeigh to settle estate

1827 15 Feb: Book 8 Page 96 Elizabeth Harden (4-82) to Townshend McVeigh for benefit of Thomas Biscoe, Deed of Trust on a slave and personal property Proved 12 Sept 1825 by Seth and Jesse McVeigh and on 6 March 1827 fully proved by Robert Rose to be recorded.

1827 15 Mar: Book 8 Page 129 John J Harding President of Board of Overseers of the poor. Deliver bond to Cyrus Burson for care of an illegitimate child.

1827 16 Mar: Book 8 Page 135 Harding vs Waltman Continued

1827 14 May: Book 8 Page 163 Elizabeth Harding (4-82) ordered her Negroes James and Ann be excepted from tax

1827 15 Jun: Book 8 Page 215 Harding vs Waltman Issue waived and judgement

1827 09 Jul: Book 8 Page 226 Harding vs Lovett Judgement

1827 09 Jul: Book 8 Page 226 Harding vs Daine

1828 04 Jan: Book 8 Page 383 Elizabeth Hardin (4-82) to E Tyler in Trust for Stephen Garrett on all her interest in undivided tract in Loudoun County purchased by said Elisabeth Harden and William Hardin and of Mary Taylor received 21 Oct 1827 and proved is admitted record.

Minute Book 1a 1829-1830

1829 10 Aug: Book 1a Page 76 William Hardin (4-82) estate account by Stephen Garrett continued

1829 11 Aug: Book 1a Page 85 Elizabeth Hardin (4-82) vs William Hardin, Elizth Harden, Sarah Jane Harden infants under the age of twenty-one years. Charles Eskridge appointed Guardian for the defendants to defend them.

1829 11 Aug: Book 1a Page 86 Elizabeth Hardin (4-82)) vs William Hardin etc. Case coming to be heard by consent. Joseph Hawkins, William Gulick and Stephen Garrett to divide in two square parts the tract of land in the bill and proceedings mentioned allotting one moiety to plaintiff and the other to the defendants.

1829 12 Sep: Book 1a Page 133 William Harden's (4-82) estate account received and recorded

1830 12 Jul: Book 1a Page 399 Catherine Harding to Alfred Belt deed received and ordered to be recorded

1830 11 Oct: Book 1a Page 470 Elizabeth Harden (4-82) last will presented and certified. On motion of Henry Harding (4-85), executor therein named present security bond.

1830 12 Oct: Book 1a Page 474 Henry Harding (4-85) vs Lewis Harding (4-84). The defendants Lewis (4-84) and Presley Harden (4-83) are not residents of the commonwealth it is ordered that publication be made against the said absent defendants according to law.

1830 12 Oct: Book 1a Page 474 Henry Harding (4-85) vs Lewis Harding (4-84). Split land one moiety to Henry Harding and the other to the defendants.

Minute Book 1 1830-1832

1832 9 Jan: Book 1 Page 359 Stephen Garrett admr of William Harden (4-82) decd ordered Jesse McVeigh Edmund Tyler and Amos Gulick to settle the amount of the administration.

Minute Book 4 1834-1836

1834 10 Mar: Book 4 Page 67 On motion of Stephen Garrett admin of William Harden (4-82) decd ordered John Moore, John Ish, and Edmund Tyler or any two of them being first qualified according to Law do make and settle the account of his administration beginning where the last settlement ended and make report to the court.

1835 08 Jun: Book 4 Page 211 An administration account on the estate of William Harding (4-82) decd having been heretofore recd and the same is ordered to be recorded.

1835 14 Sep: Book 4 Page 285 On the motion of Margaret Harding (4-85), widow of Henry Harding (4-85) decd who made oath and together with Joseph S Harding (4-135) William M Harding Joseph Combs and Sander Elgin his securities entered into and acknowledged a bond in the amount of one thousand dollars conditioned according to Law. Certificate is granted for letters of administration of the estate of the said Henry Harding decd.

1835 13 Oct: Book 4 Page 308 Margaret Harden (4-85) is appointed Guardian to Maria Harden (4-157), Mildred Harden (4-158), Robert Henry Harden (4-159), Elizabeth Ellen Harden (4-161), Eliza Jane Harden (4-162), John Ramey Harden (4-160), Susan Ann Harden (4-163), Martha Frances Harden (4-164) and Lewis Bard Harden (4-165) orphans of Henry Harden (4-85) and who therefrom together with Joseph S. Harden (4-135), William M Harden and Samuel Elgin her securities entered into and acknowledged a bond in the penalty of seven hundred dollars conditioned as the law directs.

1835 13 Oct: Book 4 Page 308 Albert Harden (4-156) orphan of Henry Harden (4-85) decd came into Court and made choice of Margaret Harden (4-85) as his guardian who therefore together with Joseph S. Hardin (4-135) William M Harden & Samuel Elgin her sureties intd into and acknowledged a bond in the penalty of one hundred and fifth dollars conditioned as the law directs.

Deed Books Index

A-298-300 Edward Harden to George Gregg
A-453-4 Edward Harden to George Gregg L&R
B-158-9 Edward Harden to George Gregg L&R
D-508-9 Edward Harden from John Hough L&R
I-299-301 Edward Harden to Henry McCabe L&R
Q-346-8 Edward Harden to Elisha Gregg L&R
U-112 Henry Taylor from Earl of Tankerville B&S

1796 23 Jan: Book X Page 74 William H. Harding and wife Ann A. Harding of Loudoun County, Virginia to William Wilson B&S for 660 Pounds 440 acres purchased of Edward Adams. Ordered to be recorded May 9 1796

1796 23 Jan: Book X, Page 297 William H. Harding from Edward Adams B&S Land in Loudoun Co., Virgnia on Goose Creek 440 acres

X-377 Henry Taylor from Joseph Taylor B&S

(William Hanby Harding is the son of Edward Harding and Elizabeth Hanby)

1797 16 Aug: Book Y Page 139 William H. Harding and wife Nancy and Wesley Adams to John Alexander Binns B&S for 700 pounds lawful money, in Loudon County on Beaver Dam Creek, purchased of Nathan Ball. Proved 20 December 1797

1796 01 Mar: Book 2C Page 55 William H. Harding of Loudoun Co., VA from Jonah Hague and wife Martha of same, B&S for 500 pounds, 170 acres in Loudoun. Proved 6 August 1802.

1802 15 Jun: Book 2C Page 235 William H. Harding of Jefferson County, commonwealth of Virginia, to George Carter of Outlands, Loudoun Co., VA Land purchased of Jonah Hague 170 acres, Mortgage for $1650. Proved 15 February 1803

1800 28 Jun: Book 2D Page 215 William H. Harding Trustee from Patrick Cavan Trust 90 acres on Broad Run Proved Dec 18 1801 180 acres

1803 Feb: Book 2D Page 223 William H. Harding Trustee to Wm. H. Harding of the county of Jefferson, Commonwealth of Virginia, B&S Purchased Deed of Trust 187 acres. Proved Oct 12 1803.

Virginia County Records

1804 10 Mar: Book 2E Page 71 William H. Harding and Ann Alexander his wife of the county of Jefferson in the commonwealth of Virginia to James Campbell of Loudoun B&S, 275 Pounds money, His interest in 9.5 acres on Broad Run, Proved May 14 1804

1796 23 Jan: Book 2E Page 107 William H. Harding and wife Ann of Loudoun County to William Witson B&S 664 Pounds money, land in Loudoun purchased of Edward Adams, 440 acres, Proved May 14 1804.

1804 29 Aug: Book 2E Page 442 Ferdinando Fairfax appoints William Hanby Harding Power of Attorney to sell and subdivide land in Loudoun Co., VA Proved 10 September 1804.

1806 21 Oct: Book 2H Page 337 Wm. H. Harding and Ann Alexander his wife Of Jefferson County, Virginia to Doctor Thomas Sim of Loudoun County VA B&S 171 acres purchased of Jonah Hague Proved 12 May 1807

1807 04 Apr: Book 2I Page 134 Elizabeth Harden (4-21) and William Harden (4-82) from Mary Taylor both of Loudoun County, B&S $1300.124 acres Proved 12 Oct 1807.

1807 14 Aug: Book 2I Page 139 William H. Harding and Ann Alexander his wife of Jefferson County VA to Sandford Ramey of Loudoun County, VA B&S $1770 Land on Kittotoctin 148 acres Proved Oct 12 1807

2K-281 Henry Taylor to John Stoutsenberger

2M-179 John J. Harding from William Noland B&S

General Index 1813-1833

1822 24 May: Book 3E-262 William (4-82) and Henry Harden (4-85) of Loudoun County to Silas Garrett of the same. $264.68. Undivided slaves in the possession of their mother Elizabeth Harden (4-21).

08 Jun: 1822 Book 3E-268 Susan P B Harding to Sanford Ramey of Loudoun County. Land of John Binns dec. 17 acres

1822 Jun: 3 Book E Page 275 Elizth P B Harding of Jefferson County VA to Sanford Ramey B&S 275 Land of John Binns

1822 09 Sep: Book 3F-252 William Randall and Rachel his wife of Fauquier County to William Harden (4-82) of Loudoun County VA. $5 Land in Loudoun 6 acres.

1824 11 Sep: Book 3H-416 Thomas N. Harding of Loudoun County to Thomas McGill of Montgomery Co., MD Personal property to pay debt.

1827 11 Sep: Book 3P-223 Elizabeth Harden (4-82) of the first part, Edmund Tyler of the second part, Stephen Garrett of the third part, all of Loudoun County VA. Elizabeth Harden (4-82) and Henry Harden (4-85) are indebted to

Stephen Garrett on a note dated 29 Jan: 1827 payable on or before 4 February 1827 for $291.92. Therefore, this indenture witnesseth that the said Elizabeth Harden (4-82) for the sum of $1 paid by the said Edmund Tyler, releases a certain tract of land in Loudoun County purchased by the said Elizabeth Harden (4-82) and William Harden (4-82) decd by deed dated 4th April 1807 totaling 123 acres the said Elizabeth Harden's (4-82)half of the said tract of land. Elizabeth Harden (4-82) and Henry Harden (4-85) will pay the note to Stephen Garrett

1830 06 Jul: Book 3U-95 Bill of Sale Catherine S. Harding of Jefferson County to Alfred Belt of Loudoun County, land assigned as one of the devisees of John A. Binns dec. 37 ½ acres

1830 15 Dec: Book 3Z-158 Division of land between Henry Harding (4-85) and the heirs of William Harding (4-82) decd. Lot #1 to Henry Harding (4-85) 65 acres and remove old houses the late residence of Elizabeth Harding (4-82) Dec. To the heirs of William Harding (4-82) dec 63 ½ acres.

General Index 1833-1857

1832 01 Oct: Book 4A-230 Henry Harding (4-85) and Margaret his wife of Loudoun County to Stephen Garrett of same, $70. Parcel of land allotted to him by the last will of his mother Elizabeth Harding (4-82) decd, 65 acres.

1839 12 Oct: Book 4N-394 William L Harding (4-132) (son of William Harding (4-82) decd.) now of Loudoun, to Joseph Garrett of Loudoun County. Consideration of certain contracts between the parties and $1 cash. Land in Loudoun on Little River, tract where his mother Elizabeth Harding (4-82) now lives 60 acres, his interest being one-third part encumbered by his mother's claim during her natural life. He also owns a lot of land 6 ¼ acres

1850 02 May: Book 5C-314 George Beatty of Loudoun owes Sarah Jane Harding of Loudoun $100. He sells to John Orr for $5 slaves and land. Orr to pay Harden $100. If not paid she can sell the property.

Federal Census Records

Loudoun Co., Virginia Census of 1810
Thomas Harden 31010 32010
Presley Harden (4-83) 30010 10100
Henry Harden (4-85) 20100 00100
Lewis Harden (4-84) 20010 20100
Elisabeth Harden (4-21) 00010 10001
Jab Harding 22210 32110
Presley Williams 00010 00200
Jos Poston 30010 30100
Nancy Harden 31000 13010

John Harden 00010 00100

Loudoun Co., Virginia Census of 1820
Page 1 Leesburg John J. Harding 300010 20020
Page 10 Leesburg Thomas Harding 211301 31210
Page 39 Middleburg Edward Harding 200010 10010
Page 61 Waterford William Harding (4-82) 200020 20110
Page 61 Waterford Henry Harding (4-85) 410010 40010
Page 61 Waterford Elizabeth Harding (4-21) 000000 00002
Page 61 Waterford Rebecca Harding 100000 01210

Loudoun Co., Virginia Census of 1830
Page 24 Middleburg Elizabeth Harding (4-82) 0001 0020001
Page 31 Leesburg John J Harding 0201001 2020011
Page 67 Leesburg Edward Harding 2210001 1010001
Page 103 Bloomfield Joseph Harding 100001 00002
Page 103 Bloomfield Thomas Harding 00010001 0020001
Page 104 Bloomfield James Harding 100001 20001

Loudoun Co., Virginia Census 1840
Page 139 Jonah Hood Albert Harding (4-156) 10001 00001
Page 145 Jonah Hood Margaret Harden (4-85) 01011 10120001
Page 148 Jonah Hood Elizabeth Harding (4-82) 0000 00010001
Page 210 District 1 Edward Harden 01131001 0000101
Page 220 District 1 John J Harding 000010001

Loudoun CO., Virginia Census 1850
Page 313 Family # 17
Margaret Harding (4-85) 62 No occupation RE $200 Born Virginia
Robert Harding (4-159) 29 Labour Born Virginia
John Harding (4-160) 23 Labour Born Virginia
Lewis Harding 20 (4-165) Labour Born Virginia
Ellen Harding (4-161) 22 No occupation Born Virginia
Eliza Harding (4-162) 21 No occupation Born Virginia
Martha Harding (4-164) 20 No occupation Born Virginia
Catherine Harding 13 No occupation Born Virginia

Middlesex County, Virginia Records

Formed 1669 from Lancaster County

Deed Books

1709 18 Sep: Deed Book B (or 2) Page 211 Bond George (9-1) Harding and Richard Bailey bound to John Smith. Condition that George Harding is (9-1) Executor of the last will and testament of Thomas Baynes

Will Books

1744 10 Oct: probated 2 April 1745, will of George Hardin (9-1), Gent, names wife Elizabeth (9-1), daughter Mary (9-4), son Thomas (9-1), land in Orange County, niece Elizabeth Stapleton. Humphrey Keeble Executor. Keeble renounced being executor and wife Elizabeth became executor Estate appraised by Armestead Churchil April 1745. Estate in Caroline County appraised by Robert George, John George, Richard George and Wm Smithworth. April 1745

1758/ 9 20 Jan: probated 05 June 1759. Will of Elizabeth Hardin (9-1). Mentions son Thomas Hardin, Daughter Mary Blacknall (9-4), granddaughter Elizabeth Keebles, granddaughters Betty, Ann and Mary Blacknall. Executors, son Thomas Hardin and Charles Blacknall. Witnesses Walter Keeble and John Clarcey

1759 07 Nov: probated 4 Dec 1759 will of Thomas Hardin (9-2), to wife Lucy (9-2) land in Orange Co.

From Spotsylvania County, Virginia: 4 September 1733 William Johnston of Spotsylvania Co to Geoge Hardin (9-1) of Middlesex County 1020 acres in Spots Co.

Christ Church Parish Register

1709 27 Apr: Page 73 Peter Harding (8-4), son of Nicholas (8-3) and Elizabeth (8-3) born

1712 03 May: Page 77 Thomas (9-2), son of George (9-1) and Elizabeth Hardin (9-1) born

1716 21 Dec: Page 96 Anne (9-3) , daughter of George (9-1) and Elizabeth Hardin (9-1) born

1722 07 Nov: Page 111 Mary (9-4) daughter of George (9-1) and Elizabeth Hardin (9-1) born

Marriage Records

1733 21 Sep: Lucy Hardin married William Stapleton
1745 03 Oct: Mary (9-4) Hardin married Charles Blacknall
1747 5 Jan: Thomas Harding (9-2) married Lucy Billups (9-2)
1765 22 Oct: Lucy Hardin (9-2) widow married John Morgan

Northumberland Co., Virginia Records

Formed 1646 from Indian Territory

Deeds and Wills A 1650-1652

Deeds and Wills B 1652-1658

1655/6 02 Jan: Page 67 In a deposition Mrs. Elizabeth Newman is age 80 or so and a midwife.

Deeds and wills C 1658-1666

1658 22 Nov: Page 13 Richard Rice recorded His Pattent To all and whereas ( ) Esq & give & (---) of land situate ( ) in the southwest ( ) easterly upon the ( ) northwesterly upon ( ) Cameron and a man (---)south westerly upon the ( ) of Mr. Thomas Bre ------- the first lands three hundred and ------ the main having for length into the woods -------boring unto him the sd Richard Rice by and for the transportation of eight persons in the Colony whose names are --- of Records maintained under the ---- dated this --- of Jan: 1656. W. Claiborne Sec.

1658 22 Nov: Page 13 Be it known unto all men by these presents that I Richard Rice with the consent of my wife assign and sett over all my right title and interest of this Pattent with all privileges of ye Land herein mentioned to Thomas Harding (1-1) and James Johnson their heires and assigns forever. Witness our hands the 22 November 1658. Richard Rice (his mark) Anne Rice (her mark) Witnesses Thomas Stoughton, Robert Kempe.

1658 22 Nov: This Afft was acknowledged in Northumberland County Court by the said Richard Rice unto the sd Thomas Harding (1-1) and James Johnson and so recorded with the patent.

1659 13 Apr: Page 21 Elizabeth Newman widow gives personal items to Peter Presley Jr., Martha Haynie and Elizabeth Haynie. Witnesses William Presley and John Haynie.

1659 10 Mar: Page 22bJohn Haynie deed to his children, daughters Martha and Elizabeth Haynie and daughter-in-law Susanna Ware. ---- Presley or his brother-in-law -----.

1661 24 Aug Page 63 recorded 9 September 1661 Know all men that we James Johnson and Anne my wife doe hereby affirme now unto James Claughton his heires exers and admrs the one-half of the land wherein mentioned in this patt it being two hundred acres of Land the halfe of four hundred acres

In Witness whereof we have hereunto set our hands this 24 of August 1661. Mark of James Johnson. Mark of Anne Johnson. Witnesses Daniel Roberts, Thomas Harding (1-1) his mark, Linton's mark.

1661 09 Sep: This assignment was (missing) by James Johnson and Thomas Hardin (1-1). (missing) and is recorded.

1661 09 Sep: Page 63 recorded Thomas Harding (1-1) his assignment of pattent to James Johnson. Know all men that I (---) Anne (1-1) my wife doo here (---) of the wherein mentioned (---) hovels and for --- In (---) sett my hand and sould and (---) signed sealed and delivered (---) the presence of us Daniel Roberts and James Claughton.

1661 09 Sep: The (---) ed in Court by Thomas Harding (1-1) and (---). Recd by him assigned to the (---) ames Johnson and is recorded in folio (&c)

1661 09 Sep: Page 63 Recorded James Johnson sale of land to Thomas Harding (1-1). Know all men by these presents that I James Johnson (--------) hereby bargain and sell unto Thomas Harding (1-1) the quantity of one hundred and fifty acres of land lying and being situate in the County of Northumberland wherein nobody dwell, the sd land beginning at a chestnut tree marked four ---- and from that tree --- upon a line of marked trees into the woods south southwest and being on the eastward side of a patent of four hundred acres formerly belonging to Richard Rice being part thereof sold to Johnson for myself, my heires &c. Doo hereby warrant the said land unto the sd Harding his heires &c from ye claims or ------ forever. In witness whereof wee have here set our hands and seales this ninth of September 1661. Mark of James Johnson and seale. Signed and sealed in the presence of us John Cantaraceau and Daniell Roberts. 9 Sept 1661, this sale of land was acknowledged in Court by the said James Johnson and recorded.

1661 04 Aug: Page 64 recorded 9 September 1661 James Claughton sale of land to Thomas Harding (1-1) 100 acres part of a pattent of 400 acres dated 13 October 1651 granted unto Robert Bradshaw, ye said 100 acres beginning at a farm formerly belonging to ---- Williams and upon a swamp lying ----- Beaver Dam Swamp and soo running southwest and northwest to ye aforesaid pattent the sd land being in Northumberland County and the sd James Claughton do hereby for myself my heires and execs --- make and --- ye sd land good unto the heires of Thomas Harding, his heires (much legal language) I have hereunto set my hand this 24 day of August 1661. Ordered recorded 9 September 1661

1663 12 Mar: Page 125a --- Harding (1-1) witnessed deed Geo Medcalf to John Tyngey 100 acres

1665 18 Aug: Page 170A To all &c Whereas &c Know ye yt I ye sd William Berkeley doe --- and grant unto James Johnson four hundred acres of land situate, lying and being in Northumberland County and on the southwest side of Mattapony River bound on ye north by and upon ye land of Robert Bradshaw and John Bradshaw. North ye & upon ye sd land ye land of Lawrence Dawson and ye ---- swamps being a branch of Broad Creek, Southerly upon ye --- woods above ye head of ye land of Mr. Thomas Claughton and running from ye --- lands 320 poles parallel to ye ----- into the woods ye sd lands belonging formerly unto Richard Rice as and pattent dated ye 28 June 1656 & by ye said Richard Rice assigned and sett over to Thomas Harding and James Johnson as ye record of Northumberland County dated ye 22 of 9ber 1658 now falls appeareth and by ye sd Thomas Harding assigned & --- unto James Johnson as by ye records of Northumberland County dated ye 9 of September 1661 now fully appeareth &c dated 8 of October 1662.

1665 18 Aug: Page 170A I Anne Hardinge (1-1) wife of Thomas Hardinge (1-1) as is mentioned doo make over all my right of dower to ye land herein mentioned unto ye herein mentioned James Johnson his heirs &c for --- do empower ---- and acknowledge ye same in Northumberland County Court. I set my hand and seale this 18 of August 1665. At Court 20 November 1665 ordered recorded.

1665 19 Aug Page 170a James Johnson sells 100 acres to Thomas Harding (1-1) on Beaver Dam Swamp

1665 06 Sep: Page 156 John Tyngey gives to Ann Harding (1-2), daughter of Thomas Hardinge (1-1), one cow calf

Deeds and Wills D 1666-1672

1667 01 Aug: Page 30 proved 27 Nov 1667 will of John Tyngey, son-in law William Moseley one heifer and a bull, to John Moseley, Henry Moseley, "I bequeath unto Thomas Harding (1-1), his eldest boy, one heifer three yrs old, if he dye ye heifer shall be given to ye youngest boy" Wife Elizabeth also Mary Hardwood

1667 18 May: Page 126 proved 19 November 1669 Will of John Moseley mentions brother William Moseley, executor, brother Henry Moseley, cosen Thomas (1-3) Harden one cow with Browning, cosen Ann Harden (1-2) one heifer, to Robert Pennell and his wife. Brother Henry Moseley the plantation. Witnesses Henry Moseley, Robert Pennell, Jane Pennell.

1668/9 26 Jan: Page 45 Elizabeth Tyngey, widow of John Tyngey, enters into agreement to protect her rights to property after marrying William Shoares.

1671 10 Oct: Page 200 Ralph Waddington bought land from Francis Roberts.

1670 27 Oct: Sir William Berkeley granted to Thomas Harding (1-1) 575 acres between Mattapony and Yeocomico rivers Grants

Deeds and Wills E 1707-1720 (re-recorded)

1703 26 Mar: Probate 21 June 1704 Page 9 Will of Joseph Palmer of Wiccomico, Northumberland Co., VA. Names sons John, Joseph, Thomas, Benjamin, Isaac, wife Alice, executors, friend Richard Wright and brother Robert Palmer, and Thomas Downing.

1708/9 08 Feb: Page 91 Henry Harding (3-1) witnesses deed from Thomas Leachman to Thomas Smith

1707/8 10 Feb: Page 97 Probated 21 Jan 1708/9 Will of Thomas Gill mentions son William, daughter Dinah Gill, son Thomas Gill, daughter Susanna Robinson, daughter Frances Waddington.

1700/1 13 Jan Probated 19 Feb 1700/1 Page 108 Will of John Robinson mentions eldest son Richard, sons Anthony and Thomas, youngest sons Joseph and Benjamin.

1707 07 Apr Page 116 Deed Mark Harding (5-1), carpenter from heirs of John Mutton 50 Acres in Wicomico Parish

1678 20 Oct: Page 118 Ralph Waddington of Fairfield Parish deed of gift to son Ralph Waddington, land bought of James Allen. Also mentions son George Waddington.

Deeds and Wills F 1710-1713

1713 19 May: Page 283 Deed from William Harding (1-9) planter of St. Stephens Parish to Samuel Robinson conveys land in Wicomico Parish, said land lately in the occupation of the said William Harding, it being part of a patent formerly granted to Edward Saunders, decd. called Saunder's Quarter, which said Sanders devised to his son Ebenezer, who sold 200 acres to John Evans by deed dated 12 May 1685 who sold 100 acres of it to Richard Lewis on the 3rd day of June 1689 and the said Lewis --- by deed of assignment dated the 2nd day of March 1694 to Thomas Harding III (1-8) from whom the said one hundred acres of land hereby bargained and sold descends unto the said William Harding (1-9)

Deeds and Wills G 1718-1725

1719 28 Apr: Page 53 probated 19 Aug 1719, Thomas Harding III (1-8) witnessed will of William Nelms

Virginia County Records

1719/20 17 Feb: Page 96 Pursuant to an order of the Northumberland County Court dated ye 20th Day of January 1719/20 wee the subscribers being sworn by Capt. Richard Spann did appraise the Estate of Frances Harding (2-1), formerly Robertson, decd. in money as follows: (List of estate items valued at 30 pounds, 7 shillings, 2 pence.) Taken by Thomas Gille, Charles Nelms, Samuel Blackwell, Samuell Robinson.

1719/20 17 Feb: Page 96 This inventory of Frances Harding (2-1), decd., formerly Frances Robertson, was exhibited into Northumberland County Court by Samuell Robinson, admr of the said dec upon oath and on his motion it" admitted to record.

1720 14 Nov: Page 145 Mark Harding (5-1) and wife Mary (5-1) of Richmond County, 50 acres in Wicomico Parish, Northumberland Co. to John Pope. Recorded 15 February 1720-21.

1721 27 Sep: Page 253 John Bird of Stafford Co., VA to Thomas Harding III (1-8) of St. Stephens Parish, Northumberland County. 50 acres in Northumberland County, bounded by Richard Bradley and Johnson's land. Recorded 21 February 1721/22

1722 17 Oct Page 290 probated 19 Dec 1722 Will of Thomas Harding III (1-8) of St. Stephens Parish, wife Mary, to every one of my children, six in number. To three sons William Harding (1-14), Thomas Harding (1-15), Samuel Harding (1-16), personal property, to two sons William Harding (1-14) and Samuel Harding (1-16) land on Mattapony joining Clayton and Johnson, equally divided, to son Thomas Harding (1-15) plantation I live on together with a piece of land purchased of James Palmer, to daughter Jane Harding (1-17) rest of land in Mattapony, 250 acres, to daughter Judah Harding (1-18), land in North Farnham Parish, Richmond County, 100 acres, part of patent to Henry Corbin, wife two negroes, one unnamed daughter.

1722 19 Dec: Page 296 James Palmer of Richmond Co., VA to Thomas Harding (1-15), son of Thomas Harding III (1-8) lately decd. of Northumberland Co., VA Consideration is 120 acres in Richmond Co., VA which I had by way of exchange with sd Harding decd. Property is 120 acres in Northumberland Co., VA bounded by John Harris, Thomas Harding and John Smith. Signed by James and Mary Palmer. On 19 Dec 1722 the court gave Livery and seize to the within Thomas Harding and Mary Harding (1-8) his mother during his minority.

1724 24 Sept Page 390 probated 15 Dec 1725 Will of Thomas Barecraft, sons John, land, son Thomas, plantation, son Simon Peter, plantation, daughter Jane Hardin (1-10), two ewes and 600 pounds tobacco, daughters Martha Haynie, Winifred Gill, and -- Pew, each two ewes.

1725 18 Aug: Page 404 Rosten Betts and Mary his wife to George Ball for love and affection of her daughter Mary Harding (1-19), ½ part of land sold September 20 1671 by Robert Burrell to William Berry, father of Mary Betts, late Mary Harding (1-8), granted on behalf of Mary Harding (1-19). Recorded August 1725.

1723 17 Jul: Page 408 Additional inventory of Thomas Harding III (1-8) dec, filed consists of debts of estate and amounts due estate. Includes an amount due to James Erwin for schooling of Mary Harding. The document itself is not dated. This is the date of document recorded before this one.

Deeds and Wills H 1726-1729

1724 24 May: Page 4 We the subscribers being desired by Mary Harden (1-8) and John Humphries and Elinor his wife to settle and make a line of Division between the said Mary Harden (1-8) and John Humphries and Elinor his wife of a parcel of land lying and being in Great Wicomico Parish formerly the land of William Berry decd. father to the said Mary Harden and grandfather to the said Elinor Humphries. We accordingly met on the said land on the 25 day of March 1724 with all persons therein concerned and (divided the land). Recorded 24 May 1724.

1722 19 Dec: Page 19 Per an order of the Court dated 19 December 1722, an inventory of the estate of Thomas Harden (1-8) decd. was filed on 6 January 1722/3 and ordered recorded. Executors are Mary Harden (1-8) and George Ball.

1725/6 16 Feb: Page 19 Inventory of Thomas Bearcraft filed by John Bearcraft.

1721 20 Nov: Page 35a probated 18 Jan 1726/7 Will of Richard Smith Sr., son Richard Smith, daughter Elizabeth Dameron, daughter Anne Smith, Francis Harding (2-3) both witnessed and proved the will

1728 13 Jul: Page 99 Alice Palmer of Wiccomico to daughter Rebecca Snow wife of Samuel Snow and Isaac Palmer, her youngest son, 60 acres in Great Wiccomico conveyed to Alice Palmer by Thomas Downing 16 January 1710. Recorded 17 July 1728.

1726 02 Sept Page 109 probate 16 Oct 1728 Will of Richard Lattimore. Names sons Clement, John, William, daughter Mary, Martha, Anne, Leanne, wife, son David and Grandson Richard.

1729 20 Nov: Page 121 Inventory of William Humphries filed in court. Signed by Elinor Humphries.

1726/7 06 Mar: Page 143a probated 18 Feb 1729/30 will of Pitts Curtis witnessed by Thomas Hardin

Deeds and Wills I 1737-1743

1740 12 May: Page 77 In obedience to an order of Court dated the 10 March 1739, We the subscribers having met has allocated Judith Harding (1-18) her share of her father Thomas Harding III (1-8) decd. estate and likewise her share of her brother Samuel Harding (1-16) Decd. estate as follows: Items listed. Samuel Blackwell, Samuel Nelms, Thomas Haynie, John Hudnall Mary 12, 1740 this division of the estate of Thomas Harding III (1-8) and Samuel Harding (1-16) decd. estate to Judith Harding (1-18) was ordered returned unto Northumberland County Court by Samuel Blackwell, Samuel Nelms, Thomas Haynie and John Hudnall. Ordered to be recorded

1741 10 Aug: Page 134 Moses Lunsford of Prince William County, power of attorney to William Boggess of Northumberland to acknowledge deeds dated 28 and 29 July 1741 to Thomas Harding (2-4) of Northumberland Co., dated 29 July 1741. Witness Charles Harding (2-2). 10 August 1741 Proved in Northumberland County Court by Charles Harding (2-2).

1741 28 Jul: Page 134 Moses Lunsford to Thomas Harding (2-4) of Northumberland County, for 5 shillings, land in Wicomico, 50 acres bounded by James Davison and Robert Angel. Witnesses Charles Harding (2-2), Joseph Whitehead, Francis Ballinger.

1741 29 Jul: Page 134a Moses Lunsford to Thomas Harden (2-4) of Wicomico, Northumberland Co., VA for 3500 pounds of tobacco, land in Wiccomico, 50 acres by the land of James Davison and Robert Angell. Witnesses Charles Harden, Joseph Whitehead, Francis Ballinger.

1741 29 Jul: Page 173 Moses Lunsford and Charles Harding (2-2) of Overwharton Parish, Stafford County, VA are bound to Thomas Harding (2-4) of Wicomico Parish, Northumberland County for 800 pounds tobacco, dated 29 July 1741. Consideration of bond is to complete deeds dated 28 and 29 July 1741. Filed in Court 10 May 1742.

Deeds and Wills J 1743-1747

1744 Martha Lunceford, wife of William Lunceford of Wicomico, names in will God-child Hannah Harding (2-4) and brother Joseph Robinson

1744 07 Oct: Page 52 Two deeds George Ball to son Richard Ball 150 acres bought of mother-in-law Sarah Haynie by deed dated 17 February 1714 and to son John Ball 120 acres bought of mother-in-law Sarah Waddy in St. Stephens Parish by deed dated 9 April 1739, Witness to both deeds William Harding (1-14)

1746 13 Oct: Page 156 Isaac Palmer of Wiccomico, Northumberland County, deed to Rebecca Snow, land in Wiccomico 60 acres. Witnesses Alice and Judith Palmer. Dated 30 May 1745, Recorded 13 October 1746.

1746 Page 165 Morris Gibbons mentions daughter Jane Harding (1-15), dau Jemima Cook, dau Kathleen Haynie, son John Gibbons, daus Elizabeth and Judith

1747 13 Apr: Page 193 Spencer Ball of Northumberland County deed to the children of brother-in-law William Harding (1-14) by his present wife Sarah Harding (1-14). Three negroes to be divided and given to the children present and future as they reach age 20 or marry. Recorded 13 April 1747

1747 15 Sep: Page 245 William Hughlett and Mary of St. Stephens Parish, Northumberland County, to William Harding (1-14) of same, for 225 Pounds, land on the Coen River, totaling 393 acres.

Deeds and Wills K 1747-1749

1747 13 Apr: Page 50 William Harding (1-14) bond to Spencer Ball for deed of gift ordered recorded at court of 14 March 1747.

1748 14 May: Page 148 Will of Isaac Palmer mentions cousins Nargale Serazer Palmer and Spencer Snow, dividing the estate between them. Proved 8 August 1748.

Deeds and Wills Book 1 1750-1751

1750 06 Aug Page 229 Will of Samuel Denney, brother Mark Harding (2-16), Mother Hannah Harding (2-4), Hopkins Harding (2-15)

1750 10 Dec Thomas Harding (2-4) Estate adm by Hannah Harding (2-4)

Deeds and Wills Book 2 1752-1754

1751 11 Nov Page 66 Deed William Harding (1-14) of St Stephens Parish Northumberland County from John Evins 12 ½ acres 1200 Pounds of Tobacco next to Harding's land on Claughton Creek

1752 Page 105 William Harding (1-14) deed of gift to daughter Sarah provided he has no son by his present wife now living.

Deeds and Wills Book 3 1754-1756

1755 11 Nov Page 251 William Harding (1-14) and wife Sarah (1-14) deed of gift to daughter Mary, wife of Mathew Neale

1756 08 Mar: Thomas Harding (1-15) to administer est of Joseph Robinson

Deeds and Wills 4 1756-1758

1757 01 Mar: Page 48 In obedience to an order of the Northumberland County Court dated February the 14 1757 with the subscribers being appointed in the same order to possess Thomas Harding (1-15) and Hezekiah Haynie Securities of Joseph Roberson Jr. with one third part of the estate of Jos Roberson Sr. Estate in the hands of Mary Robinson accordingly mett on the 25 day of February 1757 and allotted as follows: one-third of estate valued at 19 pounds 10 sh 5p Signed by Beverly Shreve, John Corbell and John Hobson. Court on 1 March 1757 ordered it to be recorded.

1757 01 Mar: Page 51 Inventory of the estate of Joseph Roberson dec.

Wills and Deeds 5 1758-1762

1759 09 Apr: Page 62 Deed Hopkins Harding (2-15) of Wicomico Parish, Northumberland Co., to John Tipper and Hannah his wife of the same, for 15 pounds, 50 acres bounded on south by William Angel, east by James Davison, North and west by the Creek from the Wiccomicco River. Recorded 9 April 1759.

1759 10 Sep: Page 122 Expenses of the estate of John Harding (2-19) orphan, December 7 1758. Accounting of estate. Built a shed at John Blundell's house. Bought shoes made by Benjamin Haynie. On September 10 1759, recorded by Samuel Blackwell, guardian to John Harding (2-19).

1760 01 Mar: Page 186 Pursuant to Court Order dated 11 February 1760, subscribers (David Lattimer, William Angel and Charles James) possessed Hopkins Harding (2-15) with Mark Harding (2-16) part of his decd. father's estate as also with a Legacy of 5 pounds bequeathed to the sd Mark by will of Samuel Denney. On Mar: 1, 1760 said items were sold by Hopkins Harding (2-15) for 21 pounds 21 shillings. Recorded 1 March 1760

1761 13 Apr: Thomas Harding (1-15) estate administered by Jane Harding (1-15) and William Harding (1-14)

1761 15 Nov: Page 496 Proved 8 February 1762 Will of William Harding (1-14) of St. Stephens Parish, sons in law Mathew Neale (1-28), John Cralle (1-27) Jr., Joseph Wildey (1-24), son William Harding (1-32) all my land, if he dies land goes to daughter Frances Harding (1-31), son William Harding (1-32) four negroes, wife Sarah (1-14), to have all land so long as she is a widow to bring up my four children, Jane Harding (1-30), Molley (1-29), Frances (1-31) and William Harding (1-32), sons in law John Lewis, Griffin Fauntleroy, daughters Jane (1-30), Molley (1-29) and Frances Harding (1-31). Executors Col. Spencer Ball, Matthew Neale and William Eskridge.

Wills and Deeds 6 1762-1766

1762 12 Apr: Page 19 Jean Harding (1-15), adm of Thomas Harding (1-15) dec and Henry Boggess and Elisha Betts of Northumberland Co., bond to Matthew Neale and William Eskridge, execs of William Harding (1-14) decd. for 1200 pounds dated 10 March 1762. Whereas the above bound Jean was jointly concerned with the above-named William Harding (1-14) decd. in the admin of her decd. husband Thomas Harding (1-15) estate, she wishes to take all of the estate of Thomas Harding (1-15) into her hands and clears the executors and heirs of William Harding (1-14) decd. of any claims against his estate. At a court of 12 April 1762 bond was acknowledged and ordered recorded.

1762 10 May: Page 36 At a court held 13 April 1761, a committee was appointed to appraise the estate of Thomas Harding (1-15) decd. Inventory was made by William Hudnall, Eben Nelms and John Humphries. Presented at court 10 May 1762 and ordered recorded.

1762 10 Aug: Page 96 Pursuant to Court order of 12 July 1762 ordered Hopkins Harding (2-15) to possess the estate of Aaron Nelmes, orphan of Aaron Nelmes decd. that was in the hands of John Nutt, his guardian. On 10 Aug 1762 Court ordered it recorded.

1763 13 Jun: Page 229 Deed dated 22 November 1762 Hopkins Harding (2-15) of Wicomico, Northumberland Co., to Joseph Moore of same, for 2500 Pounds and tobacco and one house, lease for 21 years, 50 acres on Wicomico River. Ordered recorded 13 June 1763.

1763 12 Dec: Page 316 Dated 13 June 1763 Will of Sarah Harding (1-14) of St. Stephens Parish Northumberland Co., VA. Divides estate between three daughters Jane Harding (1-30), Molley Harding (1-29) and Frances Harding (1-31) and son William Harding (1-32) to have a desk and press and a young man. Executors Friends Matthew Neale, John Cralle (1-27) Jr., and Griffin Fauntleroy. Witnesses were John Lewis, Mary Eskridge and Hannah Lewis. Proved in Court 12 December 1763.

1764 09 Jan: Page 340 Sarah Harding (1-14) inventory taken 23 November 1763 and ordered recorded 9 Jan 1764.

1763 12 Dec: Page 360 Court ordered division of Negroes given by Spencer Ball to the legal representatives of William (1-14) and Sarah Harding (1-14) decd. The men that married some of the daughters of said Hardings being present and the guardians of the children of said Hardings being likewise present, the estate is divided into nine parts. Receiving shares are men who married daughters, Mathew Neale (1-28), John Cralle (1-27) Jr., Joseph Wildey (1-24), Griffin Fauntleroy (1-25), John Lewis (1-26). Guardians are John Cralle Jr. for Jane Harding (1-30), Molley Harding (1-29) and Frances Harding (1-31). Guardian for William Harding (1-32) is Matthew Neale.

1765 11 Feb: Page 512 By Court order dated 13 November 1764, John Harding (2-19) to get part of deceased father Thomas Harding's estate in the hands of John Blackwell. Recorded 11 Feb 1765.

1765 21 Page 585 Deed Mark Harding (2-16) from John Tiffee

1765 12 Aug: Page 590 Inventory of William Harding (1-14) decd. ordered recorded. Court ordered said inventory on 8 February 1762.

1765 12 Aug: Page 591 Sale list of estate of William Harding (1-14) decd. ordered recorded.

1765 02 Sep: Page 613 recorded 9 Sept 1765, deed from John Harding (2-19) of St. Stephens Parish, Northumberland Co. to John Worman of same for 202 pounds, 100 acres in St. Stephens Parish, which came into my possession as follows: 100 acres was given by Ralph Waddington to my grandfather John Waddington, who took up 98 ½ acres surplus land. At death all 198 ½ acres went to Ralph Waddington, son of John. Ralph in his will gave it to his cozen John Harding (2-14), elder brother to the aforesaid John Harding (2-19) first part named in the presents and half to him and his heirs, other half Ralph Waddington gave to his sister Sarah Ann and Isaac Palmer. The said John Harding (2-14), elder brother to the said John Harding (2-19) first party named above and Sarah Ann and Isaac Palmer deceased with no heirs and the said present John Harding (2-19) came into possession of 198 1/2 acres as heir at law. Land is on the Wicomico River.

Wills and Deeds 7 1766-1770

1767 12 Jan: Page 7 Division of slaves to three youngest daughters of William Harding (1-14) Deceased. To Jane Harding (1-30) who married Parish Garner (1-30). Molley Harding (1-29) and Frances Harding (1-31) with guardian John Cralle (1-27).

1767 15 Oct: Wooldridge Smith has land bounded by William Nelms and Thomas Harding

1769 01 Feb: Samuel Harding (1-38) wit will of Jesse Ball

1769 10 Sep: Page 443 Will of Joseph Wildey (1-24) of Northumberland County. To son Joseph Wildey Part of land he lives on. Son William Wildey rest of land, To son Heli Wildey (1-57). Rest of estate divided between seven children Salley, Molley, William, Joseph, Heli, Jane, and Betty. Wife Judith Wildey. Proved 11 December 1769.

Wills and Deeds 8 1770-1772

1770 14 May: Samuel Harding (1-38) adm est of William Greenwood

Wills and Deeds 9 1772-1776

1774 23 Apr: Page 532 Proved 13 Feb 1775 Will of Mark Harding (2-16) names wife, son Thomas Harding (2-52), daughter Betty (2-53), son Charles (2-54), Son Mark (2-55), child wife is now with, Brother Hopkins Harding (2-15) and wife to raise daughter Betty (2-53). Witnesses Thomas Copridge, Ephraim Hughlett, Elizabeth Copridge.

12 Jun: 1775 Page 588 Deed Hopkins Harding (2-15) and wife Jemima (2-15) to Robert Walker

Wills and Deeds 10 1776-1780

03 Nov: 1777 Page 387 William Harding (1-32) and Milly his wife of St. Stephens Parish Northumberland County to Thomas Downing of the same, 50 acres in Northumberland County.

Wills and Deeds 12 1782-1785

22 Jun: 1784 Page 238 Estate to Catherine Harding. In obedience to an order of Northumberland County Court Dated the 15th June 1784 We the subscribers being appointed by the court to Possess Catharine Harding with the estate bequeathed to her under the will of Elizabeth Nelms Decd in the Hands of Lindsy Opie Gent Execr of said decd have met and Possessed the sd Catherine Harding with a Negro woman Cate. We also Report that the sd ecectr pay unto the sd Catharine Harding Rent for four years Including the Present year for the use of the Room and Land Bequeathed the said Harding by the sd Decd six pounds Current Money of Virginia and that the sd Catherine Harding have a Right to the sd Room and Land during her Maiden Life given under our hands this 22 Day June 1784. Kenner Cralle, William Nutt, Spencer M Ball, Hudson Muse.

05 Mar: 1785 Page 409 William Neale and Nancy his Wife to William Harding (1-32) of St Stephens Parish, Northumberland County for 50,500 pounds of Crop tobacco. 210 acres.

Wills and Deeds 13 1785-1787

12 Jun: 1786 Page 198 Will William Harding (1-32) of St. Stephens Parish, Will written 11 March 1786, proved 12 June 1786. Plantation whereon I now

live and the plantation I purchased of John Cralle, my negro slaves, stock of cattle, hogs, and horses, shall be kept together by my executors until my son James Harding (1-60) arrives at the age of twenty-one, to support and educate my several children. Son James Harding (1-60) to have my land. All my negroes, slaves, stock of cattle, hogs, horses, and all my personal estate, to be equally divided between my sons and daughters, viz James (1-60), William (1-61), Thomas (1-62), Sarah (1-63), Ann (1-64), Easter (1-65), Alcey (1-66) and Milly Harding (1-67). In case my son James (1-60) should departed this life before the age of twenty-one, the lands go to my son William (1-61). The land I purchased of Wm. Neale that was Lewis's, shall be sold to pay my debts. Friends James Cox and Peter Cox, Executors Witnesses: John Harford, Sarah Smith, and Charles William Kester

1799 Inventory of William Harding (1-32) filed

Wills and Deeds 14 1787-1793

13 Sep: 1790 Page 557 Accounting of estate of Thomas Harding Deceased. Last item, by Samuel Harding Recd from Mrs. Hurst of the Estate

Wills and Deeds 15 1794-1799

31 Mar: 1797 Page 372 James Harding (1-60) and Ann his wife of Cherry Point, St Stephens Parish, Northumberland Co. to William Harding (1-57) of the same for the natural love and affection he hath unto the said William Harding his son, land where he now lives given him by will from his father William Harding on Coan River bounding Pemberton Claughton 120 acres, William to have possession of the property after death of himself and his wife Ann. Witnesses John Cralle, Ann Henrietta Leland, John Cralle (1-27) Jr, Mary Cralle.

11 Sep: 1797 Page 408 James Harding (1-60) of Northumberland County to Catesby Jones bill of sale for three Negroes plus animals and furniture. For 200 pounds

14 Feb: 1798 Page 464 James Harding (1-60) and Nancy his wife of Northumberland County, St. Stephens Parish to Charles Fallin of same, for 120 pounds, 58 acres on Cherry Point Neck. Witness John Cralle, William Claughton, William Harding (1-61), Catesby Jones.

13 Feb: 1798 Page 467 James Harding (1-60) and Nancy his wife of Ste Stephens Parish Northumberland County to James Cox of same. For 67 Pounds. 32 ¾ acres of land. Witnesses William Claughton, Samuel Cralle, Pemberton Claughton, Catesby Jones.

03 Mar: 1799 page 618 James Harding (1-60) of Northumberland County VA in consideration of the natural love and affection which I bear to John Glasscock of Richmond Co., Virginia plus 140 pounds of lawful money, 150 acres on which he now lives. Witnesses William Smith Jr, William Meskell, Thomas M. Glasscock

22 Apr: 1804 Page 181 William Claughton from James Harding (1-60), both of Northumberland County Virginia, 150 acres given to James by his father William Harding (1-32), for payment of $40 per annum for seven years.

Wills and Deeds 17 1803-1808

16 Jan: 1805 Book 16 Page 415 Will of Cyrus Harding (2-43) of Northumberland County, Wicomico Parish. To my two youngest children, Polly and the other not yet baptized his five negroes. Executors William Goodridge and Billy Harding (2-45). Proved 3 June 1806.

Wills and Deeds 19 1811-1815

1812 12 Oct: Book 19 Page 278 Will of Hopkins Harding: (2-15) To wife Jemima. To granddaughters Polly (2-77) and Nancy (2-78), daughters of son Cyrus Harding (2-43) dec. Granddaughter Rebecca (2-76), daughter of Cyrus, To daughter Lucy (Pitman) (2-51), wife of Edward Pitman (2-51). To son Billy Harding (2-45). To daughter-in-law Sally Harding (2-47), widow of son John Harding (2-47). To grandson John H. Harding (2-84). To grandson Hiram Harding (2-79). To grandson Cyrus Harding (2-86). Neice Hannah H. Carter. To Winifred Edwards. To Thomas Trance. To Susanna Webb. Grandson Thomas E. Harding (2-80). Proved 14 December 1812.

Wills and Deeds 22 1819-22

1819 15 Jun: Page 447 Will of Samuel Harding (1-38)
Estate to sister Jane Harding, (1-41) To grand-nephews William Jett (1-63), Joseph Jett (1-64), John H. Jett (1-65). William Jett (1-68) executor, William Harding (1-61) Jr and Thomas Towles his securities. Proved 11 December 1820.

1822 28 Jul: Book 23 Page 257 Jane Harding (1-41) from William Jett (1-68) Deed

Wills and Deeds 25 1831-1833

1827 13 Mar: Page 316 Will of William Harding (2-45) of Northumberland County. To son Hiram Harding (2-79) land in Lancaster County. To son Thomas E. Harding (2-80). To son William Harding. To Daughter Eliza Cole. To son John H. Harding (2-84). To son Cyrus Harding (2-86). To son James Harding (2-87). To three granddaughters Hannah, Elizabeth, and Sally. To Samuel

Pitman. Under 12. To niece Mary Pitman. Grandsons William Edward Coles and John H. Coles. Sons Hiram, John H and William to be executors. Proved 11 March 1833.

Northumberland County VA Order Books

Order Book 1 1652-1657

1650 22 Nov: Record Book 14 Page 31 Grant: Sir William Berkeley to George Nott Sr., 200 acres in Northumberland "on the west side of the head of the Youocomocoe River abutting Southeast upon head of the said river southwest upon an Indian Bridge and a Valleye Northwest and Northeast upon the maine woods. 50 acres due by assignment of George Berry and the other 150 acres granted for transportation of 3 persons into this colony. Nott assigned the patent to Peter Knight 30 January 1652/3, recorded 20 September 1653.

1651 24 May: Book 14 Page 14 John Bennett witnesses deed for sale of a cow from John Mottrom to Richard White.

1651 18 Nov: A grant made near George Knott's land

1651 21 Nov: George Nott acknowledged a deed

1651 25 Nov: Book 2 Page 7 John Bennett on a jury

1652/3 20 Jan: George Nott paid 4549 pounds of tobacco to Peter Knight.

1652/3 20 Jan: Book 2 Page 8 John Bennett Carpenter gets 50 acres for transporting William Spense to the colony

1653 20 Sep: Book 2 Page 16 Thomas Hawkins vs John Bennet Seaman referred to next court

1653/4 26 Feb: Page 24 Geo Nott on committee to settle a difference between Nicholas Morris and Isabel Salisbury

1654 20 May: Book 2 Page 14 John Bennett on a Jury

1655 20 Aug: Book #14 Page 52 A dispute between Thomas Litton and his brother-in-law Thomas Shaue over payment for land. Among deponents were George Nott aged 36 or thereabouts, Elizabeth Nott aged 36 years of thereabouts, George Berry aged 32 years of thereabouts. Others also testified. Including John Haynie aged 31 years or thereabouts.

1655 20 Aug: Page 32 George Nott to administer estate of John Kaye deceased.

1655 20 Aug: Page 33 Geoge Nott on panel to solve dispute between John Hayles and John Trussell

1655 18 Nov: Will of George Knott of Northumberland County, VA. To wife Elizabeth Nott 100 acres, Son George Nott 100 acres, son John Nott 100 acres, son William Nott 100 acres, daughter Ann Nott one brass kettle, to Henry Lenton son of Anthony Lenton, to brother George Berry, to Thomas Hall (indentured servant). Proved 20 March 1655

1655 20 Nov: Book 2 Page 34 John Bennett named in case Cole vs Morris

1655 20 Nov: Book 2 Page 55 John Bennett executor of John Foster

1655 20 Nov: Page 70 William Harding, convicted of witchcraft and sorcery, sentenced to 10 stripes on his bare back and banished from Colony.

Book 2 1657-1661

1658/9 20 Jan: Petition of John Bennett, who married the sister of George Berry now deceased, granted administration of George Berry's estate.

1660 17 Nov: Elizabeth Bennett, relict and adm of John Bennett, who was adm of George Berry. In court.

Book 3 1661-1666

1663 Apr: C 20 John Motley transported Elizabeth Harding to colony

1665: C 20 Elizabeth Harding, age about 20, confirms deposition of Rich Thompson

Book 4 1666-1678

1668/9 27 Jan: Page 27 Thomas Hardinge (1-1) serves on a jury in case of John Gaylord vs. John Saffin

1668/9 27 Jan: Page 29 Thomas Hardinge (1-1) gives evidence on behalf of John Saffin vs. Rich Thompson. Saffin ordered to pay 180 pounds tobacco to Thompson

1669 06 Apr: Page 31 this day in Court makes Choyce of Thomas Harding (1-1) to be his guardian

1669 P 26 Dec: age 43 Thomas Hardinge (1-1) on a jury, John Mottrom vs Thomas Mathieu, with Ralph Waddington and 10 others.

1670 10 Oct: Page 52 Thomas Hardinge (1-1) on a jury

Virginia County Records

1671 15 Nov: Page 68 Thomas Hardinge (1-1) on a jury, Matthew Rhodon vs Rich Cox

1672 17 Apr: Page 74 Thomas Harding (1-1) Constable for Mattapony

1673 18 Aug: Page 92 This day ye last will and testament of Stephen Thomas was proved in Court by ye oathes of Richard Browne and Rich Pemberton witnesses to ye said will.

1675 16 Jun: Page 116-B Upon ye motion of Anne Harding (1-1) ye relict of Thomas Harding (1-1) a comm of admin is granted to the said Anne Harding (1-1), admin of her said deceased husband she giving Caution according to law.

1675 16 Jun: Page 116-B Anne Harding (1-1), James Claughton, and James Johnson doo oblige themselves ye --- bond of sixty thousand pounds of tobacco to ensure ye said Anne Harding (1-1) shall own Administration of ye estate of Thomas Harding (1-1) deceased and that she shall exhibit an inventory thereof until this court.

1675 16 Jun: Page 116-B William Shear, Anthony Lynton, Thomas Perry and James Moore are appointed to appraise ye estate of Thomas Harding (1-1) deceased being sworn by ye next Justice of ye Peace.

1675/6 19 Jan: Page 126 "Whereas it appears to this court that there is due unto Mr. Rich Parrott Esq Attorney for Ann Harding, Mary Harding, George Harding, Mary Harding and Thomas Orley, the heires of Thomas Orley, late of this County decd. an estate according to appraisement amounting to the sum of fourteen thousand five hundred twenty-four pounds of tobacco, judgment is granted the said Mr. Richard Parrott, attorney as aforesaid for ye yet same agst the estate of William Jolland decd. who married the Relict of ye said Thomas Orley and ordered ye the Sheriff possess ye said Mr. Parrott with the ---- of the sd Thomas Orley in right of the said prayers.

Book 5 1678-1698

1679 20 Aug: Page 41 "Upon ye petition of Thomas Harding II (1-3), son of Thomas Harding (1-1) dec, who is of fourteen years of age, prayes that his mother Ann Harding (1-1) might be his guardian. It is ordered that the said Ann (1-1), now the wife of Richard Bradley (1-1), be guardian to the said Thomas (1-3)."

1683 09 Aug: Page 198 1 "Upon ye petition of Anne Bradley (1-1) ye Executor of Richard Bradley (1-1) decd. of probate is granted her of ye last will and testament of sd Rich and will being probated by the oaths of James Johnson and Thomas Miller witnesses of ye sd will."

Harding Families of the Northern Neck of Virginia

1689 18 Jul: Page 476 "Thomas Harding II (1-3) agst James Claughton referred to next court"

1690 19 Nov: Page 525 "Upon ye second of Thomas Harding II (1-3) it is ordered that Geo Cog --- layout and survey an hundred acres of land situated in Mattapony in this County according to ye courses mentioned in the bill of sale conveyed by James Claughton to Thomas Harding (1-1) Decd., father of the said Thomas Harding II (1-3). The said Harding giving release to ye land according to Act."

1690 19 Nov: Page 528 Whereas Luke Rowland (1-3) was summoned to this Court by a note left at ye suit of Thomas Harding II (1-3) for four thousand pounds of tobacco and excess damages pleaded to be sustained by ye Thomas Harding II (1-3) from ye sd Rowland (1-3) and fayling of his appearance to answer ye said suit or attachment is therefore awarded ye said Harding (1-3) against ye said Rowland (1-3) for ye said sum returnable at next the court."

1690 21 Nov: Page 529 "Henry Harding (1-6) and John Harding (1-7) have in court made choice of their brother Thomas Harding II (1-3) to be their guardian"

1690 17 Dec: Page 534 Thomas Harding II (1-3) having brought by action agst Luke Rowland (1-3) for five thousand pounds of tobacco damages awarded to ye said by for entering into the possession of the land in possession of ye said land pay costs of its execution.

1690/1 19 Mar: Page 549 The differences depending upon an injunction in Chancery obtained by Luke Rowland (1-3) agst an order obtained by Thomas Harding II (1-3) agst ye said Rowland ye 17 day of December 1690 is dismissed and ordered ye the said former order be confirmed and ye the said Luke Rowland (1-3) pay costs of suit and Exch.

1691 20 Aug: Page 564 William Harding (1-5) on ye behalf and as next friend to John Harding (1-7) and Henry Harding (1-6), orph of Thomas Harding (1-1) dec against Luke Rowland (1-3) Referred

1691 20 Aug: Page 564 Cha Harris and Luke Rowland (1-3) doo oblige themselves their heirs, executors, administrators jointly and severally in the sum of 20,000 pounds of tobacco and ???? that ye said Rowland shall appear at the next court and answer the suit of William Harding (1-5).

1691 02 Sep: Page 566 Whereas John Haynie Sr. petitioned court that Thomas Harding II (1-3) dec died intestate leaving an estate in Lands and Chattels and had issue by said Haynie's daughter dec also a son named Thomas Harding III (1-8) who hath from his birth being three years since been sustained by him and prayed for guardianship of said child. It is therefore ordered that ye sd Mr. Haynie be guardian of the sd Thomas Harding III (1-8), that he exhibit an inventory of the sd Harding's estate by the next court and enter into bond the surety to be acceptable for the said estate wn ye orpht comes of age.

1691/2 19 Feb: Page 581 "Ordered that sometime between this and the next court that Richard Fflynt and Thomas Bushrod and George Hutton and ye James Soburn or any three of them meet and etc. and state ye accts of William Harding (1-9) and others ye orphans of Thomas Harding II (1-3) decd. against Luke Rowland (1-3) and make report of their proceedings at the next court."

1692 10 May: Page 592 Ordered that Mr. Richard Fflynt and George Hutton and James Soburn and Thomas Bushrodd or any three of them being sworn by the next Justice meet sometime before the next court and take an appraisement of the estate of Thomas Harding II. (1-3) Sr decd. and make returns to the next court and also that Luke Rowland (1-3) at that time make exhibition oath to the same.

1692 10 Oct: Page 603 Elizabeth Price, a svt to Thomas Flint, gave birth to an illeg. Child and swore William Harding (1-5) was the father.

1693/4 19 Jan: Page 646 Whereas William Harvey was arrested at ye land of Capt John Haynie, guardian of Thomas Harding III (1-8) for ye said (number) of pounds of tobacco. Of ye said building and more etc."

Page 660 Will of Ralph Waddington proved

1696 22 May: Page 728 "Captain John Haynie, guardian of Thomas Harding III (1-8), orphan to Thomas Harding Sr. (1-3), against Luke Rowland (1-3), who married Anne (1-3) the Administrator of Thomas Harding II (1-3). Referred"

1696 16 Jul: Page 736 "Capt. John Haynie, guardian to the orphans of Thomas Harding II (1-3) dec vs Luke Rowland (1-3) who has married Anne (1-3), admx of the said Harding (1-3). Continued until the next court."

1696 17 Sep: Page 742 "Mr. John Haynie Sen, guardian of the orphans of Thomas Harding II (1-3) decd. against Luke Rowland (1-3), who married Ann (1-3) the admx of said Harding (1-3). Continued by consent.

1696 16 Dec: Page 753 "Upon the petition of Henry Harding (1-6), commission of Adm is granted him on the estate of William Harding (1-5), decd., he giving Caution for his due administration on the said estate according to law."

1696 17 Dec: Page 754 "Upon the motion of Henry Harding (1-6) admr of William Harding (1-5) decd. it is ordered that Richard Fflynt Jr., Thomas Barcroft, Hugh Stathan, and John Lawrence or any three of them being first sworn by the next Justice meete and appraise the estate of the said decd. and return an appraisal thereof under law at the next court."

Harding Families of the Northern Neck of Virginia

1697 21 Apr: Page 761 "Upon petition of Mary Rowland, relict of Luke Rowland decd. a commission of administration on the Estate of her said husband also giving Caution for ---- administration on the said estate according to law."

1697 21 Apr: Page 761 "Whereas it appears to this court that the Estate of William Harding (1-5) decd. is indebted to Henry Harding (1-6) his admr by account for sundry charges and other expenses which this court esteems reasonable eight hundred pounds of tobacco ---- Judgment is granted the said Harding adm against the said decd. estate for the said funds."

1697 22 Apr Page 764 "Mr. James Johnson vs Henry Harding (1-6) adm of William Harding (1-5) continued to the next court."

1697 22 Apr: Page 765 "Mr. John Cralle agst Henry Harding (1-6), adm of William Harding (1-5), continued to the next court."

1697 20 May: Page 774 "James Johnson agst Henry Harding (1-6), admr of William Harding (1-5) decd. continued."

1697 20 May: Page 774 "Mr. John Cralle against Henry Harding (1-6) admr of William Harding (1-5) continued.

1697 18 Aug: Page 781 "Upon the motion of Jane Harding (1-6), widow and relict of Henry Harding (1-6), decd., a commission of Adm is granted her on the estate of her said deceased husband and had giving (---) for her did administer on the said estate according to law.".

1697 18 Aug: Page 781 "Upon the motion of Jane Harding (1-6), admr of Henry Harding (1-6) decd., Mr. Richard Fflynt and Thomas Miller and William Brand and John Lewis and John Cralle or any four of them, are by the Court appointed to appraise the estate of the said decd. being first summoned by the next justices and ordered that said Jane exhibit an inventory thereof to the next court upon oath."

1697 16 Sep: Page 792 "Charles Harris against Mary Rowland, adm of Luke Rowland referred"

1697/8 18 Feb: Page 809 Richard Robinson and Frances his wife brought suits against Edward Watkins and Anne his wife executors of Ralph Warrington decd for a third part or filial portion of the said decd Estate pled the said Frances being daughter to the said Warrington and the said Watkins and his wife not appearing to answer the sd suit Order is therefore granted the said Robinson and his wife agst Capt William Jones, Sheriff, for a third part of the said estate according to law.

1697/8 19 Feb: Page 814 Upon the motion of Charles Ashton (1-6) and Jane (1-6) his wife, Com of Adm is granted them on est of William Harding (1-5) dec., they giving Caution for their due administration on the said estate according to law.

1697/8 18 Feb: Page 816 Robert Rowland age 4 the 31st of Jan. last by the consent of his mother Mary Rowland to serve Edward Woodridge until 21

1698 19 May: Page 825 Charles Ashton (1-6) having noted to the court that William Harding (1-5) to whom he is administrator did begin and work carpentry works for and towards building a house for Richard Thompson who refuseth satisfaction for the said work not being finished. The Court doe therefore appoint Mr. Richard Flynt, John Lawrence and Thomas Miller to view the said Worke, compute the value thereof and make a report to the next court.

1698 21 Jul: Page 835 "Judgment is granted Mr. John Cralle agst Charles Ashton (1-6) and Jane (1-6) his wife, admr of William Harding (1-5) deced for the payment of three hundred and four pounds of tobacco on balance of a bill for four hundred and fifty founds of tobacco dated November 29 169- and ordered to pay the said summe of three hundred and four pounds of tobacco to the said Cralle our of the said deced estate."

1698 21 Jul: Page 835 "Whereas it appears to the court that William Harding (1-5) estate is indebted to James Johnson by accounts for diff and other expenses in his lifetime and after his death 712 pounds of tobacco is granted to said Johnson against Charles Ashton and Jane (1-6) his wife, admr of the said decd. Ordered that the administrator pay the said funds out of said decd. estate."

Book 6 1699-1713

1700 23 Aug: Page 128 John Cockrell and his servant Henry Harding (1-6) having each attended this court three days as Evidence on the behalfe of John Scott against James White as the said Cockrell hath made oath It's therefore ordered the said Scott pay the said Cockrell for the same two hundred and forty pounds of tobacco.

1700/1 15 Jan: The last will of Charles Ashton (1-6) was this day proved by the oaths of Trigue Allen and Charles Carpenter, witnesses thereto and recorded.

1700/01 19 Feb: Page 143 Mary Laurence Sevt to Capt Thomas Windor having had a bastard child in the time of her Service by William Harding and thus hath made oath in court and that said Capt Windor having in court affirmed the paymt of her ssins He therefore ordered she serve her said Master one yeare and a halfe after her time of Indenture be expired according to law and further ordered that the said William Enter into bond with good and sufft security to hold the xxx harmless.

1705/6 Mar: C 21 250 acres to Capt George Eskridge for transportation of Henry Harding (3-1) and others.

1706 23 Nov: Page 412 Anne Belcher (3-1) wid agt Fergus att Timothy Swillivant dismissed

1706/7 19 Mar: Page 433 Thomas Hardinge (1-8), Thomas Webb petitioning this court that they sent their tythables according to law the fourth of June last past by John Haynie Jun. That they knew nothing to the contrary but that they were entered until Mr. John Haynie Sr. informed them to ye contrary and prayed to have Liberty and be admitted tythables being ready to pay the same to such persons appointed to recv ye same and ye set John Haynie Jun making oath in Court they desired him to enter their titheables but through forgetfulness he did it not and the court consider that they have Liberty to pay their levies this sent Colletons to such persons as are appointed to recv ye said. They being accountable to ye courts and at they laying ye levy.

1708 20 May: Page 519 20 Upon the petition of Henry Harding (3-1) and Anne (3-1) his wife, com of Adm is granted them on the estate of William Beltcher Jr. decd. they giving Caution for their due admin on ye sd deced estate according to law.

1708 20 May: Page 519 Hugh Callan enters himself security in the sum of ten thousand pounds of tobacco to ye Justices of Northumberland Court that Henry Harding (3-1) and Anne (3-1) his wife shall duly administer the estate of Wm. Beltcher Jr. decd.

1709 19 Aug: Page 623 Judgment is granted William Winder for Six hundred forty-seven pounds of Tobacco against the Estate of Richard Williams in the hands of Anne Harding Widow and relict of William Harding deceased And Ordered she forthwith deliver and pay the same unto the said Winder.

Book 7 1713-1719

1713 18 Nov: Page 4 William Humphries having sold drink contrary to law and having been presented by the Grand Jury for the same it is ordered that he be fined for his said offense according to law and ordered he pay ye same with costs at Execution

1713/14 12 Mar: Page 21 Eliza Callan, orphan daughter of Hugh Callan decd. seven years old the first day of July next is bound and apprenticed to Thomas Harding III (1-8) in all such lawfull services and imployment as he shall imploy until she shall attain the age of eighteen years. Ye said Thomas Harding his heirs or assns in consideration thereof during the said term funding and allowing for her sufficient apparell Dyet and Lodging and educating her according to law for his said performances where he ye said

Thomas Harding III (1-8) and William Botts doe hereby oblige themselves, their heirs exers and admins jointly severally in ye penall sum of five thousand pounds of tobb to be pd to ye Justices of this county for the time being to ye life of ye said orph in case of the sd Thomas Harding III (1-8) noncompliance with the Act of Assembly in that case provided.

1713/14 18 Mar: Page 24 Joseph Robinson and Frances his wife late Frances Waddington, relict of John Waddington decd., granted probate. No will existed.

1713 18 Mar: Mark Harding (5-1) Page 26 examined for evidence.

1714 19 May: Page 34 John Waddington inventory filed.

1714 17 Jun: Page 46 Thomas Hobson, adm of ye will annexed of William Windsor decd. against William Humphries (1-7) and Ann (1-7) his wife Continued till ye next court.

1714 14 Sep: Page 73 An indenture between William Humphries (1-7) and Ann (1-7) his wife (on behalf of their son Thomas Harding (1-11)) and Grant Jewsbury being acknowledged in Court by Richard Wright attorney of the sd William and Ann unto the sd Grant and allso by the sd Grant unto the sd attorney and also the sd William and Ann's power of atty to ye sd Wright to perform the same being proved in Court on the motion of the said Grant Jewsbury are admitted to record.

1716 16 Jun: Page 188 the Last will and Testament of Richard Robinson dec presented by Frances Robinson, his exec and proved by John Wortham, Thomas Robinson and Samuel Robinson

1717 05 May: Page 209 Joseph Robinson and Frances his wife acknowledge deed to John Lunsford.

1717 16 May: Page 215 Thomas Harden (1-8) is appointed Constable in the stead and place of Clement Corbell for the Middle part of St. Stephens Parish Including Keesmans Neck and ordered that he Presente his said office within his precinct and that he be sworn to perform the same by the next Justice.

1717 21 Aug: Page 234 Thomas Harding (1-11) orphan son of John Harding (1-7) dec, having moved to the Court for Liberty to make a choice of a guardian which is granted he hath made Choice of his Cosin Thomas Harding III (1-8) who is admitted he giving Caution for the sd performance of his said trust.

1717 19 Sep: Page 241 John Harding (1-10) and Jane Harding (1-10) his wife late Jane Trussell, relict of John Trussell decd came into court and made oath that the said John Trussell departed this life without making any will so far as they knew or believe and on their motion and giving Security for their

Harding Families of the Northern Neck of Virginia

Inst and faithfull Admin of the said Decd Estate, Certificate is granted them for obtaining letters of administration.

19 Sep: 1717 Page 241 Upon motion of John Harding (1-10) and Jane Harding his wife admin of John Trussell Decd, Mr. Rodham Neale, Gilbert Harold, John Shirley and Henry Dawson or any of three of them are appointed to meet sometime before the next Court being full sworn by Capt Christopher Neale or Mr. Thos. Highlet and appraise the said Decd estate ---- and ordered that the said Admin Exhibit an Inventory thereupon oath to the next Court.

Page 276 20 Aug: 1718 William Humphries (1-7) and Anne (1-7) his wife, next of kin to Cuthbert Bennett Decd came into court and made oath that the said Cuthbert departed this life without making any will so far as they knew or believe and on their motion and giving Security for their Inst and faithfull Admin of the said Decd Estate, Certificate is granted them for obtaining letters of administration.

1718 20 Aug: Page 276 Upon motion of William Humphries (1-7) and Anne (1-7) his wife admin of Cuthbert Bennett Decd, Mr. Robert Jones, Mr. Edward Lee, John Coles and Thomas Smith or any of three of them are appointed to meet sometime before the next Court being full sworn by Mr. Peter Presley or Capt Richard Speer and appraise the said Decd estate ---- and ordered that the said Admin Exhibit an Inventory thereupon oath to the next Court.

1718 18 Sep: Page 294 Mark Harding (5-1) vs Curtis dismissed.

1718 19 Nov: Page 296 John Haynie having acknowledged a deed of indenture to Thomas Harding III (1-8) on ye motion of the said Harding (1-8) ye said deed is admitted to record.

1719 20 Aug: Page 330 Thomas Harding (2-4) and Frances Harding (2-1) being summoned to this Court by noat att the suit of John Froman for the sum of three hundred and thirteen pounds of tobacco by account and not appearing an attachment is therefore granted the said Froman against the estates of the said Thomas Harding (2-4) and Frances Harding (2-1) for the said sum with costs returnable to the next court.

1719 17 Sep: Page 343 Thomas Harding (2-4) and Frances Harding (2-1) being summoned to this Court by noat att the suit of John Froman for the sum of three hundred and thirteen pounds of tobacco due by a bill bearing ye date Anno 1718 and not appearing an attachment is therefore granted the said Froman against the estates of the said Thomas Harding (2-4) and Francis Harding (2-1) for the said sum with costs returnable to the next court.

1719/20 20 Jan: Page 353 Samuel Robinson in administration?? Of Frances Harding (2-1 came into court and made oath that the said Frances died with no will (probate granted)

Book 8 1719-1729

1719/20 17 Feb: Page 1 Cuthbert Bennett, orphan to Cuthbert Bennett decd is apprenticed to Meredith Mahain. He is ten years old next September.

1719/20 17 Feb: Page 1 Inventory of the estate of Frances Harding (2-1) formerly Frances Robinson was presented to the Court by Samuell Robinson and on his motion it admitted to record.

1720 16 Jun: Page 19 Judgment is granted to Thomas Harding III (1-8) against estate of Frances Harding (2-1) dec, in the hands of Samuel Robinson, admr of the said decd for the sum of three hundred pounds of tobb to which he hath made oath. Ordered that the said Samuell Robinson adm as aforesaid pay the said sum of three hundred pounds of tobb to the said Thomas Harding III (1-8) with costs at Execution.

1720 16 Jun: Page 20 Judgment is granted to Mr. Charles Hobson executor of Thomas Hobson against the estate of Frances Harding (2-1) in the hands of Samuel Robinson admr of the sd deced in the sum of 400 pounds of tobacco.

1721/22 21 Feb: Page 61 Grace and Edward Orphs of Cuthbert Bennett being by this court bound to Thomas Toulson William Toulson being his Security Thomas Worman and the William Requests came into Court and with the said Thomas Toulson entered into a Recognizance of Five thousand pounds Tobb penalty for performance of the said Toulson's time in behalf of each Orphan.

1722 06 May: 6 Page 75 Whereas William Humphreys has made it appears to this Court that he has paid One thousand Six hundred- and three-pounds Tobacco of the Estate of Cuthbert Bennit dec, this County was of opinion this will be allowed (illegible) the said tobacco.

1722 06 May: 6 Page 75 Lovely Bennit Orphan of Cuthbert Bennit decd being six years old the Second Day of next January is bound apprentice to John Norman until he attains the age of twenty-one years to serve the said Norman in all such lawfull Employments as he shall have occasion Vis finding the said orphan Sufficient Diet apparels washing and lodging and to teach him to read and write and the trade of a Cooper. John Rogers came into court and with the said Norman acknowledged Jointly and severally with the said Norman in the Penalty of Five Thousand pounds tobacco Such to be paid to the Justices in behalf of the orphans in case the said Norman should be any ways Deficient in his promises.

1722/3 16 Jan: Page 95 An inventory of the Estate of Thomas Hardin (1-8) decd presented into Court by Mr. George Ball and Mary Hardin (1-8) and on their motion it's admitted to record.

1722/3 20 Feb: Page 99 Upon petition of Richard Vanlandegam, judgment is granted against Mary Harding (1-8) and George Ball, executors of Thomas Harding III (1-8) decd for 400 lbs tobacco.

1722/3 20 Feb: Page 99 Upon petition of Elizabeth Nelms, judgment is granted against Mary Harding (1-8) and George Ball, executors of Thomas Harding III (1-8) decd for 9-2-10 Sterling.

1724 16 Sep: Page 160 Joseph Robinson named guardian of Warrington Robinson

1726/ 27 15 Mar: Page 256 Upon petition of Isaac Palmer ordered that Joseph Robinson, adm of John Warrington decd pay to the said Isaac Palmer and his wife Sarah Anne part of the said decd father's estate.

1728 21 Aug: Page xx Robert Million against the estate of Dennis Fallin dec'd who was admr. of Cuthbert Bennett, dec'd for his wife Grace's portion (formerly Grace Benett) which is ordered to be paid by Ann Fallin Exc. of the said Dennis Fallin out of the said dec'd estate with cost.

1728 Sep: Page 310 Elinor Humphries granted administration of William Humphries estate.

1729 06 Jul: Page 346 Morris Gibbons vs. William Wye. Gibbons awarded 2550 pounds tobacco

Book 9 1729-1737

1730 20 Aug: Page 21 Ralph Warrington paid for attending court.

1732 16 Aug: Page 64 Upon the petition of William Harding (1-14) ordered that Charles Nelms, John Hudnal, Samuel Blackwell and Samuel Nelms meet sometime before the next court having first sworn by the next Justice and Value the Negroes belonging to the orphans of Thomas Harding III (1-8) decd and Divide them Equally between the Said orphans and if it shall happen upon Such Division that the Negro assigned to the said William Harding (1-14) shall be of greater Value than his share he shall be obliged to give bond to the execs of the said Harding Decd at the delivery of the slave for the overplus of the value.

1733 16 Aug: Page 111 Upon the Petition of Thomas Harden (1-15), orphan of Thomas Harden (1-8) late of this county decd, Charles Nelms, John Hudnal, Samuel Blackwell and Sam Nelms meet sometime before the next court having first sworn by the next Justice and Value the Negroes belonging to the orphans of Thomas Harding III (1-8) decd and Divide them Equally between the Said orphans and if it shall happen upon Such Division that the Negro assigned to the said Thomas Harding (1-15) shall be of greater Value than his share he shall be obliged to give bond to the execs of the said Harding Decd at the delivery of the slave for the overplus of the value.

1733 23 Nov: Page 129 Upon the petition of George Humphries setting forth that he married Jane Harding (1-17), daughter of Thomas Harding III (1-8) decd by which he is entitled to a child's part of the estate of the said decd ordered that Mr. George Ball, Executor of the said decd deliver to the said George Humphries his part according to a late division made by John Hudnal, Samuel Nelms and Samuel Blackwell and it is agreed that the said George Humphries have the Negro man of the value of seventy-eight pounds upon his giving security to the said executor for the money he amounts to more than his wives part of the said estate.

1734 16 May: Page 149 Nelms vs Thomas Harden. Judgment to Nelms for 400 lbs tobacco

1735 19 Nov: Page 202 Ralph Waddington will probated by administer Joseph Robinson.

1737 11 Apr: Page 255 Thomas Harding having made oath that he attended eleven days as an Evidence for Robert Clark, ordered that the said Robert Clark pay him for his said attendance according to law at Execution.

Book 10 1737-1743

1737 10 Oct: Page 6 Hester Flood servant of William Barret Came into Court and of her free will and consent agreed to serve Thomas Harding one year after her Indented time Expired for Consideration of the sd Harding's buying her from ye sd William Barret Which is ordered to be recorded.

1738 Page 48 Samuel Snow vs. Isaac Palmer and Thomas Palmer.

1738 11 Jul: Page 57 Hornby vs Thomas Harding. Judgment to Hornby for 320 lbs tobacco

1739 12 Jun: Page 99 William Harding (1-14) vs Henry Dawson Judgment is granted the sd Harding agst the said Dawson for ye sum of four hundred and thirty-four pounds of tobacco Ordered the sd Dawson pay ye same to ye sd Harding with costs.

1739 09 Oct: Page 109 Thomas Harding (1-15) vs Thomas Machen ensuit and one attorney's fee.

1739 10 Dec: Page 116 Thomas Harding (1-15) having obtained an attachment under the hand of John Waughop Gent one of the Magistrates of this County against the estate of Thomas Machen for the sum of 1275 pounds of tobacco and the Sheriff of this County having thereupon Returned at Northumberland on November 13, 1739 then attached the estate of Thomas Machen for the use of Thomas Harding (1-15) as much corn and tobacco as will satisfy ye debt and costs. Joseph Nutt: : and the debt appears to be justly due from ye sd Machen the sd Thomas Harding (1-15) having made oath thereto judgment is granted the sd Thomas Harding (1-15) for ye sd sum of 1275 pounds of tobacco and costs and ordered the sd Sheriff sell to ye highest bidder the sd attached goods and chatles to satisfy ye sd Debt and Costs and pay ye same to ye sd Thomas Harding (1-15).

1739 10 Dec: Page 116 Morris Gibbons having obtained an attachment under the hand of John Waughop Gent one of the Magistrates of this County against the estate of Thomas Machen for the sum of 1275 pounds of tobacco and the Sheriff of this County having thereupon Returned at Northumberland on November 13, 1739 then attached the estate of Thomas Machen for the use of Morris Gibbons as much corn and tobacco as will satisfy ye debt and costs. Joseph Nutt and the debt appears to be justly due from ye sd Machen the sd Morris Gibbons having made oath thereto judgment is granted the sd Morris Gibbons for ye sd sum of 1275 pounds of tobacco and costs and ordered the sd Sheriff sell to ye highest bidder the sd attached goods and chatles to satisfy ye sd Debt and Costs and pay ye same to ye sd Morris Gibbons.

1739/40 11 Feb: Page 121 Moses Lunsford vs the estate of John Lunsford, George Mills admr, Report ordered.

1739/40 10 Mar: Page 124 Thomas Dameron Jr., Richard Haynie and Thomas Harding (1-15) processioners appointed to procession the 6th Precinct of St. Stephens Parish and report.

1739/40 10 Mar: Page 124 William Trussell, William Harding (1-14) and George Lamkin processioners appointed to procession the 1st Precinct of St. Stephens Parish and report.

1739/40 10 Mar: Page 125 Judith Harding (1-18) vs George Ball continued for report.

1740 13 May: Page 139 Judith Harding (1-18) vs George Ball Gent, Samuel Blackwell Gent, Samuel Nelms, Thomas Haynie and John Hudnall herein partitioned ye sd Judith (1-18) her part of Thomas Harding III (1-8) Decd estate. Returned and report of ye same which was ordered to be recorded and ye prosecution dismissed.

1742 13 Apr: Page 259 Robert Warrington and Joseph Robinson gave evidence for Isaac Palmer vs John Corbin. Paid for attending court.

1742/3 25 Jan: Page 321 At a Court called and held for Northumberland County for the examination of Thomas Harding (2-4) of this County on suspicion of feloniously burning an outhouse belonging to Joseph Robinson of this County. Witnesses on behalf of our Sovereign Lord the King against the sd Thomas Harding (2-4) wit Isaac Palmer, Sarah Thomas, John Thomas, and William Walker being sworn and examined by the Court the sd evidences not proving any matter of fact or giving sufficient evidence to commit the sd prisoner to the General Court for his further tryall concerning the sd felony. He is aquited of the sd crime, but it is the Court's opinion and ordered by the sd Court that the sd Thomas Harding (2-4) pay the costs of this prosecution.

Book 11 1743-1749

Page 26 John Gorham vs Thomas Harding judgment 334 pounds tobacco

1745 09 Jul: Page 74 In the Suit between William Harding (1-14) Pet vs Richard Gorham deft, by attachment against the Estate of the sd Defd the sd Plt made oath to the truth of his Petition and Judgment is granted him against the sd defendant for the sum of two pounds four shillings and two pence half in current money and the attachment being returned served on his crop of corn in the field and the use of the home and plantation Ordered the Sheriff sell and pay the sd debt and costs out of the same.

1746 11 Mar: Page 168 Cornelius Todd vs Thomas Harding, judgment awarded to Todd for 291 pounds of tobacco.

1746 10 Feb: Page 171 Elizabeth Gawkins vs. John Harden, petition dismissed

1746 06 Mar: Page 179 Spencer Ball to William Harding (1-14) children, deed ordered recorded

Page 231 Campbell vs. Harding

1747 09 Nov: Page 260 William and Mary Hughlett deed to William Harding (1-14) ordered recorded.

1747/8 12 Jan: Page 272 William Jones vs. Thomas Harding continued.

1747/8 14 Mar: Page 281 Bond William Harding (1-14) to Spencer Ball ordered recorded.

1748 18 Aug: Page 368 Isaac Palmer's will ordered recorded

1748 18 Feb: Page 411 Isaac Palmer's inventory ordered recorded

1748/9 13 Feb: Page 416 Winnifred Harding, (2-17) orphan of Thomas Harding (2-4) decd, is by the Court bound to Maximilian Haynie until she arrive at the age of 18 and said Haynie is to learn her to sew, read and spin.

1748/9 13 Mar: Page 429 Frances Ann Harding, (2-18) orphan of Thomas Harding (2-4) decd, is by the Court bound to Benjamin Haynie to learn her to read, sew and spin.

1749 08 May: Page 469 John Downing, executor of Samuel Snow vs Gnarl Serazer Palmer, executor of Isaac Palmer Decd, Judgment of 400 pounds tobacco

1749 13 Jun: Page 481 Colson vs Thomas Harding dismissed

1749 11 Jul: Page 500 John Smith, executor of John Smith decd, vs. Thomas Harding, In Detinue, Jury is out.

1749 12 Jul: Page 509? John Smith, executor of John Smith decd, vs Thomas Harding, In Detinue.

Book 12 1750 to 1753

1750 10 Sep: Page 80 William Harding (1-14) is appointed guardian to Mary Appleby, orphan of John Appleby.

1750 10 Sep: Page 81 Ordered that William Haynie, Moseley Mott, John Humphries, Thomas Cottrell or any three of them Possess William Harding (1-14) with Mary Appleby's part of her decd Father's estate / first allowing the widow her dower / and make their report to the Court.

750 10 Dec: 1 Page 111 Ordered that William Harding (1-14), Matthew Neale, William Humphries and David Straughn appraise the estate of Timothy Paydon.

1750 10 Dec: Page 111 On the motion of Hannah Harding (2-4), who made oath according to law, Certificate is granted her for obtaining letters of Administration of the Estate of Thomas Harding (2-4) decd she giving bond and security. Whereupon she together with Chas Coppedge and Edwin Fielding securities. Entered into and acknowledged bond for the due admin of the said estate. Ordered that Robert Angell, David Lattimore, John Berry, and William Berry appraise the estate of Thomas Harding (2-4) decd.

1751 13 May: Page 162 An inventory and appraisement of the estate of Thomas Harding (2-4) deceased was this day returned and ordered to be recorded.

1751 13 May: Page 162 An inventory and appraisement of the estate of Samuel Denney deceased was this day returned and ordered to be recorded.

1751 12 Nov: Page 245 William Harding (1-14) vs Samuel Partridge, in debt for 128 pounds of tobacco.

1752 13 Apr: Page 268 A bond from William Harding (1-14) to Sarah Humphries was proved by the oaths of John Pace and Francis Gordon, witnesses thereto, and ordered recorded.

1752 14 Apr: Page 276 William Harding (1-14) vs. John Evans, dismissed.

1752 18 Jun: Page 299 Thomas Harding (1-15) appointed Overseer of the Road in the Room of Thomas Dammeron and it is ordered that he clean and keep the same in good repair.

1752 15 Jul: Page 320 The petition of Thomas Harding (1-15) against William Johnston is continued.

1752 25 Sep: Page 344 Harry Piper, assignee of Richard Jackson vs William Harding (1-14). Judgment of 1-18-11 granted.

1753 13 Feb: Page 383 The petition of Thomas Harding (1-15) against William Johnson is dismissed being agreed the parties.

1753 13 Feb: Page 383 The petition of William Johnson against Thomas Harding (1-15) is dismissed being agreed the parties.

Book 13 1753-1756

1753 09 Jul: Page 14 William Harding (1-14) attachment

1753 13 Aug: Page 36 Thomas Harding (1-15) appointed surveyor of highway from Smith Oldfield to Coan Warehouse.

1753 14 Aug: Page 42 Thomas Ball vs Thomas Harding (1-15) judgment granted.

1753 14 Aug: Page 42 William Harding (1-14) attachment against the estate of William Hughlett.

1754 11 Feb: Page 74 Thomas Harding (1-15) et al to appraise estate of Robert Rowland

1754 13 Mar: Page 91 William Harding (1-14) attachment against estate of William Hughlett

1754 04 Jul: Page 173 Thomas Harding (1-15) witness for Spencer Haynie gets 150 pounds tobacco for 6 days at court.

1754 14 Oct: Page 226 William Harding (1-14) as inspector reports.

1755 10 Mar: Page 273 Bond from William Harding (1-14) to Matthew Neale ordered recorded

1755 12 May: Page 312 John Harding (2-19), orphan of Thomas Harding (2-4) decd, bound to Peter Chapman until he is of 21 years to learn the trade of taylor.

1755 13 May: Page 324 Sarah Harding (2-20), John Harding (2-19) and Hannah Harding (2-21), orphans of Thomas Harding (2-4) decd choose Joseph Robinson Jr. as their guardian. Security is Joseph Robinson Sr.

1755 13 Oct: Page 381 William Harding (1-14) witness for James Crane, earns 25 pounds of tobacco for one day at Court.

1755 13 Nov: Page 410 Deed William Harding (1-14) to Matthew Neale proved.

1756 08 Mar: Page 464 Petition of Frances Harding (2-18) for her part of deceased father Thomas Harding (2-4) estate in the hands of Presley Thornton Esq.

1756 10 Mar: Page 483 William Harding (1-14) witness for James Wilkins gets 100 pounds of tobacco for four days in court.

Book 14 1756-1758

1756 10 May: Page 7 Hopkin Harding, (2-15) orphan of Thomas Harding (2-4) decd made choice of Swan Pritchard for his guardian. Joshua Palmer Security

1756 11 Oct: Page 62 William Harding (1-14) and John Meath, Inspectors of the TOB at the Coan Warehouse in this County produced in court an account upon Oath of the transfer Notes that were not by the sd inspectors taken in and received before the 1st Day of October which amounts to three thousand and eight hundred and eighteen pounds of Tob. There is also remaining in their hands twelve pounds Eighteen shillings Current money.

1757 14 Feb: Page 120 On motion of Thomas Harding (1-15) and Hezekiah Haynie Securities for the administration of the estate of Joseph Robinson decd, James Daughity, Beverly Hacum and John Hobson are appointed to process the sd Harding and Haynie with the third part of the movable estate of Joseph Robinson Jun decd in the hands of Mary Robinson and make report thereof to the next court.

1757 14 Mar: Page 121 A report of processing Thomas Harding (1-15) and Hezekiah Haynie with the estate of Joseph Robinson decd was this day returned and ordered to be recorded.

1757 09 May: Page 150 Hopkins Harding (2-15) witness ordered to be paid 25 pounds of tobacco for attending court.

1757 10 Oct: Page 228 Swan Pritchard appeared for not rendering report on Guardianship of the Estate of Hopkins Harding, (2-15) orphan of Thomas Harding (2-4) decd.

1757 10 Oct: Page 228 William Harding (1-14) and John Meath account of Coan warehouses

1758 13 Mar: Page 272 Mark Harding (2-16) orphan of Thomas Harding, bound to Robert Balvard

1758 11 Sep: Page 341 Thomas Harding (1-15) Plaintiff v Jonathan Edwards Defendant

1758 19 Oct Page 348 William Harding (1-14) sworn to his inspector's account

1758 19 Oct: Page 349 William Harding (1-14) v Jonathan Edwards continued

1758 17 Nov: Page 356 Samuel Blackwell Gent produced in court an account of his Guardianship of the Estate of John Harding (2-14) orphan of Thomas

Harding (2-4) decd which being Examined and Allowed by the Court and sworn to by the said Blackwell was ordered to be recorded.

Book 15 1758-1762 Partial Index from Page 362

1762 12 Apr: Page 367 A bond from Jane Harding (1-15) Henry Boggess and Elisha Betts to Matthew Neale and William Eskridge Acknowledged and ordered to be recorded.

1762 10 May: Page 377-8 The last will and testament of William Harding (1-14) was this day by Oath of Thomas Smith one of the Witnesses thereto

1762 Jun: Page 428 Ordered that Onesephorus Harvey pay unto Mark Harding (2-16) Two Hundred pounds Tobc for Eight days attendance at this Court as a Witness for the sd Harvey against Robert Balvard

1762 13 Jul: Page 455 Moses Lunsford, William Copedge, Richard Taylor and Jesse Robinson or any three of them are appointed to Possess Hopkins Harding (2-15) with the Estate of Arom Nelms orphan of Aron Nelms Decd in the hands of John Nutt and make report thereof to the court.

1762 09 Aug: Page 466 Report of possessing Hopkins Harding (2-15) with the Estate of Aron Nelms was this day returned and ordered to be recorded.

1762 13 Sep: Page 515 Report of the Valuations of a negro left by the will of William Harding (1-14) decd to Griffin Fauntleroy was this day returned and ordered to be recorded.

1762 11 Oct: Page 538 A Deed of Bond from John Harding (2-14) and Mary his wife of the one part to Pemberton Claughton of the other part was proved by the Witnesses and Admitted to Record.

Census Records

1810 Federal Census
Page 982 Thomas Harding (2-52) 21001 10010
Page 982 William Harding (2-45) 31010 11010
Page 983 Hopkins Harding (2-15) 00101 10101
Page 985 Samuel Harding (1-38) 11001 00020

1820 Federal Census
Page 7 William Harding (2-81) 102200 00100
Page 8 Hiram Harding (2-79) 000010 30200
Page 8 Sam'l Harding (1-38) 000001 02001
Page 8 William Harding (2-45) 020101 00010
Page 9 Charles Harding (2-54) 000000 00000
Page 9 Thomas G. Harding 200100 00200

Page 9 Thomas Harding (2-52) 210001 01001

1830 Federal Census Page 205
William Harding (2-45) 00001001 000101
William Harding (2-81) Jr 010121 000101
Hiram Harding (2-79) 000001 203002001
Thomas E Harding (2-80) 000011 00003
John H Harding (2-84) 20001 00010
Cyrus Harding (2-86) 0001100110001
Jane Harding (1-41) 00000001 0000110001
Page 208 Chas Harding (2-54) 00001 100110001

Personal Property Tax Lists

1782 Thomas Edwards List
Page 1 Hopkins Harding (2-15) 5 Persons 14 Cattle 2 Horses

1782 Thomas Downing's List
Samuel Harding (1-38) 7 Persons 14 Cattle 3 Horses 2 Wheels

1782 Peter Cox List
William Harding (1-32) 15 Persons 20 Cattle, 4 Horses 2 Wheels

1783 Personal Property Tax List
Hopkins Harding (2-15) 1 male over 21, 4 slaves, 16 Cattle, 2 Horses
Page 12 Thomas Harding (2-52) 1 male over 21, 2 Horses
Page 12 Samuel Harding (1-38) 1 male over 21 8 slaves, 19 cattle, 3 horses
Above two next to each other.
Page 16 William Harding (1-32) 1 male over 21 13 slaves, 20 cow 4 horse 2 wheel

1784 Personal Property Tax List
Hopkins Harding (2-15) 1 male, 5 slaves, 2 horse 14 cows
Samuel Harding (1-38) 1 male 8 slaves, 13 cow 5 horse 4 wheels
William Harding (1-32) 1 male, 15 slaves, 16 cattle 3 horses

1785 Personal Property Tax List
Hopkins Harding (2-15)1 male, 7 slaves, 12 cow 2 horse
Samuel Harding (1-38) 1 male, 9 slaves, 13 cow 5 horse 4 wheels
Thomas Harding (2-52) 1 male, 3 slave, 4 cow 3 horse
William Harding (1-32) 1 male, 10 slave, 16 cow, 6 horse

1786 Personal Property Tax List
Pg 2 Thomas Harding (2-52) 1 male 3 slave 1 cow I horse
Pg 5 Hopkins Harding (2-15) 1 male 8 slave 12 cow 2 horse

Virginia County Records

Pg 15 Samuel Harding (1-38) 1 Male, 6 slave, 16 cow 3 horse
Pg 20 William Harding (1-32)'s Estate 16 slave 19 cow 6 horse

1787 Personal Property Tax List
Thomas Harding (2-52) 1 21 0 16-21 4 blacks 2 horse 5 cattle
Hopkins Harding (2-15) and Cyrus Harding ov 21 1 16-21 9 slave 2 horse 18 cow
Sam'l Harding (1-38) 8 blacks 2 horse 18 cow

1788 Personal Property Tax List
Jane Harding (1-41) 2 blacks over 16
William Harding (1-32) Estate 8 blacks 1 horse
Samuel Harding (1-38) 5 blacks 1 horse 3 cows 2 wheels
Hopkins Harding (2-15) and Cyrus Harding 1 16-21 5 blacks 3 horse
Thomas Harding (2-52) 3 blacks 1 horse (same page as Hopkins)

1789 Personal Property Tax List
Thomas Harding (2-52) No assets
Maryanne Harding 1 male under 21 1 black 3 horses
William Harding (1-32) Estate 8 slaves 3 horse
Jane Harding (1-41) 2 blacks over 16
Samuel Harding (1-38) 6 blacks 2 horses

1790 Personal Property Tax List
Hopkins Harding (2-15) and Cyrus Harding 2 16-21 6 blacks 4 horses
Thomas Harding (2-52) 1 male 16-21 1 black 2 horse
William Harding (1-32) Estate 6 blacks 3 horses
Jane Harding (1-41) 1 black over 16
Samuel Harding (1-38) 7 blacks 2 horses

1791 Personal Property Tax List
Hopkins Harding (2-15), with Cyrus, Billey & John Harding 8 blacks 3 horses
William Harding (1-32)'s Estate 8 blacks 2 horses
Samuel Harding (1-38) 8 blacks 2 horses

1792 Personal Property Tax List
Thomas Harding (2-52) No assets
Hopkins Harding (2-15) with Billy and John Harding 8 blacks 3 horses
Cyrus Harding (2-43) 2 blacks 1 horse
William Harding (1-32) Estate 8 blacks 2 horses
Samuel Harding (1-38) 8 blacks 2 horses

1793 Personal Property Tax List
Billy Harding (2-45) 3 blacks
Thomas Harding (2-52) No assets

Harding Families of the Northern Neck of Virginia

Hopkins Harding (2-15) 8 blacks 3 horses
Cyrus Harding (2-43) 2 blacks 1 horse
William Harding (1-32)'s Estate 9 blacks 2 horses
Samuel Harding (1-38) 7 blacks 1 horse

1794 Personal Property Tax List
Billy Harding (2-45)
Hopkins Harding (2-15)
Cyrus Harding (2-43)
Thomas Harding (2-52)
William Harding (1-32)'s estate

1795 Personal Property Tax List
Cyrus Harding (2-43)
Hopkins Harding (2-15)
William Harding (2-45)
Thomas Harding (2-52)
William Harding (1-32)'s Estate
Samuel Harding (1-38)

1796 Personal Property Tax List
William Harding (1-32)'s Estate
Samuel Harding (1-38)
William Harding (2-45)
Hopkins Harding (2-15)
Cyrus Harding (2-43)
Charles Harding (2-54)

1797 Personal Property Tax List
Samuel Harding (1-38)
James Harding (1-60) (on same list as Samuel) 7 slaves 3 horses now of age
Thomas Harding (2-52)
William Harding (2-45)
Cyrus Harding (2-43)
Hopkins Harding (2-15)
Charles Harding (2-54)

1798 Personal Property Tax List
William Harding (2-45)
Cyrus Harding (2-43)
Hopkins Harding (2-15)
Thomas Harding (2-52)
Samuel Harding (1-38)
William Harding (2-45)

James Harding (1-60)
Thomas Harding (2-52) These three together on list

1799 Personal Property Tax List
List 1 Hopkins Harding (2-15)
List 1 Cyrus Harding (2-43)
List 1 William Harding (2-45)
List 1 Thomas Harding (2-52)
List 1 John Harding
List 2 James Harding (1-60)
List 2 William Harding (1-61)
List 2 Samuel Harding (1-38)

1800 Personal Property Tax List
List 1 Cyrus Harding (2-43)
List 1 Billy Harding (2-45)
List 1 Hopkins Harding (2-15)
List 1 Thomas Harding (2-52)
List 2 Samuel Harding (1-38)
List 2 William Harding (1-61)
List 2 James Harding (1-60)

1801 Personal Property Tax List
List 1 Samuel Harding (1-38)
List 1 James Harding (1-60)
List 2 Hopkins Harding (2-15)
List 2 Thomas Harding (2-52)
List 2 Cyrus Harding (2-43)
List 2 Billy Harding (2-45)

1802 Personal Property Tax List
List 1 Thomas Harding (2-52)
List 1 Billy Harding (2-45)
List 1 Cyrus Harding (2-43)
List 1 Hopkins Harding (2-15)
List 2 James Harding (1-60)
List 2 William Harding (1-61)
List 2 Samuel Harding (1-38)

Northern Neck Land Grants

9 Dec: 1746 Book F Page 260 Costillo Hill of Northumberland County 125 acres, adjacent William Harding (1-14).

Marriage Records of Northumberland

1757 Dec: Joseph Wildey (1-24) and Judith Harding (1-24)
1759 Mar: Griffin Fauntleroy (1-25) and Betty Harding (1-25)
1759 03 Jul: John Cralle and Spilman Garner
1760 John Lewis (1-26) and Hannah Harding (1-26)
1765 19 Jan: Parish Garner (1-30) and Jane Harding (1-30)
1765 27 May: Ellis Hudnall (1-39) and Judith Harding (1-39)
1767 19 Dec: William Gaskins and Mary Harding
1771 20 Mar: James Hudnall (1-36) and Jemima Harding (1-36)
1773 04 Dec: Samuel Lewis (1-31) and Frances Harding (1-31)
1774 07 Dec: John Anderson (1-24) and Judith Wildy (1-24)
1777 Aug: James Cox and Mary Harding
1778 Sally Wildy (1-52) and William Coles
1784 30 Aug: Thomas Gaskins, Gent and Sally Harding spinster
1790 26 Apr: Heli Wildy (1-57) and Betty S. Nelms

St. Stephens Parish Register

Children of Thomas Harding (1-1)
1664 04 Sep: Thomas Harding II (1-3) born
1669 20 Jul: William Harding (1-5) born

Children of Thomas Harding II (1-3)
1710 21 Feb: Thomas Harding IV (1-15) born
1690 15 Feb: William Harding (1-9) born

Children of Phebe Harding:
1704 26 Jul: John born

Children of William Harding (2-1):
1704 02 Jul: Charles Harding (2-2)
1704 02 Jul: Francis Harding (2-3)
1706 02 Feb: Thomas Harding (2-4)

Children of William Harding (1-9)
1717 06 Oct: Thomas Harding (1-20)
1721 16 Jul: Juddaydah Harding (1-21)

Children of Thomas Harding (1-15)
1734 21 Apr: John Harding (1-33) born
1737 09 Sep: Thomas Harding (1-34) born
1737 09 Sep: Frances Harding (1-35) born
1739 03 May: Jemayma Harding (1-36) born

1741 06 Apr: Mary Harding (1-37) born
1744 06 Mar: Samuel Harding (1-38) born
1745 18 Jul: Judith Harding (1-39) born
1748 05 Apr: Hatte Harding (1-40) born

Children of Frances Harding:
1759 15 Dec: Peggy Harding born

Children of Joseph Wildey and Judith Wildey: (1-24)
1757 Dec: Jos Wildey married Judith Harding (1-24)
1758 02 Sep: Sarah Wildey (1-52) born
1760 09 Apr: William Wildey (1-42 born
1761 14 Sep: Molly Wildey (1-54) born
1763 17 Mar: Judith Wildey (1-55)

Children of William Harding (1-32) and Milly Harding: (1-32)
1775 18 Nov: James Harding (1-60) born
1778 07 Jan: William Harding (1-61) born
1778 07 Jan: Thomas Harding (1-62) born

Children of Edward Bennett:
1676 20 Sep: Ann Bennett (1-7)
1678 15 Dec: John Bennett
1780 15 Jan: Cuthbert Bennett
1682 10 Dec: Elizabeth Bennett
1684 30 Jan: Dorothy Bennett
1687 27 Mar:Edward Bennett

Children of Cuthbert Bennett:
1708 25 Nov: Edward Benn(ett)

Children of Edward Bennett:
1707 15 Aug: Ann Bennett dau to Edward born
1709 03 Dec: Joseph Bennett son to Edward born
1731 16 Mar: Judy Bennett dau to Edward born
1732 02 Feb: Winifred Bennett dau to Edward born

1696 31 Mar: John Barecraft, son to Thomas born
1701 08 Aug: Martha Barecraft daughter to Thomas born
1756 03 Dec: Presley Barecraft son to John and Mary born
17 Nov: 1758 Kezia Barecraft daughter to Martrum and Alice born
1758 12 Oct: John Barecraft son to John and Mary born
1760 06 Mar: Sarahan Barecraft, daughter to John and Mary born
1761 17 Apr: Katy Barecraft, daughter to Martrum and Alice born

1757 18 Dec: Lucretia Nelms Barecraft daughter to Winifred born (a bastard)
1767 28 Feb: Rodham Neale Barecraft son to George and Susannah born
1755 20 Apr: Sarah Ann Barecraft, wife to John, died
1755 21 Apr: John Barecraft son to John died
1759 12 May: John Barecraft, son to John and Mary died

1710 21 Nov: George Trussell, son to John, born
1715 19 Oct: Mathew Trussell, son to John, born

Orange County, Virginia Records

Formed From Spotsylvania County in 1734

Court Records

1736 25 Nov: Book 1 Page 134 The suit brought by William Crossthwaite against Benjamin Hardin is dismissed.

1738 26 Oct: Book 1 Page 403 Robert Green Gent produced a certificate granted to John Ashby dated 9 May 1733 for taking up two runaway Negroes belonging to John Diggs in Prince Wiliam County.

1740 27 Nov: Book 2 Page 303 The suit of attachment brought by John Ashby plaintiff against the Estate of Nicholas Copeland Defendant is dismissed.

1740 28 Nov: Book 2 Page 288 Benjamin Hardin having made oath that he had attended three days as an evidence for Valentine Sevier against Sameul Bason his Motion ordered that he pay him for the same Seventy-five pounds of tobacco according to law.

1741 09 May: Book 2 Page 366 The order for making laying and marking the road petitioned for by Benjamin Hardin and others being returned, appointed an overseer.

1741 25 Jul: Book 2 Page 427 Petition from Thomas Ashby Jr for road from Howell's Ford to the top of Blue Ridge, It is ordered that all the inhabitants that live on the Lowlands on both sides of the River from Lidwells to Scotts Hills clear the same under Robert Ashby who is appointed overseer of the said road.

1741 25 Sep: Book 3 Page 113 Thomas Ashby Jr having made oath that he had attended four days as an evidence for Joseph Combs agst Samuel Timmons. On his Motion ordered that he pay him for same one hundred pounds of tobacco according to law.

1741 26 Sep: Book 3 Page 30 In the Action of trespass upon the Case between Thomas Ashby Jr Plaintiff and Henry Halkenburgh Defendant. A Motion of a Special imparlance is granted him until the next court.

1741 28 Nov: Book 3 Page 89 The suit by petition brought by John Hardin (5-2) plaintiff against James Scott Neither party appearing is dismissed.

1741 28 Feb: Book 3 Page 113 On petition by John Hardin (5-2) and others for clearing road from John Knaillands to Ashbys road at the fox trap liberty is granted the petitioners. Ordered that they assist on Ashbys road to top of ridges and help to clear same.

1742 26 Mar: Book 3 Page 125 Action between Thomas Ashby Jr plaintiff and Henry Halkenburgh Defendant, Plaintiff won the case.

1742 26 Mar: Book 3 Page 127 On motion of Thomas Ashby Sr an evidence for Thomas Ashby Jr against Henry Holkenburgh to be paid for two days attendance. On motion of John Ashby as evidence for Thomas Ashby Jr against Henry Holkenburgh It is ordered he pay him for two days attendance according to law.

1742 25 Aug: Book 3 Page 232 The suit by attachment brought by William Roberts against the Estate of Joseph Hardin is dismissed

1742 24 Sep: Book 3 Page 242 Action of trespass between William Roberts and Joseph Harden, defendant not appearing judgement is granted to the plaintiff unless defendant appears at next court.

1742 25 Sep: Book 3 Page 287 The suit by petition brought by John Mercer Plaintiff against John Hardin (5-2) defendant. Continued.

1742 27 Jan: Book 3 Page 319 The action of trespass upon the case between William Roberts plt and Joseph Hardin Deft the Judgement of last September Court agst the said deft and Sheriff of this county is confirmed for what of the sum sued for in Declaration Shall appear to be justified upon execution of a writ of inquiry to be executed the next court.

1742 21 Mar: Book 3 Page 394 Thomas Ashby sworn to Military commission as a Captain.

1743 26 Mar: Book 3 Page 409 The action between William Roberts and Joseph Hardin defdt continued to July Court.

1743 25 Jun: Book 3 Page 493 Joseph Hardin ads William Roberts case continued

1743/4 22 Mar: Book 4 Page 64 William Roberts vs Jos Harding dismissed, plaintiff removed from country and defendant did not show up.

1743 John Hardin (5-2) vs John Grant 4-65

1744 28 Jun: Book 4 Page 145 John Hardin (5-2) ads John Grant Trespass

1746 23 May: Book 4 Page 481 John Hardin (5-2) vs James Brown case dismissed.

1746 23 May: Book 4 Page 481 John Hardin (5-2) to pay Marquis Calmes witness for two days attendance 260 pounds of tobacco

1746 John Harding vs James Brown DB9 74

1747 Thomas Hardin vs Michael Whatley DB9 161

1747 25 Jul: Book 5 Page 27 Elizabeth Hardin Plaintiff vs Michael Whatley Defendant. In debt. George Wythe Atty for Plaintiff asked for special bail from defendant.

1747 18 Aug: Book 5 Page 47 Elizabeth Hardin Plaintiff vs Michael Whatley Defendant. Defendant claims debt was paid.

1747 22 Oct: Book 5 Page 64 Elizabeth Hardin vs Michael Whatley Case Continued Page 77

1747 24 Mar: Book 5 Page 105 Elizabeth Hardin vs Michael Whatley Jury Trial of case, ruled for defendant, allowed plaintiff to present bill of Exceptions to the Opinion.

1748 27 May: Book 5 Page 117 Elizabeth Hardin vs Michael Whatley. Bill of exceptions introduced.

1748 18 Jul: Book 5 Page 149 Thomas Hardin (9-2) and wife Indenture of lease and release to John Boutwell acknowledged and ordered to be recorded

1753 26 Apr: Book 5 Page 415 John Harding (5-2) vs Henry Franklin Trespass and battery Plaintiff won.

1769 22 Jun: Book 8 Page 14 William Harding (3-9), executor of George Harding (3-3) by Attorney John Gibbs, vs Thomas Kendall Judgement for plaintiff. 8-14

Deed Abstracts

1740 22 Nov: Book 5 Page 182 Nathaniel Thomas of Opeckon in Orange County to John Hardin (5-2) of Shenando of same county, for 5 shillings, lease a parcel of land in Opeckon 380 acres for one year.

1740 24 Nov: Nathaniel Thomas releases property to John Hardin (5-2) payment 47 pounds same land as above.

1745 25 Nov: Book 10 Page 258 Thomas Hardin (9-2) of Middlesex County appoint James McColough of Orange County, Power of Attorney to bargain sell Deliver and Receive either Corns Tobacco Cattle Hoggs Horses or anything whatsoever in my Absence as well as if I were present and shall extend to any commodity whatsoever of mine in the said county as far as necessary for my benefit.

1748 26 Jul: Book 11 Page 60 Thomas Hardin (9-2) of the Parish of Christ Church in the County of Middlesex and Lucy (9-2) his wife to John Boutwell of St Mary's Parish in Caroline County, Lease for 5 shillings with one-year term. A Tract of land containing 1000 acres being a tract of land granted to George Hardin (9-1), father of said Thomas (9-2) by Patent and in his last will and testament.

1748 27 Jul: Book 11 Page 61 Thomas Hardin (9-2) and Lucy (-2) his wife to John Boutwell Release of same property to John Boutwell.

Northern Neck Land Grants

1742 01 Feb: Book 7 Page 397 Josh Hite of Orange County, VA to Thomas Ashby of Orange Co., VA Lease 200 acres of land in Orange County, VA Term of Lease, one year.

Prince William County, Virginia Records

Formed From Stafford and King George Counties in 1731

Northern Neck Land Grants

1751/2 2 Jan: Page F-343 Isaac Judd of Prince William Co., 798 acres in Prince William County, on Aquia and Cannon Run on Road from George Harding's (3-2) to Prince William Courthouse

Will and Deed Abstracts

1734 16 Mar: Book C, Page 36, Will of Mark Hardin (5-1) Wife Mary, Eldest son John Hardin (5-2), 250 acres, Son Martin Hardin (5-3) 200 acres, Son Mark Hardin (5-13) 200 acres, son Henry Hardin (5-5) 200 acres. Daughters Martha McDonhill Abigail, Mary, Ann, Alis, Elizabeth (100 acres). Proved 1 May 1735 All land in Prince William County.

1741 Henry Harding (5-5) voted for Valentine Peyton and Thomas Harnson for Burgesses

1743/4 16 Feb: Book C Page 458 Will of Thomas Jordan of Prince William County. To John Jordan's two sons Thomas Jordan and Francis Jordan 104 acres. To son John Jordan tract of land. To two daughters 287 acres. To Isom Royalti?

Two-year-old heffer. To George Hardin a five-year-old horse. Proved 6 March 1744

1748/9 Charles Harding witnessed a deed for Walters

1756 George Harding witnessed a deed from Young to Latimore

1761 Charles Harding voted in the Burgesses election

1763 Edward Harding witnessed a deed.

Deed Abstracts

1733 02 Oct: Book B Page 176 Mark Hardin (5-1) lease to James McDonnell Book B Page 176-180

1733 12 Oct: Book B Page 173-175 Mark Hardin (5-1) of same from James McDonnell of Hamilton Parish Prince William Co VA Lease for one year. East side the South Branch of Kettle Creek

1734 10 Jun: Book B Page 174 James McDonnell of Prince William release to Mark Hardin (5-1) of same 300 acres John Hardin mentioned in title on side of page. Also release and bond

1750 21 Oct: Book M Page 121 Thomas Ashby Jr of Frederick Co., Virginia to William Hand of same. Lease of land, 108 acres in Prince William Co granted to Ashby by patent 30 May 1748 from Proprietors of the Northern Neck of Virginia. Lease for term of one year. Witness John Ashby.

1775 11 Sep: Book T Page 167 Martin Hardin (5-3) of Augusta Co., VA to son John Hardin (5-27) of Prince William County Deed (Note on side: Delivered William Hardin Sept 8, 1784) "for the love and affection which he hath and for the better maintenance and livelihood for him the said John Hardin" two half acre lots in Dumfries, Prince William County lots 127 and 126 in the tenure and occupation of Christen Bowers and Nathaniel Vollum. Proved 2 October 1775

1780 10 Feb: Book U Page 180 John Hardin (5-27) of Virginia to William Carr of Dumfries, Prince William Co VA 3000 pounds Virginia money, two lots on one acre of land in Dumfries number 126 and 127 tenanted by Christian Bower. Proved 4 Sept 1780 (Delivered Mr. Hardin Sept 8, 1784)

1784 10 Sep: Book W Page5 76 Deed John Harding (5-27) and Jane (5-27) his wife of Fayette Co, and William Carr of Prince William Co and Margaret his wife to William McDaniel of Prince William County 2 Lots in Dumfries, Prince William County VA.

1785 02 May: Book W Page 109 Thomas Bland of Prince William Co., VA to Nancy Harding (2-13) wife of George Harding (2-13) of Stafford County, VA, for love and good will. Deed for one negro boy named Peter.

1797 07 Jun: Book Z Page 127 Indenture Edward Hardin Sr of Prince William Co., VA binds his son Edward Hardin Jr as an apprentice to John Henry of same county. Tenure to end when Edward Hardin Jr reaches age of 22 on 6 June 1801.

Court Order Books

1751 08 Aug: Book 1 Page 19 Martin Hardin (5-3) vs Frances Ball, Administrator of John Ball. It is considered that the said Martin ought to recover against the said Frances four pound and also his goods etc to be levied of the goods and chattles of the said John in the hands of the said Frances unadministered

1752 28 Jul: Book 1 Page 42 John Hardin (5-2) vs Humphrey Calvert for Trespass assault and battery. Continued to next court.

1752 29 Jul: Book 1 Page 47 John Hardin (5-2) vs Humphrey Calvert continued.

1752 29 Jul: Book 1 Page 51 Martin Hardin (5-3) vs Philomon Waters. Waters didn't show up. Hardin wins case.

1752 24 Aug: Book 1 Page 62 License is granted to Martin Hardin (5-3) to keep an Ordinary

1753 30 May: Book 1 Page 120 Lydia Hardin (5-3) having attended four days for Maximilian Berryman as an Evidence on the above complaint ordered that he do pay her for the same according to law.

1753 21 May: Book 1 Page 147 John Hardin (5-2) vs Humphrey Calvert Defendant ordered to appear in court.

1753 21 May: Book 1 Page 150 John Hardin (5-2) vs Philemon Waters continued

1753 29 Aug: Book 1 Page 242 John Hardin (5-2) vs Humphrey Calvert. Suit resolved with defendant paying Cash,

1753 29 Aug: Book 1 Page 244 Martin Hardin (5-3) vs Philemon Waters Jr, in Debt. Defendant admitted he owed the money. Judgement for plaintiff.

1753 27 Nov: Book 1 Page 311 Hardin vs Hardin On the motion of Marquis Calmes by William Elzey his attorney as trustee for Betty Harding (5-13) on a decree of alimony against her husband Mark Harding (5-13) who failing to comply with this Court's decree ordered that the said Harding be attached to comply with the same.

Book 2 Page 132, 271 Ordinary License

1754 24 Sep: Book 2 Page 149 Martin Hardin (5-3) vs Maximilian Berryman Debt

1754 27 Nov: Book 2 Page 186 Mark Hardin (5-13) acknowledged Deeds of Lease Release and receipt endorsed to Martin Hardin.

1755 27 Mar: Book 2 Page 219 Martin Hardin's (5-3) Claim received no satisfaction for taking up a servant man.

Richmond Co., VA Records

Formed from Old Rappahannock County in 1692

North Farnham Parish

1730/1 14 Feb: William Harding (1-14) married Sarah Ball (1-14)

Deeds Book 8

1720 26 Jan: Page 16 Thomas Harding (1-11) of Stafford Co., VA to Thomas Harding III (1-8) of St. Stephens Parish, Northumberland County, Virginia, for 5 shillings, 200 acres in Richmond County, Virginia. Land that was granted formerly unto Mathew Wilcocks from ye honorable Henry Corbin, sold by deed dated 15 April 1672 to Stephen Thomas and by said Stephen Thomas devised by his last will dated 2 June 1675 unto John Harding (1-7), father of ye first named above Thomas Harding (1-11) and descended by right of inheritance unto the said Thomas Harding (1-11), first party above. Signed by mark: Deed acknowledged in court 1 Mar: 1720 by Thomas Harding (1-11) of Stafford County.

1722 03 Oct: Page 152 Thomas Harding III (1-8) of Northumberland County, VA to James Palmer of Richmond County, 200 acres of land sold by Thomas Harding (1-11) of Stafford County to Thomas Harding III (1-8) of Northumberland County. Signed without a mark. Acknowledged in court 3 October 1722 by Thomas Harding III (1-8).

Court Order Book 9 1721-1732

1722 03 Oct: Page 74 Thomas Harding III (1-8) came into court and acknowledged his deed for land, the livery of Seizen thereon endorsed and bond for performance of Covenants unto James Palmer, which was admitted to Record.

Will Book 2

1709 25 Dec: Book 2 Page 31 Will of James Innis. To daughter Sarah land lying beyond the main run that runs up to Jackson's Plantation, To daughter Sarah the mulatto child, one feather bed, furniture, 3 cows. To daughter Elizabeth land I took up later on the Fall run, two cows 1000 pounds of tobacco. To daughter Hannah one cowe and 500 pounds tobacco. To son Enoch plantation where I now live. To son James the remainder of land lying between the Eastern branch main run and Mr. Jacksons land. My will is that the said land be rented out till he comes of age of 18 years. Rest of estate equally divided between son Enoch and son James and that if either dye before they come of age that the survivor have the whole. Daughter Sarah Executor. Grey horse to my wife. Proved 6 December 1710

Will Book 7

1784 5 Feb: Page 459 Will of William Glascock of North Farnham Parish, Richmond County. To son-in-law William Harding (1-32) the use of two Negro Girls and the use of 100 Pounds current money to until my grandchildren, the children of my daughter Milly Harding (1-32) Decd arrive at the age of twenty-one years. Rest of Negroes to my following children: George, Priscilla, Ann and son-in law William Harding. Son John Glascock. Son Richard Glascock to pay 475 Pounds to estate for land given to him. John Glascock to be executor. Proved 7 March 1785.

Russell County, Virginia Records

Formed 1786 from Washington County

United States Census Records

1850 Census 24th District, Russell County, Virginia Page 112

Res	Fam	Name	Age	Sex	Occupation	Birthplace
754	754	Abner Harding (3-79)	46	M	Farmer	SC
754	754	Susan Harding Sr	87	F	(3-33)	PA
754	754	Susan Harding Jr	46	F	(3-80)	S Carolina
754	754	Phoebe Harding	41	F	(3-81)	S Carolina
754	754	William Skeene	24	M	Labourer	Russell Co
754	754	James K. P. Harding	4	M		Russell Co

1850 Census 54th District, Russell County, Virginia Page 28

Res	Fam	Name	Age	Sex	Occupation	Birthplace
179	179	William Harding	48	M	Farmer	SC (3-78)
179	179	Thomas Mason	50	M		Fairfax Co

Harding Families of the Northern Neck of Virginia

179	179	Eliza Mason	37	F			Russel Co
179	179	Robert Mason	18	M	Labourer		Russell Co
179	179	Margaret Mason	15	F			Russell Co
179	179	John Mason	14	M			Russell Co
179	179	Drewry Mason	12	M			Russell Co
179	179	Edward Mason	3	M			Russell Co

1850 Census 54th District, Russell County, Virginia Page 244

Res	Fam	Name	Age	Sex	Occupation	Birthplace
346	347	Retty Monk (3-78)	45	F		Russell Co
346	346	Joseph Monk	19	M	Labouror	Russell Co
346	346	John Monk (3-131)	17	M	Labourer	Russel Co
346	346	George Monk (3-132	13	M	Labourer	Russell Co
346	346	James P Monk	8	M		Russell Co

1860 Census Kanawha County, Virginia Page 107

Res	Fam	Name	Age	Sex	Occupation	Birthplace
744	744	John Mank (3-131)	25	M	Laborer	Virginia
744	744	Amanda Mank	23	F		Virginia
744	744	Beverly J. Mank	3	M		Virginia
744	744	Isabella Mank	2	F		Virginia
744	744	Not Named Mank	1/12	F		Virginia
744	744	James Mank	15	M		Virginia
745	745	George Hardin(3-132	25	M	Laborer	Virginia
745	745	Mary Hardin	20	F		Virginia
745	745	James Hardin	8	M		Virginia

1860 Census Gibsonville, Russell County, Virginia Page 199-200

Res	Fam	Name	Age	Sex	Occupation	Birthplace
1343	1343	Abner Harding (3-79)	55	M	Farmer	SC
1343	1343	Phebe Harding	50	F		SC
1343	1343	William Skeene	37	M	Farm Labor	(Virginia)
1343	1343	James P Harding	15	M	Farm Labor	(Virginia)
1343	1343	Betsy Skeene	24	F	Domestic	(Virginia)
1344	1344	Jonathan Skeene	71	M	Farm Labor	SC
1344	1344	Fanny Skeene	64	F		SC
1344	1344	Sally Skeene	39	F		(Virginia)
1344	1344	James E. Skeene	12	M		(Virginia)
1344	1344	Thomas Skeene	5	M		(Virginia)
1345	1345	William Harding	58	M	Farmer	SC
1345	1345	Eliza Harding	47	F		(Virginia)
1345	1345	Edward Harding	13	M		(Virginia)
1345	1345	Elijah Harding	8	M		(Virginia)

1345	1345	Henry Harding	2	M			(Virginia)
1345	1345	Drewry Mason	20	M	Farm Labor		(Virginia)
1345	1345	Nancy Bailey	30	F	Domestic		(Virginia)
1346	1346	Robert Mason	28	M	Farmer		(Virginia)
1346	1346	John Mason	23	M	Farmer		(Virginia)
1346	1346	Margaret Mason	26	F			(Virginia)

1870 Census Poca, Kanawha County, West Virginia Page 236

Res	Fam	Name	Age	Sex	Occupation	Birthplace
171	171	James Monk	26	M	Farmer	VA
171	171	Catharine Monk	26	F		VA now WV
171	171	Alice J. Monk	4	F		WV
171	171	Tressa M. Monk	3	F		WV
171	171	Arreta F. Monk	1	F		WV
171	171	James Monk	3/12	M		WV
171	171	Ransom Adkins	10	M		WV
172	172	George W. Harding	38	M	Farmer	VA now WV
172	172	Mary S. Harding	37	F	Keep House	VA now WV
172	172	Joana Monk	14	F	Dom Svt	VA now WV
173	173	Elizabeth Monk	40	F	Keep House	VA now WV
173	173	Sarah C. Monk	12	F		VA now WV
173	173	Charles M. Monk	10	M		VA now WV
173	173	Frans S Monk	6	M		VA now WV

1870 Census Poca, Kanawha County, West Virginia Page 234

Res	Fam	Name	Age	Sex	Occupation	Birthplace
156	156	John Harding (3-131	42	M	Farmer	VA
156	156	Amanda Harding	36	F	Keep House	VA
156	156	Beverly J. Harding	13	M		VA now WV
156	156	Izabell Harding	12	F		VA now WV
156	156	Ellen N. Harding	10	F		VA now WV
156	156	Mary J. Harding	8	F		VA now WV
156	156	James F. Harding	6	M		WV
156	156	Victora Harding	4	F		WV
156	156	Octava Harding	11/12	F		WV

Marriage Records

1855 11 Oct: John Hardin (3-131), Age 23, Single, born 1832 Russell Co., VA, mother Aretta Monk, married Amanda M. Fields Russell Co., Virginia. She born 1835 Russell Co, daughter of Joel Fields and Eliza A. Fields.

Probate Records

1859 02 Jul: Will Book 7, Page 211 Will of William Harding (3-78). Proved 4 September 1860. To beloved wife Eliza, all my estate. If she remarries, divide my estate among my three children Edward K (3-133), Elijah,(3-134) and Henry (3-135). Although two of my aforesaid children Edward K and Elijah were born before the marriage of myself and my said wife Yet I have since the marriage and now do recognize them as my children. Wife Eliza to be executor.

Revolutionary War Pension Filed Russell Co.

1848 9 Aug: North Carolina Service of Peter Skeen, Widow Sarah Skeen R9360. Applied in Russell Co., Virginia at a quarterly court. Statement of Witness Susannah Harding (3-33): Susannah Harding another witness being duly sworn states she is 84, she was the sister of Peter Skeen, the husband of the applicant for pension. She says she cannot now speak with perfect certainty as to the number of tours nor as to the length of time her brothers Peter and James were in the war of the Revolution. She has perfect recollection in that Peter served two if not more tours about the year 1779 and 1780, and she thinks that they were the regular tours that men performed in the army but cannot say how long. She says the 15th October 1779 as she now thinks Peter Skeen and his present widow Sarah, the applicant for a pension, were lawfully married by Esquire Douglass of Caswell Co., NC and lived together as man and wife, till Peter's death 1826, and that since that time his wife Sarah has remained a widow. Widow says that her brother James above mentioned died before Peter. She also says that she has been intimately acquainted with her brother Peter and Family ever since his marriage in North Carolina, South Carolina and in Virginia, that Peter Skeen before his death has been a resident of this county about 24 or 25 years. Signed Susannah Harding. Statement of Sarah Skeen, Age 85, widow of Peter Skeen. She states that she and Peter were married October 15,1779 in Caswell Co., North Carolina and remained in that county six years after their marriage and removed to South Carolina and remained there about 13 years and then removed to this county of Russell Co., VA where they remained.

Shenandoah Co., Virginia Records

Formed 1772 from Frederick County

Will and Probate Records

- 1779 28 Sep: Will Book A Page 233 Will of Henry Harding (3-2) of the County of Shenando, Virginia. To wife Wilmouth Harding (3-2), to sons George Harding (3-4), Henry Harding (3-8) and Nicholas Harding (3-6). To Daughter Nanny Combs (3-7), Daughter Wilmouth Smith (3-5). Proved 25 November 1779.

- 1786 22 May: Book B Page 250 Appraisal of the estate of Joseph Fetheringil deceased. Taken by John Netherton, Nicholas Harding (3-6) and James Mathews

- 1794 14 Dec: Book D, Page 474 Will of Wilmouth Harding. Wilmouth Harding (3-2) bequeaths to daughters Nancy Combs (3-7) and Willmuth Smith (3-5): entire estate split equally. Executors to be John Caveland Robert McKay. Witnesses James Matthews Sr., Thomas G. Martin, Henry Harding (3-8). Proved 8 December 1795.

Deed Books

- 1775 27 Nov: Book B Page 266 Henry Harding (3-2) Sr of Dunmore County (now Shenandoah) for natural love and affection to his son Nicholas Harding (3-6) of same county, Lot #5 of Thomas Marshall's Survey of 5 April 1775, 250 acres. Signed Henry Harding, Wilmouth Harding. Witnesses John Netherton, Reubin Padget Sr, Henry Calfee.

- 1775 27 Nov: Book B Page 269 Henry Harding (3-2) of Dunmore County VA to son-in-law John Smith (3-5) of same county, for love and affection, Lot #4 of Thomas Marshall's Survey of 5 April 1775 386 acres, Signed Henry Harding Sr and Wilmouth Harding. Witnesses Henry Calfee, John Netherton, Reuben Padgett Sr.

- 1775 27 Nov: Book B Page 271 Henry Harding (3-2) of Dunmore County VA to son George Harding (3-4) of same county, for love and affection, Lot #3 of Thomas Marshall's Survey of 5 April 1775 400 acres, Signed Henry Harding Sr and Wilmouth Harding. Witnesses Henry Calfee, John Netherton, Reuben Padgett Sr.

- 1775 27 Nov: Book B Page 302 Henry Harding (3-2) of Dunmore County VA to son Henry Harding (3-8) Jr. of same county, for love and affection, Lot #3 of Thomas Marshall's Survey of 5 April 1775 556 acres, Signed Henry Harding Sr and Wilmouth Harding. Witnesses Henry Calfee, John Netherton, Reuben Padgett Sr.

- 1777 04 Jan: Book B Page 502 John Smith of Dunmore County to Thomas Allen of same. 50 pounds. Parcel containing 386 acres which he lives on. Granted to him as deed of gift from Henry Harding his father-in-law. Mortgage, terms that John Smith will repay Thomas Allen 50 pounds by 4 January 1780. Signed by John Smith. Witness Nicholas Harding. No wife signed

Harding Families of the Northern Neck of Virginia

1777 05 Jan: Book B Page 504 Nicholas Harding (3-6) of Dunmore County VA to Thomas Allen of same County. 50 pounds current money, 250 acres received by deed of gift from his father Henry Harding (3-2). Condition is he will repay the 50 pounds with lawful interest by 4 January 1780 and from thenceforth this deed will be void. Signed Nicholas Harding, Witnesses Cornelius Thompson, John Smith, John Ridley.

1778 09 Jan: Book C Page 52 John Hardin (5-2) of Monongalia County, VA to Thomas Allen of Dunmore County VA. 90 pounds current money. 290 acres granted to the said John Hardin, dated 18 February 1773.

1779 05 Oct: Book C Page 206 George Harding (3-4) of Shenandoah County VA to Thomas Allen of same, 700 pounds current money 131 acres on south side of Shenandoah River. Term of 500 years. Condition is George Harding (3-4) will repay the 700 pounds 10 October 1782. Signed George Hardin. Witnesses Mary Jennings, Sarah Hopewell, Deborah Allen, Will Conyer?

1778 13 Dec: Book C Page 439 Henry Harden (3-2) Sr and Wilmouth (3-2) his wife of Shenandoah County VA to Reuben Padgit Jr of same, 5 shillings current money, 86 acres, part of larger parcel he bought from George Evins 26 May: 1761. Lease for one whole year. Signed Henry Harden Sr and Wilmouth Harden. Witnesses John Netherton, Samuel Berry, Theophilus Pagett.

1778 14 Dec: Book C Page 440 Henry Harden (3-2) and Wilmouth (3-2) his wife of Shenandoah County, VA to of Reuben Padgit of same. For 200 Pounds current money,

1780 20 Nov: Book E Page 106 John Smith and Wilmouth his wife of Shenando County to Jon Reamy of same. Lease 5 shillings, Bounded by Thomas Allen, Henry Harding, Nicholas Harding. 130 acres part of 1775 deed of gift to John Smith. Term of one year.

1782 22 Jun: Book D Page 316 John Smith and Wilmouth his wife of Shenando County to Thomas Allen of same. 5 shillings. Land bounded by Hanry Hardin, John Reamy, George Harding, and Thomas Allen. 71 acres. Part from a 370-acre deed of gift from father-in-law Henry Harding, and part from 170 acres granted to him by Patent bearing the date 23 Nov 1779. Lease term of one year.

1785 20 Nov: Book E-404 Henry Harding (3-8) of Shenandoah County VA to James Roy of the same. For 5 shillings land on Shenandoah River in Shenandoah County 181 acres Lease for one year. Signed Henry Harding and Rebecca Harding.

1785 21 Nov: Book E Page 406 Henry Harding (3-8) of Shenandoah County to James Raw of same. 300 pounds current money to James Raw. Land borders on Nicholas Harding (3-6). 181 acres One year lease. Signed Henry and Rebecca Harding.

1785 24 Nov: Book E Page 409 Henry Harding (3-8) of Shenandoah County to Theophilus Padget of same for 5 shillings 266 acres of land in Parish of Beckford, Shenandoah Co VA one year lease. Signed Henry Hardin and Rebecca his wife. On page 410 is the release.

1787 25 Apr: Book F 328 George Harding (3-4) and Margaret his wife of Shenandoah County VA to Thomas Allen of same. 200 pounds current money. 130 acres. Land purchased from John Harrell. Signed George Harding and Margaret Harding.

1787 19 Feb: Book G Page 11 Nicholas Harding (3-6) of Shenandoah County VA and Ann his wife to Alexander Machie of same. 5 shillings. Part of William Russell's Patent conveyed to him by his father. 250 acres for term of one year.

1787 20 Feb: Book G Page 12 Nicholas Harding (3-6) and Ann of Shenandoah County to Alexander Machis 550 acres Release

1787 25 Jan: Book G Page 494 Nicholas Harding (3-6) to Alexander Machis. Ann his wife acknowledges her consent to this deed dated 19 and 20 February 1787

1792 27 Sep: Book H Page 446 Nicholas Harding (3-6) of Virginia to Henry Ashby and Mason Jones Bill of Sale For 400 pounds to be given them as payment on a judgement of 1500 pounds of tobacco rendered by the court, all his personal estate, listed in detail, also a division of his father Henry Harding's estate in the hands of his mother Wilmouth Harding.

1792 27 Sep: Book H Page 448 Nicholas Harding (3-6) and Ann his wife of Shenandoah Co VA to Henry Ashby and Mason Jones of Frederick Co, VA Deed For 520 Pounds current money, 572 acres in Shenandoah Co., VA except one-third part encumbered by my Mother Wilmouth Harding (3-2)'s life.

1789 09 May: Book H Page 459 John Netherton Sr of Shenandoah Co to Nicholas Harding (3-6) of same, for 140 Pounds current money, 2 slaves, one wagon, one rifle, one cow and calf.

1792 25 Oct: Book I Page 165 John Mathis and wife Mary Ann of Green Co., North Carolina to Henry Harding (3-13), known as Long Henry of Shenandoah County, Virginia. 132 acres in Shenandoah Co.

1792 07 Oct: Book I 248 Henry Ashby and Elenor his wife, Mason Jones and Mary his wife of Frederick Co Virginia, Nicholas Harding (3-6) and wife Ann Deed to Joseph Stover and Philip Spangler of Shenandoah Co. For 480 pounds current money 572 acres. Give a long rendition of how the land passed from person to person to Henry Harding Sr, who devised it in his will to Nicholas Harding who sold it to Ashby and Jones. Witness Thomas Allen

1794 08 Sep: Book I Page 407 George Harding (3-4) and wife Margaret of Shenandoah County VA to Henry Harding (3-16) Jr of the same. 444 Pounds current money. 121 acres, land conveyed from his father Henry Harding Sr in 1775. Signed George and Margaret Harding.

1794 13 Aug: Book I Page 409 George Harding (3:4) and Margaret his wife of Shenandoah County VA to Thomas Allen of same. 226 Pounds 10 shillings current money. 316 acres. Land from 1775 deed of gift from his father Henry Harding and from his brother-in-law John Smith.

1795 08 Sep: Book K Page 13 Henry Harding (3-13) and Deliliah his wife of Shenandoah Co VA to James Stinson of same. 120 pounds land on Flint Creek, the same land conveyed to Henry Harding by John Matthews 25 October 1792 132 acres.

1795 01 Oct: Book K Page 40 Henry Harding (3-16) and Mary of Shenandoah Co VA to William Allen of the same. 114 Pounds land in Shenandoah Co on Gooney Run. Goes to Thomas Allen's land that Hardin purchased of George Harding 121 acres.

1796 13 Jul: Book K Page 509 William Dyer and Nancy his wife to Henry Harding (3-16) both of Shenandoah County, Virginia for 100 pounds 154 acres in Shenandoah County on Dry Run

1799 28 Mar: Book L Page 300 Henry Harding (3-16) and Mary his wife of Shenandoah County VA to Michael Rosenberger of the same place. $1000, 154 acres on waters of Dry Run. Borders Thomas Allen land.

1798 06 Oct: Book L Page 338 Jacob Berlin and Rosina his wife of Strasburg, Shenandoah Co., VA to Henry Harding of same. For 211 Pounds. Three half-acre lots, numbered two, three, and four in Town of Strasburg.

1798 08 Oct: Book M Page 254 Henry Harding and Catherine his wife of Strasburg, Shenandoah to Christian Stover son of Jacob of the same 3 ½ acres of lots in Strasburg, lots two, three, and four conveyed to Henry Hardin 6 October 1798 by Jacob Berlin. In payment of debts to Stover and Thomas Clayton. Mortgaged to be paid by 1 October 1800.

1800 21 Jan: Book M Page 714 John Netherton of the county of Jefferson in Kentucky to John Roye and John F Roy 1000 pounds land on the north side of the South River in Shenandoah County VA 200 acres.

Marriage Records

1776 21 Nov: Nicholas Harding (3-6) married Ann Ashby (3-6) Bond Edwin Young

1782 14 Oct: Henry Harding (3-13), son of George Harding (3-3), married Delilah Allensworth (3-13) Bond Henry Harding and Nicholas Harding

1784 07 Dec: Joseph Featheringill married Mary Atwood

1785 11 Oct: Sarah Harding (3-30), daughter of Henry Harding (3-8), married William Hancock (3-30)

1786 03 Oct: Winifred Harding (3-17), daughter of George Harding (3-4), married John Netherton (3-17) Jr. Consent signed by George Harding.in 1786.

1788 27 Nov: Henry Harding (3-16) married Polly Allensworth (3-16), daughter of Philip

Personal Property Tax Lists

1782 Personal Property Tax Lists
Wilmouth Harding (3-2) (2 males)
George Harding (3-4) (4 males)
Nicholas Harding (3-6) (6 males)
Henry Harding (3-8) 3 males
Samuel Harding (1 male)
Thomas Harding (1 male)

1783 Personal Property Tax Lists
Martin Harding (1 male)
Henry Harding (3-8) (1 male)
Wilmouth Harding (3-2) and Jna Allensworth (1 male)
Henry Harding (3-13) (1 male)
George Harding (3-4) and Jos Fetheringale (2 males)
Nicholas Harding (3-6) (1 male)

1784 Personal Property Tax Lists
George Harding (3-4)
Henry Harding (3-13)
Nichlas Harding (3-6)
John Harding
Henry Harding (3-16) Jr
Wilmouth Harding (3-2)

1785 Personal Property Tax Lists
Henry Harding (3-13)
Nicholas Harding (3-6)
Wilmouth Harding (3-2)
Henry Harding (3-8) Sr
John Harding

1786 Personal Property Tax Lists
Wilmouth Harding (3-2)
Nicholas Harding (3-6)
Henry Harding (3-8)
George Harding (3-4)

1787 Personal Property Tax Lists
George Harding (3-4) (George Harding, Henry Harding)
Nicholas Harding (3-6)
Wilmoth Hardin (3-2)
Henry Harding (3-8)
Samuel Harding (levy free)

1788 Personal Property Tax Lists
Wilmouth Harding (3-2)
Henry Harding (3-16), son of George Harding (3-4)

1789 Personal Property Tax Lists
Nicholas Harding (3-6)
George Harden (3-4)
Henry Harding (3-8)
Henry Harden (3-13)
Wilmouth Harden (3-2)
Samuel Harden

1790 Personal Property Tax Lists
Henry Harding (3-8) Sr
George Harding (3-4)
Henry Harding (3-16)
Nicholas Harding (3-6)
Samuel Harding
Wilmouth Harding (3-2)

1791 Personal Property Tax Lists
George Harding (3-4) 1 male
Henry Harding (3-16) 1 male
Nicholas Harding (3-6)
Willmouth Harding (3-2)
Henry Harding (3-8) Sr
Samuel Harding Levy Free

1792 Personal Property Tax Lists
Henry Harding (3-16) 2 over 16

Henry Harding (3-8) Sr
George Harding (3-4)
Nicholas Harding (3-6)
Willmouth Harding (3-2)
Samuel Harding

1793 Personal Property Tax Lists
March 14 George Harding (3-4) 1 white over 16
March 14 Henry Harding (3-16) 2 whites over 16
Apr 1 Samuel Harding (levy free)
Apr 1 Henry Harding (3-8) 1 over 16
Apr 15 Wilmouth Harding (3-2) 1 over 16

1794 Personal Property Tax Lists
March 13 George Harding (3-4) 1 white over 16
March 16 Henry Harding (3-8) 1 over 16
March 13 Long Henry Harding (3-13) 1 over 16
April 30 Wilmouth Harding (3-2)
May 9 Samuel Harding (levy free)

1795 Personal Property Tax Lists
March 10 Henry Harding (3-8) 1 white 2 black
March 31 Long Henry Harding (3-13) 1 white
Apr 9 Samuel Harding (no levy)

1796 Personal Property Tax List
March 15 Henry Harding (3-16) 1 white 1 black
July 9 Long Henry Harding (3-13) 1 white

1797 Personal Property Tax List
Apr 29 Henry Harding (3-16) 1 white 1 black

1797 Personal property Tax List
April 28 Henry Harding (3-16) 1 white one horse

1798 Personal Property Tax List
Aug 20 Henry Harding (3-16) 1 over 16
Aug 20 Henry Harding

Spotsylvania County, Virginia Records

Formed 1721 from Essex, King and Queen and King William Counties

Probate Records

1872 26 Mar: Will book Y Page 433 Will of Mark Harding (4-19). Proved September 1873.

I Mark Harding (4-19) of the County of Spotsylvania, State of Virginia, do make and hereby revoking all others heretofore made by me. Article 1. I devise to all of my children to be divided equally among them four hundred dollars being a part of the money under the control of W A Little Commissioner under a decree of the Circuit Court of Spotsylvania in the Case of Honey vs Harding which said four hundred dollars was for the Sale of a Negro named George, which was devised to me by my mother.

Article 2 I devise to my son Elijah P. Harding (4-80) two hundred dollars out of the balance of said fund in the hands of the Commissioner aforesaid which said balance was the proceeds of the sale of Negroes devised to me by my brother Lewis Harding (4-18).

Article 3 I give to my daughter Engedi A Foster (4-81) wife of William E Foster (4-81) the balance of the funds in the hands and under the control of the said Commissioner together with all other property which I may possess or be entitled to, for and during the natural life of my daughter for the separate use and Benefit of my said daughter and free from the control of her said husband to dispose of as she may think proper. Article 4 I constitute and appoint my grandson O D Foster Executor of this my last will and testament. In testimony thereof, I have hereunto set my hand and affixed my seal this 26 Day of March 1872 Mark Harding (4-19)

Census Records

1860 Census of Berkeley Parish, Spotsylvania County, Virginia
Mark Harding (4-19) Age 71 Gentleman Born in Virginia
Agnes Harding (4-19) Age 70 born in Virginia
William E. Foster (4-81) Age 38 Farmer born in Virginia
Engedi Foster (4-81) 36 born in Virginia
Eight Foster Children

1870 Census Livingston, Spotsylvania Co., Virginia Page 20
Edward Foster (4-81) Age 48 VA
Engedi Foster (4-81) Age 47 VA
Mark Harding (4-19) Age 83 VA Retired

Stafford County, Virginia Records

Virginia County Records

Formed 1664 from Westmoreland County

1810 Census of Falmouth, Stafford County, Virginia
Page 42 John Harding of C 20010 20010
Page 43 Lucy Harding (2-10) 00000 00201
Page 44 Elijah Harding (4-14) 00010 00010
Page 44 John Harding Jr 11201 01101
Page 48 Clarka Harding (4-2) 00100 00001
Page 49 Enoch Harding (4-12) 21010 31010

1810 Census of Aquia, Stafford County, Virginia
Page 24 Joel Harding (2-30) 21010 01010
Page 25 Thomas Harding (2-11) 00021 20501
Page 31 Mark Harding (4-19) 00200 00010

1820 Census of Stafford County, Virginia
Page 714 Philip Harding (2-28) 100100 20100
Page 714 Mark Harding (4-19) 300020 10020
Page 717 Byram Harding (2-29) 100010 10010
Page 717 Thomas Harding (2-11) 000011 10101
(Separated by spaces)
Page 717 Clarky Harding (4-2) 000010 02211
Page 717 Elizabeth Harding 001210 00101
Page 717 Enoch Harding (4-12) 220010 12101
Page 178 William Harding 32101 10010

1830 Census of Stafford County, Virginia
Page 59 Mark Hardin (4-19) 00210 0100
Page 59 Willi Hardin 00112001 00011001
Page 60 Thomas Hardin (2-11) 00000000001 (80-90) 00001001
Page 60 Diram Hardin (2-29) 1100001 100101
Page 61 Elizth Ashby 00012 0011201
Page 61 Enos (Enoch) Hardin (4-12) 001100001 (60-70) 00021001
Page 64 Lewis Hardin 000001 No Women
Page 65 Strother Hardin (2-31) 100001 00001011 000000001

1840 Census of Stafford County, Virginia
Page 6 Strother Harding (2-31) 101001 00001
Page 7 William Harding Jr 01201 20001
Page 7 William Harding (2-27) 110010001 010010001
Page 9 Philip Harding (2-28) 0111001 002101
Page 14 Mark Harding (4-19) 00002001 00010001
Page 17 Strother Harding (2-31) Sr. 100001 00101
Page 24 Elizabeth Harding 0000 021001001

Harding Families of the Northern Neck of Virginia

Page 25 Enoch Harding (4-12) 000001 0001
Page 31 Byram Harding (2-29) 000100001 0010001

1850 Census Eastern District of Stafford Co, VA mortality
Enoch Harding (4-12) Died September 1849 age 82 Paralysis

1850 Census Eastern District, Stafford County, Virginia Page 14

Res	Fam	Name	Age	Sex	Occupation	Birthplace
226	226	John L. Harding	14	M		Virginia
226	226	John M Henry	33	M	Minister	New York
226	226	Martha F. Henry	29	F		Virginia

1850 Census Eastern District, Stafford County, Virginia Page 19

Res	Fam	Name	Age	Sex	Occupation	Birthplace
324	324	Sarah Harding	76	F		Virginia
324	324	Enoch Harding	43	M	Farmer	Virginia
324	324	Strother Harding	38	M	Merchant	Virginia

1850 Census Eastern District, Stafford County, Virginia Page 22

Res	Fam	Name	Age	Sex	Occupation	Birthplace
366	366	Thomas B. Harding	33	M	Farmer	Virginia
366	366	Thomas Harding	57	M		Virginia

1850 Census Eastern District, Stafford County, Virginia Page 25

Res	Fam	Name	Age	Sex	Occupation	Birthplace
410	410	William Harding	45	M	Laborer	Virginia
410	410	Mary A. Harding	38	F		Virginia
410	410	George R. Harding	15	M		Virginia
410	410	Ann E. T. Harding	13	F		Virginia
410	410	Caroline Harding	11	F		Virginia
410	410	Annetta T. Harding	7	F		Virginia
410	410	William J. Harding	5	M		
410	410	Alexander C. Harding	2	M		Virginia

1850 Census Eastern District, Stafford County, Virginia Page 22

Res	Fam	Name	Age	Sex	Occupation	Birthplace
438	438	Mark Harding	63	M		Virginia
438	438	Agnes Harding	55	F		Virginia

1850 Census Eastern District, Stafford County, Virginia Page 28

Res	Fam	Name	Age	Sex	Occupation	Birthplace
458	458	Phillip Harding Sr	55	M	Farmer	Virginia
458	458	Frances Harding	55	F		Virginia

Virginia County Records

458	458	Phillip Harding Jr	18	M	Cooper	Virginia
458	458	Humphrey Harding	16	M	Cooper	Virginia

1850 Census Eastern District, Stafford County, Virginia Page 40

Res	Fam	Name	Age	Sex	Occupation	Birthplace
638	638	William Harding	74	M	(2-27)	Virginia
638	638	Elizabeth Harding	75	F		Virginia
638	638	George R. Harding	40	M	Cooper	Virginia
638	638	Ellen Bradshaw	13	F	(2-70)	Virginia
638	638	Catherine Harding	25	F		Virginia
638	638	Sarina A. Harding	6	F		Virginia
638	638	Thomas W. Harding	4	M		Virginia
638	638	Sarah Harding	3	F		Virginia
638	638	James D. Harding	1	M		Virginia
638	638	John C. Bradshaw	16	M	Cooper	Virginia

1850 Census Eastern District, Stafford County, Virginia Page 40

Res	Fam	Name	Age	Sex	Occupation	Birthplace
639	639	Richard D. Harding	36	M	(2-72)	Virginia
639	639	Margaret Harding	20	F		Virginia
639	639	Josephine Harding	3	F		Virginia
639	639	Mary E. Harding	2m	F		Virginia
639	639	Ann Ennis	17	F		Virginia

1850 Census Eastern District, Stafford County, Virginia Page 42

Res	Fam	Name	Age	Sex	Occupation	Birthplace
656	656	Thomas S. Harding	46	M	Me Minister	Virginia
656	656	Mary T. Harding	34	M	Farmer	Virginia
656	656	Lemira Harding	10	F	(2-69)	Virginia
656	656	Alpheus Harding	7	M		Virginia
656	656	Rowena Harding	3	F		Virginia
656	656	Joseph C. Harding	2m	M		Virginia

1850 Census Eastern District, Stafford County, Virginia Page 45

Res	Fam	Name	Age	Sex	Occupation	Birthplace
714	714	William J. Harding	28	M	Carpenter	Virginia
714	714	Mary A. Harding	28	F		Virginia
714	714	George W. Harding	6	M		Virginia
714	714	Phillip J. Harding	4	M		Virginia
714	714	Henrietta Harding	2	F		Virginia

1850 Census Eastern District, Stafford County, Virginia Page 45

Res	Fam	Name	Age	Sex	Occupation	Birthplace
718	718	Strother B. Harding	43	M	Farmer	Virginia

718	718	Ann Harding	34	F	Virginia
718	718	Benjamin B. Harding	11	M	Virginia
718	718	Ann E. Harding	8	F	Virginia
718	718	Robert L. Harding	7	M	Virginia
718	718	Thaddeus Harding	2	M	Virginia
718	718	Susan V. Harding	4	F	Virginia

Military Pension Records

William Harding (2-27) Pension Application for service in the War of 1812, over 84 pages, refers to locations in Stafford County, Virginia and Clarke County, Iowa and to his service. Following are gleanings from that file by page number on the Fold-3 site.

Page 1: File numbers 22544 and 19792, Served in Capt. Elijah Harding Co VA Militia and Capt. George Hamilton VA militia.

Page 2: Received pension beginning 4 December 1872 in Clarke Co., Iowa

Page 3: Applied first under Act of 1855

Page 4: He served under Capt. Harding from 4 September to 3 October 1814 and under Capt. Hamilton 3 October to 5 November 1814.

Page 7: Served under Capt. Elijah Harding.

Page 10: William Harding appeared in Stafford County VA court 23 July 1852, declaration to obtain bounty land. After 5 months of service, he was taken sick and went on furlough. Also appeared Philip Harding who swore he received his bounty land warrant, said he served with William Harding 4 months 20 days and William was furloughed for illness.

Page 13: William Harding was 79 years old in appearance 28 July 1855 in Stafford County Court. Got bounty land warrant for 80 acres that he disposed of.

Page 16: He was drafted at Aquia. Stafford County July 1814 for 12 months, served six months, discharged at Camp Selden January 1815.

Page 38: In application 21 May 1872, his attorney states, "The old man is quite infirm and needs the money."

Page 41: States he is 94 years old, 21 July 1871.

Page 55: Statement from Pension office: William Harding lived 1850-1855 Stafford Co., VA and 1871-1872 Clarke Co., Iowa. He married Elizabeth Doggett (2-27) 1802 in Culpeper County, Virginia.

Page 58: Was in one battle on Aquia Creek.

Page 63: He was last paid 4 December 1873 for pension.

Philip Harding (4-77) Pension Application for War of 1812

Page 5: In service 22 August 1814. Under Capt. Elijah Harding (4-14) and and Capt J E Edmiston

Page 9: Filed for pension 6 May 1860

Page 11: In Elijah Harding's (4-14) company 22 August to 5 November 1814

Page 13: Signed required oath of allegiance 27 Apr: 1865.
Page 19: 27 Apr: 1865 stated he was age 72 living in Fredericksburg, Virginia

Northern Neck Land Grants

1713/14 03 Feb: Page ?-60 Henry Harding (3-1) of Stafford County, grant for 564 acres of land on Acquia Creek between lands of Robert Carter and Daniel Crosby

1725 20 May: Page ???? Henry Harding (3-1) of Stafford County, grant for 978 acres in Stafford County on Acquia Creek bounded by Robert Carter, George Crosby and Henry Harding

1739 28 Nov: Book E Page 113 Charles Harding (2-2) of Stafford County, 269 acres adjacent Capt. John Lee, Samuel Timmons, Joseph Combs, near S run of Chappawamsick, Brent Town Road.

1757 28 Jul: Book I Page 17 Charles Harding (2-2), 14 acres on Beaver Dam Run of Acquia, 413 acres on Rocky Run, adjacent Robert Ashley, Joseph Combs, Barber, Isaac Birdwell, Frister, Cartey, Wells, Combs, Brent Town Road.

1761 03 Aug: Book I Page 74 Charles Harding (2-2) 100 acres on Silver Mine Branch of Chappawamsick Run.

1762 16 Jul: Book I Page 85 Charles Harding (2-2) 115 acres on Chappawamsick Run

1757 15 Oct: Book K Page 15 Charles Harding (2-2) 364 acres on Beaver Dam and Great Rock Road. (Note: never taken up by grantee)

From the St. Paul's Parish Register

1740 3 Dec: George Hardin (3-3) married Jane Bunbury (3-3)

From the Overwharton Parish Register

Children of Charles Harding (2-2) and Rachel Harding (2-2):
1738 12 Mar: William Harding (2-6) born
1740 03 Feb: Ann Harding (2-7) born
1742 09 Nov: Jane Harding (2-8) born
1745 06 Apr: Charles Harding (2-9) born
1747 03 Aug: John Scott Harding (2-10) born
1749 11 Aug; Thomas Harding (2-11) born
1752 19 Mar: Moses Hardin (2-12) born
1754 03 Jul: George Harding (2-13) born

Harding Families of the Northern Neck of Virginia

Children of Henry Harding (3-2) and Wilmouth Harding (3-2)
1741 14 Apr: Wilmoth Harding (3-5) born
1743 06 Jul: Nicholas Harding (3-6) born

Children of George Harding (3-3) and Jane Harding (3-3)
1743 07 Mar: Franky Harding (3-10) born, mother Jinny
1746 01 Dec: Winny Harding (3-11) born, mother Jean
1749 29 May: Ann Harding (3-12) born, Mother Jane
1753 29 Aug: Henry Harding (3-13) born, Mother Jane
1758 23 Mar: Sarah Harding (3-14) born, Mother Jean

1746 28 Jan: William Harding (2-5) and Patty Green (2-5) married
1746 25 Oct: Hall Harden (2-22) born

1754 13 Sep: Anne Harding died

1756 20 Jul: Ann Harding married Mark Waters

1740 05 Dec: William Million, son of Robert, died
1740 07 Dec: Elizabeth Million, daughter of Robert, died
1741 08 Apr: Anne Million, Daughter of Robert and Grace, died
1745 04 Sep: Winifred Million married Elias Ashby
1745 15 Dec Clarky Million Daughter of Robert Bapt
1747 12 Dec: William Bennett Million son of Robert and Grace born
1748 22 Sep: William Bennett Million Baptized
1749 14 Dec: Robert Million married Keziah Holliday
1749 01 Oct: John Million Son of Robert died
1750 13 Nov: Jemima Million daughter to Robert born
1753 02 Apr: Sithy Million daughter of Robert of Keziah born
1756 13 Feb: Sarah Ann Million daughter of Robert and Keziah born
1758 19 Apr: Jeanny Millian daughter of Robert and Keziah born

1742 09 Jul: Elizabeth Asbee, daughter of Jean and John born
1742 20 Oct: Stephen Asbee, son of Robert and Mary born
1744 05 Sep: Stephen Asbee, son of Robert and Mary died
1745 10 Jan: Ann Asbee, daughter of Robert and Mary, born
1745 04 Sep: Elias Ashby married Winifred Million
1746 23 Apr: William Asbee, son of Elias and Winifred born
1747 17 Jan: Sarah Asbee, daughter of Robert and Mary born
1749 15 Mar: Fransisina Ashby, daughter of Winifred and Elias born
1749 05 Mar: Thomas Ashby, son of Robert and Mary, born
1750 29 May: Jess Ashby, son of Margaret born
1751 26 Dec: Elisha Ashby, son of Elias and Winifred, born
1751 14 Nov: Thomas Ashby married Mary Maccullough

1751 11 Sep: Millie Ashby, daughter of Robert and Mary, born
1752 30 Jul: Mary Ann Asbee, daughter of Thomas, born
1753 28 Oct: Wilmoth Ashby, daughter of Robert Jr., born
1754 15 Oct: Elizabeth Asbee, wife of Robert died
1754 03 Nov: Elizabeth Asbee, daughter of Mary and Thomas, born
1756 26 Feb: John Ashby married Sarah McCullough
1756 01 Jan: Catherine Ashby married Isaac Murphy
1756 06 Jun: John Ashby, son of John, born
1756 25 Jul: William Ashby, son of Robert Bapt
1757 06 Feb: Hanknsson Ashby son of Thomas and Mary, born
1858 22 Nov: Bailey Ashby, son of John and Sarah, born

Miscellaneous Records

List of Tobacco Tenders 1724
From Virginia Colonial Papers, Folder 52, Library of Congress. Tending 10,035 tobacco plants: Henry Hardin (3-1), Zenony Willson, William Jenkinson, John Leechman, age 15, Henry Harden (3-2) Jr., age 10.

Negro Slave owners in Overwharton Parish:
George Harding (3-3). 1751

Virginia Gazette Reference
1768 06 Feb: Virginia Gazette of says George Harding (3-3) of Halifax Co., VA died lately in Stafford Co. while there on business. I have not been able to find the original Virginia Gazette notice, but this record agrees with the Halifax County records of his estate.

Index to lost Deed and Will books

Hardin to Lunsford Book O-292 1747-1754
Hardin to Walters Book Q 82 1764-1773
Harding to Horton Book Q 133 1764-1773
Harding to Harding Book Q 324 1764-1773
Harding to Hooe Book Q 328 1764-1773
Harding to Harding Book Q 367 1764-1773
Charles Harding will Book W-N 385 1767-1783 (2-9)
Charles Harding deed Book R 209 1773-1779 (2-9)
Many deeds from John Scott Harding (2-10)
Harding from Mason Book L 508 1728-1731 Deed
Harding from Lunsford Book O 578 1747-1754 L&R
Harding from Combs Book Q 184 1764-1773
Harding from Fristoe Book Q 188 1764-1773
Harding from Harding Book Q 324 1764-1773

Harding from Harding Book Q 327 1764-1773

Will and Deed Book M 1729-1767

1722 07 Mar: Page 3 Valentine Payton sells land bordering on land formerly surveyed for Henry Harding (3-1).

1726 11 May: Page 253 William Allen of Overwharton Parish, to Henry Harden (3-1) of same, for 900 pounds of tobacco, 60 acres in Overwharton Parish between John Schoemack and Joseph Allen and a tract belonging to Henry Harden formerly sold to him by William Allen at the head of Elk Run, a branch of the Occoquan River

1726 03 Nov: Page 328 Joseph Allen of Overwharton Parish to Henry Harden (3-1), for 5000 pounds of tobacco, 100 acres given him by William Allen in 1723. By land of Henry Harden and John Delashemate

1727 03 May: Page 434 John Hardin witnessed deed from Cudberth Byram to Peter Byram

1731 10 May: Henry Harding (3-1) inventoried the estate of William Mason

1733 16 Nov: Henry Harding (3-1) witnessed a bond

1734 14 Aug: Inventory of Thomas Timmons lists a servant man Charles Harding (2-2)

1736 16 Oct: Will of Nicholas George, names daughter Wilmoth Harding (3-2), to get the bed and furniture in the shed where she now lies, but not the bedstead, one iron pot and ½ dozen pewter plates, one pewter dish, one small trunk, and one pewter basin.

1737 Jan: Appraisal of the estate of Henry Harding (3-1) Sr., dec, valued at 126-15-11. Estate was shown to appraisers by the widow and executors. Appraisers were George Crosby, Peter Byram, and William Kendall

1740 15 May: Remainder of the estate of Henry Harding (3-1) Sr. decd appraised at 47-3-9 by same appraisers as above.

1740 11 Nov: Estate of Elias Hore, a 1734 note to Charles Harding (2-2)

1741/2 17 Feb: Charles Harding (2-2) witnesses the will of Thomas Bowts

1742 17 Aug: Charles Harding (2-2) witnessed the will of William Brent

1744 5 Apr: Charles Harding (2-2) appraised the estate of John Holliday

1745 Jul: George Harding (3-3) bought from estate of Anthony Linton

Estate of William Mason paid money due to Charles Harding (2-2)

1747 Estate of Thomas Hampton debt of George Harding (3-3) recorded

William Jackson estate owed money to Charles Harding (2-2)

1750 14 Aug: Estate of Ann Parson paid Charles Harding (2-2)

1750 Charles Harding (2-2) was on an appraisal list

1750, George Harding (3-3) was on an appraisal list

1750 Estate of William Brent received money for corn sold to Charles Harding (2-2)

1754 11 Jun: Charles Harding (2-2) appraised the estate of James Starke

1755 13 May: George Harding (3-3) valued the estate of George Allen

Will and Deed Book P 1755-1764

1755 13 Oct: Page 86-88 Henry Harding (3-2) and Wilmoth Harding (3-2) of Frederick Co., VA leased for one year to George Harding (3-2) of Stafford Co., planter, 200 acres on Aquia Creek, formerly property of Henry Harding (3-1), dec,

1760 Page 257 Robert Million Sr. to Robert Million Jr land in Overwharton Parish Stafford Co bought of Robert Ashby Jr 100 acres 5 shillings, Witnesses Charles Harding (2-2), Leonard Always, George Folsom, Benjamin Folsom Jr, James Wigington

1760 21 Feb: Charles Harding (2-2) witnessed deed from William Fitzhugh to Richard Bristoe

1762 11 Mar: Goods of estate of Robert Burgess sold to Charles Harding (2-2)

1765 05 Oct: George Harding (3-3) valued the estate of H. Bussey

Deeds and Wills Book S 1780-1787

1784 Page 223, Marquis Calmes of Hampshire Co., VA to William Harding (4-2) of Overwharton Parish, Stafford County, rents 150 acres on south side of the north run of Aquia called Cannon's Run for the lives of William Harding (4-2) and Clerkey (4-2) and son Lewis Harding (4-18). Witnesses Cuthbert Harding (4-11) and James Holloway.

1784 24 Feb: Marquis Calmes to William Philips, 300 acres on north run of Aquia Creek.

1786 11 Sep: Page 335, William Fitzhugh has transferred land in Stafford County to Thomas Harding (2-11), dower given land from Cary's Patent and Thompson's Patent on Aquia Creek.

Deeds and Wills Book AA 1810-1813

1810 03 May: Page 162 William Walters of Stafford County, to Thomas Beach, for $399 land on Deep Run and Aquia Run, part of a tract his father Charles Walters purchased of Henry Hardine 133 acres

1810 06 Nov: Page 153 Moses Kendall to Aaron Kendall, 130 acres on Aquia Run.

1810 25 Dec: Page 226 Thomas Fristoe of Stafford County to Jesse Fristoe, bounded by land owned by Representatives of John Scott Harding (2-10) dec, William Carr, Thomas Fristoe, lands of Thomas Harding (2-11), and the north side of the south prong of Chappawamsick Run. Witnesses Henry Williams, Bernard Harding, Thomas Fristoe

1811 16 Jan: Page 225 Barnett Harding of Stafford County to Joseph Stark, 100 acres on a side of Rocky Run. Bounded by Rocky Run and Fristoe's property.

1811 27 Nov: Page 277 Enoch Harding (4-12) and Sarah Harding (4-12) his wife, Elijah Harding (4-14) and Philadelphia (4-14) his wife, Lewis Harding (4-18), Mark Harding (4-19) and Ann his wife to Moses Kendall, for $1022, land and gristmill, south side of main run of Aquia Run, conveyed to said Enoch, Elijah, Lewis and Mark by Asa Holloway and Robert Painter, executors of the last will of James Holloway, dec and widow Mary by deed on 21 May 1801. 10 acres on the south side of Aquia Run, one acre on north side.

Deeds and Wills Book GG 1825-1827

1826 22 Apr: Page 278. Proved 11 December 1826 Will of Clarky Harding(4-2). In the name of God, Amen I Clarkey Harding of the County of Stafford and Commonwealth of Virginia, being weak in body but of sound mind and memory, do make and ordain this my last Will and testament hereby revoking all former Wills by me made. Imprimis. It is my Will & desire that after my mortal remains are committed to the earth in a decent Christian manner, my just debts shall be paid. 2ndly – It is my will that the heirs of my son Elijah (4-14) shall not receive the fifty dollars which I assumed to pay them, as a free gift by an obligation now in the possession of my son Enoch, nor any part thereof; and instead of the said fifty dollars, they shall receive the portion hereinafter bequeathed to them. 3rdly, I give and bequeath my said servant Fenton and her future increase to my son Mark (4-19) for & during his natural life, for the exclusive use and benefit of his children lawfully begotten and after the death of my said son Mark, the said servant maid shall belong to his surviving children and to their heirs forever. 4thly I desire that all my property of every description be sold to the highest bidder at public auction on a credit of twelve months, and the proceeds of such sale, when collected, be divided among my following named children and grandchildren in manner following to wit: The said proceeds are to be divided into ten equal parts and my son John (4-10) is to take one part, Cuthbert (4-11) another part, Enoch (4-12) a third part, Frances (4-13) a fourth part, the heirs of the body of my son Elijah (4-14) share and share alike, a fifth part, Selah (4-15) a sixth part, Nancy (4-16) a seventh part Adah (4-17) an eighth part, Lewis (4-18) a ninth part and Mark (4-19) the tenth part. It is of course my wish that my maid servant herein bequeathed to my son Mark should not be sold by my Executor: and I also direct that my son Lewis shall take his choice of one of my horses in addition to the part herein before bequeathed him and have the same to his use forever. Lastly, I constitute and appoint my son Mark executor to this my last will and testament. Witness my hand and seal this 22nd day of April one thousand eight hundred and twenty-six. Clarkey Harding her mark. Signed sealed and acknowledged by the testator in our presence who in her presence and at her request subscribed the same as witnesses. Edward Barber Wm Moore.

1826 11 Dec: Page 279 Stafford County Court December the 11th 1826 The last will and testament of Clarky Harding (4-2) decd was proved by the oaths of the witnesses thereto and ordered to be recorded. And on motion of Mark Harding the executor therein named who made oath thereto and entered into bond with security conditioned as the law directs. Certificate is granted him for obtaining a probate thereof in due form.

1827 01 Feb: Page 309 Inventory of Clarky Harding made and submitted to court by Mark Harding executor.

Court Order Book 1790-1793

1791 November Court Page 216 Thomas Harding (2-11) ordered to pay witnesses for being a witness for him vs Jordan's Administrator. Pay Joseph Franklin, William Divien, Ann Divan, Mary Lotes, Philip Foxworthy, Vincent Foxworthy, Benjamin Million and wife

1792 June Court Page 274. Thomas Harding (2-11) is appointed a Commissioner for the Valuation of property take//n by Execution Vice Willam Gant who is not eligible from his not being a free holder.

Land Tax Records

1782 Land Tax Records
List 1
John Harden (2-10) 70 acres $8/acre 2.3 tax
Thomas Harding (2-11) 50 acres $7/acre Tax 2.3
George Harding (2-1 65 acres 10/acre Tax 9.0

1783 Land Tax Records

Harding Families of the Northern Neck of Virginia

List 1 John Harden (2-10) 70 acres
List 1 Thomas Harden (2-11) 90 acres
List 1 George Harding (2-13) 69 acres

1784 Land Tax Records
John Scott Harding (2-10) 70 acres
Thomas Harding (2-11) 50 acres
George Harding (2-13) 65 acres

1786 Land Tax Records
Land transfer Will Fitz Hugh to Thomas Harding (2-11) 130 acres

1787 Land Tax Records
John Harding (2-10) 70 acres
George Harding (2-13) 65 acres
Thomas Harding (2-11) for William Fitzhugh

1788 Land Tax Records
John Harding (2-10) 70 acres
George Harding (2-13) 65 acres
Thomas Harding (2-11) for William Fitzhugh 130 acres)

1789 Land Tax Records
John Harding (2-10) 70 acres
George Harding (2-13) 65 acres
Thomas Harding (2-11) for William Fitzhugh 130 acres

1790 Land Tax Records
John Harding (2-10) 70 acres
George Harding (2-13) 65 acres
Thomas Harding (2-11) for William Fitzhugh 130 acres

1791 Land Tax Records
John Harding (2-10) 70 acres
George Harding (2-13) 65 acres
Thomas Harding (2-11) for William Fitzhugh 130 acres

1792 Land Tax Records
John Harding (2-10) 70 acres
George Harding (2-13) 65 acres
Thomas Harding (2-11) for William Fitzhugh 130 acres
Enoch Harding (4-12) for William Phillips 104 acres

1793 Land Tax Records

John Harding (2-10) 70 acres
George Harding (2-13) 65 acres
Thomas Harding (2-11) for William Fitzhugh 130 acres
Enoch Harding (4-12) for William Phillips 104 acres

1794 Land Tax Records
John Harding (2-10) 70 acres
George Harding (2-13) 65 acres
Thomas Harding (2-11) for William Fitzhugh 130 acres
Enoch Harding (4-12) for William Phillips 104 acres

1795 Land Tax Records
Lucy Harding (2-10) for John S. Harding 70 acres
George Harding (2-13) 65 acres
Thomas Harding (2-11) for William Fitzhugh 130 acres
Enoch Harding (4-12) for William Phillips 104 acres

1796 Land Tax Records
Lucy Harding (2-10) for J. Scott Harding 70 acres
George Harding (2-13) 65 acres
Thomas Harding (2-11) for William Fitzhugh 130 acres
Enoch Harding (4-12) for William Phillips 104 acres

1797 Land Tax Records
Lucy Harding (2-10) 70 acres
George Harding (2-13) 65 acres
Thomas Harding (2-116 130 acres)
Enoch Harding (4-12) for William Phillips 104 acres

1798 Land Tax Records
Lucy Harding (2-10) 70 acres
George Harding (2-13) 65 acres
Thomas Harding (2-11) 130 acres
Enoch Harding (4-12) for William Phillips 104 acres
Thomas Harding (2-11) for W Carr 100 acres
Joel Harding (2-30) for Jos Kendall 116 2/3 acres
George Harding (2-13) for W Carr 90 acres

1799 Land Tax Records
Lucy Harding (2-10) 70 acres
Thomas Harding (2-11) 130 acres
Enoch Harding (4-12) 104 acres
Thomas Harding (2-11) for W Carr 100 acres
Joel Harding (2-30) for Jos Kendall 116 2/3 acres

Harding Families of the Northern Neck of Virginia

George Harding (2-13) for W Carr 90 acres

1800 Land Tax Records
Lucy Harding (2-10) 70 acres
Thomas Harding (2-11) 130 acres
Enoch Harding (4-12) 104 acres
Thomas Harding (2-11) 100 acres for W Carr
Joel Harding (2-30) for Jos Kendall 116 2/3 acres
George Harding for W Carr 90 acres (2-13)

1801 Land Tax Records
Lucy Harding (2-10) 70 acres
Thomas Harding (2-11) 130 acres
Enoch Harding (4-12) 104 acres
Thomas Harding (2-11) for William Carr 100 acres
Joel Harding (2-30) for Jos Kendall 116 2/3 acres
George Harding (2-13) for William Carr 90 acres

1802 Land Tax List
Lucy Harding (2-10) 70 acres
Thomas Harding (2-11) 130 acres
Enoch Harding (4-12) 104 acres
Thomas Harding (2-11) for William Carr 100 acres
Joel Harding (2-30) for Jos Kendall 116 2/3 acres
George Harding (2-13) for Carr 90 acres
Enoch Harding, (4-12) Elijah Harding, Lewis Harding, Mark Harding for James
    Holloway Executors 10 acres

1803 Land Tax List
Lucy Harding (2-10) 70 acres
Byram Harding (2-29) for Thomas Harding 130 acres
Enoch Harding (4-12) 104 acres
Thomas Harding (2-11) for William Carr 100 acres
Joel Harding (2-30) for Geo J Kendall 116 2/3 acres
George Harding (2-13) for Carr 90 acres
Enoch Harding (4-12), Elijah Harding, Lewis Harding, Mark Harding for James
    Holloway Executors 10 acres

1804 Land Tax List
Lucy Harding (2-10) 70 acres
Byram Harding (2-29) for Thomas Harding 130 acres
Enoch Harding (4-12) 104 acres
Thomas Harding (2-11) for William Carr 100 acres
Joel Harding (2-30) for Geo J Kendall 116 2/3 acres)
George Harding (2-13) for Carr 90 acres

Virginia County Records

Enoch Harding (4-12), Elijah Harding, Lewis Harding, Mark Harding for James Holloway Executors 10 acres

1805 Land Tax List
Lucy Harding (2-10) 70 acres
Byram Harding (2-29) for Thomas Harding 130 acres
Enoch Harding (4-12) 104 acres
Enoch Harding (4-12) with others for Holloway's Executors 10 acres
Joel Harding (2-30) for Geo J Kendall 116 2/3 acres
Thomas Harding (2-11) for William Carr 100 acres
George Harding (2-13) for Carr 90 acres

1806 Land Tax List
John Carr for George Harding (2-13) Lease 90 acres
Lucy Harding (2-10) 70 acres
Byram Harding (2-29) for Thomas Harding 150 acres
Enoch Harding (4-12) 104 acres
Enoch Harding (4-12) with others for Holloway's Executors 10 acres
Joel Harding (2-30) for Geo J Kendall 116 2/3 acres
Benjamin Tolson for Jordan and Harding (not in former sheet)

1807 Land Tax List
Lucy Harding (2-10) 70 acres
Thomas Harding (2-11) 50 acres
Byram Harding (2-29) for Thomas Harding 100 acres
Enoch Harding (4-12) 104 acres
Enoch Harding (4-12) with others for Holloway's Executors 10 acres
Joel Harding (2-30) for Geo J Kendall 116 2/3 acres

1809 Land Tax List
Lucy Harding (2-10) 70 acres
Mrs Lucy Haarding (2-10) (never before listed) 40 acres
Thomas Harding 50 acres (2-11)
Byram Harding (2-29) for Thomas Harding 100 acres
Enoch Harding 104 acres (4-12)
Enoch Harding (4-12) with others for Holloway's Executors 10 acres
Joel Harding (2-30) for Joshua Kendall 116 2/3 acres
Alienations: Thomas Fristoe for Lucy Harding (2-10) and others 7 2/3 acres

1810 Land Tax List
Thomas Fristoe for Lucy Harding (2-10) and others 7 2/3 acres
Lucy Harding (2-10) 70 acres and 40 acres
Thomas Harding (2-11) 50 acres
Byram Harding (2-29) for Thomas Harding 100 acres

Harding Families of the Northern Neck of Virginia

Byram Harding (2-29) for Richard Fristoe 30 acres
Enoch Harding (4-12) 104 acres
Enoch Harding (4-12) with others for Holloway's Executors 10 acres
Joel Harding (2-30) for Joshua Kendall 116 1/2 acres
Lewis Harding for Haman McInteer 40 acres

1811 Land Tax List
Thomas Fristoe for Lucy Harding (2-10) and others 7 2/3 acres
Lucy Harding (2-10) 70 acres and 40 acres
Barnett Harding 100 acres for R Hord
Thomas Harding (2-11) 50 acres
Byram Harding (2-29) for Thomas Harding 100 acres
Byram Harding (2-29) for Richard Fristoe 30 acres
Enoch Harding (4-12) 104 acres
Enoch Harding (4-12) with others for Holloway's Executors 10 acres
Joel Harding (2-30) for Joshua Kendall 116 1/2 acres
Alienation: Lewis Bridewell for Haman McInteer and Lewis Harding 176 7/8 acres
Alienation: Bernard Harding for Rhoda Hord 100 acres

1812 Land Tax List
Thomas Fristoe for Lucy Harding (2-10) and others 7 2/3 acres
Lucy Harding (2-10) 70 acres and 40 acres
Thomas Harding (2-11) 120 acres
Byram Harding (2-29) for Thomas Harding 80 acres
Byram Harding (2-29) for Richard Fristoe 30 acres
Enoch Harding (4-12) 104 acres
Joel Harding (2-30) for Joshua Kendall 116 1/2 acres
Joel Harding (2-30) For Catherine Kendall 28 acres

1813 Land Tax List
Edward Barber 120 acres adjoining Robert Beaty, Lewis Bridewell, J Harding William McInteer

Mrs. Seth Combs for John Combs Wavy land adjoining Mrs Tibbs Mrs. Harding t Peyton T Henford

Thomas Fristoe for R Fristoe three lots 41 ½ acres wavey adjoining each other and bounded by Mrs. Tebbs, William Williams, Benjm Tolson, the heirs of Robert William Jacobs, Harding

Elijah Hambrough 78 ½ acres Broken and bounded by H McInteer G Lane M Kendall, Harding

Lucy Harding (2-10) 70 acres and 40 acres, Broken and adjoining each other and bounded by Harding Mrs. Combs, T Fristoe and Mrs. Tebbs

Thomas Harding (2-11) 120 acres wavey adjoining Thomas Harding Thomas Fristoe Mrs. Tebbs and Byram Harding

Byram Harding (2-29) for T Harding 80 acres, for R Fristoe 30 acres, wavey and adjoining Thomas Harding, Thomas Fristoe, Lyles heirs, Mrs. Tebbs etc.

Peter Hambrough for James Hambrough 300 acres, wavey and adjoined by George Lane, J Read, Mrs. Tebbs, Harding, Kendall

Enoch Harding (4-12) 104 acres, wavey and adjoined by George Lane, M Kendall, Hansbrough, Mrs. Tebbs

Elijah Harding (4-14) for A Holloway, 117 acres and 100 acres, wavey and adjoining each other and a part of the Parke Tract

Joel Harding (2-30) 116 ½ acres, for Catherine Kendall 28 acres, wavey and adjoined by Moses Kendall, Lucy Kendall, T Harrison, James Thornton, and Gaddes, for John C Edrington and others 239 acres wavey and adjoined by M Kendall, E Barber, McInteer Mrs. Phillips

Thomas Harrison for P Harrison 600 acres wavey and bounded by Kendall, Sewart, L Kendall Harding etc. (2-11)

Alterations: Joel Harding (2-30) from J C Edrington 239 acres

Alterations Elijah Harding (4-14) from Aaron Holloway 117 acres and 180 acres

1814 Land Tax Lists
Lucy Harding (2-10) 70 acres bounded Tebbs, Fristoe and Harding 10 miles north of courthouse; 40 acres bounded by Tebbs, Fristoe, Harding, Pritchard, Lane and McInteer
Thomas Harding (2-11), 120 acres bounded by L Harding, Tebbs, Fristoe
Byram Harding (2-29) 80 acres bounded by L Harding, Fristoe etc. 30 acres bounded by L Harding, Fristoe etc.
Enoch Harding (4-12) 100 acres lease for life bounded by Euztace, Tebbs, Hooe etc.
Elijah Harding (4-14) 117 acres a part of the Parke Tract
Joel Harding (2-30) 116 ½ acres, a part of J Kendall; 28 acres Aquia Run and Cannon's Run; 239 acres on Beaver Dam by Tebbs, Combs etc

1815 Land Tax Lists
Lucy Harding (2-10) 70 acres Stafford County by Tebbs Fristoe and Harding. CH 10 miles north; 40 acres, same bounds, CH 10 miles north
Thomas Harding (2-11) 120 acres Stafford Co, South Run Harding and Tebbs 10 miles north
Byram Harding (2-29) 80 acres same bounds, CH 10 miles north, 30 acres same bounds

Harding Families of the Northern Neck of Virginia

Enoch Harding (4-12) 104 acres, bound by Hansborough, Kendall CH 12 Miles N
Elijah Harding (4-14) 117 acres lease for life Parke etc. CH 10 miles north; 100 acres CH 10 miles north
Joel Harding (2-30) 116 ½ acres bound Kendall and others CH 8 miles N, 28 acres Aquia Run and Cannon's Run; 239 acres on Beaver Dam by Tebbs, Combs etc

1816 Land Tax Lists
Lucy Harding (2-10) deceased, resides in Stafford, 70 acres and 40 acres
Thomas Harding (2-11) of Stafford 120 acres
Byram Harding (2-29) of Stafford 80 and 30 acres
Enoch Harding (4-12) of Stafford 104 acres
Elijah Harding (4-14) deceased 117 acres leased, and 100 acres leased
Joel Harding (2-30) of Stafford Fee land 116 ½ acres, 28 acres, 239 acres, 33 acres all on Aquia Run

1817 Land Tax Lists
Thomas Harding (2-11) of Stafford 120 acres Fee on South Run
Byram Harding (2-29) of Stafford 110 acres Fee, 170 acres on South Run
Enoch Harding (4-12) of Stafford 104 acres fee
Heirs of Elijah Harding (4-14) 117 acres Lease for Life and 100 acres Lease for Life
Joel Harding (2-30) of Stafford, of Stafford, 116 ½ acres, 28 acres, 239 acres all Fee Owned

1818 Land Tax Lists
Mark Harding of Stafford 200 acres on Potomac River bought from Philip Jones
Byram Harding (2-29) of Stafford 110 acres on South Run Fee
Thomas Harding (2-11) of Stafford 120 acres South Run
Enoch Harding (4-12) 104 acres Cannons run
The heirs of Elijah Harding (4-14) Lease 117 acres and 100 acres
Joel Harding (2-30) of Stafford 116 ½, 28, 239 acres Aquia Run

Personal property tax lists 1783
Page 11 Before 12 May George Harding (2-13) 1 male 0 slaves 2 horses 4 cattle
Page 11 Before 12 May Benjamin Million 1 male 0 slaves 1 horse 7 cattle
Page 11 Before 12 May Charles Harding (2-9) 1 male 1 horse 3 cattle
Page 14 Robert Million 1 Tithe 1 over 21 13 cattle 6 horses
Page 14 Harden Kendall 2 cattle 1 horse
Page 15 Thomas Harding (2-11) 1 tithe 1 over 21 1 black 7 cattle 2 horse
Page 15 John S Harding (2-10) 1 tithe 1 over 21 7 cattle 2 horse
New List of John R Dayton:
Page 16 William Harding (4-2) 2 whites over 21 2 Negroes 4 horses 16 cattle 12 in family

Virginia County Records

Page 18 Charles Harding (2-9) No items at all

Personal Property Tax Lists 1784
NOTE: Page 1 horse and cattle column may be reversed
Page 1 Thomas Harding (2-11) 1 white 1 slaves 2 cattle 6 horse
Page 1 John S. Harding (2-10) 1 white 0 slaves 2 cattle 9 horse
Page 1 George Harding (2-13) 1 white 1 slave 2 cattle 6 horse
Page 1 Benjamin Million 1 white 1 slave 1 cattle 7 horse
Page 1 Robert Million 1 white 5 cattle 13 horse
Page 11a William Harding (4-2) 1 white 2 negroes 5 horse 18 cattle
Page 11a Charles Harding (2-9) 1 white 0 negroes 5 horse cattle unreadable
NOTE: Page numbers 10 and 11 are microfilmed twice

Personal Property Tax List 1785
Charles Harding (2-9) 1 over 21 4 horse 4 cattle
Cuth Harding (4-11) 1 over 21 2 horse 1 cattle (same page as above)
William Harding (4-2) 1 over 21 1 over 16 4 slaves 4 horse 15 cattle
John Harding (4-10) (next line) 1 over 21 1 horse 1 cow
Four pages later in alpha listing:
John S. Harding (2-10) over 21 3 horse 9 cattle
Thomas Harding (2-11) 1 over 21 1 slave 2 horse 7 cattle
Geo Harding (2-13) 1 over 21 1 slave 2 horse 4 cattle

Personal Property Tax List 1786
Page 6 John Harding (4-10) 1 over 21 2 horse 1 cow
Page 6 Cuthbert Harding (4-11) 1 over 21 2 horse 2 cow
Page 8 William Harding (4-2) 1 over 21 1 16-21 5 slaves 4 horse 15 cow
Page 14 George Harding (2-13) 1 over 21 1 slave 3 horse 6 cow
Page 14 Thomas Harding (2-11) 1 over 21 1 slave 2 horse 6 cow
Page 15 J S Harding (2-10) 1 over 21 4 horse 9 cow
Page 15 Charles Harding (2-9) 1 over 21 1 16-21 1 horse 3 cow

Personal Property Tax List 1787
March 12 George Harding (2-13) over 21 1 slave 3 horse 5 cow
March 12 John Scott Harding (2-10) over 21 3 horse 9 cattle
March 24 William Harding (4-2) over 21 1 16-21 6 slave 5 horse 15 cattle
March 24 John Harding (4-10) over 21 2 horse 2 cow
March 24 Cuthbert Harding (4-11) over 21 3 slaves 1 horse 3 cow
April 9 Thomas Harding (2-11) over 21 1 slave 2 horse 8 cow

Personal Property Tax 1788
March 14 Cuthbert Harding (4-11) 1 black 2 horses
March 15 John Harding (4-10) 2 horses
March 15 Thomas Harding (2-11)

Harding Families of the Northern Neck of Virginia

March 15 (unreadable) (ends with -es) Harding 1 horse
March 28 George Harding (2-13) 3 horses
March 28 John Scott Harding (2-10) 3 horses
April 12 William Harding (4-2) and Enough Harding over 21, 1 16-21

Personal Property Tax 1789
March 21 John Harding (4-10) 1 over 16 3 livestock
March 21 Cuthbert Harding (4-11) 1 over 16 1 black 2 horses
March 28 George Harding (2-13) 1 over 16 1 black 2 livestock
March 30 Thomas Harding (2-11) 1 over 16 1 black 3 livestock
March 30 John Scott Harding (2-10) 2 over 16 4 livestock
April 13 William Harding (4-2) 3 over 16 2 black 7 livestock
June 29 William Harding (Chapawamsick) 1 over

Personal Property Tax 1790
March 27 William Harding (4-2) (5 over 16) 3 black 7 livestock
March 27 John Harding (4-10) 1 black 4 livestock
April 3 George Harding (2-13) 2 over 16 1 livestock
April 5 Thomas Harding (2-11) 1 black 2 livestock
April 12 George Harding (2-13) 1 black 2 horse
April 12 John S. Harding (2-10) (2 over 16) 3 livestock
May 15 Cuthbert Harding (4-11) 2 livestock

Personal Property Tax 1791
March 14 Cuthbert Harding (4-11) 1 black 2 livestock
March 14 William Harding (4-2) (3 over 16) 3 black 6 livestock
March 14 Thomas Harding (2-11) (Constable) 1 black 3 livestock
March 14 John S Harding (2-10) (2 over 16) 1 black 3 livestock
March 14 William Harding (4-2) 1 livestock
March 15 George Harding (2-13) 1 black 2 livestock
April 2 Enoch Harding (4-12) 1 livestock
July 29 John Harding (4-10) 1 black 3 livestock

Personal Property Tax 1792
March 12 Enoch Harding (4-12) 1 black 1 livestock
March 12 Cuthbert Harding (4-11) 2 black 3 livestock
March 12 Thomas Harding (2-11) Const 1 black 3 livestock
March 17 George Harding (2-13) 1 black 2 livestock
March 17 William Harding (4-2) (3 over 16) 3 black 6 livestock
March 31 John S. Harding (2-10) 2 over 16 1 black 3 livestock
July 9 John Harding (4-10) 3 livestock

Personal Property Tax 1793
March 11 William Harding (4-2) (3 over 16) 3 black 6 livestock

March 11 Thomas Harding (2-11) Constable 1 black 3 livestock
March 18 Enoch Harding (4-12) 1 black 1 livestock
April 8 George Harding (2-13) 1 black 4 livestock
August 1 John S. Harding (2-10) 2 over 16 3 livestock
August 21 John Harding (4-10) 2 livestock

Personal Property Tax 1794
March 10 Thomas Harding (2-11) Const 1 black 3 livestock
March 10 George Harding (2-13) 2 blacks 4 livestock
March 10 Enoch Harding (4-12) 1 black 1 livestock
March 15 William Harding (4-2) (3 over 16) 3 black 6 livestock
March 22 John Harding (4-10) 3 livestock
April 5 George Harding (2-42) 3 livestock

Personal Property Tax 1795
April 4 Thomas Harding (2-11) Const 1 livestock
April 13 George Harding (2-42) Jr 1 livestock
April 13 Lucy Harding (2-10) 3 livestock
April 13 George Harding (2-13) Sr 1 black 6 livestock
May 15 John Harding (4-10) 3 livestock
May 15 Enoch Harding (4-12) 1 black 1 livestock
May 26 William Harding (4-2) (4 over 16) 3 black 8 livestock

Personal Property Tax 1796
May 9 Enoch Harding (4-12) 2 livestock
May 9 George Harding (2-42) Jr 1 black 1 livestock.
May 9 Lucy Harding (2-10) 3 livestock
May 12 George Harding (2-13) 2 black 3 livestock
May 12 John Harding (4-10) 4 livestock
May 16 Wiliam Harding (4-2) (2 over 16) 3 black 8 livestock
May 16 Joel Harding (2-30) 1 black 1 livestock
August 8 Thomas Harding (2-11) Cons 1 black 3 livestock

Personal Property Tax 1797
May 10 George Harding (2-13) 2 black 2 livestock
May 10 Enoch Harding (4-12) 2 livestock
May 10 George Harding (2-42) Jr 1 black 2 livestock
May 10 Thomas Harding (2-11) (Constable) 2 black 3 livestock
May 10 John Harding (4-10) 1 black 4 livestock
May 20 William Harding (4-2) (2 over 16) 4 black 7 livestock
May 20 Joel Harding (2-30) livestock 1 black 1
August 12 Lucy Harding (2-10) 1 over 16 1 black 1 livestock

Personal Property Tax 1798

Harding Families of the Northern Neck of Virginia

Apr 14 George Harding (2-42) 1 black 1 livestock
May 17 George Harding (2-13) Sr 1 black 1 livestock
May 17 Lucy Harding (2-10) 2 livestock
May 17 William Harding (4-2) Executor 5 black 7 livestock
May 17 John Harding (4-10) (2 over 16) 6 livestock
May 17 Joel Harding (2-30) 1 black 1 livestock
September 15 Enoch Harding (4-12) 2 livestock

Personal Property Tax 1799
May 16 John Harding (4-10) (2 over 16) 1 black 5 livestock
May 16 Joel Harding (2-30) 1 black 1 livestock
May 16 George Harding (2-42) Jr 1 livestock
May 16 Clarkey Harding (4-2) (2 over 16) 7 black 7 horses
May 16 Enoch Harding (4-12) 1 black 2 livestock
July 18 Lucy Harding (2-10) 2 over 16 2 horses

Personal Property Tax 1800
April 6 Thomas Harding (2-11) 2 blacks 5 horses
April 6 Elijah Harding (4-14) (2 over 16) 6 blacks 8 horses
April 6 Thomas Harding Jr 1 livestock
May 8 Joel Harding (2-30) 1 black 1 horse)
Sept 19 John Harding (4-10) (2 over 16) 2 over 16 1 black 5 Horses

Personal Property Tax 1801
March 21 Enoch Harding (4-12) 2 black 4 horse
March 21 John Harding (4-10) (2 over 16) 4 horses
June 13 Thomas Harding (2-11) 2 blacks 5 horses
September 1 Clerky Harding (4-2) (2 over 16) 7 black 5 horse
October 4 Joel Harding (2-30) 1 black 1 horse)
October 4 Thomas Harding Jr.
October 4 Lucy Harding (2-10) 1 horse

Personal Property Tax 1802
April 9 Thomas Harding Jr 1 horse
May 11 Thomas Harding (2-11) Sr. 1 black 1 horse
May 11 Joel Harding (2-30) 1 black 2 horse)
May 20 John Harding 1 horse
May 20 Clarky Harding (4-2) (2 over 16) 1 black 9 horse
August 9 Enoch Harding (4-12) 2 black 3 horse
August 9 John Harding (4-10) (2 over 16) 2 horses
August 10 Thomas Harding
August 10 Lucy Harding (2-10) 1 horse

Personal Property Tax 1803

May 13 Clarky Harding (4-2) 2 over 16 7 black 8 horses
May 13 Thomas Harding (2-11) 1 black 5 horse
May 13 John Harding (4-10) Sr.5 horse
May 13 Enoch Harding (4-12) 2 black 2 horse
May 13 John Harding 1 horse
August 5 John Harding 1 horse
August 5 Lucy Harding (2-10) 1 over 16, 2 horse
August 9 Joel Harding (2-30) 1 lack 2 horse)
Second List

Personal Property Tax 1804
March 10 John Harding Jr 1 horse
March 10 Lucy Harding (2-10) 2 horses
March 10 Joel Harding (2-30) 1 black 2 horse)
April 1 John Harding (4-10) Sr 2 over 16, 5 horse
April 1 Enoch Harding (4-12) 1 black 3 horse
May 21 Thomas Harding (2-11) Sr. 1 black 5 horse
May 30 Clarky Harding (4-2) 3 over 16 7 black 8 horse
July 9 Thomas Harding Jr. 1 horse
May 14 Byram Harding (2-29) 1 horse

Personal Property Tax for 1805
March 12 Thomas Harding none
April 8 Thomas Harding (2-11) Sr Constable 1 black 4 horse
May 13 Mason Harding (4-52) 2 horses
May 18 Clerkey Harding (4-2) 6 black 6 horse
May 18 Elijah Harding (4-14) 2 black 1 horse
May 18 Enoch Harding (4-12) 2 black 3 horse
May 18 Charles Harding
May 18 Thomas Harding
July 6 John Harding (4-10) 3 over 16
September 4 John Harding Jr.1 horse
September 4 Lucy Harding (2-10) 1 horse

Personal Property tax list for 1806
March 13 John S. Harding 1 male 1 black 1 horse
Aprill 4 Lucy Harding (2-10) 1 male 1 black 3 horse
April 12 Clarky Harding (4-2) 3 males 8 black 8 horse
April 12 Enoch Harding (4-12) 1 male 2 black 3 horse
April 12 Joel Harding (2-30) 1 male 1 black 2 horse)
Aprill 14 Thomas Harding (2-11) (Constable) 2 males 1 black 4 horse
May 24 Elijah Harding (4-14) 1 male 2 black 2 horse
May 24 John Harding (4-10) 3 males 4 horse
July 12 Mason Harding (4-52) 1 male 2 horse

Harding Families of the Northern Neck of Virginia

Personal Property tax list for 1807
March 21 John S. Harding 1 male 1 black 1 horse
March 21 Thomas Harding (2-11) Constable 2 males 2 black 3 horse
April 4 Mrs. Lucy Harding (2-10) 1 male 3 horse
April 11 Mrs. Clarkey Harding (4-2) 2 males 9 black 8 horse
April 11 Elijah Harding (4-14) 1 male 2 black 1 horse
April 11 Enoch Harding (4-12) 1 male 2 black 2 horse
April 13 Joel Harding (2-30) 1 male 2 horse)
June 8 John Harding (4-10), son of William 3 white males 1 horse

Personal Property tax list for 1809
March Mark Harding (4-19) 1 male
Second list
March 10 Mason Harding (4-52) 1 male 1 horse
March 14 Elijah Harding (4-14)
March 14 Joel Harding (2-30) 1 male 4 horse)
March 17 Mrs. Clarkey Harding (4-2) 1 male 9 black 7 horse
April 1 Byram Harding (2-29) 1 male 2 horse
April 1 John S. Harding 1 male 1 horse
April 1 Lucy Harding (2-10) 1 horse
April 1 Thomas Harding (2-11) (exempt) 2 black 2 horse
April 1 Barnett Harding 1 male 1 horse
April 8 Enoch Harding (4-12) 1 male 2 black 2 horse
April 8 Bennett Harding (4-53) 1 male
April 26 John Harding (4-10) 2 males 1 horse

Personal Property Tax List for 1810
Bennett Harding (4-53) List #1 1 male 1 horse
Mark Harding (4-19) List #1 1 male 2 black 1 horse
List #2
Mason Harding (4-52) 1 male
John Harding (4-10) Sr. 2 males 2 horse
Enoch Harding (4-12) 1 male 2 black 2 horse
Thomas Harding (2-11) (constable) 3 black 3 horse
Barnett Harding 1 male
Byram Harding (2-29) 1 male 1 horse
Joel Harding (2-30) 1 male 3 horse)
Elijah Harding (4-14) 1 male 4 black 3 horse
John S. Harding 1 male 1 horse
Mrs. Clarkey Harding (4-2) 1 male 10 black 7 horse
Lucy Harding (2-10) 1 horse

1811 Personal Property Tax List

Bennett Harding (4-53) 1 male 1 horse
Mark Harding (4-19) 1 male 2 black 2 horse
March 9 Joel Harding (2-30) 1 male 2 horse)
March 9 Thomas Harding (2-11) exempt 3 black 3 horse
March 9 Barnett Harding 1 male
March 9 Byram Harding (2-29) 1 male 1 horse
March 12 John S. Harding 1 male
April 13 Elijah Harding (4-14) 1 male 4 black 4 horse
April 13 Mrs. Clarkey Harding (4-2) 1 male 8 black 5 horse
April 13 Enoch Harding (4-12) 1 male 3 black 3 horse
April 23 John Harding (4-10) 1 male 2 horse

1812 Personal Property Tax List (in land tax files)
March 4 Bernard Harding, I black
March 9 Mrs. Clarkey Harding (4-2) 5 blacks 4 horse
March 9 Joel Harding (2-30) 1 black 3 horse)
March 10 Thomas Harding (2-11) exempt 3 black 4 horse
March 23 John S. Harding
March 23 Byram Harding (2-29) 2 horses
March 27 William Harding (2-27) 2 horses
April 4 Bennett Harding (4-53) 1 horse
April 4 John Harding (4-10) 2 horses
April 4 Nelson Harding 1 horse
April 11 Enoch Harding (4-12) 5 black 3 horse
April 11 Elijah Harding (4-14) 4 black 4 horse

1813 Personal Property Tax Listing
Mark Harding (4-19) 2 male 3 black 3 horse
March 6 Elijah Harding (4-14) 1 male 5 black 4 horse
March 6 Bernard Harding 1 male
March 6 John S. Harding 1 male
March 6 Joel Harding (2-30) 2 Males 2 black 3 horse)
March 6 William Harding (2-27) 1 male 1 horse
March 8 Mrs. Clarkey Harding (4-2) 1 male 5 black 4 horse
March 8 Enoch Harding (4-12) 1 male 6 black 4 horse
March 19 Thomas Harding (2-11) Exempt 3 black 2 horse
March 25 Byram Harding (2-29) 1 male 2 horse
April 24 Bennett Harding (4-53) 1 male 2 horse

1814 Personal Property Tax Listing
March 1 Byram Harding (2-29)
March 3 Bernard Harding
March 3 William Harding (2-27) son of Scott (2-10)

Harding Families of the Northern Neck of Virginia

March 3 Joel Harding (2-30)
March 4 Thomas Harding (2-11) exempt
March 14 Elijah Harding (4-14)
March 14 Enoch Harding (4-12)
March 17 Bennett Harding (4-53)
March 17 Mrs. Clarkey Harding (4-2)
March 24 William Harding Sr.
March 30 John S Harding
Mark Harding (4-19)

1815 Personal Property Tax List
February 23 Bernard Harding
March 1 Thomas Harding (2-11) Exempt
March 1 Byram Harding (2-29)
March 13 William Harding (2-27) Sr
March 13 Joel Harding (2-30)
March 13 Enoch Harding (4-12)
March 14 William Harding (Forest)
April 1 John S. Harding
April 10 Mrs. Clarkey Harding (4-2)
April 19 Philadelphia Harding (4-14)

1816 Personal Property Tax Lists
March 15 Byram Harding (2-29)
March 16 Thomas Harding (2-11) Exempt
March 16 John S. Harding
March 16 William Harding (2-27) Jr
April 4 William Harding Sr
April 28 Joel Harding (2-30) 2 whites
April 28 Mrs. Clarkey Harding (4-2)
May 13 Enoch Harding (4-12)
May 13 Philadelphia Harding (4-14)
April 15 Mark Hardin 2 males (4-19)

1817 Personal Property Tax Lists
May 28 Mark Harding (4-19)
March 6 William Harding (2-27)
March 17 Thomas Harding (2-11) exempt
March 17 Byram Harding (2-29)
April 14 Joel Harding (2-30)
April 14 Enoch Harding (4-12)
April 26 Mrs. Clarkey Harding (4-2)

1818 Personal Property Tax Lists

March 7 Mrs. Clarkey Harding (4-2)
March 7 Thomas Harding (2-11) exempt
March 7 Joel Harding (2-30)
March 10 William Harding (2-27)
March 15 Byram Harding (2-29)
March 23 Philip Harding (2-28)
April 13 Enoch Harding (4-12)
March 4 Mark Harding (4-19)

1819 Personal Property Tax Lists
March 1 Thomas Harding (2-11) exempt
March 13 Byram Harding (2-29)
March 24 Clarkey Harding (4-2)
March 24 Joel Harding (2-30)
March 29 Enoch Harding (4-12)
April 18 William Harding (2-27)
April 30 Phillip Harding (2-28)
March 6 Mark Harding (4-19) 2 males
March 8 Harrison Harding

1820 Personal Property Tax Lists
March 1 William Harding 2 males
March 10 Byram Harding (2-29)
March 10 Thomas Harding (2-11) exempt
March 27 Mrs. Elizabeth Harding
March 27 Enoch Harding (4-12)
March 1 Mark Harding (4-19)

Westmoreland Co., VA Records

Formed from Northumberland in 1653

"Virginia Colonial Soldiers" by L D Bookstruck

1756 Jul: Page 62 Pay Roll of Capt. Henry Woodward's Company Peter Hardin, corporal.

1756 13 Jul: Page 81 Size Roll of Capt. Harry Woodward's Company

Peter Hardin, enlisted Oct 1755 Westmoreland Co., Virginia, age 23, 5' 7" planter, born Virginia, brown hair, slim made.

Joseph Cockrill enlisted Oct 1755 Westmoreland Co., Virginia, age 23, 5' 4" planter, born Virginia, well made, fair, red hair.

1756 31 Jul: Page 83 Payroll of Capt. Woodward's Co.: Peter Harding on furlough

1756 31 Jul: Page 89 Payroll of Capt. Woodward's Co.: Peter Harding on furlough

Court Order Book

John Harding (1-7) gave evidence

Court Order Book 1698-1705

John Harding (1-7) witnessed the will of Philip Hearn

John Harding (1-7) owes debt to William Clark estate

1704 06 Jul: Page 231a John Harding (1-10), son of William Harding (1-5) and Elizabeth (1-5) his wife, aged 11 years, is by the Court bound apprentice to John Harding (1-7) his uncle with him to live after the manner of an apprentice until he has attained the age of 18 years. In consideration whereof the said John Harden (1-7) doth hereby assume and obligate himself to find his said apprentice sufficient meat and drink and Lodging and apparel during the said term and in the meanetyme to instruct or cause him to bee instructed in reading and to gett perfectly by heart the church catechisms and the rudiments of the Christian Religion according to his quality and capacity.

Court Order Books

1720 30 Mar: Page 386 John Harden (1-12), orphan, bound to Henry Garner

1720 30 Mar: Page 286 William Harden (1-13), orphan, bound to Edmund Jeoffries

1734 26 Mar: Page 131 Book 1731-1739 Matthew Trussell came into court and made oath that his father-in-law John Harding (1-10), decd, departed this life without making any will so far as he knows or believes and upon his motion a giving Peter Rust and Geo Jeffries for his securities according to law certificate is granted him for obtaining Letters of Administration on the said decedent's estate in due form and it is ordered that Jos Garland, Thomas Butler, James Coleman and John Curtcher or any three of them being first sworn before a magistrate of the said County do sometime before the next court to be held for the County aforesaid value and appraise the said decedent's estate in money and make report thereof to the said next court.

1734 28 May: Page 137 Book 1731-39 Matthew Trussell, administrator of John Harding (1-10) decd, returned upon oath an Inventory of the said Hardin's estate, which is admitted to record.

1736 25 May: Page 197-a Book 1731-39 On motion of Geo Jeffries, it is considered by this court that Willoughby Harding (1-22), an orphan son of John Harding (1-10) decd, be bound to him the said Jeffries until he the said Willoughby shall attain the age of twenty-one years (he being nine years old the twenty-third day of February last). (Legal language follows)

1754 28 May: Abraham Garrard to pay Thomas Harden (1-23) for appearing in court

1755 24 Jul: Richard Jackson to pay Charles Harding (2-2) 17 pounds of tobacco for coming from Stafford County 64 miles to prove two deeds.

1759 Page 87a Book 1758-61 Thomas Hardin (1-23) and Sarah (1-23) his wife came into court and Personally acknowledged together with the Lien of Seizen thereon endorsed, a deed of testament by them issued to John Brown to be their proper act and deed, the said same being first sworn according to law and relinquished her rights &c and ordered recorded.

Deed and Will Book

1733/4 18 Jan: Will of William Butler witnessed by John Harding (1-10).

Deed and Will Book 11

1753 27 Mar: Page 482 Thomas Blundell and wife Jemima of Cople Parish Westmoreland Co. to Thomas Hardin (1-23) of some 50 acres in Nomony Forest, Cople Parish

Deed and Will Book 12

1753 20 Jan: Page 75 rec 26 Mar: 1754 Nathaniel Jones will mentions land where John Clift now lives, bought of George Harding (3-3) in Stafford County, said land devised to son John Jones.

1755 Mar: 01 Thomas Harden (1-23) witnesses a deed from Edwin Turner to Peter Presley Cox 50 acres in Cople Parish, Westmoreland Co., VA

Deed and Will Book 13

1759 24 Oct: Page 253 Thomas Hardin (1-23) and Sarah (1-23) his wife of unknown, to John Brown of Westmoreland Co., VA 50 acres in Cople Parish. Witnesses were Richard Beard, Vincent Lewis, Garrard Hutt.

Deed and Will Book 14

1761 27 Sep: Page 120 Peter Harding to Robert Middleton Bond

1764 03 Jul: Page 272 Peter Harding to Robert Middleton Deed

Deed and Will Book 14

1761 07 Sep: Page 120 Peter Harden of Couple Parish, Westmoreland Co., VA and and Zachariah White of Lunenburg, Richmond County enter into a bond. The Condition is that Peter Harding and Mary Jeffries his wife, daughter and one of the coheirs of Benjamin Walker, late of the County of Westmoreland, have sold to Robert Middleton their title to 150 acres in Couple Parish Westmoreland Co., VA that belonged to Thomas Walker, grandfather of Mary Jeffries Thomas Walker and from him descended to his three daughters Seleashea, Mary Jeffries, and Alice as coheirs. Mary is not as yet of full age to pass a conveyance to Robert Middleton. Bond accepted by court 30 March 1762.

Chapter 5
North Carolina County Records

Caswell Co., NC Records

Federal Census Records

1786 State Census
Presley Harden (1-43) 2 males 21-60, 3 males 0-21 & 60-up, three females.

1790 Federal Census
Prestley Harding (1-43) Hillsborough District or St. Davids Dist. Page 82

1800 Federal Census
Henry Harden (1-49) 00010 30010
John Windsor 02001 00111

1810 Federal Census
Henry Harden (1-49) 10010 03010

Deed Records

1783 13 Oct: Page B 299 State of North Carolina, Alexander Martin, Grant to William Hardin (5-111) for 257 acres on Hico and Gents Creeks

1786 13 Jan: Page C-153 William Harding (5-111) of Caswell Co., NC to Henry Graves of Granville Co., NC 100 acres

1786 07 Jun: Page ??? William Johnson of Caswell Co., NC to Thomas Hornbuckle of Fairfax Co., VA, witnesses Thomas Harden (1-23) and William Hornbuckle (1-42)

1786 10 Oct: Page E-144 James Scott and wife Mary of Caswell Co., NC to Thomas Harden (1-23) of Rockingham Co., NC for 150 Pounds, 188 acres on Country Line Creek adj Jeremiah Poston, Rockingham Co. line, Daniel Gwynn, Nathan Rice, Waddy Tate. Witnesses Presley Harden (1-43) and Jeremiah Harden (1-45).

1787 20 Feb: Page E-168 William Harding (5-111) to Joseph Beadles of Halifax Co., VA, 511 acres

Harding Families of the Northern Neck of Virginia

1786 01 Jun: Page E-288 Daniel Johnston to John Harden (1-44) for 150 Pounds, 600 acres on Moon's Creek adjacent to William Johnson, Henry Dixon, Cobb. Witness William Hornbuckle (1-42) and Thomas Harden (1-23).

1786 04 Nov: Page F-312 John Murphy and wife Nancy of Caswell Co., NC and wife to Jeremiah Hardin (1-45) of the same county, for 80 Pounds Sterling, 200 Acres adjacent Atkinson, Rice, Walker, Jesse Oldham. Signed John and Anne Murphy. Witness: John Harden (1-44)

1789 14 Aug: Page F-322 Daniel Gwynn and wife Zipporah of Caswell Co., NC to Thomas Hardin (1-23) of Guilford Co., NC for 150 Pounds Sterling, 158 acres adjacent to Guilford Co. Line, Nathan Rice and Em Eaks. Signed Daniel and Zipporah Gwynn. Witnesses, Jere Poston, William Hornbuckle, David Poyner.

1790 04 Nov: Deed Rowland Hughes to William Brown, witness John Harden (1-44)

1790 30 Nov: Page H-80 Jeremiah Harden (1-45) and wife Sarah (1-45) of Caswell Co., NC to Lewis Pike of Caswell, for 80 Pounds Sterling 200 acres adjacent Adkinson, Walker, Jesse Oldham. Signed Jeremiah (1-45) and Sarah Hardin (1-45). Witnesses Presley Hardin (1-43) and John Robertson.

1789 22 Sept Page H-151 John Harden (1-44) and wife Sarah of Orange Co., NC to Thomas Hornbuckle of Caswell Co., NC for 100 Pounds, 20 acres on Moon's Creek adjacent to Daniel Johnson and Noah Cobb. Witnesses Richard Hornbuckle, William Williams, Henry Harden (1-49)

1792 14 Jan: Deed Hugh Larimore to George Hornbuckle, witness P. Harden (1-43)

1794 02 Dec: Page H-433 Thomas Harden (1-23) Sr. of Rockingham Co., NC to son Henry Harden (1-49). 145 acres on Country Line Creek, part of purchase of James Scott. Signed Thomas Hardin (1-23). Witnesses Jere Poston, P. Hardin (1-43).

1795 18 Jan: Page H-417 Thomas Harden (1-23) Sr. of Rockingham Co., NC to son Thomas Harden (1-48) Jr., 100 acres on Country Line Creek adjacent to Henry Harden and Tapscott. Signed Thomas Hardin (1-23). Witnesses Jere Poston, William Hornbuckle (1-42), Henry Harden (1-49)

1795 08 Jan: Page ???? Deed John Lenox to Lewis Pike. Witness Jeremiah Harden (1-45)

1795 19 Jul: Division of the estate of Waddy Tate, Witness Presley Harden (1-43)

1796 Sep: Page K-915 Thomas Harden (1-48) of Caswell County to Samuel Cobb of the same, for 50 Pounds, 100 acres on Country Line Creek adjacent

Thomas Harden, Henry Harden (1-49), Tate's Line. Witnesses: P. Harden (1-43), James Cobb.

1799 07 Jan: Page L-18 Thomas Hornbuckle to Henry Harden (1-49) his son-in-law, for 5 shillings, love and affection, 200 acres on Moon's Creek adjacent to Samuel Walker, James Johnston, and Noah Cobb. Witnesses Richard and George Hornbuckle.

1799 15 Apr: Page L-61 Jesse Dickens of Person Co., NC to Thomas Harden (1-23) of Rockingham Co., NC, for 37 Pounds, 168 acres on Haw River adjacent Eaks Corner, Walker, Rockingham Co. line, Taylor. Witnesses Robert Mitchell and Iverson Gwyn

1799 15 Apr: Deed Jesse Dickens to Iverson Gwynn, witness Peter Harden (1-50)

1806 29 Jul: Deed John Windsor Jr. to Aaron Simpson, witness Henry Harden (1-49)

1813 03 Jun: Page R-32 Samuel Cobb of Caswell Co., NC to Peter Harden (1-50) of Rockingham Co., NC for $250 100 acres on Country Line Creek, part of the land of Thomas Harden (1-23), adjacent Tapscott. Witnesses Thomas and Anthony Williamson.

1816 27 Dec: Page S-25 John Harden (1-44) of Orange Co., NC to Peter Harden (1-50) of Rockingham Co., NC, for $400 162 acres on Moon's Creek adjacent William Orr, Henry Dixon, Joseph Rowe, William Paschall. Witnesses Iverson Gwyn and James Foster

1816 29 Nov: Page S-34 Allotment of the lands of Henry Harden (1-49) estate to his three children, Deborah (1-92) who married John P. Freeman (1-92) 64.8 acres, Thompson Harden (1-93) 64.8 acres, and James Foster (1-91) and Nancy (1-91) 64.8 acres

1818 02 Sep: Division of the land of James Simpson, 146 acres each to James Foster (1-91), Sally Simpson, Milly Simpson, Polly Simpson and Sally Simpson Jr.

1819 07 Oct: John P. Freeman and Deborah (1-78) his wife of Caswell Co., NC to John Windsor of Rockingham Co., NC for $647.50, 64.8 acres on Moon's Creek adjacent to Thompson Harden (1-93)

1823 10 Oct: John Windsor of Rockingham Co., NC, guardian of Thompson Harden (1-93), to Azariah Graves, 192 acres in Carroll Co., Tennessee, 166 acres in Hatchie Creek, Tennessee and 2 tracts of 132 acres on Moon's Creek, adjacent to Thompson Harden (1-93).

1826 18 Oct: Page X-149 Power of Attorney Thompson Harden (1-93) of Logan Co., KY to Joseph Windsor of Caswell Co., NC to demand money due him by conveyance deed to Henly Humphries, his interest in 65 or 66 acres.

1827 12 May: Page X-304 Peggy Harden (1-51) of Rockingham Co., NC to Frances Hornbuckle of Caswell Co., NC, for $150 a Negro girl Julia, aged 8 years.

1831 31 Dec: Joseph Windsor, attorney for Thompson Harden (1-93) of Logan Co., KY to James Wilson of Caswell Co., NC for $160 ½ of undivided 162 acres belonging to Thompson Harden (1-93) and John Harden (1-79) on Moon's Creek adjacent to Joseph Rowe.

1832 26 May: Page AA-333 John Harden (1-79) of Orange Co., NC to William M. Harralson of Caswell Co., NC for $200 a tract on Moon's Creek

1837 29 Apr: Page DD-276 Margaret Harden (1-51) of Rockingham Co., NC to Bernard H. Boswell of Caswell Co., NC for $34.80 25 1/5 acres adjacent Iverson Gwynn

William Walker to E. J. Harding Page HH-574

Guilford Co., NC Records

Federal Census

1790 Federal Census
Page 497 Charles Hardin 22400
Page 505 Thomas Hardin 10100

1800 Federal Census
Page 677 Salisbury Charles Harden 00111 00101
Page 645 Salisbury Thomas Harden 10010 20010
Page 621 Salisbury Stewart Harden 30010 10011

1810 Federal Census
Page 424 Greensboro John Harden 00010 10111
Page 92 Greensboro Steward Hardin 32010 30010

1820 Federal Census
Page 79 Stewart Harden 111201 11101
Page 87 Charles Hardin 020010 60001]
Page 87 John Harden 200101 21012

1830 Federal Census
Page 121 John Hardin 01110001 20101101
Page 155 Charles Hardin 00002001 001220001
Page 188 John Hardin 1100001 01001

1840 Federal Census
Page 277 Chas Hardin 000000001 0000000001
Page 277 John Hardin Sr 010110001 00211001
Page 277 John Hardin 1100011 11001
Page 266 Peter Hardin 00001 00001

Deed Books Index

1779 Page A-524 Charles Hardin a Grant from the State. Tract of land of 640 acres in Guilford County on Brushy Fork

1782 2 Oct: Page C-133 John Hardin a Grant from Francis Cook 350 acres Guilford County on Alamance River

1799 Page G-405 Charles Hardin a deed from David Reynolds

Will Books

1775 15 Oct: Page A-152 Probated Nov 1775 Will of Thompson Harris, names wife Hannah, sons Robert, John, Thompson, and Christopher Harris.

1806 07 May: Page A-172 Probated August 1807 Will of Charles Hardin, mentions wife Jean Hardin to live on plantation, daughter Rebecca a colt plus $50, son Stewart 120 acres, son John 190 acres, son Charles 190 acres, daughter Catherine a colt plus $25, David Pritchett not yet of age $5, son-in-law David Braggard (Briggance) $5. Witnesses Thomas McCulloch Sr., T. McCulloch Jr.

1809 Aug: probated Page A-272, Will of Gideon McKemma mentions daughter Elizabeth Hardin 5 shillings, daughter Mary Bishop 5 shillings, son William 85 acres, son Shadrach 30 acres, son James 30 acres, wife Charity house etc.

1799 15 Oct: Page A-317 probate 19 Oct 1799, will of Robert Ramsey mentions shoe boots to Charles Hardin, clothes to Thomas McCulloch, a gown to Mary McCulloch, wife and family rest of estate.

1864 Feb: Page D-197 Will of David B. Hardin mentions Jane, Daniel, John C., Sarah J., James M., Mary E., Joseph C. Hardin and William H., Margaret, and Eve Woods.

Marriage Records

1790 30 Mar: Thomas Hardin married Mary Hancock (son of Edmund of Rutherford Co NC)

1810 26 Mar: Cattrin Hardin married Samuel Quiet

1819 12 May: Charles Hardin married Charlotte Fields

1825 25 Jun: Sally Hardin married Basil Hays

1839 31 Jan: Polly Hardin married Samuel H. Hunter John Hardin bond

1831 17 Oct: John Hardin married Elizabeth Ann Ross

1832 20 Apr: Marmaduke Swain married Jane Hardin

1833 06 Feb: Hiram Lamb married Rebecca Hardin

1835 02 Jul: Wyatt Erwin married Charlotte Hardin

1837 01 Feb: Peter Hardin married Elizabeth Hardin

1837 11 Feb: John Trogdon married Isabella Hardin

1837 15 Jun: Caroline Hardin married Samuel Harvy

1840 16 Oct: Hannah Hardin married Jabin Erwin 16 Oct: 1840 bond John Hardin

1841 03 Jun: Jane Hardin married William Forbes bond John Hardin

1842 22 Apr: Jonahan Causey married Margaret Hardin

1844 20 Aug: Charles Hardin married Mary Jane Gilbreath bond John Hardin

1846 01 Jun: John Hardin married Catharine Forbis

1849 24 Apr: Benton Fields married Martha Hardin

1849 02 Jun: Rankin Lambeth married Mary E. Hardin

1851 22 Oct: John W. Haith married Martha J Hardin

1855 19 Jul: David B. Hardin married Jane Wood

1860 24 Nov: Alson G Jones married Isabel E. Hardin

1865 23 Dec: Charlotte H. Hardin married Thomas R. Greeson

Johnston Co., NC Records

Deed Books

1759 11 Jun: Book A1 Page 77 Mark Hardin (5-31) of Johnston Co., North Carolina to Thomas Robertson of same 10 acres for four pounds current money of Virginia, on north side of Nuse River, Part of a deed granted to Justin Farrell 9 May 1757 from the Earl of Granville for 605 acres. Witnesses Henry Hardin (5-5), Mark Hardin and William Hardin (5-33)

Orange Co., NC Records

1790 Federal Census

John Harden (1-44) Page 93 Chatham District
John Harden Page 93 Chatham District
John Harden Page 95
Nicholas Harden Page 93 Chatham District

Marriage Records

1783 14 Dec: John Hardin (1-44) married Sarah Holt (1-44) Bond Wm. Oneil

1789 03 Dec: Jeremiah Harden (1-45) married Sarah Wiley (1-45) Bond Samuel Thompson

1791 20 Dec: Thomas Harden (1-48) married Elizabeth Powell (1-48) Bond John Powell

1792 02 Nov: Edmund Hardin married Patty Davis Bond Benjamin Lacy

1806 12 Aug: William Whitsett married Joany Harden Bond James Whitsitt

1812 26 Oct: John Harden (1-79) married Rebeckah Holt (1-79) Bond Thomas Sellers

1812 26 Nov: John S. Prather (1-80) married Mary Harden (1-80) Bond William Whitsitt

1816 24 Sep: Lewis Holt (1-82) married Elizabeth Harden (1-82) Bond Simpson Haris

1823 28 Feb: George Hurdle (1-83) married Peggy Hardin (1-83) Bond John Harden

1835 14 Nov: Daniele Harden (1-112) married Kitty Garrison (1-112) Bond G. Hurdle

1843 07 Feb: Daniel C. Harden (1-112) married Mrs. Rebecca C Foust (1-112)

1844 12 Nov: William M. Mebane (1-116) married Margerite Jane Harden (1-116)

1848 03 Apr: Peter Harden (1-115) married Sarah E. Holt (1-115) Bond George Hurdle

Deed Records

c 1790 John Harden (1-44) from Michael Holt et al Deed Book 3 Page 140

1795 Mar: 1 John Harden (1-44) from Benjamin Raney et al Deed Book 5 Page 289

1803 Sep: 13 John Harden (1-44) from Thomas Powell Deed Book 13 Page 139

1812 Sep: 09 Deed Book 14 Page 474 John Harden (1-79) from Andrew Gibson

1817 10 Jun: Deed Book 18 Page 318 John Harden (1-79) and Rebecca Harden (1-79) to John Holt

1819 29 Aug: Deed Book 19 124 John Harden (1-79) et al from William Holt

1819 29 Aug: Deed Book 19 Page 124 John Harden (1-79) et al from Jas Thomas

1821 17 Oct: Deed Book 21 Page 268 John Harden (1-79) from J S Prather (1-92)

1837 26 Nov: Deed Book 28 Page 120 John Harden (1-79) to Daniel Harden (1-112)

1845 13 Sep: Daniel Harden (1-112) from Henry Foust Est Deed Book 32 page 474

1845 01 Apr: Deed Book 33, page 245 John Harden (1-79) from John Holt

Will and Probate Records

1769 20 Aug: Will of Edmund Hardin mentions wife Mary, three children and unborn child. Executors, wife Mary and Thomas Cate. Witnesses John Baskett, Jonathan Hardin, and Moses Rice.

1798 23 Jan: Probate August 1799 Will of Michael Holt, mentions children by first wife, wife Jean, son Joseph, daughters Margaret Powell, Elizabeth Smith, Sarah Harden (1-44), sons Joshua Holt and Isaac Holt, daughter Mary Thompson, daughter Catherine Holt, sons Michael Holt and William Holt. Executors, wife Jean, sons Isaac and Joshua. Witnesses J Scott, William Rainey, and John Holt.

1807 24 Oct: Probate August 1808 Page D-235 Will of John Harden (1-44) Orange County, North Carolina. In the name of God Amen I John Harden (1-44) of the County of Orange and State of North Carolina do make and appoint this my last will and testament as follows (to wit) I commit my body to the earth to be decently buried and my soul to the hands of Almighty God who gave ---- And my worldly estate property and goods has been his will to bestow upon me I bestow and commit as follows (viz) First I give and bequeath unto my son John Harden (1-79) Part of a tract of land lying on the waters of Moon Creek With the wood Land part and one negro girl by the name of Cloe & one man Cott which is now called his ----- And I give and bequeath unto my loving wife Sarah (1-44) all the remaining property which I possess With the tract of land whereon I now live and part of the before mentioned tract of land on Moon Creek called the old part one negroe man named Louis two negro wenches named pat and Clary one set of Smith Tools all my stock of Cattle Horses Hogs Sheep. One tract of land called the Powel tract one negroe girl by the name of Lydia to have during her life and dispose of at her death them and their increase as she thinks best and proper, Except the tract of land whereon I now live. It is my will and desire to be divided between my four youngest daughters at my wife Death Polly (1-80) Sally (1-81) Betsy (1-82) & Peggy (1-83) as my wife Deems best and most suitable. In witness whereof I have hereunto set my hand and seal this 24th Day of October in the year of Our Lord one thousand eight hundred & seven. John Harden. Witnesses Jean Hoth William Hoth. Orange County August Term 1808 Page 236 The execution of the foregoing last will and Testament of John Harden (1-44) decd was duly proved in open Court by the oath of William Hoth subscribing witness thereto and ordered to be recorded.

1814 20 Sep: Page D-418-20 Probate November 1814 Will of Sarah Harden (1-44) mentions, son John Harden (1-79) provided for in will of his father, daughter Mary Prather (1-80) 150 acres at Powell's Place, youngest daughters Sarah (1-81), Betsy (1-82) and Peggy (1-83). Peggy to have tract I live on and Rainey tract. Executors Archibald D. Murphy, John L. Prather (1-80), John Harden (1-79). Witnesses Thomas Scott, Rebeckah Harden (1-79).

1819 14 Mar: Probated May 1819 Will of Benjamin Whidbee, mentions wife Sally, son Joseph, all my children. Executors, wife Sally and brother-in-law William Holt. Witnesses John Harden (1-79) and Lewis Holt.

1830 04 Nov: Estate of Thomas Harden (1-23) Order issued 24 Jan 1831: "The Sheriff of Orange County Greeting, You are hereby commanded to summon John Harden (1-79), Executor if found in your county to appear before the Justices and Court of Please and Quarter Sessions to be held for the at the courthouse in Hillsborough on the fourth Monday of February next then and there to answer the petition of Elizabeth (Powell) Harden (1-48), guardian of Joshua Harden (1-90), a copy thereof accompanies this subpoena." The petition of Joshua Hardin by his next friend Elizabeth (Powell) Harden (1-48) against John Harden (1-79) Executor of Peter Hardin (1-50) deceased: "Respectfully represents to your Worship that Peter Harden (1-50) late of Rockingham County, departed this life sometime in the year ---- having first duly made and published his last will and testament in writing in which he bequeathed a legacy to one Joshua Harden, son of one Thomas Harden (1-48) who was brother of said Peter Harden (1-50). That said Peter (1-50) died without reworking said will and that at the session of Rockingham County Court the same will was offered for probate by the Deft John Harden (2-19) as one of the executors named therein, that the Deft John Harden (2-19) took upon himself the burthen of executing same. (Part crossed out: "Your petitioner that her late husband Thomas Harden (1-48) aforesaid moved to the State of Tennessee --- time in the year and died Intestate sometime in the month of in AD 182-, that the legacy left him in his father's will was not all paid to him that your petitioner succeeded by the laws of distribution to a share of his father's Thomas Harden (1-23) personal estate. That at the session of Giles County Court in the state of Tennessee petitioner Elizabeth (Powell) Harden (1-23) was appointed Guardian of the person and estate of said Joshua-- that as one of the distributees of his father Thomas Harden (1-48) as aforesaid, the said **Joshua** was entitled to the sum of eighty-five dollars on the 1st day of November 1821, then in the hands of the Deft John Harden (2-19) and Exr as aforesaid."(Balance of the document is a request for payment. John Harding filed a response saying he didn't know anything about Joshua Harding

Randolph Co., NC Records

Federal Census Records

1790 Federal Census
Robert Harden Page 99 12100
Mark Hardin Page 98 11400

1800 Federal Census
Hannah Harden Page 318 01000 11101
Benjamin Harden Page 19 20010 10010
Gabrile Hardin Page 19 00001 00000

1810 Federal Census
Mark Harden Page 25 00010 01021

1830 Federal Census
Mark Hardin Page 25 0203001 1020001

1840 Federal Census
Charles Hardin Page 105 0012001 1000010001
Mark Hardin Page 106 0001100101 00101001
Amaziah Hardin Page 106 10001 02001
Zimri Hardin Page 88 11001 20001

1850 Federal Census

Page 249 Family 1272
Mark Hardin 63 Farmer $325 Real Estate Born North Carolina
Sarah Hardin 65 born in North Carolina

Page 249 Family 1273
John Hardin 37 Farmer born NC
Sabra Hardin 20 born NC
Sarah Hardin 19 born NC
Zach Hardin 13 born NC

Page 250 Family 1274
Zimri A. Hardin 38 Farmer 200 Real Estate born NC
Lucy Hardin 26 NC
William 17 NC
Mary 15 NC
John 13 NC
Sarah 11 NC
Josephine 9 NC
Louisa Hardin 7 NC

Deed Books

1793 Book 1 Page 211 Mark Harden from John and Jean Welborn deed 50 acres

1793 Book 1 Page 212 Mark Harden from John Welborn Deed 100 acres

1795 01 Aug: Book 6 Page 128 Mark Hardin to John Welborn both of Randolph County NC Deed 3 3/4 acres

1796 14 Apr: Book 7 Page 295 Mark Hardin to Eli York, both of Randolph County NC Deed 50 acres Part of land conveyed to Mark Hardin by John Welborn.

1795 Book 7 Page 296 Mark Hardin to Samuel York Both of Randolph County NC Deed 26 acres part of land conveyed to him by John Welborn

1816 Book 13 Page 407 Mark Harden from Letten Roach deed 40 acres

1820 Book 20 Page 458 Mark Harden from William York deed 109 acres

1841 Book 27 Page 103 Mark Harden from Enoch S. Craven deed 15 acres

Rockingham Co., NC Records

Federal Census Records

1790 Federal Census

William Hardin (5-33) Salisbury District 11100
Henry Hardin) Salisbury District 11403
Thomas Hardin (1-23) Salisbury District 30207

1800 Federal Census

Thomas Harden (1-23) 00011 00011
Mark Harden (5-112) 20010 00110

Marriage Record Index

1796 26 Jan: Mark Harden (5-112) married Frances Hill

Deed Records

1786 Page A-123 Zachariah Standley of Louisa County, Virginia to Henry Harden (5-37) of Rockingham County NC, 200 acres on Beaver Island Creek

1786 25 Mar: Page A-144 Watson Gentry of Rockingham Co., NC to Henry Harden (5-37) of same, 50 acres. Witnesses Benjamin Cook, Mark Hardin (5-31)

1787 17 May: State of North Carolina to William Hall, 250 acres Country Line Creek, adjacent to Thomas Harden (1-23)

1789 28 Aug: Book B-250 William Hall of Montgomery Co. to William Williams of Guilford Co., NC for 150 Pounds 150 acres on Country Line Creek adjacent to Thomas Harden (1-23), and Haggard. Witnesses William Hornbuckle (1-42), Henry Harden (1-49) and Hugh Gwyn.

1790 Page C-40 Peter O'Neal to Thomas Harding (1-23) for 60 Pounds 60 acres Country Line Creek adjacent to Jeremiah Poston and William Walker. Witnesses Henry Harden (1-49) and John Cox

1787 10 Nov: Page C-135 Benjamin Cook to Henry Harden (5-37) for 100 Pounds 100 acres on Mayo River

1793 12 Oct: Page C-331 Henry Harden (5-37) of Wilkes Co., GA to Mark Harden (5-31) of Rockingham Co., NC 200 acres on Beaver Island Creek of Dan River

1793 05 Jun: Page D-12 Andrew Wilson and wife Margaret to Thomas Hornbuckle of Caswell Co., NC for 20 Pounds, 35 acres on Haw River. Witnesses William Hornbuckle (1-42), Henry Harding (1-49) and Thomas Harding (1-48).

1793 Page D-166 Henry Harden (5-37) of Wilkes Co., GA by attorney M. Harden (5-31) to John Mathews of Rockingham Co NC 150 acres Mayo Creek. (Initial is hard to read)

1793 14 Oct: George Hornbuckle to William Hornbuckle (1-42), Land on Country Line Creek by Jere Poston. Witnesses Henry Harden (1-49) and Jeremiah Harden (1-45).

1795 16 Nov: William Hornbuckle (1-42) to Cagebeth White, land adjacent Thomas Harden (1-23).

1797 Page E-236 Absalon Harvey to Peter Hardin (1-50) for 20 Pounds 45 acres on Country Line Creek adjacent to Thomas Harden (1-23). Witnesses Henry Harden (1-49) and George Hornbuckle.

1797 16 Oct: Henson Humphrey to Absalom Harvey, land on Country Line Creek adjacent to Thomas Harden (1-23). Witnesses Peter Harden (1-50), Henry Harden (1-49).

1799 Page F-106 Elizabeth and John Glenn Jr. to Mark Hardin (5-112) 133 ½ acres Dan River

1800 Page G-31 Daniel Gwynn to Thomas Harden (1-23) 84 ¾ acres

1801 Page H-40 Charles Sillivan to Peter Harden (1-50) 62 acres Country Line Creek

1795 Page H-50 John Hill to Mark Harden (5-112) 500 acres on Elk River

1803 Page L-167 Robert Williams to Peter Harden (1-50) 404 acres Wolf Island Creek

1806 Page M-142 Hugh Gwyn to Peter Harden (1-50) 96 acres Country Line Creek

1808 Page N-2 Hugh Gwyn to Peter Harden (1-50) and Thomas Harden (1-23) 200 acres Country Line Creek

Will Records

1794 09 Oct: Old Wills-35 No probate date, Will of William Harden (5-111) mentions wife Elizabeth, brother Mark Harden (5-112), brother-in-law Thornton P. Guinn. Executor Almond Guinn, Thornton P. Guinn. Witnesses Adam Crafford and --- Darnel.

1784 02 Jun: Old Wills-183 No probate date, Will of William Williams of Guilford Co., NC, mentions sons John, James and William Taylor Williams, daughters Margaret Appleton, Nancey Foot, Elender Appleton, Susanner Harden (1-43), Jeane Williams, Frances Williams. Executors, sons James and William Williams. Witness Henry Harden (1-49) and Elisha Rice.

1798 09 Feb: Old Wills-202 Will of Hedgebeth White witnessed by P. Harden.

1809 25 May: Page A-86 no probate date, Will of Thomas Harden (1-23). "In the name of God, I Thomas Harden of the County of Rockingham and state of

Harding Families of the Northern Neck of Virginia

North Carolina, being of perfect sound mind and memory I on this twenty-fifth day of May in the year of our lord 1809 make and publish this my last will and testament in manner and form following: First I give to my two sons Henry Harden (1-49) and Peter Harden (1-50) and also to my daughter Peggy harden and to my beloved wife ten Negroes of their choice out of my stock of slaves to be equally divided between them and at the death of my said wife Eleanor Harden (1-23) that her part be equally divided between Henry Harden (1-49), Peter Harden (1-50) and Peggy Harden (1-51). Secondly, I give to my daughter Peggy Harden (1-51) during her life 150 acres of land of Gwynn's tract and after her death to return to my son Peter Harden (1-50). I also give to my said daughter Peggy harden her bed and furniture, one horse saddle and bridle forever. Thirdly I give to son Peter Harden (1-50) the Plantation whereon I now live with 50 acres of Gwynn's tract one bed and furniture and also two horses, a wagon and grain. Fourthly I lend to my said wife Eleanor Harden (1-23) during her life all my household and kitchen furniture with my stock of every kind and at her Death to be equally divided between my two sons Henry Harden (1-49) and Peter Harden (1-50) and my daughter Peggy Harden (1-51). Fifthly I give the remainder of my Negroes to be equally divided amongst my other children, viz, To Ann Read (1-46) lawful begotten children, to Presley Harden (1-43), John Harden (1-44) and Jeremiah Harden (1-45) lawful begotten children, to Thomas Harden (1-48), Sarah Rogers (1-47) and William Hornbuckle (1-42) to be equally divided between them. It is to be observed that the children of Ann Read (1-46), John Harden (1-44), and Jeremiah Harden (1-45) is to have each only a share equal to a real legatee. Sixthly I do constitute and appoint my two sons Henry Harden (1-49) and Peter Harden (1-50) Executors of this my last will and testament signed sealed published and delivered by me Thomas Harden (1-23) the testator as my last will and testament in the presence of us who were by when it was perfected. Witnesses John Reid, John Windsor Jr., Travis Scathers. Signed Thomas Harden (1-23).

1821 9 Mar: Page A-135 probate November 1821 Will of Elizabeth Black mentions children Polly Jackson, Leanne Wright, Pleasant Black, Elizabeth Webster, Joseph Black, John Black, Caroline Matilda Black. Executor son Pleasant Black. Witnesses Mark Hardin (5-112) and Frances Harden

1819 27 Jan: Page A-179 Probate Feb 1819, Will of Peter Hardon (1-50) mentions sister Peggy Hardon (1-51) and her heirs, nephews Thompson Hardon (1-93) and John Hardon (1-79), executors: friends and nephews Thompson (1-93) and John Hardon (1-79). Witnesses Joseph McCain and Hezekiah Boswell.

1819 11 Dec: Page A-257 probate August 1821 Will of Miles Murphy mentions daughters Sally Murphy, Patsy Murphy and Nancy Harden. John Brockman.

All the rest of my children. Executors John Brockman and Sally Murphy. Witnesses James Rauley and Allen Nichols.

1834 04 Jan: Page B-213 Codicil 2 July 1839, Probate Nov 1839, Will of Mark Hardin (5-112) mentions sons William H. Hardin, Pleasant G. Hardin, Larriston B. Hardin, daughter Cynthia Hardin, Executors friends William Fervel and Peter Cardwell. Witnesses A. Henderson, T. Searcy, John G. Wingfield.

1826 29 Jul: Page B-235 Probate May 1840 Will of Peggy Harden mentions nephews John Harden and Thompson Harden, nieces Deborah Freeman wife of Patman Freeman, Peggy Hardle wife of George Hardle, Elizabeth Rice daughter of Jeremiah Rice, Rebecca Hardin wife of John Harden. Also mentioned are Elizabeth Hornbuckle, widow of Richard Hornbuckle and her daughter Frances Hornbuckle, brother John Harden's children, Presley Harden and his children. Executors are nephews John Harden and Thompson Harden. Witnesses William Holt and Joseph Holt.

1842 22 Apr: Page B-297 probated August 1843 Will of George Hardin mentions wife Mary Hardin, to Jinny and Sally Mathews who I raised from infancy. Executor wife Mary Hardin. Witness Robert L. Corum.

1844 17 Sep: Page C-16 probated November 1844, Will of Thomas Harding mentions wife Martha C. Harding, sons Thomas J., Elisha J., James H., and Robert C. Harding. Six youngest children are Mary Ann Pearsons, Thomas J. Harding, Elisha J. Harding, Martha J. Bailey, Saruke B. Jeffries, James H. Harding. Executors wife Martha and son James H. Harding. Witnesses, F. W. Watson, H. L. Patricks, J. D. Reed.

Chapter 6
Tennessee County Records

Giles Co., Tennessee Records

Federal Census Records

1820 Census, Pulaski, Giles County, TN
All of these are together on page 17:
Elizabeth Harden (1-48) 010100 01001
Jeremiah Harden (1-86) 110010 100010
William Harden (1-87) 0001 0001
James McCutchen 020001 10500

1830 Census, Giles County, Tennessee Page 178
Thomas J Hardin 200001 110010001

Deed Records

1818 27 Aug: Book C Page 378 Deed of gift Thomas Hardin (1-48) to Hiram Hardin (1-88) Registered 30 Jan 1819. "To all whom these presents may come I Thomas Hardin (1-48) do send greeting Know ye that I the said Thomas Hardin (1-48) of the County of Giles and State of Tennessee for and in consideration of the love good will and affections which I have and do bear towards my son Hiram Hardin (1-88) of the County and State aforesaid have given and granted and by these presents, do freely give and grant, unto the said Hiram Hardin and his heirs executors administrators Viz all and singular my claim interest in and to the following species of property, viz Two improvements on the Congressional reservation in the County and State aforesaid including one Grist mill and the presents crops now growing on said improvements five head horse beasts six head of Cattle, fifty head of hogs one sett blacksmith tools together with all my household and Kitchen furniture including Beds. now in possession of me the said Thomas Hardin also all plantation utensils all of which before the signing of these presents I have delivered to him the said Hiram Hardin an Inventory signed with my hand, and bearing even date to have and to hold all the before recited property to him the said Hiram Hardin his heirs executors from henceforth as his and their property absolutely without any manner of condition. In witness Whereof I have herewith put my hand and seal this

27th day of August in the year of our lord One thousand eight hundred and eighteen."

Signed Sealed and Delivered in the presence of John Wright

Thomas Hardin (1-48)

State of Tennessee Giles Circuit Court September Term 1818

I Henry Hazen Clerk of said court do hereby Certify that the within Deed of Gift from Thomas Hardin (1-48) to Hiram Hardin (1-88) was produced in Court and proven to be the act and deed of the said Thomas Hardin by the oath of John Wright the subscribing Witness thereto and ordered to be certified for registration.

In testimony whereof I have hereunto set my hand and private seal there being no seal of office this 19th day of January 1819

H Hazen Clerk

1843 10 Apr: Giles County, Tennessee land grants. Grant to D. A. Alexander, assignee of Hiram Harden (1-88), 154 acres

Shelby Co., Tennessee Records

Probate Records

1856 26 Sep: Book 3E Page 81-82 Will of John L. Woodson. To heirs of Edward Woodson decd 50 acres bounded by Henry Williams and J. Harden. Sell 26 acres and give J Harden's (1-90) daughter by his dec'd wife Mary Harden $50. Give to Joshua Harden (1-90) my jack and trunk and desk and horse. Joshua Harden (1-90) executor. Proved August 1857.

Deed Records

1845 13 Jun: State of Tennessee grant to Joshua Hardin (1-90), recorded, filed with Deed Register 14 Feb 1853 Noted in Note Book No 3, page 59, Recorded 16 Feb 1853

1852 13 Jan: Joshua Harden (1-90) deed to George W. Williams for $375, both of Shelby Co., TN, Range three Sections 5 of the 11th Surveyors District of the County, part of 280 acres tract entered in the name of Joshua total sold 141 acres. Harden Proved Feb 12, 1853.

Marriage Records

Harding Families of the Northern Neck of Virginia

1848 15 Jun: Book 1 Page 191 Joshua Harden (1-90) married Lucy E. M. J. Woodson by Minister George M. Williams Filed July 14 1848

1857 7 Feb: Book 1 Page 410 Joshua Harding (1-90) married Eliza O'Quin

Taxation Records

1837 Tax List: William Harden (1-87)
1837 Tax List: Joshua Harden (1-90)
1837 Tax List: Hiram Harden (1-88)
1838 Tax List: William Harden (1-87)
1838 Tax List: Joshua Harden (1-90)
1838 Tax List: Hiram Harden (1-88)

Federal Census Records

1840 Census Shelby County, Tennessee
Page 39 (Enumerated together)
Josh Hardin (1-90) 00001 0000000001 (female age 70 to 80)
Hiram Hardin (1-88) 1210001 012001

1850 Census District 8, Shelby County, Tennessee Page 154

Res	Fam	Name	Age	Sex	Occupation	Birthplace
	1122	Joshua Harding	38	M	Farmer	Tennessee
	1122	Elizabeth Harding	82	F		N Carolina
	1122	Lucy Harding	37	F		Virginia
	1122	Thomas Harding	39	M	Farmer	Tennessee

1860 Census District 8, Shelby County, Tennessee Page 149

Res	Fam	Name	Age	Sex	Occupation	Birthplace
1233	1206	Joshua Hardin	51	M	Farmer	Tennessee
1233	1206	Eliza Hardin	33	F		Tennessee
1233	1206	Marion Hardin	18	M		Tennessee
1233	1206	Allen Hardin	15	M	Farmer	Tennessee

1870 Census District 8, Shelby County, Tennessee Page 16

Res	Fam	Name	Age	Sex	Occupation	Birthplace
134	134	Joshua Hardin	61	M	Farmer	Tennessee
134	134	Elizy Hardin	48	F		Tennessee

1880 Census District 8, Shelby County, Tennessee Page 38

Res	Fam	Name	Age	Sex	Occupation	Birthplace
352	360	Joshua Hardin	68	M	Farmer	VA VA VA
352	360	Elizy Hardin	54	F		VA VA VA

Williamson Co., Tennessee Records

Taxation Records

1800 Tax Lists
Thomas Harding (1-48) No Land, 2 Town Lots

1801 Tax Lists
Thomas Hardin (1-48) No Land 1 white
Presley Hardin (1-43) No Land 2 whites, one slave
Giles Harding 100 acres on Little Harpeth no tithables

1802 Tax Lists
Giles Harden 100 acres on Little Harpeth no tithables
Presley Hardin (1-43) No land 1 tithable 1 slave
Thomas Hardin (1-48) no land 1 tithable

1803 Tax Lists
Presley Harding (1-43) no land 1 white 1 slave
Thomas Harding (1-48) no land 1 white

1804 Tax Lists
Presley Hardin (1-43) 640 acres Five Mile Creek 1 white 1 slave

1805 Tax Lists
Presley Harden **(1-43)** 210 acres Big Harpeth 1 white
John Harding (1-72) No Land 1 White
Thomas Harden (1-48) No Land 1 white
Page 15 Thomas Harden (1-48) 1 Free Poll No slaves (To Bedford County by 1812)
Page 15 Samuel McCutchan

Census Records

1820 Census of Franklin, Williamson County Tennessee
Presley Harden (1-43) Page 646 000011 00110
John Harden (1-72) Page 646 100200 11010
Gregory Wilson (1-76) Page 646 100010 00010
Jeremiah Harden (1-75) Page 534 000011 -00101

Marriage Records

1807 07 Aug: Thomas H. Hardin married Lucy Nolen (This man's parentage is unknown at present. He and Lucy later lived in Marshall Co., TN and left records there.)

1812 25 Sep: Peggy Harden (1-73) married Samuel Shelburne (1-73) (Bond with Nathaniel Smiths)

1814 26 Jul: Jeremiah Harden (1-86) married Sally McCutchin (1-86) (Bond with Jeremiah harden)

1815 17 Aug: Sally Harden (1-76) married Gregory Wilson (1-76) (Bond with David Huston)

1815 29 Dec: John Harden (1-72) married Susanna Appleton (1-72) (Bond with NP Hardeman)

1816 22 May: Horace H. Harding married Susan McMullen (Bond with James McComb)

1818 19 Jan: John Harden (1-72) Married Mary Tilman (1-72) (Bond with James Nowlen, brother of Lucy Nolen above)

1839 24 Sep: Presley W Harden (1-102) married Mary L. Williams (1-102) Bond with Josephus Williams)

Deed Records

1803 14 Mar: Book A Page 325, Presley Harden (1-43) of Williamson County, Tennessee from James Anderson of same, Lease land on Land on Murphy's Fork 640 acres for a term of two years beginning the next January 1., Proved in court May 1803, Recorded Dec 28 1803.

1804 09 Jul: Book A Page 522 recorded 15 Sep 1804, Presley Harden (1-43) of Williamson Co., TN from Reuben Parks of same for $525 210 acres on waters of the Big Harpeth Proved in Court July 1804

1807 25 Jul: Book B Page 514 recorded 26 Dec 1807 Presley Harden (1-43) of Williamson Co to John Harden (1-72) of Williamson Co TN 105 acres on the Big Harpeth $275

1807 25 Jul: Book B Page 515, recorded 26 Dec 1807 Presley Harden (1-43) of Williamson County TN to Jeremiah Harden (1-75) of same 105 acres on Big Harpeth $225.00

1811 05 Oct: Book B Page 670 Recorded 5 November 1811 Samuel Shelburn (1-73) of Williamson County, Tennessee to Thomas Harden (1-48) of Williamson County, Tennessee $370 102 acres on the Waters of the Harpath bordering John Parker and James Williams. Witnesses Elijah Williams, William Meason Acknowledged October Court 1811

1815 05 Nov: Book D Page 125 Recorded 11 March 1816 Thomas Harden (1-48) of the County of Williamson TN to John Harden (1-72) of same, $1000, land on Big Harpeth, 102 acres

1819 28 May: Book F Page 100 recorded 1 Nov 1819 John Harden (1-72) of Williamson Co. TN from David McElwee of Warren Co., TN $2730, Land on Big Harpeth River, 210 acres

Book F Page 321. Certification of plat of land for John Harden (1-72) and others surveyed Sept 29, 1819, 2,711 acres on Big Harpeth River land granted to James Scurlock by the state.

1820 23 Apr: Book G. Page 59 recorded 27 Aug 1821 John Harden (1-72) of Williamson Co to Henry Cook of same. $133 6 acres on Big Harpeth River

1821 29 Dec: Book G. Page 134, recorded 20 Apr 1722 Jeremiah Harden (1-75) of Williamson Co., to Gregory Wilson (1-76) of Williamson $650 50 acres

1821 29 Dec: Book G, page 154 rec 14 June 1822 John Harden (1-72) of Williamson Co to Jeremiah Harden (1-75) of Williamson County, $500 70 acres on Big Harpeth River,

1823 11 Oct: Book G. Page 438, rec 6 May 1824 John Harden (1-72) to Thomas A. Jones, land on Big Harpeth River, $1015, 101 acres on Big Harpeth River

1824 10 Oct: Book H, page 70 John Harden (1-72) of Williamson Co TN to Jacob Halfacre of Williamson, $478 Land on Big Harpeth River 53 acres

1824 13 Oct: Book H, page 71 Proved Oct 1824 court John Harden (1-72) to Thomas A. Jones, both of Williamson Co. NC $428, 47 acres,

1825 04 Dec: Book H page53 John Horden (1-72) of Williamson Co TN to Thomas Old of same, $1800 dollars, Land on Big Harpeth River on Jeremiah Harden's Line, 150 acres.

1825 Dec: Book H page 666 Recorded 20 Nov 1827 John Harden (1-72) of Williamson Co TN to Thomas Old of same, $1800, Land on Big Harpeth River, 150 acres

1828 21 Oct: Book J Page 427 recorded 27 Apr 1829 Jeremiah Harden (1-75) to Alfred Gee Land on Big Harpeth River 154 ¾ acres, $1550

Will and Probate Records

1815 Jan: Presley Harden (1-43) bought one bed in estate sale

1816 Apr: Presley Harden (1-43) bought items from estate.

Apr: 1819 John Harden (1-72), Guardian of the children of John Appleton settlement. Agreeable to an order of the Honourable Court of Williamson

County at April Session 1819 to us directed We have proceeded to settle with John Hardin, Guardian for the Estate of John Appleton Decd. (Settlement items 1815-1818 Total $2332,82) The above settlement with John Harden, Guardian for the Estate of John Appleton Decd this 3rd Day of July 1819 by us John Thompson, James Neelley, Peter Burton, whole settlement as above recited was produced in open court at July session 1819 and the same was ordered to be recorded

1828 24 Nov: Jeremiah Harden (1-75) Will made, presented to court January 1829. In the name of God Amen. I Jeremiah Harden in sound mind and (unreadable) hath this day the Twenty fourth of November one thousand eight hundred and twenty-eight make this last will and testament as follows viz. I give to my beloved wife Elizabeth (1-75) after paying all legal demands all my real and personal property to dispose of as she thinks proper among my children viz. Susan Taylor Harden (1-108), John Click Harden (1-109), Peter Harden, (1-110) and Margaret Jane Harden (1-111) as they become of age or marry and at her deceased to be equally divided among my children and further it is my desire that John Click Senr and John Click Jr should be my Executors to this my last will and testament. Given under my hand seal the day and date above written. Signed and sealed in the presence of Jas Harrison Thomas Merritt Signed: Jere Harden. January Court 1829, January 7, 1829 executors approved and will filed.

Wife Elizabeth Harden (1-75) later Mrs. Lewis Baldwin

June 1831, cash paid to T Harden

XXLegal action

Susan Taylor Harden (1-108) et al vs Lewis Baldwin and wife 5 aug 1835

Jeremiah Harden (1-75) had land in Henry Co., TN

He sold land to Alfred Gee before he died for $1550, which remained unpaid. Was paid to Elizabeth and Lewis Baldwin, who spent and wasted it.

Chapter 7
Alabama, Arkansas, Georgia County Records

Lauderdale County, Alabama Records

Will and Probate Records

1831 19 Sep: Will of Polly Harden (1-77) dated Lauderdale County, Alabama Will Book A-B 1833-1897 page 33-34 Proved 7 August 1837 Lauderdale Co, Alabama. "In the name of God Amen being in a low state of health the () of mind and knowing Certainty of Death and the uncertainty of life make this my last will and testament. Item 1st I give unto my beloved mother Susannah Hardin (1-43) a twenty dollar note that owing of me for a horse. Item 2nd I lend my beloved mother a negro girl named Rachael during her life and then said negro girl sold and equally divided between Jeremiah H Shelborne (1-103), Polly Shelborne (1-104), Nancy Shelborne (1-105), Thomas R. Shelborne (1-106) and Peggy Taylor Shelborne (1-107) and John Wilson Item 3rd I give to my sister Susannah Hardin (1-78) one Spotted Vane bed cover. Item 4th I give my horse to Jeremiah H. Shelborne (1-103) and Prestley Hardin (1-102) equally I give two beds to my sisters Peggy Shelborne and Sally Wilson all my bed clothing to be equally divided between them. Item 5th I give my two trunks to Polly Shelborne and Nancy Shelborne. Item 6th I give my large chest to Thomas R. Shelborne. Item 7th I give my large table to Presley Hardin (1-102) my History to Polly Shelborne and my hymn book to Nancy Shelborne. Item 8th I wish my clothing Equally divided between Peggy Shelborne Sally Wilson Polly Shelborne Nancy Shelborne and Peggy Shelborne. Item 9th It is my will that Samuel Shelborne Senr and John Harden (1-72) execute this my last will and testament. Given under my hand and seal this 19th day of September 1831. Signed Polly Hardin (1-77)" Witnesses J P Shelborne, Mark Trousdale, William Kitchens. The State of Alabama, Lauderdale County. The foregoing will was this day produced in open court and produced in open court and proven by the oaths of the subscribing Witnesses J P Shelborne William N Trousdale and William Hutchens and ordered to admitted to probate the 17 August 1837.

Gravestone Records

Harden Cemetery, Center Star, Lauderdale Co., Alabama
Susan Harden (1-43) Born 27 June 1757 died 27 Mar: 1844, Inscription: Wife of Presley Harden (1-43).

John Harden (1-72) Born 30 Sept 1775 died 15 Aug 1846.

Arkansas County Records

Federal Census Records

1840 Census Languile, Poinsett County, Arkansas
Jeremiah Harden (1-86) 0011101 0010101
1840 Census Griggs, Van Buren County, Arkansas
William Harden (1-87) 001001 0000001

1850 Census Jefferson, Carroll County, Arkansas Page 172

Res	Fam	Name	Age	Sex	Occupation	Birthplace
667	667	William Hardin	55	M	Farmer	N Carolina
667	667	Agnes Hardin	49	F		Tennessee
667	667	Thomas P Hardin	30	M	Farmer	Tennessee
667	667	Rebecca Hole	78	F		Unknown
667	667	Rebecca A. Hole	8	F		Arkansas
667	667	Sarah A. Hole	7			Arkansas

1850 Census Bolivar Poinsett County, Arkansas Page 213

Res	Fam	Name	Age	Sex	Occupation	Birthplace
200	200	John Hardin	28	M		Tennessee
200	200	Emily Hardin	21	F		Alabama
201	201	Thomas Hardin	24	M		Tennessee
201	201	John Daley	20	M		Unknown
201	201	Nancy Daley	21	F		Tennessee
202	202	James Hardin	35	M		Tennessee
202	202	Loucey Hardin	29	F		Tennessee
202	202	Mary C. Hardin	8	F		Arkansas
202	202	William B. Hardin	6	M		Arkansas
202	202	John Thule Hardin	4	M		Arkansas
202	202	Sarah S. Hardin	2	F		Arkansas

1860 Census Washington, Carroll County, Arkansas Page 64

Res	Fam	Name	Age	Sex	Occupation	Birthplace
1138	430	William Hardin	65	M	Farmer	N Carolina
1138	431	Agnes Hardin	60	F		Tennessee

Warren County, Georgia Records

Will and Probate Records

1813 13 Apr: Book 1810-1826, Page 43 Will of Mark Hardin (5-112) Probated November 1817. Bequests to wife Frances, sons Henry, Mark, Martin, James, John, and William, daughters Sally, Patsy, Nancy, Polly (married James George), Judith Willis. Executors Isaiah Tucker, Richard Fletcher

Chapter 8
Indiana County Records

Clark Co., Indiana Records

19 Jan: 1865 Original on Ancestry no book or page # Will of William Hardin (3-50). No wife mentioned. Children: Grandson John Pate. Seven children now living: Lucy Hardin (3-83) wife of John B. Rankin (3-83), Lewis Hardin (3-84), Emily Hardin (3-89) wife of Lawrence Barachman, Jane Hardin (3-88) wife of Peter Mitchel (3-88), Paulina Hardin (3-90) wife of Eli Burt, James Hardin (3-91) and Owen Hardin (3-85). Son-in-law Eli Burt executor. Probated 2 September 1865.

Census Records

1850 Census Utica, Clark County, Indiana Page 390
641-691 Amasa Burt 75 M Farmer 5000 Md
641-691 Eli Burtt (3-90) 33 M Farmer Indiana
641-691 Paulina Hardin (3-90) Burt F 24 Kentucky
641-691 Alonzo Johnston M 19 KY
641-691 Mary Johnston F 17 Indiana

711 762 William Hardin (3-50) 63 M Farmer 5500 VA
711-762 Rhoda Hardin (3-50) 64 F VA
711-762 Owen Hardin (3-85) 35 Farmer KY
711-762 James Hardin (3-91) 19 Farmer KY

1860 Census Utica, Clark County, Indiana
1 1 William Hardin (3-50) 70 M Farmer 9000 500 Virginia
1 1 Jemima Hardin (3-50) 65 F KY
1 1 Sarah Beges 67 KY
1 1 Persyla Chapel 10 IN

2 2 Owen Hardin (3-85) 42 M Farmer 2000 300 KY
2 2 Anna Hardin (3-85) 26 IN
2 2 Nora Hardin 9 IN
2 2 Ella Hardin 5 IN

Charlestown, Clark Co., Indiana
44-41 Peter Mitchell (3-88) 52 M Indiana
44-41 Rebecca J. Mitchell (3-88) 38 F Kentucky
44-41 Marietta. Mitchell 11 Kentucky
44-41 John F Mitchell 9 Kentucky
44-41 Wiliam T. Mitchell 1 mo Kentucky
44-41 Missouri Wheeler 23 Housework Indiana

Marriage Records

1850 15 Oct: Owen G. Hardin (3-85) married Ann Eliza Prather
1858 29 Nov: Page 377 William Hardin (3-50) married Jemima Coombs

Cemetery Records

Burtt Cemetery, Utica, Clark Co., Indiana
William Hardin (3-50) born 15 Mar: 1788 died 23 August 1865

Rhoda Wilhoit Hardin (3-50) born 23 May 1785 VA died 22 July 1856 first wife

Jemima Hardin (3-50) born 27 May 1795 died 27 Nov 1861 (married first Jesse Coombs 2 Feb 1854)

Presley Hardin (3-86) born 1817 Jefferson County, Kentucky d 10 August 1847

Paulina Hardin (3-90) Burtt born 5 July 1826 died 25 September 1871 Utica Clark Co IN married Eli Burtt (3-90) 1817-1797

Mary Ann Hardin (3-87) Pate born 10 April 1820 died 28 September 1855 Wife of Hartwell Pate

Dearborn Co., Indiana Records

From History of Dearborn County

Compiled by Archibald Shaw, Published 1915 B.F. Bowen & Co Indianapolis

Page 110: "The same year (1796) Henry Hardin (3-13) and family, consisting of William, Mary, James, Catherine, John, and Philip, settled on the site of the hamlet of Hardinsburg. Other families settling in the vicinity in the same year were those of William Allensworth and Isaac Allen, who occupied the land subsequently known as the Samuel Morrison farm."

Marriage Records

1824 Caty Hardin (3-45) to Jacob Dennis (3-45) Daughter of Henry Hardin (3-13) Dearborn County Deed Book BB Page 567

Elizabeth Hardin (3-48) to John St. Clear same reference as Caty

Mary Hardin (3-41) to Elijah Dawson c 1824 Same reference as Caty

Nancy Hardin (3-49) to Ephraim Morrison (3-49) same reference as Caty

Federal Census Records

1820 Federal Census Dearborn County, Indiana
Page 93 Henry Hardin (3-13) 010201 00101
Hardinsburg Page 24 Jacob Dennis (3-45) 300010 01010
Hardinsburg Page 24 Elijah Dawson (3-41) 230010 20010
Lawrenceburg Page 95 Ephraim Morrison (3-49) 200010 00100

1830 Federal Census Indiana
Dearborn Co, Lawrenceburg Page 34 Jacob Dennis (3-45) 1111201 000001
Marion Co Wayne Elijah Dawson (3-41) 2110101 0121001
Marion Co., Lawrence Page 218 Henry Harden (3-13) 21002 00001
Marion Co Lawrence Page 218 Ephraim Morrison (3-49) 1120001 210101

1840 Federal Census Indiana
Marion Co, Washington Page 360 Elijah Dawson (3-41) 002101001 22010001

1850 Federal Census Washington, Marion Co., Indiana
1011 1011 Elijah Dawson (3-41) 69 M Farmer VA
1011 1011 Mary Dawson (3-41) 64 VA
1011 1011 Amanda Dawson 28 Ind
1011 1011 Charles Dawson 26 IND
1011 1011 Jefferson Dawson 23 IND
1011 1011 James Wells 18 IND

Marion Co., Indiana Records

Revolutionary War Pension Records

Henry Hardin (3-13) applied for a Revolutionary War Pension in Marion Co., Indiana 13 September 1832. In his application he states he was 80 years old and was born in Stafford County, Virginia. He lived on Hyco Creek in Halifax County Virginia near the North Carolina Line when he enlisted in early fall of 1775 for six months under Capt. Peter Rogers and Col Lewis. He served again in Hillsborough, North Carolina in 1776 for six months under Capt.

Moore and later moved to Woodstock, Shenandoah County, Virginia where he enlisted in August 1780 and served eighteen months. The actual document contains many pages of details on where he fought during his service. He lived at Woodstock until 1796, when he moved to Dearborn County, Indiana as one of the early settlers with his wife and family. By 1830 he lived in Marion County, Indiana. At the end of his declaration summary of his testimony, the Marion Co., Indiana court document stated, "He was born in Stafford County in Old Virginia in the year 1752 from which his father removed to Hico where he first volunteered and from that to Woodstock, where he enlisted for the last 18 months. Since the war he resided in Woodstock until 1796 when he removed to Dearborn County Indiana, from which place he removed to this county. He has no record of his age. Said Isaac Way of Ripley County can testify about his service. According to the Indiana Pensioners list, he was paid through September 1834. 1832 16 October Ripley County Indiana statement of Isaac Way: He knew Henry Harding during the Revolution. Henry Harding is 80 years old. Private from Virginia for 18 months. Believes he served under Green at siege of Ninety-Six. Believes he served other terms of service

Chapter 9
Kentucky County Records

Anderson Co., Kentucky Records

Personal Property Tax Records

1827 Personal Property Tax Lists
John Hardin 74 acres KY River patent to Taylor
William McMannaway No land

1828 Personal Property Tax Lits
Johanna Hardin 70 acres Gilberts Creek Patent Hoomes

1830 Personal Property Tax List
Hannah Hardin 72 acres Gilberts Creek Patent Entered to Homes? 0 21 1 horse
Powel Hardin no land 1 male 1 horse

1833 Personal Property Tax List
Hannah Harden 75 acres G Creek Entered to Taylor 3 horses
Powell Hardin 100 acres Fox Creek Entered to Tilford
Henry Hardin No land Next on list.

1835 Personal Property Tax List
Hannah Hardin 80 acres on Ky River Patent Hoomes
Powell Hardin 209 acres Gilberts River
Henry Hardin no land close by.

1837 Personal Property Tax lists
Powell Hardin 109 acres Fax Creek
James D. Hardin No land

Deed Records

1834 19 Sep: Book C. Page 69 Powell Hardin from James Tilford 100 acres on Fox River

1835 24 Oct: Book C Page 216 Johanna Hardin, Mark G. Hardin, Mary Hardin and William H. Hardin to Allen N. McAlister, all of Anderson County, $294 73 ½ acres

3 Mar: 1837 Book C Page 429 Powell Hardin and Susan his wife to Grayson B. Taylor, both of Anderson County. Land on Fox Run 100 acres.

Bath Co., Kentucky Records

Will and Probate Records

1849 09 Sep: Book E Page 128 Will of Lewis Hardin (4-84) Appraisement E-385 Sale Bills E-282 Settlement E-381 E-160. Of Bath County. To wife Edat (4-84) His entire estate. Two sons George (4-152) and John Edgar (4-153) $250 each. Remainder divided between sons Manly Hardin (4-146), William Hardin (4-145), Fielding Hardin (4-147), Joseph Hardin (4-148), Presley Hardin (4-150), James Hardin (4-151), George Hardin (4-152) and John Edgar Hardin (4-153). Daughter Lucinda Young (4-149) wife of David B. Young (4-145) of Missouri to get equal part if she outlives her husband and not otherwise. Proved October Court 1849.

1849 04 May: Book F Page 54 Will of Presley Harden (4-83), proved 20 March 1858 In the name of God amen I Presley Hardin of the County of Bath and State of Kentucky being sick and weak in body but of sound mind and disposing memory for which I thank God and calling to mind the uncertainty of human life and being desirous to dispose of all such worldly Estate as it hath pleased God to bless me with I give and bequeath the same in manner following that is to say. 1st I desire that a sufficiency of the perishable part of my property be sold after my decease to pay all my just debts and funeral expenses. 2nd I desire at my death that there shall be a sale made of all the personal property made after keeping Say what is actually necessary for Keeping up the farm Say two head of horses Two Cows and Gears and ploughs and Such other necessary farming utensils also I wish my Black boy Dick (if not previously sold) Sold at my decease and the proceeds of him and the personal property above named the Money loaned out and the interest of same I wish my wife Sarah Hardin (4-83) shall have the use of during her life. 3rd I desire that my grand Son Raney Burnes shall be paid out of the Sale of my land after my wife's death Two Hundred and fifty Dollars together with a horse Saddle and bridle I have already given him. 4th I wish my wife Sarah Hardin to have the use and benefit of all my land and the balance of my Salves during her Natural life to have the use and full Control of Same. 5th I wish at my wife's death my land to be sold and also my Blacks unless the Blacks Can be amiably divided between My Natural heirs according to appraisement and the proceeds of same and also the Sale of my boy Dick and any personally property that may be sold at my decease after my wife's decease to be divided among my Natural heirs as follows to wit. I wish all of my Estate at my wife's death to be divided equally among my children or their heirs after in the first place paying my Grand Son Ramey Burnes Two hundred and fifty dollars as above named. The names of my children are as follows: Joseph S. Hardin (4-135) Lewis Hardin (4-136) Wesley Hardin (4-137) the heirs of Elizabeth Burnes (4-138) Decd which are Joseph P. Burnes Enock P. Burnes Susan R. Burnes, William T Burnes and Sanford "Raney" Burnes Sarah Baird (4-139) Jane Baird (4-142) Emily Amos (4-141) Milford Baird (4-143) Presley Hardin (4-140) and William E. Hardin (4-144) the above property or The proceeds to be equally divided among all the heirs except William T. Hardin as I have already given him a piece of land where he now lives which I Consider his full share also my daughter Sarah Baird(4-139) I have paid to or for her husband Ratliff Baird some money as security and he owes me some for horses sold to him. Also, my son Lewis Hardin (4-136) has paid some money for the said Ratliff Baird any amount that may be due me or my Son Lewis Hardin by Ratliff Baird at my wife's death I wish kept out of my daughter Mrs. Sarah Baird's part of my Estate the balance to be equally divided between my other Children and the heirs of my daughter Elizabeth E. Burnes Decd her heirs drawing their mother's one share of the Estate. I wish it to be however distinctively understood that any portion going to each one of my daughters is to go to them and their Natural heirs. 6th I desire and appoint my son Presley Hardin My Executor and wish him to attend to all the business of the Estate hereby revoking all other or former wills or testaments by me heretofore made. In witness whereof I have hereunto set my hand and affixed my Seal this fourth day of May in the Year of our Lord Eighteen hundred and forty-nine. Signed Sealed published and declared as and for the last will and testament of the above-named Presley Hardin Sen in the presence of us: Isaac Menchy and Charles Taylor. Proved in Court 20 May 1858

Clark Co., Kentucky Records

Deed Records

1795 27 Nov: Book 1 Page 591 Benjamin Ashby to Enos Hardin (4-7) of Clarke County Power of attorney. Be it known to all those whom it may concern that I Benjamin Ashby of Frederick County in the State of Virginia reposing especial Trust and Confidence in my friend Enos Hardin of Clark County in the State of Kentucky do appoint and constitute the said Enos Hardin my True and lawful Attorney for me my Heirs etc to transmit and execute every kind of Business I may have with in the State of Kentucky in my absence respecting any lands I may have within the said state as well as any other matter or concern hereby for me and my heirs authorizing and impowering my said attorney to sell and execute deeds for any tract of Land I may have within the said state of Kentucky for such prices and Condition as he may think proper hereby ratifying and confirming every such sales Deed by him done by these presents in as full and ample a manner as if done by myself were I personally present. In testimony of which I have hereunto set my hand and seal this twenty-seventh Day of November one thousand seven hundred and ninety-five. Signed B Ashby Witnesses James Hardin (4-8) and Evangelist Hardin (4-6)

1795 26 Nov: Book 1 Page 592 Benjamin Ashby to Nathaniel Ashby Power of Attorney Benjamin Ashby of Frederick County, Virginia owns 652 acres on the Kentucky River in Franklin County, Kentucky, part of a 1250-acre tract granted to Francis Berry 21 September 1787. Appoints Nathaniel Ashby of Fayette County KY lawful attorney to sell the land in the following manner. 250 acres to Daniel Stephens, two hundred acres to Evangelist Hardin (4-6), 200 acres to Enos Hardin (4-7), all inhabitants of Kentucky. Signed B Ashby, witnesses James Hardin (4-8) and Nancy Field.

1802 09 Mar: Book 4 Page 357 Benjamin Ashby revokes power of attorney given to Enos Hardin (4-7) 22 November 1795.

1805 22 Apr: Book 7 Page 85 Enos (Innis) Harden (4-7) of Franklin Co., KY Agreement with Peter Scholl of Clarke Co., KY Innis Hardin sold land to Peter Scholl 28 Sept 1798 100 acres. Agree to resolve all claims regarding said sale.

1810 27 Jun: Book 7 Page 410 Enos Hardin (4-7) of Franklin Co KY to John Johnson. Land in Clarke County KY 100 acres obtained from Scholl's heirs.

1802 Jun: Book 7 Page 414 Enos Hardin (4-7) of Franklin County KY to John Johnson 100 acres from Scholl's heirs Filed 24 June 1810

1803 03 Sep: Book 7 Page 417 Innis Hardin (4-7) of Franklin County KY to Peter Scholl, Abraham Scholl, and Joseph Scholl of the County of Clarke KY legatees of William Scholl deceased. Innis Hardin claims preemption of 1000 acres the legatees of sd Scholl claim, a different preemption obtained in the name of Daniel Boone and the two claims interfere with each other. Innis Hardin gives up all that part that interferes except 200 acres which the Scholls relinquished to him.

1803 03 Sep: Book 7 Page 419 Peter Scholl, Abraham Scholl, and Joseph Scholl heirs of William Scholl deceased to Innis Hardin (4-7) of Franklin Co KY. Settles conflict in land ownership referred to in previous deed.

1793 Personal Property Tax Lists
Enos Hardin (4-7)

1794 Personal Property Tax Lists

Harding Families of the Northern Neck of Virginia

Benjamin Hardin (4-9)
Enos Hardin (4-7)

1795 Personal Property Tax Lists
Ennis Hardin 1000 acres in Clark County, Stoner Creek (4-7)
Ennis Hardin (4-7)
Benjamin Hardin (4-9)
James Hardin (4-8)

1796 Personal Property Tax Lists and land Lists
Benjamin Hardin (4-9) 50 acres on Flat Creek Clark Co, William Anderson
Benjamin Hardin (4-9) 200 acres on Kentucky R Franklin Co Fran Berry
Ennis Hardin (4-7) Table of land owned

Acres First Class	Acres second class	Acres Third Class	On Which Watercourse	County	Entered by
1000	0	0	Stoner	Clark	E Hardin
	200		Kentucky	Franklin	Ben Ashby
	2666 2/3		Treadwater	Franklin	Ben Ashby
		700	N Dikson	Mason	John Brownly
		652	Kentucky	Franklin	Frank Berry
		325	Kentucky	Franklin	M W Conroy
	250		Cedar Cr	Franklin	John Marshall
		250	Kentucky	Franklin	John Marshall
	310		Kingston	Clark	William Flemming
	150		Kingston	Clark	Sam Moore
	325		Stoner	Clark	John Marshall
	51		Howards Cr	Clark	Thomas Marshall
	250		Little Mountain	Clark	Ben Ashby
	1500		N Licking	Mason	John Brownly
	1400		Cabin Cr	Mason	Frem Ash
	134		Kentucky	Franklin	Robert Ashby

1797 Personal Property Tax Lists and Land lists
Benjamin Harden (4-9) 50 Acres on Flatt Creek Montgomery Co W Anderson
Benjamin Hardin (4-9) 200 Acres Kentucky R Franklin Co., F Berry

1797 Personal Property and Land Lists
Samuel Harding No land

1798 to 1801 No Hardins

Franklin Co., Kentucky Records

Formed from Woodford, Mercer, and Shelby Counties in 1794

Federal Census Records

1810 Federal Census
Page 52 Richard Hardin 20001 00101
Page 53 James Hardin (4-8) 11001 31020 (Next to Enos)
Page 53 Enos Hardin (4-7) 12001 01000 (Next to Vengelist)
Page 53 Vengelist Hardin (4-6) 32301 01101 (Next to Enos)
Page 55 Mark. Hardin 11110 10100
Page 55 Martin D. Hardin (5-99) 10010 00010

1820 Federal Census
Page 74 Richard Hardin 201001 01100
Page 76 Martin D. Hardin (5-99) 110010 10100
Page 27 Wesley Hardin 000010 00010

Court Records

1813 21 Jun: Book E Page 335 On the motion of Benjamin Hardin (4-9) administration of the goods, chattles, rights and credits of James Hardin (4-42) decd is granted him whereupon he took oath required by law and entered into bond with William S. Quarles his security in the penalty of two hundred dollars conditioned as the law directs.

1813 21 Jun: Book E Page 335 On the motion of Benjamin Hardin (4-9) administration of the goods chattles rights and credits of Benjamin Hardin (4-43) Jr decd is granted him whereupon he took the oath required by law and entered into bond with William E. Quarles his security in the penalty of two hundred dollars conditioned as the law directs.

1813 21 Jun: Book E. Page 335 Ordered that Enos Hardin (4-7), James Hardin (4-8), Wilford Stephens and Benjamin Stephens or any three of them being first duly sworn do appraise the personal estate of James Hardin (4-42) decd and make report thereof to court.

1813 21 Jun: Book E. Page 335 Ordered that Enos Hardin (4-7), James Hardin (4-8), Wilford Stephens and Benjamin Stephens any three of them being first duly sworn to appraise the personal estate of Benjamin Hardin (4-43) decd and make report thereof to Court.

1813 20 Sep: Book H Page 345 On the motion of Vangelous Hardin (4-6) administration of the goods chattles rights and credits of John Hardin (4-24) Deceased granted him whereupon he took the oath required by law and entered into bond with John Scr (name unreadable) his security in the penalty of one hundred fifty dollars conditioned

Harding Families of the Northern Neck of Virginia

1813 20 Sep: Book H 346 Ordered that Enos Hardin (4-7), James Hardin (4-8), Wilford Stephens and Benjamin Stephens or any three of them being first sworn do appraise the personal estate of John Hardin (4-24) decd and make report thereof to the court.

1813 16 Nov: Book H Page 367 It is ordered that a judgement be entered up against James Hardin (4-8) Constable of this County for the sum of thirty dollars fifteen of which was impound on Reuben Jackson and fifteen dollars on Benjamin Stephens for a breach of the peace and that he pay the costs of prosecution before William Quarles Esq.

1814 18 Apr: Book E Page 398 An inventory of the estates of James Hardin (4-42), Benjamin Hardin (4-43) and John Hardin (4-24) was returned to Court and ordered to be recorded.

1814 19 Sep: Book F Page 27 On motion of James Hardin (4-8) he is permitted to renew his bond as constable in this County thereupon he executed acknowledgement the same with William E. Quarles his security conditions as the law directs.

1814 19 Dec: Book F Page 42 On the motion of Westly Hardin leave is given him to keep a tavern at his house in this county having entered into bond with Thomas Long his Security conditioned as the law directs.

1816 19 Aug: Book F Page 199 On the motion of Westly Hardin leave is given him to keep a tavern at his house in the county whereupon he entered into bond with Alexn Wilson his security conditioned as the law directs.

1816 19 Aug: Book F Page 203 On the motion of James Hardin (4-8) leave is given him to renew his bond as constable in this county Whereupon he entered into a bond with William Rowlett senr his security conditioned as the law directs.

1817 19 May: Book F Page 288 Benjamin Hardin (4-9) came into court and give his list of Taxable property for the year 1816 which being sworn to is ordered to be certified.

1818 15 Jun: Book F Page 397 On the motion of James Hardin (4-8) and John Scrinnher administration of the estate of Enos Hardin (4-33) Decd is granted them. Whereupon the said James Hardin (4-8) and John Scrimher entered into bond with John Bartlett and Clement Bell their securities in the penalty of $5000 conditioned as the law requires and thereupon took the oath required by law.

1818 15 Jun: Book F Page 397 Ordered that Charles Tyler, Tavener Branham, Marmaduke Betts and Peter Landon being sworn be appointed to appraise the estate of Enos Hardin (4-33) Decd and make report to this court.

1818 17 Aug: Book F. Page 412 On the motion of James Hardin (4-8) leave is given him to renew his bond as constable in this County. Whereupon the said Hardin entered into bond with Peter Sanders and John Williams his securities in the penalty of $1000 conditioned as the law directs.

Deed Records

1809 09 Oct: Book C Page (after 139) Martin D. Hardin (5-99) from J Dudley

1814 06 May: Book D Page 330 Martin D. Hardin (5-99) to Franklin County Court

1815 14 Apr: Book E Page 19 Mark Hardin to Hunt and Blanton

1814 04 Nov: Book E. Page 21 M. D. Hardin (5-99) to George Madison

1811 02 Mar: Book C Page 363 Enos Hardin (4-7) of Franklin County KY from Benjamin Ashby of Frederick County, Virginia, part of a tract of land Ashby purchased from Miles Conway 2 January 1802 on the Kentucky River in Franklin County KY.318 ¾ acres. In 1807 he sold about 200 acres to Toliver Craig. Balance now goes to Enos Harding. (4-7)

1813 23 Oct: Book D Page 233 Martin D. Hardin (5-99) from Cover Franklin C

1814 18 Apr: Book D. Page 415 Mark Hardin from Hugh McIlvain

1816 23 May: Book E Page 364 Mark Hardin to Will S. Waller

1815 17 Jul: Book E Page 84 Mark Hardin from County Sheriff

1816 07 Feb: Book E Page 218 Mark Hardin from Isham Talbut

1816 04 Mar: Book E 240 Mark Hardin from Benjamin Hickman

1816 22 May: Book E Page 352 Mark Hardin from Benjamin Hickman

1815 02 Oct: Book E Page 470(5?) Martin D. Hardin (5-99) from J Dudley

1819 09 Jun: Book G Page 354 Westley Hardin and Frances his wife of Franklin County KY to Othneil Kerrick of same county, for $1150 55 acres

1818 01 Sep: Book G Page 529 Mark Hardin &c to Humphrey Marshall

Marriage Bond Records

1801 26 May: Richard Hardin married Joanna McAlister

1808 08 Oct: Wesley Hardin married Frances Bartlett

1809 20 Jan: Martin D. Hardin (5-99) married Elizabeth Logan (5-99)

1814 21 Mar: Elizabeth Hardin (4-25), daughter of Evangelist Hardin (4-6), married Jacob Kelly (4-25). Over 21 Gabriel Woodfill Presided

1814 21 Mar: Sarah Hardin (4-26), daughter of Evangelist Hardin (4-6), married Orlander Lindsey (4-26) Over 21 Gabriel Woodfill presided.

1814 02 Apr: Lucy Harding (4-32), daughter of James Harding (4-8), married Celus B. Calvert (4-32) over 21 W. Hickman presided

1818 28 Apr: George Hardin (4-28) married Jemima Hawkins (4-28) Bond George Hardin and Benjamin Hawkins no father given

1818 29 Dec: Lewis Hardin (5-95) married Elizabeth Sheets

1820 20 Dec: Haydon Hardin married Polly Tracey

1822 12 Oct: Mark Hardin (4-45) married Loucinda Douthitt (4-45)

1824 15 Nov: William Hardin (5-81) married Caroline C. Innes

1825 05 Apr: Mary Ann Hardin married Lewis C. Wright

1829 16 Sep: Sarah Ann Hardin married Jonathan A. Holderby

1830 28 Jan: James Sanders married Jane Hardin

1830 05 Apr: Eliza Hardin married Porter Clay

1835 10 Jan: William Hardin married Eliza Milam

1837 31 Oct: William Hardin married Amanda C. Richardson

Personal Property Tax Lists

1801 Tax Lists of Franklin County, Kentucky
James Hardin (4-8) 100 acres Franklin County Cedar Creek 1 over 21
Enus Harden (4-7) 200 acres Franklin Co Ky River Entered Jos Berry Patent Francis Berry
Enos Harden (4-7) 1000 acres Clark Co., KY Entered to Enous Hardin
Benjamin Harden 200 acres Franklin Co Ky River Entered Jos Berry Patent Francis Berry

1802 Tax Lists of Franklin Co., Kentucky
Richd Hardin 120 acres Franklin Co Ky River Entered to Marshal
Enos Harden (4-7) 700 acres Clark Co Entered to Enos Hardin
Enos Hardin (4-7) 277 acres Franklin Co Entered to F Berry
Enos Hardin (4-7) 200 acres Franklin Co
Benja Hardin 200 acres Franklin Co Twin River Entered to F Berry

1803 Tax Lists of Franklin Co., Kentucky
Richd Hardin 100 acres Franklin Co W Ky River Patent Thomas Marshall
James Hardin (4-8) 100 acres Franklin Co
Mark Hardin 50 acres Franklin Patent A Easten

Venjalous Hardin (4-6) 200 acres Franklin Co Kentucky R Entered Berry
Enos Hardin (4-7) 200 acres Franklin Co Kentucky River Entered Francis Berry
Enos Hardin (4-7) 99 acres Hardin Co Panther Creek Part of Suttons
Enos Harden (4-7) 700 acres Clark Co., Stones R Enter Enos Hardin
Enos Hardin (4-7) 77 acres Franklin Co Ky River Enter Francis Berry

1804 Tax Lists Franklin Co., Kentucky
Richard Hardin Acres in Franklin Co Patent Heirs of James Marshall
Enos Hardin (4-7) 200 acres Franklin Co KY Entered Francis Berry
Enos Hardin (4-7) 77 acres Franklin Co Francis Berry
Enos Hardin (4-7) 500 acres Clark Co E Hardin
Enos Hardin (4-7) 800 acres Henry Co Ky River E Hardin
Enos Hardin 100 acres Hardin Co Painter Creek Sutton
Enos Hardin (4-7) 200 acres Christian Co Tradewater Hardin and Shales
Venjlous Hardin (4-6) 200 acres Franklin Co Ky Francis Berry
James Hardin (4-8) Franklin Co
Mark Hardin 500 acres Washington Co Jn Hardin

1805 Tax Lists Frankllin Co., Kentucky
Richard Hardin 50 acres Franklin Co Thomas Marshall heirs.
Mark Hardin Property in Washington, Lincoln, Madison and Nicholas counties 500
    acres patented to John Hardin
James Hardin (4-8) no land
Venjelist Harden (4-6) 200 acres Franklin Co Entered to Berry
Venjelist Hardin (4-6) 200 acres Henry Co., Ky Entered to Lewis Hedge

1806 Tax Lists Franklin Co., Kentucky
Richard Harden 50 acres Franklin Co Thomas Marshall heirs
Mark Hardin Thousands of acres of land in several counties
Enos Hardin (4-7) Land in Franklin, Hardin, Henry, Henderson counties
James Hardin (4-8) no land
Evengelist Hardin (4-6) 200 acres Franklin Co
Evengelist Hardin (4-6) 200 acres Henry Co KY

1807 Tax Lists Franklin Co., Kentucky
Rchard Harden 50 acres Franklin Co., Marshall heirs
Mark Hardin Thousands of acres in many counties.
James Hardin (4-8) no land
Enos Hardin, (4-7) land in Franklin, Henry and Henderson counties
Vengelist Hardin (4-6) 200 acres Franklin Co 200 acres Henry Co

1808 Tax Lists Franklin Co., Kentucky
Richard Harden 50 acres
Ennis Hardin (4-7) land in Franklin, Herny and Henderson Counties

Harding Families of the Northern Neck of Virginia

James Harden (4-8) no land
Mark Hardin lots of land
Martin D. Hardin (5-99) land in Washington and Logan Counties
Evangelist Harden (4-6) land in Henry and Franklin counties Berry J Ashley

1809 Tax Lists of Franklin Co., Kentucky
Richard Hardin
Mark Hardin
Enose Hardin (4-7) land in Franklin, Henry, Henderson and Hardin County
Martin D Hardin
Martin D Hardin Jr
Evangelist Hardin (4-6)
James Hardin Jr (4-8) no land
Daniel Harden no land

1810 Tax Lists of Franklin Co., Kentucky
M. D. Hardin
Rossan Hardin ad MD Hardin Jr
Mark Hardin
Richard Hardin
James Hardin (4-8)
Daniel Hardin
Evangelist Hardin (4-6)
Enos Hardin (4-7)
Webb Hardin

1811 Tax Lists of Franklin Co., Kentucky
Richard Hardin
Daniel Hardin
James Hardin (4-8)
Evangelist Hardin (4-6)
James Hardin Sr.
Enos Hardin (4-7)
Martin D Hardin
Mark Hardin

1812 Tax Lists of Franklin County, KY
Richard Hardin
Martin D.Hardin (5-99)
Mark Hardin
James Harding (4-8)
James Harden
Benjamin Hardin
Enos Hardin (4-7)

1813 Tax Lists of Franklin Co., Kentucky
Martin D. Hardin (5-99)
Mark Hardin
James Hardin (4-8)
Enos Hardin (3 over 16) (4-7)
Evangelist Hardin (4-6)
Westley Hardin

1814 Tax Lists of Franklin Co., Kentucky
Martin D. Hardin (5-99)
Mark Hardin
Richard Hardin
Evangelious Hardin (4-6)
Enos Hardin (4-7)
James Hardin (4-8)
William Hardin

1815 Tax Lists of Franklin Co., Kentucky
Mark Hardin
Martin D Hardin (5-99)
Richard Hardin
Westley Hardin
Robert Hardin
James Hardin (4-8)
Enos Hardin (4-7)
Evangelist Hardin (4-6)

1816 Tax Lists of Franklin Co., Kentucky
Richard Hardin
M D Hardin (5-99)
James Harding Jr 700 acres
James Hardin (4-8) 100 acres
Enos Hardin (4-7)
Westley Hardin
Robert Hardin

1817 Tax Lists of Franklin Co., Kentucky
Robert Hardin
Richard Hardin
Wesley Hardin Land in Franklin, Shelby Co. Town lot South Franklin
George Hardin
Enos Hardin (4-7)

1818 Tax Lists of Franklin Co., Kentucky
Martin Hardin (5-99)
Land held by Mrs. Hardin
James Hardin (4-8)
Lewis Hardin
Richard Hardin

1819 Tax Lists of Franklin Co., Kentucky
Martin D Hardin (5-99)
Richard Hardin
Hardin Hardin???
James Hardin (4-8)
Richard Hardin

1820 Tax Lists of Franklin Co., Kentucky
Westley Hardin
Richard Hardin

Henry Co., Kentucky Records

Federal Census Records

1810 Federal Census
Page 472 Jacob Kelly 02001 10011

1820 Federal Census
Page 256 New Castle Jacob Kelly (4-46) 100010 20100
Page 257 New Castle Jacob Kelly 000001 00001

1830 Federal Census
Page 269 Ennis Hardin (4-29) 00001 00001
Page 269 John Hardin (5-56) 000110001 (60-70) 00000001 (50-60)
Page 271 Benjamin Hardin (4-9) 0010010001 001
Page 271 Daniel Hardin (4-41) 0011101 1111001
Page 271 Mark Hardin (4-45) 10001 21001
Page 302 Eli P. Hardin 210001 120001
Page 302 Peter Hardin (5-132) 000011 0110001

1850 Federal Census
Page 447-8 Household 103: John Woodin 69, James Hardin 7, Tho W. Harding 5, Mary Harding 39, Sarah Woodin 66

Marriage Records

1815 22 Jan: Benjamin Hardin (4-9) married Rebecca Jackson (4-9)

1816 19 Oct: Peter Hardin (5-132) married Sally Hardin. Son of John Hardin (5-42) and Barbara Rowner.

1840 23 Dec: Pluright Hardin married Polly Woodin (see 1850 Census above)

1838 08 Apr: William Hardin married Nancy Sparks

1812 09 Jun: Daniel Hardin (4-41) married Rebecca Kelley (4-41), daughter of John Kelley

1827 05 Dec: Ennis Hardin married Eliza Smith, daughter of Robert Smith

1847 14 Feb: Ben Hardin Jr, son of Ben, married Elvina Combs, daughter of William T. Combs.

Revolutionary War Pension Applications

From National Archives Records Service information File number S-31100

Benjamin Hardin (4-9) States he served as a private in the company of Captain Ashby in regiment of Col Neville in the Virginia Line for 10 months and subsequently a private in the same company two months. He enlisted in Hampshire County, Virginia in June 1777. Served until 1779 when he was discharged when he was discharged from service at Winchester Virginia. Was in MacIntosh's Campaign and at the siege of Yorktown. He gives conflicting dates of service in his various filings. Another says he enlisted in July 1776 and served until May or June 1778. Another document says he served about one year and was discharged in consequence of his selling a substitute for him to serve the balance of the time. He was discharged in Virginia. 19 August 1818, Mordecai Battson declared he served in the Revolutionary War in 1776 and that he served in the same company with Benjamin Hardin for one year.

1820 02 Oct: In Scott County, Kentucky Court Summary Benjamin Hardin (4-9) lived in Owen County, Kentucky in 1820. Served in Capt. Stephen Ashby's company on Pennsylvania Frontier two years, discharged on way to Winchester. Has not disposed of any property to meet qualifications for pension, Owns 250 acres of land and horses, cattle, sheep, hogs, total value $912. By profession a blacksmith but not able to work. Family is six persons and himself, Rebecca Hardin age 43, William Jackson, age 7, John Jackson, age 13, and Samuel Jackson age 11, R. Ann Hardin aged 5, W. Hardin Age 3.

1823 01 Sep: In Henry County Court Benjamin Hardin (4-9) Stated that he had living with him only three children, Beckey Ann aged 7, Washington age 5 years, and Nancy age 2.

1832 Aug: In Henry County Court On the sixth day of August 1832 came personally into Open Court (being a Court of record having the power of fine and imprisonment) Benjamin Hardin (4-9) who upon his oath declares that he is seventy-nine years of age that he was once on the pension roll under the Act of March 1818 and the 18th of said month and was dropped therefrom on account of property. He further declares that he was a private in Capt. Stephen Ashby under Col Nevill that his present place of residence is Henry County, Kentucky and that he resided in Franklin or Scott County at the time he first made application for pension.

Will Records

1824 22 Jul: Book 2 Page 330 Will of William Kelly, Executor to sell land in Scott Co. Mentions wife, children to have schooling. Father Joseph Kelly executor. Proved August 1824.

1825 08 Jan: Book 2 Page 329, Wife Sarah Kelly, at her death all equally divided between children. Son Amos. William Kelly and Joshua Wallace executors. Proved August 1825

1824 30 Sep: Book 1 Page 242 William Kelly Inventory

1830 19 Dec: Book 4 Page 464 Will of Wiliam Kelly, mentions wife Jane all estate, his children not named. Brother James F. Kelly to be executor. Proved January Court 1831.

Deed Records

1801 19 Jan: Book 1 Page 96 New Castle Trustees to John Hardin (5-56) 6 pounds current money, Two lots in New Castle #25 and #63

1804 05 Jul: Book 2 Page 163 John Harden (5-56) to Poindexter Thomison $200 Lot 25 in the Town of New Castle

1804 05 Jul: Book 2 Page 163 John Hardin (5-56) to John McKinley $200 East half of Lot 24 in New Castle

1812 05 Feb: Book 4 Page 123 Benjamin Hughes of Fayette Co KY to Benoni Hardin of Washington County, KY for $122 Land in Henry County 145 acres *(son of Absolom Hardin (5-43))*

1813 09 Aug: Book 4 Page 372 Benoni Hardin and Elizabeth his wife of Washington Co., KY to Moses Lancaster of Henry Co KY $307.50 145 acres *(son of Absolom Hardin (5-43))*

Kentucky County Records

1874 01 Jun: Book 4 Page 500 A list of deeds recorded in the Court of Appeals subsequent to 1st of January and prior to 1 June 1874 for lands in Henry County. Dated Oct 9, 1873. Filed Apr 18 1874 David Laughead to Enos Hardin (4-7) 300 acres on Waters of Ky River and 500 acres same. (No idea why this is placed in this book)

1823 13 May: Book 10 Page 239 John P. Thomas of Franklin Co KY to Peter Hardin (5-132) of Washington Co., KY $250 100 acres in Henry Co KY

1826 18 Sep: Book 12 Page 185 Heirs of Enos Hardin (4-7): George Hardin (4-28) and Jemima (4-28) his wife, Enos Hardin (4-29) and Elizabeth (4-29) his wife, Thomas Hardin (4-30) and Rachael (4-30) his wife, Benjamin Hawkins (4-31) and Ann (4-31) his wife, of the County of Owen KY to Evangelist Hardin (4-6) of Henry Co., KY for $200 Land in Henry Co., KY on Kentucky River 200 acres

1825 05 Mar: Book 11 Page 165 William Taylor of Jefferson Co KY to John Hardin (5-56) of Henry Co KY $560.50 280 ¼ acres in Henry Co.

1827 05 Nov Book 12 Page 410 Benjamin Hardin (4-9) of Henry Co., KY to Mark Hardin (4-45), William Hardin (4-44), Daniel Hardin (4-41), Henry Hardin (4-48), Nathaniel Hardin (4-47) George Washington Hardin (4-50) and Nancy Hardin (4-51) and Jacob Kelly (4-46), the parties of the second part all being children of said Benjamin except Jacob Kelly (4-46) who married Elizabeth Hardin (4-46), daughter of said Benjamin Hardin (4-9). Where one Laughead was entitled to a claim in Henry Co on Kentucky River containing 900 acres, resurveyed at 1020 acres. The said Benjamin Hardin (4-9) and his brother Ennis Hardin (4-7) purchased of said Laughead 800 acres of land one McCord purchased the other 200 acres. Benjamin Hardin (4-9) purchased 200 acres for his share and since traded his land in Owen Co., KY 200 acres for the 600 acres from the said Ennis. Benjamin gave the land to his children and is now dividing it between them.

1830 29 Sep: Book 14 Page 53 John Hardin (5-56) of Henry Co., KY and wife Elizabeth (5-56) to John Owen 194 acres in Henry Co KY

1830 29 Sep Book 14 Page 54 John Hardin (5-56) and wife Elizabeth (5-56) of Henry Co., KY to William Thompson of Shelby Co KY $700 100 acres Henry Co

1832 08 Mar: Book 14 Page 477 James McDonald to Peter Hardin (5-132) one cabin and animals as security for debts.

1831 19 Apr: Book 14 Page 205 Lynch Terrell of Henry County KY to Peter Hardin (5-132) of same county $175 for 8 ¼ acres in Henry Co., KY

1832 Book 14 Jun: 15 Page 154 Mary Clark, Benjamin Clark and Sarah Clark his wife, Archibald Clark and Isaac Clark of Coles Co IL to Mark Hardin (4-45) and Nathaniel Hardin (4-47) of Henry Co., KY $50 100 acres in Henry Co., KY

1835 15 Dec Book 17 Page 109 Henry Hardin (4-48) and Charlotte (4-48) his wife of White Co, Illinois to William Hardin (4-44) of Henry Co KY $200 Land known as Henry Hardin's Part of Lots #7 and #8

1840 08 Dec: Book 18 Page 108 Jacob Kelly (4-46) and Elizabeth Kelly his wife late Elizabeth Hardin (4-46) of the State of Illinois, by Henry G Kelly their attorney to William Hardin (4-44) of Henry County, Kentucky. $114 Land in Henry County in Hardin's Bottom on Kentucky River 12 acres, the same land conveyed to said Kelly's by Benjamin Hardin (4-9) on the 5 day of November 1827 and lying adjoining 200 acres now belonging to said William as purchased of Stephens or and lots No 7 & 8 allotted to Henry Hardin (4-48) and now owned by said William (4-44).

1840 P Hardin to A Eddy 19 428 105 A Ky River
1843 P Hardin to T Smith 20 7 150 A Ky River
1843 J R Hardin from C Fears 20 11 34 acres
1840 William Hardin from W Stephens 20 346 100 acres
1845 M Hardin from N Hardin 21 438 100 acres
1846 M Hardin heirs to J Lecompte 21 448 50 acres
1846 Hardin Plot land 23 59
N Hardin from R Sanford 23 37 109 acres
M Hardin from R Sanford 23 40 24 acres
P Hardin from R Sanford 23 38 109 acres
A H Hall from R Sanford 23 39 109 acres
M Hardin from E S Bayley 24 338 Land on Ky River
1852 J R Hardin from T Smith Exec 24 555 180 acres
1851 D Hardin from Clements Exec 24 299 104 acres Ky River
1851 D Hardin from Clements Exec 24 300 68 acres Kentucky River

Personal Property Tax Lists

1825 Tax Lists of Henry County, Kentucky
Page 26 Peter Hardin 100 acres Kentucky River Patent Powell
Page 26 Ennis Hardin No Land
Page 26 John Hardin 180 acres Kentucky River Patent Taylor
Page 28 Henry Hardin No Land
Page 28 Will Hardin No Land
Page 28 Benja Hardin 500 acres Kentucky River Patent Henton
Page 29 Danl Hardin 100 acres Kentucky River Patent Henton

1826 Tax Lists of Henry County, Kentucky

Page 27 Daniel Hardin 100 acres on Kentucky River Patent Lawhead
Page 27 Mark Hardin 100 acres Kentucky River Patent Lawhead
Page 27 William Hardin 80 acres Kentucky River Patent Lawhead
Page 27 Henry Hardin 100 acres Kentucky River Patent Lawhead
Page 27 Nathaniel Hardin 50 acres Kentucky River Patent Lawhead
Page 28 Evangelist Hardin 150 acres Kentucky River Patent David Lawhead
Page 28 Eli P. Hardin No Land
Page 29 John Hardin 180 acres Kentucky River Patent Taylor
Page 29 Dennis Hardin No Land
Page 30 Peter Hardin 100 acres Green River Patent Taylor
Page 31 Mark Hardin No Land

1827 Tax Lists of Henry County, Kentucky
Page 27 Daniel Hardin 148 acres Kentucky River Patent Lawhead
Page 27 Mark Hardin 100 acres Kentucky River Patent Lawhead
Page 27 Henry Hardin 100 acres Kentucky River Patent Lawhead
Page 27 William Hardin 200 acres Kentucky River
Page 27 Evangelist Hardin No Land
Page 28 Eli P. Hardin No Land
Page 28 Ennis Hardin No Land
Page 28 John Hardin 180 acres Kentucky River Patent Taylor
Page 30 Peter Hardin 100 acres Kentucky River

1828 Tax Lists of Henry County, Kentucky
Page 26 Mark Hardin No Land
Page 26 Eli P Hardin No Land
Page 27 William Hardin 140 acres Kentucky River Patent Lawhead
Page 27 Mark Hardin 100 acres Kentucky River Patent Lawhead
Page 28 Peter Hardin 100 acres Kentucky River
Page 28 Mark Hardin No Land
Page 28 Daniel Hardin 248 acres Kentucky River
Page 28 Benjamin Hardin 200 acres Kentucky River
Page 28 John Hardin 180 acres Kentucky River Patent Taylor

Hopkins Co., Kentucky Records

Formed 1806 from Henderson County, Kentucky

Federal Census Records

1810 Federal Census
Page 1 Nicholas Hardin (3-6) 01111 01301 Hardinville
Page 2 Nathaniel Hardin (3-22) 20100 00100
Page 2 John Ashby 30010 21010
Page 2 Stephen Ashby 30010 20100
Page 2 Reuben Berry 02101 41001 County

1820 Federal Census
Page 249 George Hardin (3-20) 200010 00100
Page 250 Nathaniel Hardin (3-22) 020010 20010
Page 250 Nicholas Hardin (3-6) 000101 00121

1830 Federal Census
Nicholas Hardin (3-6) 00000100001 0000120001
Page 45 Nathaniel Hardin (3-22) 0001101 1120001

1840 Federal Census
Page 356 Herod Harding (3-23) 0000001 00011
Page 381 Nathaniel Hardin (3-22) 01000001 0110001
Page 381 Nancy Hardin (3-6) 0000 01000200001
Page 362 Silas Hardin 00001 0001
Page 376 Isham Hardin 110001 10001

Deed Records

1816 22 Jan: Deed Book 1 Page 367 Reuben Berry to William Berry Personal Property One Negro Man

1821 10 May: Book 3 Page 392 Nicholas Harding (3-6) of Hopkins County Ky to Bank of the Commonwealth of Kentucky a mortgage for $600 payable in 180 days.

1825 06 Jan: Book 4 Page 394 Reuben Berry Sr to Bartheney Berry, Lucinda Berry, and Hannah Bleu, wife of John Blew Deed For love and affection and a bond executed to Reuben in penalty of 2000 dollars conditioned on the support and maintenance of "myself and Sinah my wife during our natural lives for five Negro slaves.

1825 Feb: Deed Book 4 Page 416 Reuben Berry of Hopkins County to John Blue of same. For $100 50 acres in Hopkins County.

1825 05 Feb: Deed Book 4 Page 424 Nicholas Harding (3-6) of Hopkins Co., KY to his daughter Elizabeth Harding (3-25) one negro girl.

1825 26 Feb: Deed Book 4 Page 416 Reuben Berry of Hopkins co., KY for $300 to Barthianna Berry and Lewenda Berry 150 acres.

1830 Book 5 Page 422 Parthena Lucinda, Linah and Reuben Berry Estate to Joseph Robertson Power of Attorney

1842 08 Jul: Book 14 Page 373. Everybody named below to Elizabeth and Eleanor Harding, 180 acres from Nicholas Harding (3-6) estate as below. Similar deed on page 376 to James Prather et al.

1847 Book 12 Page 414 Heirs of Nicholas Harding (3-6) to Herod Harding (3-23). Whereas Nicholas Harding of Hopkins Co KY died 12 February 1833 and left a will left land 86 acres to his wife Nancy (3-6). Children of Nicholas Harding are Mary Ashby wife of John Ashby, Nathaniel Harding, Herrod Harding, Nancy Harding, now Nancy Downey wife of Robert Downey, Elizabeth Harding, Wilmoth Harding now Wilmoth Prather wife of James Prather and Eleanor Harding, Nancy Harding relinquished Property 1 Dec 1834 to Children Then daughter Mary Ashby (3-21) and her husband John Ashby died. Their heirs are Enos J. Ashby, Stephen Ashby, William J. Ashby, Nancy Howel wife of Vincent Howel, Sally Ashby wife of Daniel Ashby, Emily Ashby wife of Enos G. Ashby, Betsy Stodghill wife of John Stodghill, Lucinda Crabtree, wife of John Crabtree and Matilda Robertson, wife of Edwin Robertson all of them sell to Herod Harding.

1848 22 Sep: Book 13 Page 433 Isham Harding of Hopkins County to Nathaniel Harding for $75.75 his 1848 crop of tobacco a mortgage for 12 months.

Will Records

1829 Will of Reuben Berry of Hopkins County, KY To daughter Hanah 100 acres where (Reuben) now lives to convey at her mother's death. Balance of land to daughters Lucinda and Parthena. Wife Sina. Daughter Polly Williams $100. To sons Bouns, William, Joseph, Thomas, Reuben one dollar each as they got their part of the estate. To four oldest daughters Anne, Becky, Elizabeth, Sally one dollar each as they got their part of the estate. Executor Gen Stephen Ashby and John White. Proved December 1829.

1826 24 Mar: Proved April 1833 Will of Nicholas Harding (3-6). To wife (3-6) all personal and real property for her lifetime. After her death property to be divided among children Mary Ashby (3-21), Nathaniel Harding (3-22), Herrod Harding (3-23), Nancy Harding (3-24), Elizabeth Harding, Wilmoth Harding and Elinor Harding. To Daughter Sarah Jones (3-19) one shilling and to son George Harding the same. Executors to be son-in-law John Ashby and son Nathaniel Harding. Inventory signed by John Ashby Jr, Vincent Harvell and John Combs and filed May 1833.

Jefferson Co., Kentucky Records

Federal Census Records

1850 Census Division 2 Jefferson County, Kentucky Page 265 (3- 115413)

Res	Fam	Name	Age	Sex	Occupation	Birthplace
256	258	John W. Hardin	29	M	Farmer	Kentucky
256	258	Asberine Hardin	26	F	(3-106)	Kentucky
256	258	William H. Hardin	8	M		Kentucky
256	258	Elizth Hardin	4	F		Kentucky
256	258	Arnett Hardin	1	M		Kentucky
256	258	James W. Antle	23	M	Laborer	Kentucky
256	258	Thomas G. Antle	18	M	Laborer	Kentucky
256	258	Jeremiah Antle	21	M	Laborer	Kentucky

Will Books

1790 12 Oct: Book 1 Page 70 Will of Henry Harding (3-8). To wife Rebeckah (3-8) entire estate during her widowhood. Seventy Pounds of estate be paid to son Henry Harding and to daughter Caty Harding. At decease of wife Rebeckah, estate equally divided among five children: John, Wilmouth, Sarah, Henry, and Caty. Also, free one Negro gal named Pol. Proved November 1, 1796.

1821 15 Oct: Proved 12 November 1821 Book 2 Page 141 Ann Harding of Jefferson County KY. To Sarah Ann Wren, daughter of John and Verlinda Wren three negroes. To my niece Verlinda Wren half f the land I own to be equally divided between Verlinda and Hezekiah Magruder. To nephew Hezekiah Magruder the other half of the land. To Nephew Josiah Harding Magruder. The nephews and nieces are children of Daniel Magruder. Witnesses Enoch Magruder, William Duerson, Benjamin W. Jones. *(Ann married Jonah Harding also Ann wife of Isaiah Harding. Not related)*

1822 21 Aug: Book 2 Page 241 Will of Rebecca Harding (3-8) of Jefferson County, Kentucky. Daughters Sally Hancock and Caty Schreader her clothes. Balance equally divided between son Henry Hardin, Sally Hancock, and Caty Schraeder. Proved 15 July 1823. Witness Harding Hancock. William Handcock administrator.

1822 17 Jun: Book 2 Page 248 Will of Henry Hardin (3-31) Sen. To son John 100 acres, to son Henry 50 acres. Wife Polly. Other children to receive up to $350 as they marry or come of age: Nancy, Polly, William, Allien, Eliza, Rebecca Jane, and Ann. Proved 13 October 1823.

1839 08 Jul: Proved 7 October 1839 Book 3 Page 192 Will of Sarah Harding. To granddaughter Mary Margaret Owen, daughter of Shapley Owen. Daughter Margaret Barker. Grandsons John and Jacob Owen, sons of Shapley Owen.

(Sarah was wife of Zephaniah Hardin died 1811 in Louisville. Not related to the Hardins in this book)

1864 02 Jul: Book 6 Page 230 John Hardin of Louisville. Wife Gertrude Hardin Residence occupied by us on Second Street between Gran and Walnut. Half a farm in Shelby Co. Sister Mrs. Jane Logan, sons Mark Hardin and John Adair Hardin. *(Son of Mark Hardin #6:26)*

1867 14 Jul: 19 Aug: 1867 Book 6 Page 531 Elizabeth J Harding. To sister-in-law Nelly Hardin wife of Benoni Hardin. Mother Nancy Hardin, sister Lucinda K Anderson, grandfather Benoni Hardin, land lying in Washington County Ky, Grandmother Rachel Hardin. Brother Benoni Hardin, Neice Lillian B. Anderson, daughter of sister Lucinda K and brother-in law B S Anderson. *(This is part of Family 6, Mark Hardin (5-1) and Mary (MNU) (5-1). Benoni Hardin is the son of Absolom Hardin (5-43)).*

Deed Books

1799 07 Feb: Book 5 Page 24 Mark Hardin (5-26) and Susannah (5-26) his wife of Washington County KY to John Strother of Culpeper Co VA, for two negroes, 501 A Culpeper County

1801 25 Mar: Book 6 Page 16 Charles Catlett and Catherine of Frederick County VA to Edward Dorsey. $900 Three-fifths parts of 500 acres in Jefferson County, a moiety of the entire tract of 1000 acres patented on 23 April 1785 to James Catlett, now deceased, who conveyed 500 acres to Charles Catlett who sold it to Rowley, Smith and Hardin and Edward Dorsey purchased said Smith's part 3/5 or 300 acres. Land on Floyds Fork. Bordering Joseph Jones survey of 1250 acres.

1801 01 Aug: Book 6 Page 34 Edith Catlett to Edward Dorsey both of Kentucky. $250. Land on Floyds Creek 1/6 part of a tract of 500 acres,

1800 30 Jun: Book 6 Page 311 John Catlett, Nathaniel McPherson and Elizabeth his wife, James Catlett, Charles Catlett, Jane Gosney, children and heirs of James Catlett dec to Susannah Dorsey, wife of Edward Dorsey of Anne Arundel Co MD, land on Floyds Fork near Goose Creek, 500 acres for $1125

1801 04 Dec: Book 6 Page 245 Joseph Strother (brother of Joseph Strother) and Nancy Strother to Mark Harden (5-26) of Washington Co., KY 200 acres Prather Creek, one moiety of a tract patented 23 August 1785 and granted to James Catlett, grandfather of said Edy Catlett, from whom the land descended to Edy Catlett in common with five other heirs each holding equal parts.

Harding Families of the Northern Neck of Virginia

1803 13 Jan: Book 6 Page 391 John Gwathney and Ann Buckhannon Gwathney of Jefferson County to John Netherton Jr of same. $225 25 acres. No location given

1803 13 Jan: Book 6 Page 392 John Gwathney and Ann Buckhannon Gwathney his wife of Jefferson Co., KY to Henry Hardin (3-16) of Jefferson County KY for $800 100 A Jeff Co on Harrods Creek Start at corner of Temple Gwathney and John Gwathney, part of David Williams survey between the fork of Harrods Creek. Recorded 6 April 1803.

1803 28 Feb: Book 6 Page 393 Jane Breckinridge, devisee, of Jefferson County to William Arterburn Jr. 100 acres. For $1.

This property has quite a history. It started with Alexander Breckinridge on 20 September 1784 issuing a bond to ensure payment given to John Stewart of Amherst Co VA, Condition was that Breckinridge sold to Stewart 200 acres on Harrods Creek, part of a 1000-acre survey in Breckinridge's name. Two hundred acres in a square to be laid off. The bond contains these endorsements:

1. J Stewart assigns the bond to Mr. John Johnston. Witness Thomas Wharton, Joseph Crenshaw, William Mayo. No Date
2. Johnston assigns the bond to Benjamin Johnston 20 January 1790, witness William Kenser
3. Benjamin Johnston assigned the bond to Henry Harding (3-8) 29 January 1795. Witness John Netherton, John Hardin.
4. Henry Hardin (3-31) assigned the note to John Netherton 09 February 1798. Witness John Pringle
5. 07 September 1798 John Netherton Jr assigned the bond to John Mathews and Henry Netherton. Witness Will Stevens
6. 14 Jun: 1799 Henry Netherton assigned his rights to Owen Gwathney. Witness John Netherton.
7. 11 February 1800 John Mathews assigned his rights to John Mackey. Witness Jeremiah Mathews.
8. 04 December 1801 John Mackey assigned his rights to William Arterburn. Witness Owen Gwathney
9: Owen Gwathney and William Arterburn Jr divided the land into two parcels of 100 acres each 10 William
10: Alexander Breckinridge died and left all his land to his wife Jane Breckinridge.to end this bond, Jane Breckinridge sells her part to William Arterburn for $1.

1804 03 Sep: Book 7 Page 75 Henry Hardin (3-16) and Polly his wife of Jefferson Co KY to Thomas Mason of same county for $681 106 A Floyds Creek, part of James Catlett's 1000-acre survey. Bounded by Edward Dorsey.

Kentucky County Records

1807 24 Sep: Book 8 Page 188 Charles Lynch of Shelby Co KY to John Harding of Shelby County KY for 5 shillings, On Floyds Fork part of survey of James Kemp for 9250 acres, 100 at Harrods Creek.

1808 18 Jul: Book 8 Page 342 John Young and Peggy his wife of Jefferson County KY to John Harding of Shelby County KY for 50 pounds, 100 a Prather Creek

1808 30 Aug: Book 8 Page 357 Henry Harding (3-16) and Mary his wife of Jefferson Co., KY to heirs of Edward Dorsey Deceased (Patience Dorsey Luckett, Polly Ann Hibbs, Matilda Dorsey, Urith Owings Dorsey) 60 Pounds current money. 61 ¾ Acres on Floyds Fork, Part of 1/5 share of James Cattlett's 1000-acre survey purchased of the heirs of James Cattlett. Witnesses Susanna Dorsey, Owen Gwathney, Thomas Ramey, George Harding (3-15)

1812 07 Dec: Book 9 Page 494 Owen Gwathney and Ann his wife to William Harding (3-50) borders on Henry Harding (3-16) property. For $238 34 acres Jeff Co

1812 07 Dec: Book 9 Page 495 Owen Gwathney and Ann his wife to Henry Harding (3-16) for $672 96 acres Jeff Co adjoining William Harding (3-50) land.

1814 07 Feb: Book 10 Page 444 Samuel H, Luckett and Catherine his wife of Louisville, KY to George Hardin (3-15) of Jefferson Co KY. for $50. ½ acre in Transylvania #15 Ohio St.

1814 Apr: Book 10 Page 497 Reuben Ross and Betsy his wife of Jefferson County KY to William Harding (3-50) (son of George) of the same place $154.17 46 ½ acres Harrods Creek bounded by John Wilhoit

1814 09 Aug: Book H Page 310 John Dicken of Ohio County to George Harden (3-15) of Jefferson County KY. For 50 Pounds, Tract of 50 acres on Harrods Creek. Witnesses John Netherton, Henry Netherton, Julius Wilhoit. Sworn by oaths of Henry Hardin and Julius Wilhoit.

1815 09 May: Book I Page 251 Henry Hardin (3-31) and Polly (3-31) his wife late Polly Smith, Anna Smith, James Archer and Hannah his wife late Hannah Smith, Nathan Stevens and Rebecca his wife late Rebecca Netherton, the heirs of Benjamin Smith Deceased to Stephen Smith of Jefferson Co., KY For $1 to each person, all interest in the estate of Benjamin Smith deceased. (Nathan Stephens married Rebecca Netherton 4 April 1814 Henry Co. KY (James Archer married Hannah Smith 1 Dec 1813 Jefferson Co., KY)

1806 Book I. Page 309 Henry Hardin (3-31) and Polly (Mary) (3-31)his wife of Jefferson County to Charles Smith of same county For $588 98 A Floyds Fork. Filed 13 April 1812

Harding Families of the Northern Neck of Virginia

1812 12 Apr: Book I. Page 311 Henry Hardin (3-31) and Mary (3-31) his wife of Jefferson Co., KY to John Wilhoit of same. For $87 11 ¾ A Harrods Creek

1815 20 Jun: Book I Page 364 George Hardin (3-15) of Jefferson County KY to Samuel H Luckett of same, For $50 ½ A Lot 15 in Transylvania.

1817 04 Aug: Book M Page 269 Paul Skidmore and Frances M his wife of Louisville, to George Harden (3-15) of Jefferson County KY for $100 Lot 15 Ohio Street in Transylvania

1815 30 Aug: Book M Page 310 George Hardin (3-15) of Jefferson Co KY to William Hardin (3-50) of same county for $1 Land on Harrods Creek Witnesses Owen Gwathney, William Harding Jr, Julius Wilhoit. No acreage given.

1820 08 Jul: Book R. Page 509 William Hardin and Ann his wife to Jonathan Elston and Leaven Laurence for $895.10 Lots 53 54 Middletown mortgage to be repaid by the first of January 1820

1822 09 Apr: Book U Page 285 William Hardin and his wife to Nathan Marders. Marders and James Taylor endorsed a note to United States Bank for $3850 for accommodation of John Evans Co, which firms William Harden was a member. Bank got judgement against the said Hardin and others on the note in court and levied the lands of said Harding in Middletown at the sale Marders purchased the Lot 53 54 and 73 Main St, Middletown to settle the case.

1819 01 Jan: Book U Page 341 William A Harding (3-51) from Elizabeth Wilhoit 165 A Harrods Creek. This is a very complicated deed in which the heirs of John Wilhoit distribute the estate so will summarize carefully. Party of the first part: Lewis Wilhoite of Jefferson County KY, administrator of estate of John Wilhoite deceased with will annexed. Party of the second part: Elizabeth Wilhoite of same, widow of John and Executrix of the estate. Party of the third part: Aaron Wilhoite, Simion Wilhoite, Elliott Wilhoite, Julius Wilhoite, all of same county, Abraham Wilhoite of Woodford Co, sons of John Wilhoite dec., Mary Miller of VA, a widow and daughter of John Wilhoite, Adam Schreader and Anne his wife, William Broylis and Elizabeth his wife, and William Harding (3-50) and Rhoda Harding (3-50) his wife, daughters of John Wilhoite dec., all of Jefferson Co KY. Party of the fourth part: Nancy Wilhoite, Executrix and Medly Shelton, executors of the will of Elijah Wilhoite dec (a son of John Wilhoite dec), all of Woodford Co KY. Party of the fifth part: Johnathan Harding (3-52) and William A. Harding (3-51) of Jefferson Co., KY. Then the will is transcribed into the deed. Dated 3 December 1814 Proved 13 Mar: 1815. Witnesses were Owen Gwathney, Henry Harding, William Harding Jr. The deed continues: John Wilhoite held 165 acres on Harrods Creek bordering H Harding and William Harding property, sold on the 30th day of April to Johnathan Harding and William A. Harding under terms outlined in the deed.

- 1822 24 Jun: Book U Page 398 Norbourne and Ann Beall, William and Matilda Galt, and Richard Maupin of Jefferson County to Henry Harding (3-31) of the same county. 50 A Herrods Creek

- 1822 11 May: Book V Page 381 Lewis Wilhoite etc (same as earlier deed) to Jonathan Harding (3-52) and William A. Harding (3-51) 165 A Harrods Creek to clear title on 1 January 1819 deed.

- 1826 18 Apr: Book Z Page 327 George Hardin (3-15) of Oldham County, KY to Christian Barrell of Jefferson County, For $60 Lot 15 on Ohio Street in Transylvania.

- 1834 01 Mar: Book MM Page 347 William Hardin and Ann Hardin his wife of Jefferson County, KY to John W. Yeager of Jefferson Co KY for $5,340 257 A Goose Creek

- 1837 08 Jun: Book 49 Page 147 John W. Athey and Phebe his wife and Elisha Athey to William Hardin and eight others. For $20. House on West First St Louisville. Mortgage.

Benjamin Harding to Trevor Lawrence 54-594

William Harding to Leaven E Hall 55-106

William Harding to Robert N Miller 55 109

William Harding to Thomas T Haggin 55 110

William Hardin to Thomas R Parrent 56 80

William Hardin to Thomas R Parrent 56-84

William Hardin to John N McMichael 56-254

David R Harding to Nancy Kendall 57-8

Benjamin Harding to Sallie T. Dixon 58-582

James M Harding to James Rudd 66-628

Court Records

- 1796 Oct: Book 5 Page 30 Last will of Henry Harding dec (3-8) proved by the oaths of Jose Keller and John Netherton. Executors approved

- 1798 07 Aug: Book 6 Lyman Harding admitted to practice as an attorney at law in this court

1810 12 Mar: Book 9 Page 85 Administration of estate of William W. Harding granted to Zephaniah Harding

1810 11 Jun: Book 9 Page 104 Inventory and appraisement of the estate of William W. Harding dec received and filed.

1811 11 Mar: Book 9 Page 184 Administration account of Zephaniah Harding as admin of William W Harding ordered to be examined.

1814 08 Aug: Book 11 Page 75 Administration of the estate of Zephaniah Harding granted to Sarah Harding widow of deceased and Edmund Sale.

1815 13 Mar: Book 11 Page 160 Inventory and appraisal of the estate of Zephaniah Harding received

1815 08 May: Book 11 Page 193 Eli Harding, infant orphan of Zephaniah Harding deceased being above the age of fourteen years, chose Sarah Harding his mother as his guardian.

1815 08 May: Book 11 Page 194 The Court appoints Leavin Lawrence James Edwards William Hite and James Boston to divide the slaves belonging to the estate of Zephaniah Harding decd between Mary Sale Ann Thornton Margaret Harding John D. Harding Eli Harding and Lucy Harding and make a report

Federal Census Records

1810 Federal Census Jefferson County, Kentucky
Page 558 Middletown Henry Hardin (3-16) 31201 01010
Page 558 Middletown George Hardin (3-4) 00011 00001
Page 558 Middletown William Hardin (3-50) 00100 10100

1820 Federal Census Jefferson County, Kentucky
Page 35 Middletown William Hardin (3-50) 200011 21010
Page 57 Ann Hardin 000010 00101

1850 Federal Census Jefferson County, KY District 1 Page 193
282 282 Hartwell Pate (3-87) M 32 Wagon Maker Georgia
282-282 M. A. Pate (3-87) F 23 Kentucky
282-282 L. A. Pate F 7 Kentucky
282-282 John Pate M 4 Kentucky

Marriages

1785 27 May: Register Page 2 James Hardin married Margaret Wells Spinster (Many researchers place this James as a son of Jack Hardin of the Mark Hardin (5-1) Mary (MNU) (5-1) family. However, no James is mentioned in Jacks will and he seems to be too old to be Jack's son.)

1797 18 Jan: Register Book 1 Page 25 William Shrader married Catha Hardin (3-32)

1798 15 May: Register Book 1 Page 30 Nancy Harding (3-18) married Henry Netherton (3-18) George Harding written and signed consent for the marriage of his daughter.

1803 21 May: Register Book 1 Page 44 License Married 26 May 1803 Caspar Young married Nancy Harding

1808 02 Jan: Register Book 1 Page 59 William Hardin (3-50) married Rody Wilhite. Witnesses Julius Willhite and Henry Netherton (3-18). Daughter of John Wilhite

1811 08 Apr: Register Book 1 Page 69 Edmund Sale married Nancy Harding. Daughter of Zephaniah Harding. Married 11 April 1811 Consent given. (Not related to the Hardins in this book)

1813 19 Jan: Register Book 1 Page 74 Jonathan Harding (3-52) to Lucy Wilhoite (3-52) Daughter of John Wilhoite, consent given. Married 28 January 1813

1815 23 Feb: Ann Harding married William H. Honiton. Daughter of Sarah Hardin (widow of Zephaniah Hardin)

1816 25 Mar: Register Book 1 Page 87 Alexander Harding to Louisa Hite. Father John Hite consent given. Married 28 March 1816. (Descended from John Harding of Frederick Co., Maryland. Not related)

1816 16 May: Register Book 1 Page 87 John Hardin (3-67) married Nancy Phillips (3-67) daughter of Samuel Phillips

1817 17 Dec: Register Book 1 Page 95 Henry C. Hardin married Lucy Bridges daughter of Benjamin Bridges Sr.

1817 25 Dec: Register Book 1 Page 95 Shapley Owen married Lucy Hardin, daughter of Sarah Harding (widow of Zephaniah Hardin)

1819 07 Jan: Register Book 1 Page 101 Margaret Harding married He H Barken. Daughter of Sarah Harding (widow of Zephaniah Hardin)

1819 15 Jan: Register Book 1 Page 101 Lawrence Byrne married Elizabeth Harding (of lawful age) No marriage return.

1821 27 Feb: Register Book 1 Page 122 Henry Hardin (3-68) Jr to Mary Phillips (3-68), daughter of Samuel Phillips.

1821 12 Sep: Register Book 1 Page 122 Thomas Callahan married Nancy Hardin (3-69), daughter of Henry Harding (3-31).

Harding Families of the Northern Neck of Virginia

1823 27 Feb: Register Book 1 Page 122 Abm Souther (3-54) married Catherine Hardin (3-54), daughter of Henry Hardin (3-16). Proved by the affirmation of James Hardin.

1825 06 Dec: Register Book 1 Page 168 Thomas H Jones married Henrietta F Hardin, daughter of William Hardin

1826 01 Jun: Register Book 1 Page 172 Edward G. Harding married Ann Lewis, daughter of James Lewis, (Son of Vachel Harding and Descended from Robert Harding of Talbot County Maryland)

1827 01 Sep: Register Book 2 Page 13 Albert G. Harding married Flora N. E. Wigginton, daughter of James Wigginton

1827 26 Jul: Register Book 2 Page 13 William Harding married Mary Ann Vembly, daughter of Jacob Vembly

1828 25 Dec: Register Book 2 Page 28 Frances Harding widow married Thomas Parrent

1829 27 Apr: Register Book 2 Page 32 Solomon Harding married Susan Taylor, daughter of Benjamin Taylor

1829 19 Aug: Register Book 2 Page 37 Anna Harding married David B. Phillips. Widow of Edward Greenberry Harding deceased.

1832 15 May: Register Book 2 Page 84 Nancy C. Hardin married John A McMichael. Daughter of William Hardin

1833 27 Feb: Register Book 2 Page 103 James Allen Hardin married Mary Ann Lucinda Elston, daughter of Mary Bell late Eston

1833 27 Feb: Register Book 2 Page 103 Honora Harding married Thomas Kelley. Daughter of Henry Harding decd and Ellen Harding who gave consent

1833 26 Mar: Register Book 2 Page 104 Maria Louise Hardin married Geo A Frederick. Daughter of William Hardin

1834 16 May: Register Book 2 Page 107 David T. Hardin married Mary K. Davis, daughter of Robert Davis

1834 24 Jun: Register Book 2 Page 133 Davis R. Harding married Susan Kendall, daughter of Rouzey Kendall

1834 25 Jul: Register Book 2 Page 135 Vachel M D Harding married Elizabeth Ann Brown, daughter of James Brown decd and Priscilla Brown (Descended from Robert Harding of Talbot County Maryland)

1834 08 Dec: Register Book 2 Page 142 Harriet Harding married William Norton, daughter of Vachel Harding (Descended from Robert Harding of Talbot County Maryland)

1834 29 Dec: Register Book 2 Page 144 Rebecca W. Harding married George H. Jones. Daughter of Vachel Harding (Descended from Robert Harding of Talbot County Maryland)

1835 27 Aug: Register Book 2 Page 158 Thomas W. Harding married Milly Harrison, daughter of William Harrison

1836 03 Sep: Register Book 2 Page 187 Lemuel Harding married Sarah Wilkinson, widow of William Wilkinson decd

06 Jun: 1844 Register 1844 Page 94 Elizabeth Sebolt married George B. Yenowine She is ward of Thomas Morris, proved by Amos Sebolt her uncle where she resides. She had a son George Hardin Yenowine and Margaret Hardin Yenowine. George H. Yenowine death record in 1901(Deaths Page 347 in Milwaukee Wisconsin) gave his mother's name as Elizabeth Hardin.

Personal Property and Land Tax Records

1794 Personal and Land Tax Lists
1794 June 28 John Netherland 1334 ¼ acres Fayette County

1796 Personal and Land Tax Lists
1796 June 3: Henry Harding Sr, (3-8) no land, 1 male over 21, 1 black over 16, 2 total Blacks 6 horses 3 cattle
1796 June 16 John Harding (3-28) no land, 1 over 21, 5 blacks, 3 Horse 5 cattle
1796 June 2 John Netherton 100 acres Harrods Creek Jefferson Co
1796 June 2 Henry Netherton

1797 Personal and Land Tax Lists
1797 May: 12 Henry Hardin (3-31) Jr no land 1 over 21 1 black 3 cattle
1797 May: 12 Rebecca Hardin (3-8) (widow) no land 2 blacks 3 cattle

1799 Personal and Land Tax Lists
1799 June 13 Henry Hardin (3-31) no land 1 over 21 5 horses
1799 June 24 Zephaniah Harding no land, 1 over 21 1 over 16 6 blacks two livestock
1799 June 27 Rebecca Harding (3-8) (widow) 2 blacks 2 livestock
1799 June 28 George Harding (3-4) Sr no land 1 over 21 1 over 16 3 blacks 2 livestock

1800 Personal and Land Tax Lists
1800 Mar 31 Zephaniah Harding 1 over 21 1 16-20
1800 May 26 Henry Harding (3-16) Sr. 614 acres Floyds Fork Patent to James Catlett 1 male 1 horse

Harding Families of the Northern Neck of Virginia

1800 May 29 George Harding (3-4) Sr, no land 1 over 21, 1 over 16, 3 blacks 2 livestock
1800 June 6 Henry Harding (3-31) Jr, 100 acres Jefferson Co on Harrods Creek, Entered Survey Patented to Samuel Beale 1 over 21 2 Livestock
1800 June 7 Rebecca Harding (3-8) 2 blacks 1 livestock

1801 Personal and Land Tax Lists
1801 July 16 George Harding (3-4) Sr No land 1 male, 3 blacks 2 livestock
1801 July 16 George Harding (3-15) Jr 1 male
1801 July 16 Henry Harding (3-16) Sr Land: 272 acres Jefferson County, Floyds Ford Entered Surveyed Patented Robert Catlett. 1 over 21 2 livestock
1801 July 16 Henry Harding (3-31) Jr No land 1 male 4 livestock
1801 July 18 Zephaniah Harding 2 over 21 7 blacks 2 livestock

1802 Personal and Land Tax Lists
1802 May 15 George Harding (3-4) Sr 1 male, 3 blacks 1 livestock
1802 May 15 George Harding (3-15) Jr 1 male
1802 May 27 Zephaniah Harding 1 male 8 black 3 livestock
1802 June 10 Henry Hardin (3-16) 150 acres Jefferson Co Floyds Creek Entered, Surveyed, Patented James Catlett
1802 July 15 Henry Hardin (3-31) Jr 100 acres Jefferson Co Harrods Creek Entered Surveyed Patented to Samuel Beale
1802 July 15 Rebecca Hardin (3-8) 1 black 1 livestock

1803 Personal and Land Tax Lists
1803 May 5 William Harding 1 male
1803 May 5 Zephaniah Harding 1 male 8 blacks 5 livestock
1803 June 21 Rebecca Hardin (3-8) widow 1 black 1 livestock
1803 June 21 Henry Harding (3-16) Sr 100 acres Jefferson County Harrods Creek Enter Survey Patent Joel Stephens
1803 June 21 Henry Harding (3-16) Sr 98 acres Jefferson County Floyd's Fork Enter Survey Patent James Catlett,
1803 June 21 George Harding (3-4) Sr 1 male 3 black 3 livestock
1803 June 21 George Harding (3-15) Jr 1 male 1 livestock
1803 June 23 Henry Harding (3-31) Jr 100 acres Jefferson County Harrods Creek Enter Survey Patent Samuel Beall

1804 Personal and Land Tax Lists
1804 Apr 25 Zephaniah Harding 1 male 5 blacks 5 livestock
1804 May 24 George Harding (3-15) Jr 1 male 1 livestock
1804 June 30 George Harding (3-4) Sr 1 male 3 blacks 3 livestock
1804 June 30 Henry Harding (3-31) Sen 100 acres Jefferson County Harrods Creek Enter Survey Patent David Williams 1 male 3 livestock

Kentucky County Records

1804 June 30 Henry Harding (3-31) Jr 150 acres Jefferson County, Goose Creek Enter Survey Patent John Willis 1 male 2 livestock
1804 July 19 Rebecca Harding (3-8) widow 2 blacks 1 livestock

1805 Personal and Land Tax Lists
1805 June 19 Henry Harding (3-31) Jr 150 acres Jefferson County Goose Creek Enter Survey Patent Willis 1 male 3 livestock
1805 June 19 William Harding (3-50) 1 male 2 livestock
1805 June 20 Zephaniah Harding 1 male 8 black 5 livestock
1805 Aug 26 Rebecca Hardin (3-8) widow 2 blacks 1 livestock
1805 Aug 25 Henry Harding (3-16) Sr 100 acres Jefferson County Harrods Creek Enter Survey Patent David Williams
1805 George Harding (3-4) Sr 1 male 3 black 3 livestock

1806 Personal and Land Tax Lists
1806 May 24 George Hardin (3-4) Sr 1 male 3 blacks 4 livestock
1806 May 28 George Harding (3-15) Jr 1 male
1806 July 5 William Harding 1 male 3 livestock
1806 July 5 Zephaniah Harding 1 male 8 blacks 6 livestock
1806 July 31 Henry Harding (3-16) Sr 100 acres Jefferson Co Harrods Creek Enter Survey Patent David Williams
1806 Aug 1 William Harding (3-50) Jr 1 male 3 livestock
1806 Aug 16 Henry Harding (3-31) Jr 130 acres Jefferson County Goose Creek Enter Survey Patent John Willis
1806 Aug 16 Henry Harding (3-31) Jr 100 acres Harrods Creek Enter Survey Patent Samuel Beale
1806 Aug 16 Rebecca Harding (3-8) 2 blacks 1 livestock

1807 Personal and Land Tax Lists
1807 July 15 W William Harding 1 male 1 horse
1807 July 17 Zephaniah Harding 1 male 8 blacks 7 livestock
1807 Aug 4 Henry Harding (3-16) Sr 100 acres Jefferson County Harrods Creek Enter Survey Patent David Williams
1807 Aug 12 Henry Harding (3-31) Jr 10 acres Jefferson County Harrods Creek enter survey patent Samuel Beall
1807 Aug 12 Henry Harding (3-31) Jr 130 acres Jefferson County Goose Creek Enter Survey Patent John Willis
1807 Aug 14 Rebecca Hardin (3-8) 2 blacks 1 livestock
1807 Aug 21 Geo Harding (3-4) Sr 2 males 3 blacks 7 livestock
1807 Aug 21 Geo Harding (3-15) Jr 1 male

1808 Personal and Land Tax Lists
1808 June 4 W William Harding 1 male 2 livestock
1808 June 4 Zephaniah Harding 1 male 8 blacks 7 livestock

Harding Families of the Northern Neck of Virginia

1808 July 27 Henry Harding (3-16) Sr 100 acres Jefferson County Harrods Creek Entry Survey Patent David Williams
1808 July 28 George Harding (3-4) Sr 1 male 3 blacks 4 livestock
1808 July 28 George Harding (3-15) Jr 1 male
1808 Aug 12 William Harding (3-50) 1 male 1 livestock
1808 Aug 13 Rebecca Harding (3-8) widow 2 blacks 2 livestock
1808 Aug 13 Henry Harding (3-31) Jr 100 acres Jefferson County Harrods Creek Entry Survey Patent Samuel Beall
1808 Aug 13 Henry Harding (3-31) Jr 120 acres Jefferson County Goose Creek Entry Survey Patent John Willis

1809 Personal and Land Tax Lists
1809 July 7 George Harding (3-4) Sr 1 male 2 blacks 2 livestock
1809 July 7 George Hardin (3-15) Jr 1 male
1809 July 7 William Hardin (3-50) Jun 1 male 1 livestock
1809 July 12 Henry Hardin (3-31) Jr 100 acres Jefferson County Harrods Creek Entry Survey Patent Samuel Beall 1 male 3 livestock
1809 July 12 Henry Hardin (3-31) Jr 130 acres Jefferson Co Harrods Creek entry Survey Patent John Willis
1809 July 15 Rebecca Hardin (3-8) widow 2 blacks 1 livestock
1809 July 28 Henry Hardin (3-16) Sr. 100 acres Jefferson Co Harrods Creek Entry Survey Patent David Williams
1809 Aug 1 W William Hardin 1 male 1 livestock
1809 Aug 8 Zephaniah Hardin 1 male 10 blacks 8 livestock

1810 Personal and Land Tax Lists
1810 July 23 Henry Hardin (3-31) 100 acres Jefferson County Harrods Creek Entry Survey Patent Samuel Beall 1 male 1 male over 16 2 Blacks 4 livestock
1810 July 23 Henry Hardin (3-31) 130 acres Jefferson County Goose Creek Entry Survey Patent John Willis
1810 July 23 George Hardin (3-15) 1 male over 21 one male over 16 2 blacks 2 livestock
1810 July 23 William Hardin (3-50) 1 male 2 livestock
1810 July 23 Henry Hardin (3-16) Sr. 213 acres Jefferson County Harrods Creek Entry Survey Patent Samuel Beall
1810 July 23 William Hancock (3-30) 150 acres Jefferson County Harrods Creek Entry Survey Patent Samuel Bealle
1810 July 14 Zephaniah Harding 1 male over 21 3 males over 16 10 black 8 livestock

1811 Personal and Land Tax Lists
1811 No Day Henry Harding (3-16) 100 acres no details 1 male 1 black 4 livestock
1811 No Day William Hancock (3-30) 150 acres Harrods Creek Entry Survey Patent E Stevens

1811 No Day George Harding (3-15) 3 over 21 4 livestock
1811 No Date William Hardin (3-50) 1 over 21 3 livestock (all the above together on the list
1811 July 20 Henry Harden (3-31) 130 acres Jefferson County Goose Creek Entry Survey Patent Willis 1 male 2 black 7 livestock
1811 July 20 Henry Hardin (3-31) 100 acres Jefferson County Harrods Creek Entry Survey Patent S Beall
1811 July 20 Zephaniah Harding 1 male 10 black 9 livestock
1811 Sept 12 Richard H Hardin 1 male 3 black 1 livestock

1812 Personal and Land Tax Lists
1812 No Date George Hardin (3-15) 1 male 2 black 4 livestock
1812 No Date Henry Hardin (3-16) 180 acres Jefferson County Harrods Creek Patent etc. D Williams
1812 No Date William Hancock (3-30) 140 acres Patent etc. Edward Stephens 1 male 5 livestock
1812 No Date William Hardin (3-50) 1 male 2 livestock
1812 August 10 Zephaniah Hardin 1 male 10 black 10 livestock
1812 August 8 Henry Hardin (3-31)130 acres Jefferson County Goose Creek Patent etc. Willis 1 male 2 blacks 6 livestock
1812 August 8 Henry Hardin (3-31) 100 acres Harrods Creek Patent etc. Beall
1812 Apr 25 H R Hardin 1 male 3 black 1 tavern

1813 Personal and Land Tax Lists
1813 June 26 Henry Hardin (3-31) 100 acres Jefferson County H Creek Patent etc. Beall 1 over 21, 1 16-21 2 black 6 livestock
1813 June 26 Josiah Harding 1 male 12 black 6 livestock
1813 May 4 Zephaniah Hardin 1 male 9 black 4 livestock
1813 August 1 George Hardin (3-15) 1 male 2 black 9 livestock
1813 August 1 William Hardin (3-50) 44 acres Jefferson County Harrods Creek Patent etc. Leavin Powell
1813 August 1 George Hardon 1 male
1813 August 1 Harry Hardin (3-16) 140 acres Jefferson County Harrods Creek Patent etc David Williams 1 over 21 2 16-26. 4 livestock

1814 Personal and Land Tax Lists
1814 Harry Hardin (3-31) 50 acres Jefferson County Harrods Creek Patent Beall 1 over 21 8 blacks 5 livestock
1814 Rebecca Hardin (3-8) 2 black 1 livestock
1814 William Hardin (3-50) 34 Acres Jefferson County Harrods Creek Patent Samuel Hoke
1814 William Hardin (3-50) 80 acres Jefferson County Harrods Creek 1 male 2 black 9 livestock
1814 Jona Hardin (3-52) 1 male 1 livestock

Harding Families of the Northern Neck of Virginia

1814 Henry Harden (3-16) 180 acres Jefferson County Harrods Creek Patent David Williams 1 male 3 livestock
1814 Josiah Hardin 325 acres Jefferson Co, Ohio River Patent Hugh Mercer 1 male 14 blacks 7 livestock
1814 Zephaniah Hardin 1 male 8 black 10 livestock
1814 Richard H. Hardin dec

1817 Personal and Land Tax Lists
1817 Vachel Harden 7 acres Jefferson County Mill Creek Patent William Pope 1 male 5 livestock *(Descended from Robert Harding of Talbot County Maryland)*
1817 Josiah Hardon 325 acres Floyds Fork Patent John Mercer
1817 Jonathan Hardin (3-52) 95 acres Jefferson County Harrods Creek Patent Moses Kirkpatrick
1817 Henry Hardin (3-16) Jr 213 acres Jefferson County Harrods Creek Patent David Williams
1817 William Hardin Jr no land 1 white
1817 William Hancock (3-30) 135 acres Jefferson County Harrods Creek Patent M Kuykendall
1817 George Hardin no land 1 male
1817 William Hardin (3-50), son of George 200 acres Jefferson County, Harrods Creek Patent M Kuykendall
1817 George Hardin Jun, Henry Hardin (3-16), Henry Fenby?? 250 acres Jefferson County, Harrods Creek Patent N B Beall 1 male 10 blacks 3 livestock
1817 Alexr Harding 1 male 1 black 3 livestock
1817 John Hardin 1 male 2 livestock
1817 Sarah Hardon 5 blacks 6 livestock
1817 William Hardin 591 acres Shelby County Long Run Patent W Chisham 1 male 4 black 1 livestock
1817 William Hardin 59 acres Shelby County Long Run
1817 Richard H. Hardin Town Lots same for 1816

1818 Personal and Land Tax Lists
1818 Josiah Hardin 325 acres Jefferson County Taylor Creek Patent Mercer 1 male 11 black 8 livestock
1818 Vachel Hardin 8 ¼ acres Jefferson County Mill Creek Patent William Pope 1 male 4 livestock (Descended from Robert Harding of Talbot County Maryland)
1818 John Hardin 1 male 4 livestock
1818 George Hardin (3-15) Jr 1 male 1 lot in Transylvania
1818 Jonathan Hardin (3-52) 20 acres Jefferson Co Harrods Creek Patent Kirkpatrick 1 male 2 black 2 livestock
1818 Henry Hardin (3-16) Sr 215 acres Jefferson County Harrods Creek Patent D Williams 1 male 1 black 2 livestock

1818 William Hardin Jr 1 male 1 livestock
1818 George Hardin (3-15) 1 male 2 black 2 livestock
1818 William Hardin (3-50) 177 acres Jefferson County Harrods Creek Patent Kirkpatrick 1 male 2 black 2 livestock
1818 Henry Hardin (3-31) 250 acres Jefferson County Harrods Creek Patent N B Beall 1 male 11 black 4 livestock
1818 William Harding 58 ¾ acres 1 male 2 blacks

1819 Personal and Land Tax Lists
1819 Vachel Hardin 84 ¼ acres Jefferson County Mill Creek Patent Pope 1 male 3 livestock (Descended from Robert Harding of Talbot County Maryland)
1819 Josiah Hardin 320 acres 1 male 10 black 7 livestock
1819 Sarah Hardin 2 black 1 livestock
1819 William Harding 3 acres 1 male 5 livestock
1819 William Hancock (3-30) Sr 135 acres
1819 William Hancock (3-30) No land
1819 George Hardin (3-15) 1 male
1819 James Harden (3-53) 1 male l livestock
1819 Henry Harding (3-31) 200 acres
1819 Jonathan Harding (3-52) 155 acres
1819 William A. Harding (3-51)
1819 Henry Harding (3-16) 250 acres
1819 John Harding 200 acres
1819 Eli Harding
1819 Rebecca Harding (3-8)
1819 William Hardin Town Lots
1819 Richard H Hardin Town lots 4 lots in Portland ½ acre Louisville

1820 Personal and Land Tax Lists
1820 Sarah Hardin
1820 Sigh Hardin 325 acres
1820 William Hardin 300 acres Name might be Hardson
1820 William Hardin Sr 300 acres

1821 Personal and Land Tax Lists
1821 William Hancock (3-30) 135 acres Jefferson County Harrods Creek Patent to Stephens
1821 Jonathan Hardin (3-52) 155 acres Jefferson County Horrods Creek Patent Williams
1821 Geo Hardin (3-15)
1821 William Hardin (3-50) 300 acres Jefferson County Harrods Creek Patent Kirkpatrick
1821 Henry Hardin (3-16) 200 acres Jefferson Co Harrods Creek patent Williams
1821 James Hardin (3-53)

Harding Families of the Northern Neck of Virginia

1821 John Hardin 100 acres Jefferson County Harrods Creek Beall
1821 Henry Hardin (3-68) 50 acres Jefferson Co Harrods Creek Beall
1821 Henry C. Hardin
1821 Ann Hardin 200 acres Jefferson Co. Ohio River
1821 Rebecca Hardin (3-8)
1821 Henry Hardin Jr 130 acres Jefferson County Harrods Creek Beall

1822 Personal and Land Tax Lists
1822 William Hardin two lots in Middletown #53 #54
1822 Vachel Hardin 80 ¼ acres Jefferson co Mill Creek William Pope *(Descended from Robert Harding of Talbot County Maryland)*
1822 William Hardin three lots in Middletown
1822 Vachel Hardin 8 acres Mill creek *(Descended from Robert Harding of Talbot County Maryland)*
1822 Henry Hardin
1822 Albert Hardin 1 lot in Portland
1822 Frances B Harden
1822 Henry Harden (3-68) 50 acres Jefferson Co Harrods Creek Beall
1822 John Harden 202 acres Jefferson Co Floyds Fork Nichols
1822 Henry Hardin (3-31) Sr 100 acres Jefferson Co Harrods Creek Beall
1822 Henry Harden (3-16) Sr 200 acres Jefferson Co Harrods Creek D Wiliamson
1822 James Harden (3-53)
1822 Jonathan Harden (3-52) 150 acres Jefferson Co Harrods Cr Ross

1823 Personal and Land Tax Lists
1823 Henry Hardin (3-68) 50 acres Jefferson Co Goose Creek Beall
1823 Henry Hardin
1823 Henry Hardin (3-16) Sr 200 acres Jefferson Co Harrods Creek
1823 James Hardin (3-53)
1823 William Hardin (3-50) 200 acres Jefferson Co Harrods Creek
1823 Benjamin Hardin (second list)
1823 William Hardin
1823 Albert Harding one lot in Portland
1823 Henry Hardin one lot in Shepherdsville

1824 Personal and Land Tax Lists
1824 Frances M Harden
1824 Henry C Harden
1824 Benjamin Hardin
1824 Vachel Hardin 8 acres Jefferson Co Mill Creek *(Descended from Robert Harding of Talbot County Maryland)*

Livingston Co., Kentucky Records

Will Books

1839 17 September Book B Page 128 Will of Absolom Hardin (5-43). To son Henry Hardin 200 acres where Frithins Say lives, To son George Hardin 100 acres. To son Andrew S. Hardin 50 acres where he lives. Son Hiram Hardin 70 acres he sold to Samuel Hardin. To son Samuel Hardin 50 acres. To son Benoney Hardin 70 acres where I now live. Executors are son Andrew S. Hardin and son Samuel Hardin. Proved 7 April 1851.

Mercer Co., Kentucky Records

Will and Probate Records

1795 08 Oct: Book 1 Page 214 Will of John Berry of Mercer Co., KY Wife Anne 1/3 of property, Daughters Peggy and Rachel when they come of age. Rachel Berry and Robert Mitchael Executors Proved October 1795. Witnesses: Thomas Gash, Richard Berry, Elizabeth Ewing, Polly Berry. Codicil gives use of 50 acres to James B. Sparrow and his wife.

1795 Nov: Book 2 Page 6-7 Inventory of John Berry

1801 26 Oct: Book 2 Page 274 Richard Berry Account of John Berry Decd. Among other items, "To Cash pd the surveyor for dividing the land between the orphan and widow." "To attending the sale after the marriage of the widow."

1797 19 May: Book 2 Page 36 Will of Stephen Ashby He is of Mercer Co., KY. Sons Daniel, Absolom, John, Stephen, and Enos. Daughters Lettice Nealle, Rosy Timmons, Anna Prather. Proved July 1797. Executors, his sons. Witnesses Thomas Adams, John Wagner, Enos Harden Mason Jones.

1797 25 Feb: Book 2 Page 80 Will of Henry Ashby of Mercer Co., KY. To Wife Ellender Ashby, daughter Elizabeth. Children named were sons Argyle Ashby, Robert Ashby, Bounds Ashby, Grandchildren Mary and Mitildy heirs of Stephen Ashby deceased, grandsons Lewis and John Robason, daughter Mary Jones, daughter Nancy Hardin, son George Ashby, daughter Sinoe, daughter Sarah Fields, Executors Mason Jones, and Bounds Ashby. Witnesses Danl Ashby, John Ashby, Stephen Ashby. Proved

Marriage Records

Harding Families of the Northern Neck of Virginia

1786 18 Aug: Book 1 Page 2 John Berry to Anne Mitchell, No Bondsman, James Mitchell, her father, certifies she is over 21

1787 28 Feb: Marriage of Anney Ashby and Thomas Prather, Bond Barney Stagner, Bride's consent Stephen Ashby, Witness Absalom Ashby

1787 07 September Marriage of George Timmons and Rose Ashby, bond Daniel Ashby Consent for bride Stephen Ashby

1789 23 Jun: Marriage of Daniel Ashby and Mary ? Bond Peter Casey

1789 (21 Dec: Filed) Elizabeth Berry to Wiley Brassfield, Bond Thomas Berry Jr, Father Thomas Berry, Witness Sarah Harris and John Berry

1790 09 Jan: (Filed) Nancy Berry to Daniel McGary Bond John Berry, Groom Consent Hugh McGary, Teste Robert McGary and John Ray

1792 15 Jun: Marriage of Henry Hardin (5-55) and Mary Davis (5-55) Bond: James Davis. Consent: Edward Davis Mark Hardin (5-13) and Ann Hartley

1793 30 Jan: Marriage of Enos Hardin (4-7) and Martha Ann Ashby. Bond by Enos Hardin (4-7) and George Ashby (also certified bride over 21)

1794 20 Feb: Book 1-24 Reuben Berry to Syner Fetheringille. Bond: Daniel Ashby

1794 22 Oct: Book 1-32 Richard Berry to Polly Ewing. Archibald Bilba certifies bride over 21

1796 30 Mar: Book 1 Page 42 Anne Berry to Jacob Durham Bond: Robert Mitchell

1808 Book 2-224 William Berry to Nancy Hale

1795 H C Harding

1795 14 Aug: Marriage of James Hardin (4-8) and Hanna Berry (4-8) (Reuben Berry and Sinai Ashby) Bond: Reuben Berry

1796 10 Aug: Marriage of Nicholas Harding and Marim Ashby Bond John Resley, Bride's father George Ashby, Test: Margaret Resley

1797 09 Jan: Marriage of Bounds Ashby and Elizabeth Cardwell. Bond Vincent Fuget, Bride's father John Cardwell Note in margin: Went to Hopkins Co with his mother, brothers etc.

1797 10 Apr: Page 4 Marriage of Polly Hardin (3-21) and John Ashby Bond Nicholas Hardin (3-6)

1797 27 May: Marriage of Joseph Warden and Sarah Ashby Bond George Ashby, Father Jesse Ashby

1798 07 Feb: Marriage of Jesse Ashby and Sally Lucas Bond Lawrence Lowe, bride's father Abraham Lucas

1798 30 Jun: Marriage of Absalom Ashby and Jenny Sheumate, Bond Henry Ashby also certified bride is 21

1800 18 Feb: Marriage of Hannah Ashby and Benjamin Shumate, Bond Jesse Ashby, Father George Ashby, Witness Henry Ashby

1801 05 Sep: Marriage of Peggy Ashby and John Colvin, Bond John Ashby

1804 27 Nov: Page 11 Marriage of Rebecca Hardin (4-27) and Jeremiah Bunnel (4-27), Bond by Samuel B. Robertson. (Her death record says her parents were Ennis (4-7) and Sophia Hardin (4-7) and she was born in Maryland. Died 7 Jan 1856 Hart Co KY. Age 70 years 7 months, born about 1785. She is not among the heirs of Enos Hardin (4-7), who died in 1826 in Henry Co., Kentucky)

1805 27 Feb Marriage of Anne Ashby and Thomas Anderson. Bond Henry Ashby

1806 30 Jun: marriage of Martin Hardin (5-106) and Rosannah Fisher (parents Martin Hardin (5-29) and Letitia Stull) Bond Elijah Fisher who certifies bride over 21

1806 14 Oct: Marriage of Mark Hardin (5-88) and Mary Adair (5-88) Parents John Hardin (5-27) and Jane Davies (5-27) (Bond John L. Bridges)

Personal Property Tax Lists

1794 List 1 George Ashby
1794 List 1 Silas Ashby
1794 List 1 John Berry
1794 List 2 Argile Ashby
1794 List 2 Daniel Ashby
1794 List 2 George Ashby
1794 List 2 Henry Ashby
1794 List 2 Jesse Ashby
1794 List 2 John Ashby
1794 List 2 Nicholas Hardin (0 over 21 1 16-21) 4 Slaves 3 Horses

1795 Nicholas Nardin (2 over 21)
1795 Jesse Ashby
1795 Henry Ashby
1795 Stephen Ashby
1795 George Ashby
1795 Hanry Ashby
1795 Stephen Ashby
1795 Daniel Ashby
1795 Peter Ashby
1795 John Ashby

1796 Nicholas Hardin No land 1 over 21

Nelson Co., Kentucky Records

Will and Probate Records

1788 04 Jun: Will of John Hardin (5-2) of Nelson Co., Kentucky. Mentions sons John (5-12), Mark (5-13), William(5-15) and Benjamin Hardin (5-14), daughters Abigail Lynch (5-17), Mary Thomas (5-18), Catherine Bennett (5-119), Elizabeth Hardin (5-20), Susannah Walker (5-21). Polly Hardin the daughter of Margaret Huby, grandson Henry Hardin, son of John, granddaughter Katy Thomas, granddaughter Cassandra Hardin. Executors William Hardin and Benjamin Hardin. Proved 13 October 1789. (Note: This is one of the sons of Mark Hardin (5-1) and Mary (MNU) (5-1)

1790 31 Mar: Will of Mark Hardin (5-13) of Nelson Co., Kentucky Mentions wife Ann (5-13), sons Henry (5-55), John (5-56), Mark (5-59), Benjamin (5-60), gives them "land I live on" Daughters Mary (5-61), Lydia (5-62), and Sarah (5-63). Daughter Catherine Hallett (5-57), Daughter Hannah Stalcup (5-58), Daughter Ann (5-54). Witnesses Benjamin and John Hardin. Proved 8 May 1792.

Personal Property Tax Lists

1785 Personal Property Tax lists
Stephen Harden
John Harden Sr. (5-2)
Hector Hardin (5-50)
William Harden (5-44)

1786 Personal Property Tax Lists
---- Harden 80 years of age (5-2)
John Harding (5-12)
Mark Hardin (5-13)
John Hardin

1787 Personal Property Tax Lists
William Hardin (5-44)

1788 Personal Property Tax Lists
William Hardin (5-44)
Stephen Harding

Oldham Co., Kentucky Records

Formed 1823 from Jefferson, Shelby, Henry Counties, Kentucky

Deed Records

1826 04 Apr: Book A Page 229 Eliab White and Julia his wife to Henry Hardin (3-16) both of Oldham County KY 81 ½ acres HC $600 surveyed to Samuel Beall on South Harrods Creek

NOTE: The family in next two deeds originated in Montgomery Co., Maryland and has no connection with any of the families discussed in this book

1827 01 Dec: Book A Page 431 Joshua G. Barclay and Sarah his wife to of Louisville to William N. Harding and Josiah Harding and Josiah H Wheeler. $500 75 A on Taylors Creek. Land was devised by Josiah Hardin to Josiah H Wheeler by will dated 2 May 1820 in Jefferson Co, Land went ot Josiah Harding's wife Ann and to his sister Deborah Wheeler

1827 29 Dec: Book A Page 432 Same group as above William N Harding, Josiah Harding, and Josiah H Wheeler to Joshua D Barclay 60 acres on Taylor's creek

1830 16 Jan: Book B Page 167 Henry Harding (3-16) and Mary Harding of Oldham County to William Harding of same county. $525 35 acres. Part of 100 acres bought of John Gwathmey. Bounded by Henry Harding, Jonathan, and William Harding. Witnesses Jonathan Harding, Warner Harding, Rowley Harding

1831 04 Jan: Book B Page 217 Jonathan Harding (3-52) from William Ingram 149 ½ acres

1833 06 Jul: Book C Page 121 Norbonne B Beale of the first part, Norbonne A Galt and Elizabeth his wife of the second part, and Levi Taylor and Samuel Gwathney trustees and executors of Matilda A. Maupin decd of the third part. and Wlliam J Hardin (3-72) of the fourth part. Whereas 400 acres on South Fork of Harrods patented to Samuel Beall, since deceased, On 15 April 1816, Norborne Beall, William Galt and Richard Maupin sold 286 acres to one Henry Hardin (3-31), who sold 87 acres to William B. Russell, who sold them to Noah Dorsey, who sold them to John Hardin (3-67). Henry Hardin made payments in 1816, 1818, and 1823, then departed this life. John Hardin paid $51.71 on 13 February 1824, leaving a balance due which William J Hardin (3-72) agreed to pay for the heirs of his father Henry Hardin dec for 200 acres and also to purchase 52 acres for himself in addition, John Hardin (3-67) administered his estate, leaving a debt which William J Hardin (3-72), son of Henry Hardin (3-31) has agreed to pay.

Harding Families of the Northern Neck of Virginia

1834 05 May: Book C Page 209 Henry Hardin (3-68): and Polly his wife to William Yager, both of Oldham Co., KY. $193.75 19 acres on Curry's Fork of Floyd's fork.

1834 21 Feb: Book C Page 213 Jonathan Hardin (3-52) and Lucy his wife to William A. Hardin (3-51), both of Oldham Co., KY 165 acres $1. Land bounded by Henry Netherton and Henry Hardin and William Hardin.

1834 26 Sep: Book C Page 258-259 Hanson &C to William N. Harding 60 acres

1834 30 Oct: Book C Page 280 William N Harding to Wesley Schrader 101 acres

1835 01 Aug: Book C Page 419 Henry Hardin (3-68) and wife Mary of Oldham County to Henry N. Brown of Jefferson County KY. $850 175 acres on Curry's Fork of Floyd's Fork.

1836 16 Feb: Book C Page 453 Allen Yewell to William A Hardin (3-51) both of Oldham County KY.$100 on Harrods Creek 1 acre by Lawrence O. Hickman's blacksmith shop.

1836 13 Feb: Book 6 Page 505 William Trigg of Jefferson County KY to William A. Hardin (3-51) of Oldham County KY $400 All interest in the estate of his father Thomas Trigg decd in the possession of his mother Mary Trigg on waters of Pond Creek consisting of land negroes and livestock.

1836 12 May: Book C Page 531 William J Hardin (3-72) and Emily his wife of Oldham Co., KY to John Hardin (3-67) of Oldham Co KY $30 100 acres from corner of John Hardin down Woodson's line

1836 17 May: Book C Page 534 William J Hardin (3-72) and Emily his wife to Calvin E. Stoddard, both of Oldham County KY. $207. Land on Horrod's Creek, part of a tract purchased by W J Hardin of N Bealle and sold to James A Hardin under certain conditions fully complied with. Borders CE Stoddard No acreage given.

1836 30 Mar: Book C Page 537 William J Hardin (3-72) and Emily his wife to Calvin E. Stoddard, both of Oldham County KY, For $1000. Land on waters of South Harrod's Creek, bounded by Jacob Shrader, and William J Hardin and John Hardin 100 acres

1836 17 May: Book C Page 544 Henry Hardin (3-68) and Mary his wife to Charity Boulware both of Oldham County KY. $20 2 acres on road of Flat Rock.

1836 05 Apr: Book C Page 545 Rosanna Smith to William Hardin (3-72), both of Oldham County KY, $12.50 a lot in Rollington.

1836 15 Aug: Book C Page 618 William N Hardin of Shelby Co KY to James Duerson of Oldham Co Kentucky 61 acres. $600 bounded by Henry Schrader.

Kentucky County Records

1836 18 Jul: Book C Page 625 Sheriff ordered to find 20 inhabitants of Oldham County not related to Henry Hardin Jr, Sarah Ann Hardin, J W. Hardin, Mary J Hardin, Amanda Hardin, Oldham Hardin, America Hardin and Emaline F Hardin, infant children and heirs of John Hardin (3-67) decd and Mrs. Nancy Hardin, widow of the said John Hardin decd.to decided from a survey of the construction of the Ohio and Lexington Railroad to determine damages from construction of the railroad. In court Paschal Wilhoite adm of John Harding's estate and railroad agents. Jury set damages at $62.75. Parcel to be used for railroad is bounded by Nancy Hardin, John Connier and Nathaniel Brown.

1837 29 Apr: Book D Page 98 William A. Harding (3-51) and Sarah his wife to Henry Netherton all of Oldham County $333 Land on Harrods Creek 10 acres. Begin at David Wilhoit's settlement.

1837 29 Apr: Book D Page 99 William Harding (3-50) and Rhoda Harding (3-50) his wife to Henry Netherton both of Oldham County KY $800 Land on Harrods Creek 106 ½ acres

1837 29 Apr: Book D Page 101 Henry Netherton and Nancy his wife to William A. Harding (3-51) $45.50 land on Harrods Creek on the corner of the land purchased by Jonathan Harding and William A. Harding from the heirs of John Wilhoyte total of five acres.

1836 18 Nov: Book D Page 217 William J Hardin (3-72) and Emily his wife to William K Allen both of Oldham County, $30. Lot in the town of Rollington. ¼ acre.

1838 11 Jun: Book D Page 289 William A. Hardin (3-51) of Oldham Co KY to John B. Rankin (3-83) of same. $120 land on Harrods Creek NE of William A Hickman blacksmith shop, one acre of land. No wife named.

1834 30 Oct: Book D Page 339 Jacob Souther and Katherine his wife of Oldham County to Jonathan Hardin (3-52) $2068 land on Waters of Harrods Creek. Start at corner of Isaac Smith to Reuben Ross corner, 145 acres.

1841 10 May: Book E page 117 John Hardin (3-106) of Oldham County KY to James Antle of same county. Payoff of mortgage from Antle to Hardin on personal property, Hardin releases all interest in the property.

1841 10 May: Book E 130 John Hardin (3-106) to James Antel satisfaction of debt.

1839 01 Oct: Book E Page 138 Henry Hardin (3-68) and Mary his wife of Oldham County KY to Joseph M Beard of Fayette County KY $5400 263 acres on Floyd's Creek, bounded by John Connyers, William Arrowsmith and Hardin's spring.

1843 13 Mar: Book E Page 411 Rowley Hardin (3-55) to Warner Hardin (3-55) both of Oldham County KY 88 acres $1 on Harrods Creek bound by Robert W Lewis, Henry Netherton, William A. Hardin.

1843 13 Mar: Book E. Page 413 Warner Hardin (3-56) and Catharine Ann his wife of Oldham County KY to Rowla Hardin (3-55) of same. $1 Land on Harrods Creek bounded by A Carpenter, Christian Sears, W. Hardin Warner Hardin William A Hardin, Jonathan Hardin 88 acres

1843 05 Apr: Book E Page 484 Rowley Hardin (3-55) to Warner A Hardin (3-56) both of Oldham Co KY 90 acres $2500 land on Harrods Creek. Bounded by William A Hardin, Jonathan Hardin, Abel Carpenter, Warner A Hardin 90 88/100 acres.

1843 08 Apr: Book F 9 William A. Hardin (3-51) and Sarah his wife to John B. Rankin (3-83) all of Oldham County Ky 30 acres on Harrods Creek $900 Borders on Mr Netherton. Jonathan Hardin certifies that Sarah Hardin appeared and consented to deed.

1845 25 Jul: Book F Page 120 John Hardin (3-67) Division of Land 192 acres divided to heirs. To Nancy Hardin as dower 60 acres, Lot 1, 20 acres to Abner Hardin, infant heir of Henry Hardin decd, an heir of John Hardin dec. Lot #2 28 ½ acres to John Hardin. Lot #3 26 acres to Amanda Brown. Lot #4 24 acres to Sarah Ann Buckner Late Sarah Ann Hardin. Lot #5 24 acres to Katherine Brown, late Katherine Hardin.

1846 16 Mar: Book F Page 166 John F Locke of Oldham County KY to William A. Hardin (3-51) one negro boy named Jack and girl named Jack. $550 to pay off debt to Samuel Reedy

1846 13 Dec: Book F Page 262 Lewis Hardin (3-84) from James Clore and Eliza his wife and Jesse Clore, all of Oldham County. 206 acres

1847 17 Feb: Book F Page 310 William Hardin (3-50) and Rhoda Harding (3-50) his wife to Jesse Y Clore 102 ¼ acres on South Harrods Creek. for $2,781

1848 05 Jul: Book F Page 497 Presley N. Yager to Warner Hardin (3-56), both of Oldham Co KY for $123.75 6 ¾ acres and 20 poles, part of the home farm of Christian Sears decd.

1848 12 Dec: Book G Page 26 William Hardin (3-50) Sr (hard to read) and Jesse Clore, both of Oldham Co., KY to Philip PCS Barbour of same county. 202 1/3 acres on Harrods Creek, 101 acres of which on the north end of the tract recently acceded to Jesse Clore. For $6000. Signed William Hardin (3-50), Rhoda Harding (3-50), Jesse Y, Clore, Mildred A Clore. Witnesses George Harbold, John B. Rankin (3-83).

1851 04 Feb: Book G Page 471 John W. Hardin (3-106) and Azbarene Hardin his wife of Jefferson Co., Kentucky to William Lee White of the same county.

For $493.50 two tracts in Oldham County. First is 28 ½ acres, being that portion of the farm of John Hardin decd assigned by the County Commissioners to the said John W. Hardin on the line of the dower right. Second part being one fifth of the undivided part of said Dower, about 60 acres.

1851 14 Oct: Book G Page 596 Abram Clore and Caroline G. Clore his wife of Oldham County KY to Warner Hardin (3-56) of same place. For $3300 all interest we have in a parcel on Harrods Creek. Beginning point at land at corner of P. N. Yager. 115 acres.

Personal Property tax lists

1825 Personal Property Tax Lists
1825 J (3-52) & W (3-50) Harding 155 acres Oldham Co Harrods Creek 2 over 21
1825 William Hancock (3-30) 100 acres Harrods Creek
1825 Henry Harding (3-16) 210 acres Harrods Creek Patent Williams
1825 James Harding (3-53) no land
1825 William Harding 203 acres Harrods Creek Patent Kirkpatrick
1825 Henry Harding (3-68) Jr 50 acres Harrods Creek Patent Beall
1825 John Hardin (3-67) 100 acres Curry Fork Patent Norbonne Beall
1825 Mary Hardin (3-31) 150 acres Curry Fork Patent N Beall

1826 Personal Property Tax Lists
1826 Henry Harding (3-68) 50 acres Harrods Creek Patent S Beall
1826 John Harding (3-67) 181 acres Harrods Creek S Beall
1826 Mrs. Polly Harding (3-31) 157 acres Harrods Creek Patent S Beall
1826 Henry Hardin (3-16) 200 acres Harrods Creek Patent D Williams
1826 Jona (3-52) and William Hardin (3-50) 190 acres Harrods Creek D Williams and
1826 James Hardin (3-53) no land

1827 Personal Property Tax Lists
1827 Henry Hardin (3-16) 180 acres Harrods Creek Entered Williams Survey Hite
1827 Rowly Harden (3-55) No land
1827 James Harden (3-53) no land
1827 William Hardin (3-50) and Jonathan Hardin (3-52) 190 acres survey Williams
1827 William Hardin 203 acres
1827 Miss Polly Harding (3-31) 157 acres Harrods Creek entered Beall
1827 Henry Harding (3-68) 120 acres Harrods Creek Beall
1827 John Harding (3-67) 180 acres Harrods Creek Beall

1828 Personal Property Tax Lists
1828 Warner Harding (3-56) no land

1828 Roley A Harding (3-55) no land
1828 Henry Harding Senr (3-16) 200 acres Harrods Creek Williams
1828 Jonathan Harding (3-52) and William Harding (3-50) 150 acres Harrods Creek Williams
1828 William Harding Senr 203 acres Harrods Creek Kirkpatrick
1828 Isaac Harding 60 acres Taylors Creek
1828 Mary Hardin (3-31) 150 acres Beall
1828 William Hardin no land
1828 Henry Hardin (3-68) 130 acres Harrods Creek Beall

Will and Probate Records

1829 12 Nov: Book 1 Page 167 Will of Henry Harding (3:16) of Oldham County KY. To wife Polly Hardin all of estate. Two sons Jonathan (3-52) and William (3-51) to be executors of the will. At death of wife, equally divide estate between my six eldest children: Jonathan Hardin (3-52), William Hardin (3-51), James A. Hardin (3-53), Katharine Souther (3-54), Rowley Hardin (3-55), Warner Hardin (3-56). Tract of land to Rowley and Warner Hardin. Sums of money to pay other children: $500 to son Butlar Hardin (3-57). Eldest four children Jonathan Hardin, William Hardin, James A. Hardin, Katherine Souther $300 each. To son James A. Hardin negro girl Margaret. To son Butler Hardin negro woman. Bedding to my four sons James A Hardin, Rowley Hardin, Warner Hardin and Butlar Hardin. William Hardin and Abram H. Keller to be guardian of son Butlar Hardin. Proved 19 July 1830.

1835 25 Nov: Book Page 215 John Hardin dec Inventory, Value $300

1835 04 Dec: Book 2 Page 84 John Hardin Sale. Most items sold to Ann Hardin. By Paschal Wilhoit and John Hardin Administrators

1843 05 Apr: Book 2 Page 405 Will of Rowley Hardin (3-55). William A. Hardin Trustee. $250 to school district to buy a library, globes, surveying instruments to be selected by Jonathan Hardin (3-52), William A. Hardin (3-51) and John S. Million. Witnesses John S. Million, William T Hardin. Proved 15 May 1843.

1850 26 Oct: Book 3 Page 348, 349, 496 Estate of Nancy Hardin. Sale bill: Among purchasers John Hardin. Note on John Hardin, John W. Hardin. Distribution: to Hiram Ritter guardian for Abner Hardin $340, to E. A. Brukner guardian for John B and Mary Jane Brukner, To John W. Hardin for papers, Balance to John W. Hardin. More details in the books.

1867 22 May: Book 5 Page 288 Will of Jonathan Harding (3-52). To wife Lucy Harding (3-52), daughter Eleanor Ann Clore wife of Allen Clore, son William Temple Harding, daughter Elizabeth Yager wife of A. C. Yager, Mary Jane

Yager, wife of P. N> Yager, granddaughter Elizabeth Onorah Yager, son A. H. Harding, son John Warner Harding, Susan Frances Yager, second wife of P. N. Yager. William Temple Harding and P. N. Yager executors. Proved April 1869.

Marriage Records

1824 10 Mar: Marriage bonds: William Hardin (3-51) married Sarah Trigg (3-51)

1825 22 Sep: William H. Brown (3-71) married Wilmouth Hardin (3-71). Mrs. Mary Hardin her mother gave consent her father being dead. Henry Hardin bond

1826 22 Dec: Marriage Bonds: William Harding (3-72) married Emily Brown (3-72), daughter of Nathan Brown. Bond was Henry Hardin and William Hardin

1833 28 Feb: Eleanor Ann Hardin (3-93) married Allen Clore

1835 05 Jun: Amanda Hardin (3-76) m Gipson Wilhoit. Mother Mary Hardin, Witness Henry Hardin, James A Hardin, Hyrum Ritter

1836 20 Oct: Catharine Harding (3-94) married Richard Clore Her father Jonathan Harding consented

1836 28 Nov: bond Richard Jobe and Gabriel Wilhite to ensure marriage of Richard Jobe (3-75) and Rebecca Hardin (3-75), daughter of Mary Hardin

1837 Jan: Marriage Bonds: John B. Rankin (3-83) married Lucy Hardin (3-83). Bond John B. Rankin and Jonathan Hardin. She is daughter of William Hardin.

1837 20 Feb: Simeon Wilhite and Richard Jobe bond for Simeon Wilhite to marry Mildred Ann Hardin (3-77) with consent of her guardian Henry Hardin and Mary Hardin.

1838 21 Mar: Marriage Bonds: Warner Hardin (3-56) married Catherine Ann Hitt (3-56)

1839 21 Mar: Sarah Ann Hardin (3-105) married Edmund A. Buckner

1840 31 Mar: Marriage Bonds: Mary Ann Hardin (3-87), daughter of William Hardin (3-50) of Oldham County, married Hartwell Pate (3-87). Bond Hartwell Pate and J R Hardin

1840 04 May: Elizabeth Hardin (3-96) daughter of Jonathan Hardin married Abraham C. Yager bond William F Hardin

1840 20 Aug: Lewis Hardin (3-84) married Margaret Clore, infant ward of Willis Snyder

1840 25 Oct: Bond for marriage of Henry Harden (3-104) and Emily Ritter, daughter of John Ritter.

1840 17 Dec: Marriage Bonds. John W. Hardin (3-106) married Asbrene Antle, daughter of James Antle

1841 07 Aug: Peter Hardin married Rachel B Pennington

1842 31 Mar: Marriage Bonds Emelin Hardin (3-89), daughter of William Hardin married Lawrence Barrickman (3-89). Bond Lawrence Barrickman and Owen Hardin

1843 23 Nov: Mary Jane Harding (3-97) married P N Yager

1844 03 Oct: Catherine D. Hardin (3-112) license to marry Thomas E. Brown

1845 Nov: Marriage Permission Ann Sanderson give permission for John Hardin to marry her daughter Mary Susannah Drady. Stepdaughter of James Sanders

1845 28 Dec: John Hardin married Susanna Drady

1846 06 Feb: Amanda Hardin (3-108) married David Flint. Her age proven by Thomas C. Brown.

1847 05 Apr: Marriage Bonds Rebecca Jane Hardin (3-88), of Oldham Co., Kentucky, daughter of William Hardin, married Peter Mitchell (3-88). Bond Peter Mitchell and Presley Hardin, brother of Rebecca Jane Hardin.

1852 03 Feb: Mrs. Emily Hardin (3-104) married James A Featheringill Bond Hiram Ritter

1853 24 Oct: Jack Hardin age 35 of Washington Co KY married Nannie Harris age 19 born Washington County KY

1854 29 Nov: Abraham H Hardin (3-98) married Louisa F. Yager daughter of Henry C. Yager

Federal Census Records

1830 Federal Census Oldham County, Kentucky
Page 262 Archibald Harding 000001 0000100001
Page 269 John Harding (3-67) 021001 0001
Page 269 William Harding (3-72) 10001 0001
Page 271 Henry Harding (3-68) 01001 11001
Page 272 Laurence Clore 01110001 1010101
Page 272 Evan Wilhoite 01020101 0111101
Page 272 Lewis Wilhoite 000000001 0001100101
Page 272 William Hardin (3-50) 0022001 1121001 (listed twice)
Page 272 Elijah Clore 00211001 01011
Page 273 James Harding (3-53) 000031 0000001
Page 274 William A. Harding (3-51) 200001 10001

Kentucky County Records

Page 274 Zechariah Willhoite 100001 01001
Page 274 Hanson Harding 10001 20001
Page 275 Henry Netherton (3-18) 000100001 000010001
Page 275 Jonathan Harding (3-52) 101001 111101
Page 279 Mary Harding (3-16) 0001 01210001
Page 282 William Harding (3-50) 0022001 1210101 (listed twice)

1840 Federal Census Oldham County, Kentucky
Page 158 William Hardin (3-50) 01003001 0120001
Page 158 William A. Hardin (3-51)0011101 010001
Page 158 Jonath Hardin (3-52) 0110101 011000100001
Page 158 Warner Hardin (3-56) 100001 00001
Page 158 Mary Harding (3-16) 000001 0000000001
Page 170 Nancy Hardin (3-67) 0021 011201

1850 Census Division 1 Odham County, Kentucky Page 50

Res	Fam	Name	Age	Sex	Occupation	Birthplace
150	156	Emily Hardin	32	F	(3-104)	Kentucky
150	156	Abner Hardin	8	M	(3-136)	Kentucky
245	256	Lawrence Barrickman	33	M	Farmer (3-89)	Kentucky
245	256	Emily Barrickman	25	F		Kentucky
245	256	William J Barrickman	7	M		Kentucky
245	256	Thomas H Barrickman	5	M		Kentucky
245	256	Mildred Barrickman	3	F		Kentucky
245	256	Louisa Barrickman	2	F		Kentucky
245	256	John R Barrickman	6m	M		Kentucky
255	266	Lewis Hardin	39	M	(3-84) Farmr	Kentucky
255	266	Margaret Harding	24	F		Kentucky
255	266	Mary F Harding	8	F		Kentucky
255	266	W. R. Harding	7	M		Kentucky
255	266	Sarah Hardin	5	F		Kentucky
255	266	Mildred Harding	3m	F		Kentucky
258	269	Jona Hardin	58	M	Farmer (3-52)	Virginia
258	269	Lucy Hardin	57	F		Virginia
258	269	Abn Hardin	21	M	Farmer	Kentucky
258	269	John Harding	18	M		Kentucky
258	269	Susan Harding	16	F		Kentucky
304	316	David Flint	39	M	Farmer	Kentucky
304	316	Amanda Flint	39	F	(3-108)	Kentucky
304	316	John Flint	4	M		Kentucky
304	316	Henry Flint	3	M		Kentucky
304	316	Cordelia Flint	1	F		Kentucky
304	316	Nancy Hardin	53	F		Kentucky
354	366	William A. Hardin	56	M	Farmer (3-51)	Virgnia

354	366	Sarah Hardin	49	F			Kentucky
354	366	Albert Harding	20	M	Farmer		Kentucky
354	366	Mary Trigg	74	F			Virginia
354	366	Samuel Frederick	60	M	Farmer		Virginia
355	367	Evan M. Netherton	32	M	Farmer		Kentucky
355	367	Nancy Netherton	56	F			Kentucky
355	367	Geo Hardin	58	M	Laborer		Virginia
368	368	John Rankin	41	M	Farmer		Ohio
368	368	Lucy Rankin	41	F			Kentucky
368	368	Robert Rankin	25	M	Carpenter		Kentucky
368	368	John Rose	23	M	Capenter		Kentucky
368	368	William Coons	21	M	Carpenter		Kentucky
370	382	Warner Hardin	44	M	Farmer (3-56)		Kentucky
370	382	Catharine Hardin	32	F			Kentucky
370	382	Geo Hardin	12	M			Kentucky
370	382	Jane B. Hardin	9	F			Kentucky

1860 Census, Odham County, Kentucky Page 104

Res	Fam	Name	Age	Sex	Occupation	Birthplace
760	756	John B. Rankin	51	M	Farmer	Ohio
760	756	Lucy Rankin	51	F		Kentucky

1870 Census Brownsboro, Odham County, Kentucky Page 8

Res	Fam	Name	Age	Sex	Occupation	Birthplace
62	62	John B. Rankin	61	M	Farmer	Ohio
62	62	Lucy Rankin	61	F		Kentucky
62	62	Ann E. Ward	8	F		Kentucky

Owen Co., Kentucky Records

United States Census Records

1820 Federal Census Owen Co., Kentucky
Page 100 Lewis Hardin (4-34) 000100 00100
Page 104 Benjamin Hardin (4-9) 120001 10001
Page 105 James Hardin (4-8) 210001 02100
Page 106 George Hardin (4-28) 100300 01000

1830 Federal Census Owen Co., Kentucky
Page 314 Lewis Hardin (4-34) 010001 300001

Kentucky County Records

Page 320 Ennis Hardin (4-29) 100210 10001
Page 328 Absalom Hardin (4-36) 11000 10100
Page 328 James Hardin (4-8) 001110001 (60-70)
Page 322 Jacob Kelley (4-46) 20101 00011

1840 Federal Census Owen Co., Kentucky
Page 205 Lewis Hardin (4-34) 101001 0220001
Page 208 Thomas Hardin (4-30) 112001 21001
Page 208 James Hardin (4-8) 2010210001 (70-80) 10001
Page 211 Enos Hardin (4-29) 101001 121001

1850 Census District 1 Owen County, Kentucky Page 76

Res	Fam	Name	Age	Sex	Occupation	Birthplace
381	381	Enos Hardin Sen	53	M	Farmer	Kentucky
381	381	Elizabeth Hardin	50	F		Kentucky
381	381	Amanda Ann Hardin	18	F		Kentucky
381	381	George Hardin	12	M		Kentucky
381	381	Sally Ann Hardin	12	F		Kentucky
381	381	America Hardin	4	F		Kentucky
381	381	Enos Hardin	7	M		Kentucky

1850 Census District 1 Owen County, Kentucky Page 71

Res	Fam	Name	Age	Sex	Occupation	Birthplace
536	536	Samuel Sanders	45	M	Farmer	Kentucky
536	536	Baylis G. Hardin	33	M	Laborer	Kentucky
536	536	Livingston Hardin	24	M	Laborer	Kentucky

1850 Census District 1 Owen County, Kentucky Page 72

Res	Fam	Name	Age	Sex	Occupation	Birthplace
548	548	Enos Hardin Jr.	26	M	Farmer	Kentucky
548	548	Eliza Hardin	20	F	Laborer	Kentucky
548	548	Alonzo Hardin	1	M		Kentucky

1850 Census District 1, Owen County, Kentucky Page 72

Res	Fam	Name	Age	Sex	Occupation	Birthplace
549	549	Thomas Hardin	49	M	Farmer	Kentucky
549	549	Rachael Hardin	43	F	(4-30)	Kentucky
549	549	George W. Hardin	19	M	Laborer	Kentucky
549	549	Thomas Hardin	17	M	Laborer	Kentucky
549	549	Martha Hardin	15	F		Kentucky
549	549	Adaline Hardin	13	F		Kentucky
549	549	William Hardin	7	M		Kentucky
549	549	Alice Hardin	4	F		Kentucky

1850 Census District 1 Owen County, Kentucky Page 83

Res	Fam	Name	Age	Sex	Occupation	Birthplace
642	642	Edward C. Hardin	57	M	Laborer	Kentucky
642	642	Eliza O Hardin	36	F		Kentucky
642	642	Mary F. Hardin	14	F		Kentucky
642	642	George A Hardin	10	M		Kentucky
642	642	Nancy J. Hardin	8	F		Kentucky

Personal Property Tax Books

1819 Personal Property Tax Lists
Innis Hardin (4-29) No Land
William Hardin No Land
James Hardin (4-8) 100 acres Owen Co. Entered William Boyd
Lewis Hardin (4-34) No Land
George Hardin (4-28) No Land
Evangelist Hardin (4-6) 200 Acres Owen Co Entered to B Ashby
Evangelist Hardin (4-6) 50 Acres Henry Co Entered to Lowhead

1820 Personal Property Tax Lists
George Hardin (4-28) 50 acres on Ky River Henty Co
Enos Hardin (4-29) No Land
Benjamin Hardin (4-9) 200 acres on Ky River Owen Co Entered to F Berry
Benjamin Hardin (4-9) 50 acres on Ky River Henry Co Entered to Loyhead
James Hardin (4-8) 100 acres on Cedar River Owen)
Lewis Hardin (4-34) No Land

1821 Personal Property Tax Lists
Ennis Hardin (4-29) No Land
William Hardin 200 acres on Ky River Owen Co 2 over 21 Entered Ashly
Lewis Hardin (4-34) No Land
James Hardin (4-8) 100 acres on Cedar River Owen Co Entered to Boyd
George Hardin (4-28) 600 acres on Ky River Henry Co

1822 Personal Property Tax Lists
William Hardin 200 acres Owen Co Patent to Ashby
Ennis Hardin **(4-29)** 2347 acres on Ky River Owen Co Patent Ashby
Ennis Hardin (4-29) 1443 acres Franklin Co Ky River Patent Ashby
Ennis Hardin (4-29) 600 acres Henry Co Patent Lauhead
George Hardin (4-28) 550 acres Owen Co Patent Berry
Lewis Hardin (4-34) No Land
James Hardin (4-8) 100 acres on Elkhorn Owen Co

1823 Personal Property Tax Lists
Ennis Hardin (4-29) 234 acres Owen Co Ky River Patent Ashby
Ennis Hardin (4-29) 144 acres Franklin Co Patent Ashby
Ennis Hardin (4-29) 600 acres Henry Co Patent Laufhead
Lewis Hardin (4-34) No Land
George Hardin (4-28) 215 acres Owen Co Patent Berry
George Hardin (4-28) 100 acres Owen Co
Thomas Hardin (4-30) 900 acres on Ky River Owen Co Patent Berry
James Hardin (4-8) 100 acres Owen Co on Cedar River

1824 Personal Property Tax Lists
Lewis Hardin (4-34) No Land
James Hardin (4-8) 100 Acres Cedar River Owen Co
Thomas Hardin (4-30) 500 acres on Ky River Owen Co Entered Francis Berry
George Hardin (4-28) 250 acres Ky Rover Owen Co Entered Francis Berry
George Hardin (4-28) 100 acres Owen Co Green River Entered John Ashby
Eanos Hardin (4-29) 218 acres Ky River Owen Co Entered Francis Berry
Eanos Hardin (4-29) 234 acres Cedar River Owen Co Entered Robert Ashby
James Hardin (4-8) Senr 100 acres Cedar River Entered JP Crittenden
Absolom Hardin (4-36) No Land

1825 Personal Property Tax Lists
Lewis Hardin (4-34) No Land
Thomas Hardin (4-30) 600 acres Owen Co Ky River Patent Berry
George Hardin (4-28) 400 acres Owen Co Ky River Patent Berry
Enos Hardin (4-29) 550 acres Ky River Owen Co Patent Berry
James Hardin (4-8) 100 acres Cedar River Owen Co Patent Boyd

1826 Personal Property Tax Lists
Thomas Hardin (4-30) 1 over 16 650 acres Owen Co Ky River Patent Berry
George Hardin (4-28) 400 acres Ky River Owen Co Patent Berry
Ennis Hardin (4-29) 200 acres Owen Co Ky River Patent Berry
Ennis Hardin (4-29) 234 acres Owen Co Ky River Patent Ashby
James Hardin (4-8) 100 acres Owen Co Cedar Creek Patent Boyd
Lewis Hardin No Land

1827 Personal Property Tax Lists
Thomas Hardin (4-30) 800 acres Owen Co Ky River Patent Berry
Absolem Hardin No Land
Ennis Hardin (4-29) 200 acres Owen Co Ky River patent Berry
George Hardin (4-28) 200 acres Owen Co Ky River Patent Berry
George Hardin 100 acres Owen Co
James Hardin (4-8) 100 acres Owen Co Cedar Cr Patent Boyd

Harding Families of the Northern Neck of Virginia

Lewis Hardin (4-34) No Land

1828 Personal Property Tax Lists
Ennis Hardin (4-29) 200 acres Owen Co Ky River Patent Berry
James Hardin (4-8) 100 acres Owen Co Cedar Cr Patent Boyd
Lewis Hardin (4-34) No Land
Thomas Hardin (4-30) 1000 acres Owen Co Ky River Patent Ashby
Absolom Hardin (4-36) No Land

1829 Personal Property Tax Lists
Ennis Hardin (4-29) 200 acres Owen Co Ky River Patent Ashby
Thomas Hardin (4-30) 1000 acres Owen Co Ky River Patent Ashby
James Hardin (4-8) 100 acres Owen Co Cedar Cr Patent Boyd
Absolom Hardin (4-36) No Land
Lewis Hardin (4-34) No Land

1830 Personal Property Tax Lists
Lewis Hardin (4-34) No Land
Thomas Hardin (4-30) 1000 acres Owen Co Ky River Patent Berry
James Hardin (4-8) 100 acres Owen Co Cedar Cr Patent Boyd
Absolom Hardin (4-36) No Land
Enos Hardin (4-29) No Land

1831 Personal Property Tax Lists
Absolom Hardin (4-36) No Land
Thomas Hardin (4-30) 1000 acres Owen Co Ky River Patent Ashby
Lewis Hardin (4-34) No Land
Ennis Hardin (4-29) 200 acres Owen Co Ky River Patent Ashby
James Hardin (4-8) 100 acres Owen Co Cedar Cr Patent Boyd

1832-1833 No Personal Property Tax Lists

1834 Personal Property Tax Lists
James Hardin (4-8) 100 acres Owen Co Cedar Cr Patent Boyd
Absolom Hardin (4-36) No Land
Lewis Hardin (4-34) No Land
Thomas Hardin (4-30) 1000 acres Owen Co Ky River Patent Ashby
Enos Hardin (4-29) 200 acres Owen Co., Ky River Patent Ashby

1835 Personal Property Tax Lists
James Hardin (4-8) 100 acres Owen Co Cedar Cr Patent Boyd
Absolom Hardin (4-36) No Land
Lewis Hardin (4-34) No Land
Thomas Hardin (4-30) 1000 acres Owen Co Ky River Patent Ashby

Kentucky County Records

Enos Hardin (4-29) 200 acres Owen Co., Ky River Patent Ashby

1836 Personal Property Tax Lists
James Hardin (4-8) 100 acres Owen Co Cedar Cr Patent Boyd
Absolom Hardin (4-36) No Land
Thomas Hardin (4-30) 1000 acres Owen Co Ky River Patent Ashby
Ennis Hardin (4-29) 200 acres Owen Co., Ky River Patent Ashby

1837 Personal Property Tax Lists (No List for 1838)
James Hardin (4-8) 100 acres Owen Co Cedar Cr Patent Boyd
Absolom Hardin (4-36) No Land
Enos Hardin (4-29) 200 acres Owen Co., Ky River Patent Ashby
Thomas Hardin (4-30) 1000 acres Owen Co Ky River Patent Ashby

1839 Personal Property Tax Lists
B Hardin No Land
Lewis Hardin (4-34) No Land
James Hardin (4-8) 100 acres Owen Co Cedar Cr Patent Boyd
Enos Hardin (4-29) 380 acres Owen Co
Thomas Hardin (4-30) 1000 acres Owen Co Ky River Patent Ashby
A Hardin (4-36)
J B Hardin (4-40)

1840 Personal Property Tax Lists
Lewis Hardin (4-34) No Land
Absolem Hardin (4-36) No Land
B G Hardin (4-39) No Land
Jas B Hardin (4-40) No Land
Thomas Hardin (4-30) 1000 acres Owen Co Ky River Patent Ashby
Ennis Hardin (4-29) 378 acres Owen Co

1841 Personal Property Tax Lists
Absolom Hardin (4-36)
James Hardin (4-8) 100 acres Owen Co Cedar Cr Patent Boyd
Enis Hardin (4-29) 400 acres Owen Co Ky River
James B Hardin (4-40)
Lewis Hardin (4-34)
Balis Hardin (4-39)
Thomas Hardin (4-30) 1000 acres Owen Co Ky River Patent Ashby

1842 Personal Property Tax Lists
Lewis Hardin (4-34) No Land
James Hardin (4-40) No Land
Absolem Hardin (4-36)

Enis Hardin (4-29) 424 acres Owen Co Ky River
Enis Hardin (4-29) 64 acres Owen Co Clarke Branch
Thomas Hardin (4-30) 1000 acres Owen Co Ky River Patent Ashby
James Hardin (4-8) 100 acres Owen Co Cedar Cr Patent Boyd
B G Hardin (4-39)

1843 Personal Property Tax Lists
Balies Hardin (4-39) No Land
Thomas Hardin (4-30) 1000 acres Owen Co Ky River Patent Ashby
Absolem Hardin (4-36) No Land
Enos Hardin (4-29) 424 acres Owen Co Ky River
Lewis Hardin (4-34) No Land
William Hardon No Land

1844 Personal Property Tax Lists
Absolom Hardin (4-36) No Land
Enos Hardin (4-29) 430 acres Owen Co Ky River
Thomas Hardin (4-30) 1000 acres Owen Co Ky River Patent Ashby
Balis Hardin (4-39) No Land
Lewis Hardin (4-34) No Land

1845 Personal Property Tax Lists
Lewis Hardin (4-34) No Land
Absolum (4-36) Hardin No Land
B G Hardin (4-39) No Land
Thomas Hardin No Land
Thomas Hardin (4-30) 1000 acres Owen Co Ky River Patent Ashby

1846 Personal Property Tax Lists (No books 1847-1849)
Absolem Hardin (4-36) No Land
B G Hardin (4-39) No Land
Enos Hardin (4-29) 400 acres Owen Co Ky River
Enos Hardin (4-101) Jr No Land
Thomas Hardin (4-30) 1000 acres Owen Co Ky River Patent Ashby

1850 Personal Property Tax Lists
Thomas Hardin (4-30) 1000 acres Owen Co Ky River Patent Ashby
Enos Hardin (4-101) Jr No Land
Absalom Hardin (4-36) No Land
J A Hardin (4-102) No Land
Enos Hardin (4-29) Sr. 100 acres Owen Co Ky River
Enos Hardin (4-29) Sr. 400 acres Owen Co Ky River
John W Hardin No Land
Balis G. Hardin (4-39) No Land

A L Hardin No Land

1851 Personal Property Tax Lists
A L Hardin No Land
Balis G Hardin (4-39) No Land
Thomas Hardin (4-30) 1000 acres Owen Co Ky River Patent Ashby
Ennis Hardin (4-101) Jr No Land
Absalom Hardin (4-36) No Land
J A Hardin (4-102) No Land
Ennis Hardin (4-29) Sr. 100 acres Owen Co Ky River
Ennis Hardin (4-29) Sr. 400 acres Owen Co Ky River
J W Hardin No Land

Will Books

1843 18 Feb: Book C Page 127 Will of James Hardin (4-8) Sr of Owen Co. Daughter Harriet Hawkins (4-35) to have $10. To her three daughters $9 to be divided among them. Son Bales Hardin (4-39) one feather bed and a cow. Sell farm and divide among all my children: Lucy Calvert (4-32), Lewis Hardin (4-34), Harriet Hawkins (4-35), Absolum Hardin (4-36), Mary Ellis (4-38), Bales Hardin (4-39), Sarah Thornton (4-37), James B. Hardin (4-40). Executor James E. Duvall. Proved March 1843

1849 22 Aug: Book D Page 150 Report of Balis G. Hardin (4-39) Guardian of heirs of Milton Sparks decd.

1750 16 Apr: Book D Page 223 Final settlement of James Hardin (4-8) estate by executor James E. Duvall.

1853 21 Mar: Book D Page 403 Final settlement of the guardian estate of Milton Sparks by Balis G, Hardin (4-39), guardian.

1855 30 Nov: Book D Page 524 Inventory of the estate of Thomas Hardin (4-30) presented.

1855 01 Dec: Book D. Page 542 Sale bill of Thomas Hardin (4-30) filed. Among buyers Mrs. Hardin and G. W. Hardin.

Deed Books

1821 Book A Page 88 Martin D. Hardin (5-99) from Peter G. Voorhies & wife Mortgage 2 Lots Frankfort and 5 tracts Cedar Cr

1823 25 Dec: Book A Page 416 Robert Ashby of Henderson Co KY by atty to George Hardin (4-28), James Hardin (4-8), and Thomas Hardin (4-30) and Ann Hawkins (4-31) Deed Tract Ky R

Harding Families of the Northern Neck of Virginia

- 1825 03 Aug: Book B Page 49 Benjamin Hardin (4-9) of Henry Co Ky to Enos Hardin (4-7) of Owen Co KY Deed 214 A Ky R Land he swapped for a parcel in his county.

- 1825 12 Sep: Book B 77 George Hardin (4-28), Enos Hardin (4-29), Benjamin Hawkins (4-31), and Thomas Hardin (4-30), heirs of Enos Hardin (4-7) deceased to Tom, alias Tom Frazier, a man of color. Set free from service. Emancipated.

- 1829 27 Aug: Book C Page 366 William Warner Estate by sheriff to Thomas Hardin (4-30) Deed 120 A Cedar Cr

- 1832 14 Dec: Book D Page 277 Jacob H Holeman to John J Hardin exr et al 804 Acres Liberty and Marion Rd. Mortgage due 1st of January

- 1835 01 Jun: Book E. Page 232 Livingston S. Guthrie and Hannah his wife, Ennis (4-29) and Elizabeth Hardin (4-29), John and Amanda Brewer, and Marticia Guthrie, widow of Alexander Guthrie, heirs of Alexander Guthrie of Henry County, KY to Sydner? D. Hanks of Gallatin Co., KY $700 Deed Tract on Cedar Cr

- 1837 25 Apr: Book F Page 53 Enos Hardin (4-29) and Elizabeth Hardin (4-29) to Johnson Ballard $700 200 A Ky R

- 1839 01 Oct: Book F Page 331 James Ross and wife of Franklin County KY to Enos Hardin (4-29) of Owen County KY. $400 Deed 168 acres Cedar Creek etc.

- 1839 03 Jan: Book F Page 333 Robert Ashby of Union County KY to Enos Hardin (4-29) of Owen County KY $150 Deed Tract Ky R

- 1840 10 Aug: Book G Page 119 William E. Ball of Owen County Ky to James Hardin (4-8) Personal Property furniture and tools. Paid with a note from Thomas Berryman.

- 1840 11 Apr: Book G Page 181 William Cave and wife of Boone Co MO to James Hardin (4-8) of Owen County. $420 Land in Owen Co on Cedar Creek 96 acres.

- 1841 11 Sep: Book G Page 382 Henley Roberts and John Bennett of Owen Co KY to Enos Hardin (4-29) of Owen County KY $280 Personal Property loan to be redeemed before 1 June 1842.

- 1842 03 Aug: Book H. Page 316 William J. Spires and Eliza Spires his wife of Owen County to Enos Hardin (4-29) of Owen County. $299 29 A Ky R

- 1843 26 Apr: Book H Page 448 John Warner, William Warner and Thomas Hardin (4-30) sold by commissioners to John C. Bates 101 A Cedar Cr. In satisfaction of court order.

1843 19 Jul: Book I Page 31 Absolom Hardin (4-36) of Owen Co KY to George C. Branham and George C. Branham all his right and title claim interest and demand in the estate of his father James Hardin (4-8) and all the claim he has against Lewis Hardin (4-34) and William Thornton which claims are in suit in Owen County Court.

1843 01 Jul: Book I Page 32 Lewis Hardin (4-34) of Owen County for $219.66 sells to George C. Branham and George C. Branham all right and claim to deceased father James Hardin's Estate.

1848 25 Jan: Book J Page 261 Balis Hardin (4-39) and Sarah (4-39) his wife to George C. Branham, all of Owen County for one dollar, 24 acres the portion of Joshua Spires farm which was allocated to said Sarah as one of his children and her dower rights to a tract of 27 acres near the tract which formerly belonged to Milton Sparks Dec'd which descended to his heirs at his death and three Negro slaves. Milton Sparks Est to Henry S (4-131) and Sarah Hardin Personal Property and 24 A and 27 A Ky R. Said Branham to hold such property in trust for use and benefit of Sarah Hardin and her three infant children viz Mary V Sparks, Milton Sparks and Henry S Hardin during her life, the same property at no time subject to the payment of the debts of the said Balis Hardin (4-39). Branham will sell on terms he sees fit all the property conveyed to him and collect the proceeds to pay the debts of Balis Hardin (4-39) and Sarah Hardin whether created before or after their marriage and pay the residue to Balis and Sarah Hardin.

1845 22 Feb: Book J Page 430 Jacob Swigert and John J. Hardin to Frank Johnson Release Mortgage obligation

1849 08 Mar: Book J Page 476 William Sandford to Enos Hardin (4-29) both of Owen County $57 28 A Ky R

1846 28 Jan: Book K Page 31 James Sewall, executor of the estate of James Hardin (4-8) decd late of Owen Co, to John W. Smith of same county. James Hardin died 18 February 1843 100 acres Cedar Creek. Smith bought estate for $1140 by notes payable in two years. Paid not and sold land.

1850 25 Aug: Book K Page 238 G C Branham, proprietor of the town of Monterey in Owen Co KY to Enos Hardin (4-101) Jr $30 Lot #23 in Monterey

1851 26 Apr: Book K Page 428 Enos Hardin (4-101) Jr and wife Eliza Ann Hardin (4-101) to Thomas Hardin (4-30) both of Owen County $350 Lot 23 in Monterey

1852 25 Sep: Book L Page 294 John Harrod and Mary Harrod, Enos Hardin (4-29), A.L. Hardin (4-94) and N. D. Tyler and Elizabeth Tyler his wife of Franklin and Owen Counties to James Long of Owen County 50 acres of land for $250.in Caves Creek with interest from 1 January 1849

Harding Families of the Northern Neck of Virginia

1852 27 Sep: Book L Page 296 John Harrod and Mary Harrod, Enos Hardin (4-29), A.L. Hardin (4-94) and N. D. Tyler and Elizabeth Ann Tyler to Thomas Long 50 acres Caves Creek

1856 15 Feb: Book M Page 338 Enos Hardin (4-29) of Owen Co KY to Rachel Hardin (4-30), widow of Thomas Hardin (4-30) decd, (These are all children of Thomas) Enos Hardin Jr, (4-101) J. V. V. Hardin (4-102), Nancy Hardin (4-103), Martha E. Hardin (4-106), George W. Hardin (4-103), Thomas J. Hardin (4-105), Adaline Hardin (4-107), William D. Hardin (4-108), and Alice Hardin (4-109), heirs of Thomas Hardin (4-30) Decd of Owen County. $200 64 A Ky R

1856 10 May: Filed 4 July 1856 Book M Page 510 Benjamin T. Hawkins (4-31) and Alcey (4-31) his wife, James Humphry and Martha (4-110) his wife late Hawkins, Jane Emmerson (4-111) late Hawkins and her husband Z.T. Emmerson, John S. Smith (4-112) and Amanda (4-112) his wife late Hawkins, Enos Hawkins (4-113), George Hardin (4-28) and Jemima (4-28) his wife late Hawkins, of Pike County Missouri, Enos Hardin (4-29) of Owen Co KY of the first part, and Rachel Hardin (4-30), widow of Thomas Hardin (4-30) decd, (all are children of Thomas and Rachel Hardin) Enos Hardin Jr, (4-101) J A.A. Hardin (4-102), Nancy A. Hardin, George W. Hardin (4-104), Thomas J. Hardin (4-105), Martha E. Hardin (4-106), Adaline Hardin (4-107), William D. Hardin (4-108), and Alice Hardin (4-109) of Owen Co KY of the other part. Witnesseth, the parties of the first part the heirs at law of Ann Hawkins (4-31) decd late Ann Hardin and Enos Hardin, for $1800 convey to the heirs at law of Thomas Hardin (4-30) decd tracts of land in Owen Co KY. First tract 218 acres borders Evangelist Hardin (4-6), part of a tract of 1250 acres patented to Francis Berry. Second tract also part of same patent 144 acres. Signed by Enos Hardin, B T Hawkins (4-31), Alcey Hawkins(4-31), James Humphrey, Martha Ann Hawkins, John S, Smith (4-112), Amanda A. Smith, Z.T. Emmerson, James Emmerson, Enos Hawkins, Cassander Hawkins, Jesse A. Hardin, Nancy Ann Hardin, George Hardin, Minney Hardin

1856 10 Mar: Book M 512 Rachel Hardin (4-30), widow of Thomas Hardin (4-30), Enos Hardin (4-101), J A A Hardin (4-102), Thomas J. Hardin, George Hardin (4-104) and Jemima Hardin (4-28) his wife, J. M. Gatewood and Milinda Gatewood his wife, Elizabeth Hardin, Martha A Hardin and William E. Hardin, Benjamin T. Hawkins (4-31) and Alsey his wife, Martha Humphrey and James Humphrey, Zachariah T Emmerson and Jane Emmerson (4-111) his wife, John S. Smith (4-112) and Amanda A. Smith his wife, Enos Hawkins and Cassandra Hawkins his wife, parties of the first part to Enos Hardin (4-29) of the second part. 243 A Ky R in consideration of another tract of land and one dollar.

1856 20 Sep: Book M Page 553 Theodore W. Bates of the first part, John C. Bates and his wife Elizabeth M Bates of the second part and to Enos Hardin (4-101) of the third part. For $200 98 acres on Cedar Cr.

1856 11 Aug: Book M Page 608 John S. Smith (4-112) of Pike County Missouri to Jesse AA Hardin (4-102) Power of Atty to collect all monies from the estate of Thomas E. Smith Dec.

1857 08 Sep: Book N 4 Page 308 RE Williams of Owen Co Ky to B A Hughes and G W Hardin (4-104) of same 3 acres Pond Br

1857 Book N Page 332 T W Bates of Carroll County to John Harrod, Norville D Tyler and Enos Hardin (4-29) of Franklin and Owen Co KY

Marriage Records

1821 27 Sep: John Hawkins (4-35) married Harriett Hardin (4-35).

1823 9 Jun: Thomas Hardin (4-30) married Rachel Allen (4-30)

1823 12 Jun: Ennis Hardin (4-29) married Elizabeth Guthrie (4-29)

1826 06 Dec: Polly Hardin (4-38) married Israel Ellis (4-38)

1827 29 Oct Absolom Hardin (4-36) married Elenor Warner (4-36)

1828 04 Aug: Sallie Hardin (4-37) married William P. Thornton (4-37)

1833 14 May: Catharine Hardin married George Hutchison

1833 20 Sep: Absolam Hardin (4-36) married Catharine Henderson (4-36)

1844 16 Dec: Baylis G. Hardin (4-39) married Sarah Sparks (4-39)

1847 01 Apr: J. E. Hardin (4-87) married Nancy Ann Hardin (4-103)

1869 16 Feb: Bales Hardin (4-39) married Mary E. Evans (4-39)

Find A Grave Index

Enos Hardin (4-101) Born 18 Oct 1824 died 1 November 1901 Hardin Cemetery

Eliza A. Hardin (4-101) Born 16 Oct 1830 died 31 October 1902 Hardin Cemetery

J. A. Hardin (4-102) born 1827 Hardin Cemetery

M. A. Hardin (4-90) Wife of J. A. Hardin (4-102) Born 1827 Died 1896 Hardin Cemetery

Rachel Allen Hardin (4-30) born 23 December 1804 Bourbon Co., KY Died 19 December 1876 Monterey, Owen Co., KY Hardin Cemetery

Thomas Hardin (4-30) born 24 Nov 1801 died 6 Oct 1855 Kentucky Hardin Cemetery

Washington Co., Kentucky Records

Marriage Records

1798 27 Aug: John Hardin (2-34) married Jenny Keeling (2-34)

1801 06 Jan: Sarah Hardin (2-40) married John Hendrickson (2-40). Daughter of Moses Harding (2-12) and Mary

1802 08 Apr: Jane Harding (2-38) married James Thompson (2-38)

1802 29 Sep: Richard Pyburn (2-36) married Mary Harden (2-36)

1806 18 Mar: William Harden (2-37) married Peggy Keeling (2-37)

1810 26 Jun: James Hardin (2-39) married Susannah Tubman (2-39)

1831 28 Mar: Thomas A. Hardin married Nancy E. Head Bond Edward Berry

Deed Records

1796 03 Mar: Book A Page 323 Anthony Hundley of Washington Co KY and Charlotte his wife to Moses Hardin (2-12) of same county and state. For 18 pounds. 100 acres on Chaplin Waters.

1802 03 Aug: Book B Page 579 Anthony Hundley and Charlotte his wife of Washington County KY to Moses Hardin (2-12) of same. For 37 Pounds, 200 acres on Chaplin Waters and Long Lick Creek. Part of 9355 acres patented to Hundley and Walton.

1811 19 Feb: Book C. Page 513 (501 typescript) William Meredith and Milla Meredith his wife to Moses Hardin (2-12) and John Hardin (2-34), all of Washington County, Kentucky, $400 134 acres on Lick Creek.

1814 19 Oct: Book D Page 522 Moses Hardin (2-12) and Mary (2-12) his wife of Washington County KY to William Hardin of same. For $90. 31 acres and 38 poles between Chaplin's Waters and Long Lick Creek Part of Moses Hardin 200-acre survey. Witnesses Benjamin Keeling, John Keeling, James Hardin (2-39)

1817 14 Apr: Book E. Page 337 Matthew Walton and Frances his wife to Moses Hardin (2-12), both of Washington County, Kentucky 25 pounds 4 shillings 127 acres.

1818 09 Aug: Book F Page 38 Moses Hardin (2-12) and Mary his wife and John Hardin (2-34) and wife Jane (2-34) to Daniel Cheatham 134 acres

1819 02 Oct: Book F Page 304 Henry H. Bayne and Susannah his wife to Moses Hardin Moses Hardin (2-12), both of Washington County, Kentucky. $102 18 acres (hard to read)

1821 01 Jul: Book G. Page 298 John Pope and Frances his wife of Washington Co KY to Moses Hardin Moses Hardin (2-12) of the same for $140 plus interest, 19 acres on Chaplin's Fork and Long Lick Creek

1821 Jun: Book G. Page 299 John Pope and Frances his wife of Washington Co KY to Moses Hardin (2-12) of the same for $152 land on Lick Creek bounding John Hardin's land 19 acres and 8 poles.

1821 20 Jan: Book G Page 371 Moses Hardin (2-12) and wife Mary of Washington Co KY to James Harding of same. For $120, 38 acres on Chaplin's Creek and Long Lick Creek on John Harding's line.

1821: 20 Jan: Book G. Page 372 Moses Hardin (2-12) and Mary his wife of Washington Co KY to John Hardin of same. For $120 86 and ½ acres on Chaplin's Fork and Long Lick Creek

1822 12 Dec: Book H Page 139 Moses Hardin (2-12) and Mary his wife of Washington Co., KY to William Hardin of same. For $304 two tracts in Washington County 120 acres,

1822 12 Dec: Book H Page 142 William Hayden (later in the deed is William Hardin (2-37) and signed Hardin) and Margaret (2-37) his wife of Washington County KY to Moses Hardin (2-12) $524 31 acres and 30 poles

1823 14 Jul: Book H Page 248 Moses Hardin (2-12) of Washington County, KY to John Pope of same, returning land transferred to him in error.

Wills and Inventories

06 Apr: 1826 Book D Page 181 Inventory of Moses Hardin (2-12),

1826 13 Apr: Book D Page 176 Sale list of Moses Hardin (2-12). Purchasers include James Hardin Jr, Moses Hardin, John Hardin Jr. Signed James Hardin (2-39) Administrator of Moses Hardin.

1826 11 Nov: Book D Page 214 Sale List of Moses Hardin (2-12) Dec. Purchasers include James Hardin (2-39), William Hardin (2-37).

1829 01 May: Book H Page 16 Will of John Hardin (2-34) of Washington County, KY. To wife Jain (2-34), the plantation, furniture, animals. She is to give and make every Child equal proportion with William Hardin, Nancy Keeling, Fanna Keeling, John Hardin, Thomas Hardin $67. Executor James Hardin (2-

39). Witnesses John Keeling, James Hardin (2-39), Jaine Hardin (2-34). Proved 22 December 1845.

1848 18 Sep: Book H Page 328 settlement of estate of John Hardin (2-34). Note payments from Thomas Hardin, Wesley Hardin, J W Gordon. Paid receipts from Dorman Chesers, and W. H. Chesers three from Julia Hardin

Federal Census Records

1850 Washington County, Kentucky
795 795 John Keeling 60 Farmer VA with 7 children
796 796 Lawson Duncan 28 Farmer KY with wife and two children
797 797 Harrison Harden 39 Farmer born KY with wife and 9 children
798 798 Henry Cheatham 49 Farmer born Ky with wife and 9 children
799 799 John Hickerson 58 born VA with wife and 6 children
800 800 Thomas Hardin 41 Farmer born KY with wife Sarah P 31, Eliza B 10, Mary P 1
801 801 John W. Hardin 22 Farmer born Ky with Elizabeth 21 and Susan 8/12
802 802 Bailey Hardin 27 Farmer born Ky wife two children
803-803 Wesley Hardin 35 wife Elizabeth and 5 children
804 804 Thomas Nantz 30 born KY three children
805 805 Reubin Cobbs 43 born VA with wife three children
806 806 James Hardin (2-39) Sr age 61 wife Susannah 63 and four others
807 807 John Cutsmeier 65 wife Catherine 55
809 809 Sanford Cutsmeier 29 wife and child

810 810 John J Hardin 34 Farmer KY
810-810 Elizabeth Hardin 32 born Ky
810 810 Marion Hardin 12 born Ky
810 810 George D. Hardin 6 born KY
810-810 Susan E. Hardin 3 born Ky

811 811 Jane Harden (2-34) age 67 land $700 born Ky
811 811 Julia A. Hardin Age 23 Born KY
811 811 Charles Buford 17 none born KY

812 812 Hardin Cheser 40 and Jane Hardin 40 Farmer
813 813 Thomas Bird 53 wife and children
814 814 Elizabeth Scott 33 born KY wit

815 815 Mahala Hardin 39 born KY
815-815 Daniel Hardin 8 born KY
815-815 Mary E. Hardin 6 born KY
815 815 Julia A. Hardin age 1 born KY

Kentucky County Records

Followed by 4 Cheser families.

841 841 John Hardin 46 Farmer born KY with Sarah Hardin 39 and children John B, James W, Henderson, Alfred, Howell, Eras, Berry and Cyntha.
842 842 Charles Hardin 39 Farmer, Calvin Hardin 11

Personal Property Tax Lists

NOTE: Most of the unnumbered names on this list are descendants of Family #6 Mark Hardin (5-1) and Mary (MNU) (5-1). I have not attempted to determine which person is which because others have done so.

1792 Personal Property Tax Lists
Benjamin Hardin
John Hardin
Martin Hardin
Henry Hardin
Ann Hardin
John Hardin Jr
Big John Hardin
John Harding (lower on the list, others are together at the top)
Thomas Harding
Robert Harding
Jane Hardin (separated)
Stephen Harding (2 over 21)
Mark Hardin
Absalom Hardin (5-43)
Moses Hardin (2-12)
Ede? Hardin

1794 Personal Property Tax Lists
Baly Harding (2-33)
Martin Hardin
Ead Harding
Moses Hardin (2-12)
Benjamin Hardin
Ann Hardin
Absolum Hardin (5-43)
Jain Hardin
Jain Hardin
John Hardin
John Hardin B
John Hardin

Harding Families of the Northern Neck of Virginia

Robert Harding
Thomas Harding
Mark Hardin
Stephen Harding

1795 Personal Property Tax Lists and Land ownership
Stephen Harding Land in Washington Co Rolling Fork 180 acres
John Harding No Land
Absalom Harding (5-43) Land in Washington Co on Beech Fork 119 acres
Big John Hardin No Land
John Hardin Jr Land in Washington Co., on Beech Fork 150 acres
John Hardin Jr Land in Washington Co on Toad Run 100 acres
Ann Hardin Land in Washington Co on Toad run 100 acres
Martin Hardin Land in Washington Co on Pleasant Run 1000 acres
Martin Hardin Land in Harding Co on Jewels Creek 1000 acres
Henry Hardin Land in Washington Co on Toad Run 100 acres
Robert Harding Land in Washington Coon Rolling Fork 100 acres
Ede Hardin No Land
Thomas Harding land on Cissel River 90 acres
Jean Hardin Land in Washington Co Pleasant Run 300 acres
John Hardin's heirs Land in Washington Co Pleasant Run 1500 acres
John Hardin's heirs Land in Washington Co Pleasant Run 400 acres
John Hardin's heirs Land in Washington Co Beech Fork 250 acres
John Hardin Senr Land in Washington Co Pleasant Run 96 acres
John Hardin Senr Land in Hardin Co Jewels Creek 400 acres
Bailey Hardin (2-33) No land
Moses Hardin (2-12) Land in Washington Co Beech Fork 100 acres
Benjamin Hardin Land in Washington Co Saverne Run 800 acres
Benjamin Hardin Land in Hardin Co on Jewels Creek 800 acres
Benjamin Hardin Land in Hardin Co on Sinking Creek 500 acres
Cassander Hardin Land in Hardin Co on Hardin's Settlement 200 acres
Mark Hardin Land in Washington Co Hardin's Creek 1250 acres
Mark Hardin Land in Washington Co Beech Fork 200 acres
Mark Hardin land in Hardin Co Jewels Creek 1500 acres

1796 Personal Property Tax Lists and Land Ownership
John Harding No Land
Mark Hardin 3 parcels 1250, 1500 200 Washington and Hardin Co
C John Harding No Land
Ede Harding No Land
Bailey Hardin (2-33) No Land
Moses Hardin (2-12) 2 parcels 100, 100 Washington Co
Tobert Harding 100 acres Washington Co
Absalom Harding (5-43) 120 acres on Beach Fork Washington Co

Kentucky County Records

Ann Hardin 100 acres Washington Co Patent to Mark Hardin
Mark Hardin 100 acres toad run Washington Co Patent Mark Hardin
Henry Hardin 100 acres Washington Co Patent to Mark Hardin
Martin Hardin 1000 acres Washington Co Patent Martin Hardin
Martin Hardin 1000 acres Hardin co Patent Martin Hardin
John Hardin Sr 96 acres Washington Co Patent Joseph Lewis
John Hardin Sr 400 acres Hardin Co Patent John Hardin
John Hardin 100 acres toad run Washington Co Patent Mark Hardin
John Hardin 150 acres Washington Co Patent to John Lewis
Jane Hardin 300 acres Pleasant Run Washington Co Patent John Hardin
Benjamin Hardin 600 & 200 acres Washington Co 800 & 500 &200 Hardin Co
      Patent to Benjamin Hardin, John Hardin, Lydia Hardin
Cassander Hardin 200 acres Hardin Co Patent John Hardin
Martin Hardin and son 1000 acres Shelby Co Patent Martin Hardin
Thomas Harding 100 acres Cissel River Washington Co Patent Robert Vaughan

1797 Personal Property Tax Lists and Land Ownership (Very hard to read)
Benjamin Hardin Jr
Jean? Hardin
Mark Hardin
Ede Hardin
Cassandra Hardin
Benjamin Hardin
Thomas Harding
Moses Hardin (2-12)
Bailey Hardin (2-33)
B John Hardin
Robert Hardin
John T Hardin
Martin Hardin Jr

1799 Personal Property Tax Lists and Land Ownership
Thomas Hardin 100 acres
Benjamin Hardin Jr 100 acres
Mark Hardin Jr 100 acres
Benjamin Hardin
Martin Hardin
Jeptha Hardin
John Hardin Sr
Rob Hardin
John Hardin Jr
Henry Hardin
Martin Hardin Sr
Moses Hardin (2-12)

Bailey Hardin (2-33)
John Hardin
Robert Hardin
Mark Hardin Jr
William Hardin
Moses Hardin (2-12)
John Hardin
Bailey Hardin (2-33)
William Hardin of M
Mark Hardin

1800 Personal Property Tax Lists and Land Ownership
Mark Hardin
Thomas Hardin
Moses Hardin (2-12)
Bailey Hardin (2-33)
Martin Hardin Jr
Henry Hardin
John Hardin
Mark Hardin
Robert Hardin
Benjamin Hardin Jr
John Hardin Sr
John Hardin Jr
Martin Hardi
Benjamin Hardin

Chapter 10
Missouri County Records

Pike Co., Missouri Records

Federal Census Records

1830 Census Pike County, Missouri
Page 241 John Hawkins 21001 20001 (4-35)
Page 242 Benjamin F. Hawkins (4-31) 210011 111001
Page 242 Hermin Hawkins 000010001 000010001 *(Father of John and Benjamin)*

1840 Census Pike County, Missouri
Page 66 William C. Hardin 10021 20010
Page 85 Benjamin Hawkins (4-31) 0012001001 0011110001
Page 86 John R. Hawkins (4-35) 2111001 102001
Page 86 William G Hawkins 200001 10011 *(Brother of John and Benjamin)*
Page 92 George Hardin (4-28) 0100101 1221001

1850 Census Cuivre, Pike Co, Missouri Page 75-76

Res	Fam	Name	Age	Sex	Occupation	Birthplace
200	200	William G. Hawkins	41	M	Farmer	Kentucky
200	200	Martha Hawkins	37	F		Kentucky
200	200	Benjamin C. Hawkins	13	M		Missouri
200	200	Edward D. Hawkins	12	F		Missouri
200	200	Nancy M. Hawkins	10	M		Missouri
200	200	Martha A. Hawkins	8	M		Missouri
200	200	Richard J. Hawkins	6	M		Missouri
200	200	John W. Hawkins	4	M		Missouri
200	200	Infant Hawkins	4m	F		Missouri
200	200	Herman Hawkins	82	M	None	Virginia

1850 Census Cuivre, Pike Co, Missouri Page 166

Res	Fam	Name	Age	Sex	Occupation	Birthplace
91	91	John R. Hawkins	48	M	To the mines	Kentucky
91	91	Harriet Hawkins	48	F		Kentucky
91	91	Nancy Hawkins	22	F		Kentucky
91	91	Sally Hawkins	20	F		Kentucky
91	91	John L. Hawkins	18	M	Farmer	Missouri
91	91	Benjamin T. Hawkins	16	M		Missouri

Harding Families of the Northern Neck of Virginia

Res	Fam	Name	Age	Sex	Occupation	Birthplace
91	91	Rebecca A. Hawkins	14	F	Mail Carrier	Missouri
91	91	George Hawkins	10	M		Missouri
91	91	Lucy Jane Hawkins	8	F		Missouri

1850 Census Cuivre, Pike Co, Missouri Page 168

Res	Fam	Name	Age	Sex	Occupation	Birthplace
104	104	Benjamin T. Hawkins	54	M	Farmer	Virginia
104	104	Ailsie Hawkins	45	F	(4-31)	Kentucky
104	104	Jane Hawkins	26	F		Kentucky
104	104	Amanda Hawkins	25	F		Kentucky
104	104	Ennis Hawkins	22	M	Farmer	Missouri
104	104	Cassandra Hawkins	22	F		Missouri
104	104	George M McCollum	20	M	Mail Carrier	Missouri

1850 Census Cuivre, Pike Co, Missouri Page 172-4

Res	Fam	Name	Age	Sex	Occupation	Birthplace
175	175	Elizabeth Jasper	38	F		Kentucky
175	175	Emeline Jasper	14	F		Missouri
175	175	Terrell Jasper	12	M		Missouri
175	175	Mary Jasper	10	F		Missouri
175	175	Belvedere Jasper	8	F		Missouri
175	175	Merrill Jasper	5	m		Missouri
175	175	William Hawkins	23	M		Missouri
175	175	Catherine Hawkins	16	F		Missouri
175	175	Mary Hawkins	3m	F		Missouri

1850 Census Cuivre, Pike Co, Missouri Page 173-4

Res	Fam	Name	Age	Sex	Occupation	Birthplace
176	176	J. E, Hardin	30	M	Farmer	Kentucky
176	176	Nancy Ann Hardin	21	F		Kentucky
176	176	Minerva B. Hardin	2	F		Missouri
176	176	George Hardin	57	M	Farmer	Kentucky
176	176	Jemima Hardin	55	F		Kentucky
176	176	Elizabeth Hardin	24	F		Kentucky
176	176	Martha A Hardin	22	F		Kentucky
176	176	William Hardin	21	M	Laborer	Missouri
176	176	Maria L. Hardin	18	F		Missouri
176	176	Ailsie J Hardin	14	F		Missouri

1860 Census Bowling Green, Pike Co., Missouri Page 39

Res	Fam	Name	Age	Sex	Occupation	Birthplace
258	257	J. E. Hardin	40	M	Miller	Kentucky
258	257	Nancy A, Hardin	30	F	Dom	Kentucky
258	257	Mary B. Hardin	8	M		Missouri
258	257	Janetta Hardin	4	F		Missouri
258	257	Infant Hardin	2m	M		Missouri

258	257	Thomas Scrimpshire	25	M	Day Labor		Missouri

1860 Census Bowling Green, Pike Co., Missouri Page 41

Res	Fam	Name	Age	Sex	Occupation	Birthplace
275	275	J. A.A. Hardin	33	M	Hotel	Kentucky
275	275	M. A, Hardin	33	F	Dom	Kentucky
275	275	C. E. Hardin	2	M		Missouri
275	275	Jessie A. Hardin	3m	F		Missouri
275	275	George Hardin	65	M	Out of Business	Missouri
275	275	Elizabeth Hardin	35	F	Dom	Missouri
275	275	William E. Hardin	28	M		Missouri
275	275	Ezra Hunt	75	M	Attorney	Virginia
275	275	Mariah E. Hunt	48	F		NC

Marriage Records

1833 06 Jun: Benjamin Hawkins (4-31) married Ailsey Lowry (4-31) Book 1 Page 79 both of Pike County

1834 13 Mar: William C. Hardin (born in Virginia, no known relationship) married Louisa Margaret Pettibone Book 1 Page 88

1836 19 Jul: William Hawkins married Martha Bondurant Book 1 Page 126

1838 31 May: John Hawkins Jr to Rachel Stevenson Book 2 Page 17

1841 30 Aug: Martha Ann Hawkins (4-110) married James Humphrey (4-110)

1845 27 Nov: James Hawkins and Susan Hedges Book 2 Page 139

1849 08 Apr: William Hawkins (4-114) to Catherine Jasper (4-114) Book 2 page 257

1849 24 Dec: Ennis Hawkins (4-113) to Cassander Doyle (4-113) Book 2 Page 259

1849 06 Dec: William Hardin (born in Virginia, no known relationship) to Louisa Beasley Book 2 Page 261

1850 07 Mar: Humphrey Hawkins To Mary McMillin Book 2 Page 267

1850 12 Sep: Zachariah T Emerson (4-111) to Jane Hawkins (4-111) Book 2 Page 274

1851 06 Mar: Jesse A. A Hardin (4-102) to Martha Ann Hardin (4-90) Book 2 Page 288

1851 22 May: Moses Hawkins of Ralls Co Mo to Susan C Davis Book 2 Page 294

1851 23 Oct: Samuel B Hardin to Catherine G. Waugh Book 2 Page 306

1852 Dec: John S Smith (4-112) and Amanda M Hawkins (4-112) Book 3 Page 30

1853 01 Dec: William Hardin (4-91) to Susan Jones (4-91) Book 3 Page 55

1853 16 Nov: Littleberry Hawkins to Mary Jane Miller Book 3 Page 55

1856 01 Jul: Robert Hawkins to Virginia M Bristow Book 3 Page 138

1857 02 Apr: William G Hawkins Susan Mackey Book 3 Page 172

1857 19 Mar: James Emerson and Susan Hawkins Book 3 Page 174

1858 Aug: James M Hawkins to Eliza J Farquar Book 3 Page 225

J (Isaac)? W Hawkins to Catherine Baird Book 3 Page 362

1863 17 Nov: William E Hardin (4-91) and Mollie Gray (4-91) Book 3 Page 559

Will and Probate Records

1837 17 May: Book 2 Page 152 Benjamin T. Hawkins (4-31) appointed guardian of James Humphrey a minor of age 13 and up.

1850 11 Jun: Book 4 Page 147 Hiram Edwards, Jesse E Hardin (4-87) and Levi Pettibone security bond for Hiram G. Edwards appointed guardian of George Hardin (4-28), a person of unsound mind

1856 17 Mar: Book 4 Page 506, 507 Estate of Susan Hardin (4-91). William E. Hardin (4-91), Jesse E Hardin (4-87) and Benjamin T. Hawkins (4-31) bond to administer the estate of Susan Hardin deceased. Susan O. Hardin (4-166) a minor is the only heir of Susan Hardin deceased. William E Hardin gets letters of administration for her estate.

1859 10 Aug: Book 5, Page 161 William E. Harding appointed guardian of William A. Harding a minor. *(This and the three records pertain to a different William Harding, who married Louisa Beasley and died in Pike County in 1861.)*

1861 25 Apr: Book 5 Page 304, Louisa Harding, bond to become administrator.

1861 18 Mar: Book 5 Page 312 Will of William E. Hardin deceased. All of property to his wife. Probated 4 April 1861.

1861 25 Apr: Book 5 Page 358 Estate of William E. Hardin. Louisa Harding given letters of administration.

1866 23 Apr: Book 6 56 Letters 57 Estate of Benjamin T. Hawkins (4-31) David L. Caldwell, James Humphrey (4-110) and John S. Smith (4-112) and Zachariah Emerson (4-111) as securities bond for David Caldwell to administer estate. States that Alcy Hawkins (4-31) (widow) Martha Humphrey (4-110), Jane

Emerson (4-111), Amanda Smith (4-112) and Enos Hawkins (4-113) are the only heirs. He died with no will. David L. Caldwell administrator.

1866 27 Oct: Book 6 Page 92 Will of Alcy Hawkins (4-31). To Nephew Benjamin T Humphrey house in Bowling Green, Pike County which she occupies. To Benjamin T Hawkins son of Enos Hawkins (4-113) all her cash and money due her. To Benjamin L Smith, son of John Smith (4-112) one bed and bedclothes. To James Humphrey (4-110) the brown mare Barney. To the children of my deceased husband Benjamin T Hawkins (4-31), any other personal property and effects to divide among themselves. Proved 28 November 1866

1869 22 Aug: Book 6 Page 453 Estate of Benjamin T Hawkins, minor. Enos Hawkins (4-113) principal and William G Hawkins as security, bond. Enos Hawkins appointed curator of estate.

Cemetery Records

Eolia Cemetery, Eola, Pike County, Missouri:
W. E. Harding Jan 5 1824-Mar 15 1861

Lewisa his wife Sept 8 1830-Feb 13 1897

(This record is about William Harding and Louisa Beasley and is unrelated to the families in this book.

Chapter 11
Ohio and South Carolina County Records

Belmont Co., Ohio Records

Census Records

1820 Union Township
Bennett Harden (4-53) 300010 20010

Guernsey Co., Ohio Records

Marriage Records

1824 12 Jan: Book 1810-1863 Page 206 Nelson Hardon (4-58) married Lucy Oder (4-58)

Probate Records

1824 24 Jan: Book A Page 105 Will of Thomas Harden. To wife Janet Harden, to daughter Bula Casterlain. To sons James Harden and Gideon Harden. To son John. To son Joshua. To son Denman Harden. Proved 27 June 1824 *(From Sussex County, New Jersey, no parentage known)*

1872 01 Feb: Book 3 Page 434 Will of Bennett Harden (4-53). To son Benet and his wife Mary. Daughter Mariah Stockdale. Children Joseph, John, Benet, Jeremiah, Hiram, Mason, James. Daughters Meriah Stockdale, Sarah Douglas, Martha Jane Harper, heirs of Mary Stockdale deceased, William Stockdale, Bennet, James, Martha, Mary Ann Proctor, Fanny McPeek. Proved 26 January 1883

Census Records

Missouri County Records

1820 Federal Census (All on neighboring lines) *(All from the family of Thomas Hardin in the will above.)*

Page 180 Madison Thomas Harden 000001 00001
Page 180 Madison James Hardin 000100 20700
Page 180 Madison John Harden 10001 20100

1830 Federal Census
Page 404 Londonderry Nelson Harding (4-58) 2000001 00001
Page 404 Londonderry Bennett Harding (4-53) 1212001 2 2 00001
Page 416 Madison John Hardin 210001 101001*(Both John and Thomas are from the family of Thomas Hardin in the will above.)*
Page 417 Madison James Harden 021001 212001

1840 Federal Census
Page 347 Madison Margaret Hardin 01211 0100001
Page 348 Madison Bennett Hardin (4-53) 11112001 00210001
Page 378 Washington John Hardin 0110101 112101 *(From Maryland, unrelated to Bennett Harding)*

1850 Federal Census Beaver Township
(The ancestry of this man is unknown, possibly from Isaac of Somerset PA)
777 778 James Harden 28 Farmer Born Pennsylvania
777 778 Mary Harden 24 born Ohio
777 778 Rebecca Harden 7 born Ohio
777 778 James Harden 3 born Ohio
777 778 Edward Harden 1 born Ohio

1850 Federal Census Madison Township
262 264 Bennett Hardin 63 (4-53) Farmer 1600 born VA
262 264 Martha Hardin (4-53) 55 born Virginia
262 264 John Hardin 33 born Virginia
262 264 Mason Hardin 28 Farmer born Ohio
262 264 Hiram Hardin 24 Farmer born Ohio
262 264 Sarah Hardin 20 born Ohio
262 264 Bennet Hardin 19 Farmer born Ohio
262 264 Joseph Hardin 16 Farmer born Ohio
262 264 James Hardin born Ohio
262 264 James Stockdale born Ohio

(The ancestry of this man is not known but not connected to Bennett Harding)
279 281 William Hardin 25 Farmer born Ohio
279 281 Harriet Hardin 21 born Ohio
With Matthew and Eliza Hughes

1850 Federal Census Washington Township
Note: This family is from Frederick County Maryland, unrelated to Bennett Harding)
1780 1797 John Hardin 54 Farmer 2000 Born unknown
1780 1797 Martha Hardin 47 born Ohio
1780 1797 Margaret Hardin 22 born Ohio
1780 1797 Sarah Hardin 20 born Ohio
(Continuation of the above family from Frederick County MD)
1781 1798 Charles Hardin 27 Farmer born Ohio
1781 1798 Elizabeth Hardin 25 born Ohio
1781 1798 Amelia Hardin 11 born Ohio
1781 1798 Geo Hardin 16 born Ohio
1781 1798 Ann Hardin 14 born Ohio
1781 1798 John Hardin 6 born Ohio
1781 1798 Basil Hardin 8 born Ohio

1850 Federal Census Washington Township
(NOTE: Descended from Isaac Hardin of Somerset Pennsylvania. No relation to Bennett Harding)
1018 1029 Westley Hardin 37 born Ohio
1018 1029 Rebecca Hardin 38 born Ohio
1018 1029 Mary Hardin 11 Born Ohio
1018 1029 David Hardin 9 born Ohio
1018 1029 Eliza Hardin 7 born Ohio
1018 1029 Emily Hardin 5 born Ohio
1018 1029 John Hardin 3 born Ohio

Laurens Co., South Carolina Records

Will and Probate Records

1809 22 May: Book 1802-1809 Page 345 Will of William Harding (3-9) Inventory 29 July 1809, gives slaves to his wife (not named). Bequests to son Abner Harding (3-33)'s widow Susannah (3-33) and his children when they come of age. Bequests to son Abraham Harding (3-34), Daughter Salley (3-35), son William Harding (3-36), daughter Elizabeth (3-37), son Nicholas Harding (3-38), son George Harding (3-39), son Henry Harding (3-40). Nicholas Harding and George Harding appointed executors.

1800 Census for Laurens County, South Carolina
Abner Harding (3-33) 20010 20010

Deed Records

Missouri County Records

1788 14 Aug: Book B Page 437 Henry Harding of Laurens County 96 District from William Cason and Ann $6 100 acres on Saluda River

1788 15 Aug: Book B. Page 438 Henry Harding of Laurens County 96 District from William Cason and Ann 75 acres 15 Pounds on Saluda River

1790 19 Aug: Book C Page 281 Henry and Clary Harding of Laurens County 96 District to John Meek 200 acres $5 on Saluda River

1790 19 Aug: Book C. Page 282 Henry and Clary Harding of Laurens County 96 District to John Meek 100 acres 50 Pounds on Saluda River

1805 05 Nov: Book H Page-238 William Harding (3-36) Jr of Laurens District SC to John McClure 75 acres $250 on Brush River he got by deed from John Gray. Recorded 1 August 1807.

1802 30 Jan: Book J Page 269 William Harding (3-36) of Laurens Dist SC from Thomas Broughton of Edgefield District 100 acres $100 Recorded July 6, 1812

1812 20 Jun: Book J Page 269 William Harding (3-36) of Laurens Dist SC to Northam Vance 100 acres $100 Recorded 38 June 1812

1819 03 Aug: Book K Page 256 On Brushy Creek William Harding (3-36) and John Munro, executors of William Johnson Deceased to Thomas Dalrymple 213 ½ acres $324

Chapter 12
Comments on published articles

Article 1: Mrs. O. A. Keach, Tyler's Quarterly

After trying to make sense of the various reconstructions of the descendants of Thomas Harding of Northumberland County, VA, I decided that there were so many contradictions and errors of fact in the published materials that the family trees were hopelessly inaccurate. Many non-existent individuals appeared on the charts, dates were changed to suit the convenience of the compiler, children were assigned to parents with no documentary evidence and dates were incorrect.

The only solution was to go back to the original records and see how much of the published data could be proven.

The source of most of the errors is an article by Mrs. O. A. Keach, which appeared in Tyler's Quarterly Magazine one hundred years ago. The article proposed an English connection for Thomas Harding and the names of his children and grandchildren. With virtually no change, this article has been copied and recopied for over a century and the errors in it have been perpetuated until they are considered fact.

In 1971 Lucy Lemoine Waring published a book concerned mostly with the family of Hopkins Harding of Northumberland Co., VA, which gives an incorrect ancestry for his family.

Fredna Tweedt Irvine in 1976 published Henry Hardin of California, showing in detail the family of the Henry Hardin of Stafford County, VA, giving him an incorrect connection to Thomas Harding of Northumberland County.

Another Harding family record was published in 1981 by Eva Hardin Benning in her book *Francois Benin, His Descendants and Allied Families*, in which the first three generations are mostly copied from Mrs. Keach's work. However, she added a lot of material, which contains many errors of fact and incorrect connections.

In July and August 1998, I searched all the extant deed, will and court record books of Northumberland County, VA and extracted all the Harding and related data I could find from 1648 to about 1770 to make sense of the family relationships. This amounts to several hundred individual citations, some of them never quoted before, which taken together produce a radical reconstruction of the family of Thomas Harding of Northumberland and other Harding families in the same county unrelated to Thomas.

Since the Keach article is crucial to the currently accepted structure of the family, I will begin by commenting on each of the errors and purported proofs in that article so that it is clear exactly where Mrs. Keach went wrong. The original article is in italics. My comments are in bold regular type.

HARDINGS OF LONDON and VIRGINIA
By Mrs. 0. A. Keach
(Tyler's Quarterly Magazine, Vol. 2: 104-110 Oct. 1920)

This short chapter in the history of the Hardings is designed to record and preserve the interesting and definite proofs of descent from the London Family of that name.

(Note: Mrs. Keach starts with the assumption that she has proved her case, which as we will see is far from the truth.)

Thomas Harding, founder of this distinguished Virginia family, probably came to Northumberland Co., with his uncle, Thomas Orley. Both came from London as the court records at Heathsville, conclusively prove.

In the Cavaliers and Pioneers series, Thomas Orley appears several times as being transported from England or as transporting others from England. In none of those records does Thomas Harding appear. Several Thomas Hardings do appear in the records, however none of them can be conclusively identified with Thomas Harding of Northumberland.

Thomas Orley is first mentioned in the will of Thomas Keen, b. 27 Nov., 1652, as one of the friendly "overseers" of the estate of his wife and children.

On 20 May, 1653, he claimed a tract of land for his own transportation and acquired other land in "Cherry Point Neck." He was appointed constable for the Chicacone district 20 Jan., 1657, and was generally active in community life until his early death. Thos. Orley's will, d. 11 Aug. 1662, pr. 8 Oct., 1662, names his wife Rebecca - Sister Mary Harden wife of George Harden, John Harden son ---- and Mary Harden his wife.

The will of Thomas Orley is badly damaged, which the quote above does not make clear. In fact, only about one quarter of the bequest section has survived and is written exactly as quoted in the first part of this book Each line in the middle of the will is missing about six to ten words. The will concludes by naming John Tyngey, Nicholas Owen and one other as executors. Note that there is a bequest to --- Orley of White Chappel. The significance of this is shown in part 1.

Harding Families of the Northern Neck of Virginia

He does not mention his nephew, Thomas Harding, in his will and had doubtless made generous provision for him, but a later record mentions legacies from Thos. Orley which the children of Thos. Harding claimed.

It is true that Thomas Harding is not named in the will. We will deal with the record mentioned above later in this article. It is sufficient to say now that nowhere in that record is Thomas Harding mentioned.

Rebecca, the widow of Thomas Orley, m. Wm. Jalland.

Two years after the death of Thos. Orley, on 22 Sept., 1664, a power of attorney was recorded from "George Harding citizen and grocer of London and Mary Harding his wife," The latter is described as daughter. of Thos. Orley of London and Anne his wife deceased, and sister of Thos. Orley, late of Cherry Poynt, in Va., planter, dec'd.

The power of attorney was given to Capt. Wm. Hall of London, Mariner, who was to "demand, recover and receiv"e from Rebecca Orley late wife of Thos. Orley and from William Jalland of Cherry Point, planter, her now husband, her now husband, all goods due sd Harding from sd Orley's estate. A certificate of baptism accompanies the power of attorney as follows: These are to certify to all whomme It may concern that Mary Orley the daughter of Thos. and Anne Orley was baptized at the parish church (charge) of St. Mary's White Chappel on the 25 of April 1622, this being a true copy Taken out of the Register by me.

John Johnson D D Rect.

Fran. Fielder Church wardens

Thomas Slightholm

20 April 1665 Recorded.

Note that the actual document demands that Thomas Orley's widow and her new husband William Jollins hand over the estate to the London family. Nowhere do they mention Thomas Harding. These records are entirely about the London family of George Harding attempting to collect their legacy.

Thomas Harding, son of George and Mary Orley Harding of London had many descendants in Northumberland Co. *

Thomas was not the son of George and Mary Orley Harding of London.

* 20 Nov., 1653, upon supposition of witchcraft against William Harding with (Rev.) David Lyndsay as witness, the Court ordered 10 stripes on the bare back, and forever banished (the sd Harding) from the county. He was ordered to depart in the space of three months. There is no further mention of this Harding, as he doubtless obeyed the order of the Court as soon as possible. The Southern colony was decidedly more lenient in its dealings with persons accused of witchcraft than the Massachusetts colony.

Young Thomas, the immigrant, with James Johnson, bought or traded for a "pattent" of land containing 400 acres on 22 Nov., 1658, from the original patentee, Richard Rice. One half of this patent was assigned 24 Aug., 1661, by James Johnson and Annie his wife unto James Claughton - the sd 200 acres * * * abutting N. E. on Mattapony River - with Thos. Harding as one of the witnesses. On the same day James Claughton made a deed to Thos. Harding for 100 acres of this patent on the Mattapony river. As this was Thomas Harding's first independent transaction, he may have recently come of age.

This latter assumption that he was recently of age is unjustified. This is an assumption of the author to support her contention that Thomas could be the son of George and Mary Orley Harding.

On 9 Sept., 1661, James Johnson and Anne his wife made a deed to Thos. Harding for 150 acres "where the said Johnson now dwells" from this 400-acre patent in Mattapony. Later records show that Mattapony became the home place of the older line of Hardings for several generations.

In Nov., 1661, Thos. Harding and Anne his wife made a deed to James Johnson.*

This deed was recorded 9 September 1661 (Deeds and Wills 1658-1666 page 63) Much of the deed is missing but it is clear that Thomas Harding and his wife Anne made the deed prior to the date given by Mrs. Keach and that Thomas was married by this date.

*The birth certificate of Thos. Harding's mother shows that John Johnson D. D. was rector of St. Mary's Parish church in London and the frequent association of James Johnson with Thos. Harding and his children raises an interesting question of probable relationship between Dr. Johnson and James Johnson, who was a prominent early citizen of St. Stephen's parish and left many descendants.

This is a wild assumption with no basis in fact.

Thomas Harding m. Anne Moseley, dau. of Henry and Anne Mosely.

The will of Henry Moseley, d. 26 March, 1655, pr. 20 Sept.9 1656, names his wife and sons Henry and John. A son William was evidently a posthumous child. Henry Moseley was about 42 years of age at the time of his death, and his home was on Moseley's Creek. His widow, Anne Moseley, m. second, John Lyngey.

On 25 Feb., 1660, Anne Lyngey, wife of John Lyngey, gave a power of attorney to her son Henry Mosely.

On 6 Sept., 1665, John Lyngey, who had married the child's grandmother, made a deed of gift to Anne Harding, the dau. of Thos. Harding, "for one cow calf." In his will, d. 1 Aug.,1667, Mr. Lyngey left a legacy to Thom. Harding's oldest boy. He also mentions his sons in law (stepsons) William, John and Henry Moseley. Mary Hardwood is named as a legatee, and this may have been a mistake in copying the name of Mary Harding.

The name of the testator was John Tyngey. I have not been able to locate the deed of gift to Anne Harding mentioned above despite searching page by page from 1665 to 1667. The Sporacio abstracts of the deed and will books also do not contain mention of this item. The attempt to equate Mary Hardwood with Mary

Harding is a weak attempt to add this woman to Thomas Harding's family. In fact, this legacy to Mary Hardwood is several lines away from the legacies to Thomas Harding's sons. She is not specifically stated to be a relative, as Tyngey has done with all his other legatees.

The will of John Moseley, d. 18 May, 1669, mentions his cousins Thos. and Ann Harding and brothers William and Henry Moseley.

As one of the churchwardens, Thomas Harding attended a vestry meeting 25 March, 1671, called by the minister Mr. John Farnefold to determine the bounds of the globe lands.

Thomas Harding died intestate, probably in 1674, **(actually the year was 1675)** as on June 16 of that year Anne Harding was by the court granted administration on the estate of her deceased husband, Thomas Harding. James Johnson was one of her securities. Somewhat later Mr. Richard Parrot was attorney for Anne and Mary Harding, heirs of Thos. Orley, deceased.

This citation from the Order Book establishes the Orley-Harding relationship.

This record is so crucial to Mrs. Keach's argument that I will quote it in full. It is found in Court Order Book 4, 1666-1678, Page 126:

"Page 126 19 January 1675/6 "Whereas it appears to this court that there is due unto Mr. Rich Parrott Esq Attorney for Ann Harding, Mary Harding, George Harding, Mary Harding and Thomas Orley, the heires of Thomas Orley, late of this County decd an estate according to appraisement amounting to the sum of fourteen thousand five hundred twenty-four pounds of tobacco, judgment is granted the said Mr. Richard Parrott, attorney as aforesaid for ye yet same agst the estate of William Jolland decd who married the Relict of ye said Thomas Orley and ordered ye the Sheriff possess ye said Mr. Parrott with the ---- of the sd Thomas Orley in right of the said prayers."

In addition, I will quote from the Parish Register of St. Mary Whitechapel, London, England, the children of George and Mary Harding:

Anne Harding ba 27 Feb 1647 St. Mary Whitechapel, Stepney
Mary Harding ba 25 October 1651 St. Mary Whitechapel, Stepney
Elizabeth Harding ba 1 July 1655 St. Mary Whitechapel, Stepney
Samuel Harding ba 2 February 1661 St. Mary Whitechapel, Stepney
John Harding ba 7 March 1665 St. Mary Whitechapel, Stepney

In the will of Thomas Orley above, Orley mentions George and Mary Harding and a Mr. Orley. In the court record above, George and Mary Harding, Ann Harding, Mary Harding, and Thomas Orley hired an attorney to collect their estate. The heirs listed in the court record match the London family and the heirs listed in Thomas Orley's will. In addition, there is no mention of Thomas Harding, or any of Thomas Harding's sons in the court record. Far from proving that Thomas Harding's family claimed the legacy, this record proves that the London

Comments on Published Articles

family claimed it and that Thomas Harding's family had no part in the legacy and no connection with the London family.

The children of (1) Thomas and Anne Moseley Harding were:
Anne mentioned in court records
Mary mentioned in court records
Thomas, b. 4 Sept., 1664 St. Stephens Par. Register
Henry mentioned in court records
William, b. 20 July, 1669, Parish Reg.

Of the children listed above, Ann is mentioned in John Moseley's will. Mary is mentioned only in the 1675 court record mentioned above and is erroneously taken to be a daughter of Thomas Harding by Keach when she is in fact a daughter of George and Mary Harding of London. Therefore, Thomas Harding had no daughter Mary. In addition, Henry Harding was born after William and Thomas, and Thomas Senior had another son John Harding not mentioned in Mrs. Keach's article, proven by court records to be quoted in the discussion of Henry Harding's family.

The order of births is not certain, but it would seem that Thomas was the eldest son.

On 20 Aug., 1679, Anne Harding, now wife of Richard Bradley (1-1), was by the court appointed guardian to her son, Thomas Harding, 14 years of age.

Richard Bradley **(1-1)** died and Anne (1-3), his widow, m. a third time, Luke Rowland (1-3).

The Anne Harding (1-3) who married Luke Rowland (1-3) was in fact the widow of Thomas Harding II (1-3) (number 4 below), according to the following Court order from Book 5 1678-1698 Page 742: 17 Sept 1696 "Mr. John Haynie Sen, guardian of the orphans of Thomas Harding decd against Luke Rowland (1-3), who married Ann (1-3) the admx of said Harding Continued by consent." As is clear from the record quoted below, John Haynie was guardian of the orphans of Thomas Harding II (1-3), who died in 1691.

4. Thomas Harding (Thomas II) (1-3) came of age in 1685, and probably shortly thereafter married a daughter of Capt. John Haynie. In March, 1691, Thos. Harding was member of a jury. On 20 May, 1691, he was appointed constable for Mattapony. Both Thos. Harding and his wife ----Haynie Harding, were dead before Sept., 1691, as the following record of that date shows. Whereas, Mr. John Haynie, Sr., petitions this court that Mr. Harding late of this county deceased died intestate, leaving an estate in lands and chattels and had issue by the said Mr. Haynie's daughter deceased also a son named Thomas Harding, who hath from his birth, being three years old, since been sustained by him, prayed that he right have the guardianship of the said child, Captain Haynie was by the court appointed guardian of the child.

Harding Families of the Northern Neck of Virginia

The next records refer to Mr. Thomas Harding, the immigrant, and the final settlement of his estate.

On 19 Feb., 1692, the Court appointed a jury to audit the accounts of William Harding (recently of age) and other orphans of Thomas Harding, decd.

This record (from Book 5 1678-1698 Page 581 reads as follows: 19 Feb 1691/2 "Ordered that sometime between this and the next court that Richard Fflynt and Thomas Bushrod and George Hutton and ye James Soburn or any three of them meet and etc. and state ye accts of William Harding and others ye orphans of Thomas Harding decd against Luke Rowland (1-3) and make report of their proceedings at the next court." As you can see, there is no mention that William was recently of age. The William referred to here is William, born 1690, the son of Thomas Harding II.

18 May, 1692, the Court ordered the appraisement of the estate of Thomas Harding Sr., decd. The appraisers to make return to the next Court thereof, and also that Luke Rowland (1-3) at that time exhibit his oath to the same.

On 22 May, 1696, Capt. John Haynie, guardian of Thomas Harding, orphan of Thomas Harding, Sr., brought suit against Luke Rowland (1-3), who married Anne (1-3) the Administratrix (and widow) of Thomas Harding (1-3), decd. Capt. Haynie died in 1697, leaving a will which was burned with other Court records in 1710. His son, John Haynie, Sr., was one of his executors, and on 19 Nov. 1718, gave a "deed of Indenture with Livery and Seizen" to Thomas Harding (1-8). This was probably a bequest from Capt. Haynie to his grandson.

The children of (4) Thomas and Haynie Harding were:

7. Thomas, b. 1688, Court record

8. William, b. 15 Feb., 1690, Parish record

There may have been other children who have not been identified,

7. Thomas Harding (Thomas2, Thomas1) came of age about 1709. He m. Mary Berry, dau. of William Berry. The will of Elizabeth Bledsoe, d, 13 Feb., 1708, names her granddaughter Mary Berry and her son-in-law Wm. Berry.

The third Thomas Harding d. in 1722. His will dated 17 Oct., 1722, and pro. 11 Dec., 1722, names his wife Mary, gives his son William a tract of land in Mattapony, joining on the land of Claughton and Johnson.

Son Samuel land in Mattapony.

Son Thomas homestead and tract of land bought of James Palmer.

Daughter Jane 250 acres in Mattapony.

Daughter Judah (Judith) 100 acres in North Farnham Parish, Richmond Co., part of Henry Corbin's patent. Wife Mary and George Ball executors.

The wife of Capt. George Ball was Grace, dau. of Anthony Haynie and first cousin of Thomas Harding.

The issue of Thomas and Mary Berry Harding were:

9. William m. Sarah, dau. of Joseph and Mary Mattrom Ball.

Comments on Published Articles

Samuel

Thomas

Jane m. George Humphreys

Judah

Mary This last named dau. was b. after the death of her father, as Mary Harding on 19 Aug., 1727, made a deed to George Ball for property for her dau. Mary Harding.

Mary, the widow of Thomas Harding, m. second Roston Betts.

I have no problem with the above material on Thomas Harding II (1-3) and Thomas Harding III and their families. I do have material on the children of William and Thomas Harding above as well as material on the William Harding who was born in 1690, which will be covered later.

5. Henry, son of Thomas and Anne Moseley Harding, was doubtless the namesake of his grandfather, Henry Moseley. The date of his birth is not known. It may have been 1666 or 67.

He m. Jane and had issue: probably Henry, William, Thomas, John.

The following court records, from Book 5 1678-1698, show the approximate age and time of majority for Henry Harding and prove the existence of the last son of Thomas Harding I, John Harding:

Page 529 21 Nov 1690 "Henry and John Harding have in court made choice of their brother Thomas to be their guardian"

Page 564 20 August 1691 "William Harding on ye behalf and as next friend to John and Henry Harding, orph of Thomas Harding dec against Luke Rowland (1-3) Referred"

This means that Henry Harding was born no earlier that 1670 and most likely 1671 given that his brother William was born in July 1669. Thus Henry Harding married most likely in 1692 or 1693. The latest date for his death (8 August 1697) is proven by the following orders from Book 5 1678-1698:

Page 761 21 April 1697 "Whereas it appears to this court that the Estate of Will Harding decd is indebted to Henry Harding his admr by account for sundry charges and other expenses which this court esteems reasonable eight hundred pounds of tobacco ---- Judgment is granted the said Harding adm against the said decd estate for the said funds."

Page 764 22 Apr 1697 "Mr. James Johnson vs Henry Harding adm of William Harding continued to the next court."

Page 765 22 Apr 1697 "Mr. John Cralle agst Henry Harding, adm of William Harding, continued to the next court."

Page 774 20 May 1697 "James Johnson agst Henry Harding, admr of William Harding decd continued."

Page 774 20 May 1697 "Mr. John Cralle against Henry Harding admr of William Harding continued.

Page 781 8 August 1697 "Upon the motion of Jane Harding, widow and relict of Henry Harding, decd, a commission of Adm is granted her on the estate of her said deceased husband and had giving (---) for her did administer on the said estate according to law.".

Page 781 8 August 1697 "Upon the motion of Jane Harding, admr of Henry Harding decd, Mr. Richard Fflynt and Thomas Miller and William Brand and John Lewis and John Cralle or any four of them, are by the Court appointed to appraise the estate of the said decd being first summoned by the next justices and ordered that said Jane exhibit an inventory thereof to the next court upon oath."

20 Nov., 1696, upon the Motion of Henry Harding, adm. of William Harding decd, it is ordered that Richard Flynt, Jr., Thomas Bearcroft et al appraise the estate of the sd deceased.

6. William Harding was b. Jul 20,1669 and was the brother of Henry.

Again 19 Feb., 1698, an appraisement was ordered of the estate of Wm. Harding, deceased.

Henry Harding probably d. in 1698, as on 19 May of that year the court appointed a jury to view work done on house of Richard Thompson by Wm. Harding.

Note the above orders. Henry was dead by August 1697. The text of the above order is as follows (Book 5 1678-1698):

Page 781 8 August 1697 "Upon the motion of Jane Harding (1-6), widow and relict of Henry Harding (1-6), decd., a commission of Adm is granted her on the estate of her said deceased husband and had giving (---) for her did administer on the said estate according to law.".

Page 814 19 Feb 1697/8 Upon the motion of Charles Ashton and Jane his wife, Com of Adm is granted them on est of William Harding dec., they giving Caution for their due administration on the said estate according to law.

Page 825 19 May 1698 Charles Ashton having noted to the court that William Harding to whom he is administrator did begin and work carpentry works for and towards building a house for Richard Thompson who refuseth satisfaction for the said work not being finished. The Court doe therefore appoint Mr. Richard Flynt, John Lawrence and Thomas Miller to view the said Worke, compute the value thereof and make a report to the next court.

Page 835 21 July 1698 "Judgment is granted Mr. John Cralle agst Charles Ashton and Jane his wife, admr of William Harding deced for the payment of three hundred and four pounds of tobacco on balance of a bill for four hundred and fifty founds of tobacco dated November 29 169- and ordered to pay the said summe of three hundred and four pounds of tobacco to the said Cralle our of the said deced estate."

Page 835 21 July 1698 "Whereas it appears to the court that William Hardings estate is indebted to James Johnson by accounts for diff and other expenses in his lifetime and after his death 712 pounds of tobacco is granted to said Johnson against Charles Ashton and Jane his wife, admr of the said decd. Ordered that the administrator pay the said funds out of said decd estate."

Jane is mentioned as relict of Henry Harding, and she became the adm. of Wm. Harding's estate.

On 21 July, 1698, Jane is mentioned as the wife of Charles Ashton, and they were both sued by John Cralle as administrators of Wm. Harding.

It is believed by the writer that one of the sons of Henry and Jane Harding was William who lived in St. Stephen's Parish. On 19 May, 1713, Wm. Harding, of St. Stephens Parish made a deed to Samuel Robinson for 100 acres of land In Wicomico Parish, part of Saunder's bought by Thomas Harding from whom it descends by inheritance.

As to the purported children of Henry and Jane Harding, note that Mrs. Keach says Henry "probably" had sons Henry, William, Thomas and John. This "probably" has been omitted in later writers. There is no proof in any of the records concerning Henry and Jane Harding that they had any children. There are no guardianships of records nor are there any apprenticeships for any children of Henry Harding. Taking each child one by one:

Henry Harding II. This man is usually identified as the Henry Harding who married Anne Belcher about 1715 and moved to Stafford County, Virginia, where he had a large family. In fact, the Henry Harding who moved to Stafford married Ann Belcher in 1708, proven by the following records from Order Book 6 1699-1713:

Page 412 23 November 1706 Anne Belcher wid against Fergus att Timothy Swillivant continued

Page 519 20 May 1708 Upon the petition of Henry Harding and Anne his wife, com of Adm is granted them on the estate of William Beltcher Jr. decd they giving Caution for their due admin on ye sd deced estate according to law.

Page 519 20 May 1708 Hugh Callan enters himself security in the sum of ten thousand pounds of tobacco to ye Justices of Northumberland Court that Henry Harding and Anne his wife shall duly administer the estate of Wm. Beltcher Jr. decd.

If Henry Harding I could only have children between 1693 and 1697, any son would have been at most 15 years old, far too young to be married and administering an estate in 1708.

This Henry Harding who married Anne Belcher and moved to Stafford County is most likely the same man who was transported by Capt. George Eskridge, who received 250 acres for the transportation of Henry Harden and others 21 March 1705/6.

William Harding: Mrs. Keach assumes that the William who sold land in 1713 was a son of Henry. The deed citation actually reads as follows (Deed and Will

Book 1710-1713): Page 283 19 May 1713 "Deed from William Harding planter of St. Stephens Parish to Samuel Robinson conveys land in Wicomico Parish, said land lately in the occupation of the said William Harding, it being part of a patent formerly granted to Edward Saunders, decd called Saunder's Quarter, which said Sanders devised to his son Ebenezer, who sold 200 acres to John Evans in 1685 who sold 100 acres of it to Richard Lewis on the 3rd day of June 1689 and the said Lewis --- by deed of assignment dated the 2nd day of March 1691 (4?) to Thomas Harding from whom the said one hundred acres of land hereby bargained and sold descends unto the said William Harding"

Note that Thomas Harding got the land in 1691. This therefore refers to Thomas Harding II, not Thomas Harding I. The William who sold the land must therefore be the William Harding born 1690, son of Thomas Harding II.

Some published articles assign three children to William Harding, son of Henry, namely Charles, Francis and Thomas. According to St. Stephens Parish Register, these sons of William were born in 1704, 1704 and 1706 respectively (the first two being twins). The articles change these dates to 1714 and 1716 to make this William fit as a son of Henry. This is a blatant and unnecessary manipulation of the records. I believe the William who had these three children is unrelated to Thomas Harding I of Northumberland County, VA and that Charles is the man of the same name in Stafford County and that Thomas is the father of Hopkins and Mark Harding referred to in Lucy Waring's book.

Thomas Harding and John Harding are simply guesses by Mrs. Keach. No such sons can be documented, and none are needed. Her John is most likely Henry's brother John Harding, and the Thomas is one of many Thomas Hardings in the area. No son of Henry's named Thomas is needed nor did one exist.

It is therefore my contention that Henry Harding and Jane Harding had no children and that it is not necessary to postulate children for them since all the Hardings in the county can be accounted for in other ways.

The early Hardings were short-lived, as Thomas, the immigrant, and his sons were all dead before 1700. There are numerous records of the Hardings in the old court books, and much valuable material for the family historian. **(Except the youngest son John)**.

However, Thomas Harding was not ancestor of all of that name in Northumberland.

No further mention is found of William Harding, accused of witchcraft and ordered to leave the county in 1653. But among the headrights of Capt^{l}. George Eskridge, recorded 21 March, 1706 and assigned to him by Jno. Cottrell is Henry Harding who had doubtless been transported to VA several years before this date. He may have been the Henry Harding who on 23 Aug., 1700, was a witness in a case before the court and is mentioned as the servant of John Cockrell.

This Henry Harding is likely the one mentioned above who married Anne Belcher and moved to Stafford County, VA.

The older line of descent from Thomas Harding is traceable through the inheritance of land. Later wills and court orders help identify his other descendants.

Article 2: Eva Hardin Benning, Francois Benin

FRANCOIS BENIN (Francis Benning)
His Descendants and Allied Families
By Eva Hardin Benning (1981)

This material on the Harding family is an 18-page section of a book on the descendants of Francois Benin written and published by Eva Hardin Benning in 1981. This book is available in the original at the Mormon Family History Library in Salt Lake City, (US-Can 929.273 B437b) or by microfilm (Film # 1033867, Item #2).

This item is important because Mrs. Benning purports to cover all the descendants of Thomas Harding I of Northumberland Co., VA, many into the early 1800s. In many cases her later work is valuable. However, her early work depends in large measure on the material of Mrs. Keach discussed in the article above. As is readily apparent, this work contains many errors.

Essentially this book is a rehash of Mrs. Keach's material so includes virtually all the errors Mrs. Keach made. As my research has shown, many of the records were misread and many of the personal connections were fabricated.

I am not quoting specific portions of the book because it is under copyright.

Article 3: Lucy Lemoine Waring, "Hardings of Northumberland Co., VA"

There is little to comment on this book, published in 1971, since we have discussed the first generations quite thoroughly in other sections of this book. However, the areas of concern are in the second and third generations as presented here. First, this material is presented with no documentation of any kind. Mrs. Waring makes assertions and expects us to believe them without proof.

First, she gives William Harding (1-5) a son Thomas. The only known son for William Harding (1-5) is John Harding, (1-10) born about 1693, who was apprenticed to his uncle John Harding (1-7) in Westmoreland County, VA in 1704. (See Westmoreland County records). There is a Thomas Harding, (2-4) son of William Harding (2-1) listed in the St. Stephens Parish Register, born in 1706, ten years after William the son of Thomas Harding I died. I have listed this William as Family Number 2 above and do include this Thomas Harding in his family.

Second, she has Thomas Harding (2-4) marrying Hannah Hopkins, daughter of Robert and Hannah Hopkins of Lancaster County. There was a Hopkins family in Lancaster County, however, other records indicate that Hannah was the daughter of John Warrington of Northumberland County. (See County records above)

Again, she has used material from Mrs. Keach's article as if it were true, which makes her treatment of the early generations of the family inaccurate. For the first three or four generations, this book is not to be relied upon. Material on later generations is valuable but must be used with the greatest caution and research in the original records.

Article 4: Fredna Tweedt Irvine, "Henry Hardin of California"

HENRY HARDIN OF CALIFORNIA
BY Fredna Tweedt Irvine
Belmont, Massachusetts
1976

Most of my comments on this book are the same as on the previous books. She used material from Keach and Dorothy Ford Wulfeck and a genealogist Mrs. F. Everett Bowen as reliable sources, which they are not. Again, these are flawed sources and must not be relied upon

Article 5: J. Oran Hardin, "Hardin USA"

I discovered this treasure trove of Harding information at the Family History Library in Salt Lake City in June 1998. This multi-volume set contains a huge amount of information on the family. Due to limited time, I was only able to read through small portions containing data on the families I was interested in, which is only a small portion of the data contained here.

This set is a must first stop for anyone researching the Harding family.

The cautions expressed in my comments on Mrs. Wulfeck's book apply here as well. Private researchers supplied much of the data, giving rise to many contradictions, precisely what gives the books so much value. The researcher will find varying opinions on a given line and see what research has been done in the past. They are free to pursue work in original records and make an informed decision as to which interpretation, if any, they will accept.

Article 6: Dorothy Ford Wulfeck, "Hardings in Virginia and Kentucky"

This book has the virtue of being one of the most important and one of the most maddening of the Harding books in print, precisely because she makes no representation that any of the material in the book is accurate.

In her introduction, Mrs. Wulfeck states that this material is drawn from many sources, none of which she will vouch for. She states that her book is a resource for further research, a workbook and not a genealogy. Many of the records are drawn from published sources, which themselves contain errors. Many others are based on the personal research of the contributors.

Anyone using this book is well advised not to accept any statement made therein as fact without doing further research in original records, as I have done for this book.

Having given this caution, I believe that this is a valuable resource for researchers precisely because Mrs. Wulfeck has brought together conflicting opinions on several lines as well as details of later generations which might have remained in private hands and thus be unavailable to us.

I do not intend to do a line-by-line critique of her book. However, any data in her book concerning the Harding families of Northumberland, Stafford, Westmoreland, Fairfax, and Fauquier counties must be compared to the data in this book and to original records since the errors in these lines recorded here are massive.

In the Fairfax County section on page 56, the deeds she quotes from Bayless Hardin are not Fairfax deeds. Possibly they are from Frederick County or another Virginia county. Since I have not followed this family in detail, I do not know where these deeds belong.

A large part of the book is concerned with the descendants of Mark Hardin of Prince William County, many of whose descendants went to Kentucky. Another large part concerns the descendants of Henry Harding of Stafford County, again with many descendants in Kentucky.

Index
Including Individual Numbers

Each person who has a number is numbered in the index. Non-Harding persons show the name of the person they married in the index. Persons with no numbers could not be placed in one of the five families featured in this book. However, they lived in the area I have covered or were families with strong connections to the Hardin families. I have not indexed miscellaneous names such as persons who bought land or witnesses or persons mentioned in records who are not connected to the Hardings.

Adair
  Mary (Mark Hardin) (5-88), 349
Allen
  Rachel (Thomas Hardin) (4-30), 325, 370, 371
Allensworth
  Deliliah (Henry Harding) (3-13), 247
  Polly (Mary) (Henry Harding) (3-16), 246, 247, 356, 359
Anderson
  John (Judith Harding) (1-24), 230
  Mary (3-42), 95
Appleton
  Susanna (John Harden) (1-72), 300
Arledge
  Jane (1-6), xv, 212, 213
Ashby, 93, 99, 100, 118, 151, 169, 171, 172, 173, 174, 236, 246, 251, 256, 257, 313, 314, 317, 329, 347, 348, 349, 362, 363, 364, 365, 366, 367
  Ann (Nicholas Harding) (3-6), 246, 328, 329
  Benjamin, 117, 118, 119, 120, 169, 312, 313, 317
  Elizabeth (4-2) (William Hardin) (4-2), 42, 111, 114, 115, 169
  Henry, 93, 169, 172, 174, 245, 347, 349
  John, 93, 99, 100, 136, 137, 139, 166, 169, 171, 172, 232, 233, 236, 257, 328, 329, 347, 348, 349, 363
  John (4-5), 114
  Martha, 112
  Martha Ann, 118
  Martha Ann (Enos Hardin) (4-7), 348
  Nathaniel, 117, 120, 313
  Robert, 117, 120, 126, 127, 128, 138, 139, 171, 172, 232, 259, 314, 347, 363, 367, 368
  Stephen, 99, 118, 150, 169, 174, 323, 324, 328, 329, 347, 348, 349
  Thomas, 111, 136, 137, 151, 169, 171, 172, 173, 232, 233, 235, 236, 256
  Thomas), 54
Ashton
  Charles (Jane Arledge) (1-6), 212, 213
Ball
  Anastasia (Stacy) (William Harding) (2-5), 161, 165
  Mary (Moses Harding) (2-12), 372, 373
Barecraft, xiii, 21, 53, 54, 197, 231, 232
  Jane (John Harding) (1-10), 197, 215, 216
Barrickman
  Lawrence (Emily Harding) (3-89), 103, 358, 359
Beard
  Isabella (Martin Harding) (4-65), 123
Belcher
  Anne (Henry Harding) (3-1), 32, 37, 38, 46, 89, 214, 397
Bennett, 9, 41, 51, 115, 127, 172, 231, 256, 274, 275, 276, 384, 385
  Ann (John Harding) (1-7), 215, 216, 231
  Cuthbert, 52, 216, 217, 218, 231
  Elizabeth, 122, 208, 231
  John, 12, 13, 207, 208, 231, 368

404

Index

Berry, 12, 52, 53, 111, 120, 151, 169, 171, 172, 198, 207, 208, 222, 244, 313, 314, 318, 319, 320, 328, 329, 347, 348, 349, 362, 363, 364, 370, 372, 375, 394
  Elizabeth (Knott, Bennett, Mann, Tyngey, Shoares), 12, 13, 14
  Hanna (James Hardin) (4-8), 119, 348
  Mary (Thomas Harding III) (1-8), 197, 198, 217, 218
Binion
  William B. (Margaret Harden) (1-85), 63
Bland
  Nancy (George Harding) (2-13), 237
Bradley
  Richard (1-1), 209, 393
Brown
  Emily (William Harding) (3-72), 357
  William H. (Wilmouth Harding) (3-71), 357
Bullitt
  Seth (4-3), 114
Bunbury
  Jane (George Harding) (3-3), 255
Bunnel
  Jeremiah (Rebecca Hardin) (4-27), 118, 349
Burtt
  Eli (Paulina Harding) (3-90), 103, 306, 307
Callahan
  Thomas (Nancy Harding) (3-69), 100, 102, 337
Calvert
  Silas B. (Lucy Harding) (4-32), 318
Clarissa (Clarkey)
  Million, 41, 112, 115
Clarissa Million (4-2) (William Harding), 32
Clements
  Sarah (John Samuel Harding) (4-69), 123
Click
  Elizabeth (Jeremiah Harden) (1-75), 302
Clore, 104, 105, 106, 354, 355, 356, 357, 358
  Margaret (Lewis Hardin) (3-84), 103, 357
Cloud
  Catherine (3-43), 96
  Jane (3-44), 96
Combs
  Jane (4-5), 114
  John (4-3), 114
  Joseph (4-22), 117
  Joseph (4-4), 40, 42, 111, 114, 116

  Joseph I (1-23), 28
  Joseph I (4-1), 15, 16, 17, 32, 39, 40, 42, 75, 110, 111, 113
  Joseph II (4-4), 16
  Robert Ashby (4-20), 117
  Stephen (4-23), 117
Cox
  Peter, 24, 205, 226
  Peter Presley, 23, 24, 59, 279
  Sarah (1-23), 28
Cox?
  Sarah (Thomas Harden) (1-23), 23, 25, 32, 58, 279
Cralle
  John (Sarah Harding) (1-27), 201, 202, 203, 205
Daily
  Thomas P. (Amanda Ann Hardin) (4-96), 126
Daniel
  John (Nancy Harding) (2-62), 168
Davies
  Jane (John Hardin) (5-27), 138, 142, 236, 349
Davis
  Mary (Henry Hardin) (5-55), 348
Dawson
  Elijah (Mary Harding) (3-41), 95, 308
Denney, 77, 81, 82, 86, 200, 201, 222
Dennis
  Jacob (Catherine Harding) (3-45), 96, 308
Doggett
  Elizabeth (William Harding) (2-27), 20, 253, 254
Douthitt
  Loucinda (Mark Hardin) (4-45), 318
Downey
  Robert (Nancy Harding (3-24), 93
Doyle
  Cassandra (Enos Hawkins) (4-113), 128, 381
Elizabeth Hardin
  Elizabeth (5-34), 139
Ellis
  Israel (Mary Hardin) (4-38), 120, 371
Emerson
  Zachariah T. (Jane Hawkins) (4-111), 128, 370, 381, 382
Evans
  Mary E. (Baylis G. Hardin) (4-39), 371
Everett
  Jemima (Hopkins Harding) (2-15), 204

Harding Families of the Northern Neck of Virginia

Fauntleroy
  Griffin (Betty Harding) (1-25), 203, 230
Foster
  James (Nancy Harden) (1-91), 65, 283
  William E. (Ada Engedi Harding) (4-81), 250
Foust
  Rebecca C. (Daniel Clapp Harden) (1-112), 287
Freeman
  John Patman (Deborah Harden) (1-92), 65, 283
Garner
  Parish (Jane Harding) (1-30), 203, 230
Garrison
  Kitty (Daniel C Harden) (1-112), 287
George
  Wilmouth (Henry Harding) (3-2), 166, 167, 168, 243, 244, 245, 247, 248, 249, 256, 258, 259
Gibbons, 56, 57, 200, 218, 220
  Jane (Thomas Harding IV) (1-15), 200, 201, 225
Giles
  Mary (Thomas Harding) (unrelated), 11, 12
Glasscock
  Milly (William Harding (1-32), 60, 204, 231, 239
Gray
  Mollie (William E. Hardin) (4-91), 382
Green
  Patty (William Harding) (2-5), 36, 256
Guthrie
  Elizabeth (Enos Hardin) (4-29), 325, 368, 371
Hale
  Agnes (William Presley Harden) (1-87), 70
Hancock
  William (Sarah Harding) (3-30), 247, 342, 343, 344, 345, 355
Harden
  America Lackland (1-137), 73
  Ann (Reid) (1-46), 22, 58, 294
  Anthony (2-25), 161, 184
  Barbara Holt (1-117), 69
  Betsy (Holt) (1-82), 63, 287, 289
  Bledsoe (5-128), 145
  Caroline (1-139), 73
  Charles (2-23), 77, 161
  Daniel Clapp (1-112), 68, 287, 288
  Deborah (Freeman) (1-92), 65, 72, 283

Emma R. (Williams) (1-103), 67
George Monroe (1-121), 69
George Washington (1-138), 73
Hall (2-22), 77, 83, 161, 164, 165, 168
Harriet Eliza (2-67), 83, 151
Henry (1-49), 22, 23, 58, 64, 281, 282, 283, 292, 293, 294
Henry (3-104), 107, 110, 357
Henry (5-37), 139, 145, 292
Henry Roger (1-131), 72
Hiram (1-88), 24, 25, 26, 27, 34, 64, 70, 296, 297, 298
James M. (1-123), 70, 304
Jane (Whitsett) (1-84), 63
Jane (William Hornbuckle) (1-42), xiii, 58, 61
Jeremiah (1-45), 22, 58, 63, 160, 164, 165, 281, 282, 287, 293, 294
Jeremiah (1-75), 62, 68, 299, 300, 301, 302
Jeremiah (1-86), 27, 64, 70, 124, 296, 300, 304
Jeremiah Holt (1-113), 69
John (1-125), 70, 304
John (1-44), 22, 26, 58, 62, 282, 283, 287, 288, 289, 294
John (1-72), 62, 67, 299, 300, 301, 303, 304
John (1-79), 26, 63, 68, 284, 287, 288, 289, 294
John Click (1-109), 68, 302
John Milton (1-136), 73
John William (1-120), 69
Joseph (4-154), 132
Joshua (1-90), 26, 27, 64, 71, 297, 298
Margaret (1-85), 63
Margaret (Hurdle) (1-83), 63, 287, 289
Margaret Eleanor (1-134), 72
Margaret Jane (1-111), 68, 302
Margaret Jane (1-116), 287
Margaret Jane (1-16), 69
Margery (1-124), 70
Martha Frances (4-164), 133, 180, 187
Mary (Prather) (1-80), 63, 287, 289
Mary Ann (2-68), 83, 151
Mary Ann (Ball) (2-24), 78, 161
Mary Catherine (1-118), 69
Mary Elizabeth (1-135), 73
Mary Lyddey (Yancey) (1-128), 71
Nancy (2-62), 83, 168
Nancy (2-65), 83, 151
Nancy (Foster) (1-91), 65, 72, 283
Nancy Ann (1-122), 69
Peggy (1-51), 66
Peggy (Margaret) (1-51), 22, 58, 284, 294

Index

Peggy (Samuel Shelborne) (1-73), 62, 67, 300
Peter (1-110), 68, 302
Peter (1-50), xiii, 21, 22, 23, 26, 58, 65, 283, 293, 294
Peter Holt (1-115), 287
Peter Ray (1-115), 69
Philip (1-140), 73
Polly (1-77), 62, 303
Presley (1-43), xiii, 20, 21, 22, 23, 26, 58, 61, 131, 281, 282, 283, 294, 299, 300, 301, 304
Presley W. (1-102), 67, 300, 303
Rebecca Adeline (1-119), 69
Sally (1-81), 63, 289
Sally (Gregory Wilson) (1-76), 62, 300, 303
Sally H. (1-114), 69
Sarah (Rogers) (1-47), 22, 58, 294
Susan Taylor (1-108), 68, 302
Susanna (Pope) (2-60), 83, 168
Susannah (1-78), 62, 303
Susannah (2-63), 83, 151
Thomas (1-23), xiii, xv, 20, 21, 22, 23, 24, 25, 26, 28, 32, 33, 34, 38, 46, 57, 124, 160, 161, 163, 164, 180, 279, 281, 282, 283, 292, 293, 294
Thomas (1-48), 22, 25, 26, 27, 34, 58, 64, 282, 287, 294, 296, 297, 299, 300, 301
Thomas (1-74), 62
Thomas (1-89), 64
Thomas Green (2-26), 36, 78, 83, 151, 161, 164, 165
Thomas Jefferson (1-126), 34, 70, 304
Thomas Jefferson (1-130), 71
Thomas Presley (1-127), 26
Thomas Presley (5-60), 304
Thomas Presley) (1-127), 70
Thomas Sinclair (2-66), 83, 151
Thompson (1-93), 65, 72, 283, 284, 294
Walter Elias (1-132), 72
William (4-2), 28
William L. (4-132), 131, 182, 190
William Presley (1-129), 71
William Presley (1-87), 24, 25, 26, 27, 64, 70, 296, 298, 304, 305
William Thompson (1-133), 72
Willliam (2-64), 83, 151

Hardin
Abigail (5-17), 136, 350
Abigail (5-7), 135
Abraham H (3-98), 106, 358
Absolom (4-36), 119, 129, 361, 363, 364, 365, 366, 367, 369, 371
Absolom (5-43), 140, 324, 331, 347, 375, 376
Adeline (4-107), 127, 370
Ailcey (4-93), 126
Alexander Livingston (4-94), 126, 369, 370
Alice (5-51), 140
Alis (5-10), 135
Amanda (Flint) (3-108), 107, 358
Amanda Ann (Daily) (4-96), 126
Amelia (5-74), 141
America (3-110), 107
America Elizabeth (4-100), 126
Ann (5-54), 140, 350
Ann (5-9), 135
Ann (Hawkins) (4-31), 118, 128, 325, 367, 370, 380
Avarilla (5-38), 139
Bailey (2-33), 80, 375, 376, 377, 378
Baylis G. (4-39), 120, 130, 361, 365, 366, 367, 369, 371
Benjamin (4-9), 16, 32, 41, 42, 111, 112, 115, 121, 168, 314, 315, 316, 322, 323, 324, 325, 326, 360, 362, 368
Benjamin (5-14), 136, 137, 141, 350
Benjamin (5-72), 141
Benjamin (Stiller Ben) (5-60), 140, 350
Benjamin Jr (4-43), 121, 315, 316
Burgess (5-131), 145
Cassandra (5-69), 141
Catherine (5-19), 136, 350
Catherine (5-28), 138
Catherine (5-57), 140, 350
Catherine (5-64), 141
Catherine Ann Hardin (Clore) (3-94), 106, 357
Catherine D. (Brown) (3-112), 108, 358
Cato (5-53), 140
Celia (5-83), 142
Clara (5-129), 145
Cynthia (5-127), 145
Daniel (4-41), 121, 322, 323, 325
Daniel (5-84), 142
Daniel (5-86), 142
Daniel Stull (5-89), 142
Davis (5-101), 143
Davis (5-93), 142
Eleanor Ann (Clore) (3-93), 105, 357
Elijah (5-78), 141
Eliza A. (Enos Hardin Jr) (4-101), 369, 371
Elizabeth (4-89), 126, 381
Elizabeth (5-11), 135
Elizabeth (5-20), 136, 350
Elizabeth (5-47), 140
Elizabeth (Kelly) (4-25), 117, 121, 317
Elizabeth (Kelly) (4-46), 121, 325, 326
Elizabeth (Yager) (3-96), 106, 357
Emaline F. (3-111), 108

Harding Families of the Northern Neck of Virginia

Enos (4-101), 127, 134, 361, 366, 367, 369, 370, 371
Enos (4-29), 118, 126, 322, 325, 361, 362, 363, 364, 365, 366, 367, 368, 369, 370, 371
Enos (4-33), 119, 316
Enos (4-7), 16, 32, 41, 111, 112, 113, 115, 118, 150, 151, 174, 184, 312, 313, 314, 315, 316, 317, 318, 319, 320, 321, 325, 348, 349, 368
Enos (4-99), 126
Enos David (4-155), 132
Evangelist (4-6), 16, 41, 111, 112, 115, 117, 121, 174, 313, 315, 317, 318, 319, 320, 321, 325, 362, 370
George (4-28), 118, 125, 318, 325, 360, 362, 363, 367, 368, 379, 380, 381, 382
George (5-52), 140
George Thomas (4-98), 126
George W. (4-103), 370
George W. (4-104), 127, 370, 371
George Washington (4-125), 130
George Washington (4-50), 121, 325
Hannah (5-24), 137
Hannah (5-58), 140, 350
Harriet (Hawkins) (4-35), 119, 129, 367, 371, 379
Hector (5-50), 140, 350
Henry (3-47), 96
Henry (4-48), 121, 325, 326
Henry (5-121), 145
Henry (5-5), 44, 45, 135, 139, 173, 235, 286
Henry (5-55), 140, 348, 350
Henry (5-79), 141
Henry Edward (5-110), 144
Henry S. (4-131), 130, 369
Isabel (5-48), 140
James (2-39), 80, 372, 374
James (4-122), 130
James (4-42), 121, 315, 316
James (4-8), 16, 41, 112, 113, 115, 119, 313, 314, 315, 316, 317, 318, 319, 320, 321, 322, 348, 360, 361, 362, 363, 364, 365, 366, 367, 368, 369
James (5-114), 144
James (5-71), 141
James B. (4-40), 120, 365, 367
Jane (Thompson) (2-38), 80, 372
Jehu (5-75), 141
Jesse (5-16), 136, 142
Jessie Allen (4-102), 127, 134, 366, 367, 370, 371, 381
Jessie Allen (4-98), 126

Jessie E. (4-87), 126, 127, 133, 371, 380, 382
John (3-44), 96
John (4-24), 117, 315, 316
John (5-105), 143
John (5-117), 144
John (5-12), 136, 139, 350
John (5-2), 45, 135, 136, 167, 169, 170, 171, 172, 175, 176, 233, 234, 235, 237, 244, 350
John (5-27), 138, 142, 236, 349
John (5-42), 140, 146
John (5-56), 140, 174, 324, 325, 350
John (5-88), 142
John (Jack) (5-40), 139
John E. (5-76), 141
John L. (5-130), 145
John Stephen (2-34), 80, 372, 373, 374
John W. (3-106), 107, 110, 330, 358
Joseph (4-21), 117
Joseph Sanford (4-135), 131
Judith (5-116), 144
Judith (5-35), 139
Latitia S. (5-96), 142
Letitia (5-109), 143
Lewis (4-34), 119, 360, 361, 362, 363, 364, 365, 366, 367, 369
Lewis T. (5-95), 142
Lucy (4-123), 130
Lydia (5-108), 143
Lydia (5-25), 137
Lydia (5-62), 140, 350
Lydia (5-65), 141
Lydia Ann (5-103), 143
Malinda (4-88), 126
Maria (4-92), 126
Mariam (5-45), 140
Mark (4-45), 121, 318, 322, 325, 326
Mark (5-1), 17, 32, 33, 41, 43, 44, 45, 46, 111, 113, 116, 135, 196, 197, 215, 216, 235, 236, 331, 336, 350, 375
Mark (5-100), 143
Mark (5-112), 144, 292, 293, 294, 295, 305
Mark (5-123), 145
Mark (5-13), 136, 140, 174, 176, 177, 235, 237, 238, 348, 350
Mark (5-26), 137, 142, 331
Mark (5-31), 44, 139, 143, 286, 292
Mark (5-4), 41, 46, 111, 135, 138, 171, 172
Mark (5-59), 140, 350
Mark (5-88), 349
Mark (5-91), 142
Martha (4-95), 126

Index

Martha (5-118), 144
Martha (5-15), 135
Martha Ann (Jessie Hardin) (4-90), 126, 127, 371, 381
Martha E. (4-128), 130
Martha Elizabeth (4-106), 127, 370
Martin (5-106), 143
Martin (5-113), 144
Martin (5-124), 145
Martin (5-29), 138, 143
Martin (5-3), 135, 137, 166, 167, 168, 235, 236, 237, 238
Martin (5-36), 139, 145
Martin (5-87), 142
Martin D. (5-99), 143, 315, 317, 320, 321, 322, 367
Martin L. (5-70), 141
Mary (5-102), 143
Mary (5-18), 136, 350
Mary (5-22), 137, 166, 168
Mary (5-32), 139
Mary (5-61), 140, 350
Mary (5-68), 141
Mary (5-8), 135
Mary (5-82), 142
Mary (Ellis) (4-38), 120, 367, 371
Mary (Pyburn) (2-36), 80, 372
Mary Alice (4-109), 127, 370
Mary Ann (5-46), 140
Mary Hunter (5-115), 144
Mary J. (3-107), 107
Matilda (5-49), 140
Melinda Ann (5-80), 141
Moses (2-12), 36, 75, 80, 165, 255, 372, 373, 375, 376, 377, 378
Nancy (4-51), 121, 325
Nancy (5-119), 144
Nancy Ann (4-103) (Jessie Hardin) (4-87), 127, 133, 370, 371
Nancy Ann (4-96) (Jessie Hardin) (4-87), 126
Nathaniel (4-47), 121, 325, 326
Nestor (5-41), 140
Oldham (3-109), 107
Peter (5-132), 146, 322, 323, 325
Philip (3-46), 96
Polly (5-85), 142
Presley (4-83), 20, 125, 131, 180, 181, 187, 190, 311
Rebecca (3-75), 101, 357
Rebecca (Jeremiah Bunnell) (4-27), 118, 349
Rebecca Ann (4-49), 121
Richard (5-126), 145
Richard Calvin (4-129), 130

Rosanna (5-30), 138
Rosanna (5-67), 141
Rosannah (5-104), 143
Sally (5-107), 143
Sally Ann (4-97), 126
Samuel Lee (4-126), 130
Sarah (5-118), 144
Sarah (5-39), 139
Sarah (5-63), 140, 350
Sarah (5-66), 141
Sarah (5-98), 143
Sarah (Benjamin Hardin) (5-23), 141
Sarah (Hendrickson) (2-40), 80, 372
Sarah (Lindsey) (4-26), 117, 318
Sarah (Thornton) (4-37), 119, 367, 371
Sarah Ann (Buckner) (3-105), 107, 357
Sarah Ellen (Benjamin Hardin) (5-23), 137
Sarah White Stull (5-90), 142
Simeon T. (4-127), 130
Sophia (Enos Hardin) (4-7), 118, 349
Susan (5-125), 145
Susan O. (4-166), 134, 382
Susannah (5-21), 136, 350
Susannah Mary (5-97), 142
Swan (5-122), 145
Thomas (4-30), 118, 127, 325, 361, 363, 364, 365, 366, 367, 368, 369, 370, 371, 372
Thomas (5-92), 142
Thomas Jefferson (4-105), 127, 370
Warren (5-73), 141
William (2-37), 80, 372
William (4-130), 130
William (4-145), 132, 311
William (4-44), 121, 325, 326
William (5-111), 144, 281, 293
William (5-15), 136, 141, 350
William (5-33), 139, 145
William (5-81), 142, 318
William (5-94), 142
William Cregg (4-124), 130
William David (4-108), 127, 370
William E (4-91), 126, 133, 381, 382
William Henry (5-44), 140, 350
William S. (5-121), 144
Winnie Ann (5-77), 141
Hardin (Middlesex Co VA)
Anne (9-3), 192
Anne (9-4), 192
Elizabeth (8-3), 192
Elizabeth (9-1), 192
George (9-1), 192, 235
Lucy (Billups (9-2)), 192
Lucy (Billups) (9-2), 192, 235
Mary (9-4), 192

409

Harding Families of the Northern Neck of Virginia

Nicholas (8-3), 192
Peter (8-4), 192
Thomas (9-1), 192
Thomas (9-2), 192, 234, 235

Hardin (Orange Co VA)
Benjamin, 232
Elizabeth, 234
Joseph, 233

Harding
Abner (3-136), 110, 359
Abner (3-33), 95, 102, 239, 386
Abner (3-79), 103, 240
Abraham (3-34), 95, 386
Ada Engedi (Foster) (4-81), 124, 250
Adah (McInteer) (4-17), 116, 261
Albert (4-156), 132, 188, 191
Alcey (1-66), 60, 205
Amnah (Shackelford) (2-57), 83, 168
Amy (4-64), 123
Ann (1-64), 60, 205
Ann (2-7), 75, 255
Ann (3-12), 91, 256
Ann Eliza (3-120), 108
Ann L. (3-127), 109
Anne (1-2), 3, 8, 195
Anne (Cheatham) (2-41), 80
Anne (Thomas Harding, Luke Rowland) (1-3), 8, 10, 11, 49, 211, 393, 394
Benjamin A. (3-129), 109
Bennett (4-53), 122, 274, 275, 276, 384, 385
Betty (2-53), 82, 204
Betty (Griffin Fauntleroy) (1-25), 55, 230
Butlar (3-57), 97, 356
Byram (2-29), 79, 251, 252, 264, 265, 266, 267, 268, 273, 274, 275, 276, 277
Catherine (3-128), 109
Catherine (Jacob Dennis) (3-45), 96, 308
Catherine (William Shrader) (3-32), 94, 337
Charles (2-2), 14, 15, 16, 19, 36, 41, 46, 74, 75, 111, 199, 230, 255, 258, 259, 279
Charles (2-54), 82, 204, 225, 226, 228
Charles (2-9), 75, 255, 257, 268, 269
Cuthbert (4-11), 116, 122, 259, 261, 269, 270
Cyrus (2-43), 81, 84, 206, 227, 228, 229
Cyrus (2-86), 85, 206, 226
Daniel (4-55), 122
Easter (1-65), 60, 205
Edward K. (3-133), 110, 242
Elijah (3-134), 110, 242
Elijah (4-14), 20, 116, 123, 251, 254, 260, 261, 267, 268, 272, 273, 274, 275, 276

Elijah Parkinson (4-80), 124, 250
Elinor (3-27), 93, 329
Eliza (3-74), 101
Eliza Jane (4-162), 133, 187, 191
Elizabeth (2-32), 79
Elizabeth (2-35), 80
Elizabeth (2-73), 84
Elizabeth (2-83), 85
Elizabeth (3-25), 93, 328
Elizabeth (3-37), 95, 386
Elizabeth (4-133), 131
Elizabeth (4-60), 122
Elizabeth (Burnes) (4-138), 132, 312
Elizabeth (John St Clear) (3-48), 96, 308
Elizabeth (William Harding) (4-82), 19, 182, 186, 187, 189, 190, 191
Elizabeth Ellen (4-161), 133, 187, 191
Emily (Amos) (4-141), 132, 312
Emily (Barrickman) (3-89), 103, 306, 358, 359
Emily J. (3-126), 109
Enoch (4-12), 116, 251, 252, 260, 261, 262, 263, 264, 265, 266, 267, 268, 270, 271, 272, 273, 274, 275, 276, 277
Enoch (4-74), 123
Female (2-75), 84
Fielding (4-147), 132, 311
Frances (1-35), 56, 230
Frances (2-59), 83, 168
Frances (4-71), 123
Frances (4-86), 125, 181
Frances (Samuel Lewis) (1-31), 55, 201, 202, 203, 230
Frances (Shackleford) (4-13), 116, 261
Frances Ann (2-18), 76, 221, 223
Francis (2-3), 14, 15, 46, 74, 76, 198, 230
Francis Marion (3-121), 109
Franky (3-10), 91, 256
Garland (4-66), 123
George (2-13), 75, 80, 237, 255, 262, 263, 264, 265, 268, 269, 270, 271, 272
George (2-42), 271
George (2-58), 83, 165, 168
George (3-15), 92, 96, 333, 334, 335, 340, 341, 342, 343, 344, 345
George (3-20), 93, 328, 329
George (3-3), 37, 89, 90, 167, 173, 234, 247, 255, 256, 257, 258, 259, 279
George (3-39), 95, 386
George (3-4), 90, 92, 170, 172, 173, 243, 244, 245, 246, 247, 248, 249, 336, 339, 340, 341, 342
George Jr (2-42), 81, 271, 272
George R. (2-70), 84, 253
George W. (3-132), 110, 240, 241

Index

George Washington (4-152), 132, 311
Gilbert (4-73), 123
Hannah (1-26), 55, 230
Hannah (2-21), 76, 223
Hatte (1-40), 56, 231
Henry (1-6), xv, 7, 8, 11, 14, 17, 18, 48, 50, 210, 211, 212, 213, 396
Henry (3-1), 17, 18, 22, 29, 32, 37, 38, 46, 89, 168, 196, 214, 255, 257, 258, 259
Henry (3-13), 91, 95, 245, 246, 247, 248, 249, 256, 308
Henry (3-135), 110, 242
Henry (3-16), 92, 97, 246, 247, 248, 249, 332, 333, 336, 338, 339, 340, 341, 342, 343, 344, 345, 346, 351, 355, 356
Henry (3-2), 89, 166, 167, 168, 170, 172, 243, 244, 256, 257, 259
Henry (3-31), 94, 100, 246, 330, 332, 333, 334, 335, 337, 339, 340, 341, 342, 343, 345, 346, 351
Henry (3-40), 95, 386
Henry (3-68), 100, 108, 337, 346, 352, 353, 355, 356, 358
Henry (3-8), 90, 94, 243, 244, 245, 247, 248, 249, 330, 332, 335, 339
Henry (4-85), 125, 132, 181, 187, 188, 189, 190, 191
Henry Andrew (3-117), 108
Henry Wildy (4-72), 123
Herod (3-23), 93, 328, 329
Hiram William (2-79), 85, 206, 225, 226
Hopkins (2-15), 14, 15, 76, 81, 200, 201, 202, 204, 224, 225, 226, 227, 228, 229
Hopkins (2-85), 85
Irene Francis (3-115), 108
James (1-60), 60, 66, 205, 206, 228, 229, 231
James (3-43), 96
James (3-53), 345, 355
James (3-91), 104, 306
James (4-151), 132, 311
James (4-59), 122
James A. (3-124), 109
James A. (3-53), 97, 345, 346, 355, 356
James Allen (3-116), 108
James Allen (3-73), 101
James Orion (2-87), 85, 206
Jane (1-17), 197, 219
Jane (1-30), 55, 201, 202, 203, 230
Jane (1-41), 56, 206, 226, 227
Jane (2-8), 75, 255
Jane Amanda (4-79), 124
Jemayma (1-36), 56, 230
Jemima (James Hudnall) (1-36), 230
Jeremiah (1-86), 17

Joel (2-30), 79, 251, 263, 264, 265, 266, 267, 268, 271, 272, 273, 274, 275, 276, 277
John (1-$), 18
John (1-10), xiii, 8, 18, 21, 50, 53, 215, 216, 278, 279
John (1-12), 9, 51, 278
John (1-33), 56, 230
John (1-7), 7, 8, 9, 21, 29, 48, 51, 53, 210, 215, 238, 278
John (2-14), 15, 76, 81, 203, 224, 225
John (2-19), 15, 76, 82, 201, 203, 223
John (2-47), 81, 206
John (3-131), 110, 240, 241
John (3-28), 339
John (3-67), 100, 107, 337, 351, 352, 353, 354, 355, 358
John (4-55), 122
John Bennett (4-10), 40, 41, 116, 122, 260, 269, 270, 271, 272, 273, 274, 275
John Edgar (4-153), 132, 311
John Hopkins (2-84), 85, 206, 226
John J. (3-130), 109
John Ramey (4-160), 133, 180, 187, 191
John Samuel (4-69), 123
John Scott (2-10), 19, 20, 36, 75, 78, 255, 257, 260, 261, 262, 263, 268, 269, 270, 271, 275
Jonathan (3-52), 97, 103, 105, 334, 335, 337, 343, 344, 345, 346, 351, 352, 353, 355, 356, 357, 359
Joseph (4-21), 16, 18, 20, 32, 36, 38, 40, 41, 111, 113, 124, 165, 179, 181, 183, 184
Joseph I (4-21), 16, 17
Joseph S. (4-148), 132, 311
Joseph Sanford (4-135), 187, 188, 312
Judah (1-18), 197, 199, 220
Judah (1-21), 230
Judith (Ellis Hudnall) (1-39), 56, 61, 230, 231
Judith (Joseph Wildey) (1-24), 55, 60, 203, 230, 231
Julia Ann (3-118), 108
June Amanda (3-76), 357
June Amanda (3-76), 101
Katharine (Souther) (3-54), 97, 338, 356
Larkin (4-54), 122
Lewis (3-84), 103, 306, 354, 357, 359
Lewis (4-136), 131, 312
Lewis (4-18), 116, 250, 259, 260, 261
Lewis (4-56), 122
Lewis (4-84), 125, 132, 180, 181, 187, 190, 311
Lewis Bard (4-165), 133, 180, 187, 191

Harding Families of the Northern Neck of Virginia

Lewis G. (4-78), 124
Louisa Jane (Baird) (4-142), 132, 312
Lucinda (Young) (4-149), 132, 311
Lucy (Calvert) (4-32), 119, 318, 367
Lucy (John Scott) (2-10), 20, 251, 263, 264, 265, 266, 267, 268, 271, 272, 273, 274
Lucy (Pitman) (2-51), 81, 206
Lucy (Rankin) (3-83), 103, 306, 357
Manley (4-146), 132, 311
Marcus (4-62), 122
Maria (4-157), 132, 187
Marissa (4-70), 123
Mark (2-16), 15, 76, 82, 200, 201, 203, 204, 224, 225
Mark (2-55), 82, 204
Mark (4-19), 41, 116, 124, 250, 251, 252, 260, 261, 274, 275, 276, 277
Martha (4-67), 123
Martha Frances (4-164), 191
Martin (4-65), 123
Mary (1-19), 198
Mary (1-28), 55
Mary (1-37), 56, 231
Mary (4-68), 123
Mary (4-75), 123
Mary (Elijah Dawson) (3-41), 95, 308
Mary (Polly) (Ashby) (3-21), 93, 99, 329, 348
Mary Ann (Pate) (3-87), 103, 336, 357
Mary E. (3-123), 109
Mary Jane (3-119), 108
Mary Jane (Yager) (3-97), 106, 358
Mason (4-52), 122, 273, 274
Mildred (4-158), 133, 187
Mildred (Baird) (4-143), 132, 312
Mildred Ann (Simeon Wilhoit) (3-77), 101
Mildred Ann (Simeon Wilhoite) (3-77), 357
Milly (1-67), 60, 205
Molley (1-29), 55, 201, 202, 203
Nancy (2-78), 85, 206
Nancy (3-24), 93, 329
Nancy (4-16), 116, 261
Nancy (Callahan) (3-69), 100, 337
Nancy (Ephraim Morrison) (3-49), 96, 308
Nancy (Netherton) (3-18), 92, 337, 359
Nanny (Nancy) (3-7), 90, 243
Nathaniel (3-22), 93, 328, 329
Nelson (4-58), 122, 384, 385
Nicholas (3-38), 95, 386
Nicholas (3-6), 38, 90, 93, 243, 244, 245, 246, 247, 248, 249, 256, 328, 329, 348
Owen G. (3-85), 103, 306, 307
Paulina (Burtt) (3-90), 103, 306, 307
Phebe (3-81), 103
Philadelphia (Elijah Harding) (4-14), 260, 276
Philip (2-28), 79, 251, 277
Philip (2-61), 83, 168
Philip (2-74), 84
Philip (4-77), 123, 254
Polly (2-77), 85, 206
Presley (3-86), 103, 307
Presley (4-140), 132, 312
Presley (4-150), 132, 311
Rebecca (Netherton) (3-8), 330, 339, 340, 341, 342, 343, 345, 346
Rebecca Jane (Mitchell) (3-88), 103, 306, 307, 358
Rebecca K. (2-76), 84, 206
Richard (2-50), 81
Richard (2-72), 84, 253
Robert Henry (4-159), 133, 187, 191
Robert Wesley (4-137), 131, 312
Rowley (3-55), 97, 107, 354, 355, 356
Salley (3-35), 95, 386
Sally (John Harding) (2-47), 206
Sally Coppedge (2-82), 85
Samuel (1-16), 52, 197, 199
Samuel (1-38), 56, 61, 203, 204, 206, 225, 226, 227, 228, 229, 231
Samuel Hopkins (2-48), 81
Sarah (1-27), 55
Sarah (1-63), 60, 205
Sarah (2-20), 76, 223
Sarah (3-14), 91, 256
Sarah (4-15), 116, 261
Sarah (4-61), 122
Sarah (Baird) (4-139), 132, 312
Sarah (Ball) (1-14), 200, 201, 202, 238
Sarah (Hancock) (3-30), 94, 100, 247
Sarah (Jones) (3-19), 93, 329
Sarah A. (3-125), 109
Sarah Ann (3-115), 108
Sarah Ann (4-134), 131, 182
Strother (4-76), 123
Strother B. (2-31), 79, 251, 252
Susan (3-80), 103
Susan Ann (4-163), 133, 187
Thomas (1-1), xiii, xiv, xv, 1, 3, 6, 7, 8, 12, 13, 14, 17, 18, 21, 22, 32, 33, 34, 46, 47, 48, 156, 193, 194, 195, 196, 208, 209, 210, 230
Thomas (1-11), 9, 21, 51, 54, 215, 238
Thomas (1-20), 230
Thomas (1-23), 17, 54
Thomas (1-34), 56, 230
Thomas (1-48), 17
Thomas (1-62), 60, 205, 231

Index

Thomas (2-11), 75, 79, 251, 255, 259, 260, 261, 262, 263, 264, 265, 266, 267, 268, 269, 270, 271, 272, 273, 274, 275, 276, 277
Thomas (2-4), 14, 15, 36, 46, 199, 200, 216, 220, 221, 222, 223, 224, 225, 230
Thomas (2-52), 82, 204, 225, 226, 227, 228, 229
Thomas (Mary Giles) (unrelated), 11, 12
Thomas Everett (2-46), 81
Thomas Everett (2-80), 85, 206, 226
Thomas G., 225
Thomas II (1-3), 3, 8, 9, 10, 11, 47, 49, 195, 196, 209, 210, 211, 230, 393, 395
Thomas III (1-8), 8, 11, 49, 52, 196, 197, 198, 199, 210, 211, 214, 215, 216, 217, 218, 219, 220, 238
Thomas IV (1-15), 52, 56, 197, 201, 202, 218, 219, 220, 222, 223, 224, 230
Thomas Sharp (2-69), 84, 252, 253
Warner A. (3-56), 97, 107, 354, 355, 356, 357, 359
William (1-13), 9, 51, 278
William (1-14), 52, 54, 197, 199, 200, 201, 202, 203, 218, 219, 220, 221, 222, 223, 224, 225, 229, 238
William (1-32), 55, 60, 176, 201, 202, 203, 204, 205, 206, 226, 227, 228, 231, 239
William (1-5), xv, 8, 18, 21, 48, 50, 210, 211, 212, 213, 230, 278
William (1-57), 205
William (1-61), 60, 205, 206, 229, 231
William (1-9), 8, 11, 49, 53, 196, 211, 230
William (1-94), 66
William (2-1), 14, 15, 16, 18, 19, 22, 32, 34, 36, 38, 41, 46, 74, 230
William (2-27), 18, 19, 20, 36, 79, 84, 130, 153, 251, 253, 254, 275, 276, 277
William (2-5), 15, 36, 46, 74, 77, 160, 161, 162, 163, 164, 165, 256
William (2-6), 16, 75, 255
William (2-81), 85, 225, 226
William (3-36), 95, 103, 386, 387
William (3-50), 96, 103, 306, 307, 333, 334, 336, 337, 341, 342, 343, 344, 345, 346, 353, 354, 355, 356, 357, 358, 359
William (3-78), 103, 109, 239, 240, 242
William (3-82), 103
William (3-9), 37, 38, 91, 94, 167, 173, 234, 386
William (4-2), 15, 16, 32, 38, 39, 40, 41, 42, 110, 111, 112, 114, 115, 259, 268, 269, 270, 271, 272
William (4-82), 19, 20, 36, 125, 130, 181, 185, 186, 187, 189, 190, 191
William (Billy) (2-45), 81, 85, 206, 225, 226, 227, 228, 229
William A. (4-63), 123
William Allensworth (3-42), 95
William Allensworth (3-51), 97, 105, 334, 335, 345, 352, 353, 354, 356, 357, 358, 359
William Edgar (4-144), 132, 312
William H. (2-71), 84, 252
William J (3-72), 101, 109, 351, 352, 357, 358
William Jefferson (3-113), 108
William McClelland (3-122), 109
Willoughby (1-22), 21, 53, 279
Wilmouth (3-26), 93, 329
Wilmouth (3-29), 94
Wilmouth (Brown) (3-71), 101, 357
Wilmouth (Smith) (3-5), 90, 243, 256
Winifred (Netherton) (3-17), 92, 247
Winnifred (2-17), 76, 221
Winny (3-11), 91, 256

Harding (Essex Co VA)
Andrew, 158
John, 157
LeRoy (7-2), 154
Nicholas (8-3), 158
Richard, 158
Thoma (7-1)s, 155
Thomas, 158, 159
Thomas (7-1), 154, 155, 157
William, 159
William (8-2), 154, 155, 156, 157, 158, 159

Harding of London, xiv, 1, 2, 3, 4, 5, 6

Harrison
Elizabeth (4-4), 114

Hartley
Ann (Mark Hardin) (5-13), 140, 177, 348, 350

Hawkins
Amanda M. (John Smith) (4-112), 128, 370, 382, 383
Benjamin S. (4-118), 129
Benjamin T. (4-31), 325, 368, 370, 379, 380, 381, 382, 383
Enos (4-113), 128, 370, 381, 383
George (4-120), 129
Jane (Emerson) (4-111), 128, 370, 381, 383
Jemima (George Hardin) (4-28), 318, 325, 370, 380
John (Harriet Hardin) (4-35), 371, 379
John S. (4-117), 129
Lucy Jane (4-121), 129

Harding Families of the Northern Neck of Virginia

Martha (Humphrey) (4-110), 128, 370, 381, 382
Nancy (4-115), 129
Rebecca A. (4-119), 129
Sally (4-116), 129
William (4-114), 129, 381

Haynie, 8, 9, 10, 11, 49, 52, 53, 57, 76, 77, 193, 197, 199, 200, 201, 207, 210, 211, 214, 216, 220, 221, 222, 223, 224, 393, 394

Henderson
Catherine (Absolom Hardin) (4-36), 130, 371

Hendrickson
John (Sarah Harding) (2-40), 372

Hitt
Catherine Ann (Warner Harding) (3-56), 357

Holt
Lewis (Betsy Harden) (1-82), 287
Rebecka (John Harden) (1-79), 287, 288, 289
Sarah (John Harden) (1-44), 58, 287, 288, 289
Sarah E. (Peter Ray Harden) (1-115), 69, 287

Holtzclaw
Winifred Ann (William Hardin) (5-15), 141

Hord
Agnes (Mark Harding) (4-19), 250

Hornbuckle
Elizabeth (Henry Harden) (1-49), 58
William (Jane Harden) (1-42), xiii, 23, 281, 282, 292, 293, 294

Housley
Sarah (Philip Harding) (3-46), 96

Hudnall
Elizabeth (William Jett) (1-68), 61, 66
Ellis (1-70, 61
Ellis (Judith Harding) (1-39), 56, 61, 230
Frances (1-69, 61
James (Jemima Harding) (1-36), 56, 230
John (1-71, 61

Humphrey
Frances (Philip Harding) (4-77), 123
James (Martha Hawkins) (4-110), 128, 381, 382, 383

Humphries
George (Jane Harding) (1-17), 52, 219
William (Anne Bennett) (1-7), 214, 215, 216, 218

Hurdle
George (Margaret Harden) (1-83), 287

Jackson
Rebecca (Benjamin Hardin) (4-9), 323

Jasper
Catherine (4-114), 129, 381

Jett
Jane (1-67, 67
John H. (1-65), 206
John H. (1-97), 67
Joseph (1-64), 206
Joseph (1-96), 67
Judith (1-101, 67
Thomas Harding (1-99, 67
William (1-63), 206
William (1-68), 66, 206
William (1-95, 66

Jobe
Richard (Rebecca Jane Harding) (3-75), 357

Jones
Susan (William E Hardin) (4-91), 126, 382

Keeling
Jenny (John Stephen Hardin) (2-34), 372, 373, 374
Margaret (Peggy) (William Hardin) (2-37), 372

Kelley
Rebecca (Daniel Hardin) (4-41), 323

Kelly
Jacob (Elizabeth Hardin) (4-25), 117, 317
Jacob (Elizabeth Hardin) (4-46), 121, 322, 325, 326, 361

Kendall
Sarah (Enoch Harding) (4-12), 260

Knott, 12, 13, 14, 207, 208

Lackland
Margery (Thompson Harden) (1-93), 65

Lewis
John (Hannah Harding) (1-26), 203, 230
Samuel (Frances Harding) (1-31), 230

Lindsey
Orlando (Sarah hardin) (4-26), 117, 318

Logan
Elizabeth (Martin D. Hardin) (5-99), 317

Lowry
Alcey (Benjamin Hawkins) (4-31), 370, 381, 382, 383

Ludwick
Catherine (3-47), 96

Lunsford, 15, 75, 77, 87, 199, 215, 220, 225, 257
Rachel (Charles Harding) (2-2), 41, 255

Lynch

Index

Judith (Henry Harding) (5-5), 139
Mann
    Samuel (Elizabeth Berry), 14
McCutchin
    Sally (Jeremiah Harden) (1-86), 300
McInteer
    William (Adah Harding) (4-17), 116
Mebane
    Rebecca C. (Daniel Clapp Harden) (1-112), 68
    William M. (Margaret Jane Harden) (1-116), 69, 287
Million, 218, 256, 259, 261, 268, 269, 356
    Clarissa (Clarkey) (William Harding) (4-2), 15, 16, 41, 251, 259, 260, 261, 272, 273, 274, 275, 276, 277
Mitchell
    Peter (Rebecca Harding) (3-88), 103, 306, 358
Monk
    Aretta (Retty) (William Harding) (3-78), 240, 241
Montgomery
    John (Martha Hardin) (4-95), 126
Morrison
    Ephraim (Nancy Harding) (3-49), 96, 308
Moseley
    Anne (Thomas Harding I) (1-1), xiii, xv, 3, 12, 13, 17, 22, 32, 33, 34, 46, 194, 195, 209
    Henry, 12, 13, 14, 195, 391, 392, 395
Neale
    Mathew (Mary Harding) (1-28), 201, 203
Netherton
    Henry (Nancy Harding) (3-18), 92, 337, 359
    John (Winifred Harding) (3-17), 92, 247
O'Quin
    Eliza (Joshua Harden) (1-90), 71, 298
Oder
    Lucy (Nelson Harding) (4-58), 384
Orley, xiv, 1, 2, 3, 4, 5, 6, 7, 209, 389, 390, 391, 392
Palmer, 57, 83, 86, 87, 88, 196, 197, 198, 200, 203, 218, 219, 220, 221, 224, 238, 394
Pate
    Hartwell (Mary Hardin) (3-87), 103, 336, 357
Payne
    Elizabeth (John Hardin) (5-56), 140

Phillips
    Mary (Henry Harding) (3-68), 337
    Nancy (John Harding) (3-67), 337, 359
    Samuel, 337
Pitman
    Edward (Lucy Harding) (2-51), 206
Pope
    Frances (Philip Harding) (2-61), 168
    William (Susanna Harding) (2-60), 168
Powell
    Elizabeth (Thomas Harden) (1-48), 25, 26, 27, 34, 58, 287
Prather
    James (Wilmouth Harding) (3-26), 93
    John L. (Mary Harden) (1-80), 287, 289
Pressley
    Elizabeth (Joseph Harding) (4-21), 19, 181, 189, 190, 191
Price
    Elizabeth (1-5) (William Harding) (1-5), 18
Price?
    Elizabeth (1-5), 21, 278
Pyburn
    Richard (Mary Harding) (2-36), 372
Rankin
    John B. (Lucy Hardin) (3-83), 103, 306, 353, 354, 357, 359, 360
Ritter
    Emily (Henry Hardin) (3-104), 110, 358
Robinson, 15, 53, 57, 74, 76, 77, 82, 85, 86, 87, 137, 138, 166, 196, 197, 199, 201, 212, 215, 216, 217, 218, 219, 220, 223, 224, 225, 397, 398
Routt
    Nancy (Benjamin Hardin) (4-9), 168
Rowland
    Luke (1-3), 8, 10, 11, 49, 50, 51, 210, 211, 212, 393, 394, 395
Royster
    Lucy (Jeremiah Holt Harden) (1-113), 69
Sanford
    Martha (George Washington Hardin) (4-50), 121
    Sarah (Nathaniel Hardin) (4-47), 121
Sarratt
    Dickerson (2-63), 151
Sears
    Margaret (Henry Harding) (4-85), 181, 187, 188, 191
    Sarah (Presley Hardin) (4-83), 180, 311
Shackelford
    Daniel (Amnah Harding) (2-57), 168

Harding Families of the Northern Neck of Virginia

Shelborne
    Jeremiah H. (1-103), 67, 303
    Nancy (1-105), 68, 303
    Peggy Taylor (1-107), 68, 303
    Polly (1-104), 68, 303
    Samuel (1-73), 300, 303
    Thomas R. (1-106), 68, 303

Shoares
    William (Elizabeth Berry), 14, 195

Shockley
    Judith (Marcus Harding) (4-62), 122

Shrader
    William (Catherine Harding) (3-32), 337

Skeen
    Susannah (Abner Harding) (3-33), 242, 386

Smith
    John (Wilmouth Harding) (3-5), 243
    John S. (Amanda Hawkins) (4-112), 370, 371, 382, 383
    Mary (Henry Hardin) (3-31), 333, 334, 355, 356

Souther
    Abraham (Katherine Harding) (3-54), 338

Sparks
    Sarah (Baylis G. Hardin) (4-39), 369, 371

St. Clear
    John (Elizabeth Harding) (3-48), 96, 308

Starkey
    MInerva (Thomas Presley Harden) (1-127), 70

Strawbridge
    Isabella (John Hardin) (5-12), 139

Stull
    Susannah (Mark Hardin) (5-26), 137, 331

Taylor
    Eleanor (Thomas Harden) (1-23), 22, 58, 294

Thatcher
    Edith (Lewis Harding) (4-84), 180, 311

Thomas
    Stephen, 48, 51, 156, 157, 209, 238

Thompson
    James (Jane Hardin) (2-38), 372

Thornton
    William P. (Sarah Hardin 4-37), 119
    William P. (Sarah Hardin) (4-37), 371

Tilden
    Mary(JohnHarden) (1-72), 67

Tilman
    Mary (John Harden) (1-72), 300

Trigg
    Sarah (William Harding) (3-51), 357

Trussell, 53, 54, 208, 215, 216, 220, 232, 278, 279

Tubman
    Susannah (James Hardin) (2-39), 372

Tyngey
    John, 8, 12, 13, 14, 47, 48, 194, 195, 389, 391

Votaw
    Martha (Garland Harding) (4-66), 123

Waddington, 15, 74, 76, 81, 83, 85, 86, 87, 88, 196, 203, 208, 211, 212, 215, 218, 219, 220, 401
    Frances (William Harding) (2-1), 15, 197, 216, 217
    Hannah (Thomas Harding) (2-4), 15, 179, 199, 200, 222

Warner
    Eleanor (Absolom Hardin) (4-36), 130, 371

Warre, 9, 10, 11

Waters
    Lydia (Martin Hardin) (5-3), 137, 167, 237

Whitworth
    James (Amy Harding) (4-64), 123
    Samuel (Mary Harding) (4-68), 123

Wickliffe
    Robert (Mary Hardin) (5-22), 137

Wildey
    Elizabeth (1-59), 60
    Heli (1-57), 60, 203
    Jane (1-58), 60
    Joseph (1-56), 60
    Joseph (Judith Harding) (1-24), 201, 203, 230, 231
    Judith (1-55), 60, 231
    Molly (1-54), 60, 231
    Sarah (1-52), 60, 230, 231
    William (1-53), 60, 231

Wiley
    Sarah (Jeremiah Harden) (1-45), 58, 282, 287

Wilhoite, 93, 96, 101, 102, 103, 104, 105, 106, 333, 334, 335, 337, 353, 356, 357, 358
    Gipson (June Amanda Harding) (3-76), 357
    Lucy (Jonathan Harding) (3-52), 337, 356
    Rhoda (William Harding) (3-50), 306, 307, 334, 353, 354
    Simeon (Mildred Ann Harding) (3-77), 357

Williams

Index

Mary L. (Presley W. Harden) (1-102), 67, 300
Susannah (Presley Harden) (1-43), 58, 293, 303, 304
Wilson
Gregory (Sally Harden) (1-76), 299, 300
Woodson

Lucy (Joshua Harden) (1-90), 71, 298
Yancey
Sterling Mann (Mary Lyddey Harden (1-128), 71
Young
David B. (Lucinda Harding) (4-149), 132, 311

www.ingramcontent.com/pod-product-compliance
Lightning Source LLC
Chambersburg PA
CBHW071257110426
42743CB00042B/1083